AMERICAN GOVERNMENT

AMERICAN GOVERNMENT

Readings and Cases

FOURTEENTH EDITION

Peter Woll
Brandeis University

New York   San Francisco   Boston
London   Toronto   Sydney   Tokyo   Singapore   Madrid
Mexico City   Munich   Paris   Cape Town   Hong Kong   Montreal

Publisher: Priscilla McGeehon
Senior Acquisitions Editor: Eric Stano
Marketing Manager: Megan Galvin-Fak
Production Manager: Joseph Vella
Project Coordination, Text Design, and Electronic Page Makeup: Shepherd, Inc.
Senior Cover Design Manager: Nancy Danahy
Cover Designer: Joel Zimmerman
Cover Photo: © Peter Grindley/FPG International
Manufacturing Buyer: Al Dorsey
Printer and Binder: Maple-Vail Book Manufacturing Group
Cover Printer: Phoenix Color Corp.

Library of Congress Cataloging-in-Publication Data

American government : readings and cases / [edited by] Peter Woll.—14th ed.
    p. cm.
  Includes bibliographical references.
  ISBN 0-321-07999-X
  1. United States—Politics and government. I. Woll, Peter, 1933–
JK21 .A445 2001
320.473—dc21   00-053475
                                                              CIP

Please visit our website at http://www.ablongman.com

ISBN 0-321-07999-X

2 3 4 5 6 7 8 9 10—MA—04 03 02

This book is dedicated to
my brother John and to the memory of L

————————

CONTENTS

the right to be free from crimes of violence motivated by gender." Gender-motivated crimes of violence are not economic activity that Congress can regulate under the commerce clause. Nor can Congress sustain the legislation under its Fourteenth Amendment enforcement authority (#5) which applies only to state action.

evolving meaning and should be strictly interpreted in textual terms. Issues of the court's legitimacy and public approval or disapproval should in no way influence constitutional interpretation.

PREFACE

This is an exciting new edition of *American Government: Readings and Cases*. The text takes into account recent developments, cases, and debates over campaign finance reform; the new Supreme Court imposed limits on congressional power over the states and other rulings; and political trends that are reshaping government and politics at the national and state levels.

As always, the text updates key Supreme Court decisions that affect the political process and public policy as well as civil liberties and rights. Other than cases, a wide variety of new selections cover such hot issues as the growing importance of citizen initiatives in the states and how they replace Madison's constitutional design, as well as regulation of campaign finance, including how political parties have taken a major role in campaign finance. Other new readings illustrate fresh approaches to such topics as the Madisonian model and interest group power, covering the role of interest groups in the political process from elections to Capitol Hill and public policy. A new selection on the presidency applies and expands James David Barber's analysis of presidential style to the Clinton presidency. Other additions focus on the many paradoxes of presidential politics and leadership and the media's role in presidential politics.

The Supreme Court has taken an activist stance in crucial areas of constitutional law, politics, and public policy. The new edition contains the Court's major cases decided in its 1999–2000 term that add new dimensions to our civil liberties and rights. Also added to this edition are the landmark cases that establish constitutional rules governing hate speech, university and college speech codes and harassment policies, school prayer, and the death penalty. Other important cases new to this edition illustrate how the Court has applied the Constitution to the political process in campaign finance and party primaries in ways that will have a profound effect on the political system. An important aspect of litigation has always been politics by other means, and nowhere is this better illustrated than in the new edition of this text.

Cases involving politics by other means and judicial activism added to this edition include major Supreme Court decisions that:

- limit of the power of Congress under the commerce clause to enact legislation to help prevent violence against women.
- protect political parties' First Amendment rights of association by preventing states from adopting blanket primaries open to all voters regardless of party affiliation; and
- expand political party power to make indirect expenditures in behalf of candidates.

In the area of civil liberties and civil rights, exciting and controversial cases new to this edition are Supreme Court rulings on:

- how the First Amendment applies to fighting words and hate speech;
- university speech codes and harassment policies;
- congressional attempts to regulate sexually explicit programming by cable television;
- student-led prayers at high school football games; and
- the death penalty

The text continues to provide key classic and contemporary readings and cases that introduce students to the underpinnings and current practices of American government. It complements regular textbooks by illustrating and amplifying important issues and concepts, and at the same time, due to the organization and design of the book, it is suitable for use as a core textbook. Included are extensive notes that prepare for, connect, and comment on the selections and point out their significance within the broader context of American government.

The core readings and cases have always given students a real sense of their great heritage. Without detailing each and every selection, the highlights of what students learn from this text are:

- John Locke's theory of government by consent
- Madison's constitutional model of balance and deliberative government in the national interest
- Hamilton's model of strong presidential government, energy in the executive being the definition of good government
- The Supreme Court's role in constitutional interpretation and how it shapes our government and politics
- The Bill of Rights and how the Supreme Court has interpreted it
- The constitutional and political basis of our federal system
- The importance of *Federalist 10* and Madison's view of factions and special interests
- The party model of government and the role of parties in the political process
- Interest group theory and its critics
- The nature of PACs and their role in the political process
- The characteristics of the Presidency and contrasting theories of presidential power
- Edmund Burke's Speech to the Electors of Bristol
- The theories of David Mayhew, Richard Fenno, Morris Fiorina, Lawrence Dodd, and Nelson Polsby that explain Congress and the electoral connection
- The views of Supreme Court Justices William H. Rehnquist, Sandra Day O'Connor, and Antonin Scalia on the proper interpretation of the Constitution

An instructor's manual and a student manual accompany the text. Students and professors can access the student manual on the Web at http://www.unet. brandeis.edu/~woll. My website also has my introductory American Government course syllabus and extensive lecture notes using this reader.

LongmanParticipate.com
(www.longmanparticipate.com)

Also available is access to Longman Participate.com, a new website for American government courses. A six-month subscription to the site is FREE when the access card is ordered packaged with this Woll's reader. More interactive, more comprehensive, and more media-rich than any American government web site currently available, LongmanParticipate.com offers instructors and students an exciting new resource for teaching and learning about our political system that's easy to integrate into any course. For each major topic in American Government, there are five highly interactive, in-depth exercises (Simulations, Visual Literacy, Interactive Timelines, Participation, and Comparative) and much more!

Contact your local Allyn&Bacon/Longman representative to find our how to order the reader packaged with the LongmanParticipate.com subscription card.

ACKNOWLEDGMENTS

My Longman editor Eric Stano has skillfully and professionally guided the new edition from the beginning. It's comforting to have an editor who immediately answers my e-mail to him even at 8 A.M.! That is the kind of support every author appreciates.

I would also like to thank the other talented professionals at Longman and Shepherd who helped this text move smoothly through the production process.

My colleague and co-author on other books, Stephen J. Rockwell, researched the readings for the new edition, and as always his suggestions were invaluable. Stephen is a real professional. He has continued to author the instructor's and student manuals for the text.

Political scientists nationwide have helpfully reviewed the text and made suggestions for the new edition. I would particularly like to thank Robert S. Friedman at California State University-Sacramento; Mark S. Jendrysik at University of North Dakota; Mark R. Joslyn at Universityof Kansas; William J. Kubik at Hanover College; William Taggart at New Mexico State University, and D. Stephen Voss at University of Kentucky.

PETER WOLL

AMERICAN GOVERNMENT

PART ONE

THE SETTING OF THE AMERICAN SYSTEM

CHAPTER 1

CONSTITUTIONAL GOVERNMENT

The Founding Fathers were consummate politicians, but also brilliant political philosophers in their own right. They did not hesitate to draw upon the rich Western tradition of political philosophy as they searched for an ideal model of government. Above all, they wanted a government responsive to the people but also one of balanced and limited powers.

Constitutional Democracy: The Rule of Law

The Western political heritage has emphasized the importance of democracy and the rule of law. Aristotle's *Politics* stressed the viability of democracy, provided there are sufficient checks upon unlimited popular rule.

The American constitutional tradition reflects the beliefs of many political philosophers. One of the most dominating figures is John Locke. It is not suggested that Locke was read by most of the colonists, but only that his ideas invariably found their way into many writings of eighteenth-century America, most importantly the Declaration of Independence. In a letter to Henry Lee in 1825, Thomas Jefferson wrote:

"When forced . . . to resort to arms for redress, an appeal to the tribunal of the world was deemed proper for our justification. This was the object of the Declaration of Independence. Not to find out new principles, or new arguments, never before thought of, not merely to say things which had never been said before; but to place before mankind the common sense of the subject, in terms so plain and firm as to command their assent, and to justify ourselves in the independent stand we are compelled to take. Neither aiming at originality of principle or sentiment, nor yet copied from any particular and previous writing, it was intended to be an expression of the American mind, and to give to that expression the proper tone and spirit called for by the occasion. All its authority rests then on the harmonizing sentiments of the day, whether expressed in conversation, in letters,

3

printed essays, or in the elementary books of public right [such] as Aristotle, Cicero, Locke, Sidney, etc. . . ."

In May 1790, Jefferson wrote: "Locke's little book on government is perfect as far as it goes." Although Jefferson's admiration of Locke was perhaps greater than that of many other colonists, his views did reflect a mood of eighteenth-century America. Locke's *Second Treatise, Of Civil Government* attempted to trace the reasons why people enter into political societies in the first place. The eighteenth century, no less than the twentieth, was an era characterized by attempts to be "scientific" in political formulations. Locke's *Second Treatise,* first published in 1690, reflected the scientific emphasis that was to prevail so widely beginning in the eighteenth century. To Locke, natural law was objectively valid, and therefore once ascertained, governments based upon it would have a superior claim to legitimacy. Locke is notable for his discussions of natural law, from which he derived the "best" form of government. In reading Locke, one should observe how much importance he placed upon property rights and the right of the people to dissolve government once it no longer meets their legitimate expectations.

1

SECOND TREATISE, OF CIVIL GOVERNMENT

John Locke

∽

Of the State of Nature

To understand political power aright, and derive it from its original, we must consider what estate all men are naturally in, and that is, a state of perfect freedom to order their actions, and dispose of their possessions and persons as they think fit, within the bounds of the laws of Nature, without asking leave or depending upon the will of any other man.

A state also of equality, wherein all the power and jurisdiction is reciprocal, no one having more than another, there being nothing more evident than that creatures of the same species and rank, promiscuously born to all the same advantages of Nature, and the use of the same faculties, should also be equal one amongst another, without subordination or subjection, unless the lord and master of them all should, by any manifest declaration of his will, set one above another, and confer on him, by an evident and clear appointment, an undoubted right to dominion and sovereignty. . . .

But though this be a state of liberty, yet it is not a state of license; though man in that state have an uncontrollable liberty to dispose of his person or possessions, yet he had not liberty to destroy himself, or so much as any creature in his possession, but where some nobler use than its bare preservation calls for it. The state of Nature has a law of Nature to govern it, which obliges every one, and reason, which is that law, teaches all mankind who will but consult it, that being all equal and independent, no one ought to harm another in his life, health, liberty or possessions. . . . And, being furnished with like faculties, sharing all in one community of Nature, there cannot be supposed any such subordination among us that may authorize us to destroy one another, as if we were made for one another's uses, as the inferior ranks of creatures are for ours. Every one as he is bound to preserve himself, and not to quit his station wilfully, so by the like reason, when his own preservation comes not in competition, ought he as much as he can to preserve the rest of mankind, and not unless it be to do justice on an offender, take away or impair the life, or what tends to the preservation of life, the liberty, health, limb, or goods of another.

And that all men may be restrained from invading others' rights, and from doing hurt to one another, and the law of Nature be observed, which willeth the peace and preservation of all mankind, the execution of the law of Nature is in that state put into every man's hands, whereby every one has a right to punish the transgressors of that law to such a degree as may hinder its violation. For the law of Nature would, as all other laws that concern men in this world, be in vain if there were nobody that in the state of Nature had a power to execute that law, and thereby preserve the innocent and restrain offenders; and if any one in the state of Nature may punish another for any evil he has done, every one may do so. For in that state of perfect equality, where naturally there is no superiority or jurisdiction of one over another, what any may do in prosecution of that law, every one must needs have a right to do.

And thus, in the state of Nature, one man comes by a power over another, but yet no absolute or arbitrary power to use a criminal, when he has got him in his hands, according to the passionate heats or boundless extravagancy of his own will, but only to retribute him so far as calm reason and conscience dictate, what is proportionate to his transgression, which is so much as may serve for reparation and restraint. . . .

Every offence that can be committed in the state of Nature may, in the state of Nature, be also punished equally, and as far forth, as it may, in a commonwealth. For—though it would be beside my present purpose to enter here into the particulars of the law of Nature, or its measures of punishment, yet it is certain there is such a law, and that too as intelligible and plain to a rational creature and a studier of that law as the positive laws of commonwealths, nay, possibly plainer; as much as reason is easier to be understood than the fancies and intricate contrivances of men, following contrary and hidden interests put into words. . . .

Of the Ends of Political Society and Government

If man in the state of Nature be so free as has been said, if he be absolute lord of his own person and possessions, equal to the greatest and subject to nobody, why will he part with his freedom, this empire, and subject himself to the dominion and control of any other power? To which it is obvious to answer, that though in the state of Nature he hath such a right, yet the enjoyment of it is very uncertain and constantly exposed to the invasion of others; for all being kings as much as he, every man his equal, and the greater part no strict observers of equity and justice, the enjoyment of the property he has in this state is very unsafe, very insecure. This makes him willing to quit this condition which, however free, is full of fears and continual dangers; and it is not without reason that he seeks out and is willing to join in society with others who are already united, or have a mind to unite for the mutual preservation of their lives, liberties, and estates, which I call by the general name—property.

The great and chief end, therefore, of men uniting into commonwealths, and putting themselves under government, is the preservation of their property; to which in the state of Nature there are many things wanting.

Firstly, there wants an established, settled, known law, received and allowed by common consent to be the standard of right and wrong, and the common measure to decide all controversies between them. For though the law of Nature be plain and intelligible to all rational creatures, yet men, being biased by their interest, as well as ignorant for want of study of it, are not apt to allow of it as a law binding to them in the application of it to their particular cases.

Secondly, in the state of Nature there wants a known and indifferent judge, with authority to determine all differences according to the established law. For every one in that state being both judge and executioner of the law of Nature, men being partial to themselves, passion and revenge is very apt to carry them too far, and with too much heat in their own cases, as well as negligence and unconcernedness, make them too remiss in other men's.

Thirdly, in the state of Nature there often wants power to back and support the sentence when right, and to give it due execution. They who by any injustice offended will seldom fail where they are able by force to make good their injustice. Such resistance many times makes the punishment dangerous, and frequently destructive to those who attempt it.

Thus mankind, notwithstanding all the privileges of the state of Nature, being but in an ill condition while they remain in it are quickly driven into society. Hence it comes to pass, that we seldom find any number of men live any time together in this state. The inconveniences that they are therein exposed to by the irregular and uncertain exercise of the power every man has of punishing the transgressions of others, make them take sanctuary under the established laws of government, and therein seek the preservation of their property. It is this makes them so willingly give up every one his single power of punishing to be exercised by such alone as shall be appointed to it amongst them, and by such rules as the community, or those authorised by them to that purpose, shall agree on. And in this we have the original right and rise of both the legislative and executive power as well as of the governments and societies themselves.

For in the state of Nature to omit the liberty he has of innocent delights, a man has two powers. The first is to do whatsoever he thinks fit for the preservation of himself and others within the permission of the law of Nature; by which law, common to them all, he and all the rest of mankind are one community, make up one society distinct from all other creatures, and were it not for the corruption and viciousness of degenerate men, there would be no need for any other, no necessity that men should separate from this great and natural community, and associate into lesser combinations. The other power a man has in the state of Nature is the power to punish the crimes committed against that law. Both these he gives up when he joins in a private, if I may so call it, or particular political society, and incorporates into any commonwealth separate from the rest of mankind.

The first power—viz., of doing whatsoever he thought fit for the preservation of himself and the rest of mankind, he gives up to be regulated by laws made by the society, so far forth as the preservation of himself and the rest of that society shall require; which laws of the society in many things confine the liberty he had by the law of Nature.

Secondly, the power of punishing he wholly gives up, and engages his natural force, which he might before employ in the execution of the law of Nature, by his own single authority, as he thought fit, to assist the executive power of the society as the law thereof shall require. For being now in a new state, wherein he is to enjoy many conveniences from the labor, assistance, and society of others in the same community, as well as protection from its whole strength, he is to part also with as much of his natural liberty, in providing for himself, as the good, prosperity, and safety of the society shall require, which is not only necessary but just, since the other members of the society do the like.

But though men when they enter into society give up the equality, liberty, and executive power they had in the state of Nature into the hands of the society, to be so far disposed of by the legislative as the good of the society shall require, yet it being only with an intention in every one the better to preserve himself, his liberty and property (for no rational creature can be supposed to change his condition with an intention to be worse), the power of the society or legislative constituted by them can never be supposed to extend farther than the common against those three defects above mentioned that made the state of Nature so unsafe and uneasy. And so, whoever has the legislative or supreme power of any commonwealth, is bound to govern by established standing laws, promulgated and known to the people, and not by extemporary decrees, by indifferent and upright judges, who are to decide controversies by those laws; and to employ the force of the community at home only in the execution of such laws, or abroad to prevent or redress foreign injuries and secure the community from inroads and invasion. And all this to be directed to no other end but the peace, safety, and public good of the people. . . .

Of the Extent of the Legislative Power

The great end of men's entering into society being the enjoyment of their properties in peace and safety, and the great instrument and means of that being the laws established in that society, the first and fundamental positive law of all commonwealths is the establishing of the legislative power, as the first and fundamental natural law, which is to govern even the legislative itself, is the preservation of the society and (as far as will consist with the public good) of every person in it. This legislative is not only the supreme power of the commonwealth, but sacred and unalterable in the hands where the community have once placed it. Nor can any edict of anybody else, in what form soever conceived, or by what power soever backed, have the force and obligation of a law which has not its sanction from that legislative which the public has chosen and appointed it; for without this the law could not have that which is absolutely necessary to its being a law, the consent of the society, over whom nobody can have a power to make laws but by their own consent and by authority received from them. . . .

These are the bounds which the trust that is put in them by the society and the law of God and Nature have set to the legislative power of every commonwealth, in all forms of government. First: They are to govern by promulgated established laws, not to be varied in particular cases, but to have one rule for rich and poor, for the favorite at Court and the countryman at plough. Secondly: These laws also ought to be designed for no other end ultimately but the good of the people. Thirdly: They must not raise taxes on the property of the people without the consent of the people given by themselves or their deputies. And this properly concerns only such governments where the legislative is always in being, or at least where the people have not reserved any part of the legislative to deputies, to be from time to time chosen by themselves. Fourthly: Legislative neither must nor can transfer the power of making laws to anybody else, or place it anywhere but where the people have. . . .

Of the Dissolution of Government

The constitution of the legislative [authority] is the first and fundamental act of society, whereby provision is made for the continuation of their union under the direction of persons and bonds of laws, made by persons authorised thereunto, by the consent and appointment of the people, without which no one man, or number of men, amongst them can have authority of making laws that shall be binding to the rest. When any one, or more, shall take upon them to make laws whom the people have not appointed so to do, they make laws without authority, which the people are not therefore bound to obey; by which means they come again to be out of subjection, and may constitute to themselves a new legislative, as they think best, being in full liberty to resist the force of those who, without authority, would impose anything upon them. . . .

Whosoever uses force without right—as every one does in society who does it without law—puts himself into a state of war with those against whom he so uses it, and in that state all former ties are cancelled, all other rights cease, and every one has a right to defend himself, and to resist the aggressor. . . .

Here it is like the common question will be made: Who shall be judge whether the prince or legislative act contrary to their trust? This, perhaps, ill-affected and factious men may spread amongst the people, when the prince only makes use of his due prerogative. To this I reply, The people shall be judge; for who shall be judge whether his trustee or deputy acts well and according to the trust reposed in him, but he who deputes him and must, by having deputed him, have still a power to discard him when he fails in his trust? If this be reasonable in particular cases of private men, why should it be otherwise in that of the greatest moment, where the welfare of millions is concerned and also where the evil, if not prevented, is greater, and the redress very difficult, dear, and dangerous? . . .

To conclude. The power that every individual gave the society when he entered into it can never revert to the individuals again, as long as the society lasts, but will always remain in the community; because without this there can be no community—no commonwealth, which is contrary to the original agreement; so also when the society hath placed the legislative in any assembly of men, to continue in them and their successors, with direction and authority for providing such successors, the legislative can never revert to the people whilst that government lasts; because, having provided a legislative with power to continue for ever, they have given up their political power to the legislative, and cannot resume it. But if they have set limits to the duration of their legislative, and made this supreme power in any person or assembly only temporary; or else when, by the miscarriages of those in authority, it is forfeited; upon the forfeiture of their rulers, or at the determination of the time set, it reverts to the society, and the people have a right to act as supreme, and continue the legislative in themselves or place it in a new form, or new hands, as they think good.

———————————— ℰℱ ————————————

The influence of John Locke goes far beyond his impact on the thinking of the founding fathers of the United States, such as Thomas Jefferson. Some scholars (among them, Louis Hartz, *The Liberal Tradition in America*) have interpreted the American political tradition in terms of the pervasive attachment to the ideas and values set forth in the writings of Locke. There is little question that American political life has been uniquely characterized by widespread adherence to the fundamental principles about the relations among people, society, and government expressed in Locke's writings.

It is not just that we have representative government, with institutions similar in structure and function to those of the constitutional democracy described in Locke's *Second Treatise,* but that through the years we have probably maintained, more than any other society, a widespread agreement about the fundamental human values cherished by Locke. His emphasis upon the sanctity of private property has been paramount in the American political tradition from the very beginning. Moreover, Locke's views on the nature of man are shared by most Americans. All our governmental institutions, processes, and traditions rest upon principles such as the primacy of the individual, man's inborn ability to exercise reason in order to discern truth and higher principles of order and justice, and a political and social equality among people in which no person shall count for more than another in determining the actions of government and their application. We may not have always practiced these ideals, but we have been *theoretically* committed to them.

Framing the Constitution: Elitist or Democratic Process?

A remarkable fact about the United States government is that it has operated for two hundred years on the basis of a written Constitution. Does this suggest unusual sagacity on the part of the Founding Fathers, or exceptional luck? What was involved in framing the Constitution?

In the following selection John P. Roche suggests that the framing of the Constitution was essentially a democratic process involving the reconciliation of a variety of state, political, and economic interests. Roche writes that "the Philadelphia Convention was not a College of Cardinals or a council of Platonic guardians working in a manipulative, predemocratic framework; it was a *nationalist* reform caucus that had to operate with great delicacy and skill in a political cosmos full of enemies to achieve one definitive goal—popular approbation." Roche recognizes that the framers, collectively, were an elite, but he is careful to point out that they were a political elite dedicated for the most part to establishing an effective and at the same time controlled national government that would be able to overcome the weaknesses of the Articles of Confederation. The framers were not, says Roche, a cohesive elite dedicated to a particular set of political or economic assumptions beyond the simple need to create a national government that would be capable of reconciling disparate state interests. The Constitution was "a vivid demonstration of effective democratic political action, and of the forging of a national elite which literally persuaded its countrymen to hoist themselves by their own bootstraps."

------------------------------ **2** ------------------------------

THE FOUNDING FATHERS: A REFORM CAUCUS IN ACTION

John P. Roche

Over the last century and a half, the work of the Constitutional Convention and the motives of the Founding Fathers have been analyzed under a number of different ideological auspices. To one generation of historians, the hand of God was moving in the assembly; under a later dispensation, a dialectic (at various levels of philosophical sophistication) replaced the Deity: "relationships of production" moved into the niche previously reserved for Love of Country. Thus in counterpart to the *zeitgeist*, the framers have undergone miraculous metamorphoses: at one time acclaimed as liberals and bold social engineers, today they appear in the guise of sound Burkean conservatives, men who in our time would subscribe to *Fortune*, look to Walter Lippmann for political theory, and chuckle patronizingly at the antics of Barry Goldwater. The implicit assumption is that if James Madison were among us, he would be President of the Ford Foundation, while Alexander Hamilton would chair the Committee for Economic Development.

The "Fathers" have thus been admitted to our best circles; the revolutionary ferocity which confiscated all Tory property in reach and populated New Brunswick with outlaws has been converted by the "Miltown School" of American historians into a benign dedication to "consensus" and "prescriptive rights." The Daughters of the American Revolution have, through the ministrations of Professors Boorstin, Hartz, and Rossiter, at last found ancestors worthy of their descendants. It is not my purpose here to argue that the "Fathers" were, in fact, radical revolutionaries; that proposition has been brilliantly demonstrated by Robert R. Palmer in his *Age of the Democratic Revolution*. My concern is with the future position that not only were they revolutionaries, but also they were democrats. Indeed, in my view, there is one fundamental truth about the Founding Fathers that *every* generation of zeitgeisters has done its best to obscure: they were first and foremost superb democratic politicians. I suspect that in a contemporary setting, James Madison would be Speaker of the House of Representatives and Hamilton would be the *eminence grise* dominating (*pace* Theodore Sorensen or Sherman Adams) the Executive Office of the President. They were, with their colleagues, *political men*—not metaphysicians, disembodied conservatives or Agents of History—and as recent research into the nature of American politics in the 1780s confirms, they were committed (perhaps willy-nilly) to working within the democratic framework, within a universe of public approval. Charles Beard *and* the filiopietists to the contrary notwithstanding, the Philadelphia Convention was not a College of Cardinals or a council of Platonic guardians working within a manipulative, predemocratic framework; it was a *nationalist* reform caucus which had to operate with great delicacy and skill in a political cosmos full of enemies to achieve the one definitive goal—popular approbation.

Perhaps the time has come, to borrow Walton Hamilton's fine phrase, to raise the framers from immortality to mortality, to give them credit for their magnificent demonstration of the art of democratic politics. The point must be reemphasized: they *made* history and did it within the limits of consensus. There was nothing inevitable about the future in 1787; the *zeitgeist*, that fine Hegelian technique of begging causal questions, could only be discerned in retrospect. What they did was to hammer out a pragmatic compromise which would both bolster the "national interest" and be acceptable to the people. What inspiration they got came from their collective experience as professional politicians in a democratic society. As John Dickinson put it to his fellow delegates on August 13, "Experience must be our guide. Reason may mislead us."

In this context, let us examine the problems they confronted and the solutions they evolved. The Convention has been described picturesquely as a counter-revolutionary junta and the Constitution as a coup d'état, but this has been accomplished by withdrawing the whole history of the movement for constitutional reform from its true context. No doubt the goals of the constitutional elite were "subversive" to the existing political order, but it is overlooked that their subversion could only have succeeded if the people of the United States endorsed it by regularized procedures. Indubitably they were "plotting" to establish a much stronger central government than existed under the Articles, but only in the sense in which one could argue equally well that John F. Kennedy was, from 1956 to 1960, "plotting" to become President. In short, on the fundamental *procedural* level, the Constitutionalists had to work according to the prevailing rules of the game. Whether they liked it or not is a topic for spiritualists—and is irrelevant: one may be quite certain that had Washington agreed to play the de Gaulle (as the Cincinnati once urged), Hamilton would willingly have held his horse, but such fertile speculation in no way alters the actual context in which events took place.

I

When the Constitutionalists went forth to subvert the Confederation, they utilized the mechanisms of political legitimacy. And the roadblocks which confronted them were formidable. At the same time, they were endowed with certain potent political assets. The history of the United States from 1786 to 1790 was largely one of a masterful employment of political expertise by the Constitutionalists as against bumbling, erratic behavior by the opponents of reform. Effectively, the Constitutionalists had to induce the states, by democratic techniques of coercion, to emasculate themselves. To be specific, if New York had refused to join the new Union, the project was doomed; yet before New York was safely in, the reluctant state legislature had *suasponte* to take the following steps: (1) agree to send delegates to the Philadelphia Convention; (2) provide maintenance for these delegates (these were distinct stages: New Hampshire was early in naming delegates, but did not provide for their maintenance until July); (3) set up the special ad hoc convention to decide on ratification; and (4) concede to the decision of the ad hoc convention that New York should participate. New York admittedly was a tricky state, with a strong interest in a status quo which permitted her to exploit New Jersey and Connecticut, but the same legal hurdles existed in every state. And at the risk of becoming boring, it must be reiterated that the *only* weapon in the Constitutionalist arsenal was an effective mobilization of public opinion.

The group which undertook this struggle was an interesting amalgam of a few dedicated nationalists with the self-interested spokesmen of various parochial bailiwicks. The Georgians, for example, wanted a strong central authority to provide military protection for their huge, underpopulated state against the Creek Confederacy; Jerseymen and Connecticuters wanted to escape from economic bondage to New York; the Virginians hoped to establish a system which would give that great state its rightful place in the councils of the republic. The dominant figures in the politics of these states therefore cooperated in the call for the Convention. In other states, the thrust towards national reform was taken up by opposition groups who added the "national interest" to their weapons system; in Pennsylvania, for instance, the group fighting to revise the Constitution of 1776 came out four-square behind the Constitutionalists, and in New York, Hamilton and the Schuyler *ambiance* took the same tack against George Clinton. There was, of course, a large element of personality in the affair: there is reason to suspect that Patrick Henry's opposition to the Convention and the Constitution was founded on his conviction that Jefferson was behind both, and a close study of local politics elsewhere would surely reveal that others supported the Constitution for the simple (and politically quite sufficient) reason that the "wrong" people were against it.

To say this is not to suggest that the Constitution rested on a foundation of impure or base motives. It is rather to argue that in politics there are no immaculate conceptions, and that in the drive for a stronger general government, motives of all sorts played a part. Few men in the history of mankind have espoused a view of the "common good" or "public interest" that militated against their private status; even Plato with all his reverence for disembodied reason managed to put philosophers on top of the pile. Thus it is not surprising that a number of diversified private interests joined to push the nationalist public interest; what would have been surprising was the absence of such a pragmatic united front. And the fact remains that, however motivated, these men did demonstrate a willingness to compromise their parochial interest in behalf of an ideal which took shape before their eyes and under their ministrations.

As Stanley Elkins and Eric McKitrick have suggested in a perceptive essay [76 *Political Science Quarterly* 181 (1961)], what distinguished the leaders of the Constitutionalist caucus from their enemies was a "Continental" approach to political, economic and military issues. To the extent that they shared an institutional base of operations, it was the Continental Congress (thirty-nine of the delegates to the Federal Convention had served in Congress), and this was hardly a locale which inspired respect for the state governments. Robert de Jouvenal observed French politics half a century ago and noted that a revolutionary Deputy had more in common with a nonrevolutionary Deputy than he had with a revolutionary non-Deputy; similarly one can surmise that membership in the Congress under the Articles of Confederation worked to establish a Continental frame of reference, that a Congressman from Pennsylvania and one from South Carolina would share a universe of discourse which provided them with a conceptual common denominator vis-à-vis their respective state legislatures. This was particularly true with respect to external affairs: the average state legislator was probably about as concerned with foreign policy then as he is today, but Congressmen were constantly forced to take the broad view of American prestige, were compelled to listen to the reports of Secretary John Jay and to the dispatches and pleas from their frustrated envoys in Britain, France, and Spain. From considerations such as these, a "Continental" ideology developed which seems to have demanded a revision of our domestic institutions primarily on the ground that only by invigorating our general government could we assume our rightful place in the international arena. Indeed, an argument with great force—particularly since Washington was its incarnation—urged that our very survival in the Hobbesian jungle of world politics depended upon a reordering and strengthening of our national sovereignty.

The great achievement of the Constitutionalists was their ultimate success in convincing the elected representatives of a majority of the white male population that change was imperative. A small group of political leaders with a Continental vision and essentially a consciousness of the United States' *international* impotence, provided the matrix of the movement. To their standard other leaders rallied with their own parallel ambitions. Their great assets were (1) the presence in their caucus of the one authentic American "father figure," George Washington, whose prestige was enormous; (2) the energy and talent of their leadership (in which one must include the towering intellectuals of the time, John Adams and Thomas Jefferson, despite their absence abroad), and their communications "network," which was far superior to anything on the opposition side; (3) the preemptive skill which made "their" issue The Issue and kept the locally oriented opposition permanently on the defensive; and (4) the subjective consideration that these men were spokesmen of a new and compelling credo: *American* nationalism, that ill-defined but nonetheless potent sense of collective purpose that emerged from the American Revolution.

Despite great institutional handicaps, the Constitutionalists managed in the mid-1780s to mount an offensive which gained momentum as years went by. Their greatest problem was lethargy, and paradoxically, the number of barriers in their path may have proved an advantage in the long run. Beginning with the initial battle to get the Constitutional Convention called, the delegates appointed, they could never relax, never let up the pressure. In practical terms, this meant that the local "organizations" created by the Constitutionalists were perpetually in movement building up their cadres for the next fight. (The word *organization* has to be used with great caution: a political organization in the United States—as in contemporary England—generally consisted of a magnate and his following, or a coalition of magnates. This did not necessarily mean that it was "undemocratic" or "aristocratic," in the Aristotelian sense of the word: while a few magnates such as the Livingstons could draft their followings, most exercised their leadership without coercion on the basis of popular endorsement. The absence of organized opposition did not imply the impossibility of competition any more than low public participation in elections necessarily indicated an undemocratic suffrage.)

The Constitutionalists got the jump on the "opposition" (a collective noun: oppositions would be more correct) at the outset with demand for a Convention. Their opponents were caught in an old political trap: they were not being asked to approve any specific program of reform, but only to endorse a meeting to discuss and recommend needed reforms. If they took a hard line at the first stage, they were put in the position of glorifying the status quo and of denying the need for *any* changes. Moreover, the Constitutionalists could go to the people with a persuasive argument for "fair play"—"How can you condemn reform before you know precisely what is involved?" Since the state legislatures obviously would have the final say on any proposals that might emerge from the Convention, the Constitutionalists were merely reasonable men asking for a chance. Besides, since they did not make any concrete proposals at that stage, they were in a position to capitalize on every sort of generalized discontent with the Confederation.

Perhaps because of their poor intelligence system, perhaps because of overconfidence generated by the failure of all previous efforts to alter the Articles, the opposition awoke too late to the dangers that confronted them in 1787. Not only did the Constitutionalists manage to get every state but Rhode Island (where politics was enlivened by a party system reminiscent of the "Blues" and the "Greens" in the Byzantine Empire) to appoint delegates to Philadelphia, but when the results were in, it appeared that they dominated the delegations. Given the apathy of the opposition, this was a natural phenomenon: in an ideologically nonpolarized political atmosphere those who get appointed to a special committee are likely to be the men who supported the movement for its creation. Even George Clinton, who seems to have been the first opposition leader to awake to the possibility of trouble, could not prevent the New York legislature from appointing Alexander Hamilton—though he did have the foresight to send two of his henchmen to dominate the delegation. Incidentally, much has been made of the fact that the delegates to Philadelphia were not elected by the people; some have adduced this fact as evidence of the "undemocratic" character of the gathering. But put in the context of the time, this argument is wholly specious: the central government under the Articles was considered a creature of the component states and in all the states but Rhode Island, Connecticut, and New Hampshire, members of the national Congress were chosen by the state legislatures. This was not a consequence of elitism or fear of the mob; it was a logical extension of states' rights doctrine to guarantee that the national institution did not end-run the state legislatures and make direct contact with the people.

II

With delegations safely named, the focus shifted to Philadelphia. While waiting for a quorum to assemble, James Madison got busy and drafted the so-called Randolph or Virginia Plan with the aid of the Virginia delegation. This was a political masterstroke. Its consequence was that once business got underway, the framework of the discussion was established on Madison's terms. There was no interminable argument over agenda; instead the delegates took the Virginia Resolutions—"just for purposes of discussion"—as their point of departure. And along with Madison's proposals, many of which were buried in the course of the summer, went his major premise: a new start on a Constitution rather than piecemeal amendment. This was not necessarily revolutionary—but Madison's proposal that this "lump sum" amendment go into effect after approval by nine states (the Articles required unanimous state approval for any amendment) was thoroughly subversive.

Standard treatments of the Convention divide the delegates into "nationalists" and "states' righters" with various improvised shadings ("moderate nationalists," etc.), but these are *a posteriori* categories which obfuscate more than they clarify. What is striking to one who analyzes the Convention as a case study in democratic politics is the lack of clear-cut ideological divisions in the Convention. Indeed, I submit that the evidence—Madison's *Notes*, the correspondence of the delegates, and debates on ratification—indicates that this was a remarkably homogeneous body on the ideological level. Yates and Lansing, Clinton's two chaperones for Hamilton, left in disgust on July 10. (Is there anything more tedious than sitting through endless disputes on matters one deems fundamentally misconceived? It takes an iron will to spend a hot summer as an ideological *agent provocateur*.) Luther Martin, Maryland's bibulous narcissist, left on September 4 in a huff when he discovered that others did not share his self-esteem; others went home for personal reasons. But the hard core of delegates accepted a grinding regimen throughout the attrition of a Philadelphia summer precisely because they shared the Constitutionalist goal.

Basic differences of opinion emerged, of course, but these were not ideological; they were *structural*. If the so-called "states' rights" group had not accepted the fundamental purposes of the Convention, they could simply have pulled out and by doing so have aborted the whole enterprise. Instead of bolting, they returned day after day to argue and to compromise. An interesting symbol of this basic homogeneity was the initial agreement on secrecy: these professional politicians did not want to become prisoners of publicity; they wanted to retain that freedom of maneuver which is only possible when men are not forced to take public stands in the preliminary stages of negotiation. There was no legal means of binding the tongues of the delegates: at any stage in the game a delegate with basic principled objections to the emerging project could have taken the stump (as Luther Martin did after his exit) and denounced the Convention to the skies. Yet Madison did not even inform Thomas Jefferson in Paris of the course of the deliberations and available correspondence indicates that the delegates generally observed the injunction. Secrecy is certainly uncharacteristic of any assembly marked by strong ideological polarization. This was noted at the time: the *New York Daily Advertiser*, August 14, 1787, commented that the "profound secrecy hitherto observed by the Convention [we consider] a happy omen, as it demonstrates that the spirit of party on any great and essential point cannot have arisen to any height."

Commentators on the Constitution who have read *The Federalist* in lieu of reading the actual debates have credited the Fathers with the invention of a sublime concept called "Federalism." Unfortunately, *The Federalist* is probative evidence for only one proposition: that Hamilton and Madison were inspired propagandists with a genius for retrospective symmetry. Federalism, as the theory is generally defined, was an improvisation which was later promoted into a political theory. Experts on "federalism" should take to heart the advice of David Hume, who warned in his *Of the Rise and Progress of the Arts and Sciences* that "there is no subject in which we must proceed with more caution than in [history], lest we assign causes which never existed and reduced what is merely contingent to stable and universal principles." In any event, the final balance in the Constitution between the states and the nation must have come as a great disappointment to Madison, while Hamilton's unitary views are too well known to need elucidation.

It is indeed astonishing how those who have glibly designated James Madison the "father" of Federalism have overlooked the solid body of fact which indicates that he shared Hamilton's quest for a unitary central government. To be specific, they have avoided examining the clear import of the Madison-Virginia Plan, and have disregarded Madison's dogged inch-by-inch retreat from the bastions of centralization. The Virginia Plan envisioned a unitary national government effectively freed from and dominant over the states. The lower house of the national legislature was to be elected directly by the people of the states with membership proportional to population. The upper house was to be selected by the lower and two chambers would elect the executive and choose the judges. The national government would be thus cut completely loose from the states.

The structure of the general government was freed from state control in a truly radical fashion, but the scope of the authority of the national sovereign as Madison initially formulated it was breathtaking—it was a formulation worthy of the Sage of Malmesbury himself. The national legislature was to be empowered to disallow the acts of state legislatures, and the central government was vested, in addition to the powers of the nation under the Articles of Confederation, with plenary authority wherever "the separate States are incompetent or in which the harmony of the United States may be interrupted by the exercise of individual legislation." Finally, just to lock the door against state intrusion, the national Congress was to be given the power to use military force on recalcitrant states. This was Madison's "model" of an ideal national government, though it later received little publicity in *The Federalist*.

The interesting thing was the reaction of the Convention to this militant program for a strong autonomous central government. Some delegates were startled, some obviously leery of so comprehensive a project of reform, but nobody set off any fireworks and nobody walked out. Moreover, in the two weeks that followed, the Virginia Plan received substantial endorsement *en principe*; the initial temper of the gathering can be deduced from the approval "without debate or dissent," on May 31, of the Sixth Resolution which granted Congress the authority to disallow state legislation "contravening *in its opinion* the Articles of Union." Indeed, an amendment was included to bar states from contravening national treaties.

The Virginia Plan may therefore be considered, in ideological terms, as the delegates' Utopia, but as the discussions continued and became more specific, many of those present began to have second thoughts. After all, they were not residents of Utopia or guardians in Plato's Republic who could simply impose a philosophical ideal on subordinate strata of the population. They were practical politicians in a democratic society, and no matter what their private dreams might be, they had to take home an acceptable package and defend it—and their own political futures—against predictable attack. On June 14 the breaking point between dream and reality took place. Apparently realizing that under the Virginia Plan, Massachusetts, Virginia, and Pennsylvania could virtually dominate the national government—and probably appreciating that to sell this program to "the folks back home" would be impossible—the delegates from the small states dug in their heels and demanded time for a consideration of alternatives. One gets a graphic sense of the inner politics from John Dickinson's reproach to Madison: "You see the consequences of pushing things too far. Some of the members from the small States wish for two branches in the General Legislature and are friends to a good National Government; but we would sooner submit to a foreign power than . . . be deprived of an equality of suffrage in both branches of the Legislature, and thereby be thrown under the domination of the large States."

The bare outline of the *Journal* entry for Tuesday, June 14, is suggestive to anyone with extensive experience in deliberative bodies. "It was moved by Mr. Patterson [*sic*, Paterson's name was one of those consistently misspelled by Madison and everybody else] seconded by Mr. Randolph that the further consideration of the report from the Committee of the whole House [endorsing the Virginia Plan] be postponed till tomorrow and before the question for postponement was taken. It was

moved by Mr. Randolph and seconded by Mr. Patterson that the House adjourn."
The House adjourned by obvious prearrangement of the two principals: since the
preceding Saturday when Brearley and Paterson of New Jersey had announced their
fundamental discontent with the representational features of the Virginia Plan, the
informal pressure had certainly been building up to slow down the steamroller.
Doubtless there were extended arguments at the Indian Queen between Madison
and Paterson, the latter insisting that events were moving rapidly towards a probably disastrous conclusion, towards a political suicide pact. Now the process of accommodation was put into action smoothly—and wisely, given the character and
strength of the doubters. Madison had the votes, but this was one of those situations
where the enforcement of mechanical majoritarianism could easily have destroyed
the objectives of the majority: the Constitutionalists were in quest of a qualitative
as well as a quantitative consensus. This was hardly from deference to local Quaker
custom; it was a political imperative if they were to attain ratification.

III

According to the standard script, at this point the "states' rights" group intervened
in force behind the New Jersey Plan, which has been characteristically portrayed as
a reversion to the status quo under the Articles of Confederation with but minor
modifications. A careful examination of the evidence indicates that only in a marginal sense is this an accurate description. It is true that the New Jersey Plan put the
states back into the institutional picture, but one could argue that to do so was a
recognition of political reality rather than an affirmation of states' rights. A serious
case can be made that the advocates of the New Jersey Plan, far from being ideological addicts of states' rights, intended to substitute for the Virginia Plan a system
which would both retain strong national power and have a chance of adoption in
the states. The leading spokesman for the project asserted quite clearly that his
views were based more on counsels of expediency than on principle; said Paterson
on June 16: "I came here not to speak my own sentiments, but the sentiments of
those who sent me. Our object is not such a Government as may be best in itself,
but such a one as our Constituents have authorized us to prepare, and as they will
approve." This is Madison's version; in Yates's transcription, there is a crucial sentence following the remarks above: "I believe that a little practical virtue is to be
preferred to the finest theoretical principles, which cannot be carried into effect."
In his preliminary speech on June 9, Paterson had stated "to the public mind we
must accommodate ourselves," and in his notes for this and his later effort as well,
the emphasis is the same. The *structure* of government under the Articles should be
retained:

> 2. Because it accords with the Sentiments of the People.
> [Proof:]   1. Coms. [Commissions from state legislatures defining the jurisdiction of the
> delegates]
>   2. News-papers—Political Barometer. Jersey never would have sent Dele-
> gates under the first [Virginia] Plan—

Not here to sport Opinions of my own. Wt. [What] can be done. A little practical
Virtue preferable to Theory.

This was a defense of political acumen, not of states' rights. In fact, Paterson's notes
of his speech can easily be construed as an argument for attaining the substantive
objectives of the Virginia Plan by a sound political route, i.e., pouring the new wine
in the old bottles. With a shrewd eye, Paterson queried:

> Will the Operation, and Force of the [central] Govt. depend upon the mode of
> Representn.—No—it will depend upon the Quantum of Power lodged in the leg.
> ex. and judy. Departments—Give [the existing] Congress the same Powers that you
> intend to give the two Branches, [under the Virginia Plan] and I apprehend they
> will act with as much Propriety and more Energy. . . .

In other words, the advocates of the New Jersey Plan concentrated their fire on
what they held to be the *political liabilities* of the Virginia Plan—which were matters
of institutional structure—rather than on the proposed scope of national authority.
Indeed, the Supremacy Clause of the Constitution first saw the light of day in
Paterson's Sixth Resolution; the New Jersey Plan contemplated the use of military
force to secure compliance with national law; and finally Paterson made clear his
view that under either the Virginia or the New Jersey systems, the general government would ". . . act on individuals and not on states." From the states' rights
viewpoint, this was heresy: the fundament of that doctrine was the proposition that
any central government had as its constituents the states, not the people, and could
only reach the people through the agency of the state government.

Paterson then reopened the agenda of the Convention, but he did so within a
distinctly nationalist framework. Paterson's position was one of favoring a strong
central government in principle, but opposing one which in fact *put the big states in
the saddle*. (The Virginia Plan, for all its abstract merits, did very well by Virginia.)
As evidence for this speculation, there is a curious and intriguing proposal among
Paterson's preliminary drafts of the New Jersey Plan:

> Whereas it is necessary in Order to form the People of the U.S. of America in to a
> Nation, that the States should be consolidated, by which means all the Citizens
> thereof will become equally intitled to and will equally participate in the same
> Privileges and Rights . . . it is therefore resolved, that all the Lands contained
> within the Limits of each state individually, and of the U.S. generally be consid-
> ered as constituting one Body or Mass, and be divided into thirteen or more inte-
> gral parts.
> Resolved, That such Divisions or integral Parts shall be styled Districts.

This makes it sound as though Paterson was prepared to accept a strong unified central government along the lines of the Virginia Plan if the existing states were eliminated. He may have gotten the idea from his New Jersey colleague Judge David
Brearley, who on June 9 had commented that the only remedy to the dilemma over
representation was "that a map of the U.S. be spread out, that all the existing
boundaries be erased, and that a new partition of the whole be made into 13 equal

parts." According to Yates, Brearley added at this point, "then a government on the present [Virginia Plan] system will be just."

This proposition was never pushed—it was patently unrealistic—but one can appreciate its purpose: it would have separated the men from the boys in the large-state delegations. How attached would the Virginians have been to their reform principles if Virginia were to disappear as a component geographical unit (the largest) for representational purposes? Up to this point, the Virginians had been in the happy position of supporting high ideals with that inner confidence born of knowledge that the "public interest" they endorsed would nourish their private interest. Worse, they had shown little willingness to compromise. Now the delegates from the small states announced that they were unprepared to be offered up as sacrificial victims to a "national interest" which reflected Virginia's parochial ambition. Caustic Charles Pinckney was not far off when he remarked sardonically that "the whole [conflict] comes to this": "Give N. Jersey an equal vote, and she will dismiss her scruples, and concur in the Natl. system." What he rather unfairly did not add was that the Jersey delegates were not free agents who could adhere to their private convictions; they had to take back, sponsor and risk their reputations on the reforms approved by the Convention—and in New Jersey, not in Virginia.

Paterson spoke on Saturday, and one can surmise that over the weekend there was a good deal of consultation, argument, and caucusing among the delegates. One member at least prepared a full-length address: on Monday Alexander Hamilton, previously mute, rose and delivered a six-hour oration. It was a remarkably apolitical speech; the gist of his position was that *both* the Virginia and New Jersey Plans were inadequately centralist, and he detailed a reform program which was reminiscent of the Protectorate under the Cromwellian *Instrument of Government* of 1653. It has been suggested that Hamilton did this in the best political tradition to emphasize the moderate character of the Virginia Plan, to give the cautious delegates something really to worry about; but this interpretation seems somehow too clever. Particularly since the sentiments Hamilton expressed happened to be completely consistent with those he privately—and sometimes publicity—expressed throughout his life. He wanted, to take a striking phrase from a letter to George Washington, a "strong well mounted government"; in essence, the Hamilton Plan contemplated an elected life monarch, virtually free of public control, on the Hobbesian ground that only in this fashion could strength and stability be achieved. The other alternatives, he argued, would put policy-making at the mercy of the passions of the mob; only if the sovereign was beyond the reach of selfish influence would it be possible to have government in the interests of the whole community.

From all accounts, this was a masterful and compelling speech, but (aside from furnishing John Lansing and Luther Martin with ammunition for later use against the Constitution) it made little impact. Hamilton was simply transmitting on a different wavelength from the rest of the delegates; the latter adjourned after his great effort, admired his rhetoric, and then returned to business. It was rather as if they had taken a day off to attend the opera. Hamilton, never a particularly patient man or much of a negotiator, stayed for another ten days and then left, in considerable disgust, for New York. Although he came back to Philadelphia sporadically and attended the last two weeks of the Convention, Hamilton played no part in the laborious task of hammering out the Constitution. His day came later when he led the New York Constitutionalists into the savage imbroglio over ratification—an arena in which his unmatched talent for dirty political infighting may well have won the day. For instance, in the New York Ratifying Convention, Lansing threw back into Hamilton's teeth the sentiments the latter had expressed in his June 18 oration in the Convention. However, having since retreated to the fine defensive positions immortalized in the *The Federalist*, the Colonel flatly denied that he had ever been an enemy of the states, or had believed that conflict between states and nation was inexorable! As Madison's authoritative *Notes* did not appear until 1840, and there had been no press coverage, there was no way to verify his assertions, so in the words of the reporter, "a warm personal altercation between [Lansing and Hamilton] engrossed the remainder of the day [June 28, 1788]."

IV

On Tuesday morning, June 19, the vacation was over. James Madison led off with a long, carefully reasoned speech analyzing the New Jersey Plan which, while intellectually vigorous in its criticisms, was quite conciliatory in mood. "The great difficulty," he observed, "lies in the affair of Representation; and if this could be adjusted, all others would be surmountable." (As events were to demonstrate, this diagnosis was correct.) When he finished, a vote was taken on whether to continue with the Virginia Plan as the nucleus for a new constitution: seven states voted "Yes"; New York, New Jersey, and Delaware voted "No"; and Maryland, whose position often depended on which delegates happened to be on the floor, divided. Paterson, it seems, lost decisively; yet in a fundamental sense he and his allies had achieved their purpose: from that day onward, it could never be forgotten that the state governments loomed ominously in the background and that no verbal incantations could exorcise their power. Moreover, nobody bolted the Convention: Paterson and his colleagues took their defeat in stride and set to work to modify the Virginia Plan, particularly with respect to its provisions on representation in the national legislature. Indeed, they won an immediate rhetorical bonus; when Oliver Ellsworth of Connecticut rose to move that the word "national" be expunged from the Third Virginia Resolution ("Resolved that a *national* Government ought to be established consisting of a *supreme* Legislative, Executive and Judiciary"), Randolph agreed and the motion passed unanimously. The process of compromise had begun.

For the next two weeks, the delegates circled around the problem of legislative representation. The Connecticut delegation appears to have evolved a possible compromise quite early in the debates, but the Virginians and particularly Madison (unaware that he would later be acclaimed as the prophet of "federalism") fought obdurately against providing for equal representation of states in the second chamber. There was a good deal of acrimony and at one point Benjamin Franklin—of all people—proposed the institution of a daily prayer; practical politicians in the gathering, however, were meditating more on the merits of a good committee than on the utility of Divine intervention. On July 2, the ice began to break when through a number of fortuitous events—and one that seems deliberate—the majority against equality of representation was converted into a dead tie. The Convention had reached the stage where it was "ripe" for a solution (presumably all the therapeutic speeches had been made), and the South Carolinians proposed a committee. Madison and James Wilson wanted none of it, but with only Pennsylvania dissenting, the body voted to establish a working party on the problem of representation.

The members of this committee, one from each state, were elected by the delegates—and a very interesting committee it was. Despite the fact that the Virginia Plan had held majority support up to that date, neither Madison nor Randolph was selected (Mason was the Virginian) and Baldwin of Georgia, whose shift in position had resulted in the tie, was chosen. From the composition, it was clear that this was not to be a "fighting" committee: the emphasis in membership was on what might be described as "second-level political entrepreneurs." On the basis of the discussions up to that time, only Luther Martin of Maryland could be described as a "bitter-ender." Admittedly, some divination enters into this sort of analysis, but one does get a sense of the mood of the delegates from these choices—including the interesting selection of Benjamin Franklin, despite his age and intellectual wobbliness, over the brilliant and incisive Wilson or the sharp, polemical Gouverneur Morris, to represent Pennsylvania. His passion for conciliation was more valuable at this juncture than Wilson's logical genius, or Morris's acerbic wit.

There is a common rumor that the framers divided their time between philosophical discussions of government and reading the classics in political theory. Perhaps this is as good a time as any to note that their concerns were highly practical, that they spent little time canvassing abstractions. A number of them had some acquaintance with the history of political theory (probably gained from reading John Adam's monumental compilation *A Defense of the Constitutions of Government,* the first volume of which appeared in 1786), and it was a poor rhetorician indeed who could not cite Locke, Montesquieu, or Harrington *in support* of a desired goal. Yet up to this point in the deliberations, no one had expounded a defense of states' rights or the "separation of powers" on anything resembling a theoretical basis. It should be reiterated that the Madison model had no room either for the states or for the "separation of powers": effectively *all* governmental power was vested in the national legislature. The merits of Montesquieu did not turn up until *The Federalist;* and although a perverse argument could be made that Madison's ideal was truly in the tradition of John Locke's *Second Treatise of Government,* the Locke whom the American rebels treated as an honorary president was a pluralistic defender of vested rights, not of parliamentary supremacy.

It would be tedious to continue a blow-by-blow analysis of the work of the delegates; the critical fight was over representation of the states and once the Connecticut Compromise was adopted on July 17, the Convention was over the hump. Madison, James Wilson, and Gouverneur Morris of New York (who was there representing Pennsylvania!) fought the compromise all the way in a last-ditch effort to get a unitary state with parliamentary supremacy. But their allies deserted them and they demonstrated after their defeat the essential opportunist character of their objections—using "opportunist" here in a nonpejorative sense, to indicate a willingness to swallow their objections and get on with the business. Moreover, once the compromise had carried (by five states to four, with one state divided), its advocates threw themselves vigorously into the job of strengthening the general government's substantive powers—as might have been predicted, indeed, from Paterson's early statements. It nourishes an increased respect for Madison's devotion to the art of politics, to realize that this dogged fighter could sit down six months later and prepare essays for *The Federalist* in contradiction to his basic convictions about the true course the Convention should have taken.

V

Two tricky issues will serve to illustrate the later process of accommodation. The first was the institutional position of the Executive. Madison argued for an executive chosen by the national legislature and on May 29 this had been adopted with a provision that after his seven-year term was concluded, the chief magistrate should not be eligible for reelection. In late July this was reopened and for a week the matter was argued from several different points of view. A good deal of desultory speech-making ensued, but the gist of the problem was the opposition from two sources to election by the legislature. One group felt that the states should have a hand in the process; another small but influential circle urged direct election by the people. There were a number of proposals: election by the people, election by state governors, by electors chosen by state legislatures, by the national legislature (James Wilson, perhaps ironically, proposed at one point that an Electoral College be chosen by lot from the national legislature!), and there was some resemblance to three-dimensional chess in the dispute because of the presence of two other variables, length of tenure and reeligibility. Finally, after opening, reopening, and re-reopening the debate, the thorny problem was consigned to a committee for absolution.

The Brearley Committee on Postponed Matters was a superb aggregation of talent and its compromise on the Executive was a masterpiece of political improvisation. (The Electoral College, its creation, however, had little in its favor as an *institution*—as the delegates well appreciated.) The point of departure for all discussion about the presidency in the Convention was that in immediate terms, the problem was nonexistent; in other words, everybody present knew that under any system devised, George Washington would be President. Thus they were dealing in the future tense and to a body of working politicians the merits of the Brearley proposal were obvious: everybody got a piece of cake. (Or to put it more academically, each viewpoint could leave the Convention and argue to its constituents that it had *really* won the day.) First, the state legislatures had the right to determine the mode of selection of the electors; second, the small states received a bonus in the Electoral College in the form of a guaranteed minimum of three votes while the big states got acceptance of the principle of proportional power; third, if the state legislatures agreed (as six did in the first presidential election), the people could be involved directly in the choice of electors; and finally, if no candidate received a majority in the College, the right of decision passed to the national legislature with each state exercising equal strength. (In the Brearley recommendation, the election went to the Senate, but a motion from the floor substituted the House; this was accepted on the ground that the Senate already had enough authority over the executive in its treaty and appointment powers.)

This compromise was almost too good to be true, and the framers snapped it up with little debate or controversy. No one seemed to think well of the College as an *institution*; indeed, what evidence there is suggests that there was an assumption that once Washington had finished his tenure as President, the electors would cease to produce majorities and the Chief Executive would usually be chosen in the House. George Mason observed casually that the selection would be made in the House nineteen times in twenty and no one seriously disputed this point. The vital aspect of the Electoral College was that it got the Convention over the hurdle and protected everybody's interests. The future was left to cope with the problem of what to do with this Rube Goldberg mechanism.

In short, the framers did not in their wisdom endow the United States with a college of Cardinals—the Electoral College was neither an exercise in applied Platonism nor an experiment in indirect government based on elitist distrust of the masses. It was merely a jerry-rigged improvisation which has subsequently been endowed with a high theoretical content. When an elector from Oklahoma in 1960 refused to cast his vote for Nixon (naming Byrd and Goldwater instead) on the ground that the Founding Fathers intended him to exercise his great independent wisdom, he was indulging in historical fantasy. If one were to indulge in counter-fantasy, he would be tempted to suggest that the Fathers would be startled to find the College still in operation—and perhaps even dismayed at their descendants' lack of judgment or inventiveness.

The second issue on which some substantial practical bargaining took place was slavery. The morality of slavery was, by design, not at issue; but in its other concrete aspects, slavery colored the arguments over taxation, commerce, and representation. The "Three-Fifths Compromise," that three-fifths of the slaves would be counted both for representation and for purposes of direct taxation (which was drawn from the past—it was a formula of Madison's utilized by Congress in 1783 to establish the basis of state contributions to the Confederation treasury), had allayed some Northern fears about Southern overrepresentation (no one then foresaw the trivial role that direct taxation would play in later federal financial policy), but doubts still remained. The Southerners, on the other hand, were afraid that Congressional control over commerce would lead to the exclusion of slaves or to their excessive taxation as imports. Moreover, the Southerners were disturbed over "navigation acts," i.e., tariffs, or special legislation providing, for example, that exports be carried only in American ships; as a section depending upon exports, they wanted protection from the potential voracity of their commercial brethren of the Eastern states. To achieve this end, Mason and others urged that the Constitution include a proviso that navigation and commercial laws should require a two-thirds vote in Congress.

These problems came to a head in late August and, as usual, were handed to a committee in the hope that, in Gouverneur Morris's words, "these things may form a bargain among the Northern and Southern States." The Committee reported its measures of reconciliation on August 25, and on August 29 the package was wrapped up and delivered. What occurred can best be described in George Mason's dour version (he anticipated Calhoun in his conviction that permitting navigation acts to pass by majority vote would put the South in economic bondage to the North—it was mainly on this ground that he refused to sign the Constitution):

> The Constitution as agreed to till a fortnight before the Convention rose was such a one as he would have set his hand and heart to. . . . [Until that time] The 3 New England States were constantly with us in all questions . . . so that it was these three States with the 5 Southern ones against Pennsylvania, Jersey and Delaware. With respect to the importation of slaves, [decision-making] was left to Congress. This disturbed the two Southern-most States who knew the Congress would immediately suppress the importation of slaves. Those two States therefore struck up a bargain with the three New England States. If they would join to admit slaves for some years, the two Southern-most States would join in changing the clause which required the 2/3 of the Legislature in any vote [on navigation acts]. It was done.

On the floor of the Convention there was a virtual love-feast on this happy occasion. Charles Pinckney of South Carolina attempted to overturn the committee's decision, when the compromise was reported to the Convention, by insisting that the South needed protection from the imperialism of the Northern states. But his Southern colleagues were not prepared to rock the boat and General C. C. Pinckney arose to spread oil on the suddenly ruffled waters; he admitted that:

> It was in the true interest of the S[outhern] States to have no regulation of commerce; but considering the loss brought on the commerce of the Eastern States by the Revolution, their liberal conduct towards the views of South Carolina [on the regulation of the slave trade] and the interests the weak Southn. States had in being united with the strong Eastern states, he thought it proper that no fetters should be imposed on the power of making commercial regulations; *and that his constituents, though prejudiced against the Eastern States, would be reconciled to this liberality.* He had himself prejudices against the Eastern States before he came here, but would acknowledge that he had found them as liberal and candid as any men whatever. (Italics added.)

Pierce Butler took the same tack, essentially arguing that he was not too happy about the possible consequences, but that a deal was a deal. Many Southern leaders were later—in the wake of the "Tariff of Abominations"—to rue this day of reconciliation; Calhoun's *Disquisition on Government* was little more than an extension of the argument in the Convention against permitting a Congressional majority to enact navigation acts.

VI

Drawing on their vast collective political experience, utilizing every weapon in the politician's arsenal, looking constantly over their shoulders at their constituents, the delegates put together a Constitution. It was a makeshift affair; some sticky issues (for example, the qualification of voters) they ducked entirely; others they mastered with that ancient instrument of political sagacity, studied ambiguity (for example, citizenship); and some they just overlooked. In this last category, I suspect, fell the matter of the power of the federal courts to determine the constitutionality of acts of Congress. When the judicial article was formulated (Article III of the Constitution), deliberations were still in the stage where the legislature was endowed with broad power under the Randolph formulation, authority which by its own terms was scarcely amenable to judicial review. In essence, courts could hardly determine when "the separate States are incompetent or . . . the harmony of the United States may be interrupted"; the national legislature, as critics pointed out, was free to define its own jurisdiction. Later the definition of legislative authority was changed into the form we know, a series of stipulated powers, *but the delegates never seriously reexamined the jurisdiction of the judiciary under this new limited formulation.* All arguments on the intention of the framers in this matter are thus deductive and *a posteriori*, though some obviously make more sense than others.

The framers were busy and distinguished men, anxious to get back to their families, their positions, and their constituents, not members of the French Academy devoting a lifetime to a dictionary. They were trying to do an important job, and do it in such a fashion that their handiwork would be acceptable to very diverse constituencies. No one was rhapsodic about the final document, but it was a beginning, a move in the right direction, and one they had reason to believe the people would endorse. In addition, since they had modified the impossible amendment provisions of the Articles (the requirement of unanimity which could always be frustrated by "Rogues Island") to one demanding approval by only three-quarters of the states, they seemed confident that gaps in the fabric which experience would reveal could be rewoven without undue difficulty.

So with a neat phrase introduced by Benjamin Franklin (but devised by Gouverneur Morris) which made their decision sound unanimous, and an inspired benediction by the Old Doctor urging doubters to doubt their own infallibility, the Constitution was accepted and signed. Curiously, Edmund Randolph, who had played so vital a role throughout, refused to sign, as did his fellow Virginian George Mason and Elbridge Gerry of Massachusetts. Randolph's behavior was eccentric, to say the least—his excuses for refusing his signature have a factitious ring even at this late date; the best explanation seems to be that he was afraid that the Constitution would prove to be a liability in Virginia politics, where Patrick Henry was burning up the countryside with impassioned denunciations. Presumably, Randolph wanted to check the temper of the populace before he risked his reputation, and perhaps his job, in a fight with both Henry and Richard Henry Lee. Events lend some justification to this speculation: after much temporizing and use of the conditional subjunctive tense, Randolph endorsed ratification in Virginia and ended up getting the best of both worlds.

Madison, despite his reservations about the Constitution, was the campaign manager in ratification. His first task was to get the Congress in New York to light its own funeral pyre by approving the "amendments" to the Articles and sending them on to the state legislatures. Above all, momentum had to be maintained. The anti-Constitutionalists, now thoroughly alarmed and no novices in politics, realized that their best tactic was attrition rather than direct opposition. Thus they settled on a position expressing qualified approval but calling for a second Convention to remedy various defects (the one with the most demagogic appeal was the lack of a Bill of Rights). Madison knew that to accede to this demand would be equivalent to losing the battle, nor would he agree to conditional approval (despite wavering even by Hamilton). This was an all-or-nothing proposition: national salvation or national impotence with no intermediate positions possible. Unable to get Congressional approval, he settled for second best: a unanimous resolution of Congress transmitting the Constitution to the states for whatever action they saw fit to take. The opponents then moved from New York and the Congress, where they had attempted to attach amendments and conditions, to the states for the final battle.

At first the campaign for ratification went beautifully: within eight months after the delegates set their names to the document, eight states had ratified. Only in Massachusetts had the result been close (187–168). Theoretically, a ratification by one more state convention would set the new government in motion, but in fact until Virginia and New York acceded to the new Union, the latter was a fiction. New Hampshire was the next to ratify; Rhode Island was involved in its characteristic political convulsions (the legislature there sent the Constitution out to the towns for decision by popular vote and it got lost among a series of local issues); North Carolina's convention did not meet until July and then postponed a final decision. This is hardly the place for an extensive analysis of the conventions of New York and Virginia. Suffice it to say that the Constitutionalists clearly outmaneuvered their opponents, forced them into impossible political positions, and won both states narrowly. The Virginia Convention could serve as a classic study in effective floor management: Patrick Henry had to be contained, and a reading of the debates discloses a standard two-stage technique. Henry would give a four- or five-hour speech denouncing some section of the Constitution on every conceivable ground (the federal district, he averred at one point, would become a haven for convicts escaping from state authority!); when Henry subsided, "Mr. Lee of Westmoreland" would rise and literally poleax him with sardonic invective (when Henry complained about the militia power, "Lighthorse Harry" really punched below the belt: observing that while the former Governor had been sitting in Richmond during the Revolution, *he* had been out in the trenches with the troops and thus felt better qualified to discuss military affairs). Then the gentlemanly Constitutionalists (Madison, Pendleton, and Marshall) would pick up the matters at issue and examine them in the light of reason.

Indeed, modern Americans who tend to think of James Madison as a rather desiccated character should spend some time with this transcript. Probably Madison put on his most spectacular demonstration of nimble rhetoric in what might be called "The Battle of the Absent Authorities." Patrick Henry in the course of one of his harangues alleged that Jefferson was known to be opposed to Virginia's approving the Constitution. This was clever: Henry hated Jefferson, but was prepared to use any weapon that came to hand. Madison's riposte was superb: First, he said that with all due respect to the great reputation of Jefferson, he was not in the country and therefore could not formulate an adequate judgment; second, no one should utilize the reputation of an outsider—the Virginia Convention was there to think for itself; third, if there were to be recourse to outsiders, the opinions of George Washington should certainly be taken into consideration; and finally, he knew from privileged personal communications from Jefferson that in fact the latter *strongly favored* the Constitution. To devise an assault route into this rhetorical fortress was literally impossible.

VII

The fight was over; all that remained now was to establish the new frame of government in the spirit of its framers. And who were better qualified for this task than the framers themselves? Thus victory for the Constitution meant simultaneous victory for the Constitutionalists; the anti-Constitutionalists either capitulated or vanished into limbo—soon Patrick Henry would be offered a seat on the Supreme Court and Luther Martin would be known as the Federalist "bull-dog." And irony of ironies, Alexander Hamilton and James Madison would shortly accumulate a reputation as the formulators of what is often alleged to be our political theory, the concept of "federalism." Also, on the other side of the ledger, the arguments would soon appear over what the framers "really meant"; while these disputes have assumed the proportions of a big scholarly business in the last century, they began almost before the ink on the Constitution was dry. One of the best early ones featured Hamilton versus Madison on the scope of presidential power, and other framers characteristically assumed positions in this and other disputes on the basis of their political convictions.

Probably our greatest difficulty is that we know so much more about what the framers *should have meant* than they themselves did. We are intimately acquainted with the problems that their Constitution should have been designed to master; in short, we have read the mystery story backwards. If we are to get the right "feel" for their time and their circumstances, we must in Maitland's phrase, "think ourselves back into a twilight." Obviously, no one can pretend completely to escape from the solipsistic web of his own environment, but if the effort is made, it is possible to appreciate the past roughly on its own terms. The first step in this process is to abandon the academic premise that because we can ask a question, there must be an answer.

Thus we can ask what the framers meant when they gave Congress the power to regulate interstate and foreign commerce, and we emerge, reluctantly perhaps, with the reply that they may not have known what they meant, that there may not have been any semantic consensus. The Convention was not a seminar in analytic philosophy or linguistic analysis. Commerce was *commerce*—and if different interpretations of the word arose, later generations could worry about the problem of definition. The delegates were in a hurry to get a new government established; when definitional arguments arose, they characteristically took refuge in ambiguity. If different men voted for the same proposition for varying reasons, that was politics (and still is); if later generations were unsettled by this lack of precision, that would be their problem.

There was a good deal of definitional pluralism with respect to the problems the delegates did discuss, but when we move to the question of extrapolated intentions, we enter the realm of spiritualism. When men in our time, for instance, launch into elaborate talmudic exegesis to demonstrate that federal aid to parochial schools is (or is not) in accord with the intentions of the men who established the Republic and endorsed the Bill of Rights, they are engaging in historical Extra-Sensory Perception. (If one were to join this E.S.P. contingent for a minute, he might suggest that the hard-boiled politicians who wrote the Constitution and Bill of Rights would chuckle scornfully at such an invocation of authority: obviously a politician would chart his course on the intentions of the living, not of the dead, and count the number of Catholics in his constituency.)

The Constitution, then, was not an apotheosis of "constitutionalism," a triumph of architectonic genius; it was a patch-work sewn together under the pressure of both time and events by a group of extremely talented democratic politicians. They refused to attempt the establishment of a strong, centralized sovereignty on the principle of legislative supremacy for the excellent reason that the people would not accept it. They risked their political fortunes by opposing the established doctrines of state sovereignty because they were convinced that the existing system was leading to national impotence and probably foreign domination. For two years, they worked to get a convention established. For over three months, in what must have seemed to the faithful participants an endless process of give-and-take, they reasoned, cajoled, threatened, and bargained amongst themselves. The result was a Constitution which the people, in fact, by democratic processes, did accept, and a new and far better national government was established.

Beginning with the inspired propaganda of Hamilton, Madison, and Jay, the ideological build-up got under way. *The Federalist* had little impact on the ratification of the Constitution, except perhaps in New York, but this volume had enormous influence on the image of the Constitution in the minds of future generations, particularly on historians and political scientists who have an innate fondness for theoretical symmetry. Yet, while the shades of Locke and Montesquieu *may* have been hovering in the background, and the delegates *may* have been unconscious instruments of a transcendent *telos*, the careful observer of the day-to-day work of the Convention finds no overarching principles. The "separation of powers" to him seems to be a by-product of suspicion, and "federalism" he views as a *pis aller*, as the farthest point the delegates felt they could go in the destruction of state power without themselves inviting repudiation.

To conclude, the Constitution was neither a victory for abstract theory nor a great practical success. Well over half a million men had to die on the battlefields of the Civil War before certain constitutional principles could be defined—a baleful consideration which is somehow overlooked in our customary tributes to the farsighted genius of the framers and to the supposed American talent for "constitutionalism." The Constitution was, however, a vivid demonstration of effective democratic political action, and of the forging of a national elite which literally persuaded its countrymen to hoist themselves by their own boot straps. American pro-consuls would be wise not to translate the Constitution into Japanese, or Swahili, or treat it as a work of semi-Divine origin; but when students of comparative politics examine the process of nation-building in countries newly freed from colonial rule, they may find the American experience instructive as a classic example of the potentialities of a democratic elite.

John Roche's article on the framing of the Constitution was written as an attack upon a variety of views that suggested the Constitution was not so much a practical political document as an expression of elitist views based upon political philosophy and economic interests. One such elitist view was that of Charles A. Beard, who published his famous *An Economic Interpretation of the Constitution* in 1913. He suggested that the Constitution was nothing more than the work of an economic elite that was seeking to preserve its property. This elite, according to Beard, consisted of landholders, creditors, merchants, public bondholders, and wealthy lawyers. Beard demonstrated that many of the delegates to the convention fell into one of these categories.

According to Beard's thesis, as the delegates met, the primary concern of most of them was to limit the power of popular majorities and thus protect their own property interests. To Beard, the antimajoritarian attributes that he felt existed in the Constitution were a reflection of the less numerous creditor class attempting to protect itself against incursions by the majority. Specific provisions as well were put into the Constitution with a view toward protecting property, such as the clause prohibiting states from impairing contracts, coining money, or emitting bills of credit. Control over money was placed in the hands of the national government, and in Article VI of the Constitution it was provided that the new government was to guarantee all debts that had been incurred by the national government under the Articles of Confederation.

Ironically, Beard, like Roche, was attempting to dispel the prevailing notions of his time that the Constitution had been formulated by philosopher kings whose wisdom could not be challenged. But while Roche postulates a loosely knit practical political elite, Beard suggests the existence of a cohesive and even conspiratorial economic elite. The limitation on majority rule was an essential component of this economic conspiracy.

The Constitution does contain many provisions that limit majority rule. Beard claimed that the Constitution from initial adoption to final ratification was never supported by the majority of the people. The holding of a constitutional convention in the first place was never submitted to a popular vote, nor was the Constitution that was finally agreed upon ratified by a popular referendum. The selection of delegates to state ratifying conventions was not executed through universal suffrage, but on the basis of the suffrage qualifications that applied in the states and that were within the discretion of state legislatures. The limited suffrage in the states severely restricted popular participation in ratification of the Constitution.

Beard's thesis was startling at the time it was published in 1913. As it came under close examination, it was revealed that the evidence simply did not support Beard's hypothesis. Key leaders of the convention, including Madison, were not substantial property owners. Several important opponents to ratification of the Constitution were the very members of the economic elite that Beard said conspired to thrust the Constitution upon an unknowing public.

Before Beard presented his narrow thesis in 1913, he had published in 1912 *The Supreme Court and the Constitution.* The major theme of the book was that the Supreme Court was intended to have the authority to review acts of Congress under the terms of the original Constitution. At the same time, the book presents Beard's elitist view of the framing of the Constitution in a somewhat broader context than it was presented in *An Economic Interpretation of the Constitution* published a year later. But the earlier work clearly contains the economic theme, as in the passage where Beard states that the framers of the Constitu-

Where in the US?

tion were "anxious above everything else to safeguard the rights of private property against any levelling tendencies on the part of the propertyless masses." The following selection contains Beard's overview of the framing and adoption of the Constitution and highlights his economic theme and his belief in the antimajoritarian attributes of the Constitution.

3

FRAMING THE CONSTITUTION

Charles A. Beard

As Blackstone[1] shows by happy illustration the reason and spirit of a law are to be understood only by an inquiry into the circumstances of its enactment. The underlying purposes of the Constitution [of the United States], therefore, are to be revealed only by a study of the conditions and events which led to its formation and adoption.

At the outset it must be remembered that there were two great parties at the time of the adoption of the Constitution—one laying emphasis on strength and efficiency in government and the other on its popular aspects. Quite naturally the men who led in stirring up the revolt against Great Britain and in keeping the fighting temper of the Revolutionists at the proper heat were the boldest and most radical thinkers—men like Samuel Adams, Thomas Paine, Patrick Henry, and Thomas Jefferson. They were not, generally speaking, men of large property interests or of much practical business experience. In a time of disorder, they could consistently lay more stress upon personal liberty than upon social control; and they pushed to the extreme limits those doctrines of individual rights which had been evolved in England during the struggles of the small landed proprietors and commercial classes against royal prerogative, and which corresponded to the economic conditions prevailing in America at the close of the eighteenth century. They associated strong government with monarchy, and came to believe that the best political system was one which governed least. A majority of the radicals viewed all government, especially if highly centralized, as a species of evil, tolerable only because necessary and always to be kept down to an irreducible minimum by a jealous vigilance.

Jefferson put the doctrine in concrete form when he declared that he preferred newspapers without government to government without newspapers. The Declaration of Independence, the first state Constitutions, and the Articles of Confederation bore the impress of this philosophy. In their anxiety to defend the individual

---

[1]*Compiler's Note:* Blackstone, Sir William (1723–1780). Distinguished commentator on the laws of England, judge, and teacher.

against all federal interference and to preserve to the states a large sphere of local autonomy, these Revolutionists had set up a system too weak to accomplish the accepted objects of government; namely, national defense, the protection of property, and the advancement of commerce. They were not unaware of the character of their handiwork, but they believed with Jefferson that "man was a rational animal endowed by nature with rights and with an innate sense of justice and that he could be restrained from wrong and protected in right by moderate powers confided to persons of his own choice." Occasional riots and disorders, they held, were preferable to too much government.

The new American political system based on these doctrines had scarcely gone into effect before it began to incur opposition from many sources. The close of the Revolutionary struggle removed the prime cause for radical agitation and brought a new group of thinkers into prominence. When independence had been gained, the practical work to be done was the maintenance of social order, the payment of the public debt, the provision of a sound financial system, and the establishment of conditions favorable to the development of the economic resources of the new country. The men who were principally concerned in this work of peaceful enterprise were not the philosophers, but men of business and property and the holders of public securities. For the most part they had had no quarrel with the system of class rule and the strong centralization of government which existed in England. It was on the question of policy, not of governmental structure, that they had broken with the British authorities. By no means all of them, in fact, had even resisted the policy of the mother country, for within the ranks of the conservatives were large numbers of Loyalists who had remained in America, and, as was to have been expected, cherished a bitter feeling against the Revolutionists, especially the radical section which had been boldest in denouncing the English system root and branch. In other words, after the heat and excitement of the War of Independence were over and the new government, state and national, was tested by the ordinary experiences of traders, financiers, and manufacturers, it was found inadequate, and these groups accordingly grew more and more determined to reconstruct the political system in such a fashion as to make it subserve their permanent interests.

Under the state constitutions and the Articles of Confederation established during the Revolution, every powerful economic class in the nation suffered either immediate losses or from impediments placed in the way of the development of their enterprises. The holders of the securities of the Confederate government did not receive the interest on their loans. Those who owned Western lands or looked with longing eyes upon the rich opportunities for speculation there chaffed at the weakness of the government and its delays in establishing order on the frontiers. Traders and commercial men found their plans for commerce on a national scale impeded by local interference with interstate commerce. The currency of the states and the nation was hopelessly muddled. Creditors everywhere were angry about the depreciated paper money which the agrarians had made and were attempting to force upon those from whom they had borrowed specie. In short, it was a war between business and populism. Under the Articles of Confederation populism had a free hand, for majorities in the state legislatures were omnipotent. Anyone who reads the economic history of the time will see why the solid conservative interests of the country were weary of talk about the "rights of the people" and bent upon establishing firm guarantees for the rights of property.

The Congress of the Confederation was not long in discovering the true character of the futile authority which the Articles had conferred upon it. The necessity for new sources of revenue became apparent even while the struggle for independence was yet undecided, and, in 1781, Congress carried a resolution to the effect that it should be authorized to lay a duty of five percent on certain goods. This moderate proposition was defeated because Rhode Island rejected it on the grounds that "she regarded it the most precious jewel of sovereignty that no state shall be called upon to open its purse but by the authority of the state and by her own officers." Two years later Congress prepared another amendment to the Articles providing for certain import duties, the receipts from which, collected by state officers, were to be applied to the payment of the public debt; but three years after the introduction of the measure, four states, including New York, still held out against its ratification, and the project was allowed to drop. At last, in 1786, Congress in a resolution declared that the requisitions for the last eight years had been so irregular in their operation, so uncertain in their collection, and so evidently unproductive, that a reliance on them in the future would be no less dishonorable to the understandings of those who entertained it than it would be dangerous to the welfare and peace of the Union. Congress, thereupon, solemnly added that it had become its duty "to declare most explicitly that the crisis had arrived when the people of the United States, by whose will and for whose benefit the federal government was instituted, must decide whether they will support their rank as a nation by maintaining the public faith at home and abroad, or whether for the want of a timely exertion in establishing a general review and thereby giving strength to the Confederacy, they will hazard not only the existence of the Union but those great and invaluable privileges for which they have so arduously and so honorably contended."

In fact, the Articles of Confederation had hardly gone into effect before the leading citizens also began to feel that the powers of Congress were wholly inadequate. In 1780, even before their adoption, Alexander Hamilton proposed a general convention to frame a new constitution, and from that time forward he labored with remarkable zeal and wisdom to extend and popularize the idea of a strong national government. Two years later, the Assembly of the State of New York recommended a convention to revise the Articles and increase the power of Congress. In 1783, Washington, in a circular letter to the governors, urged that it was indispensable to the happiness of the individual states that there should be lodged somewhere a supreme power to regulate and govern the general concerns of the confederation. Shortly afterward (1785), Governor Bowdoin, of Massachusetts, suggested to his state legislature the advisability of calling a national assembly to settle upon and define the powers of Congress; and the legislature resolved that the government under the Articles of Confederation was inadequate and should be reformed; but the resolution was never laid before Congress.

In January, 1786, Virginia invited all the other states to send delegates to a convention at Annapolis to consider the question of duties on imports and commerce in general. When this convention assembled in 1786, delegates from only five states were present, and they were disheartened at the limitations on their powers and the lack of interest the other states had shown in the project. With characteristic fore-sight, however, Alexander Hamilton seized the occasion to secure the adoption of a recommendation advising the states to choose representatives for another conven-tion to meet in Philadelphia the following year "to consider the Articles of Confed-eration and to propose such changes therein as might render them adequate to the exigencies of the union." This recommendation was cautiously worded, for Hamil-ton did not want to raise any unnecessary alarm. He doubtless believed that a com-plete revolution in the old system was desirable, but he knew that, in the existing state of popular temper, it was not expedient to announce his complete program. Ac-cordingly no general reconstruction of the political system was suggested; the Arti-cles of Confederation were merely to be "revised"; and the amendments were to be approved by the state legislatures as provided by that instrument.

The proposal of the Annapolis convention was transmitted to the state legisla-tures and laid before Congress. Congress thereupon resolved in February, 1787, that a convention should be held for the sole and express purpose of revising the Arti-cles of Confederation and reporting to itself and the legislatures of the several states such alterations and provisions as would when agreed to by Congress and confirmed by the states render the federal constitution adequate to the exigencies of govern-ment and the preservation of the union.

In pursuance of this call, delegates to the new convention were chosen by the legislatures of the states or by the governors in conformity to authority conferred by the legislative assemblies.[2] The delegates were given instructions of a general nature by their respective states, none of which, apparently, contemplated any very far-reaching changes. In fact, almost all of them expressly limited their representatives to a mere revision of the Articles of Confederation. For example, Connecticut au-thorized her delegates to represent and confer for the purpose mentioned in the res-olution of Congress and to discuss such measures "agreeable to the general principles of Republican government" as they should think proper to render the Union adequate. Delaware, however, went so far as to provide that none of the pro-posed alterations should extend to the fifth part of the Articles of Confederation guaranteeing that each state should be entitled to one vote.

It was a truly remarkable assembly of men that gathered in Philadelphia on May 14, 1787, to undertake the work of reconstructing the American system of government. It is not merely patriotic pride that compels one to assert that never in the history of assemblies has there been a convention of men richer in political ex-perience and in practical knowledge, or endowed with a profounder insight into the springs of human action and the intimate essence of government. It is indeed an as-tounding fact that at one time so many men skilled in statecraft could be found on the very frontiers of civilization among a population numbering about four million whites. It is no less a cause for admiration that their instrument of government

---

[2]Rhode Island alone was unrepresented. In all, sixty-two delegates were appointed by the states; fifty-five of these attended sometime during the sessions; but only thirty-nine signed the finished document.

should have survived the trials and crises of a century that saw the wreck of more than a score of paper constitutions.

All the members had had a practical training in politics. Washington, as commander-in-chief of the Revolutionary forces, had learned well the lessons and problems of war, and mastered successfully the no less difficult problems of administration. The two Morrises had distinguished themselves in grappling with financial questions as trying and perplexing as any which statesmen had ever been compelled to face. Seven of the delegates had gained political wisdom as governors of their native states; and no less than twenty-eight had served in Congress either during the Revolution or under the Articles of Confederation. These were men trained in the law, versed in finance, skilled in administration, and learned in the political philosophy of their own and all earlier times. Moreover, they were men destined to continue public service under the government which they had met to construct—Presidents, Vice-Presidents, heads of departments, Justices of the Supreme Court were in that imposing body. . . .

As Woodrow Wilson had concisely put it, the framers of the Constitution represented "a strong and intelligent class possessed of unity and informed by a conscious solidarity of interests."[3] . . .

The makers of the federal Constitution represented the solid, conservative, commercial and financial interests of the country—not the interests which denounced and proscribed judges in Rhode Island, New Jersey, and North Carolina, and stoned their houses in New York. The conservative interests, made desperate by the imbecilities of the Confederation and harried by state legislatures, roused themselves from the lethargy, drew together in a mighty effort to establish a government that would be strong enough to pay the national debt, regulate interstate and foreign commerce, provide for national defense, prevent fluctuations in the currency created by paper emissions, and control the propensities of legislative majorities to attack private rights. . . . The radicals, however, like Patrick Henry, Jefferson, and Samuel Adams, were conspicuous by their absence from the convention.[4] . . .

[The makers of the Constitution were convened] to frame a government which would meet the practical issues that had arisen under the Articles of Confederation. The objections they entertained to direct popular government, and they were undoubtedly many, were based upon their experience with popular assemblies during the immediately preceding years. With many of the plain lessons of history before them, they naturally feared that the rights and privileges of the minority would be insecure if the principle of majority rule was definitely adopted and provisions made for its exercise. Furthermore, it will be remembered that up to that time the right of all men, as men, to share in the government had never been recognized in practice.

---

[3]Woodrow Wilson, *Division and Reunion* (New York: Longmans, Green, & Co., 1893), p. 12.

[4]*Compiler's Note:* The contents of this paragraph have been taken from positions on pp. 75–76 and 88 of the original text of *The Supreme Court and the Constitution* and placed here to emphasize the economic theme.

Everywhere in Europe the government was in the hands of a ruling monarch or at best a ruling class; everywhere the mass of the people had been regarded principally as an arms-bearing and tax-paying multitude, uneducated, and with little hope or capacity for advancement. Two years were to elapse after the meeting of the grave assembly at Philadelphia before the transformation of the Estates General into the National Convention in France opened the floodgates of revolutionary ideas on human rights before whose rising tide old landmarks of government are still being submerged. It is small wonder, therefore, that, under the circumstances, many of the members of that august body held popular government in slight esteem and took the people into consideration only as far as it was imperative "to inspire them with the necessary confidence," as Mr. Gerry frankly put it.[5]

Indeed, every page of the laconic record of the proceedings of the convention preserved to posterity by Mr. Madison shows conclusively that the members of that assembly were not seeking to realize any fine notions about democracy and equality, but were striving with all the resources of political wisdom at their command to set up a system of government that would be stable and efficient, safeguarded on one hand against the possibilities of despotism and on the other against the onslaught of majorities. In the mind of Mr. Gerry, the evils they had experienced flowed "from the excess of democracy," and he confessed that while he was still republican, he "had been taught by experience the danger of the levelling spirit."[6] Mr. Randolph in offering to the consideration of the convention his plan of government, observed "that the general object was to provide a cure for the evils under which the United States labored; that, in tracing these evils to their origin, every man had found it in the turbulence and follies of democracy; that some check therefore was to be sought for against this tendency of our governments; and that a good Senate seemed most likely to answer the purpose."[7] Mr. Hamilton, in advocating a life term for Senators, urged that "all communities divide themselves into the few and the many. The first are rich and well born and the other the mass of the people who seldom judge or determine right."

Gouverneur Morris wanted to check the "precipitancy, changeableness, and excess" of the representatives of the people by the ability and virtue of men "of great and established property—aristocracy; men who from pride will support consistency and permanency. . . . Such an aristocratic body will keep down the turbulence of democracy." While these extreme doctrines were somewhat counter-balanced by the democratic principles of Mr. Wilson who urged that "the government ought to possess, not only first, the force, but second the mind or sense of the people at large," Madison doubtless summed up in a brief sentence the general opinion of the convention when he said that to secure private rights against majority factions, and at the same time to preserve the spirit and form of popular government, was the great object to which their inquiries had been directed.[8]

---

[5]Jonathan Elliot, *The Debates in the Several State Conventions on the Adoption of the Federal Constitution* (Washington, D.C.: The Editor, 1827–1830), vol. v, p. 160.

[6]*Ibid.*, vol. v, p. 136.

[7]*Ibid.*, vol. v, p. 138.

[8]*The Federalist*, No. 10.

When?

They were anxious above everything else to safeguard the rights of private property against any leveling tendencies on the part of the propertyless masses. Gouverneur Morris, in speaking on the problem of apportioning representatives, correctly stated the sound historical fact when he declared: "Life and liberty were generally said to be of more value than property. An accurate view of the matter would, nevertheless, prove that property was the main object of society. . . . If property, then, was the main object of government, certainly it ought to be one measure of the influence due to those who were to be affected by the government."[9] Mr. King also agreed that "property was the primary object of society."[10] and Mr. Madison warned the convention that in framing a system which they wished to last for ages they must not lose sight of the changes which the ages would produce in the forms and distribution of property. In advocating a long term in order to give independence and firmness to the Senate, he described these impending changes: "An increase of population will of necessity increase the proportion of those who will labor under all the hardships of life and secretly sigh for a more equal distribution of its blessings. These may in time outnumber those who are placed above the feelings of indigence. According to the equal laws of suffrage, the power will slide into the hands of the former. No agrarian attempts have yet been made in this country, but symptoms of a levelling spirit, as we have understood have sufficiently appeared, in a certain quarter, to give notice of the future danger."[11] And again, in support of the argument for a property qualification on voters, Madison urged: "In future times, a great majority of the people will not only be without landed, but any other sort of property. These will either combine, under the influence of their common situation,—in which case the rights of property and the public liberty will not be secure in their hands,—or what is more probable, they will become the tools of opulence and ambition; in which case there will be equal danger on another side."[12] Various projects for setting up class rule by the establishment of property qualifications for voters and officers were advanced in the convention, but they were defeated. . . .

His viewpoint through Madison

> The absence of such property qualifications is certainly not due to any belief in Jefferson's free-and-equal doctrine. It is due rather to the fact that the members of the convention could not agree on the nature and amount of the qualifications. Naturally a landed qualification was suggested, but for obvious reasons it was rejected. Although it was satisfactory to the landed gentry of the South, it did not suit the financial, commercial, and manufacturing gentry of the North. If it was high, the latter would be excluded; if it was low it would let in the populistic farmers who had already made so much trouble in the state legislatures with paper-money schemes and other devices for "relieving agriculture." One of the chief reasons for calling the convention and framing the Constitution was to promote commerce and industry and to protect personal property against the "depredations" of Jefferson's noble freeholders. On the other hand a personal-property qualification, high

---

[9]Elliot's *Debates, op. cit.,* vol. v, p. 279.
[10]*Ibid.,* p. 280.
[11]*Ibid.,* p. 243.
[12]*Ibid.,* p. 387.

enough to please merchant princes like Robert Morris and Nathaniel Gorham would shut out the Southern planters. Again, an alternative of land or personal property, high enough to afford safeguards to large interests, would doubtless bring about the rejection of the whole Constitution by the troublemaking farmers who had to pass upon the question of ratification.[13]. . .

Nevertheless, by the system of checks and balances placed in the government, the convention safeguarded the interests of property against attacks by majorities. The House of Representatives, Mr. Hamilton pointed out, "was so formed as to render it particularly the guardian of the poorer orders of citizens,"[14] while the Senate was to preserve the rights of property and the interests of the minority against the demands of the majority.[15] In the tenth number of *The Federalist*, Mr. Madison argued in a philosophic vein in support of the proposition that it was necessary to base the political system on the actual conditions of "natural inequality." Uniformity of interests throughout the state, he contended, was impossible on account of the diversity in the faculties of men, from which the rights of property originated; the protection of these faculties was the first object of government; from the protection of different and unequal faculties of acquiring property the possession of different degrees and kinds of property immediately resulted; from the influence of these on the sentiments and views of the respective proprietors ensued a division of society into different interests and parties; the unequal distribution of wealth inevitably led to a clash of interests in which the majority was liable to carry out its policies at the expense of the minority; hence, he added, in concluding this splendid piece of logic, "the majority, having such coexistent passion or interest, must be rendered by their number and local situation unable to concert and carry into effect schemes of oppression"; and in his opinion it was the great merit of the newly framed Constitution that it secured the rights of the minority against "the superior force of an interested and overbearing majority."

This very system of checks and balances, which is undeniably the essential element of the Constitution, is built upon the doctrine that the popular branch of the government cannot be allowed full sway, and least of all in the enactment of laws touching the rights of property. The exclusion of the direct popular vote in the election of the President; the creation, again by indirect election, of a Senate which the framers hoped would represent the wealth and conservative interests of the country;[16] and the establishment of an independent judiciary appointed by the President with the concurrence of the Senate—all these devices bear witness to the fact that the underlying purpose of the Constitution was not the establishment of popular government by means of parliamentary majorities.

---

[13]*Compiler's Note:* This single paragraph from "Whom Does Congress Represent?" *Harper's Magazine*, Jan. 1930, pp. 144–152, has been inserted here because of its value in amplifying the passages from *The Supreme Court and the Constitution*. Reprinting from this article by Beard has been done with the permission of *Harper's Magazine*.

[14]Elliot's Debates, *op. cit.*, vol. v, p. 244.

[15]*Ibid.*, vol. v, p. 203.

[16]*Compiler's Note:* Popular election of senators was achieved in 1913 through the Seventeenth Amendment to the constitution.

Page after page of *The Federalist* is directed to that portion of the electorate which was disgusted with the "mutability of the public councils." Writing on the presidential veto Hamilton says: "The propensity of the legislative department to intrude upon the rights, and absorb the powers, of other departments has already been suggested and repeated. . . . It may perhaps be said that the power of preventing bad laws included the power of preventing good ones; and may be used to the one purpose as well as the other. But this objection will have little weight with those who can properly estimate the mischiefs of that inconstancy and mutability in the laws which form the greater blemish in the character and genius of our governments. They will consider every institution calculated to restrain the excess of law-making and to keep things in the same state in which they happen to be at any given period, as more likely to do good than harm; because it is favorable to greater stability in the system of legislation. The injury which may be possibly done by defeating a few good laws will be amply compensated by the advantage of preventing a number of bad ones."

When the framers of the Constitution had completed the remarkable instrument which was to establish a national government capable of discharging effectively certain great functions and checking the propensities of popular legislatures to attack the rights of private property, a formidable task remained before them—the task of securing the adoption of the new frame of government by states torn with popular dissensions. They knew very well that the state legislatures which had been so negligent in paying their quotas [of money] under the Articles [of Confederation] and which had been so jealous of their rights, would probably stick at ratifying such a national instrument of government. Accordingly they cast aside that clause in the Articles requiring amendments to be ratified by the legislatures of all the states; and advised that the new Constitution should be ratified by conventions in the several states composed of delegates chosen by the voters.[17] They furthermore declared—and this is a fundamental matter—that when the conventions of nine states had ratified the Constitution the new government should go into effect so far as those states were concerned. The chief reason for restoring to ratifications by conventions is laid down by Hamilton in the twenty-second number of *The Federalist:* "It has not a little contributed to the infirmities of the existing federal system that it never had a ratification by the people. Resting on no better foundation than the consent of the several legislatures, it has been exposed to frequent and intricate questions concerning the validity of its powers; and has in some instances given birth to the enormous doctrine of a right of legislative repeal. Owing its ratification to the law of a state, it has been contended that the same authority might repeal the law by which it was ratified. However gross a heresy it may be to maintain that a party to a compact has a right to revoke that compact, the doctrine itself has respectable advocates. The possibility of a question of this nature proves the necessity of laying the foundations of our national government deeper than in the mere sanction of delegated authority. The fabric of American empire ought to rest on the

---

[17]*Compiler's Note:* The original text, p. 75, comments: "It was largely because the framers of the Constitution knew the temper and class bias of the state legislatures that they arranged that the new Constitution should be ratified by conventions."

solid basis of the consent of the people. The streams of national power ought to flow immediately from that pure original foundation of all legitimate authority."

Of course, the convention did not resort to the revolutionary policy of transmitting the Constitution directly to the conventions of the several states. It merely laid the finished instrument before the Confederate Congress with the suggestion that it should be submitted to "a convention of delegates chosen in each state by the people thereof, under the recommendation of its legislature, for their assent and ratification; and each convention assenting thereto and ratifying the same should give notice thereof to the United States in Congress assembled." The convention went on to suggest that when nine states had ratified the Constitution, the Confederate Congress should extinguish itself by making provision for the elections necessary to put the new government into effect. . . .

After the new Constitution was published and transmitted to the states, there began a long and bitter fight over ratification. A veritable flood of pamphlet literature descended upon the country, and a collection of these pamphlets by Hamilton, Madison, and Jay, brought together under the title of *The Federalist*—though clearly a piece of campaign literature—has remained a permanent part of the contemporary sources on the Constitution and has been regarded by many lawyers as a commentary second in value only to the decisions of the Supreme Court. Within a year the champions of the new government found themselves victorious, for on June 21, 1788, the ninth state, New Hampshire, ratified the Constitution, and accordingly the new government might go into effect as between the agreeing states. Within a few weeks, the nationalist party in Virginia and New York succeeded in winning these two states, and in spite of the fact that North Carolina and Rhode Island had not yet ratified the Constitution, Congress determined to put the instrument into effect in accordance with the recommendations of the convention. Elections for the new government were held; the date March 4, 1789, was fixed for the formal establishment of the new system; Congress secured a quorum on April 6; and on April 30 Washington was inaugurated at the Federal Hall in Wall Street, New York.

─────────────────── ✑ ───────────────────

Charles A. Beard suggests that there is a dichotomy between the values of the Constitution and those of the Declaration of Independence, between Jefferson and his followers on the one hand, and Madison and Hamilton on the other. He suggests that Jefferson and the Revolutionists supported political equality and individual freedom and opposed a strong central government. The spirit of the Revolution, argues Beard, spawned the Articles of Confederation, which purposely created a weak and ineffective government. The Revolutionists, in general, were not men of property and thus did not believe that a strong central government was necessary to protect their interests. By contrast, the framers of the Constitution reflected the spirit of Alexander Hamilton, who ironically was not a man of substantial property himself, but who advocated an energetic and dominant national government. Hamilton, like many of the framers, was a strong proponent of governmental protection of property interests.

Limitation of Governmental Power
and of Majority Rule

The most accurate and helpful way to characterize our political system is to call it a constitutional democracy. The term implies a system in which the government is regulated by laws that control and limit the exercise of political power. In a constitutional democracy people participate in government on a limited basis. A distinction should be made between an unlimited democratic government and a constitutional democracy. In the former, the people govern through the operation of a principle such as majority rule without legal restraint; in the latter, majority rule is curtailed and checked through various legal devices. A constitutional system is one in which the formal authority of government is restrained. The checks upon government in a constitutional society customarily include a division or fragmentation of authority that prevents government from controlling all sectors of human life.

Hamilton noted in *Federalist 1*, "It seems to have been reserved to the people of this country, to decide by their conduct and example, the important question, whether societies of men are really capable or not, of establishing good government from reflection and choice, or whether they are forever destined to depend, for their political constitutions, on accident and force." The framers of our Constitution attempted to structure the government in such a way that it would meet the needs and aspirations of the people and at the same time check the arbitrary exercise of political power. The doctrine of the separation of powers was designed to prevent any one group from gaining control of the national governmental apparatus. The selections reprinted here from *The Federalist*, which was written between October 1787 and August 1788, outline the theory and mechanism of the separation of powers.

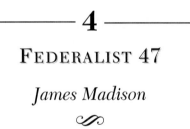

4

FEDERALIST 47

James Madison

I proceed to examine the particular structure of this government, and the distribution of this mass of power among its constituent parts.

One of the principal objections inculcated by the more respectable adversaries to the constitution, is its supposed violation of the political maxim, that the legislative, executive, and judiciary departments, ought to be separate and distinct. In the structure of the federal government, no regard, it is said, seems to have been paid to this essential precaution in favor of liberty. The several departments of power are distributed and blended in such a manner, as at once to destroy all symmetry and beauty of form; and to expose some of the essential parts of the edifice to the danger of being crushed by the disproportionate weight of other parts.

No political truth is certainly of great intrinsic value, or is stamped with the authority of more enlightened patrons of liberty, than that on which the objection is founded. The accumulation of all powers, legislative, executive, and judiciary, in the same hands, whether of one, a few, or many, and whether hereditary, self-appointed, or elective, may justly be pronounced the very definition of tyranny. Were the federal constitution, therefore, really chargeable with this accumulation of power, or with a mixture of powers, having a dangerous tendency to such an accumulation, no further arguments would be necessary to inspire a universal reprobation of the system. I persuade myself, however, that it will be made apparent to every one, that the charge cannot be supported, and that the maxim on which it relies has been totally misconceived and misapplied.

The oracle who is always consulted and cited on this subject, is the celebrated Montesquieu. If he be not the author of this invaluable precept in the science of politics, he has the merit of at least displaying and recommending it most effectually to the attention of mankind. . . .

From . . . facts, by which Montesquieu was guided, it may clearly be inferred, that in saying, "there can be no liberty, where the legislative and executive powers are united in the same person, or body of magistrates"; or "if the power of judging, be not separated from the legislative and executive powers," he did not mean that these departments ought to have no *partial agency* in, or no *control* over, the acts of each other. His meaning . . . can amount to no more than this, that where the *whole* power of one department is exercised by the same hands which possess the *whole* power of another department, the fundamental principles of a free constitution are subverted. . . .

If we look into the constitutions of the several states, we find, that notwithstanding the emphatical, and, in some instances, the unqualified terms in which this axiom has been laid down, there is not a single instance in which the several departments of power have been kept absolutely separate and distinct. . . .

The constitution of Massachusetts has observed a sufficient, though less pointed caution, in expressing this fundamental article of liberty. It declares, "that the legislative department shall never exercise the executive and judicial powers, or either of them: the executive shall never exercise the legislative and judicial powers, or either of them: the judicial shall never exercise the legislative and executive powers, or either of them." This declaration corresponds precisely with the doctrine of Montesquieu. . . . It goes no farther than to prohibit any one of the entire departments from exercising the powers of another department. In the very constitution to which it is prefixed, a partial mixture of powers has been admitted. . . .

Federalist 48

. . . I shall undertake in the next place to show, that unless these departments be so far connected and blended, as to give to each a constitutional control over the others, the degree of separation which the maxim requires, as essential to a free government, can never in practice be duly maintained.

It is agreed on all sides, that the powers properly belonging to one of the departments ought not to be directly and completely administered by either of the other departments. It is equally evident, that neither of them ought to possess, directly or indirectly, an overruling influence over the others in the administration of their respective powers. It will not be denied, that power is of an encroaching nature, and that it ought to be effectually restrained from passing the limits assigned to it. After discriminating, therefore, in theory, the several classes of power, as they may in their nature be legislative, executive, or judiciary; the next, and most difficult task, is to provide some practical security for each, against the invasion of the others. What this security ought to be, is the great problem to be solved.

Will it be sufficient to mark, with precision, the boundaries of these departments, in the constitution of the government, and to trust to these parchment barriers against the encroaching spirit of power? This is the security which appears to have been principally relied on by the compilers of most American constitutions. But experience assures us, that the efficacy of the provision has been greatly overrated; and that some more adequate defense is indispensably necessary for the more feeble, against the more powerful members of the government. The legislative department is everywhere extending the sphere of its activity, and drawing all power into its impetuous vortex. . . .

In a government where numerous and extensive prerogatives are placed in the hands of an hereditary monarch, the executive department is very justly regarded as the source of danger, and watched with all the jealousy which a zeal for liberty ought to inspire. In a democracy, where a multitude of people exercise in person the legislative functions, and are continually exposed, by their incapacity for regular deliberation and concerted measures, to the ambitious intrigues of their executive magistrates, tyranny may well be apprehended on some favorable emergency, to start up in the same quarter. But in a representative republic, where the executive magistracy is carefully limited, both in the extent and the duration of its power; and where the legislative is exercised by an assembly, which is inspired by a supposed influence over the people, with an intrepid confidence in its own strength; which is sufficiently numerous to feel all the passions which actuate a multitude; yet not so numerous as to be incapable of pursuing the objects of its passions, by means which reason prescribes; it is against the enterprising ambition of this department, that the people ought to indulge all their jealousy and exhaust all their precautions.

The legislative department derives a superiority in our governments from other circumstances. Its constitutional powers being at once more extensive, and less susceptible of precise limits, it can, with the greater facility, mask, under complicated and indirect measures, the encroachment which it makes on the coordinate departments. It is not infrequently a question of real nicety in legislative bodies, whether the operation of a particular measure will, or will not, extend beyond the legislative sphere. On the other side, the executive power being restrained within a narrower compass, and being more simple in its nature; and the judiciary being described by landmarks, still less uncertain, projects of usurpation by either of these departments would immediately betray and defeat themselves. Nor is this all: as the legislative department alone has access to the pockets of the people, and has in some constitutions full discretion, and in all a prevailing influence over the pecuniary rewards of those who fill the other departments; a dependence is thus created in the latter, which gives still greater facility to encroachment of the former. . . .

Federalist 51

To what expedient then shall we finally resort, for maintaining in practice the necessary partition of power among the several departments, as laid down in the constitution? The only answer that can be given is, that as all these exterior provisions are found to be inadequate, the defect must be supplied, by so contriving the interior structure of the government, as that its several constituent parts may, by their mutual relations, be the means of keeping each other in their proper places. . . .

In order to lay a due foundation for that separate and distinct exercise of the different powers of government, which, to a certain extent, is admitted on all hands to be essential to the preservation of liberty, it is evident that each department should have a will of its own; and consequently should be so constituted, that the members of each should have as little agency as possible in the appointment of the members of the others. . . .

It is equally evident, that the members of each department should be as little dependent as possible on those of the others, for the emoluments annexed to their offices. Were the executive magistrate, or the judges, not independent of the legislature in this particular, their independence in every other, would be merely nominal.

But the great security against a gradual concentration of the several powers in the same department, consists in giving to those who administer each department, the necessary constitutional means, and personal motives, to resist encroachments of the others. The provision for defense must in this, as in all other cases, be made commensurate to the danger of attack. Ambition must be made to counteract ambition. The interest of the man must be connected with the constitutional rights of the place. It may be a reflection on human nature, that such devices should be necessary to control the abuses of government. But what is government itself, but the greatest of all reflections on human nature? If men were angels, no government would be necessary. If angels were to govern men, neither external nor internal controls on government would be necessary. In framing a government, which is to be administered by men over men, the great difficulty lies in this: you must first enable the government to control the governed; and in the next place, oblige it to control itself. A dependence on the people is, no doubt, the primary control on the government; but experience has taught mankind the necessity of auxiliary precautions.

This policy of supplying by opposite and rival interests, the defect of better motives, might be traced through the whole system of human affairs, private as well as public. We see it particularly displayed in all the subordinate distributions of power; where the constant aim is, to divide and arrange the several offices in such a manner, as that each may be a check on the other; that the private interest of every individual, may be a sentinel over the public rights. These inventions of prudence cannot be less requisite to the distribution of the supreme powers of the state.

But it is not possible to give each department an equal power of self-defense. In republican government, the legislative authority necessarily predominates. The remedy for this inconvenience is, to divide the legislature into different branches; and to render them by different modes of election, and different principles of action, as little connected with each other, as the nature of their common functions, and their common dependence on the society will admit. It may even be necessary to guard against dangerous encroachments, by still further precautions. As the weight of the legislative authority requires that it should be thus divided, the weakness of the executive may require, on the other hand, that it should be fortified. An absolute negative on the legislature, appears, at first view, to be the natural defense with which the executive magistrate should be armed. But perhaps it would be neither altogether safe, nor alone sufficient. On ordinary occasions, it might not be exerted with the requisite firmness; and on extraordinary occasions, it might be perfidiously abused. May not this defect of an absolute negative be supplied by some qualified connection between this weaker department, and the weaker branch of the stronger department, by which the latter may be led to support the constitutional rights of the former, without being too much detached from the rights of its own department?

Interpreting the Constitution

The preceding selections have offered contrasting views on the framing, nature, and purpose of the Constitution. As background, John Locke's political philosophy expressed in his *Second Treatise, Of Civil Government* (1690) supported the political beliefs of many eighteenth-century Americans in government as a social contract between rulers and ruled to protect the natural rights of citizens to life, liberty, and, very importantly, property.

To John Roche the Constitution was a practical political document reflecting compromises among state delegations with contrasting political and economic interests among and advocates of strong national power and proponents of states' rights. Charles Beard saw the Constitution as a reflection of the interests of property owners and creditors who feared that the rule of the debtor majority would inflate currency, cancel debts, and deprive creditors of their rightful property. James Madison's selections from *The Federalist* suggest a mistrust of government, a wary view of both political leaders and the people, and an emphasis upon the need for governmental checks and balances to prevent the arbitrary exercise of political power. Madison also distrusted what he termed "faction," by which he meant political parties or special-interest groups, which he considered intrinsically to be opposed to the national interest (see *Federalist 10*, Chapter 4).

The separation of powers among the executive, legislative, and judicial branches is an outstanding characteristic of our constitutional system. A uniquely American separation of powers incorporated an *independent* executive, pitting the president against Congress and requiring their cooperation to make the government work. The separation of powers was a constitutional filter through which political demands had to flow before they could be translated into public policies.

James Madison clearly saw the separation-of-powers system, incorporating checks and balances among the branches of government, as a process that would help to prevent arbitrary and excessive governmental actions. The three branches of the government, but particularly the president and Congress, would have independent political bases, motivations, and powers that would both enable and encourage them to compete with each other.

While Madison saw the separation of powers as an important limit upon arbitrary government, Alexander Hamilton represented a different point of view. He viewed the independent presidency, a central component of the separation of powers, as an office that could make the national government energetic and effective. "Energy in the executive is the definition of good government," wrote Hamilton in *Federalist 70,* and the constitutional separation of powers would provide that energy rather than simply making the president of a co-equal branch subject to congressional whims or Supreme Court constraints.

History has, at different times, borne out the views of both Madison and Hamilton regarding the effect of the separation of powers. During times of relative political tranquility the president and Congress have often been stalemated in a deadlock of democracy. But Hamilton's imperial presidency has taken charge in times of crisis, such as during the Civil War, Franklin D. Roosevelt's New Deal in the 1930s, and the Second World War in the 1940s.

The Constitution is a frugal, bare-bones document that has, almost miraculously and with very few amendments, remained in place for over 200 years. It was not, however, a perfect governmental plan, for the nation had to fight a bloody Civil War to establish the principle of *e pluribus unum* once and for all.

While reverence for the Constitution is an important strand in our political history, it has not prevented sharp political controversy over how the Constitution should be interpreted. The framers themselves did not see eye to eye on many constitutional provisions, interpreting them in different ways. To buttress their positions political opponents have often cited the Constitution, claiming that it supports their side. For example, during George Washington's presidency Thomas Jefferson argued that the Constitution should be strictly interpreted to limit Congress to its explicit Article I powers, which did not allow establishment of a national bank. Secretary of the Treasury Alexander Hamilton took the "loose" constructionist approach in support of the bank. Hamilton argued that while Article I of the Constitution did not explicitly give Congress the authority to create a national bank, Congress could imply such authority under its enumerated power to regulate commerce among the states. Both men were using the same Constitution to support their contrasting political positions.

The historic debate over whether or not the Constitution should be read "strictly" or "loosely" has metamorphosed into another and related debate over the importance of "original intent" in constitutional interpretation. Strict constructionists argue in selection 64 that the Supreme Court has often erred in not following the original intent of the framers. The authors of the following selection, however, claim that the framers of the Constitution knew they had forged a flexible document that future generations would be able to adapt to their values and needs.

5

HOW NOT TO READ THE CONSTITUTION

Laurence H. Tribe and Michael C. Dorf

From its very creation, the Constitution was perceived as a document that sought to strike a delicate balance between, on the one hand, governmental power to accomplish the great ends of civil society and, on the other, individual liberty. As James Madison put it in *The Federalist Papers*, "[i]f men were angels, no government would be necessary. If angels were to govern men, neither external nor internal controls on government would be necessary. In framing a government which is to be administered by men over men, the great difficulty lies in this: you must first enable the government to control the governed; and in the next place oblige it to control itself. A dependence on the people is, no doubt, the primary control on the government; but experience has taught mankind the necessity of auxiliary precautions." Although Madison initially opposed the inclusion of a Bill of Rights in the Constitution, as his correspondence with Thomas Jefferson shows, he became convinced that judicially enforceable rights are among the necessary "auxiliary precautions" against tyranny.

In the Constitution of the United States, men like Madison bequeathed to subsequent generations a framework for balancing liberty against power. However, it is only a framework; it is not a blueprint. Its Eighth Amendment prohibits the infliction of "cruel and unusual punishment," but gives no examples of permissible or impermissible punishments. Article IV requires that "[t]he United States shall guarantee to every State in this Union a Republican Form of Government," but attempts no definition of republican government. The Fourteenth Amendment proscribes state abridgments of the "privileges or immunities of citizens of the United States," but contains no catalogue of privileges or immunities.

How then ought we to go about the task of finding concrete commandments in the Constitution's majestically vague admonitions? If there is genuine controversy over how the Constitution should be read, certainly it cannot be because the disputants have access to different bodies of information. After all, they all have exactly the same text in front of them, and that text has exactly one history, however complex, however multifaceted. But of course different people believe different things about how that history bears on the enterprise of constitutional interpretation. . . .

Perhaps the disputants agree on what *counts* as "the Constitution," but simply approach the same body of textual and historical materials with different visions, different premises, and different convictions. But *that* assumption raises an obvious question: How are those visions, premises, and convictions relevant to how this brief text ought to be read? Is reading the text just a *pretext* for expressing the reader's vision in the august, almost holy terms of constitutional law? Is the Constitution simply a mirror in which one sees what one wants to see?. . .

Reading the Constitution or Writing One?

The belief that we must look beyond the specific views of the Framers to apply the Constitution to contemporary problems is not necessarily a "liberal" position. Indeed, not even the most "conservative" justices today believe in a jurisprudence of original intent that looks only to the Framers' unenacted views about particular institutions or practices. Consider the following statement made by a Supreme Court justice in 1976:

> The framers of the Constitution wisely spoke in general language and left to succeeding generations the task of applying that language to the unceasingly changing environment in which they would live. . . . Where the framers . . . used general language, they [gave] latitude to those who would later interpret the instrument to make that language applicable to cases that the framers might not have foreseen.

The author was not Justice William Brennan or Justice Thurgood Marshall, but then-Justice William Rehnquist. Or consider the statement by Justice White, joined by Justice Rehnquist in a 1986 opinion for the Court: "As [our] prior cases clearly show, . . . this Court does not subscribe to the simplistic view that constitutional interpretation can possibly be limited to the 'plain meaning' of the Constitution's text or to the subjective intention of the Framers. The Constitution," wrote Justice White, "is not a deed setting forth the precise metes and bounds of its subject matter; rather, it is a document announcing fundamental principles in value-laden terms that leave ample scope for the exercise of normative judgment by those charged with interpreting and applying it."

So the "conservatives" on the Court, no less than the "liberals," talk as though *reading* the Constitution requires much more than passively discovering a fixed meaning planted there generations ago. Those who wrote the document, and those who voted to ratify it, were undoubtedly projecting their wishes into an indefinite future. If writing is wish-*projection*, is reading merely an exercise in wish-*fulfillment*—not fulfillment of the wishes of the *authors*, who couldn't have begun to foresee the way things would unfold, but fulfillment of the wishes of *readers*, who perhaps use the language of the Constitution simply as a mirror to dress up their own political or moral preferences in the hallowed language of our most fundamental document? Justice Joseph Story feared that that might happen when he wrote in 1845: "How easily men satisfy themselves that the Constitution is exactly what they wish it to be."

To the extent that this is so, it is indefensible. The authority of the Constitution, its claim to obedience and the force that we permit it to exercise in our law and over our lives, would lose all legitimacy if it really were only a mirror for the readers' ideals and ideas. Just as the original intent of the Framers—even if it could be captured in the laboratory, bottled, and carefully inspected under a microscope—will not yield a satisfactory determinate interpretation of the Constitution, so too at the other end of the spectrum we must also reject as completely unsatisfactory the idea of an empty, or an infinitely malleable, Constitution. We must find principles of interpretation that can anchor the Constitution in some more secure, determinate, and external reality. But that is no small task.

One basic problem is that the text itself leaves so much room for the imagination. Simply consider the preamble, which speaks of furthering such concepts as "Justice" and the "Blessings of Liberty." It is not hard, in terms of concepts that fluid and that plastic, to make a linguistically plausible argument in support of more than a few surely incorrect conclusions. Perhaps a rule could be imposed that it is improper to refer to the preamble in constitutional argument on the theory that it is only an introduction, a preface, and not part of the Constitution *as enacted*. But even if one were to invent such a rule, which has no apparent grounding in the Constitution itself, it is hardly news that the remainder of the document is filled with lively language about "liberty," "due process of law," "unreasonable searches and seizures," and so forth—words that, although not *infinitely* malleable, are capable of supporting meanings at opposite ends of virtually any legal, political, or ideological spectrum.

It is therefore not surprising that readers on both the right and left of the American political center have invoked the Constitution as authority for strikingly divergent conclusions about the legitimacy of existing institutions and practices, and that neither wing has found it difficult to cite chapter and verse in support of its "reading" of our fundamental law. As is true of other areas of law, the materials of constitutional law require construction, leave room for argument over meaning, and tempt the reader to import his or her vision of the just society into the meaning of the materials being considered. . . .

When all of the Constitution's supposed unities are exposed to scrutiny, criticisms of its inconsistency with various readers' sweeping visions of what it ought to be become considerably less impressive. Not all need be reducible to a single theme. Inconsistency—even inconsistency with democracy—is hardly earth-shattering. Listen to Walt Whitman: "Do I contradict myself? Very well then, I contradict myself." "I am large, I contain multitudes," the Constitution replies.

CHAPTER 2

❦

FEDERALISM

The United States government utilizes a "federal" form to secure certain political and economic objectives. This chapter identifies both the traditional and modern goals of American federalism from the writings of important theorists who have examined general and specific problems in national-state relationships. The validity of federalism is also analyzed.

Constitutional Background: National Versus State Power

No subject attracted greater attention or was more carefully analyzed at the time of the framing of the Constitution than federalism. *The Federalist* devoted a great deal of space to proving the advantages of a federal form of government relative to a confederacy, since the Constitution was going to take some of the power traditionally within the jurisdiction of state governments and give it to a newly constituted national government.

The victory of the nationalists at the Constitutional Convention of 1787, which resulted in sovereign states giving up a significant portion of their authority to a new national government, is remarkable by any standard of measurement. Today, when the creation of the Union is largely taken for granted, it is difficult to appreciate the environment of the Revolutionary period, a time when the states wanted at all costs to protect their newly won freedom from an oppressive British government. The Constitution of 1787 was accepted as a matter of necessity as much as desire.

It was against the background of the Articles of Confederation that Hamilton wrote in *The Federalist* about the advantages of the new "federal" system that would be created by the Constitution. The Articles of Confederation had been submitted to the states in 1777 and were finally ratified by all of the states in 1781, Maryland being the only holdout after 1779. The "League of Friendship" that had been created among the states by the Articles had proved inadequate to meeting even the minimum needs of union. The government of the Articles of Confederation had many weaknesses, for it was essentially a league of sov-

ereign states, joined together more in accordance with principles of international agreement than in accordance with the rules of nation states. Most of the provisions of the Articles of Confederation concerned the foreign relations of the new government and matters
of national defense and security. For this purpose a minimum number of powers were
granted to the national government, which, however, had no executive or judicial authority
and was therefore incapable of independent enforcement. National actions were dependent upon the states for enforcement, and under Article 2 "each state retains its sovereignty, freedom and independence, and every power, jurisdiction and right, which is not by
this confederation expressly delegated to the United States, in Congress assembled." The
paucity of authority delegated to the central government under the Articles left the sovereignty of the states intact. And the national government was totally dependent upon the
states as agents of enforcement of what little authority it could exercise. The government of
the Articles of Confederation then, without an executive or judicial branch, and without
such crucial authority as the power to tax and regulate commerce, required a drastic overhaul if it was to become a national government in fact as well as in name.

In the following selections from *The Federalist,* Alexander Hamilton argues the advantages of the new federal Constitution, and at the same time attempts to alleviate the fears of
his opponents that the new government would intrude upon and possibly eventually destroy the sovereignty of the states. The national government, he wrote, must be able to act
directly upon the citizens of the states to regulate the common concerns of the nation. He
found the system of the Articles of Confederation too weak, allowing state evasion of national power. Augmenting the authority of the national government would not destroy state
sovereignty, because of the inherent strength of the individual states (which at the time
Hamilton wrote were singly and collectively far more powerful than any proposed national
government). Moreover, there would be no incentives for ambitious politicians to look to
the states to realize their goals, for the scope of national power was sufficient to occupy
temptations for political aggrandizement.

6

FEDERALIST 16

Alexander Hamilton

⌒⌒

The . . . death of the confederacy . . . is what we now seem to be on the point
of experiencing, if the federal system be not speedily renovated in a more substantial form. It is not probable, considering the genius of this country, that the comply-
ing states would often be inclined to support the authority of the union, by
engaging in a war against the non-complying states. They would always be more

ready to pursue the milder course of putting themselves upon an equal footing with the delinquent members, by an imitation of their example. And the guilt of all would thus become the security of all. Our past experience has exhibited the operation of this spirit in its full light. There would, in fact, be an insuperable difficulty in ascertaining when force would with propriety be employed. In the article of pecuniary contribution, which would be the most usual source of delinquency, it would often be impossible to decide whether it had proceeded from disinclination, or inability. The pretense of the latter would always be at hand. And the case must be very flagrant in which its fallacy could be detected with sufficient certainty to justify the harsh expedient of compulsion. It is easy to see that this problem alone, as often as it should occur, would open a wide field to the majority that happened to prevail in the national council, for the exercise of factious views, of partiality, and of oppression.

It seems to require no pains to prove that the states ought not to prefer a national constitution, which could only be kept in motion by the instrumentality of a large army, continually on foot to execute the ordinary requisitions or decrees of the government. And yet this is the plain alternative involved by those who wish to deny it the power of extending its operations to individuals. Such a scheme, if practicable at all, would instantly degenerate into a military despotism; but it will be found in every light impracticable. The resources of the union would not be equal to the maintenance of any army considerable enough to confine the larger states within the limits of their duty; nor would the means ever be furnished of forming such an army in the first instance. Whoever considers the populousness and strength of several of these states singly at the present juncture, and looks forward to what they will become, even at the distance of half a century, will at once dismiss as idle and visionary any scheme which aims at regulating their movements by laws, to operate upon them in their collective capacities, and to be executed by a coercion applicable to them in the same capacities. A project of this kind is little less romantic than the monster-taming spirit attributed to the fabulous heroes and demigods of antiquity. . . . .

The result of these observations to an intelligent mind must clearly be this, that if it be possible at any rate to construct a federal government capable of regulating the common concerns, and preserving the general tranquillity, it must be founded, as to the objects committed to its case, upon the reverse of the principle contended for by the opponents of the proposed constitution [i.e., a confederacy]. It must carry its agency to the persons of the citizens. It must stand in need of no intermediate legislations; but must itself be empowered to employ the arm of the ordinary magistrate to execute its own resolutions. The majesty of the national authority must be manifested through the medium of the courts of justice. The government of the union, like that of each state, must be able to address itself immediately to the hopes and fears of individuals; and to attract to its support, those passions which have the strongest influence upon the human heart. It must, in short, possess all the means, and have a right to resort to all the methods, of executing the powers with which it is entrusted, that are possessed and exercised by the governments of the particular states.

To this reasoning it may perhaps be objected, that if any state should be disaffected to the authority of the union, it could at any time obstruct the execution of its laws, and bring the matter to the same issue of force, with the necessity of which the opposite scheme is reproached.

The plausibility of this objection will vanish the moment we advert to the essential difference between a mere noncompliance and a direct and active resistance. If the interposition of the state legislatures be necessary to give effect to a measure of the union [as in a confederacy], they have only not to act, or to act evasively, and the measure is defeated. This neglect of duty may be disguised under affected but unsubstantial provisions so as not to appear, and of course not to excite any alarm in the people for the safety of the constitution. The state leaders may even make a merit of their surreptitious invasions of it, on the ground of some temporary convenience, exemption, or advantage.

But if the execution of the laws of the national government should not require the intervention of the state legislatures; if they were to pass into immediate operation upon the citizens themselves, the particular governments could not interrupt their progress without an open and violent exertion of an unconstitutional power. No omission, nor evasions, would answer the end. They would be obliged to act, and in such a manner, as would leave no doubt that they had encroached on the national rights. An experiment of this nature would always be hazardous in the face of a constitution in any degree competent to its own defense, and of the people enlightened enough to distinguish between a legal exercise and an illegal usurpation of authority. The success of it would require not merely a factious majority in the legislature, but the concurrence of the courts of justice, and of the body of the people. . . .

FEDERALIST 17

An objection, of a nature different from that which has been stated and answered in my last address, may, perhaps, be urged against the principle of legislation for the individual citizens of America. It may be said, that it would tend to render the government of the union too powerful, and to enable it to absorb those residuary authorities, which it might be judged proper to leave with the states for local purposes. Allowing the utmost latitude to the love of power, which any reasonable man can require, I confess I am at a loss to discover what temptation the persons entrusted with the administration of the general government could ever feel to divest the states of the authorities of that description. The regulation of the mere domestic police of a state, appears to me to hold out slender allurements to ambition. Commerce, finance, negotiation, and war, seem to comprehend all the objects which have charms for minds governed by that passion; and all the powers necessary to those objects, ought, in the first instance, to be lodged in the national depository. The administration of private justice between the citizens of the same state; the supervision of agriculture, and of other concerns of a similar nature; all those things, in short, which are proper to be provided for by local legislation, can never be desirable cares of a general jurisdiction. It is therefore improbable, that there should exist a disposition in the federal councils, to usurp the powers with which they are connected; because the attempt to exercise them would be as troublesome as it would be nugatory; and the possession of them, for that reason, would contribute nothing to the dignity, to the importance, or to the splendor, of the national government.

But let it be admitted, for argument's sake, that mere wantonness, and lust of domination, would be sufficient to beget that disposition; still, it may be safely affirmed, that the sense of the constituent body of the national representatives, or in other words, of the people of the several states, would control the indulgence of so extravagant an appetite. It will always be far more easy for the state governments to encroach upon the national authorities, than for the national government to encroach upon the state authorities. The proof of this proposition turns upon the greater degree of influence which the state governments, if they administer their affairs with uprightness and prudence, will generally possess over the people; a circumstance which at the same time teaches us, that there is an inherent and intrinsic weakness in all federal constitutions; and that too much pain cannot be taken in their organization, to give them all the force which is compatible with the principles of liberty.

The superiority of influence in favor of the particular governments, would result partly from the diffusive construction of the national government; but chiefly from the nature of the objects to which the attention of the state administrations would be directed.

It is a known fact in human nature, that its affections are commonly weak in proportion to the distance of diffusiveness of the object. Upon the same principle that a man is more attached to his family than to his neighborhood, to his neighborhood than to the community at large, the people of each state would be apt to feel a strong bias towards their local governments, than towards the government of the union, unless the force of that principle should be destroyed by a much better administration of the latter.

This strong propensity of the human heart, would find powerful auxiliaries in the objects of state regulation.

The variety of more minute interests, which will necessarily fall under the superintendence of the local administrations, and which will form so many rivulets of influence, running through every part of the society, cannot be particularized, without involving a detail too tedious and uninteresting to compensate for the instruction it might afford.

There is one transcendent advantage belonging to the province of the state governments, which alone suffices to place the matter in a clear and satisfactory light—I mean the ordinary administration of criminal and civil justice. This, of all others, is the most powerful, most universal and most attractive source of popular obedience and attachment. It is this, which, being the immediate and visible guardian of life and property; having its benefits and its terrors in constant activity before the public eye; regulating all those personal interests, and familiar concerns, to which the sensibility of individuals is more immediately awake; contributes, more than any other circumstance, to impress upon the minds of the people affection, esteem, and reverence towards the government. This great cement of society, which will diffuse itself almost wholly through the channels of the particular governments, independent of all other causes of influence, would insure them so decided an empire over their respective citizens, as to render them at all times a complete counterpoise, and not infrequently dangerous rivals to the power of the union.

In *Federalist 39*, James Madison stated that the new Constitution was both federal and national. He attempted to answer arguments that the Constitution destroyed the confederacy of sovereign states and replaced it with a national government. In answering this argument Madison used the term federal as it was used by the objectors to the Constitution he was attempting to answer. They essentially used federal and confederacy interchangeably, each term referring to a system requiring agreement among the states before certain actions could be taken. Because agreement was required among the states for ratification, for example, Madison referred to the establishment of the Constitution as a federal and not a national act. Madison suggested that the character of the House of Representatives, which derives its powers from the people, was national rather than federal. Conversely, the Senate, representing the states equally, was federal, not national. With regard to the powers of the national government, Madison claimed that in operation they are national because they allow the national government to act directly upon the people, but in extent they are federal because they are limited, the states having agreed to delegate only a certain number of powers to the national government. A truly national government would not be limited in the scope of its powers.

7

FEDERALIST 39

James Madison

The last paper having concluded the observations which were meant to introduce a candid survey of the plan of government reported by the convention, we now proceed to the execution of that part of our undertaking.

The first question that offers itself is whether the general form and aspect of the government be strictly republican. It is evident that no other form would be reconcilable with the genius of the people of America; with the fundamental principles of the Revolution; or with that honorable determination which animates every votary of freedom to rest all our political experiments on the capacity of mankind for self-government. If the plan of the convention, therefore, be found to depart from the republican character, its advocates must abandon it as no longer defensible.

What, then, are the distinctive characters of the republican form? Were an answer to this question to be sought, not by recurring to principles but in the application of the term by political writers to the constitutions of different States, no satisfactory one would ever be found. Holland, in which no particle of the supreme authority is derived from the people, has passed almost universally under the denomination of a republic. The same title has been bestowed on Venice, where absolute power over the great body of the people is exercised in the most absolute manner by a small body of hereditary nobles. Poland, which is a mixture of aristocracy and of monarchy in their worst forms, has been dignified with the same appellation. The government of England, which has one republican branch only, combined with an hereditary aristocracy and monarchy, has with equal impropriety been frequently placed on the list of republics. These examples, which are nearly as dissimilar to each other as to a genuine republic, show the extreme inaccuracy with which the term has been used in political disquisitions.

If we resort for a criterion to the different principles on which different forms of government are established, we may define a republic to be, or at least may bestow the name on, a government which derives all its powers directly or indirectly from the great body of the people, and is administered by persons holding their offices during pleasure for a limited period, or during good behavior. It is essential to such a government that it be derived from the great body of the society, not from an inconsiderable proportion or a favored class of it; otherwise a handful of tyrannical nobles, exercising their oppressions by a delegation of their powers, might aspire to the rank of republicans and claim for their government the honorable title of republic. It is sufficient for such a government that the persons administering it be appointed, either directly or indirectly, by the people; and that they hold their appointments by either of the tenures just specified; otherwise every government in the United States, as well as every other popular government that has been or can be well organized or well executed, would be degraded from the republican character. According to the constitution of every State in the Union, some or other of the officers of government are appointed indirectly only by the people. According to most of them, the chief magistrate himself is so appointed. And according to one, this mode of appointment is extended to one of the co-ordinate branches of the legislature. According to all the constitutions, also, the tenure of the highest offices is extended to a definite period, and in many instances, both within the legislative and executive departments, to a period of years. According to the provisions of most of the constitutions, again, as well as according to the most respectable and received opinions on the subject, the members of the judiciary department are to retain their offices by the firm tenure of good behavior.

On comparing the Constitution planned by the convention with the standard here fixed, we perceived at once that it is, in the most rigid sense, conformable to it. The House of Representatives, like that of one branch at least of all the State legislatures, is elected immediately by the great body of the people. The Senate, like the present Congress and the Senate of Maryland, derives its appointment indirectly from the people. The President is indirectly derived from the choice of the people, according to the example in most of the States. Even the judges, with all other officers of the Union, will, as in the several States, be the choice, though a remote choice, of the people themselves. The duration of the appointments is equally conformable to the republican standard and to the model of State constitutions. The House of Representatives is periodically elective, as in all the States; and for the period of two years, as in the State of South Carolina. The Senate is elective for the period of six years, which is but one year more than the period of the Senate of Maryland, and but two more than that of the Senators of New York and Virginia. The President is to continue in office for the period of four years; as in New York and Delaware the chief magistrate is elected for three years, and in South Carolina for two years. In the other States the election is annual. In several of the States, however, no explicit provision is made for the impeachment of the chief magistrate. And in Delaware and Virginia he is not impeachable till out of office. The President of the United States is impeachable at any time during his continuance in office. The tenure by which the judges are to hold their places is, as it unquestionably ought to be, that of good behavior. The tenure of the ministerial offices generally will be a subject of legal regulation, conformable to the reason of the case and the example of the State constitutions.

Could any further proof be required of the republican complexion of this system, the most decisive one might be found in its absolute prohibition of titles of nobility, both under the federal and the State governments; and in its express guaranty of the republican form to each of the latter.

"But it was not sufficient," say the adversaries of the proposed Constitution, "for the convention to adhere to the republican form. They ought with equal care to have preserved the federal form, which regards the Union as a Confederacy of sovereign states; instead of which they have framed a national government, which regards the Union as a consolidation of the States." And it is asked by what authority this bold and radical innovation was undertaken. The handle which has been made of this objection requires that it should be examined with some precision.

Without inquiring into the accuracy of the distinction on which the objection is founded, it will be necessary to a just estimate of its force, first, to ascertain the real character of the government in question; secondly, to inquire how far the convention were authorized to propose such a government; and thirdly, how far the duty they owed to their country could supply any defect of regular authority.

First.—In order to ascertain the real character of the government, it may be considered in relation to the foundation on which it is to be established; to the sources from which its ordinary powers are to be drawn; to the operation of those powers; to the extent of them; and to the authority by which future changes in the government are to be introduced.

On examining the first relation, it appears, on one hand, that the Constitution is to be founded on the assent and ratification of the people of America, given by deputies elected for the special purpose; but, on the other, that this assent and ratification is to be given by the people, not as individuals composing one entire nation, but as composing the distinct and independent States to which they respectively belong. It is to be the assent and ratification of the several States, derived from the supreme authority in each State—the authority of the people themselves. The act, therefore, establishing the Constitution will not be a national but a federal act.

That it will be a federal and not a national act, as these terms are understood by the objectors—the act of the people, as forming so many independent States, not as forming one aggregate nation—is obvious from this single consideration: that it is to result neither from the decision of a majority of the people of the Union, nor from that of a majority of the States. It must result from the unanimous assent of the several States that are parties to it, differing not otherwise from their ordinary assent than in its being expressed, not by the legislative authority, but by that of the people themselves. Were the people regarded in this transaction as forming one nation, the will of the majority of the whole people of the United States would bind the minority, in the same manner as the majority in each State must bind the minority; and the will of the majority must be determined either by a comparison of the individual votes, or by considering the will of the majority of the States as evidence of the will of a majority of the people of the United States. Neither of these rules has been adopted. Each State, in ratifying the Constitution, is considered as a sovereign body independent of all others, and only to be bound by its own voluntary act. In this relation, then, the new Constitution will, if established, be a federal and not a national constitution.

The next relation is to the sources from which the ordinary powers of government are to be derived. The House of Representatives will derive its powers from the people of America; and the people will be represented in the same proportion and on the same principle as they are in the legislature of a particular State. So far the government is national, not federal. The Senate, on the other hand, will derive its powers from the States as political and coequal societies; and these will be represented on the principle of equality in the Senate, as they now are in the existing Congress. So far the government is federal, not national. The executive power will be derived from a very compound source. The immediate election of the President is to be made by the States in their political characters. The votes allotted to them are in a compound ratio, which considers them partly as distinct and coequal societies, partly as unequal members of the same society. The eventual election, again, is to be made by that branch of the legislature which consists of the national representatives; but in this particular act they are to be thrown into the form of individual delegations from so many distinct and coequal bodies politic. From this aspect of the government it appears to be of a mixed character, presenting at least as many federal as national features.

The difference between a federal and national government, as it relates to the operation of the government, is by the adversaries of the plan of the convention supposed to consist in this, that in the former the powers operate on the political bodies composing the confederacy in their political capacities; in the latter, on the individual citizens composing the nation in their individual capacities. On trying the Constitution by this criterion, it falls under the national not the federal character; though perhaps not so completely as has been understood. In several cases, and particularly in the trial of controversies to which States may be parties, they must be viewed and proceeded against in their collective and political capacities only. But the operation of the government on the people in their individual capacities, in its ordinary and most essential proceedings, will, in the sense of its opponents, on the whole, designate it, in this relation, a national government.

But if the government be national with regard to the operation of its powers, it changes its aspect again when we contemplate it in relation to the extent of its powers. The idea of a national government involves in it not only an authority over the individual citizens, but an indefinite supremacy over all persons and things, so far as they are objects of lawful government. Among a people consolidated into one nation, this supremacy is completely vested in the national legislature. Among communities united for particular purposes, it is vested partly in the general and partly in the municipal legislatures. In the former case, all local authorities are subordinate to the supreme; and may be controlled, directed, and abolished by it at pleasure. In the latter, the local or municipal authorities form distinct and independent portions of the supremacy, no more subject, within their respective spheres, to the general authority than the general authority is subject to them, within its own sphere. In this relation, then, the proposed government cannot be deemed a national one; since its jurisdiction extends to certain enumerated objects only, and leaves to the several States a residuary and inviolable sovereignty over all other objects. It is true that in controversies relating to the boundary between the two jurisdictions, the tribunal which is ultimately to decide is to be established under the general government. But this does not change the principle of the case. The decision is to be impartially made, according to the rules of the Constitution; and all the usual and most effectual precautions are taken to secure this impartiality. Some such tribunal is clearly essential to prevent an appeal to the sword and a dissolution of the compact; and that it ought to be established under the general rather than under the local governments, or, to speak more properly, that it could be safely established under the first alone, is a position not likely to be combated.

If we try the Constitution by its last relation to the authority by which amendments are to be made, we find it neither wholly national nor wholly federal. Were it wholly national, the supreme and ultimate authority would reside in the majority of the people of the Union; and this authority would be competent at all times, like that of a majority of every national society to alter or abolish its established government. Were it wholly federal, on the other hand, the concurrence of each State in the Union would be essential to every alteration that would be binding on all. The mode provided by the plan of the convention is not founded on either of these principles. In requiring more than a majority, and particularly in computing the proportion by States, not by citizens, it departs from the national and advances towards the federal character; in rendering the concurrence of less than the whole number of States sufficient, it loses again the federal and partakes of the national character.

The proposed Constitution, therefore, even when tested by the rules laid down by its antagonists, is, in strictness, neither a national nor a federal Constitution, but a composition of both. In its foundation it is federal, not national; in the sources from which the ordinary powers of the government are drawn, it is partly federal and partly national; in the operation of these powers, it is national, not federal; in the extent of them, again, it is federal, not national; and, finally in the authoritative mode of introducing amendments, it is neither wholly federal nor wholly national.

PUBLIUS

In *The Federalist,* Alexander Hamilton and James Madison were careful to point out the advantages of the federal form of government that would be established by the Constitution, both over the government that had existed under the Articles of Confederation and in general terms. Because many state political leaders were highly suspicious of the national government that would be created by the new Constitution, much of the efforts of Hamilton and Madison were directed toward allaying their fears. Above all, they both stated, the energy of the national government would never be sufficient to coerce the states into giving up any portion of their sovereignty. Moreover, Hamilton stated in *Federalist 17* that there would be no incentive for national politicians to take away the reserved powers of the states. The sphere of national power, although limited, was considered entirely adequate to absorb even the most ambitious politicians. And James Madison, in *Federalist 39,* was careful to point out that the jurisdiction of the national government extended only to certain enumerated objects, implying that the residual sovereignty of the states was in fact greater than the sovereignty of the national government.

Alexis de Tocqueville, an aristocratic French observer of the American political and social scene in the early 1830s, acknowledged his debt to the writers of *The Federalist* in helping him to understand American government. Many of the sanguine views of Hamilton and Madison about the prospects for the new Constitution were echoed in Tocqueville's analysis of American institutions forty years later.

Tocqueville had set out for the United States in 1831, with his friend Gustave de Beaumont, ostensibly to examine the American prison system with a view toward prison reform in France. Tocqueville was a French judicial officer, who after the July Revolution of 1830 became disenchanted with the new government of Louis Philippe, and, in a broader context, with the continual turmoil that he saw in French political institutions. While the investigation of prisons served as a ready excuse for a leave of absence from governmental duties, Tocqueville and Beaumont's real interest was in studying American society and government. It was their feeling that democracy was probably the wave of the future and that whatever lessons could be learned from the American experiment would undoubtedly be a useful guide to the future of European society.

Tocqueville was in the United States for only nine months, from May 1831 until February 1832, but during this time he traveled over most of the country east of the Mississippi, staying long enough in various places to gain wide knowledge of local customs and institutions. Most of Tocqueville's observations about the United States were objectively optimistic about the future of democracy, yet his most hopeful expectations were not always realized. In particular, after leaving the United States, he became concerned with the possibility of what he called the "tyranny of the majority," which he wrote would be an inevitable consequence of egalitarian tendencies in democratic societies such as the United States. The framers of the Constitution, too, were worried about unbridled majority rule in government, and felt that governmental tyranny by the majority would be curtailed by such institutional devices as the separation of powers, checks and balances, and federalism, the latter being a division of authority between the national government and the states. While the framers of the Constitution felt that the possibility of the tyranny of the majority was primarily a governmental problem, Tocqueville saw it as a societal dilemma, produced by the egalitarian ethic. Therefore, to Tocqueville, constitutional devices by themselves would not be sufficient to control the inevitable tendency toward majority despotism in an egalitarian society.

Tocqueville discussed the characteristics of federalism as he saw it in operation in 1831. In his discussion Tocqueville uses the terms confederation and federalism interchangeably. To him, the American federal system was one type of confederation. This is important to note because Hamilton, in his discussion of federalism in *The Federalist,* spoke of federalism in the new Constitution as replacing the "confederacy," by which he meant the government that existed under the Articles of Confederation. Most American writers on politics distinguish federalism and confederacy in the same way that Hamilton did, essentially by identifying federalism with the system of the Constitution, and a confederacy with the system of the Articles of Confederation. Under this more common definition of federalism, a federal system is one in which the national government has authority that is separate and distinct from that of the constituent states, an authority that operates directly upon the citizens of the states rather than upon the states as entities. Dual sovereignty is a characteristic of American federalism, whereas under the Articles of Confederation the national government had no authority distinct from the states, and it could not operate without their consent.

Tocqueville examined the broad social and political forces operating in society, referred to historical and comparative experience, and analyzed constitutional forms and institutional characteristics. Tocqueville recognized that while the theory of federalism may be clear, it is very difficult to apply it without some further clarification. This has certainly been true of the American federal system. As Tocqueville noted: "The sovereignty of the union is so involved in that of the states that it is impossible to distinguish its boundaries at the first glance. The whole structure of the government is artificial and conventional, and it would be ill adapted to a people which has not been long accustomed to conduct its own affairs, or to one in which the science of politics has not descended to the humblest classes of society. I have never been more struck by the good sense and the practical judgment of the Americans than in the manner in which they elude the numberless difficulties resulting from their federal constitution." Tocqueville implied that after all is said and done, federalism as well as other constitutional forms worked because of the good sense and pragmatism of the American people, which overcame constitutional ambiguity. This is why federalism worked in the United States, but, according to Tocqueville, failed in other countries that attempted to imitate the United States Constitution.

The great nineteenth-century Scotsman, scholar, politician, and world traveler, James Bryce made the great American political experiment the focus of his book, *The American Commonwealth.* Published in 1888, and later revised twice, *The American Commonwealth* was widely acclaimed and read in both England and America. Bryce and Tocqueville, somewhat ironically both Europeans, profoundly influenced nineteenth-century views of American political institutions.

Bryce's nineteenth-century analysis of American federalism in the following selection is as sharply relevant in the twenty-first century as it was at the end of the nineteenth century.

8

THE MERITS OF THE FEDERAL SYSTEM

James Bryce

. . . There are two distinct lines of argument by which their Federal system was recommended to the framers of the Constitution, and upon which it is still held forth for imitation to other countries. These lines have been so generally confounded that it is well to present them in a precise form.

The first set of arguments point to Federalism proper, and are the following:—

1. That Federalism furnishes the means of uniting commonwealths into one nation under one national government without extinguishing their separate administrations, legislatures, and local patriotisms. As the Americans of 1787 would probably have preferred complete State independence to the fusion of their States into a unified government, Federalism was the only resource. So when the new Germanic Empire, which is really a Federation, was established in 1871, Bavaria and Würtemberg could not have been brought under a national government save by a Federal scheme. Similar suggestions, as every one knows, have been made for re-settling the relations of Ireland to Great Britain, and of the self-governing British colonies to the United Kingdom. There are causes and conditions which dispose independent or semi-independent communities, or peoples living under loosely compacted governments, to form a closer union in a Federal form. There are other causes and conditions which dispose the subjects of one government, or sections of these subjects, to desire to make their governmental union less close by substituting a Federal for a unitary system. In both sets of cases, the centripetal or centrifugal forces spring from the local position, the history, the sentiments, the economic needs of those among whom the problem arises; and that which is good for one people or political body is not necessarily good for another. Federalism is an equally legitimate resource whether it is adopted for the sake of tightening or for the sake of loosening a preexisting bond.[1]

2. That Federalism supplies the best means of developing a new and vast country. It permits an expansion whose extent, and whose rate and manner of progress, cannot be foreseen to proceed with more variety of methods, more adaptation of laws and administration to the circumstances of each part of the territory, and alto-

---

[1] I have treated of this subject in an essay on the centripetal and centrifugal Forces in Constitutional Law in a book entitled *Studies in History and Jurisprudence*.

gether in a more truly natural and spontaneous way, than can be expected under a centralized government, which is disposed to apply its settled system through all its dominions. Thus the special needs of a new region are met by the inhabitants in the way they find best: its laws can be adapted to the economic conditions which from time to time present themselves; its special evils can be cured by special remedies, perhaps more drastic than an old country demands, perhaps more lax than an old country would tolerate; while at the same time the spirit of self-reliance among those who build up these new communities is stimulated and respected.

3. That Federalism prevents the rise of a despotic central government, absorbing other powers, and menacing the private liberties of the citizen. This may now seem to have been an idle fear, so far as America was concerned. It was, however, a very real fear among the ancestors of the present Americans, and nearly led to the rejection even of so undespotic an instrument as the Federal Constitution of 1789. Congress (or the President, as the case may be) is still sometimes described as a tyrant, by the party which does not control it, simply because it is a central government: and the States are represented as bulwarks against its encroachments.

The second set of arguments relate to and recommend not so much Federalism as local self-government. I state them briefly because they are familiar.

4. Self-government stimulates the interest of people in the affairs of their neighbourhood, sustains local political life, educates the citizen in his daily round of civic duty, teaches him that perpetual vigilance and the sacrifice of his own time and labour are the price that must be paid for individual liberty and collective prosperity.

5. Self-government secures the good administration of local affairs by giving the inhabitants of each locality due means of overseeing the conduct of their business. . . .

Three further benefits to be expected from a Federal system may be mentioned, benefits which seem to have been unnoticed or little regarded by those who established it in America.

6. Federalism enables a people to try experiments in legislation and administration which could not be safely tried in a large centralized country. A comparatively small commonwealth like an American State easily makes and unmakes its laws; mistakes are not serious, for they are soon corrected; other States profit by the experience of a law or a method which has worked well or ill in the State that has tried it.

7. Federalism, if it diminishes the collective force of a nation, diminishes also the risks to which its size and the diversities of its parts expose it. A nation so divided is like a ship built with water-tight compartments. When a leak is sprung in one compartment, the cargo stowed there may be damaged, but the other compartments remain dry and keep the ship afloat. So if social discord or an economic crisis has produced disorders or foolish legislation in one member of the Federal body, the mischief may stop at the State frontier instead of spreading through and tainting the nation at large.

8. Federalism, by creating many local legislatures with wide powers, relieves the national legislature of a part of that large mass of functions which might otherwise prove too heavy for it. Thus business is more promptly despatched, and the great central council of the nation has time to deliberate on those questions which most nearly touch the whole country.

All of these arguments recommending Federalism have proved valid in American experience. . . .

. . . The problem which all federalized nations have to solve is how to secure an efficient central government and preserve national unity, while allowing free scope for the diversities, and free play to the authorities, of the members of the federation. It is, to adopt that favourite astronomical metaphor which no American panegyrist of the Constitution omits, to keep the centrifugal and centripetal forces in equilibrium, so that neither the planet States shall fly off into space, nor the sun of the Central government draw them into its consuming fires. The characteristic merit of the American Constitution lies in the method by which it has solved this problem. It has given the National government a direct authority over all citizens, irrespective of the State governments, and has therefore been able safely to leave wide powers in the hands of those governments. And by placing the Constitution above both the National and the State governments, it has referred the arbitrament of disputes between them to an independent body, charged with the interpretation of the Constitution, a body which is to be deemed not so much a third authority in the government as the living voice of the Constitution, the unfolder of the mind of the people whose will stands expressed in that supreme instrument.

The application of these two principles, unknown to, or at any rate little used by, any previous federation, has contributed more than anything else to the stability of the American system, and to the reverence which its citizens feel for it, a reverence which is the best security for its permanence. Yet even these devices would not have succeeded but for the presence of a mass of moral and material influences stronger than any political devices, which have maintained the equilibrium of centrifugal and centripetal forces. On the one hand there has been the love of local independence and self-government; on the other, the sense of community in blood, in language, in habits and ideas, a common pride in the national history and the national flag. . .

The Supremacy of National Law

Tracing the historical development of nation-state relationships, one finds that there has been constant strife over the determination of the boundaries of national power in relation to the reserved powers of the states. The Civil War did not settle once and for all the difficult question of national versus state power. The Supreme Court has played an important role in the development of the federal system, and some of its most historic opinions have upheld national power at the expense of the states. In the early period of the Court, Chief Justice John Marshall in *McCulloch v. Maryland*, 4 Wheaton 316 (1819), stated two doctrines that have had a profound effect upon the federal system: (1) the doctrine of implied powers, and (2) the doctrine of the supremacy of national law. The former enables Congress to expand its power into numerous areas affecting states directly. By utilizing the commerce clause, for example, Congress may now regulate what is essentially intrastate commerce, for the Court has held that this is implied in the original clause giving Congress the power to regulate commerce among the several states. The immediate issues in *McCulloch v. Maryland* were, first, whether or not Congress had the power to incorporate, or charter, a national bank; second, if Congress did have such a power, although nowhere stated in the Constitution, did the existence of such a bank prevent state action that would interfere in its operation?

9

McCulloch v. Maryland

4 Wheaton 316 (1819)

Mr. Chief Justice Marshall delivered the opinion of the Court, saying in part:

In the case now to be determined, the defendant, a sovereign state, denies the obligation of a law enacted by the legislature of the Union; and the plaintiff, on his part, contests the validity of an act which has been passed by the legislature of that state. The Constitution of our country, in its most interesting and vital parts, is to be considered; the conflicting powers of the government of the Union and of its members, as marked in that Constitution, are to be discussed; and an opinion given, which may essentially influence the great operations of the government. . . .

If any one proposition could command the universal assent of mankind, we might expect it would be this: that the government of the Union, though limited in its powers, is supreme within its sphere of action. This would seem to result necessarily from its nature. It is the government of all; its powers are delegated by all; it represents all, and acts for all. Though any one state may be willing to control its operations, no state is willing to allow others to control them. The nation, on those subjects on which it can act, must necessarily bind its component parts. But this question is not left to mere reason: the people have, in express terms, decided it, by saying, "this Constitution, and the laws of the United States, which shall be made in pursuance thereof," "shall be the supreme law of the land," and by requiring that the members of the state legislatures, and the officers of the executive and judicial departments of the states, shall take the oath of fidelity to it. . . .

A constitution, to contain an accurate detail of all the subdivisions of which its great powers will admit, and of all the means by which they may be carried into execution, would partake of the prolixity of a legal code, and could scarcely be embraced by the human mind. It would probably never be understood by the public. Its nature, therefore, requires that only its great outlines should be marked, its important objects designated, and the minor ingredients which compose those objects be deduced from the nature of the objects themselves. That this idea was entertained by the framers of the American Constitution, is not only to be inferred from the nature of the instrument, but from the language. . . .

Although, among the enumerated powers of government, we do not find the word "bank," or "incorporation," we find the great powers to lay and collect taxes; to borrow money; to regulate commerce; to declare and conduct a war; and to raise and support armies and navies. The sword and the purse, all the external relations, and no inconsiderable portion of the industry of the nation, are entrusted to its government. It can never be pretended that these vast powers draw after them others of inferior importance, merely because they are inferior. Such an idea can never be advanced. But it may, with great reason, be contended, that a government, entrusted with such ample powers, on the due execution of which the happiness and prosperity of the nation so vitally depends, must also be entrusted with ample means for their execution. The power being given, it is the interest of the nation to facilitate its execution. It can never be their interest, and cannot be presumed to have been their intention, to clog and embarrass its execution by withholding the most appropriate means. Throughout this vast republic, from the St. Croix to the Gulf of Mexico, from the Atlantic to the Pacific, revenue is to be collected and expended, armies are to be marched and supported. The exigencies of the nation may require, that the treasure raised in the North should be transported to the South, that raised in the East conveyed to the West, or that this order should be reversed. Is that construction of the Constitution to be preferred which would render these operations difficult, hazardous, and expensive? Can we adopt that construction (unless the words imperiously require it) which would impute to the framers of that instrument, when granting these powers for the public good, the intention of impeding their exercise by withholding a choice of means? If, indeed, such be the mandate of the Constitution, we have only to obey; but that instrument does not profess to enumerate the means by which the powers it confers may be executed; nor does it prohibit the creation of a corporation, if the existence of such a being be essential to the beneficial exercise of those powers. It is, then, the subject of fair inquiry, how far such means may be employed. . . .

We admit, as all must admit, that the powers of the government are limited, and that its limits are not to be transcended. But we think the sound construction of the Constitution must allow to the national legislature that discretion, with respect to the means by which the powers it confers are to be carried into execution, which will enable that body to perform the high duties assigned to it, in the manner most beneficial to the people. Let the end be legitimate, let it be within the scope of the Constitution, and all means which are appropriate, which are plainly adapted to that end, which are not prohibited, but consist with the letter and spirit of the Constitution, are constitutional. . . .

It being the opinion of the court that the act incorporating the bank is constitutional; and that the power of establishing a branch in the state of Maryland might be properly exercised by the bank itself, we proceed to inquire:

Whether the state of Maryland may, without violating the Constitution, tax that branch? . . .

That the power of taxation is one of vital importance; that it is retained by the states; that it is not abridged by the grant of a similar power to the government of the Union; that it is to be concurrently exercised by the two governments: are truths which have never been denied. But, such is the paramount character of the Constitution, that its capacity to withdraw any subject from the action of even this power, is admitted. The states are expressly forbidden to lay any duties on imports or exports, except what may be absolutely necessary for executing their inspection laws. If the obligation of this prohibition must be conceded—if it may restrain a state from the exercise of its taxing power of imports and exports; the same paramount character would seem to restrain, as it certainly may restrain, a state from such other exercise of this power, as is in its nature incompatible with, and repugnant to, the constitutional laws of the Union. A law, absolutely repugnant to another, as entirely repeals that other as if express terms of repeal were used.

On this ground the counsel for the bank place its claim to be exempted from the power of a state to tax its operations. There is no express provision for the case, but the claim has been sustained on a principle which so entirely pervades the Constitution, is so intermixed with the materials which compose it, so interwoven with its web, so blended with its texture, as to be incapable of being separated from it, without rending it into shreds.

This great principle is, that the Constitution and the laws made in pursuance thereof are supreme; that they control the Constitution and laws of the respective states, and cannot be controlled by them. From this, which may be almost termed an axiom, other propositions are deduced as corollaries, on the truth or error of which, and on their application to this case, the cause has been supposed to depend. These are, 1. That a power to create implies a power to preserve. 2. That a power to destroy, if wielded by a different hand, is hostile to, and incompatible with, these powers to create and preserve. 3. That where this repugnancy exists, that authority which is supreme must control, not yield to that over which it is supreme. . . .

If we apply the principle for which the state of Maryland contends, to the Constitution generally, we shall find it capable of changing totally the character of that instrument. We shall find it capable of arresting all the measures of the government, and of prostrating it at the foot of the states. The American people have declared their Constitution, and the laws made in pursuance thereof, to be supreme; but this principle would transfer the supremacy, in fact, to the states. . . .

The court has bestowed on this subject its most deliberate consideration. The result is a conviction that the states have no power, by taxation or otherwise, to retard, impede, burden, or in any manner control, the operations of the constitutional laws enacted by Congress to carry into execution the powers vested in the general government. That is, we think, the unavoidable consequence of that supremacy which the Constitution has declared. . . .

Constitutional doctrine regarding the power of the national government to regulate commerce among the states to promote general prosperity has been clarified in a series of Supreme Court cases. At issue is the interpretation of the power to "regulate commerce with foreign nations, and among the several States," granted to Congress in Article I. Some of these cases have emphasized the role of the national government as umpire, enforcing certain rules of the game within which the free enterprise system functions; others have emphasized the positive role of the government in regulating the economy.

A key case supporting the supremacy of the national government in commercial regulation was *Gibbons v. Ogden,* 9 Wheaton 1 (1824). The New York legislature, in 1798, granted Robert R. Livingston the exclusive privilege to navigate by steam the rivers and other waters of the state, provided he could build a boat that would travel at four miles an hour against the current of the Hudson River. A two-year time limitation was imposed, and the conditions were not met; however, New York renewed its grant for two years in 1803 and again in 1807. In 1807 Robert Fulton, who now held the exclusive license with Livingston, completed and put into operation a steamboat that met the legislative conditions. The New York legislature now provided that a five-year extension of their monopoly would be given to Livingston and Fulton for each new steamboat they placed into operation on New York waters. The monopoly could not exceed thirty years, but during that period anyone wishing to navigate New York waters by steam had first to obtain a license from Livingston and Fulton, who were given the power to confiscate unlicensed boats. New Jersey and Connecticut passed retaliatory laws, the former authorizing confiscation of any New York ship for each ship confiscated by Livingston and Fulton, the latter prohibiting boats licensed in New York from entering Connecticut waters. Ohio also passed retaliatory legislation. Open commercial warfare seemed a possibility among the states of the union.

In 1793 Congress passed an act providing for the licensing of vessels engaged in the coasting trade, and Gibbons obtained under this statute a license to operate boats between New York and New Jersey. Ogden was engaged in a similar operation under an exclusive license issued by Livingston and Fulton, and thus sought to enjoin Gibbons from further operation. The New York court upheld the exclusive grants given to Livingston and Fulton, and Gibbons appealed to the Supreme Court. Chief Justice Marshall made it quite clear that (1) states cannot interfere with a power granted to Congress by passing conflicting state legislation, and (2) the commerce power includes anything affecting "commerce among the states" and thus may include intrastate as well as interstate commerce. In this way the foundation was laid for broad national control over commercial activity.

National Power over the States:
A Recurring Constitutional Debate

Put simply, the Constitution created federalism by delegating powers to the national government and then, in the Tenth Amendment, providing that "The powers not delegated to the United States by the Constitution, nor prohibited by it to the states, are reserved to the states respectively, or to the people."[1] The law-making powers of the national government are those enumerated powers of Congress found in Article I. The most important of these are the commerce and war powers and the power to tax and provide for the general welfare.

Constitutional and political debate during the nineteenth and much of the twentieth centuries focused upon the issue of national versus state power. Over 650,000 young men

---

[1]Interestingly, the states did not ratify the Tenth Amendment until 1798. Textually, then, the original Constitution did not reserve any powers to the states. But the states were sovereign at the time of the ratification of the Constitution, and clearly they would not have entered into any compact that would have taken away all of their sovereign powers.

lost their lives in the Civil War because of the failure of the political system to resolve national-state conflict.

Constitutional Changes in the Balance of Federalism: The Civil War Amendments

The "Civil War amendments," the Thirteenth, Fourteenth, and Fifteenth Amendments, added an important new constitutional dimension to federalism. The amendments abolished slavery (thirteenth); granted citizenship to all persons born in the United States (fourteenth); prohibited states from denying persons life, liberty, or property without due process of law or equal protection of the laws; barred states from denying the privileges and immunities of citizens of the United States (fourteenth); and prohibited both the federal government and the states from denying the right to vote on account of race, nationality, or previous condition of servitude (fifteenth).

Especially important to federalism were the enforcement clauses of the Civil War amendments which gave Congress the authority to enforce each of the amendments by "appropriate legislation." The new enforcement powers vastly expanded Congress's potential authority over the states. The Civil War had settled the question of Union once and for all time in favor of national power. The Civil War amendments were the constitutional recognition of national victory over state sovereignty in the determination of civil rights.

However, as seemingly clear as the nationalist Civil War amendments were, they did not automatically settle the political question of the scope of national power over the states. As with the original Constitution, the amendments provided an outline not a blueprint of congressional powers and protected rights. Absent a clear national majority reflected in disciplined political parties the courts once again became the supreme interpreters of the amendments and hence of the boundaries of national and state powers within their context. Litigation became politics by other means to settle disputes over national versus state power. Litigation over the constitutional authority of Congress over the states now encompassed not only the meaning of the commerce clause and other Article I powers, but also what constituted "appropriate legislation" under the enforcement clauses of the Civil War amendments.

Litigation then continues to be the avenue for the resolution of political conflict over the scope of national and state powers, particularly on the part of advocates of states' rights who were dissatisfied with what they viewed as increasing national encroachments upon state powers and rights. Of course, Congress represents, and some would argue overrepresents in the Senate, the states, and therefore is unlikely to pass legislation that unduly interferes with states' rights. But in the highly pluralistic American political system there will always be interests that are dissatisfied with national policies, and if they have the resources they will use litigation to challenge the constitutionality of congressional laws.

Commerce Clause Litigation

Over its history the Supreme Court has interpreted the commerce clause both to expand and contract the authority of the national government. After Chief Justice John Marshall's era ended in 1836, the Court gradually adopted a more restrictive view of the national commerce power, protecting state sovereignty over many areas of commercial regulation that Marshall clearly would have allowed Congress to regulate. The Supreme Court did not fully return to the broad commerce clause interpretation of the *Gibbons* case until 1937, when it reluctantly capitulated to Franklin D. Roosevelt's New Deal and the centralized government it represented. The restoration of the Marshall Court's definition of the commerce power removed constitutional restraints upon Congress.

Since 1937 the Supreme Court has essentially upheld congressional interpretations of its own authority under the commerce clause. While the commerce power is generally used to support economic regulation, Congress turned to the commerce clause for the legal authority to enact the Civil Rights Act of 1964. The public accommodations section of the bill, Title II, proscribed discrimination in public establishments, including inns, hotels, motels, restaurants, motion-picture houses, and theaters. The law declared that the "operations of an establishment affects commerce . . . if . . . it serves or offers to serve interstate travelers or a substantial portion of the food which it serves or gasoline or other products which it sells, has moved in commerce . . . [or if] it customarily presents films, performances, athletic teams, exhibitions, or other sources of entertainment which move in commerce." In *Heart of Atlanta Motel, Inc. v. United States,* 379 U.S. 241 (1964), the Supreme Court upheld the law under the commerce clause. The motel-plaintiff contended that it was in no way involved in interstate commerce, arguing that while some of its guests might be occasionally engaged in commerce, "persons and people are not part of trade or commerce . . . people conduct commerce and engage in trade, but people are not part of commerce and trade." But the Court accepted the government's argument that racial discrimination in public accommodations impedes interstate travel by those discriminated against, causing disruption of interstate commerce which Congress has the authority to prevent.

The Supreme Court did briefly resurrect the commerce clause as a limit on congressional power over the states in *National League of Cities v. Usery,* 426 U.S. 833 (1976). A sharply divided Court held that Congress could not regulate governmental activities that were an integral part of state sovereignty. The decision overturned provisions of the Fair Labor Standards Act that governed state employees. The Court's majority opinion argued that states had traditionally controlled their employees, a responsibility within state sovereignty because the states through their own democratic processes should have the autonomy to decide for themselves how they would manage their public sector.

It was not long, however, before the Court reversed the *National League of Cities* decision, holding in *Garcia v. San Antonio Metropolitan Transit Authority,* 469 U.S 528 (1985), that Congress could apply minimum-wage requirements to the states and their localities. Again the vote was closely divided, 5–4, and this time the majority opinion struck a distinct note of judicial self-restraint, concluding: "We doubt that courts ultimately can identify principled constitutional limitations on the scope of Congress' commerce clause powers over the states merely by relying on a priori definitions of state sovereignty." The Court found nothing in the Fair Labor Standards Act that violated state sovereignty, implying that it was up to Congress and not the courts to determine the extent of its power under the commerce clause. Sharp dissents were registered in the case, indicating that if in the future the issue was raised a more conservative Supreme Court majority might uphold some commerce clause restraints against national regulation of state governments. The *Garcia* decision was directly in line with Court precedents since 1937 that have supported virtually unlimited congressional authority under the commerce clause.

The *Garcia* decision appeared yet once again to have settled the constitutional question of the scope of congressional authority under the commerce clause. But, the conservative Supreme Court of the 1990s refused to grant Congress the benefit of the doubt in applying a "rational-basis" test in reviewing legislation under the commerce clause. The New Deal political victory embedded in the *Wickard v. Filburn* (1942) case doctrine where the Supreme Court deferred to congressional interpretation of its commerce power ended in *United States v. Lopez* (1995). In *Lopez* the Supreme Court by a vote of 5–4, with the conservatives in the majority, overturned the Gun-Free School Zones Act of 1990 on the ground that Congress did not have the authority to enact it under its commerce power. The law made it a federal crime "for any individual knowingly to possess a firearm at a place that the individual knows, or has reasonable cause to believe, is a school zone." Chief Justice Rehnquist's opinion for the Court flatly stated: "The Act neither regulates a commercial activity nor contains a requirement that the possession be connected in any way to interstate commerce. We hold that the Act exceeds the authority of Congress '[t]o regulate Commerce . . . among the several States. . . .' " Justice Rehnquist and his brethren in the majority were particularly concerned that Congress did not make findings that tied the possession of guns in school zones to interstate commerce. Congress merely assumed that it had the power to enact the law. The government argued before the Court that since gun possession might affect commerce among the states the law was constitutional. But, Rehnquist concluded, "To uphold the Government's contentions here, we would have to pile inference upon inference in a manner that would bid fair to convert congressional authority under the Commerce Clause to a general police power of the sort retained by the States."

The Supreme Court Redefines Congressional Power for the Twenty-first Century Limiting Congressional Authority to Regulate Violence Against Women

The Supreme Court once again confronted the question of the scope of Congress's commerce power, as well as congressional enforcement power under section 5 of the Fourteenth Amendment, when it reviewed the constitutionality of the Violence Against Women Act of 1994 in *United States v. Morrison* (2000). A vast majority of the states supported the law which reflected strong political support throughout the nation. Would a majority of only five Supreme Court Justices follow the *Lopez* precedent and overturn the law on the ground that Congress did not have the constitutional authority to enact it?

The law stated that "[a]ll persons within the United States shall have the right to be free from crimes of violence motivated by gender." The enforcement section declared: "A person . . . who commits a crime of violence motivated by gender . . . shall be liable to the party injured, in an action for the recovery of compensatory and punitive damages, injunctive and declaratory relief, and such other relief as a court may deem appropriate. . . ." The law defined a "crim[e] of violence motivated by gender" as "a crime of violence committed because of gender or on the basis of gender, and due, at least in part, to an animus based on the victim's gender."

Unlike the gun control legislation the Court voided in *Lopez* Congress made extensive findings to connect violence against women with interstate commerce.

These congressional findings are called legislative facts. They are empirical in nature and Congress uses them to make policy. Empirical findings support but do not dictate policy.

In the following case note how the dissent stresses the importance of the extensive congressional findings that connected violence against women with interstate commerce. These findings, the dissenters held, supported congressional authority under the commerce clause to enact the legislation.

10

UNITED STATES V. MORRISON (2000)

Chief Justice Rehnquist delivered the opinion of the Court.

In these cases we consider the constitutionality of 42 U.S.C. §13981 [of the Violence Against Women Act of 1994], which provides a federal civil remedy for the victims of gender-motivated violence. The United States Court of Appeals for the Fourth Circuit, sitting en banc, struck down §13981 because it concluded that Congress lacked constitutional authority to enact the section's civil remedy. Believing that these cases are controlled by our decisions in *United States v. Lopez*, we affirm.

I

Petitioner Christy Brzonkala enrolled at Virginia Polytechnic Institute (Virginia Tech) in the fall of 1994. In September of that year, Brzonkala met respondents Antonio Morrison and James Crawford, who were both students at Virginia Tech and members of its varsity football team. Brzonkala alleges that, within 30 minutes of meeting Morrison and Crawford, they assaulted and repeatedly raped her. After the attack, Morrison allegedly told Brzonkala, "You better not have any . . . diseases." In the months following the rape, Morrison also allegedly announced in the dormitory's dining room that he "like[d] to get girls drunk and. . . ." The omitted portions, quoted verbatim in the briefs on file with this Court, consist of boasting, debased remarks about what Morrison would do to women, vulgar remarks that cannot fail to shock and offend.

Brzonkala alleges that this attack caused her to become severely emotionally disturbed and depressed. She sought assistance from a university psychiatrist, who prescribed antidepressant medication. Shortly after the rape Brzonkala stopped attending classes and withdrew from the university.

In early 1995, Brzonkala filed a complaint against respondents under Virginia Tech's Sexual Assault Policy. During the school-conducted hearing on her complaint, Morrison admitted having sexual contact with her despite the fact that she had twice told him "no." After the hearing, Virginia Tech's Judicial Committee found insufficient evidence to punish Crawford, but found Morrison guilty of sexual assault and sentenced him to immediate suspension for two semesters.

Virginia Tech's dean of students upheld the judicial committee's sentence. However, in July 1995, Virginia Tech informed Brzonkala that Morrison intended to initiate a court challenge to his conviction under the Sexual Assault Policy. University officials told her that a second hearing would be necessary to remedy the school's error in prosecuting her complaint under that policy, which had not been widely circulated to students. The university therefore conducted a second hearing under its Abusive Conduct Policy, which was in force prior to the dissemination of the Sexual Assault Policy. Following this second hearing the Judicial Committee again found Morrison guilty and sentenced him to an identical 2-semester suspension. This time, however, the description of Morrison's offense was, without explanation, changed from "sexual assault" to "using abusive language."

Morrison appealed his second conviction through the university's administrative system. On August 21, 1995, Virginia Tech's senior vice president and provost set aside Morrison's punishment. She concluded that it was " 'excessive when compared with other cases where there has been a finding of violation of the Abusive Conduct Policy.' " Virginia Tech did not inform Brzonkala of this decision. After learning from a newspaper that Morrison would be returning to Virginia Tech for the fall 1995 semester, she dropped out of the university.

In December 1995, Brzonkala sued Morrison, Crawford, and Virginia Tech in the United States District Court for the Western District of Virginia. Her complaint alleged that Morrison's and Crawford's attack violated §13981 and that Virginia Tech's handling of her complaint violated Title IX of the Education Amendments of 1972, 86 Stat. 373–375, 20 U.S.C. §§1681–1688. Morrison and Crawford moved to dismiss this complaint on the grounds that it failed to state a claim and that §13981's civil remedy is unconstitutional. The United States, petitioner in No. 99-5, intervened to defend §13981's constitutionality.

The District Court dismissed Brzonkala's Title IX claims against Virginia Tech for failure to state a claim upon which relief can be granted. See *Brzonkala v. Virginia Polytechnic and State Univ.*, 935 F. Supp. 772 (WD Va. 1996). It then held that Brzonkala's complaint stated a claim against Morrison and Crawford under §13981, but dismissed the complaint because it concluded that Congress lacked authority to enact the section under either the Commerce Clause or §5 of the Fourteenth Amendment. *Brzonkala v. Virginia Polytechnic and State Univ.*, 935 F. Supp. 779 (WD Va. 1996).

A divided panel of the Court of Appeals reversed the District Court, reinstating Brzonkala's §13981 claim and her Title IX hostile environment claim. *Brzonkala v. Virginia Polytechnic and State Univ.*, 132 F. 3d 949 (CA4 1997). The full Court of Appeals vacated the panel's opinion and reheard the case en banc. The en banc court then issued an opinion affirming the District Court's conclusion that Brzonkala stated a claim under §13981 because her complaint alleged a crime of violence and the allegations of Morrison's crude and derogatory statements regarding his treatment of women sufficiently indicated that his crime was motivated by gender animus. Nevertheless, the court by a divided vote affirmed the District Court's conclusion that Congress lacked constitutional authority to enact §13981's civil remedy. *Brzonkala v. Virginia Polytechnic and State Univ.*, 169 F. 3d 820 (CA4 1999). Because the Court of Appeals invalidated a federal statute on constitutional grounds, we granted certiorari. 527 U.S. 1068 (1999).

Section 13981 was part of the Violence Against Women Act of 1994. It states that "[a]ll persons within the United States shall have the right to be free from crimes of violence motivated by gender." . . .

Every law enacted by Congress must be based on one or more of its powers enumerated in the Constitution. "The powers of the legislature are defined and limited; and that those limits may not be mistaken or forgotten, the constitution is written." *Marbury v. Madison*, 1 Cranch 137, 176 (1803) (Marshall, C. J.). Congress explicitly identified the sources of federal authority on which it relied in enacting §13981. It said that a "federal civil rights cause of action" is established "[p]ursuant to the affirmative power of Congress . . . under section 5 of the Fourteenth Amendment to the Constitution, as well as under [the Commerce Clause,] section 8 of Article I of the Constitution." We address Congress' authority to enact this remedy under each of these constitutional provisions in turn.

II

Due respect for the decisions of a coordinate branch of Government demands that we invalidate a congressional enactment only upon a plain showing that Congress has exceeded its constitutional bounds. . . . With this presumption of constitutionality in mind, we turn to the question whether §13981 falls within Congress' power under Article I, §8, [the Commerce Clause] of the Constitution. Brzonkala and the United States rely upon the third clause of the Article, which gives Congress power "[t]o regulate Commerce with foreign Nations, and among the several States, and with the Indian Tribes."

As we discussed at length in *Lopez*, our interpretation of the Commerce Clause has changed as our Nation has developed. . . . We need not repeat that detailed review of the Commerce Clause's history here; it suffices to say that, in the years since *NLRB v. Jones & Laughlin Steel Corp.*, 301 U.S. 1 (1937), Congress has had considerably greater latitude in regulating conduct and transactions under the Commerce Clause than our previous case law permitted. . . .

[Using the] principles underlying our Commerce Clause jurisprudence as reference points, the proper resolution of the present cases is clear. Gender-motivated crimes of violence are not, in any sense of the phrase, economic activity. While we need not adopt a categorical rule against aggregating the effects of any noneconomic activity in order to decide these cases, thus far in our Nation's history our cases have upheld Commerce Clause regulation of intrastate activity only where that activity is economic in nature. . . .

In contrast with the lack of congressional findings that we faced in *Lopez*, §13981 is supported by numerous findings regarding the serious impact that gender-motivated violence has on victims and their families. . . . But the existence of congressional findings is not sufficient, by itself, to sustain the constitutionality of Commerce Clause legislation. As we stated in *Lopez*, " '[S]imply because Congress may conclude that a particular activity substantially affects interstate commerce does not necessarily make it so.' " . . .

Congress found that gender-motivated violence affects interstate commerce by deterring potential victims from traveling interstate, from engaging in employment in interstate business, and from transacting with business, and in places involved in interstate commerce; . . . by diminishing national productivity, increasing medical and other costs, and decreasing the supply of and the demand for interstate products.

Given these findings and petitioners' arguments, the concern that we expressed in *Lopez* that Congress might use the Commerce Clause to completely obliterate the Constitution's distinction between national and local authority seems well founded. The reasoning that petitioners advance seeks to follow the but-for causal chain from the initial occurrence of violent crime (the suppression of which has always been the prime object of the States' police power) to every attenuated effect upon interstate commerce. If accepted, petitioners' reasoning would allow Congress to regulate any crime as long as the nationwide, aggregated impact of that crime has substantial effects on employment, production, transit, or consumption. Indeed, if Congress may regulate gender-motivated violence, it would be able to regulate murder or any other type of violence since gender-motivated violence, as a subset of all violent crime, is certain to have lesser economic impacts than the larger class of which it is a part.

Petitioners' reasoning, moreover, will not limit Congress to regulating violence but may, as we suggested in *Lopez*, be applied equally as well to family law and other areas of traditional state regulation since the aggregate effect of marriage, divorce, and childrearing on the national economy is undoubtedly significant. . . .

We accordingly reject the argument that Congress may regulate noneconomic, violent criminal conduct based solely on that conduct's aggregate effect on interstate commerce. The Constitution requires a distinction between what is truly national and what is truly local. . . .

Because we conclude that the Commerce Clause does not provide Congress with authority to enact §13981, we address petitioners' alternative argument that the section's civil remedy should be upheld as an exercise of Congress' remedial power under §5 of the Fourteenth Amendment. As noted above, Congress expressly invoked the Fourteenth Amendment as a source of authority to enact §13981. . . .

. . . [T]he language and purpose of the Fourteenth Amendment place certain limitations on the manner in which Congress may attack discriminatory conduct. These limitations are necessary to prevent the Fourteenth Amendment from obliterating the Framers' carefully crafted balance of power between the States and the National Government. . . . Foremost among these limitations is the time-honored principle that the Fourteenth Amendment, by its very terms, prohibits only state action. "[T]he principle has become firmly embedded in our constitutional law that the action inhibited by the first section of the Fourteenth Amendment is only such action as may fairly be said to be that of the States. That Amendment erects no shield against merely private conduct, however discriminatory or wrongful." *Shelley v. Kraemer*, 334 U.S. 1, 13, and n. 12 (1948). . . .

. . . Section 13981 is not aimed at proscribing discrimination by officials which the Fourteenth Amendment might not itself proscribe; it is directed not at any State or state actor, but at individuals who have committed criminal acts motivated by gender bias. . . .

. . . [W]e conclude that Congress' power under §5 does not extend to the enactment of §13981.

IV

Petitioner Brzonkala's complaint alleges that she was the victim of a brutal assault. But Congress' effort in §13981 to provide a federal civil remedy can be sustained neither under the Commerce Clause nor under §5 of the Fourteenth Amendment. If the allegations here are true, no civilized system of justice could fail to provide her a remedy for the conduct of respondent Morrison. But under our federal system that remedy must be provided by the Commonwealth of Virginia, and not by the United States. The judgment of the Court of Appeals is Affirmed.

Justice Souter, with whom Justice Stevens, Justice Ginsburg, and Justice Breyer join, dissenting.

The Court says both that it leaves Commerce Clause precedent undisturbed and that the Civil Rights Remedy of the Violence Against Women Act of 1994, 42 U.S.C. §13981, exceeds Congress's power under that Clause. I find the claims irreconcilable and respectfully dissent.

Our cases, which remain at least nominally undisturbed, stand for the following propositions. Congress has the power to legislate with regard to activity that, in the aggregate, has a substantial effect on interstate commerce. See *Wickard v. Filburn*, 317 U.S. 111, 124–128 (1942). The fact of such a substantial effect is not an issue for the courts in the first instance, but for the Congress, whose institutional capacity for gathering evidence and taking testimony far exceeds ours. By passing legislation, Congress indicates its conclusion, whether explicitly or not, that facts support its exercise of the commerce power. The business of the courts is to review the congressional assessment, not for soundness but simply for the rationality of concluding that a jurisdictional basis exists in fact. Any explicit findings that Congress chooses to make, though not dispositive of the question of rationality, may advance judicial review by identifying factual authority on which Congress relied. Applying those propositions in these cases can lead to only one conclusion.

One obvious difference from *United States v. Lopez*, 514 U.S. 549 (1995), is the mountain of data assembled by Congress, here showing the effects of violence against women on interstate commerce. Passage of the Act in 1994 was preceded by four years of hearings, which included testimony from physicians and law professors; from survivors of rape and domestic violence; and from representatives of state law enforcement and private business.

The record includes reports on gender bias from task forces in 21 States, and we have the benefit of specific factual findings in the eight separate Reports issued by Congress and its committees over the long course leading to enactment. . . .

II

The Act would have passed muster at any time between *Wickard* in 1942 and *Lopez* in 1995, a period in which the law enjoyed a stable understanding that congressional power under the Commerce Clause, complemented by the authority of the Necessary and Proper Clause, Art. I. §8 cl. 18, extended to all activity that, when aggregated, has a substantial effect on interstate commerce. . . .

Amendments that alter the balance of power between the National and State Governments, like the Fourteenth, or that change the way the States are represented within the Federal Government, like the Seventeenth, are not rips in the fabric of the Framers' Constitution, inviting judicial repairs. The Seventeenth Amendment may indeed have lessened the enthusiasm of the Senate to represent the States as discrete sovereignties, but the Amendment did not convert the judiciary into an alternate shield against the commerce power. . . .

III

As our predecessors learned then, the practice of such ad hoc review [as the majority has practiced in this case] cannot preserve the distinction between the judicial and the legislative, and this Court, in any event, lacks the institutional capacity to maintain such a regime for very long. This one will end when the majority realizes that the conception of the commerce power for which it entertains hopes would inevitably fail the test expressed in Justice Holmes's statement that "[t]he first call of a theory of law is that it should fit the facts." O. Holmes, *The Common Law* 167 (Howe ed. 1963). The facts that cannot be ignored today are the facts of integrated national commerce and a political relationship between States and Nation much affected by their respective treasuries and constitutional modifications adopted by the people. The federalism of some earlier time is no more adequate to account for those facts today than the theory of laissez-faire was able to govern the national economy 70 years ago.

A Perspective on Federalism: Present and Future

In the following selection, the role of the states in the political system is discussed from the perspective that the nature of intergovernmental relations reflects underlying political conditions and realities. As James Madison pointed out in *Federalist 39*, the original constitutional scheme of federalism represented a delicate balance between national and state ("federal") interests. But, under the original constitutional design, the national government was not to intervene directly in the affairs of state governments; and the problems of subsidiary local governments within states were not considered to be separate from the problems of the states themselves, and therefore, they were a proper matter for resolution by the individual state governments.

Morton Grodzins points out that strict separation of national and state functions has never really existed, and that even before the Constitution of 1787 a national statute passed by the Continental Congress gave grants-in-aid of land to the states for public schools. Tocqueville also comments on the difficulties of formally separating, in theory, the responsibilities of national, state, and local governments. The history of the federal system has seen the ebb and flow of national dominance over the states; centralization and decentralization have been the cyclical themes of federalism and intergovernmental relations. The thrust of the New Deal was toward centralization through the use of federal grant-in-aid programs, a philosophy that dominated the government until the emergence of the "New Federalism" of the Nixon administration, which supported decentralization of power from the national to the state governments. The move toward decentralization was broadly supported by the Republican party. Revenue sharing was inaugurated by President Nixon to transfer national funds to the states, without stipulation of how the money was to be spent. The revenue-sharing procedure was in direct contrast to the grant-in-aid programs, which allowed for state receipt of federal money upon the condition of state adherence to national standards. President Reagan's New Federalism proposed the merging of grant-in-aid programs into block grants to the states, leading eventually to a reduced federal role in financing state and local governments. The continuing conflict between the themes and realities of centralization and decentralization are examined in the following selection.

11

THE FEDERAL SYSTEM

Morton Grodzins

Federalism is a device for dividing decisions and functions of government. As the constitutional fathers well understood, the federal structure is a means, not an end. The pages that follow are therefore not concerned with an exposition of American federalism as a formal, legal set of relationships. The focus, rather, is on the purpose of federalism, that is to say, on the distribution of power between central and peripheral units of government.

I. The Sharing of Functions

The American form of government is often, but erroneously, symbolized by a three-layer cake. A far more accurate image is the rainbow or marble cake, characterized by an inseparable mingling of differently colored ingredients, the colors appearing in vertical and diagonal strands and unexpected whirls. As colors are mixed in the marble cake, so functions are mixed in the American federal system. . . .

A long, extensive, and continuous experience is . . . the foundation of the present system of shared functions characteristic of the American federal system, what we have called the marble cake of government. It is a misjudgment of our history and our present situation to believe that a neat separation of governmental functions could take place without drastic alterations in our society and system of government.

[II]. Dynamics of Sharing: The Politics of the Federal System

Many causes contribute to dispersed power in the federal system. One is the simple historical fact that the states existed before the nation. A second is in the form of creed, the traditional opinion of Americans that expresses distrust of centralized power and places great value in the strength and vitality of local units of government. Another is pride in locality and state, nurtured by the nation's size and by variations of regional and state history. Still a fourth cause of decentralization is the sheer wealth of the nation. It allows all groups, including state and local governments, to partake of the central government's largesse, supplies room for experimentation and even waste, and makes unnecessary the tight organization of political power that must follow when the support of one program necessarily means the deprivation of another.

In one important respect, the Constitution no longer operates to impede centralized government. The Supreme Court since 1937 has given Congress a relatively free hand. The federal government can build substantive programs in many areas on the taxation and commerce powers. Limitations of such central programs based on the argument, "it's unconstitutional," are no longer possible as long as Congress (in the Court's view) acts reasonably in the interest of the whole nation. The Court is unlikely to reverse this permissive view in the foreseeable future. [But note that the Supreme Court's decisions in the *Lopez* and *Morrison* (Reading 10) cases reestablished limits on Congress's power to regulate the states under the commerce clause.]

Nevertheless, some constitutional restraints on centralization continue to operate. The strong constitutional position of the states—for example, the assignment of two Senators to each state, the role given the states in administering even national elections, and the relatively few limitations on their lawmaking powers—establishes the geographical units as natural centers of administrative and political strength. Many clauses of the Constitution are not subject to the same latitude of interpretation as the commerce and tax clauses. The simple, clearly stated, unambiguous phrases—for example, the President "shall hold his office during the term of four years"—are subject to change only through the formal amendment process. Similar provisions exist with respect to the terms of Senators and Congressmen and the amendment process. All of them have the effect of retarding or restraining centralizing action of the federal government. The fixed terms of the President and members of Congress, for example, greatly impede the development of nationwide, disciplined political parties that almost certainly would have to precede continuous large-scale expansion of federal functions.

The constitutional restraints on the expansion of national authority are less important and less direct today than they were in 1879 or 1936. But to say that they are less important is not to say that they are unimportant.

The nation's politics reflect these decentralizing causes and add some of their own. The political parties of the United States are unique. They seldom perform the function that parties traditionally perform in other countries, the function of gathering together diverse strands of power and welding them into one. Except during the period of nominating and electing a President and for the essential but non-substantive business of organizing the houses of Congress, the American parties rarely coalesce power at all. Characteristically they do the reverse, serving as a canopy under which special and local interests are represented with little regard for anything that can be called a party program. National leaders are elected on a party ticket, but in Congress they must seek cross-party support if their leadership is to be effective. It is a rare President during rare periods who can produce legislation without facing the defection of substantial numbers of his own party. (Wilson could do this in the first session of the Sixty-Third Congress; but Franklin D. Roosevelt could not, even during the famous hundred days of 1933.) Presidents whose parties form the majority of the Congressional houses must still count heavily on support from the other party.

The parties provide the pivot on which the entire governmental system swings. Party operations, first of all, produce in legislation the basic division of functions between the federal government, on the one hand, and state and local governments, on the other. . . .

The party system compels administrators to take a political role. This is a third way in which the parties function to decentralize the American system. The administrator must play politics for the same reason that the politician is able to play in administration: the parties are without program and without discipline.

In response to the unprotected position in which the party situation places him, the administrator is forced to seek support where he can find it. One ever-present task is to nurse the Congress of the United States, that crucial constituency which ultimately controls his agency's budget and program. From the administrator's view, a sympathetic consideration of Congressional request (if not downright submission to them) is the surest way to build the political support without which the administrative job could not continue. Even the completely task-oriented administrator must be sensitive to the need for Congressional support and to the relationship between case work requests, on one side, and budgetary and legislative support, on the other. "You do a good job handling the personal problems and requests of a Congressman," a White House officer said, "and you have an easier time convincing him to back your program." Thus there is an important link between the nursing of Congressional requests, requests that largely concern local matters, and the most comprehensive national programs. The administrator must accommodate to the former as a price of gaining support for the latter.

One result of administrative politics is that the administrative agency may become the captive of the nationwide interest group it serves or presumably regulates. In such cases no government may come out with effective authority: the winners are the interest groups themselves. But in a very large number of cases, states and localities also win influence. The politics of administration is a process of making peace with legislators who for the most part consider themselves the guardians of local interests. The political role of administrators therefore contributes to the power of states and localities in national programs.

Finally, the way the party system operates gives American politics their overall distinctive tone. The lack of party discipline produces an openness in the system that allows individuals, groups, and institutions (including state and local governments) to attempt to influence national policy at every step of the legislative-administrative process. This is the "multiple-crack" attribute of the American government. "Crack" has two meanings. It means not only many fissures or access points; it also means, less statically, opportunities for wallops or smacks at government.

If the parties were more disciplined, the result would not be a cessation of the process by which individuals and groups impinge themselves upon the central government. But the present state of the parties clearly allows for a far greater operation of the multiple crack than would be possible under the conditions of centralized party control. American interest groups exploit literally uncountable access points in the legislative-administrative process. If legislative lobbying, from committee stages to the conference committee, does not produce results, a Cabinet secretary is called. His immediate associates are petitioned. Bureau chiefs and their aides are hit. Field officers are put under pressure. Campaigns are instituted by which friends of the agency apply a secondary influence on behalf of the interested party. A conference with the President may be urged.

To these multiple points for bringing influence must be added the multiple voices of the influencers. Consider, for example, those in a small town who wish to have a federal action taken. The easy merging of public and private interest at the local level means that the influence attempt is made in the name of the whole community, thus removing it from political partisanship. The Rotary Club as well as the City Council, the Chamber of Commerce and the mayor, eminent citizens and political bosses—all are readily enlisted. If a conference in a Senator's office will expedite matters, someone on the local scene can be found to make such a conference possible and effective. If technical information is needed, technicians will supply it. State or national professional organizations of local officials, individual Congressmen and Senators, and not infrequently whole state delegations will make the local cause their own. Federal field officers, who service localities, often assume local views. So may elected and appointed state officers. Friendships are exploited, and political mortgages called due. Under these circumstances, national policies are molded by local action.

In summary, then, the party system functions to devolve power. The American parties, unlike any other, are highly responsive when directives move from the bottom to the top, highly unresponsive from top to bottom. Congressmen and Senators can rarely ignore concerted demands from their home constituencies; but no party leader can expect the same kind of response from those below, whether he be a President asking for Congressional support or a Congressman seeking aid from local or state leaders. Any tightening of the party apparatus would have the effect of strengthening the central government. The four characteristics of the system, discussed above, would become less important. If control from the top were strictly applied, these hallmarks of American decentralization might entirely disappear. To be specific, if disciplined and program-oriented parties were achieved: (1) It would make far less likely legislation that takes heavily into account the desires and prejudices of the highly decentralized power groups and institutions of the country, including the state and local governments. (2) It would to a large extent prevent legislators, individually and collectively, from intruding themselves on behalf of non-national interests in national administrative programs. (3) It would put an end to the administrator's search for his own political support, a search that often results in fostering state, local, and other non-national powers. (4) It would dampen the process by which individuals and groups, including state and local political leaders, take advantage of multiple cracks to steer national legislation and administration in ways congenial to them and the institutions they represent.

Alterations of this sort could only accompany basic changes in the organization and style of politics which, in turn, presuppose fundamental changes at the parties' social base. The sharing of functions is, in fact, the sharing of power. To end this sharing process would mean the destruction of whatever measure of decentralization exists in the United States today. . . .

State Politics and Constitutional Government

In the following selection a celebrated national columnist and political observer finds that the growing use of initiative petitions in state politics threatens the Madisonian system of balanced government.

—— 12 ——

A REPUBLIC SUBVERTED

David Broder

✍

At the start of a new century and millennium a new form of government is spreading in the United States. It is alien to the spirit of the Constitution and its careful system of checks and balances. Though derived from a reform favored by Populists and Progressives as a cure for special interest influence, this method of lawmaking has become the favored tool of millionaires and interest groups that use their wealth to achieve their own policy goals—missing a lucrative business for a new set of political entrepreneurs.

Exploiting the public's disdain for politics and distrust of politicians, it is now the most uncontrolled and unexamined arena of power politics. It has given the United States something that seems unthinkable, not a government of laws but laws without government. The initiative process, an import now just over one hundred years old, threatens to challenge or even subvert the American system of government in the next few decades.

To be sure, change is the order of the day in the United States and elsewhere in the advanced countries of the world. The computer and the Internet are revolutionizing the economy. The speed of communications and the reduction in barriers to trade are making national boundaries less and less meaningful. The end of the Cold War has brought an outbreak of ethnic warfare and has heightened awareness of the dangers of terrorism by extremist groups on every continent.

Amid these changes, American life looks like an island of strength and stability. One reason in addition to the vitality of our business and entrepreneurial culture, the incredible productivity of our farms, the quality of our great research universities, and the energy and vigor of our people is the time tested solidity and flexibility of our system of government. The United States Constitution, in this third century of our national life, continues to provide a durable foundation for our governing institutions. The presidency, Congress, the Supreme Court, the federal system, the rule of law, have been tested by many challenges. Twice in the twentieth century we fought world wars. Twice we faced efforts to impeach and remove our chief executive. We overcame the Great Depression and led the reconstruction of Europe. Repeatedly we wrestled with the terrible legacy of the almost indelible moral stain left by slavery. And we have managed to absorb and integrate waves of immigration from lands far distant from our European roots, giving this nation a richer variety of ethnic and racial groups than ever before.

But even as the system of government invented by the founders—a system based on the separation of powers and a complex matrix of procedures designed to require the creation of consensus before the enactment of laws—has proved its worth in crisis after crisis, public impatience with "the system" has grown. Some argue that the science of public opinion and the speed of electronic communications make the political arrangements of the eighteenth century Constitution as outdated as the one horse shay. With journalism focused on the foibles in the private lives of political leaders, disdain for those in government has mounted with each new scandal. Political campaigns have become demolition derbies, in which even the winners emerge with ruined reputations. The trust between governors and governed, on which representative democracy depends, has been badly depleted. Polls consistently show an alarmingly small percentage of Americans believe the government in Washington will do what is right all or even most of the time. With the end of the Cold War, that distrust of Washington has brought about a significant shift in political power. Fewer of the decisions that determine the quality and character of our lives and communities are being made in Washington, D.C. Responsibilities are being transferred to state capitols and city halls. Except for Social Security and Medicare, federal spending is smaller than that of state and local governments. Only 13 percent of public employees are on the federal payroll. And states have become the innovators in vital areas of domestic policy, from welfare to education to growth policies.

In half our states—including the giant of them all, California—and in hundreds of municipalities, from New York City to Nome, policies are being made not by government but by initiative. In a single year, 1998, voters across America used the initiative process to pass laws or to amend state constitutions, achieving a wide variety of goals. They ended affirmative action, raised the minimum wage, banned billboards, decriminalized a wide range of hard drugs and permitted thousands of patients to obtain prescriptions for marijuana, restricted campaign spending and contributions, expanded casino gambling, banned many forms of hunting, prohibited some abortions, and allowed adopted children to obtain the names of their biological parents.

At the local level, things were even busier. No less than 226 conservation measures—for parks and greenways, open space, zoning, land use and "smart growth" regulations—were on local ballots, and 163 of them were approved. That was a 50 percent increase over 1996 and committed more than a billion dollars in local revenues. Voters in New York tried to force a referendum on building a new Yankee Stadium, and Cincinnati voted on the location of its own new ballpark. The ballpark issue was also put to a vote in Round Rock, Texas, while Kenosha, Wisconsin, voters decided on a proposed gambling initiative. Nude dancing and thong bathing suits were the issues in Seminole County, Florida. And in August of 1999, voters in Beverly Hills decided on an initiative promoted by animal rights advocates that would have required fur shops on Rodeo Drive, and other swank venues, to place on each garment a tag saying it was "made with fur from animals that may have been killed by electrocution, gassing, neck breaking, poisoning, clubbing, stomping, or drowning and may have been trapped in steel jaw leghold traps." Backers, including Sid Caesar, Jack Lemmon, and Buddy Hackett, raised $75,000 and distributed 5,000 videotapes of hidden camera scenes in which merchants assured customers the animals had died humanely. But the fur makers, bolstered by the city council and the Beverly Hills Chamber of Commerce, spent even more—$81,000. It was the only issue in an election that cost the city $60,000, and it failed, 3,363 to 1,908, with barely more than a quarter of the registered voters participating.

Not one of these decisions was made through the time-consuming process of passing and signing bills into laws—the method prescribed by the Constitution, which guaranteed the nation and each of the states "the republican form of government." Rather, they were made by the voters themselves or whatever fraction of them constituted the majority on Election Day. This is the new form of government—an increasingly popular one.

Government by initiative is not only a radical departure from the Constitution's system of checks and balances, it is also a big business, in which lawyers and campaign consultants, signature gathering firms and other players sell their services to affluent interest groups or millionaire do gooders with private policy and political agendas. These players often not even residents of the states whose laws and constitutions they are rewriting have learned that the initiative is a far more efficient way of achieving their ends than the cumbersome process of supporting candidates for public office and then lobbying them to pass or sign the measures they seek.

The process had its roots in the beginning of the last century, when Populist and Progressive reformers promoted the initiative use along with its cousin, the referendum; popular primaries; direct election of senators; and recall of errant officeholders as a remedy for the corruption rampant in the legislatures, the state capitols, and the city halls of their day. The initiative let voters, by petition, place legislation or constitutional amendments of their own devising on the ballot. The referendum made enactments of the legislature subject to up-or-down votes by the public. . . .

The great defense of [our original] scheme of government can be found in *The Federalist* papers, written to persuade the states and their people to ratify the new

Constitution. In *Federalist 10,* James Madison, one of the principal architects of the Constitution, gave the classic argument for its careful effort to balance democratic impulses with safeguards against heedless majorities.

He wrote:

> Complaints are everywhere heard from our most considerate and virtuous citizens, equally the friends of public and private faith and of public and personal liberty, that our governments are too unstable, that the public good is disregarded in the conflicts of rival parties, and that measures are too often decided, not according to the rules of justice and the rights of the minor party, but by the superior force of an interested and overbearing majority. However anxiously we may wish that these complaints had no foundation, the evidence of known facts will not permit us to deny that they are in some degree true.

Their reading of history had convinced them that the Greek city states had failed because they had tried to govern themselves by vote of the people. Madison further wrote:

> It may be concluded that a pure democracy, by which I mean a society consisting of a small number of citizens, who assemble and administer the government in person, can admit of no cure for the mischiefs of faction. A common passion or interest will, in almost every case, be felt by a majority of the whole; a communication and con-cert results from the form of government itself; and there is nothing to check the in-ducements to sacrifice the weaker party or an obnoxious individual. Hence it is that such democracies have ever been spectacles of turbulence and contention; have ever been found incompatible with personal security or the rights of property; and have in general been as short in their lives as they have been violent in their deaths.

They also argued that while direct democracy might be appropriate for a small, compact civil society, it would be impractical, let alone inconvenient, in a nation the size of the United States. Yet, as children of the Enlightenment and believers in natural law, they were convinced that individual rights preceded the formation of the state and were superior to the edicts and laws of any ruler. Thus, they wanted the government they were creating to derive its powers from "the consent of the governed."

Translating that phrase into reality became the great work of the Constitu-tional Convention. No one there argued for direct democracy. Instead, their solu-tion was representative government based on election of officials who would exercise power within the limits set forth by the constitutions of the nation and the states and under the discipline of frequent elections, which would require them to defend their actions to their constituents and allow the people to replace them if they abused their power or exercised it in ways that did not meet public approval. As Madison said at the 1788 Virginia ratifying convention, "I go on the great re-publican principle that the people will have the virtue and intelligence to select men of virtue and wisdom."

In *The Federalist,* he wrote:

> A republic, by which I mean a government in which the scheme of representation takes place, opens a different prospect and promises the cure for which we are seek-ing. Let us examine the points in which it varies from pure democracy, and we shall

comprehend both the nature of the cure and the efficacy which it must derive from the Union.

The two great points of difference between a democracy and a republic are: first, the delegation of the government, in the latter, to a small number of citizens elected by the rest; secondly, the greater number of citizens and greater sphere of country over which the latter may be extended. The effect of the first difference is, on the one hand, to refine and enlarge the public views by passing them through the medium of a chosen body of citizens, whose wisdom may best discern the true interest of their country and whose patriotism and love of justice will be least likely to sacrifice it to temporary or partial considerations. Under such a regulation, it may well happen that the public voice, pronounced by the representatives of the people, will be more consonant to the public good than if pronounced by the people themselves, convened for the purpose.

Madison conceded that there was a risk that "men of factious tempers, of local prejudices, or of sinister designs, may, by intrigue, by corruption or by other means" come to office and abuse their powers. But that risk, he said, is reduced by the size and diversity of the American Republic. "Extend the sphere and you take in a greater variety of parties and interests; you make it less probable that a majority of the whole will have a common motive to invade the rights of other citizens; or if such a common motive exists, it will be more difficult for all who feel it to discover their own strength and to act in unison with each other. . . . Hence, it clearly appears that the same advantage which a republic has over a democracy in controlling the effect of faction is enjoyed by a large over a small republic . . . [and] is enjoyed by the Union over the states composing it."

Thus, the rationale for making the United States a republic, rather than a democracy, rested on a healthy apprehension of the dangers of direct democracy and the manifold risks of relying on simple majority rule. Direct democracy, Fisher Ames of Massachusetts wrote, "would be very burdensome, subject to factions and violence; decisions would often be made by surprise, in the precipitancy of passion. . . . It would be a government not by laws but by men." The threats, as the founders envisaged them, ranged from raids on the treasury and shifting of tax burdens from one constituency to another, to the infringement of civil liberties, the submersion of minority viewpoints and interests, and even the destabilization of the entire political order.

All of those effects except the last can be seen in a number of California initiative campaigns. Proposition 13, for example, relieved many businesses and almost all apartment owners of property taxes and shifted the cost of government on to those with more transient addresses. Other initiatives commandeered high percentages of the state budget for education, requiring stringent economies in health and welfare programs that might otherwise have competed for available funds. In 1994, Proposition 187 denied education and health benefits to the families of illegal immigrants, a relatively weak minority group. And in 1996, Proposition 209 ended affirmative action, or racial and gender preferences for minorities and women, restricting education opportunities for those groups and closing down job and contract opportunities for them.

What the founders never could have foreseen, however, was the growth of a lucrative initiative industry, in which a variety of firms make handsome profits from drafting the language, collecting the signatures, managing the campaigns, and creating the media that result in the passage or defeat of these ballot measures.

A review of records for the 1998 election cycle—not one of the busiest of recent years—discloses that more than a quarter billion dollars was raised and spent on this unevenly regulated and fitfully reported arena of politics. Even more than candidate elections, initiative campaigns have become a money game, where average citizens are subjected to advertising blitzes of distortion and half truths and are left to figure out for themselves which interest groups pose the greatest threats to their self-interest.

It is a far cry from the dream of direct democracy cherished by the early nineteenth century reformers who imported this peculiar institution and installed it in this country, hoping it would cleanse our politics. They might be the first to throw up their hands in horror at what their noble experiment has produced.

Is it compatible with our form of government . . . or an alien growth? One answer comes from the distinguished historian Charles A. Beard, who was a great advocate of popular democracy in all its forms. In a book on the initiative, which he published with Birl E. Shultz in 1912, *Documents on the StateWide Initiative, Referendum, and Recall*, Beard wrote that "it is idle to speculate whether [the framers of the Constitution] would have regarded a system of initiative and referendum, such as now existing in Oregon, as repugnant to the republican form. They were not called upon to consider any such proposition."

But Beard immediately went on to quote the warnings Madison and other Founding Fathers voiced in Philadelphia about what Elbridge Gerry called "the excess of democracy." Beard wrote:

> In the face of such evidence, which may easily be multiplied by citations from the records of the convention, the *Federalist*, and other writings of this period, no one has any warrant for assuming that the founders of our federal system would have shown the slightest countenance to a system of initiative and referendum applied either to state or national affairs. If some state had possessed such a system at that time, it is questionable whether they would have been willing to have compromised with it, as they did with the slave states, in order to secure its adherence to the Union. Democracy, in the sense of simple direct majority rule, was undoubtedly more odious to most of the delegates to the convention than was slavery.
>
> When the judges of the Supreme Court are called upon to interpret the "republican" clause of the Constitution as applied to a system of initiative and referendum, it is evident they cannot discover what was the intention of the Fathers, for the latter can scarcely be said to have had any intention about a matter which had not yet come within their ken in anything approaching the form which it has now assumed. If the court, however, wishes to apply the spirit of the federal Constitution as conceived by its framers, it can readily find justification in declaring a scheme of statewide initiative and referendum contrary to the principles of that great instrument.

Beard hastened to write that such a verdict "hardly seems possible," because in a number of cases the Supreme Court said that it was up to Congress, in exercising its authority to admit states to the Union, and not to the Court, to determine whether the state constitution was satisfactory. As early as 1912, in a pair of cases challenging the constitutionality of the initiative process, *Pacific States Telephone and Telegraph v. Oregon* and *Kiernan v. City of Portland*, the justices held this was a political question, not subject to judicial review. Over the decades courts have overturned numerous individual initiatives as violating rights guaranteed by state constitutions or the Constitution. But the process itself remains constitutionally protected. And Congress has admitted to the Union states such as Oklahoma and Alaska which had the initiative process in their original constitutions.

Some legal scholars have argued that the Supreme Court rulings do not relieve state supreme courts of the right or responsibility to weigh whether the initiative process is compatible with a republican form of government, but so far no court has taken up their challenge.

The growing reliance on initiatives in the half of the country where they are available is part of the increasing alienation of Americans from the system of representative government that has served this nation for over two hundred years. As the new century begins, the reputation of elected officials at all levels has rarely been worse. Our citizens always have had a healthy skepticism about the people in public office; the whole Constitution rests on the assumption that the exercise of power is a dangerous intoxicant; hence, those in authority must be checked by clear delineation of their authority and balanced against one another, lest anyone commandeer too much power.

But what we have in the country today goes well beyond healthy skepticism to a pervasive distrust of those we ourselves have elected to exercise temporarily the authority we have given them. As a young woman attending a session of the North Carolina Institute of Political Leadership—a wonderful skills training program for community leaders who are preparing to enter elective politics—told me in 1999, "The reaction I get from people I've known for years is, 'You're such a nice person. Why would you want to go into politics?' "

The general disdain for politics and politicians is especially fierce when it comes to legislatures (including Congress) and their members. While many voters are prepared to exempt their own representative from the blanket indictment, the pervasive attitude is that our lawmakers are selfish, self-centered partisans, controlled by special interests and constantly on the lookout for ways to line their own pockets and pay off their pals and political sponsors.

One expression of that disdain has been the term-limits movement, which swept across the country during the last two decades, usually implemented by the mechanism of the initiative campaign. In that combination of initiatives and term limits, we have seen the clearest expression of the revolt against representative government. It is a command to "Clear out of there, you bums. You're none of you worth saving. We want to clean house of the lot of you. And we'll take over the job of writing the laws ourselves."

Many Americans and presumably many of those who read this will heartily endorse those sentiments and shout "Good riddance!" to the ousted legislators. In every state I visited in my reporting, the initiative process was viewed as sacrosanct. In most of them, the legislature (even though term-limited) was in disrepute.

[My] argument . . . is that representative government is not something to be discarded quite so casually. We need to examine what really happens in direct legislation by initiative. And we must ask ourselves about the implications of a weakening of our republican form of government. Is California the model we want for the nation? Or is there enduring wisdom in the founders' design?

CHAPTER 3

✌

CIVIL LIBERTIES
AND CIVIL RIGHTS

Civil liberties and civil rights cover a very broad area. Among the most fundamental civil liberties are those governing the extent to which individuals can speak, write, and read what they choose. The democratic process requires the free exchange of ideas. Constitutional government requires the protection of minority rights and, above all, the right to dissent.

The Nationalization of the Bill of Rights

It is clear from the debate over the inclusion of the Bill of Rights in the Constitution of 1787 that its provisions were certainly never intended to be prohibitions upon state action. The Bill of Rights was added to the Constitution to satisfy state governments that the same rights which they generally accorded to their own citizens under state constitutions would apply with respect to the national government and act as a check upon abridgments by the national government of civil liberties and civil rights. Proponents of a separate bill of rights wanted specific provisions to limit the powers of the national government, which, in its own sphere, could act directly upon citizens of the states.

Article X, which is not so much a part of the Bill of Rights as an expression of the balance of authority that exists between the national government and the states in the Constitution, provides that "the powers not delegated to the United States by the Constitution, nor prohibited by it to the States, are reserved to the states respectively, or to the people." Under the federal system each member of the community is both (1) a citizen of the United States and (2) a citizen of the particular state in which he or she resides. The rights and obligations of each citizenship class are determined by the legal divisions of authority set up in the Constitution. Apart from specific limits upon state power to abridge civil liberties and civil rights, as for example the prohibitions of Section 10 against state passage of any bills of attainder or ex post facto laws, there is nothing in the main body of the Constitution or the Bill of Rights that controls state action. Originally, it was up to the states to determine the protections they would give to their own citizens against state actions. The applicability of the Bill of Rights to national action only was affirmed in *Barron v. Baltimore,* 7 Peters 243 (1833).

The adoption of the Fourteenth Amendment in 1868 potentially limited the discretion that the states had possessed to determine the civil liberties and rights of citizens within their sphere of authority. The Fourteenth Amendment provided that:

> 1. All persons born or naturalized in the United States, and subject to the jurisdiction thereof, are citizens of the United States and of the state wherein they reside. No state shall make or enforce any law which shall abridge the privileges or immunities of citizens of the United States; nor shall any state deprive any person of life, liberty, or property, without due process of law; nor deny to any person within its jurisdiction the equal protection of the laws. . . .
>
> 5. The Congress shall have power to enforce, by appropriate legislation, the provisions of this article.

Although the Fourteenth Amendment appeared to be a tough restriction upon state action, its provisions were equivocal and required clarification by the Supreme Court before they could take effect. The history of the Fourteenth Amendment suggested that it was designed to protect the legal and political rights of blacks against state encroachment, and was not to have a broader application. In the *Slaughterhouse Cases,* 16 Wallace 36 (1873), the Supreme Court held that the privileges and immunities clause of the Fourteenth Amendment did nothing to alter the authority of the states to determine the rights and obligations of citizens subject to state action. Under this doctrine the Bill of Rights could not be made applicable to the states.

It was not until *Gitlow v. New York,* 268 U.S. 652 (1925), that the Court finally announced that the substantive areas of freedom of speech and of press of the First Amendment are part of the "liberty" protected by the Fourteenth Amendment due process clause; however, in Gitlow's case the Court found that the procedures that had been used in New York to restrict his freedom of speech did not violate due process. In *Near v. Minnesota,* 283 U.S. 697 (1931), the Court for the first time overturned a state statute as a violation of the Fourteenth Amendment due process clause because it permitted prior censorship of the press. *Gitlow* and *Near* were limited because they incorporated only the freedom of speech and press provisions of the First Amendment under the due process clause of the Fourteenth Amendment. The cases marked the beginning of a slow and tedious process of "incorporation" of most of the provisions of the Bill of Rights as part of the due process clause of the Fourteenth Amendment. The process of incorporation did not begin in earnest until the Warren Court, and then not until the 1960s. By the late 1970s all of the Bill of Rights was incorporated as protections against state action, with the exceptions of the rights to grand jury indictment, trial by jury in civil cases, the right to bear arms, protection against excessive bail and fines, and protection against involuntary quartering of troops in private homes.[1]

The following case presents an example of incorporation of the right to counsel under the due process clause of the Fourteenth Amendment. In cases prior to *Gideon v. Wain-*

---

[1]For an excellent discussion of the incorporation of most of the Bill of Rights under the due process clause of the Fourteenth Amendment, see Henry J. Abraham, *Freedom and the Court,* 3d ed. (New York: Oxford University Press, 1977), chap. 3.

wright, decided in 1963, the Court had upheld an ad hoc right to counsel in individual cases. That is, it had held that the facts of a particular case warranted granting the right to counsel as part of due process under the Fourteenth Amendment for that particular case only. By such ad hoc determinations, the Court was able to exercise self-restraint in relation to federal-state relations, by not requiring a general right to counsel in all state criminal cases. *Powell v. Alabama,* 287 U.S. 45 (1932), was an example of such an ad hoc inclusion of the right to counsel in a specific case, where, in a one-day trial, seven black men had been convicted of raping two white girls and sentenced to death. The Court held that under the circumstances of the case the denial of counsel by the Alabama courts to the defendants violated the due process clause of the Fourteenth Amendment. In Powell, however, the Court did not incorporate the right to counsel in all criminal cases under this due process clause. It only provided that "in a capital case, where the defendant is unable to employ counsel, and is incapable adequately of making his own defense because of ignorance, feeblemindedness, illiteracy, or the like, it is the duty of the court, whether requested or not, to assign counsel for him as a necessary requisite of due process of law. . . ." The *Powell* case was widely interpreted as nationalizing (incorporating) the right to counsel in all capital cases. The Court reaffirmed its refusal to incorporate the right to counsel in all criminal cases in *Betts v. Brady,* 316 U.S. 455 (1942). There the Court held that the Sixth Amendment applies only to trials in federal courts and that the right to counsel is not a fundamental right, essential to a fair trial, and therefore is not required in all cases under the due process clause of the Fourteenth Amendment. The Court emphasized that whether or not the right to counsel would be required depended upon the circumstances of the case in which it was requested.

In *Gideon v. Wainwright* the Court finally nationalized the right to counsel in all criminal cases under the due process clause of the Fourteenth Amendment. The case represented, in 1963, an important step in the progression toward nationalization of most of the Bill of Rights. While Justice Roberts, writing for the majority of the Court in the *Betts* case in 1942, found that the right to counsel was not fundamental to a fair trial, Justice Black, who had dissented in the *Betts* case, writing for the majority in *Gideon v. Wainwright* in 1962, held that the right to counsel was fundamental and essential to a fair trial and therefore was protected by the due process clause of the Fourteenth Amendment. In *Gideon,* Justice Black noted:

> We accept the *Brady* assumption, based as it was on our prior cases, that a provision of the Bill of Rights which is "fundamental and essential to a fair trial" is made obligatory upon the states by the Fourteenth Amendment. We think the Court in *Betts* was wrong, however, in concluding that the Sixth Amendment's guarantee of counsel is not one of the fundamental rights.

The history of Supreme Court interpretation of the Fourteenth Amendment due process clause reveals the Court acting both politically and ideologically. In the period from 1868 to 1925 the Court was careful to exercise judicial self-restraint in interpreting the Fourteenth Amendment, in part because of the conservative views of most of the justices that the Court should not impose national standards of civil liberties and civil rights upon the states. The Court did not believe in self-restraint in all areas, as is demonstrated by its use of the due process clause of the Fourteenth Amendment to impose its own views on the proper relationship between the states and business. The Court read the Fourteenth Amendment due process clause in such a way as to protect the property interests of business against state regulation. Many such laws were found to be taking the liberty or property of business without due process. Beginning with *Gitlow v. New York* in 1925, the Court for the first time added substance to the due process clause of the Fourteenth Amendment in the area of civil liberties by including First Amendment freedoms of speech and press as part of the "liberty" of the due process clause.

While the Supreme Court is sensitive to the political environment in which it functions, the ways in which it has interpreted the due process clause of the Fourteenth Amendment suggest that ideological convictions are more important than pressure from political majorities. During the era of economic substantive due process under the Fourteenth Amendment, which ended in 1937, the Court was really taking an elitist position that did not agree with the political majorities in many states that were behind the regulatory laws that the Court struck down. Nor can it be said that when the Court began to add substance in civil liberties and civil rights to the due process clause and extend procedural protection that it was supported by political majorities. In fact, the Warren Court's extension of the Fourteenth Amendment due process clause, particularly in the area of criminal rights, caused a political outcry among the states and their citizens who felt that law enforcement efforts would be unduly impeded. When the Court, in *Griswold v. Connecticut* in 1965, went beyond the explicit provisions of the Bill of Rights to find a right of privacy to strike down Connecticut's birth control statute that prevented the use of contraceptives in the state, even Justice Black, a strong supporter of incorporating the Bill of Rights under the due process clause, took objection. He found in the *Griswold* decision a return to substantive due process in a form that was unacceptable, because it was adding substance to the clause that was not explicitly provided for in the intent of the Fourteenth Amendment, which he had held in *Adamson v. California* in 1946 to be total inclusion of the Bill of Rights. The Griswold decision was not unpopular politically, but when the Court in *Roe v. Wade* in 1973 used the right of privacy to strike down a Texas abortion statute, and in effect declare all state laws that absolutely prohibited abortion to be unconstitutional, a nationwide anti-abortion movement was organized to overturn the decision by mobilizing political support behind a constitutional amendment. The Supreme Court has certainly not, in the area of interpretation of the Fourteenth Amendment, acted solely out of political motives.[2]

The following case presents an example of the way in which the Supreme Court gradually incorporated the Bill of Rights under the Fourteenth Amendment. Behind the decision to nationalize the right to counsel in *Gideon v. Wainwright* a fascinating series of events had occurred.[3] By the time the *Gideon* case was called up, the Court was purposely looking for an appropriate case from which it could incorporate the right to counsel under the due process clause of the Fourteenth Amendment. The Court felt that Gideon's case presented the kind of circumstances that would be publicly accepted as requiring the right to counsel to ensure fairness. In granting certiorari to Gideon's in forma pauperis petition ("in the manner of the pauper," a permission to sue without incurring liability for costs) the Court had in effect already made up its mind about the decision. By the appointment of attorney Abe Fortas, later to become a member of the Court (although eventually forced to resign because of conflict-of-interest charges), one of the most distinguished lawyers in the country, the Court guaranteed an eloquent and persuasive brief for the petitioner, Earl Gideon. The Court felt that the right to counsel was a right whose time had come by 1963.

---

[2]The forces affecting Supreme Court decision making are discussed in the selections by William J. Brennan, Jr., and John P. Roche in Chapter 9.

[3]The story of the case is brilliantly told by Anthony Lewis in *Gideon's Trumpet* (New York: Random House, 1964).

13

GIDEON V. WAINWRIGHT*

cf0

372 U.S. 335 (1963)

. . . Mr. Justice Black delivered the opinion of the Court, saying in part:

Petitioner was charged in a Florida state court with having broken and entered a poolroom with intent to commit a misdemeanor. This offense is a felony under Florida law. Appearing in court without funds and without a lawyer, petitioner asked the court to appoint counsel for him, whereupon the following colloquy took place:

> The Court: Mr. Gideon, I am sorry, but I cannot appoint Counsel to represent you in this case. Under the laws of the State of Florida, the only time the Court can appoint Counsel to represent a Defendant is when that person is charged with a capital offense. I am sorry, but I will have to deny your request to appoint Counsel to defend you in this case. The Defendant: The United States Supreme Court says I am entitled to be represented by Counsel.

Put to trial before a jury, Gideon conducted his defense about as well as could be expected from a layman. He made an opening statement to the jury, cross-examined the State's witnesses, presented witnesses in his own defense, declined to testify himself, and made a short argument "emphasizing his innocence to the charge contained in the Information filed in this case." The jury returned a verdict of guilty, and petitioner was sentenced to serve five years in the state prison. Later, petitioner filed in the Florida Supreme Court this habeas corpus petition attacking his conviction and sentence on the ground that the trial court's refusal to appoint counsel for him denied him rights "guaranteed by the Constitution and the Bill of Rights by the United States Government."[1] Treating the petition for habeas corpus as properly before it, the State Supreme Court, "upon consideration thereof" but without an opinion, denied all relief. Since 1942, when *Betts v. Brady*, 316 U.S. 455 . . . was decided by a divided Court, the problem of a defendant's federal constitutional right to counsel in a state court has been a continuing source of controversy and litigation in both state and federal courts. To give this problem another review here, we granted certiorari. 370 U.S. 908. . . . Since Gideon was proceeding in forma pauperis, we appointed counsel to represent him and requested both

---

*In this selection some footnotes are omitted: all are renumbered.

[1]Later in the petition for habeas corpus, signed and apparently prepared by the petitioner himself, he stated, "I, Clarence Earl Gideon, claim that I was denied the rights of the 4th, 5th and 14th amendments of the Bill of Rights."

sides to discuss in their briefs and oral arguments the following: "Should this Court's holding in *Betts v. Brady* . . . be reconsidered?"

I

The facts upon which Betts claimed that he had been unconstitutionally denied the right to have counsel appointed to assist him are strikingly like the facts upon which Gideon here bases his federal constitutional claim. Betts was indicted for robbery in a Maryland state court. On arraignment, he told the trial judge of his lack of funds to hire a lawyer and asked the court to appoint one for him. Betts was advised that it was not the practice in that county to appoint counsel for indigent defendants except in murder and rape cases. He then pleaded not guilty, had witnesses summoned, cross-examined the State's witnesses, examined his own, and chose not to testify himself. He was found guilty by the judge, sitting without a jury, and sentenced to eight years in prison. Like Gideon, Betts sought release by habeas corpus, alleging that he had been denied the right to assistance of counsel in violation of the Fourteenth Amendment. Betts was denied any relief, and on review this Court affirmed. It was held that a refusal to appoint counsel for an indigent defendant charged with a felony did not necessarily violate the Due Process Clause of the Fourteenth Amendment, which for reasons given the Court deemed to be the only applicable federal constitutional provision. The Court said:

> Asserted denial [of due process] is to be tested by an appraisal of the totality of facts in a given case. That which may, in one setting, constitute a denial of fundamental fairness, shocking to the universal sense of justice, may, in other circumstances, and in the light of other considerations, fall short of such denial. 316 U.S., at 462. . . .

Treating due process as "a concept less rigid and more fluid than those envisaged in other specific and particular provisions of the Bill of Rights," the Court held that refusal to appoint counsel under the particular facts and circumstances in the Betts case was not so "offensive to the common and fundamental ideas of fairness" as to amount to a denial of due process. Since the facts and circumstances of the two cases are so nearly indistinguishable, we think the *Betts v. Brady* holding if left standing would require us to reject Gideon's claim that the Constitution guarantees him the assistance of counsel. Upon full reconsideration we conclude that *Betts v. Brady* should be overruled.

II

The Sixth Amendment provides, "In all criminal prosecutions, the accused shall enjoy the right . . . to have the Assistance of Counsel for his defence." We have construed this to mean that in federal courts counsel must be provided for defendants unable to employ counsel unless the right is competently and intelligently waived. Betts argued that this right is extended to indigent defendants in state courts by the Fourteenth Amendment. In response the Court stated that, while the

Sixth Amendment laid down "no rule for the conduct of the states, the question recurs whether the constraint laid by the amendment upon the national courts expresses a rule so fundamental and essential to a fair trial, and so, to due process of law, that it is made obligatory upon the states by the Fourteenth Amendment." 316 U.S., at 465. . . . In order to decide whether the Sixth Amendment's guarantee of counsel is of this fundamental nature, the Court in Betts set out and considered "[r]elevant data on the subject . . . afforded by constitutional and statutory provisions subsisting in the colonies and the states prior to the inclusion of the Bill of Rights in the national Constitution, and in the constitutional, legislative, and judicial history of the states to the present date." 316 U.S., at 465. . . . On the basis of this historical data the Court concluded that "appointment of counsel is not a fundamental right, essential to a fair trial." 316 U.S., at 471. . . . It was for this reason the Betts Court refused to accept the contention that the Sixth Amendment's guarantee of counsel for indigent federal defendants was extended to or, in the words of that Court, "made obligatory upon the states by the Fourteenth Amendment." Plainly, had the Court concluded that appointment of counsel for an indigent criminal defendant was "a fundamental right, essential to a fair trial," it would have held that the Fourteenth Amendment requires appointment of counsel in a state court, just as the Sixth Amendment requires in a federal court.

We think the Court in Betts had ample precedent for acknowledging that those guarantees of the Bill of Rights which are fundamental safeguards of liberty immune from federal abridgment are equally protected against state invasion by the Due Process Clause of the Fourteenth Amendment. This same principle was recognized, explained, and applied in *Powell v. Alabama*, 287 U.S. 45 (1932), a case upholding the right of counsel, where the Court held that despite sweeping language to the contrary in *Hurtado v. California*, 110 U.S. 516 (1884), the Fourteenth Amendment "embraced" those "fundamental principles of liberty and justice which lie at the base of all our civil and political institutions," even though they had been "specifically dealt with in another part of the Federal Constitution." 287 U.S., at 67. . . . In many cases other than Powell and Betts, this Court has looked to the fundamental nature of original Bill of Rights guarantees to decide whether the Fourteenth Amendment makes them obligatory on the States. Explicitly recognized to be of this "fundamental nature" and therefore made immune from state invasion by the Fourteenth, or some part of it, are the First Amendment's freedoms of speech, press, religion, assembly, association, and petition for redress of grievances. For the same reason, though not always in precisely the same terminology, the Court has made obligatory on the States the Fifth Amendment's command that private property shall not be taken for public use without just compensation, the Fourth Amendment's prohibition of unreasonable searches and seizures, and the Eighth's ban on cruel and unusual punishment. On the other hand, this Court in *Palko v. Connecticut*, 301 U.S. 319 . . . (1937), refused to hold that the Fourteenth Amendment made the double jeopardy provision of the Fifth Amendment obligatory on the States. In so refusing, however, the Court, speaking through Mr. Justice Cardozo, was careful to emphasize that "immunities that are valid as against the federal government by force of the specific pledges of particular amendments have been found to be implicit in the concept of ordered liberty, and thus, through the Fourteenth Amendment, become valid as against the states" and that guarantees "in their origin . . . effective against the federal government alone" had by prior cases "been taken over from the earlier articles of the Federal Bill of Rights and brought within the Fourteenth Amendment by a process of absorption." 302 U.S., at 324–325, 326. . . .

We accept *Betts v. Brady*'s assumption, based as it was on our prior cases, that a provision of the Bill of Rights which is "fundamental and essential to a fair trial" is made obligatory upon the States by the Fourteenth Amendment. We think the Court in Betts was wrong, however, in concluding that the Sixth Amendment's guarantee of counsel is not one of these fundamental rights. Ten years before *Betts v. Brady*, this Court, after full consideration of all the historical data examined in Betts, had unequivocally declared that "the right to the aid of counsel is of this fundamental character." *Powell v. Alabama*, 287 U.S. 45 . . . (1932). While the Court at the close of its Powell opinion did by its language, as this Court frequently does, limit its holding to the particular facts and circum- stances of that case, its conclusions about the fundamental nature of the right to counsel are unmistakable. Several years later, in 1936, the Court reemphasized what it had said about the fundamental nature of the right to counsel in this language:

> We concluded that certain fundamental rights, safeguarded by the first eight amendments against federal action, were also safeguarded against state action by the due process of law clause of the Fourteenth Amendment, and among them the fundamental right of the accused to the aid of counsel in a criminal prosecution. *Grosjean v. American Press Co.*, 297 U.S. 233 . . . (1936).

And again in 1938 this Court said:

> [The assistance of counsel] is one of the safeguards of the Sixth Amendment deemed necessary to insure fundamental human rights of life and liberty. . . . The Sixth Amendment stands as a constant admonition that if the constitutional safeguards it provides be lost, justice will not 'still be done.' *Johnson v. Zerbst*, 304 U.S. 458 . . . (1938). To the same effect, see *Avery v. Alabama*, 308 U.S. 444 . . . (1940), and *Smith v. O'Grady*, 312 U.S. 329 . . . (1941).

In light of these and many other prior decisions of this Court, it is not surpris- ing that the Betts Court, when faced with the contention that "one charged with crime, who is unable to obtain counsel, must be furnished counsel by the state," conceded that "[e]xpressions in the opinions of this court lend color to the argument . . . " 316 U.S., at 462–463. . . . The fact is that in deciding as it did—that "appointment of counsel is not a fundamental right, essential to a fair trial"—the Court in *Betts v. Brady* made an abrupt break with its own well- considered precedents. In returning to these old precedents, sounder we believe than the new, we but restore constitutional principles established to achieve a fair system of justice. Not only these precedents but also reason and reflection require us to recognize that in our adversary system of criminal justice, any person hailed into court, who is too poor to hire a lawyer, cannot be assured a fair trial unless counsel is provided for him. This seems to us to be an obvious truth. Governments, both state and federal, quite properly spend vast sums of money to establish machinery to try defendants accused of crime. Lawyers to prosecute are everywhere deemed essential to protect the public's interest in an orderly society. Similarly, there are few defendants charged with crime, few indeed, who fail to hire the best lawyers they can get to prepare and present their defenses. That government hires lawyers to prosecute and defendants who have the money hire lawyers to defend are the strongest indications of the widespread belief that lawyers in criminal courts are necessities, not luxuries. The right of one charged with crime to counsel may not be deemed fundamental and essential to fair trials in some countries, but it is in ours. From the very beginning, our state and national constitutions and laws have laid great emphasis on procedural and substantive safeguards designed to assure fair trials before impartial tribunals in which every defendant stands equal before the law. This noble ideal cannot be realized if the poor man charged with crime has to face his accusers without a lawyer to assist him. A defendant's need for a lawyer is nowhere better stated than in the moving words of Mr. Justice Sutherland in *Powell v. Alabama:*

> The right to be heard would be, in many cases, of little avail if it did not comprehend the right to be heard by counsel. Even the intelligent and educated layman has small and sometimes no skill in the science of law. If charged with crime, he is incapable, generally, of determining for himself whether the indictment is good or bad. He is unfamiliar with the rules of evidence. Left without the aid of counsel he may be put on trial without a proper charge, and convicted upon incompetent evidence, or evidence irrelevant to the issue or other wise inadmissible. He lacks both the skill and knowledge adequately to prepare his defense, even though he have a perfect one. He requires the guiding hand of counsel at every step in the proceedings against him. Without it, though he be not guilty, he faces the danger of conviction because he does not know how to establish his innocence. 287 U.S., at 68–69. . . .

The Court in *Betts v. Brady* departed from the second wisdom upon which the Court's holding in *Powell v. Alabama* rested. Florida, supported by two other States, has asked that *Betts v. Brady* be left intact. Twenty-two States, as friends of the Court, argue that Betts was "an anachronism when handed down" and that it should now be overruled. We agree.

The judgment is reversed and the cause is remanded to the Supreme Court of Florida for further action not inconsistent with this opinion.

Chief Justice Warren, and Justices Brennan, Stewart, White, and Goldberg join in the opinion of the Court.

Mr. Justice Douglas joins the opinion, giving a brief historical resume of the relation between the Bill of Rights and the Fourteenth Amendment. Mr. Justice Clark concurs in the result. Mr. Justice Harlan concurs in the result.

Freedom of Speech and Press

There are many reasons why we should support freedom of speech and press. One of these is the impossibility of proving the existence of an Absolute Truth. No person or group can be infallible. The "best" decisions are those that are made on the basis of the most widespread information available pertaining to the subject at hand. Freedom of information is an integral part of the democratic process. In this selection from John Stuart Mill's famous essay *On Liberty*, published in 1859, the justifications for permitting liberty of speech and press are discussed.

14

LIBERTY OF THOUGHT AND DISCUSSION

John Stuart Mill

The time, it is to be hoped, is gone by when any defense would be necessary of the "liberty of the press" as one of the securities against corrupt or tyrannical government. No argument, we may suppose, can now be needed, against permitting a legislature or an executive, not identified in interest with the people, to prescribe opinions to them, and determine what doctrines or what arguments they shall be allowed to hear. This aspect of the question, besides, has been so often and so triumphantly enforced by preceding writers, that it needs not be specially insisted on in this place. Though the law of England, on the subject of the press, is as servile to this day as it was in the time of the Tudors, there is little danger of its being actually put in force against political discussion, except during some temporary panic, when fear of insurrection drives ministers and judges from their propriety; and, speaking generally, it is not, in constitutional countries, to be apprehended, that the government, whether completely responsible to the people or not, will often attempt to control the expression of opinion, except when in doing so it makes itself the organ of the general intolerance of the public. Let us suppose, therefore, that the government is entirely at one with the people, and never thinks of exerting any power of coercion unless in agreement with what it conceives to be their voice. But I deny the right of the people to exercise such coercion, either by themselves or by their government. The power itself is illegitimate. The best government has no more title to it than the worst. It is as noxious, or more noxious, when exerted in accordance with public opinion, than when in opposition to it. If all mankind minus one, were of one opinion, and only one person were of the contrary opinion, mankind would be no more justified in silencing that one person, than he, if he had the power, would be justified in silencing mankind. Were an opinion a personal possession of no value except to the owner; if to be obstructed in the enjoyment of it were simply a private injury, it would make some difference whether the injury was inflicted only on a few persons or on many. But the peculiar evil of silencing the expression of an opinion is, that it is robbing the human race; posterity as well as the existing generation; those who dissent from the opinion, still more than those who hold it. If the opinion is right, they are deprived of the opportunity of exchanging error for truth: if wrong, they lose, what is almost as great a benefit, the clearer perception and livelier impression of truth, produced by its collision with error.

It is necessary to consider separately these two hypotheses, each of which has a distinct branch of the argument corresponding to it. We can never be sure that the opinion we are endeavoring to stifle is a false opinion; and if we were sure, stifling it would be an evil still.

First: the opinion which it is attempted to suppress by authority may possibly be true. Those who desire to suppress it, of course deny its truth; but they are not infallible. They have no authority to decide the question for all mankind, and exclude every other person from the means of judging. To refuse a hearing to an opinion, because they are sure that it is false, is to assume that their certainty is the same thing as absolute certainty. All silencing of discussion is an assumption of infallibility. Its condemnation may be allowed to rest on this common argument, not the worse for being common.

Unfortunately for the good sense of mankind, the fact of their fallibility is far from carrying the weight in their practical judgment, which is always allowed to it in theory; for while every one well knows himself to be fallible, few think it necessary to take any precautions against their own fallibility, or admit the supposition that any opinion, of which they feel very certain, may be one of the examples of the error to which they acknowledge themselves to be liable. Absolute princes, or others who are accustomed to unlimited deference, usually feel this complete confidence in their own opinions on nearly all subjects. People more happily situated, who sometimes hear their opinions disputed, and are not wholly unused to be set right when they are wrong, place the same unbounded reliance only on such of their opinions as are shared by all who surround them, or to whom they habitually defer: for in proportion to a man's want of confidence in his own solitary judgment, does he usually repose, with implicit trust, on the infallibility of "the world" in general. And the world, to each individual, means the part of it with which he comes in contact; his party, his sect, his church, his class of society: the man may be called, by comparison, almost liberal and largeminded to whom it means anything so comprehensive as his own country or his own age. Nor is his faith in this collective authority at all shaken by his being aware that other ages, countries, sects, churches, classes, and parties have thought, and even now think, the exact reverse. He devolves upon his own world the responsibility of being in the right against the dissentient worlds of other people; and it never troubles him that mere accident has decided which of these numerous worlds is the object of his reliance, and that the same causes which make him a Churchman in London, would have made him a Buddhist or a Confucian in Peking. Yet it is as evident in itself, as any amount of argument can make it, that ages are not more infallible than individuals; every age having held many opinions which subsequent ages have deemed not only false but absurd; and it is as certain that many opinions, now general, will be rejected by future ages, as it is that many, once general, are rejected by the present.

The objection likely to be made to this argument, would probably take some such form as the following. There is no greater assumption of infallibility in forbidding the propagation of error, than in any other thing which is done by public authority on its own judgment and responsibility. Judgment is given to men that they may use it. Because it may be used erroneously, are men to be told that they ought not to use it at all? To prohibit what they think pernicious, is not claiming exemption from error, but fulfilling the duty incumbent on them, although fallible, of acting on their conscientious conviction. If we were never to act on our opinions, because those opinions may be wrong, we should leave all our interests uncared for, and all our duties unperformed. An objection which applies to all conduct, can be no valid objection to any conduct in particular. It is the duty of governments, and of individuals, to form the truest opinions they can; to form them carefully, and never impose them upon others unless they are quite sure of being right. But when they are sure (such reasoners may say), it is not conscientiousness but cowardice to shrink from acting on their opinions, and allow doctrines which they honestly think dangerous to the welfare of mankind, either in this life or in another, to be scattered abroad without restraint, because other people, in less enlightened times, have persecuted opinions now believed to be true. Let us take care, it may be said, not to make the same mistake: but governments and nations have made mistakes in other things, which are not denied to be fit subjects for the exercise of authority: they have laid on bad taxes, made unjust wars. Ought we therefore to lay on no taxes, and, under whatever provocation, make no wars? Men, and governments, must act to the best of their ability. There is no such thing as absolute certainty, but there is assurance sufficient for the purposes of human life. We may, and must, assume our opinion to be true for the guidance of our own conduct: and it is assuming no more when we forbid bad men to pervert society by the propagation of opinions which we regard as false and pernicious.

I answer, that it is assuming very much more. There is the greatest difference between presuming an opinion to be true, because, with every opportunity for contesting it, it had not been refuted, and assuming its truth for the purpose of not permitting its refutation. Complete liberty of contradicting and disproving our opinion, is the very condition which justifies us in assuming its truth for purposes of action; and on no other terms can a being with human faculties have any rational assurance of being right.

When we consider either the history of opinion, or the ordinary conduct of human life, to what is it to be ascribed that the one and the other are no worse than they are? Not certainly to the inherent force of the human understanding; for, on any matter not self-evident, there are ninety-nine persons totally incapable of judging of it, for one who is capable; and the capacity of the hundredth person is only comparative; for the majority of the eminent men of every past generation held many opinions now known to be erroneous, and did or approved numerous things which no one will now justify. Why is it, then, that there is on the whole a preponderance among mankind of rational opinions and rational conduct? If there really is this preponderance—which there must be, unless human affairs are, and have always been, in an almost desperate state—it is owing to a quality of the human mind, the source of everything respectable in man either as an intellectual or as a moral being, namely, that his errors are corrigible. He is capable of rectifying his mistakes, by discussion and experience. Not by experience alone. There must be discussion, to show how experience is to be interpreted. Wrong opinions and practices gradually yield to fact and argument: but facts and arguments, to produce any effect on the mind, must be brought before it. Very few facts are able to tell their own story, without comments to bring out their meaning. The whole strength and value, then, of human judgment, depending on the one property, that it can be set right when it is wrong, reliance can be placed on it only when the means of setting it right are kept constantly at hand. In the case of any person whose judgment is really deserving of confidence, how has it become so? Because he has kept his mind open to criticism of his opinions and conduct. Because it has been his practice to listen to all that could be said against him; to profit by as much of it as was just, and expound to himself, and upon occasion to others, the fallacy of what was fallacious. Because he has felt, that the only way in which a human being can make some approach to knowing the whole of a subject, is by hearing what can be said about it by persons of every variety of opinion, and studying all modes in which it can be looked at by every character of mind. No wise man ever acquired his wisdom in any mode but this; nor is it in the nature of human intellect to become wise in any other manner. The steady habit of correcting and completing his own opinion by collating it with those of others, so far from causing doubt and hesitation in carrying it into practice, is the only stable foundation for a just reliance on it: for, being cognizant of all that can, at least obviously, be said against him, and having taken up his position against all gainsayers—knowing that he has sought for objections and difficulties, instead of avoiding them, and has shut out no light which can be thrown upon the subject from any quarter—he has a right to think his judgment better than that of any person, or any multitude, who have not gone through a similar process.

It is not too much to require that what the wisest of mankind, those who are best entitled to trust their own judgment, find necessary to warrant their relying on it, should be submitted to by that miscellaneous collection of a few wise and many foolish individuals, called the public. The most intolerant of churches, the Roman Catholic Church, even at the canonization of a saint, admits, and listens patiently to, a "devil's advocate." The holiest of men, it appears, cannot be admitted to posthumous honors, until all that the devil could say against him is known and weighed. If even the Newtonian philosophy were not permitted to be questioned, mankind could not feel as complete assurance of its truth as they now do. The beliefs which we have most warrant for, have no safeguard to rest on, but a standing invitation to the whole world to prove them unfounded. . . .

We have now recognized the necessity to the mental well-being of mankind (on which all their other well-being depends) of freedom of opinion, and freedom of the expression of opinion, on four distinct grounds; which we will now briefly recapitulate.

First, if any opinion is compelled to silence, that opinion may, for aught we can certainly know, be true. To deny this is to assume our own infallibility.

Secondly, though the silenced opinion be an error, it may, and very commonly does, contain a portion of truth; and since the general or prevailing opinion on any subject is rarely or never the whole truth, it is only by the collision of adverse opinions that the remainder of the truth has any chance of being supplied.

Thirdly, even if the received opinion be not only true, but the whole truth; unless it is suffered to be, and actually is, vigorously and earnestly contested, it will, by most of those who receive it, be held in the manner of a prejudice, with little comprehension of feeling of its rational grounds. And not only this, but fourthly, the meaning of the doctrine itself will be in danger of being lost, or enfeebled, and deprived of its vital effect on the character and conduct: the dogma becoming a mere formal profession, inefficacious for good, but cumbering the ground, and preventing the growth of any real and heartfelt conviction from reason or personal experience.

Before quitting the subject of freedom of opinion, it is fit to take some notice of those who say, that the free expression of all opinions should be permitted, on condition that the manner be temperate, and do not pass the bounds of fair discussion. Much might be said on the impossibility of fixing where these supposed bounds are to be placed; for if the test be offence to those whose opinion is attacked, I think experience testifies that this offence is given whenever the attack is telling and powerful, and that every opponent who pushes them hard, and whom they find it difficult to answer, appears to them, if he shows any strong feeling on the subject, an intemperate opponent. But this, though an important consideration in a practical point of view, merges in a more fundamental objection. Undoubtedly the manner of asserting an opinion, even though it be a true one, may be very objectionable, and may justly incur severe censure. But the principal offences of the kind are such as it is mostly impossible, unless by accidental self-betrayal, to bring home to conviction. The gravest of them is, to argue sophistically, to suppress facts or arguments, to misstate the elements of the case, or misrepresent the opposite opinion. But all this, even to the most aggravated degree, is so continually done in perfect good faith, by persons who are not considered, and in many other respects may not deserve to be considered, ignorant or incompetent, that it is rarely possible on adequate grounds conscientiously to stamp the misrepresentation as morally culpable; and still less could law presume to interfere with this kind of controversial misconduct. With regard to what is commonly meant by intemperate discussion, namely, invective, sarcasm, personality, and the like, the denunciation of these weapons would deserve more sympathy if it were ever proposed to interdict them equally to both sides; but it is only desired to restrain the employment of them against the prevailing opinion: against the unprevailing they may not only be used without general disapproval, but will be likely to obtain for him who uses them the praise of honest zeal and righteous indignation. Yet whatever mischief arises from their use, is greatest when they are employed against the comparatively defenceless; and whatever unfair advantage can be derived by any opinion from this mode of asserting it, accrues almost exclusively to received opinions. The worst offence of this kind which can be committed by a polemic, is to stigmatize those who hold the contrary opinion as bad and immoral men. To calumny of this sort, those who hold any unpopular opinion are peculiarly exposed, because they are in general few and uninfluential, and nobody but themselves feels much interest in seeing justice done them; but this weapon is, from the nature of the case, denied to those who attack a prevailing opinion: they can neither use it with safety to themselves, nor, if they could, would it do anything but recoil on their own cause. In general, opinions contrary to those commonly received can only obtain a hearing by studied moderation of language, and the most cautious avoidance of unnecessary offence, from which they hardly ever deviate even in a slight degree without losing ground: while unmeasured vituperation employed on the side of the prevailing opinion, really does deter people from professing contrary opinions, and from listening to those who profess them. For the interest, therefore, of truth and justice, it is far more important to restrain this employment of vituperative language than the other; and, for example, if it were necessary to choose, there would be much more need to discourage offensive attacks on infidelity, than on religion. It is, however, obvious that law and authority have no business with restraining either, while opinion ought, in every instance, to determine its verdict by the circumstances of the individual case; condemning every one, on whichever side of the argument he places himself, in whose mode of advocacy either want of candor, or malignity, bigotry, or intolerance of feeling manifest themselves; but not inferring these vices from the side which a person takes, though it be the contrary side of the question to our own: and giving merited honor to every one, whatever opinion he may hold, who had calmness to see and honesty to state what his opponents and their opinions really are, exaggerating nothing to their discredit, keeping nothing back which tells, or can be supposed to tell, in their favor. This is the real morality of public discussion; and if often violated, I am happy to think that there are many controversialists who to a great extent observe it, and a still greater number who conscientiously strive towards it.

Mill does not justify absolute liberty of speech and press but implies that there are boundaries—although difficult to determine—to public debate. Democratic governments have always been faced with this dilemma: At what point can freedom of speech and press be curtailed? The Supreme Court has had difficulty in making decisions in areas involving censorship and loyalty and security. Freedom of speech and press cannot be used to destroy the very government that protects civil liberties.

Justice Holmes, in *Schenck v. United States*, 249 U.S. 47 (1919), stated his famous "clear and present danger" test, which subsequently was applied at both the national and state levels, for deciding whether or not Congress could abridge freedom of speech under the First Amendment:

> The most stringent protection of free speech would not protect a man in falsely shouting fire in a theatre and causing a panic. It does not protect a man from an injunction against uttering words that may have all the effects of force. . . . The question in every case is whether the words used are used in such circumstances and are of such a nature as to create a clear and present danger that they will bring about the substantive evils that Congress has a right to prevent. It is a question of proximity and degree. When a nation is at war many things that might be said in time of peace are such a hindrance to its efforts that their utterance will not be endured so long as men fight and that no Court could regard them as protected by any constitutional right.

Limiting Freedom of Speech—Hate Speech, Speech Codes, and the First Amendment

Hate speech became a major issue thorughout the country in the 1990s, particularly in schools, colleges, and universities. Educators sought to control hate speech through speech codes which attempt to define the content of hate speech and prohibit it. The ACLU notes:

> "In recent years, a rise in verbal abuse and violence directed at people of color, lesbians and gay men, and other historically persecuted groups has plagued the United States. Among the settings of these expressions of intolerance are college and university campuses, where bias incidents have occurred sporadically since the mid-1980s. Outrage, indignation and demands for change have greeted such incidents—understandably, given the lack of racial and social diversity among students, faculty and administrators on most campuses.
>
> Many universities, under pressure to respond to the concerns of those who are the objects of hate, have adopted codes or policies prohibiting speech that offends any group based on race, gender, ethnicity, religion or sexual orientation."
> HYPERLINK http://www.aclu.org/library/pbp16.html
> http://www.aclu.org/library/pbp16.html

The Supreme Court handed down its first major opinion on the constitutionality of government regulation of hate speech in the following case.

15

CHAPLINSKY V. STATE OF NEW HAMPSHIRE

∾

315 U.S. 568 (1942)

Mr. Justice Murphy delivered the opinion of the Court.

Appellant, a member of the sect known as Jehovah's Witnesses, was convicted in the municipal court of Rochester, New Hampshire, for violation of Chapter 378, Section 2, of the Public Laws of New Hampshire: "No person shall address any offensive, derisive or annoying word to any other person who is lawfully in any street or other public place, nor call him by any offensive or derisive name, nor make any noise or exclamation in his presence and hearing with intent to deride, offend or annoy him, or to prevent him from pursuing his lawful business or occupation."

The complaint charged that appellant "with force and arms, in a certain public place in said city of Rochester, to wit, on the public sidewalk on the easterly side of

Wakefield Street, near unto the entrance of the City Hall, did unlawfully repeat, the words following, addressed to the complainant, that is to say, 'You are a God damned racketeer' and 'a damned Fascist and the whole government of Rochester are Fascists or agents of Fascists' the same being offensive, derisive and annoying words and names."

Upon appeal there was a trial de novo of appellant before a jury in the Superior Court. He was found guilty and the judgment of conviction was affirmed by the Supreme Court of the State. 91 N.H. 310, 18 A.2d 754.

By motions and exceptions, appellant raised the questions that the statute was invalid under the Fourteenth Amendment of the Constitution of the United States in that it placed an unreasonable restraint on freedom of speech, freedom of the press, and freedom of worship, and because it was vague and indefinite. These contentions were overruled and the case comes here on appeal.

There is no substantial dispute over the facts. Chaplinsky was distributing the literature of his sect on the streets [315 U.S. 568, 570] of Rochester on a busy Saturday afternoon. Members of the local citizenry complained to the City Marshal, Bowering, that Chaplinsky was denouncing all religion as a "racket." Bowering told them that Chaplinsky was lawfully engaged, and then warned Chaplinsky that the crowd was getting restless. Some time later a disturbance occurred and the traffic officer on duty at the busy intersection started with Chaplinsky for the police station, but did not inform him that he was under arrest or that he was going to be arrested. On the way they encountered Marshal Bowering who had been advised that a riot was under way and was therefore hurrying to the scene. Bowering repeated his earlier warning to Chaplinsky who then addressed to Bowering the words set forth in the complaint.

Chaplinsky's version of the affair was slightly different. He testified that when he met Bowering, he asked him to arrest the ones responsible for the disturbance. In reply Bowering cursed him and told him to come along. Appellant admitted that he said the words charged in the complaint with the exception of the name of the Deity.

Over appellant's objection the trial court excluded as immaterial testimony relating to appellant's mission "to preach the true facts of the Bible," his treatment at the hands of the crowd, and the alleged neglect of duty on the part of the police. This action was approved by the court below which held that neither provocation nor the truth of the utterance would constitute a defense to the charge.

It is now clear that "Freedom of speech and freedom of the press, which are protected by the First Amendment from infringement by Congress, are among the fundamental personal rights and liberties which are protected by the Fourteenth Amendment from invasion by state [315 U.S. 568, 571] action."

Appellant assails the statute as a violation of all three freedoms, speech, press and worship, but only an attack on the basis of free speech is warranted. The spoken, not the written, word is involved. And we cannot conceive that cursing a public officer is the exercise of religion in any sense of the term. But even if the activities of the appellant which preceded the incident could be viewed as religious in character, and therefore entitled to the protection of the Fourteenth Amendment, they would not cloak him with immunity from the legal consequences for concomitant acts committed in violation of a valid criminal statute. We turn, therefore, to an examination of the statute itself.

Allowing the broadest scope to the language and purpose of the Fourteenth Amendment, it is well understood that the right of free speech is not absolute at all times and under all circumstances. There are certain well-defined and narrowly limited classes of speech, the prevention [315 U.S. 568, 572] and punishment of which has never been thought to raise any Constitutional problem. These include the lewd and obscene, the profane, the libelous, and the insulting or "fighting" words—those which by their very utterance inflict injury or tend to incite an immediate breach of the peace. It has been well observed that such utterances are no essential part of any exposition of ideas, and are of such slight social value as a step to truth that any benefit that may be derived from them is clearly outweighed by the social interest in order and morality. "Resort to epithets or personal abuse is not in any proper sense communication of information or opinion safeguarded by the Constitution, and its punishment as a criminal act would raise no question under that instrument." . . .

The state statute here challenged comes to us authoritatively construed by the highest court of New Hampshire. It has two provisions—the first relates to words or names addressed to another in a public place; the second refers to noises and exclamations. The court (91 N.H. 310, 18 A. 2d 757) said: "The two provisions are distinct. One may stand separately from the other. Assuming, without holding, that the second were unconstitutional, the first could stand if constitutional." We accept that construction of severability and limit our consideration to the first provision of the statute. . . .

On the authority of its earlier decisions, the state court declared that the statute's purpose was to preserve the public peace, no words being "forbidden except such as have a direct tendency to cause acts of violence by the person to whom, individually, the remark is addressed." It was further said: "The word 'offensive' is not to be defined in terms of what a particular addressee thinks. . . . The test is what men of common intelligence would understand would be words likely to cause an average addressee to fight. . . . The English language has a number of words and expressions which by general consent are 'fighting words' when said without a disarming smile. . . . Such words, as ordinary men know, are likely to cause a fight. So are threatening, profane or obscene revilings. Derisive and annoying words can be taken as coming within the purview of the statute as heretofore interpreted only when they have this characteristic of plainly tending to excite the addressee to a breach of the peace. . . . The statute, as construed, does no more than prohibit the face-to-face words plainly likely to cause a breach of the peace by the addressee, words whose speaking constitute a breach of the peace by the speaker—including 'classical fighting words,' words in current use less 'classical' but equally likely to cause violence, and other disorderly words, including profanity, obscenity and threats." We are unable to say that the limited scope of the statute as thus construed contravenes the constitutional right of free expression. It is a statute narrowly drawn and limited to define and punish specific conduct lying within the domain of state power, the use in a public place of words likely to cause a breach of the peace. . . . This conclusion necessarily disposes of appellant's contention that the statute is so vague and indefinite as to render a conviction thereunder a violation of due process. A statute punishing verbal acts, carefully drawn so as not unduly to impair liberty of expression, is not too vague for a criminal law. . . .

Nor can we say that the application of the statute to the facts disclosed by the record substantially or unreasonably impinges upon the privilege of free speech. Argument is unnecessary to demonstrate that the appellations "damn racketeer" and "damn Fascist" are epithets likely to provoke the average person to retaliation, and thereby cause a breach of the peace.

The refusal of the state court to admit evidence of provocation and evidence bearing on the truth or falsity of the utterances is open to no Constitutional objection. Whether the facts sought to be proved by such evidence constitute a defense to the charge or may be shown in mitigation are questions for the state court to determine. Our function is fulfilled by a determination that the challenged statute, on its face and as applied, does not contravene the Fourteenth Amendment.

Affirmed.

Hate speech was again the issue in the following case.

16

R.A.V. v. St. Paul

505 U.S. 377 (1992)

Justice Scalia delivered the opinion of the Court.

In the predawn hours of June 21, 1990, petitioner and several other teenagers allegedly assembled a crudely made cross by taping together broken chair legs. They then allegedly burned the cross inside the fenced yard of a black family that lived across the street from the house where petitioner was staying. Although this conduct could have been punished [505 U.S. 377, 380] under any of a number of laws, one of the two provisions under which respondent city of St. Paul chose to charge petitioner (then a juvenile) was the St. Paul Bias-Motivated Crime Ordinance, St. Paul, Minn., Legis.Code 292.02 (1990), which provides:

> "Whoever places on public or private property a symbol, object, appellation, characterization or graffiti, including, but not limited to, a burning cross or Nazi swastika, which one knows or has reasonable grounds to know arouses anger, alarm or resentment in others on the basis of race, color, creed, religion or gender commits disorderly conduct and shall be guilty of a misdemeanor."

Petitioner moved to dismiss this count on the ground that the St. Paul ordinance was substantially overbroad and impermissibly content based, and therefore facially invalid under the First Amendment. . . .

The trial court granted this motion, but the Minnesota Supreme Court reversed. That court rejected petitioner's overbreadth claim because, as construed in prior Minnesota cases . . . the modifying phrase "arouses anger, alarm or resentment in others" limited the reach of the ordinance to conduct that amounts to "fighting words," i.e., "conduct that itself inflicts injury or tends to incite immediate violence . . . ," . . . and therefore the ordinance reached only expression "that the first amendment does not protect,". . . . The court also concluded that the ordinance was not impermissibly content based because, in its view, "the ordinance is a narrowly tailored means toward accomplishing the compelling governmental interest in protecting the community against bias-motivated threats to public safety and order." We granted certiorari. . . .

I

In construing the St. Paul ordinance, we are bound by the construction given to it by the Minnesota court. . . .

[W]e conclude that, even as narrowly construed by the Minnesota Supreme Court, the ordinance is facially unconstitutional. Although the phrase in the ordinance, "arouses anger, alarm or resentment in others," has been limited by the Minnesota Supreme Court's construction to reach only those symbols or displays that amount to "fighting words," the remaining, unmodified terms make clear that the ordinance applies only to "fighting words" that insult, or provoke violence, "on the basis of race, color, creed, religion or gender." Displays containing abusive invective, no matter how vicious or severe, are permissible unless they are addressed to one of the specified disfavored topics. Those who wish to use "fighting words" in connection with other ideas—to express hostility, for example, on the basis of political affiliation, union membership, or homosexuality—are not covered. The First Amendment does not permit St. Paul to impose special prohibitions on those speakers who express views on disfavored subjects. . . .

In its practical operation, moreover, the ordinance goes even beyond mere content discrimination to actual viewpoint discrimination. Displays containing some words—odious racial epithets, for example—would be prohibited to proponents of all views. But "fighting words" that do not themselves invoke race, color, creed, religion, or gender—aspersions upon a person's mother, for example—would seemingly be usable ad libitum in the placards of those arguing in favor of racial, color, etc., tolerance and equality, but could not be used by those speakers' opponents. One could hold up a sign saying, for example, that all "anti-Catholic bigots" are misbegotten; but not that all "papists" are, for that would insult and provoke violence "on the basis of religion." St. Paul has no such authority to license one side of a debate to fight freestyle, while requiring the other to follow Marquis of Queensberry rules.

What we have here, it must be emphasized, is not a prohibition of fighting words that are directed at certain persons or groups (which would be facially valid if it met the requirements of the Equal Protection Clause); but rather, a prohibition of fighting words that contain (as the Minnesota Supreme Court repeatedly emphasized) messages of "bias-motivated" hatred and, in particular, as applied to this case, messages "based on virulent notions of racial supremacy." 464 N.W.2d, at 508, 511. One must wholeheartedly agree with the Minnesota Supreme Court that "[i]t is the responsibility, even the obligation, of diverse communities to confront such notions in whatever form they appear," ibid., but the manner of that confrontation cannot consist of selective limitations upon speech. St. Paul's brief asserts that a general "fighting words" law would not meet the city's needs, because only a content-specific measure can communicate to minority groups that the "group hatred" aspect of such speech "is not condoned by the majority." The point of the First Amendment is that majority preferences must be expressed in some fashion other than silencing speech on the basis of its content . . .

Let there be no mistake about our belief that burning a cross in someone's front yard is reprehensible. But St. Paul has sufficient means at its disposal to prevent such behavior without adding the First Amendment to the fire.

———————————————— ✑ ————————————————

The following case reviews the constitutionality of university speech codes under the First Amendment.

———————————— **17** ————————————

DAMBROT V. CENTRAL MICHIGAN UNIVERSITY

✑

839 F. Supp. 477; 1993

Judges: Cleland
Opinion by: Robert H. Cleland
Opinion: [*478] Memorandum Opinion and Order

I. Background

This case presents to the Court a First Amendment challenge to Central Michigan University's "discriminatory harassment policy" and a dispute over the university's decision to not renew the employment contract of its basketball coach. Plaintiff Keith Dambrot was the head basketball coach at Defendant Central Michigan

University ("CMU"). Unlike the coach, most of the members of the team (and one of the assistant coaches) are black. On at least one occasion during the 1992–93 season Dambrot used the word "nigger" in a talk he gave to the players and coaching staff, addressing several players, both black and white, and one assistant coach, by the term. Dambrot testified that he intended to use the term in a "positive and reinforcing" manner during this closed-door locker room team session. There is absolutely no evidence to the contrary. Several black members of the team testified that they use the term commonly to refer to others of their race. Mr. Dambrot testified that it was his belief that the term had a positive meaning, knowing the context in which the players used the term amongst themselves; he used the term, he says, to connote someone who is "fearless, mentally strong, and tough." . . .

Dambrot's use of the term eventually became known to certain individuals outside of the basketball team. At the request of Dambrot, Dave Keilitz, the athletic director at the university, interviewed members of the team in February, 1993. All of the black players informed him that they were not offended by their coach's use of the term. Sometime after that interview, a young man who had left the team the previous fall complained to the university's affirmative action officer of Dambrot's use of the word, claiming that he had been there during the incident. The affirmative action officer confronted Dambrot, who admitted to using the term, though in a positive manner. The officer expressed to Dambrot her opinion that the term was incapable of being used positively and that, in any case, its use was a violation of the university's "discriminatory harassment policy." After the officer recommended that Dambrot be disciplined, and Dambrot acquiesced in lieu of a more formal investigation, he was suspended without pay for five days. . . .

The Plaintiffs began this lawsuit on April 19, 1993. Dambrot alleges that his employment was terminated because he used the term "nigger," and that the termination violated his First Amendment rights to free speech and academic freedom. He has also brought claims for violation of his due process rights. . . . Several members of the basketball team have joined the lawsuit alleging violations of their First Amendment rights as well. . . .

For the reasons expressed in this opinion, the Court GRANTS summary judgment in favor of plaintiffs with respect to the challenge to the facial unconstitutionality of the CMU discriminatory harassment policy, and will permanently enjoin the defendant university from further enforcement of such policy. The Court GRANTS summary judgment in favor of defendant university with respect to plaintiff's wrongful termination claim. Finally, the Court GRANTS summary judgment in favor of defendants with respect to plaintiff's Fourteenth Amendment claim. . . .

IV. First Amendment Facial Challenge

A. Overbreadth

In order for a statute to be found unconstitutional on its face on overbreadth grounds, there must be a realistic danger that the statute itself will significantly compromise recognized First Amendment protections of parties not before the court. . . .

The CMU policy at issue seeks to prevent the following:

> any intentional, unintentional, physical, verbal, or nonverbal behavior that subjects an individual to an intimidating, hostile or offensive educational, employment or living environment by (c) demeaning or slurring individuals through . . . written literature because of their racial or ethnic affiliation; or (d) using symbols, epitaphs or slogans that infer negative connotations about an individual's racial or ethnic affiliation. [Plan for Affirmative Action at Central Michigan University, Section III(b)(1), Racial and Ethnic Harassment].

The university several times argued, albeit half-heartedly, that the policy was not a "speech code" and was not equivalent to an ordinance or statute since it contains no real penalty mechanism. The Court finds such arguments disingenuous. The introduction to the salient section of the policy states:

> Regardless of whether the courts and statutes have declared these actions unlawful, the University has declared them to be a violation of University policy: . . . Discriminatory harassment, whether or not it rises to a level of legally forbidden discrimination. [Plan for Affirmative Action at Central Michigan University, Section III. Discriminatory Harassment].

Punctuating this declaration outlawing acts which are legal in society, the affirmative action officer, in her March 30, 1993, memorandum summarizing her "Grievance Investigation," concluded with specific "Recommended Actions for Resolution." These included discipline for Dambrot involving suspension and a threat of "more severe disciplinary action" in the future should Dambrot or his staff or players not "refrain from such language." She also prescribed what plaintiff's counsel accurately identified as "sensitivity training" for everyone on ethnic terminology, such training to be conducted at the university's expense by an affirmative action officer from another institution. . . .

Is there a "realistic danger" of this policy compromising First Amendment protections? It is not much of a stretch to imagine a treatise (or a student's term paper or even a cafeteria bull session) which explores the source of conflict among residents of some middle-eastern region and posits that one tribe involved in the conflict is the more blameworthy due to some ancient ethnic traditions which give rise to barbarian combativeness or a longstanding inability to compromise. When and if it were complained of, would such a treatise (or term paper or conversation) be judged to violate the CMU policy since it potentially "demeans" or "slurs" various individuals "because of their racial or ethnic affiliation?" It would seem to be a good fit with the policy language. According to the policy, it is of no import that the author or speaker was speaking in good faith about a plausible thesis, nor that he was not intending to refer to any particular individual, either on or off CMU's campus. Any behavior, even unintentional, that offends any individual is to be prohibited under the policy. The spirit in which the words are spoken is of no moment to this policy. The intent to inform rather than harm is irrelevant. If the speech gives offense it is prohibited. . . .

As stated in *Doe v. University of Michigan*, 721 F. Supp. 852, 863 (E.D.Mich. 1989), and equally applicable here:

> What the University could not do, however, was establish an anti-discrimination policy which had the effect of prohibiting certain speech because it disagreed with ideas or messages sought to be conveyed. . . . Nor could the University proscribe speech simply because it was found to be offensive, even gravely so, by large numbers of people. . . . These principles acquire a special significance in the university setting, where the free and unfettered interplay of competing views is essential to the institution's educational mission.

Also, as noted by this District in *Doe*, "the Supreme Court has consistently held that statutes punishing speech or conduct solely on the grounds that they are unseemly or offensive are constitutionally overbroad." The policy at issue here goes even beyond suppressing "offensive" speech and suppresses "negative connotations" that are "unintentional." The policy instituted by CMU is even more overbroad than the U of M policy struck down in *Doe*, and, for that reason, all the more improper.

B. Fighting Words

CONTENT LIMITATIONS CMU has attempted to categorize the policy's prohibitions as addressing only "fighting words." This, however, even if it were true, would not save the policy. *R.A.V. v. St. Paul*, 505 U.S. 120 (1992). Such a policy, construed to reach only "fighting words," contains limitations on content and viewpoint which would render it facially unconstitutional. . . .

2. VIEWPOINT LIMITATIONS The Supreme Court in *R.A.V.*, identified constitutional problems beyond the content limitations on speech within the ordinance:

> In its practical operation, moreover, the ordinance goes even beyond mere content discrimination, to actual viewpoint discrimination. Displays containing some words—odious racial epithets, for example—would be prohibited to proponents of all views. But "fighting words" that do not themselves invoke race, color, creed, religion, or gender—aspersions upon a person's mother, for example—would seemingly be usable ad libitum in the placards of those arguing in favor of racial, color, etc. tolerance and equality, but could not be used by that speaker's opponents. *R.A.V.*, 120 L. Ed. 2d at 323 (emphasis in original).

The CMU policy similarly attempts to limit viewpoint. The policy prohibits use of "symbols, epitaphs [sic] or slogans that infer negative connotations about an individual's racial or ethnic affiliation" (emphasis added). Negative racial connotations are prohibited, but positive (or at least non-negative) connotations, based on those same racial or ethnic affiliations, are allowed. A campus speaker may thus go on at length recounting what he supposes to be the ethnic attributes of, for example, the Irish. So long as he speaks in a way which appears, from the viewpoint of the university's enforcers, to be either positive or neutral, the speaker is on safe ground so far as university policy is concerned. That speaker's tally of ethnic attributes, though, would be the only viewpoint allowed to be heard on the CMU campus, because all speakers with a differing view on that issue are prohibited by the policy from responding: in their words the speech police can "infer negative connotations about an individual's . . . ethnic affiliation" or something "hostile" on those ethnic grounds. One can, of course, remove "Irish" and substitute the "ethnic or racial affiliation" of one's choice in this example.

"If there is a bedrock principle underlying the First Amendment, it is that the Government may not prohibit the expression of an idea simply because society finds the idea itself offensive or disagreeable." The First Amendment does not recognize exceptions for bigotry, racism, and religious intolerance or ideas or matters some may deem trivial, vulgar or profane." *Iota Xi Chapter of Sigma Chi v. George Mason Univ.*, 773 F. Supp. 792, 795 (E.D.Va. 1991), quoting *Texas v. Johnson*, 109 S. Ct. at 2544.

D. Vagueness

The policy is also constitutionally void for vagueness.

Vagueness may take two forms, both of which result in a denial of due process. A vague ordinance denies fair notice of the standard of conduct to which a citizen is held accountable. At the same time an ordinance is void for vagueness if it is an unrestricted delegation of power, which in practice leaves the definition of its terms to law enforcement officers, and thereby invites arbitrary, discriminatory and overzealous enforcement. Leonardson, 896 F.2d at 196.

In the instant case, both problems—fair notice, and unrestricted delegation—are present. First, a person of ordinary intelligence would have to guess at the meaning of the prohibition. Id. The terms "offensive" and "negative" require subjective reference in order to define them; the meanings of these terms are as vastly divergent as are individual tastes and personalities. The difficulties experienced in trying to subjectively define and prohibit speech which is "offensive" become quite evident in the facts of this very case. First the reactions of the black players who testified and those whose statements were recounted in the hearings preceding this Opinion: at the interview Keilitz conducted in February, 1993, none of the players thought the term was used by their coach in a negative way. Keilitz himself may or may not have been offended, although he testified that he wouldn't have chosen to talk in that way to his own players when he was coaching. Then in March, one former player, Shannon Norris, decided that he was offended, and he complained about it. This prompted an investigation by the affirmative action officer. She was offended. Consequently, the media and public also reacted in several ways, from outrage to complacent understanding, with many variants in between, so some of them appeared to be offended, and some not. The facts of this case exemplify the vast diversity of reaction to speech which is potentially offensive. For a person, even one as perceptive and intelligent as the average college student or professor, to accurately guess what a listener's reaction will be to something potentially offensive is nigh on impossible. Emphasizing this conclusion, the Court recalls that at the preliminary injunction hearing, when asked to specify what kind of conduct would constitute a "hostile environment," the university's own President, Dr. Leonard Plachta, was utterly incapable of defining the terms of the policy. With the leader of the university unable to describe the boundaries of prohibited speech under his own policy, it becomes a daunting task for defendants to argue that the policy provides "fair notice of the standard of conduct to which a citizen is held accountable." Leonardson, supra. The policy's prohibition is vague.

This imprecision also "invites arbitrary, discriminatory and overzealous enforcement" in its application. Id. It leads to certain kinds of offensive conduct being restricted while allowing other personally offensive conduct to go unrestrained, because for the definition of its terms it depends on the viewpoint of those in charge of the affirmative action policy, the enforcement officers. Id. Although not crucial to the Court's determination of this issue, the Court is confident that a careful examination of the history of Dambrot's censure for these locker room comments would reveal an example or two of what the Supreme Court meant by "overzealous enforcement" of a "vague policy."

Summary judgment is appropriate because there are no issues of fact as to the literal content of the policy and plaintiff is entitled to judgment as a matter of law. Matsushita, supra.

V. First Amendment as Applied to Plaintiff

At oral argument and in the briefs, plaintiff relied on the following sequential analysis: (1) CMU's policy is unconstitutional because it suppresses speech that is protected by the First Amendment; (2) Plaintiff Dambrot was sanctioned pursuant to the policy and eventually terminated from employment as a result of such sanctioning; (3) therefore, plaintiff's termination was wrongful as violative of the First Amendment.

This argument is not bereft of logic; however, it misses a nuance in the required analysis which is indispensable. In order for Plaintiff Dambrot to have been harmed by the overbreadth of an improper policy, it must first be shown that his speech was protected by the First Amendment. If plaintiff's speech was not so protected, then the policy's overbreadth did not affect him. The suppression of protected speech identifies unconstitutional overbreadth in the first instance. If there is speech, but of a sort which was not constitutionally protected, the possible error of a policy would be harmless as to the speaker. . . .

It seems to the Court that Plaintiff Dambrot may be urging that the very use of the word "nigger," because its use may qualify for First Amendment shelter under other circumstances, confers upon his locker room behavior some kind of constitutional significance. If this is the logic intended, it is spurious.

Perhaps removing the contentious word from the equation will clarify: examine the hypothetical complaint of another coach from another locker room, who simply tries to motivate his troops to go out and do battle "aggressively" on the basketball court and to be "fearless, mentally strong, and tough." The coach is fired for this approach because the public university had decided upon a noncombative philosophy as to its athletic programs, consistent with the passivist outlook of an important alumnus and private benefactor, C. Milquetoast. The coach sues, claiming that his First Amendment right to speak freely has been impinged. The university stipulates that he was fired for the "aggressive battle" speech, but says that the approach a coach takes with the players is their business to regulate, and not "a matter of public concern." This Court would sustain that position because in the absence of any political or social concern, government employers are entitled to exercise discretion "without intrusive oversight by the judiciary in the name of the First Amendment." . . . Addition of the word "nigger" into this setting does not so alter the content or context so as to elevate the speech to "public concern." . . .

Dambrot's use of the term apparently stirred the interest of the public (in the form of demonstrations and letters to the editor), but this does not vitiate the requirement that the actual speech itself—as opposed to speech or media coverage or general gossip about the speech—address a matter of public concern. "What is of general interest to the public is not necessarily of public concern for First Amendment purposes." . . . Thus, although the debate about a public university employee using a word so steeped in racially negative implications is almost certainly a matter of public concern now, the question about the original speech itself stands apart.

Had Dambrot been fired simply for saying "nigger" while describing his impressions of the history of racial politics in the university community, or had the penalty come from his use of the term only while he was trying to explain or extricate himself from criticism over his alleged earlier use of it in the locker room, in either such event he would far better be able to argue that he was, at that time, injecting himself into "the marketplace of ideas"—and speaking on a matter of public concern. . . . In short, had he been doing almost anything with more intellectual content than encouraging basketball players with such terminology, he could more persuasively argue that the matter "related to a [] matter of political, social, or other concern to the community."

[The Court further dismissed plaintiff's plea that his dismissal violated his due process rights under the Fourteenth Amendment. He served at the will of the university which could dismiss him for "private" speech that concerned only university administration, not the public expression of ideas protected by the 1st amendment.]

VII. Summary and Conclusion

Because the court finds the defendant university's "discriminatory harassment" policy to be facially unconstitutional, the plaintiffs' motion for summary judgment on this question is GRANTED, and the defendant Central Michigan University is PERMANENTLY ENJOINED from enforcing said policy.

For the reasons stated herein, the defendants' motion for summary judgment is GRANTED and plaintiff's corresponding motion DENIED with respect to plaintiff's First Amendment and Fourteenth Amendment claims against the university and the individual officers of the university.

Freedom of Expression and Technological Change: Regulating the Internet

With the passage of the Communications Decency Act of 1996, the constitutional debate over the limits of freedom of expression moved from earth to cyberspace. Although the First Amendment explicitly forbids Congress from passing any law limiting freedoms of expression, Congress in response to political pressures has enacted laws restricting political and other forms of expression.

Most congressional legislation, from the infamous Sedition Act of 1798, which provided for severe punishments for those criticizing the government, through the espionage and sedition laws of World War I to the Smith Act of 1940 and the post–World War II laws dealing with the communist threat, was primarily concerned with what Congress viewed as dangerous political expression. Supreme Court Justice Oliver Wendell Holmes's clear and present danger test (see earlier discussion) allowed reasonable suppression of political speech found to be dangerous to the nation.

Congress has also responded to popular demands for the suppression of pornography and obscenity. It has passed legislation, for example, banning the transportation in interstate commerce of obscene materials. Far more than Congress, state and local governments have perennially attempted to regulate what community standards define as pornography and obscenity.

Because governmental attempts to limit freedoms of expression in whatever form pose First Amendment problems, the courts inevitably have been thrust into the center of the constitutional and political debate over the permissible scope of government action. Litigation in this area—as in so many other areas—reflects politics by other means. Congress has little to lose and everything to gain from taking positions in opposition to pornography and obscenity. A primary incentive of members of Congress is reelection, and opposing pornography and obscenity can only enhance their reelection prospects.[*]

In response to widespread concerns about pornography on the Internet, and particularly its accessibility to children, Congress in the Communications Decency Act of 1996 regulated Internet transmission of "obscene or indecent" messages directed at recipients under 18 years of age. The American Civil Liberties Union (ACLU) challenged the law on First Amendment grounds and won a victory in a three-judge district court, which declared the law to be unconstitutional. The Attorney General of the United States, Janet Reno, appealed the decision to the Supreme Court, which rendered the following opinion.

---

[*]See Chapter 8, particularly selection 57.

18

RENO V. AMERICAN CIVIL LIBERTIES UNION (1997)

Justice Stevens delivered the opinion of the Court.

At issue is the constitutionality of two statutory provisions enacted to protect minors from "indecent" and "patently offensive" communications on the Internet. Notwithstanding the legitimacy and importance of the congressional goal of protecting children from harmful materials, we agree with the three-judge District Court that the statute abridges "the freedom of speech" protected by the First Amendment.

I

The District Court made extensive findings of fact, most of which were based on a detailed stipulation prepared by the parties. . . . The findings describe the character and the dimensions of the Internet, the availability of sexually explicit material in that medium, and the problems confronting age verification for recipients of Internet communications. . . .

Sexually Explicit Material

Sexually explicit material on the Internet includes text, pictures, and chat and "extends from the modestly titillating to the hardest-core." These files are created, named, and posted in the same manner as material that is not sexually explicit, and may be accessed either deliberately or unintentionally during the course of an imprecise search. "Once a provider posts its content on the Internet, it cannot prevent that content from entering any community." Thus, for example,

> when the UCR/California Museum of Photography posts to its Web site nudes by Edward Weston and Robert Mapplethorpe to announce that its new exhibit will travel to Baltimore and New York City, those images are available not only in Los Angeles, Baltimore, and New York City, but also in Cincinnati, Mobile, or Beijing—wherever Internet users live. Similarly, the safer sex instructions that Critical Path posts to its Web site, written in street language so that the teenage receiver can understand them, are available not just in Philadelphia, but also in Provo and Prague.

Some of the communications over the Internet that originate in foreign countries are also sexually explicit.

Though such material is widely available, users seldom encounter such content accidentally. "A document's title or a description of the document will usually appear before the document itself . . . and in many cases the user will receive detailed information about a site's content before he or she need take the step to access the document. Almost all sexually explicit images are preceded by warnings as to the content." For that reason, the "odds are slim" that a user would enter a sexually explicit site by accident. . . . Systems have been developed to help parents control the material that may be available on a home computer with Internet access. . . .

Age Verification

The problem of age verification differs for different uses of the Internet. The District Court categorically determined that there "is no effective way to determine the identity or the age of a user who is accessing material through e-mail, mail exploders, newsgroups or chat rooms." The Government offered no evidence that there was a reliable way to screen recipients and participants in such fora for age. Moreover, even if it were technologically feasible to block minors' access to newsgroups and chat rooms containing discussions of art, politics or other subjects that potentially elicit "indecent" or "patently offensive" contributions, it would not be possible to block their access to that material and "still allow them access to the remaining content, even if the overwhelming majority of that content was not indecent. . . ."

VI

Regardless of whether the CDA is so vague that it violates the Fifth Amendment, the many ambiguities concerning the scope of its coverage render it problematic for purposes of the First Amendment. For instance, each of the two parts of the CDA uses a different linguistic form. The first uses the word "indecent,". . . while the second speaks of material that "in context, depicts or describes, in terms patently offensive as measured by contemporary community standards, sexual or excretory activities or organs," . . . Given the absence of a definition of either term, this difference in language will provoke uncertainty among speakers about how the two standards relate to each other and just what they mean. Could a speaker confidently assume that a serious discussion about birth control practices, homosexuality, . . . or the consequences of prison rape would not violate the CDA? This uncertainty undermines the likelihood that the CDA has been carefully tailored to the congressional goal of protecting minors from potentially harmful materials.

The vagueness of the CDA is a matter of special concern for two reasons. First, the CDA is a content-based regulation of speech. The vagueness of such a regulation raises special First Amendment concerns because of its obvious chilling effect on free speech. . . . Second, the CDA is a criminal statute. In addition to the opprobrium and stigma of a criminal conviction, the CDA threatens violators with penalties including up to two years in prison for each act of violation. The severity

of criminal sanctions may well cause speakers to remain silent rather than communicate even arguably unlawful words, ideas, and images. . . .

VII   Clear + Present Clear

We are persuaded that the CDA lacks the precision that the First Amendment requires when a statute regulates the content of speech. In order to deny minors access to potentially harmful speech, the CDA effectively suppresses a large amount
of speech that adults have a constitutional right to receive and to address to one another. That burden on adult speech is unacceptable if less restrictive alternatives
would be at least as effective in achieving the legitimate purpose that the statute
was enacted to serve. . . .

XI

In this Court, though not in the District Court, the Government asserts that—in
addition to its interest in protecting children—its "[e]qually significant" interest in
fostering the growth of the Internet provides an independent basis for upholding
the constitutionality of the CDA. . . . The Government apparently assumes that
the unregulated availability of "indecent" and "patently offensive" material on the
Internet is driving countless citizens away from the medium because of the risk of
exposing themselves or their children to harmful material.

We find this argument singularly unpersuasive. The dramatic expansion of this
new marketplace of ideas contradicts the factual basis of this contention. The
record demonstrates that the growth of the Internet has been and continues to be
phenomenal. As a matter of constitutional tradition, in the absence of evidence to
the contrary, we presume that governmental regulation of the content of speech is
more likely to interfere with the free exchange of ideas than to encourage it. The
interest in encouraging freedom of expression in a democratic society outweighs
any theoretical but unproven benefit of censorship.

For the foregoing reasons, the judgment of the district court is affirmed.

Justice O'Connor, with whom The Chief Justice joins, concurring in the judgment
in part and dissenting in part.

I write separately to explain why I view the Communications Decency Act of
1996 (CDA) as little more than an attempt by Congress to create "adult zones" on
the Internet. Our precedent indicates that the creation of such zones can be constitutionally sound. Despite the soundness of its purpose, however, portions of the
CDA are unconstitutional because they stray from the blueprint our prior cases
have developed for constructing a "zoning law" that passes constitutional muster.

Appellees bring a facial challenge to three provisions of the CDA. The first,
which the Court describes as the "indecency transmission" provision, makes it a
crime to knowingly transmit an obscene or indecent message or image to a person
the sender knows is under 18 years old. . . . What the Court classifies as a single

" 'patently offensive display' " provision, . . . is in reality two separate provisions. The first of these makes it a crime to knowingly send a patently offensive message or image to a specific person under the age of 18 ("specific person" provision). . . . The second criminalizes the display of patently offensive messages or images "in a[ny] manner available" to minors ("display" provision). . . . None of these provisions purports to keep indecent (or patently offensive) material away from adults, who have a First Amendment right to obtain this speech. . . . Thus, the undeniable purpose of the CDA is to segregate indecent material on the Internet into certain areas that minors cannot access. . . .

The creation of "adult zones" is by no means a novel concept. States have long denied minors access to certain establishments frequented by adults. States have also denied minors access to speech deemed to be "harmful to minors." The Court has previously sustained such zoning laws, but only if they respect the First Amendment rights of adults and minors. That is to say, a zoning law is valid if (i) it does not unduly restrict adult access to the material; and (ii) minors have no First Amendment right to read or view the banned material. As applied to the Internet as it exists in 1997, the "display" provision and some applications of the "indecency transmission" and "specific person" provisions fail to adhere to the first of these limiting principles by restricting adults' access to protected materials in certain circumstances. Unlike the Court, however, I would invalidate the provisions only in those circumstances. . . .

The "indecency transmission" and "specific person" provisions present a closer issue, for they are not unconstitutional in all of their applications. . . .

. . . [B]oth provisions are constitutional as applied to a conversation involving only an adult and one or more minors—e.g., when an adult speaker sends an e-mail knowing the addressee is a minor, or when an adult and minor converse by themselves or with other minors in a chat room. . . .

[But] [i]f a minor enters a chat room otherwise occupied by adults, the CDA effectively requires the adults in the room to stop using indecent speech. If they did not, they could be prosecuted under the "indecency transmission" and "specific person" provisions for any indecent statements they make to the group, since they would be transmitting an indecent message to specific persons, one of whom is a minor. . . . The CDA is therefore akin to a law that makes it a crime for a bookstore owner to sell pornographic magazines to anyone once a minor enters his store. Even assuming such a law might be constitutional in the physical world as a reasonable alternative to excluding minors completely from the store, the absence of any means of excluding minors from chat rooms in cyberspace restricts the rights of adults to engage in indecent speech in those rooms. The "indecency transmission" and "specific person" provisions share this defect.

But these two provisions do not infringe on adults' speech in all situations. And as discussed below, I do not find that the provisions are overbroad in the sense that they restrict minors' access to a substantial amount of speech that minors have the right to read and view. Accordingly, the CDA can be applied constitutionally in some situations. . . .

Thus, the constitutionality of the CDA as a zoning law hinges on the extent to which it substantially interferes with the First Amendment rights of adults. Because the rights of adults are infringed only by the "display" provision and by the "indecency transmission" and "specific person" provisions as applied to communications involving more than one adult, I would invalidate the CDA only to that extent. Insofar as the "indecency transmission" and "specific person" provisions prohibit the use of indecent speech in communications between an adult and one or more minors, however, they can and should be sustained. The Court reaches a contrary conclusion, and from that holding I respectfully dissent.

First Amendment Challenges to Renewed Congressional Attempts to Control Telecommunications Content

Political efforts to control the content of expression through telecommunications continued after and in spite of the Supreme Court's Reno decision. The Telecommunications Act of 1996 sought to regulate pornography on cable stations. It stated:

> In providing sexually explicit adult programming or other programming that is indecent on any channel of its service primarily dedicated to sexually oriented programming, a multi-channel video programming distributor shall fully scramble or otherwise fully block the video and audio portion of such channel so that one [who is] not a subscriber to such channel or programming does not receive it.

In the following case the Supreme Court reviewed the law's constitutionality after Playboy challenged it on First Amendment grounds.

19

UNITED STATES ET AL. V. PLAYBOY ENTERTAINMENT GROUP, INC.

United States Supreme Court, May 22, 2000

Justice Kennedy delivered the opinion of the Court.

This case presents a challenge to §505 of the Telecommunications Act of 1996. . . . Section 505 requires cable television operators who provide channels "primarily dedicated to sexually oriented programming" either to "fully scramble or otherwise fully block" those channels or to limit their transmission to hours when children are unlikely to be viewing, set by administrative regulation as the time between 10 P.M. and 6 A.M. . . . . Even before enactment of the statute, signal scrambling was already in use. Cable operators used scrambling in the regular course of business, so that only paying customers had access to certain programs. Scrambling could be imprecise, however; and either or both audio and visual portions of the scrambled programs might be heard or seen, a phenomenon known as "signal bleed." The purpose of §505 is to shield children from hearing or seeing images resulting from signal bleed.

To comply with the statute, the majority of cable operators adopted the second, or "time channeling," approach. The effect of the widespread adoption of time channeling was to eliminate altogether the transmission of the targeted programming outside the safe harbor period in affected cable service areas. In other words, for two-thirds of the day no household in those service areas could receive the programming, whether or not the household or the viewer wanted to do so.

Appellee Playboy Entertainment Group, Inc., challenged the statute as unnecessarily restrictive content-based legislation violative of the First Amendment. After a trial, a three-judge District Court concluded that a regime in which viewers could order signal blocking on a household-by-household basis presented an effective, less restrictive alternative to §505. 30 F. Supp. 2d 702, 719 (Del. 1998). Finding no error in this conclusion, we affirm.

I

Playboy Entertainment Group owns and prepares programs for adult television networks, including Playboy Television and Spice. Playboy transmits its programming to cable television operators, who retransmit it to their subscribers, either through monthly subscriptions to premium channels or on a so-called "pay-per-view" basis. Cable operators transmit Playboy's signal, like other premium channel signals, in scrambled form. The operators then provide paying subscribers with an "addressable converter," a box placed on the home television set. The converter permits the viewer to see and hear the descrambled signal. It is conceded that almost all of Playboy's programming consists of sexually explicit material as defined by the statute.

The statute was enacted because not all scrambling technology is perfect. . . .

These imperfections are not inevitable. The problem is that at present it appears not to be economical to convert simpler RF or baseband scrambling systems to alternative scrambling technologies on a systemwide scale. Digital technology may one day provide another solution, as it presents no bleed problem at all. Indeed, digital systems are projected to become the technology of choice, which would eliminate the signal bleed problem. Digital technology is not yet in widespread use, however. With imperfect scrambling, viewers who have not paid to receive Playboy's channels may happen across discernible images of a sexually explicit nature. How many viewers, how discernible the scene or sound, and how often this may occur are at issue in this case. . . .

II

Two essential points should be understood concerning the speech at issue here. First, we shall assume that many adults themselves would find the material highly offensive; and when we consider the further circumstance that the material comes unwanted into homes where children might see or hear it against parental wishes or consent, there are legitimate reasons for regulating it. Second, all parties bring the case to us on the premise that Playboy's programming has First Amendment protection. As this case has been litigated, it is not alleged to be obscene; adults have a constitutional right to view it; the Government disclaims any interest in preventing children from seeing or hearing it with the consent of their parents; and Playboy has concomitant rights under the First Amendment to transmit it. These points are undisputed.

The speech in question is defined by its content; and the statute which seeks to restrict it is content based. . . .

Not only does §505 single out particular programming content for regulation, it also singles out particular programmers. . . .

Since §505 is a content-based speech restriction, it can stand only if it satisfies strict scrutiny. . . . If a statute regulates speech based on its content, it must be narrowly tailored to promote a compelling Government interest. Ibid. If a less restrictive alternative would serve the Government's purpose, the legislature must use that alternative. [In *Reno v. ACLU* we stated:]

("[The CDA's Internet indecency provisions'] burden on adult speech is unacceptable if less restrictive alternatives would be at least as effective in achieving the legitimate purpose that the statute was enacted to serve"). . . .

III

The District Court concluded that a less restrictive alternative is available. . . .

When a plausible, less restrictive alternative is offered to a content-based speech restriction, it is the Government's obligation to prove that the alternative will be ineffective to achieve its goals. The Government has not met that burden here. . . .

When a student first encounters our free speech jurisprudence, he or she might think it is influenced by the philosophy that one idea is as good as any other, and that in art and literature objective standards of style, taste, decorum, beauty, and esthetics are deemed by the Constitution to be inappropriate, indeed unattainable. Quite the opposite is true. The Constitution no more enforces a relativistic philosophy or moral nihilism than it does any other point of view. The Constitution exists precisely so that opinions and judgments, including esthetic and moral judgments about art and literature, can be formed, tested, and expressed. What the Constitution says is that these judgments are for the individual to make, not for the Government to decree, even with the mandate or approval of a majority. Technology expands the capacity to choose; and it denies the potential of this revolution if we assume the Government is best positioned to make these choices for us.

It is rare that a regulation restricting speech because of its content will ever be permissible. Indeed, were we to give the Government the benefit of the doubt when it attempted to restrict speech, we would risk leaving regulations in place that sought to shape our unique personalities or to silence dissenting ideas. When First Amendment compliance is the point to be proved, the risk of non-persuasion—operative in all trials—must rest with the Government, not with the citizen. . . .

Basic speech principles are at stake in this case. When the purpose and design of a statute is to regulate speech by reason of its content, special consideration or latitude is not accorded to the Government merely because the law can somehow be described as a burden rather than outright suppression. We cannot be influenced, moreover, by the perception that the regulation in question is not a major one because the speech is not very important. The history of the law of free expression is one of vindication in cases involving speech that many citizens may find shabby, offensive, or even ugly. It follows that all content-based restrictions on speech must give us more than a moment's pause. If television broadcasts can expose children to the real risk of harmful exposure to indecent materials, even in their own home and without parental consent, there is a problem the Government can address. It must do so, however, in a way consistent with First Amendment principles. Here the Government has not met the burden the First Amendment imposes.

The Government has failed to show that §505 is the least restrictive means for addressing a real problem; and the District Court did not err in holding the statute violative of the First Amendment. In light of our ruling, it is unnecessary to address the second question presented: whether the District Court was divested of jurisdiction to consider the Government's postjudgment motions after the Government filed a notice of appeal in this Court.

The judgment of the District Court is affirmed.

─────────────────────── ⟋⟍ ───────────────────────

Equal Protection of the Laws:
School Desegregation

By now most students are thoroughly familiar with the evolution of the "separate but equal" doctrine first enunciated by the Supreme Court in *Plessy v. Ferguson,* 163 U.S. 537 (1896). Students should note that what is involved in cases in this area is legal interpretation of the provision in the Fourteenth Amendment that no state may deny "to any person within its jurisdiction the equal protection of the laws." The *Plessy* case stated that separate but equal accommodations, required by state law to be established on railroads in Louisiana, did not violate the equal protection of the laws clause of the Fourteenth Amendment. The Court went on to say that the object of the Fourteenth Amendment:

> . . . was undoubtedly to enforce the absolute equality of the two races before the law, but in the nature of things it could not have been intended to abolish distinction based upon color, or to enforce social, as distinguished from political, equality, or a commingling of the two races upon terms unsatisfactory to either. Laws permitting, and even requiring,

their separation in places where they are liable to be brought into contact do not necessarily imply the inferiority of either race to the other, and have been generally, if not universally, recognized as within the competency of the state legislatures in the exercise of their police power. The most common instance of this is connected with the establishment of separate schools for white and colored children, which has been held to be a valid exercise of the legislative power even by courts of States where the political rights of the colored race have been longest and most earnestly enforced.

Both the police power and education are within the reserved powers of the states; they are reserved, however, only insofar as they do not conflict with provisions of the Constitution. The Supreme Court, in *Brown v. Board of Education,* 347 U.S. 483 (1954), finally crystallized its interpretation of the equal protection of the laws clause in a way that resulted in a significant decrease in state power in an area traditionally reserved to states, namely, education. In addition, a general principle was established which extended far beyond the field of education.

— 20 —

BROWN V. BOARD OF EDUCATION
OF TOPEKA

347 U.S. 483 (1954)

Mr. Chief Justice Warren delivered the opinion of the Court, saying in part:

These cases come to us from the states of Kansas, South Carolina, Virginia, and Delaware. They are premised on different facts and different local conditions, but a common legal question justifies their consideration together in this consolidated opinion.

In each of the cases, minors of the Negro race, through their legal representatives, seek the aid of the courts in obtaining admission to the public schools of their community on a nonsegregated basis. In each instance, they had been denied admission to schools attended by white children under laws requiring or permitting segregation according to race. This segregation was alleged to deprive the plaintiffs of the equal protection of the laws under the Fourteenth Amendment. In each of the cases other than the Delaware case, a three-judge federal district court denied relief to the plaintiffs on the so-called "separate but equal" doctrine announced by this Court in *Plessy v. Ferguson. . . .*

The plaintiffs contend that segregated public schools are not "equal" and cannot be made "equal," and that hence they are deprived of the equal protection of the laws. Because of the obvious importance of the question presented, the Court took jurisdiction. . . .

In the first cases in this Court construing the Fourteenth Amendment, decided shortly after its adoption, the Court interpreted it as proscribing all state-imposed discriminations against the Negro race. The doctrine of "separate but equal" did not make its appearance in this Court until 1896 in the case of *Plessy v. Ferguson*, supra, involving not education but transportation. American courts have since labored with the doctrine for over half a century. In this Court, there have been six cases involving the "separate but equal" doctrine in the field of public education. . . . In more recent cases, all on the graduate school level, inequality was found in that specific benefits enjoyed by white students were denied to Negro students of the same educational qualifications. . . . In none of these cases was it necessary to reexamine the doctrine to grant relief to the Negro plaintiff. And in *Sweatt v. Painter* [339 U.S. 629 (1950)], the Court expressly reserved decision on the question whether *Plessy v. Ferguson* should be held inapplicable to public education.

In the instant cases, that question is directly presented. Here, unlike *Sweatt v. Painter*, there are findings below that the Negro and white schools involved have been equalized, or are being equalized, with respect to buildings, curricula, qualifications and salaries of teachers, and other "tangible" factors. Our decision, therefore, cannot turn on merely a comparison of these tangible factors in the Negro and white schools involved in each of the cases. We must look instead to the effect of segregation itself on public education.

In approaching this problem, we cannot turn the clock back to 1868 when the Amendment was adopted, or even to 1896 when *Plessy v. Ferguson* was written. We must consider public education in the light of its full development and its present place in American life throughout the Nation. Only in this way can it be determined if segregation in public schools deprives these plaintiffs of the equal protection of the laws.

Today, education is perhaps the most important function of state and local governments. Compulsory school attendance laws and the great expenditures for education both demonstrate our recognition of the importance of education to our democratic society. It is required in the performance of our most basic public responsibilities, even service in the armed forces. It is the very foundation of good citizenship. Today it is a principal instrument in awakening the child to cultural values, in preparing him for later professional training, and in helping him to adjust normally to his environment. In these days, it is doubtful that any child may reasonably be expected to succeed in life if he is denied the opportunity of an education. Such an opportunity, where the state has undertaken to provide it, is a right which must be made available to all on equal terms.

We come then to the question presented: Does segregation of children in public schools solely on the basis of race, even though the physical facilities and other "tangible" factors may be equal, deprive the children of the minority group of equal educational opportunities? We believe that it does.

In *Sweatt v. Painter*, supra, in finding that a segregated law school for Negroes could not provide them equal educational opportunities, this Court relied in large part on "those qualities which are incapable of objective measurement but which make for greatness in a law school." In *MacLaurin v. Oklahoma State Regents*, supras [339 U.S. 637 (1950)], the Court, in requiring that a Negro admitted to a white graduate school be treated like all other students, again resorted to intangible considerations: "his ability to study, to engage in discussions and exchange views with other students, and, in general, to learn his profession." Such considerations apply with added force to children in grade and high schools. To separate them from others of similar age and qualifications solely because of their race generates a feeling of inferiority as to their status in the community that may affect their hearts and minds in a way unlikely ever to be undone. The effect of this separation of their educational opportunities was well stated by a finding in the Kansas case by a court which nevertheless felt compelled to rule against the Negro plaintiffs:

> Segregation of white and colored children in public schools has a detrimental effect upon the colored children. The impact is greater when it has the sanction of the law; for the policy of separating the races is usually interpreted as denoting the inferiority of the Negro group. A sense of inferiority affects the motivation of a child to learn. Segregation with the sanction of law, therefore, has a tendency to retard the educational and mental development of Negro children and to deprive them of some of the benefits they would receive in a racially integrated school system.

Whatever may have been the extent of psychological knowledge at the time of *Plessy v. Ferguson*, this finding is amply supported by modern authority. Any language in *Plessy v. Ferguson* contrary to this finding is rejected.

We conclude that in the field of public education the doctrine of "separate but equal" has no place. Separate educational facilities are inherently unequal. Therefore, we hold that the plaintiffs and others similarly situated for whom the actions have been brought are by reason of the segregation complained of, deprived of the equal protection of the laws guaranteed by the Fourteenth Amendment. This disposition makes unnecessary any discussion whether such segregation also violates the Due Process Clause of the Fourteenth Amendment.

Because these are class actions, because of the wide applicability of this decision, and because of the great variety of local conditions, the formulation of decrees in these cases presents problems of considerable complexity. On reargument, the consideration of appropriate relief was necessarily subordinate to the primary question—the constitutionality of segregation in public education. We have now announced that such segregation is a denial of the equal protection of the laws. In order that we may have the full assistance of the parties in formulating decrees, the cases will be restored to the docket, and the parties are requested to present further argument on Questions 4 and 5 previously propounded by the Court for the reargument this Term [which deal with the implementation of desegregation]. The Attorney General of the United States is again invited to participate. The Attorneys General of the states requiring or permitting segregation in public education will also be permitted to appear as amici curiae upon request to do so by September 15, 1954, and submission of briefs by October 1, 1954.

On the same day the decision was announced in the Brown case (1954), the Court held that segregation in the District of Columbia was unconstitutional on the basis of the due process clause of the Fifth Amendment. [See *Bolling v. Sharpe,* 347 U.S. 497 (1954).] This situation reversed the normal one in that a protection explicitly afforded citizens of states was not expressly applicable against the national government, and could be made so only through interpreting it into the concept of due process of law.

After hearing the views of all interested parties in the *Brown* case the Court, on May 31, 1955, announced its decision concerning the implementation of desegregation in public schools.

21

BROWN V. BOARD OF EDUCATION OF TOPEKA

349 U.S. 294 (1955)

Mr. Chief Justice Warren delivered the opinion of the Court, saying in part:

These cases were decided on May 17, 1954. The opinions of that date, declaring the fundamental principle that racial discrimination in public education is unconstitutional, are incorporated herein by reference. All provisions of federal, state, or local law requiring or permitting such discrimination must yield to this principle. There remains for consideration the manner in which relief is to be accorded.

Because these cases arose under different local conditions and their disposition will involve a variety of local problems, we requested further argument on the question of relief. . . . The parties, the United States, and the states of Florida, North Carolina, Arkansas, Oklahoma, Maryland, and Texas filed briefs and participated in the oral argument.

These presentations were informative and helpful to the Court in its consideration of the complexities arising from the transition to a system of public education freed of racial discrimination. The presentations also demonstrated that substantial steps to eliminate racial discrimination in public schools have already been taken, not only in some of the communities in which these cases arose, but in some of the states appearing as amici curiae, and in other states as well. Substantial progress has been made in the District of Columbia and in the communities in Kansas and Delaware involved in this litigation. The defendants in the cases coming to us from South Carolina and Virginia are awaiting the decision of this Court concerning relief.

Full implementation of these constitutional principles may require solution of varied local school problems. School authorities have the primary responsibility for elucidating, assessing, and solving these problems; courts will have to consider whether the action of school authorities constitutes good faith implementation of the governing constitutional principles. Because of their proximity to local conditions and the possible need for further hearings, the courts which originally heard these cases can best perform this judicial appraisal. Accordingly, we believe it appropriate to remand the cases to those courts.

In fashioning and effectuating the decrees, the courts will be guided by equitable principles. Traditionally, equity has been characterized by a practical flexibility in shaping its remedies and by a facility for adjusting and reconciling public and private needs. These cases call for the exercise of these traditional attributes of equity power. At stake is the personal interest of the plaintiffs in admission to public schools as soon as practicable on a nondiscriminatory basis. To effectuate this interest may call for elimination of a variety of obstacles in making the transition to school systems operated in accordance with the constitutional principles set forth in our May 17, 1954, decision. Courts of equity may properly take into account the public interest in the elimination of such obstacles in a systematic and effective manner. But it should go without saying that the vitality of these constitutional principles cannot be allowed to yield simply because of disagreement with them.

While giving weight to these public and private considerations, the courts will require that the defendants make a prompt and reasonable start toward full compliance with our May 17, 1954, ruling. Once such a start has been made, the courts may find that additional time is necessary to carry out the ruling in an effective manner. The burden rests upon the defendants to establish such time as is necessary in the public interest and is consistent with good faith compliance at the earliest practicable date. To that end, the courts may consider problems related to administration, arising from the physical condition of the school plant, the school transportation system, personnel, revision of school districts and attendance areas into compact units to achieve a system of determining admission to the public schools on a nonracial basis, and revision of local laws and regulations which may be necessary in solving the foregoing problems. They will also consider the adequacy of any plans the defendants may propose to meet these problems and to effectuate a transition to a racially nondiscriminatory school system. During this period of transition, the courts will retain jurisdiction of these cases.

The judgments below, except that in the Delaware case, are accordingly reversed and the cases are remanded to the District Courts to take such proceedings and enter such orders and decrees consistent with this opinion as are necessary and proper to admit to public schools on a racially nondiscriminatory basis with all deliberate speed the parties to these cases. The judgment in the Delaware case—ordering the immediate admission of the plaintiffs to schools previously attended only by white children—is affirmed on the basis of the principles stated in our May 17, 1954, opinion, but the case is remanded to the Supreme Court of Delaware for such further proceedings as that Court may deem necessary in the light of this opinion.

——————————————————— ✌ ———————————————————

After the second decision of the Supreme Court in *Brown v. Board of Education* in 1955, it soon became clear that many Southern states would proceed with deliberate speed not to implement the desegregation of public schools but to obstruct the intent of the Supreme Court. The Southern Manifesto, signed by 101 members of Congress from 11 Southern states in 1956, clearly indicated the line that would be taken by many Southern members of Congress to justify defiance of the Supreme Court. The gist of the manifesto was simply that the Supreme Court did not have the constitutional authority to interfere in an area such as education, which falls within the reserved powers of the states.

After the two *Brown* decisions in 1954 and 1955, the implementation of desegregation in the South was very slow. Ten years later, less than 10 percent of the black pupils in the lower educational levels in the Southern states that had had legally segregated education before were enrolled in integrated schools. It was not until 1970 that substantial progress was made in the South. Between 1968 and 1970 the percentage of black students in all-black schools in 11 Southern states decreased from 68.0 percent to 18.4 percent. One device used to circumvent the Supreme Court's decisions was to establish de facto dual school systems, similar to those that exist in most Northern cities, whereby students are assigned to schools on the basis of the neighborhoods in which they live. Such systems are not de jure segregation because they are not based upon a law requiring segregation per se, but simply upon school board regulations assigning pupils on the basis of where they live. De facto school systems can be as segregated as were the de jure systems previously existing in the South, but the question is to what extent can courts interfere to break up de facto segregation patterns since they are not based upon legal stipulations?

In *Swann v. Charlotte-Mecklenburg County Board of Education,* 402 U.S. 1 (1971), the Supreme Court held that in Southern states with a history of legal segregated education the district courts have broad power to assure "unitary" school systems by requiring (1) reassignment of teachers, so that each school faculty will reflect a racial balance similar to that which exists in the community as a whole; (2) reassignment of pupils to reflect a racial ratio similar to that which exists within the total community; (3) the use of noncontiguous school zones and the grouping of schools for the purpose of attendance to bring about racial balance; and (4) the use of busing of elementary and secondary school students within the school system to achieve racial balance.

This case and companion cases were referred to at the time as school "busing" cases, and caused tremendous controversy within the South because communities felt they were not being treated on an equal basis with their northern counterparts, where de facto segregation is for the most part not subject to judicial intervention. The Nixon administration, which favored neighborhood schools, was firmly opposed to the transportation of students beyond normal geographic school zones to achieve racial balance. Democratic Senator Ribicoff of Connecticut attempted to attach an amendment to an administration-sponsored bill providing $1.5 billion to aid school districts in the South in the desegregation of facilities that would have required nationwide integration of pupils from intercity schools with children from the suburbs. The amendment was defeated on April 21, 1971, by a vote of 51 to 35, with most Republicans voting against it and 13 of 34 northern Democrats opposed. Busing remains a highly controversial political issue.

Swann v. Charlotte-Mecklenburg County Board (1971) held that the courts could order busing of schoolchildren within the limits of the city school district if necessary to achieve desegregated educational facilities. In the case of *Charlotte-Mecklenburg*, the limits of the city school district included the surrounding county. However, only 18 of the country's 100 largest city school districts contained both the inner city and the surrounding county. In cities such as San Francisco, Denver, Pasadena, and Boston, court-ordered busing plans pertained only to the central city school district. In 1974 the Supreme Court reviewed a busing plan for Detroit ordered by a federal district court and sustained by the court of appeals that would have required the busing of students among 54 separate school districts in the Detroit metropolitan area to achieve racially balanced schools. The decision of the lower federal court in the Detroit case set a new precedent that required busing among legally separate school districts. Proponents of the Detroit busing plan argued that the central city of Detroit was 70 percent black and that the only way integration could be achieved would be to link the school district of Detroit with the surrounding white suburban school districts. In *Milliken v. Bradley,* 418 U.S. 717 (1974), the Supreme Court held that the court-ordered Detroit busing plan could not be sustained under the equal protection clause of the Fourteenth Amendment, which was the constitutional provision relied upon in the lower court's decision to require busing. The Supreme Court found that there was no evidence of disparate treatment of white and black students among the 53 outlying school districts that surround Detroit. The only evidence of discrimination was within the city limits of Detroit itself. Therefore, since the outlying districts did not violate the equal protection clause they could not be ordered to integrate their systems with that of Detroit. Since discrimination was limited to Detroit, the court order to remedy the situation must be limited to Detroit also. The effect of the decision is to leave standing court orders for busing within school districts, but to prevent the forced merger of inner city schools with legally separate suburban school districts.

The Judicial Sources of Major Political Controversies over Civil Liberties and Rights

Chief Justice John Marshall in the early nineteenth century laid the groundwork for Supreme Court involvement in politics when he declared that "it is emphatically the province and duty of the Judicial Department to say what the law is." Ironically, in the same case he invented the doctrine of "political questions," proclaiming that the courts should not become involved in those matters more appropriately decided by legislative bodies. Marshall muted that note of judicial self-restraint, however, by his implicit recognition that the courts and not legislatures ultimately would decide what matters fell within their jurisdiction.

Chief Justice Marshall's proclamation of judicial power in *Marbury v. Madison* also incorporated the doctrine of judicial review. The authority to declare what the law is included the power to review acts of Congress and judge their constitutionality. The *Marbury* case, however, did not involve a major confrontation with Congress. The Court merely held that Congress could not grant it the mandamus power in original jurisdiction, which had been done in the Judiciary Act of 1789. Essentially the Court was interpreting the scope of its own powers, not those of Congress.

Inevitably, however, the power of judicial review pushed the Supreme Court and lower federal courts as well into political controversies as they ruled not only on congressional laws but far more importantly on the actions of state legislatures and courts. As of early 1985 the Supreme Court had held only 135 provisions of federal laws to be unconstitutional in whole or in part out of a total of approximately 91,000 public and private bills that had been passed. By contrast, the Court had overturned on constitutional grounds 970 state laws and provisions of state constitutions, 800 of these rulings coming after 1870.[5] By far the greatest political controversies have been over Supreme Court rulings affecting the states, as the nation for most of its history struggled over the question of how far national power should intrude upon state sovereignty.

Controversies surrounding Supreme Court decisions on civil liberties and civil rights have almost entirely involved Supreme Court rulings on the permissible scope of state power. In the early nineteenth century Chief Justice John Marshall's decisions in the historic cases of *McCulloch v. Maryland* (1819) and *Gibbons v. Ogden* (1823) raised the ire of states' rights advocates who widely proclaimed that the Court's actions would bring about the dissolution of the Union. The Supreme Court had unequivocally upheld national supremacy and wide congressional powers over the states.

Almost a century and a half after the *McCulloch* decision, the Supreme Court was again embroiled in a political controversy, not concerning the extent of congressional power over the states, an issue that had finally been settled in favor of the national government during the New Deal, but over how far national civil liberties and rights standards should be applied to the states. Under the chief justiceship of former California governor Earl Warren, an activist and interventionist Supreme Court in the 1960s completed the process of applying most of the provisions of the Bill of Rights to the states under the due process clause of the Fourteenth Amendment. Before the Warren era the Court had been very reluctant to extend parts of the Bill of Rights to the states, weighing heavily against such action considerations of federalism that supported state sovereignty. It nationalized only what in the view of a majority of the justices were fundamental freedoms and rights without which the democratic process and individual liberty could not survive.

The Establishment Clause and the Issue of School Prayer

As early as 1940 the Supreme Court nationalized the free exercise clause of the First Amendment, but it was not until 1947 that a majority of justices agreed that the establishment clause of the First Amendment was also a fundamental liberty protected by the due process clause of the Fourteenth Amendment.[6]

The First Amendment provision embodying the establishment and free exercise clauses states: "Congress shall make no law respecting an establishment of religion, or prohibiting the free exercise thereof." While little controversy surrounded the Supreme Court's nationalization of these provisions, its 1962 decision in *Engel v. Vitale,* given in the following selection, holding that religious freedom required a ban on prayers in public schools, caused a political backlash that continued into the 1980s, one that seemed to grow in inten-

---

[5]Henry J. Abraham, *The Judiciary: The Supreme Court in the Governmental Process,* 6th ed. (Boston: Allyn & Bacon, 1983), p. 164.

[6]The two cases nationalizing the First Amendment free exercise and establishment clauses were, respectively, *Cantwell v. Connecticut,* 310 U.S. 296 (1940) and *Everson v. Board of Education,* 330 U.S. 1 (1947).

sity as the years passed. As the Moral Majority and the Christian Right became politically active in the 1980s, one of their major goals was the restoration of prayers in public schools. They supported state efforts to pass legislation that would get around the school prayer decision by requiring moments of silence rather than prayers to open school days. However, the Supreme Court held in 1985 that an Alabama moment-of-silence statute authorizing public school teachers to hold a one-minute period of silence for "meditation or voluntary prayer" each school day violated the establishment clause of the First Amendment.[7]

Of particular concern to the Court were statements by the sponsors of the legislation that they intended the law to restore prayer to public schools. Even conservative justices, such as Sandra Day O'Connor, who supported completely voluntary moments of silence in public schools during which prayers might be given, agreed that the Alabama statute had no secular effect and was an impermissible official encouragement of prayers. The following case originated the school prayer controversy.

22

ENGEL V. VITALE

ⅇ𝒻ℴ

370 U.S. 421 (1962)

Mr. Justice Black delivered the opinion of the Court, saying in part:

The respondent Board of Education of Union Free School District No. 9, New Hyde Park, New York, acting in its official capacity under state law, directed the School District's principal to cause the following prayer to be said aloud by each class in the presence of a teacher at the beginning of each school day:

> Almighty God, we acknowledge our dependence upon Thee, and we beg Thy blessings upon us, our parents, our teachers and our country.

This daily procedure was adopted on the recommendation of the State Board of Regents, a governmental agency created by the state Constitution to which the New York Legislature has granted broad supervisory, executive, and legislative powers over the state's public school system. These state officials composed the prayer which they recommended and published as a part of their "Statement on Moral and Spiritual Training in the Schools," saying: "We believe that this Statement will be subscribed to by all men and women of good will, and we call upon all of them to aid in giving life to our program."

Shortly after the practice of reciting the Regents' prayer was adopted by the School District, the parents of ten pupils brought this action in a New York State

---

[7]*Wallace v. Jaffree,* 86 L Ed. 2d 29 (1985).

Court insisting that use of this official prayer in the public schools was contrary to the beliefs, religions, or religious practices of both themselves and their children. Among other things, these parents challenged the constitutionality of both the state law authorizing the School District to direct the use of prayer in public schools and the School District's regulation ordering the recitation of this particular prayer on the ground that these actions of official governmental agencies violate that part of the First Amendment of the federal Constitution which commands that "Congress shall make no law respecting an establishment of religion"—a command which was "made applicable to the state of New York by the Fourteenth Amendment of the said Constitution." The New York Court of Appeals, over the dissents of Judges Dye and Fuld, sustained an order of the lower state courts which had upheld the power of New York to use the Regents' prayer as a part of the daily procedures of its public schools so long as the schools did not compel any pupil to join in the prayer over his or her parents' objection. We granted certiorari to review this important decision involving rights protected by the First and Fourteenth Amendments.

We think that by using its public school system to encourage recitation of the Regents' prayer, the state of New York has adopted a practice wholly inconsistent with the Establishment Clause. There can, of course, be no doubt that New York's program of daily classroom invocation of God's blessings as prescribed in the Regents' prayer is a religious activity. It is a solemn avowal of divine faith and supplication for the blessings of the Almighty. The nature of such a prayer has always been religious, none of the respondents has denied this and the trial court expressly so found. . . .

The petitioners contend among other things that the state laws requiring or permitting use of the Regents' prayer must be struck down as a violation of the Establishment Clause because the prayer was composed by governmental officials as a part of a governmental program to further religious beliefs. For this reason, petitioners argue, the state's use of the Regents' prayer in its public school system breaches the constitutional wall of separation between church and state. We agree with that contention since we think that the constitutional prohibition against laws respecting an establishment of religion must at least mean that in this country it is no part of the business of government to compose official prayers for any group of the American people to recite as a part of a religious program carried on by government.

It is a matter of history that this very practice of establishing governmentally composed prayers for religious services was one of the reasons which caused many of our early colonists to leave England and seek religious freedom in America. The Book of Common Prayer, which was created under governmental direction and which was approved by Acts of Parliament in 1548 and 1549, set out in minute detail the accepted form and content of prayer and other religious ceremonies to be used in the established, tax-supported Church of England. The controversies over the Book and what should be its content repeatedly threatened to disrupt the peace of that country as the accepted forms of prayer in the established church changed with the views of the particular ruler that happened to be in control at the time. Powerful groups representing some of the varying religious views of the people struggled among themselves to impress their particular views upon the government and obtain amendments of the Book more suitable to their respective notions of how religious services should be conducted in order that the official religious establishment would advance their particular religious beliefs. Other groups, lacking the necessary political power to influence the government on the matter, decided to leave England and its established church and seek freedom in America from England's governmentally ordained and supported religion.

It is an unfortunate fact of history that when some of the very groups which had most strenuously opposed the established Church of England found themselves sufficiently in control of colonial governments in this country to write their own prayers into law, they passed laws making their own religion the official religion of their respective colonies. Indeed, as late as the time of the Revolutionary War, there were established churches in at least eight of the thirteen former colonies and established religions in at least four of the other five. But the successful Revolution against English political domination was shortly followed by intense opposition to the practice of establishing religion by law. . . .

By the time of the adoption of the Constitution, our history shows that there was a widespread awareness among many Americans of the dangers of a union of church and state. . . . The First Amendment was added to the Constitution to stand as a guarantee that neither the power nor the prestige of the federal government would be used to control, support or influence the kinds of prayer the American people can say—that the people's religions must not be subjected to the pressures of government for change each time a new political administration is elected to office. Under that amendment's prohibition against governmental establishment of religion, as reinforced by the provisions of the Fourteenth Amendment, government in this country, be it state or federal, is without power to prescribe by law any particular form of prayer which is to be used as an official prayer in carrying on any program of governmentally sponsored religious activity.

There can be no doubt that New York's state prayer program officially establishes the religious beliefs embodied in the Regents' prayer. The respondents' argument to the contrary, which is largely based upon the contention that the Regents' prayer is "nondenominational" and the fact that the program, as modified and approved by state courts, does not require all pupils to recite the prayer but permits those who wish to do so to remain silent or be excused from the room, ignores the essential nature of the program's constitutional defects. Neither the fact that the prayer may be denominationally neutral, nor the fact that its observance on the part of the students is voluntary can serve to free it from the limitations of the Establishment Clause, as it might from the Free Exercise Clause, of the First Amendment, both of which are operative against the states by virtue of the Fourteenth Amendment. Although these two clauses may in certain instances overlap, they forbid two quite different kinds of governmental encroachment upon religious freedom. The Establishment Clause, unlike the Free Exercise Clause, does not depend upon any showing of direct governmental compulsion and is violated by the enactment of laws which establish an official religion whether those laws operate directly to coerce nonobserving individuals or not. This is not to say, of course, that laws officially prescribing a particular form of religious worship do not involve coercion of such individuals. When the power, prestige and financial support of government is placed behind a particular religious belief, the indirect coercive pressure upon religious minorities to conform to the prevailing officially approved religion is plain. But the purposes underlying the Establishment Clause go much further than that.

Its first and most immediate purpose rested on the belief that a union of government and religion tends to destroy government and to degrade religion. The history of governmentally established religion, both in England and in this country, showed that whenever government had allied itself with one particular form of religion, the inevitable result has been that it had incurred the hatred, disrespect and even contempt of those who held contrary beliefs. That same history showed that many people had lost their respect for any religion that had relied upon the support of government to spread its faith. The Establishment Clause thus stands as an expression of principle on the part of the Founders of our Constitution that religion is too personal, too sacred, too holy, to permit its "unhallowed perversion" by a civil magistrate. Another purpose of the Establishment Clause rested upon an awareness of the historical fact that governmentally established religions and religious persecutions go hand in hand. The founders knew that only a few years after the Book of Common Prayer became the only accepted form of religious services in the established Church of England, an Act of Uniformity was passed to compel all Englishmen to attend those services and to make it a criminal offense to conduct or attend religious gatherings of any other kind—a law which was consistently flouted by dissenting religious groups in England and which contributed to widespread persecutions of people like John Bunyan who persisted in holding "unlawful [religious] meetings . . . to the great disturbance and distraction of the good subjects of this kingdom. . . ." And they knew that similar persecutions had received the sanction of law in several of the colonies in this country soon after the establishment of official religions in those colonies. It was in large part to get completely away from this sort of systematic religious persecution that the Founders brought into being our Nation, our Constitution, and our Bill of Rights with its prohibition against any governmental establishment of religion. The New York laws officially prescribing the Regents' prayer are inconsistent with both the purposes of the Establishment Clause and with the Establishment Clause itself.

It has been argued that to apply the Constitution in such a way as to prohibit state laws respecting an establishment of religious services in public schools is to indicate a hostility toward religion or toward prayer. Nothing, of course, could be more wrong. The history of man is inseparable from the history of religion. And perhaps it is not too much to say that since the beginning of that history many people have devoutly believed that "More things are wrought by prayer than this world dreams of." It was doubtless largely due to men who believed this that there grew up a sentiment that caused men to leave the crosscurrents of officially established state religions and religious persecution in Europe and come to this country filled with the hope that they could find a place in which they could pray when they pleased to the God of their faith in the language they chose. And there were men of this same faith in the power of prayer who led the fight for adoption of our Constitution and also for our Bill of Rights with the very guarantees of religious freedom that forbid the sort of governmental activity which New York has attempted here. These men knew that the First Amendment, which tried to put an end to governmental control of religion and of prayer, was not written to destroy either. They knew rather that it was written to quiet well-justified fears which nearly all of them felt arising out of an awareness that governments of the past had shackled men's tongues to make them speak only the religious thoughts that government wanted them to speak and to pray only to the God that government wanted them to pray to. It is neither sacrilegious nor antireligious to say that each separate government in this country should stay out of the business of writing or sanctioning official prayers and leave that purely religious function to the people themselves and to those the people choose to look to for religious guidance.

It is true that New York's establishment of its Regents' prayer as an officially approved religious doctrine of that state does not amount to a total establishment of one particular religious sect to the exclusion of all others—that, indeed, the governmental endorsement of that prayer seems relatively insignificant when compared to the governmental encroachments upon religion which were common-place 200 years ago. To those who may subscribe to the view that because the Regents' official prayer is so brief and general there can be no danger to religious freedom in its governmental establishment, however, it may be appropriate to say in the words of James Madison, the author of the First Amendment:

> [I]t is proper to take alarm at the first experiment on our liberties. . . . Who does not see that the same authority which can establish Christianity, in exclusion of all other Religions, may establish with the same ease any particular sect of Christians, in exclusion of all other Sects? That the same authority which can force a citizen to contribute three pence only of his property for the support of any one establishment, may force him to conform to any other establishment in all cases whatsoever?

The judgment of the Court of Appeals of New York is reversed and the cause remanded for further proceedings not inconsistent with this opinion.

Mr. Justice Frankfurter took no part in the decision of this case.

Mr. Justice White took no part in the consideration or decision of this case.

Mr. Justice Douglas concurred in a separate opinion.

Mr. Justice Stewart, dissenting:

A local school board in New York has provided that those pupils who wish to do so may join in a brief prayer at the beginning of each school day, acknowledging their dependence upon God and asking His blessing upon them and upon their parents, their teachers, and their country. The court today decides that in permitting this brief nondenominational prayer the school board has violated the Constitution of the United States. I think this decision is wrong.

The Court does not hold, nor could it, that New York has interfered with the free exercise of anybody's religion. For the state courts have made clear that those who object to reciting the prayer must be entirely free of any compulsion to do so, including any "embarrassments and pressure." Cf. *West Virginia State Board of Education v. Barnette*, 319 U.S. 624. But the Court says that in permitting school children to say this simple prayer, the New York authorities have established "an official religion."

With all respect, I think the Court has misapplied a great constitutional principle. I cannot see how an "official religion" is established by letting those who want to say a prayer say it. On the contrary, I think that to deny the wish of these school children to join in reciting this prayer is to deny them the opportunity of sharing in the spiritual heritage of our nation.

The Court's historical review of the quarrels over the Book of Common Prayer in England throws no light for me on the issue before us in this case. England had then and has now an established church. Equally unenlightening, I think, is the history of the early establishment and later rejection of an official church in our own states. For we deal here not with the establishment of a state church, which would, of course, be constitutionally impermissible, but with whether school children who want to begin their day by joining in prayer must be prohibited from doing so. Moreover, I think that the Court's task, in this as in all areas of constitutional adjudication, is not responsibly aided by the uncritical invocation of metaphors like the "wall of separation," a phrase nowhere to be found in the Constitution. What is relevant to the issue here is not the history of an established church in sixteenth-century England or in eighteenth-century America, but the history of the religious traditions of our people, reflected in countless practices of the institutions and officials of our government.

At the opening of each day's session of this Court we stand, while one of our officials invokes the protection of God. Since the days of John Marshall our Crier has said, "God save the United States and this Honorable Court." Both the Senate and the House of Representatives open their daily sessions with prayer. Each of our Presidents, from George Washington to John F. Kennedy, has upon assuming his office asked the protection and help of God.

The Court today says that the state and federal governments are without constitutional power to prescribe any particular form of words to be recited by any group of the American people on any subject touching religion. The third stanza of "The Star-Spangled Banner," made our national anthem by Act of Congress in 1931, contains these verses:

Blest with victory and peace, may the heav'n rescued land
   Praise the Pow'r that hath made and preserved us a nation!
   Then conquer we must, when our cause it is just,
   And this be our motto, "In God is our Trust."

In 1954 Congress added a phrase to the Pledge of Allegiance to the Flag so that it now contains the words "one Nation *under* God indivisible, with liberty and justice for all." In 1952 Congress enacted legislation calling upon the President each year to proclaim a National Day of Prayer. Since 1865 the words "IN GOD WE TRUST" have been impressed on our coins.

Countless similar examples could be listed, but there is no need to belabor the obvious. It was all summed up by this Court just ten years ago in a single sentence: "We are a religious people whose institutions presuppose a Supreme Being." *Zoarch v. Clauson*, 343 U.S. 306, 313.

I do not believe that this Court, or the Congress, or the President has by the actions and practices I have mentioned established an "official religion" in violation of the Constitution. And I do not believe the state of New York has done so in this case. What each has done has been to recognize and to follow the deeply entrenched and highly cherished spiritual traditions of our nation—traditions which come down to us from those who almost two hundred years ago avowed their "firm reliance on the Protection of Divine Providence" when they proclaimed the freedom and independence of this brave new world.

I dissent.

———————————————— ✌ ————————————————

Engel v. Vitale was neither the beginning nor the end of controversy over the First Amendment's establishment and free exercise clauses. Supreme Court justices have not been able to agree among themselves on the meaning of these clauses. Close decisions characterize freedom of religion cases before the Supreme Court.

Supreme Court cases concerning freedom of religion arise out of congressional and state laws that affect religion, for example, as in *Engel v. Vitale* where the New York State legislature required a nondenominational prayer at the beginning of each public school day. Other types of laws affecting religion provide for governmental aid for textbooks used in private schools, the use of public school buses to transport students to parochial schools, and the use of public school teachers to teach remedial and other special classes in nonpublic schools. Since parochial and virtually all other private schools have a religious affiliation, the use of public funds in any way to support such schools presumptively violates the separation of church and state the establishment clause of the First Amendment requires.

Generally, the Supreme Court has been very cautious in permitting government aid to parochial or private schools. However, in *Agostini v. Felton* (1997), the Court revisited and changed establishment cause case precedents to allow a closer connection between public and private education than it had previously supported. The *Agostini* case overruled *Aguilar v. Felton,* 473 U.S. 402 (1985), which had overturned a New York City program that provided public school teachers to parochial schools for remedial education. The Court found in *Agostini* that the New York program did not violate the establishment cause by advancing religion nor by causing an excessive entanglement between church and state.

On the issue of the constitutionality of prayer in public schools the Supreme Court rendered the following opinion in its term that ended in the summer of 2000.

———————————————— **23** ————————————————

SANTA FE INDEPENDENT SCHOOL DISTRICT, PETITIONER V. JANE DOE

✌

United States Supreme Court (2000)

Justice Stevens delivered the opinion of the Court.

Prior to 1995, the Santa Fe High School student who occupied the school's elective office of student council chaplain delivered a prayer over the public address system before each varsity football game for the entire season. This practice, along with others, was challenged in District Court as a violation of the Establishment Clause of the First Amendment. While these proceedings were pending in the District Court, the school district adopted a different policy that permits, but does not require, prayer initiated and led by a student at all home games. The District Court entered an order modifying that policy to permit only nonsectarian, nonproselytizing prayer. The Court of Appeals held that, even as modified by the District Court, the football prayer policy was invalid. We granted the school district's petition for certiorari to review that holding. . . .

II

The first Clause in the First Amendment to the Federal Constitution provides that "Congress shall make no law respecting an establishment of religion, or prohibiting the free exercise thereof." The Fourteenth Amendment imposes those substantive limitations on the legislative power of the States and their political subdivisions. *Wallace v. Jaffree*, 472 U.S. 38, 49–50 (1985). In *Lee v. Weisman*, 505 U.S. 577 (1992), we held that a prayer delivered by a rabbi at a middle school graduation ceremony violated that Clause. Although this case involves student prayer at a different type of school function, our analysis is properly guided by the principles that we endorsed in *Lee*. As we held in that case:

"The principle that government may accommodate the free exercise of religion does not supersede the fundamental limitations imposed by the Establishment Clause. It is beyond dispute that, at a minimum, the Constitution guarantees that government may not coerce anyone to support or participate in religion or its exercise, or otherwise act in a way which 'establishes a [state] religion or religious faith, or tends to do so.' " . . .

. . . School sponsorship of a religious message is impermissible because it sends the ancillary message to members of the audience who are nonadherants "that they are outsiders, not full members of the political community, and an accompanying message to adherants that they are insiders, favored members of the political community." . . .

Even if we regard every high school student's decision to attend a home football game as purely voluntary, we are nevertheless persuaded that the delivery of a pregame prayer has the improper effect of coercing those present to participate in an act of religious worship. . . .

The District . . . asks us to pretend that we do not recognize what every Santa Fe High School student understands clearly—that this policy is about prayer. The District further asks us to accept what is obviously untrue: that these messages are necessary to "solemnize" a football game and that this single-student, year-long position is essential to the protection of student speech. We refuse to turn a blind eye to the context in which this policy arose, and that context quells any doubt that this policy was implemented with the purpose of endorsing school prayer.

Therefore, the simple enactment of this policy, with the purpose and perception of school endorsement of student prayer, was a constitutional violation. . . .

The judgment of the Court of Appeals [which held the school prayer policy to be unconstitutional] is, accordingly, affirmed.

Chief Justice Rehnquist, with whom Justice Scalia and Justice Thomas join, dissenting.

The Court distorts existing precedent to conclude that the school district's student-message program is invalid on its face under the Establishment Clause. But even more disturbing than its holding is the tone of the Court's opinion; it bristles with hostility to all things religious in public life. Neither the holding nor the tone of the opinion is faithful to the meaning of the Establishment Clause, when it is recalled that George Washington himself, at the request of the very Congress which passed the Bill of Rights, proclaimed a day of "public thanksgiving and prayer, to be observed by acknowledging with grateful hearts the many and signal favors of Almighty God." *Presidential Proclamation, 1 Messages and Papers of the Presidents, 1789–1897,* p. 64 (J. Richardson ed. 1897).

The Court applies Lemon and holds that the "policy is invalid on its face because it establishes an improper majoritarian election on religion, and unquestionably has the purpose and creates the perception of encouraging the delivery of prayer at a series of important school events." Ante, at 26. The Court's reliance on each of these conclusions misses the mark.

First, the Court misconstrues the nature of the "majoritarian election" permitted by the policy as being an election on "prayer" and "religion." To the contrary, the election permitted by the policy is a two-fold process whereby students vote first on whether to have a student speaker before football games at all, and second, if the students vote to have such a speaker, on who that speaker will be. It is conceivable that the election could become one in which student candidates campaign on platforms that focus on whether or not they will pray if elected. It is also conceivable that the election could lead to a Christian prayer before 90 percent of the football games. If, upon implementation, the policy operated in this fashion, we would have a record before us to review whether the policy, as applied, violated the Establishment Clause or unduly suppressed minority viewpoints. But it is possible that the students might vote not to have a pregame speaker, in which case there would be no threat of a constitutional violation. It is also possible that the election would not focus on prayer, but on public speaking ability or social popularity. And if student campaigning did begin to focus on prayer, the school might decide to implement reasonable campaign restrictions.

But the Court ignores these possibilities by holding that merely granting the student body the power to elect a speaker that may choose to pray, "regardless of the students' ultimate use of it, is not acceptable." The Court so holds despite that any speech that may occur as a result of the election process here would be private, not government, speech. The elected student, not the government, would choose what to say. Support for the Court's holding cannot be found in any of our cases. And it essentially invalidates all student elections. A newly elected student body president, or even a newly elected prom king or queen, could use opportunities for public speaking to say prayers. Under the Court's view, the mere grant of power to the students to vote for such offices, in light of the fear that those elected might publicly pray, violates the Establishment Clause. . . .

The policy at issue here may be applied in an unconstitutional manner, but it will be time enough to invalidate it if that is found to be the case. I would reverse the judgment of the Court of Appeals.

—————————————————— ❧ ——————————————————

The Free Exercise of Religion

Congressional and state legislation not only may violate the establishment clause, which requires the separation of church and state, but may also impinge upon the free exercise of religion. For example, in *Reynolds v. United States* (1878), the Supreme Court upheld a federal law that made bigamy a crime against a free exercise challenge that the law interfered with the religious practices of a Mormon sect. The Court's opinion held that the interests of government in banning the "uncivilized" practice of polygamy outweighed an individual's free exercise claim. In a rather bizarre analogy, the Court wrote: "Suppose one believed that human sacrifices were a necessary part of religious worship, would it be seriously contended that the civil government under which he lived could not interfere to prevent a sacrifice?"[8]

By the 1960s the Supreme Court in free exercise cases required the government, whether Congress or state legislatures, to prove a compelling governmental interest to sustain a law that substantially burdened a religious practice.[9] But in the 1990 case, *Employment Division of Oregon v. Smith*, 494 U.S. 872 (1990), the Court dropped the requirement for the demonstration of a compelling governmental interest in reviewing an Oregon law that criminalized the use of controlled substances, including the drug peyote, which a Native American sect used during religious ceremonies. In the *Smith* case, the state of Oregon had denied unemployment benefits to Native American church members who had lost their jobs because of peyote use. The church members claimed that they were being denied their freedom to exercise religion under the First and Fourteenth Amendments. Justice Scalia's opinion for the Court held that the use of the compelling interest test to uphold laws burdening religious practices would result in anarchy. He wrote:

> . . . The rule respondents favor would open the prospect of constitutionally required religious exemptions from civic obligations of almost every conceivable kind—ranging from compulsory military service to the payment of taxes to health and safety regulation such as manslaughter and child neglect laws, compulsory vaccination laws, drug laws, and traffic laws; to social welfare legislation such as minimum wage laws, child labor laws, animal cruelty laws, environmental protection laws, and laws providing for equality for opportunity for the races. The First Amendment's protection of religious liberty does not require this.[10]

——

[8]*Reynolds v. United States*, 98 U.S. 145, 166–167 (1890).
[9]*Sherbert v. Verner*, 374 U.S. 398 (1963).
[10]*Employment Division of Oregon v. Smith*, 494 U.S. 872, 888–889 (1990).

The Religious Freedom Restoration Act of 1993 (RFRA)

Congress, while of course not supporting the use of peyote, nevertheless viewed the *Smith* decision as ominous for freedom of religion. It passed the Religious Freedom Restoration Act in 1993, overturning the *Smith* decision by requiring the restoration of the compelling governmental interest test to sustain legislative burdens upon religious practices. Not surprisingly the Supreme Court skeptically viewed the congressional attempt to dictate constitutional standards governing free exercise cases. Chief Justice John Marshall had written as far back as *Marbury v. Madison* (1803), that "It is emphatically the province and duty of the judicial department to say what the law is." In *City of Boerne v. Flores* (1997), which reviewed the Religious Freedom Restoration Act, the Court followed Marshall's dictate making it yet once again clear that the Supreme Court, not Congress, is the final arbiter of constitutional issues. The Court held that Congress could not dictate what constitutional standards govern legislative acts.

The Right to Abortion

Ironically, while the "liberal" Warren Court stirred political controversy with its school prayer and many other decisions extending civil liberties and rights to the states, it was the "conservative" Supreme Court under the chief justiceship of Warren Burger, who was appointed by Republican President Richard M. Nixon in 1969, that raised an even greater political storm by holding in the following case that the Fourteenth Amendment incorporates a right to privacy that grants women the absolute right to abortion during the first trimester of pregnancy. When the decision was handed down in 1973, a majority of states strictly regulated abortions, which could be performed if at all only to protect the life of the mother. The moral codes of many religions, particularly the Catholic church, forbid abortions under any circumstances.

Supporters of the abortion decision argued that while the issue was indeed a moral one for most people, women had a constitutionally protected right to decide whether or not they would have an abortion. Opponents not only emphatically opposed abortion on moral grounds, but also attacked the Court for acting as a supralegislature by imposing its own values upon democratically elected state legislative bodies that were regulating abortion in response to the demands of popular majorities.

The Supreme Court's abortion decision did seem to resurrect "substantive due process," a doctrine under which the Court had in the past judged the fairness of state legislation in terms not of explicitly stated constitutional standards but on the basis of its own values. The Bill of Rights does not contain a general right of privacy, although it may be fairly implied, as Justice Douglas wrote for a majority of the Court in *Griswold v. Connecticut,* 381 U.S. 479 (1965), from First Amendment freedoms of association, Fourth Amendment protections against unreasonable searches and seizures, and the Fifth Amendment shield against self-incrimination.

Whether emanating indirectly from the Bill of Rights or considered to be part of the liberty protected by the Fourteenth Amendment, the right of privacy that the Supreme Court applied in its abortion decision is highly subjective and gives the justices great leeway to impose their own concepts of privacy rights upon legislative bodies. But judicial decisions, especially those of the Supreme Court, always express the values of those making them. The justices did go beyond a strict construction of the Bill of Rights in upholding a woman's right to abortion. However, they had previously interpreted the Fourteenth Amendment due process clause just as subjectively in each case in the step-by-step process of nationalization of most of the provisions of the Bill Rights.

The Anglo-American system of law and jurisprudence has always supported the concept of a higher law that ultimately the courts must interpret and apply. In Great Britain, however, Parliament became supreme after the Glorious Revolution of 1688, preventing judicial review of parliamentary laws. Our Supreme Court, on the other hand, continues to be the final judge of what the law is, and inevitably its decisions will involve the Court in major political controversies, as has been the case in the following opinion.

24

ROE v. WADE

410 U.S. 113 (1973)

Mr. Justice Blackmun delivered the opinion of the Court:

V

The principal thrust of appellant's attack on the Texas statutes is that they improperly invade a right, said to be possessed by the pregnant woman, to choose to terminate her pregnancy. Appellant would discover this right in the concept of personal "liberty" embodied in the Fourteenth Amendment's Due Process Clause; or in personal, marital, familial, and sexual privacy said to be protected by the Bill of Rights or its penumbras, see *Griswold v. Connecticut* [1965] . . . *Eisenstadt v. Baird* [1972] . . . (White, J., concurring in result); or among those rights reserved to the people by the Ninth Amendment, *Griswold v. Connecticut*, . . . (Goldberg, J., concurring). Before addressing this claim, we feel it desirable briefly to survey, in several aspects, the history of abortion, for such insight as that history may afford us, and then to examine the state purposes and interests behind the criminal abortion laws.

VI

It perhaps is not generally appreciated that the restrictive criminal abortion laws in effect in a majority of States today are of relatively recent vintage. Those laws, generally proscribing abortion or its attempt at any time during pregnancy except when necessary to preserve the pregnant woman's life, are not of ancient or even of common-law origin. Instead, they derive from statutory changes effected, for the most part, in the latter half of the 19th century. . . .

VII

Three reasons have been advanced to explain historically the enactment of criminal abortion laws in the 19th century and to justify their continued existence.

It has been argued occasionally that these laws were the product of a Victorian social concern to discourage illicit sexual conduct. Texas, however, does not advance this justification in the present case, and it appears that no court or commentator has taken the argument seriously. The appellants and amici contend, moreover, that this is not a proper state purpose at all and suggest that, if it were, the Texas statutes are overbroad in protecting it since the law fails to distinguish between married and unwed mothers.

A second reason is concerned with abortion as a medical procedure. When most criminal abortion laws were first enacted, the procedure was a hazardous one for the woman. This was particularly true prior to the development of antisepsis. Antiseptic techniques, of course, were based on discoveries by Lister, Pasteur, and others first announced in 1867, but were not generally accepted and employed until about the turn of the century. Abortion mortality was high. Even after 1900, and perhaps until as late as the development of antibiotics in the 1940's, standard modern techniques such as dilation and curettage were not nearly so safe as they are today. Thus, it has been argued that a State's real concern in enacting a criminal abortion law was to protect the pregnant woman, that is, to restrain her from submitting to a procedure that placed her life in serious jeopardy.

Modern medical techniques have altered this situation. Appellants and various amici refer to medical data indicating that abortion in early pregnancy, this is, prior to the end of the first trimester, although not without its risk, is now relatively safe. Mortality rates for women undergoing early abortions, where the procedure is legal, appear to be as low as or lower than the rates for normal childbirth. Consequently, any interest of the State in protecting the woman from an inherently hazardous procedure, except when it would be equally dangerous for her to forgo it, has largely disappeared. Of course, important state interests in the area of health and medical standards do remain.

The State has a legitimate interest in seeing to it that abortion, like any other medical procedure, is performed under circumstances that insure maximum safety for the patient. This interest obviously extends at least to the performing physician and his staff, to the facilities involved, to the availability of aftercare, and to adequate provision for any complication or emergency that might arise. The prevalence of high mortality rates at illegal "abortion mills" strengthens, rather than weakens, the State's interest in regulating the conditions under which abortions are performed. Moreover, the risk to the woman increases as her pregnancy continues. Thus, the State retains a definite interest in protecting the woman's own health and safety when an abortion is proposed at a late stage of pregnancy.

The third reason is the State's interest—some phrase it in terms of duty—in protecting prenatal life. Some of the argument for this justification rests on the theory that a new human life is present from the moment of conception. The State's interest and general obligation to protect life then extends, it is argued, to prenatal life. Only when the life of the pregnant mother herself is at stake, balanced against the life she carries within her, should the interest of the embryo or fetus not prevail.

Logically, of course, a legitimate state interest in this area need not stand or fall on acceptance of the belief that life begins at conception or at some other point prior to live birth. In assessing the State's interest, recognition may be given to the less rigid claim that as long as at least potential life is involved, the State may assert interests beyond the protection of the pregnant woman alone.

Parties challenging state abortion laws have sharply disputed in some courts the contention that a purpose of these laws, when enacted, was to protect prenatal life. . . .

It is with these interests, and the weight to be attached to them, that this case is concerned.

VIII

The Constitution does not explicitly mention any right of privacy. In a line of decisions, however, going back perhaps as far as *Union Pacific R. Co. v. Botsford* [1891]. . . , the Court has recognized that a right of personal privacy, or a guarantee of certain areas or zones of privacy, does exist under the Constitution. In varying contexts, the Court or individual Justices have, indeed, found at least the roots of that right in the First Amendment, *Stanley v. Georgia* [1969]. . . ; in the Fourth and Fifth Amendments, *Terry v. Ohio* [1968]. . . , *Katz v. United States* [1967]. . . ; in the penumbras of the Bill of Rights, *Griswold v. Connecticut* [1965]. . . ; in the Ninth Amendments, id., at 486, . . . (Goldberg, J., concurring); or in the concept of liberty guaranteed by the first section of the Fourteenth Amendment, see *Meyer v. Nebraska* [1923]. . . . These decisions make it clear that only personal rights that can be deemed "fundamental" or "implicit in the concept of ordered liberty," *Palko v. Connecticut* [1937]. . . , are included in this guarantee of personal privacy. They also make it clear that the right has some extension to activities relating to marriage, *Loving v. Virginia* [1967]. . . ; procreation, *Skinner v. Oklahoma* [1942]. . . ; contraception, *Eisenstadt v. Baird* [1972]. . . .

This right of privacy, whether it be founded in the Fourteenth Amendment's concept of personal liberty and restrictions upon state action, as we feel it is, or, as the District Court determined, in the Ninth Amendment's reservation of rights to the people, is broad enough to encompass a woman's decision whether or not to terminate her pregnancy. The detriment that the State would impose upon the pregnant woman by denying this choice altogether is apparent. Specific and direct harm medically diagnosable even in early pregnancy may be involved. Maternity, or additional offspring, may force upon the woman a distressful life and future. Psychological harm may be imminent. Mental and physical health may be taxed by child care. There is also the distress, for all concerned, associated with the unwanted child, and there is the problem of bringing a child into a family already unable, psychologically and otherwise, to care for it. In other cases, as in this one, the additional difficulties and continuing stigma of unwed motherhood may be involved. All these are factors the woman and her responsible physician necessarily will consider in consultation.

On the basis of elements such as these, appellant and some amici argue that the woman's right is absolute and that she is entitled to terminate her pregnancy at whatever time, in whatever way, and for whatever reason she alone chooses. With this we do not agree. Appellant's arguments that Texas either has no valid interest at all in regulating the abortion decision, or no interest strong enough to support any limitation upon the woman's sole determination, is unpersuasive. The Court's decisions recognizing a right of privacy also acknowledge that some state regulation in areas protected by that right is appropriate. As noted above, a State may properly assert important interests in safeguarding health, in maintaining medical standards, and in protecting potential life. At some point in pregnancy, these respective interests become sufficiently compelling to sustain regulation of the factors that govern the abortion decision. The privacy right involved, therefore, cannot be said to be absolute. In fact, it is not clear to us that the claim asserted by some amici that one has an unlimited right to do with one's body as one pleases bears a close relationship to the right of privacy previously articulated in the Court's decisions. The Court has refused to recognize an unlimited right of this kind in the past. *Jacobson v. Massachusetts* [1905] . . . (vaccination); *Buck v. Bell* [1927] . . . (sterilization).

We, therefore, conclude that the right of personal privacy includes the abortion decision, but that this right is not unqualified and must be considered against important state interests in regulation.

Where certain "fundamental rights" are involved, the Court has held that regulation limiting these rights may be justified only by a "compelling state interest," . . . and that legislative enactments must be narrowly drawn to express only the legitimate state interests at stake. . . .

IX

The District Court held that the appellee failed to meet his burden of demonstrating that the Texas statute's infringement upon Roe's rights was necessary to support a compelling state interest. . . . Appellee argues that the State's determination to recognize and protect prenatal life from and after conception constitutes a compelling state interest. As noted above, we do not agree fully with either formulation.

A. The appellee and certain amici argue that the fetus is a "person" within the language and meaning of the Fourteenth Amendment. In support of this, they outline at length and in detail the well-known facts of fetal development. If this suggestion of personhood is established, the appellant's case, of course, collapses, for the fetus' right to life is then guaranteed specifically by the Amendment. The appellant conceded as much on reargument. On the other hand, the appellee conceded on reargument that no case could be cited that holds that a fetus is a person within the meaning of the Fourteenth Amendment.

The Constitution does not define "person" in so many words. Section 1 of the Fourteenth Amendment contains three references to "person." The first, in defining "citizens," speaks of "persons born or naturalized in the United States." The word also appears both in the Due Process Clause and in the Equal Protection Clause. "Person" is used in other places in the Constitution. . . . But in nearly all these instances, the use of the word is such that it has application only postnatally. None indicates, with any assurance, that it has any possible prenatal application.

All this, together with our observation, supra, that throughout the major portion of the 19th century prevailing legal abortion practices were far freer than they are today, persuades us that the word "person," as used in the Fourteenth Amendment, does not include the unborn. . . .

B. The pregnant woman cannot be isolated in her privacy. She carries an embryo and, later, a fetus, if one accepts the medical definitions of the developing young in the human uterus. . . . The situation therefore is inherently different from marital intimacy, or bedroom possession of obscene material, or marriage, or procreation, or education, with which *Eisenstadt, Griswold, Stanley, Loving, Skinner, Pierce,* and *Meyer* were respectively concerned. As we have intimated above, it is reasonable and appropriate for a State to decide that at some point in time another interest, that of health of the mother or that of potential human life, becomes significantly involved. The woman's privacy is no longer sole and any right of privacy she possesses must be measured accordingly.

Texas urges that, apart from the Fourteenth Amendment, life begins at conception and is present throughout pregnancy, and that, therefore, the State has a compelling interest in protecting that life from and after conception. We need not resolve the difficult question of when life begins. When those trained in the respective disciplines of medicine, philosophy, and theology are unable to arrive at any consensus, the judiciary, at this point in the development of man's knowledge, is not in a position to speculate as to the answer.

It should be sufficient to note briefly the wide divergence of thinking on this most sensitive and difficult question. . . .

X

In view of all this, we do not agree that, by adopting one theory of life, Texas may override the rights of the pregnant woman that are at stake. We repeat, however, that the State does have an important and legitimate interest in preserving and protecting the health of the pregnant woman, whether she be a resident of the State or a nonresident who seeks medical consultation and treatment there, and that it has still another important and legitimate interest in protecting the potentiality of human life. These interests are separate and distinct. Each grows in substantiality as the woman approaches term and, at a point during pregnancy, each becomes "compelling."

With respect to the State's important and legitimate interest in the health of the mother, the "compelling" point, in the light of present medical knowledge, is at approximately the end of the first trimester. This is so because of the now-established medical fact, referred to above . . . that until the end of the first trimester mortality in abortion may be less than mortality in normal childbirth. It follows that, from and after this point, a State may regulate the abortion procedure to the extent that the regulation reasonably relates to the preservation and protection of maternal health. Examples of permissible state regulation in this area are requirements as to the qualifications of the person who is to perform the abortion; as to the licensure of that person; as to the facility in which the procedure is to be performed, that is, whether it must be a hospital or may be a clinic or some other place of less-than-hospital status; as to the licensing of the facility; and the like.

This means, on the other hand, that, for the period of pregnancy prior to this "compelling" point, the attending physician, in consultation with his patient, is free to determine, without regulation by the State, that, in his medical judgment, the patient's pregnancy should be terminated. If that decision is reached, the judgment may be effectuated by an abortion free of interference by the State.

With respect to the State's important and legitimate interest in potential life, the "compelling" point is at viability. This is so because the fetus then presumably has the capability of meaningful life outside the mother's womb. State regulation protective of fetal life after viability thus has both logical and biological justifications. If the State is interested in protecting fetal life after viability, it may go so far as to proscribe abortion during that period, except when it is necessary to preserve the life or health of the mother.

Measured against these standards, Art. 1196 of the Texas Penal Code, in restricting legal abortions to those "procured or attempted by medical advice for the purpose of saving the life of the mother," sweeps too broadly. The statute makes no distinction between abortions performed early in pregnancy and those performed later, and it limits to a single reason, "saving" the mother's life, the legal justification for the procedure. The statute, therefore, cannot survive the constitutional attack made upon it here. . . .

XI

To summarize and to repeat:

1. A state criminal abortion statute of the current Texas type, that excepts from criminality only a lifesaving procedure on behalf of the mother, without regard to pregnancy stage and without recognition of the other interests involved, is violative of the Due Process Clause of the Fourteenth Amendment.

(a) For the stage prior to approximately the end of the first trimester, the abortion decision and its effectuation must be left to the medical judgment of the pregnant woman's attending physician.

(b) For the stage subsequent to approximately the end of the first trimester, the State, in promoting its interest in the health of the mother, may, if it chooses, regulate the abortion procedure in ways that are reasonably related to maternal health.

(c) For the stage subsequent to viability, the State in promoting its interest in the potentiality of human life may, if it chooses, regulate, and even proscribe, abortion except where it is necessary, in appropriate medical judgment, for the preservation of the life or health of the mother.

2. The State may define the term "physician," as it has been employed in the preceding numbered paragraphs of this Part XI of this opinion, to mean only a physician currently licensed by the State, and may proscribe any abortion by a person who is not a physician as so defined.

In *Doe v. Bolton* [1973] . . . procedural requirements contained in one of the modern abortion statutes are considered. That opinion and this one, of course, are to be read together. . . .

Mr. Chief Justice Burger concurred.

Mr. Justice Douglas concurred.

Mr. Justice Stewart, concurring:

In 1963, this Court, in *Ferguson v. Skrupa,* . . . purported to sound the death knell for the doctrine of substantive due process, a doctrine under which many state laws had in the past been held to violate the Fourteenth Amendment. As Mr. Justice Black's opinion for the Court in *Skrupa* put it: "We have returned to the original constitutional proposition that courts do not substitute their social and economic beliefs for the judgment of legislative bodies, who are elected to pass laws." . . .

Barely two years later, in *Griswold v. Connecticut,* . . . the Court held a Connecticut birth control law unconstitutional. In view of what had been so recently said in *Skrupa,* the Court's opinion in *Griswold* understandably did its best to avoid reliance on the Due Process Clause of the Fourteenth Amendment as the ground for decision. Yet, the Connecticut law did not violate any provision of the Bill of Rights, nor any other specific provision of the Constitution. So it was clear to me then, and it is equally clear to me now, that the *Griswold* decision can be rationally understood only as a holding that the Connecticut statute substantively invaded the "liberty" that is protected by the Due Process Clause of the Fourteenth Amendment. As so understood, *Griswold* stands as one in a long line of pre-*Skrupa* cases decided under the doctrine of substantive due process, and I now accept it as such.

"In a Constitution for a free people, there can be no doubt that the meaning of 'liberty' must be broad indeed." . . . The Constitution nowhere mentions a specific right of personal choice in matters of marriage and family life, but the "liberty" protected by the Due Process Clause of the Fourteenth Amendment covers more than those freedoms explicitly named in the Bill of Rights. . . .

Several decisions of this Court make clear that freedom of personal choice in matters of marriage and family life is one of the liberties protected by the Due Process Clause of the Fourteenth Amendment. *Loving v. Virginia,* . . . *Griswold v. Connecticut.* . . . In *Eisenstadt v. Baird,* . . . we recognized "the right of the individual, married or single, to be free from unwarranted governmental intrusion into matters so fundamentally affecting a person as the decision whether to bear or beget a child." That right necessarily includes the right of a woman to decide whether or not to terminate her pregnancy. "Certainly the interests of a woman in giving of her physical and emotional self during pregnancy and the interest that will be affected throughout her life by the birth and raising of a child are of a far greater degree of significance and personal intimacy than the right to send a child to private school protected in *Pierce v. Society of Sisters* [1925] . . . , or the right to teach a foreign language protected in *Meyer v. Nebraska.* . . ."

Mr. Justice Rehnquist, dissenting:

. . . I have difficulty in concluding, as the Court does, that the right of "privacy" is involved in this case. Texas, by the statute here challenged, bars the performance of a medical abortion by a licensed physician on a plaintiff such as Roe. A transaction resulting in an operation such as this is not "private" in the ordinary usage of that word. . . .

If the Court means by the term "privacy" no more than that the claim of a person to be free from unwanted state regulation of consensual transactions may be a form of "liberty" protected by the Fourteenth Amendment, there is no doubt that similar claims have been upheld in our earlier decisions on the basis of the liberty. I agree with the statement of Mr. Justice Stewart in his concurring opinion that the "liberty," against deprivation of which without due process the Fourteenth Amendment protects, embraces more than the rights found in the Bill of Rights. But that liberty is not guaranteed absolutely against deprivation, only against deprivation without due process of law. The test traditionally applied in the area of social and economic legislation is whether or not a law such as that challenged has a rational relation to a valid state objective. . . . But the Court's sweeping invalidation of any restrictions on abortion during the first trimester is impossible to justify under that standard, and the conscious weighing of competing factors that the Court's opinion apparently substitutes for the established test is far more appropriate to a legislative judgment than to a judicial one.

The Court eschews the history of the Fourteenth Amendment in its reliance on the "compelling state interest" test. . . . But the Court adds a new wrinkle to this test by transposing it from the legal considerations associated with the Equal Protection Clause of the Fourteenth Amendment to this case arising under the Due Process Clause of the Fourteenth Amendment. Unless I misapprehend the consequences of this transplanting of the "compelling state interest test," the Court's opinion will accomplish the seemingly impossible feat of leaving this area of the law more confused than it found it.

While the Court's opinion quotes from the dissent of Mr. Justice Holmes in *Lochner v. New York*, the result it reaches is more closely attuned to the majority opinion of Mr. Justice Peckham in that case. As in *Lochner* and similar cases applying substantive due process standards to economic and social welfare legislation, the adoption of the compelling state interest standard will inevitably require this Court to examine the legislative policies and pass on the wisdom of these policies in the very process of deciding whether a particular state interest put forward may or may not be "compelling." The decision here to break pregnancy into three distinct terms and to outline the permissible restrictions the State may impose in each one, for example, partakes more of judicial legislation than it does of a determination of the intent of the drafters of the Fourteenth Amendment.

The fact that a majority of the States reflecting, after all the majority sentiment in those States, have had restrictions on abortions for at least a century is a strong indication, it seems to me, that the asserted right to an abortion is not "so rooted in the traditions and conscience of our people as to be ranked as fundamental," *Snyder v. Massachusetts* [1934]. . . . Even today, when society's views on abortion are changing, the very existence of the debate is evidence that the "right" to an abortion is not so universally accepted as the appellant would have us believe.

To reach its result, the Court necessarily has had to find within the scope of the Fourteenth Amendment a right that was apparently completely unknown to the drafters of the Amendment. As early as 1821, the first state law dealing directly with abortion was enacted by the Connecticut Legislature. . . . By the time of the adoption of the Fourteenth Amendment in 1868, there were at least 36 laws enacted by state or territorial legislatures limiting abortion. While many States have amended or updated their laws, 21 of the laws on the books in 1868 remain in effect today. . . .

. . . The only conclusion possible from this history is that the drafters did not intend to have the Fourteenth Amendment withdraw from the States the power to legislate with respect to this matter. . . .

Mr. Justice White, joined by Mr. Justice Rehnquist, dissented.

The Court's decision in *Roe v. Wade* (1973) almost immediately mobilized pro-life forces who pressured Congress for a constitutional amendment to overturn the *Roe* decision. Elected officials were caught in a political vise on the issue, which they considered a no-win situation. Pro-lifers constituted a powerful political movement but not a majority of the American people who, after the *Roe* decision, favored the pro-choice position although not necessarily the practice of abortion.

For their part, politicians more often than not ducked the abortion issue by making vague statements such as, "I am personally against abortion but I must uphold and respect the Supreme Court's decision on the matter." Before the *Roe* decision, many states were well on their way toward liberalizing their abortion statutes in an environment that was relatively free of political rancor. Ironically, the *Roe* decision galvanized political opposition to abortion and forced politicians, however reluctantly, to deal with the issue. As state statutes regulating abortion were struck down one after the other, the pro-life movement gathered more steam than converts.

While pressing for a constitutional amendment, the pro-lifers knew that their best hope was to convince the Supreme Court to overturn *Roe v. Wade*. Litigation had produced the decision, and litigation could overturn it if the Court's composition changed to a more conservative, pro-life viewpoint.

Ronald Reagan's election to the presidency in 1980 gave the pro-lifers renewed hopes for change. Reagan took a strong pro-life position, putting the issue at the top of his social agenda. During his eight years as president he was able to make three conservative appointments to the Supreme Court—Sandra Day O'Connor, Antonin Scalia, and Anthony M. Kennedy. Reagan and the pro-lifers had reason to hope that these new justices might tip the Court's scale in favor of overruling *Roe v. Wade*.

The suspense on both sides of the abortion issue was almost unbearable as the Court in 1989 reviewed a circuit court decision that had struck down a Missouri abortion law on the ground that it violated the principles of *Roe v. Wade.* The law prohibited the use of public facilities or employees to perform abortions, and prohibited the use of public funds for abortion counseling. The following decision, while not overruling *Roe v. Wade,* marked the beginning of a change in the Court's attitude on the abortion issue. A plurality of justices, led by Chief Justice William H. Rehnquist, began a process of dismantling *Roe,* but did not take the final step, urged by Justice Scalia, of overturning it. Justice Blackmun, who had written the *Roe* opinion, dissented along with Justices Brennan and Marshall. Blackmun wrote, "The simple truth is that *Roe* would not survive the plurality's analysis, and that the plurality provides no substitute for *Roe*'s protective umbrella. I fear for the future. I fear for the liberty and equality of the millions of women who have lived and come of age in the sixteen years since *Roe* was decided. I fear for the integrity of, and public esteem for, this Court." He concluded, "For today, at least, the law of abortion stands undisturbed. For today, the women of this nation still retain the liberty to control their destinies. But the signs are evident and very ominous and a chill wind blows."

While it seems unlikely that the Supreme Court will overrule *Roe v. Wade* in its entirety, the Rehnquist Court has allowed states to regulate abortion to a greater degree than *Roe v. Wade* would have permitted. Chief Justice Rehnquist, Justice Antonin Scalia, and other justices have rejected much of Justice Blackmun's reasoning in *Roe v. Wade*'s majority opinion. Conservatives have broadly attacked *Roe*'s affirmation of the constitutional right to privacy, first "discovered" in *Griswold v. Connecticut* (1965), to support the right to abortion.[11]

Affirmative Action

The Supreme Court has unequivocally ruled that racial discrimination by law is unconstitutional. When the law treats racial groups differently, it is almost invariably the case that the Court will declare the law to be a violation of the equal protection clause of the Fourteenth Amendment or, where federal action is involved, the standards of equal protection required under the due process clause of the Fifth Amendment.[12]

Before the era of the Warren court, which began in 1953 and led immediately to the *Brown* decision, the Supreme Court applied a "rational-relation" or "conceivable-basis" test to determine if legislative classifications that treated separate groups of people differently constituted a violation of equal protection standards. Generally, under these tests the Court upheld the legislative classifications if it found there was a rational relationship between the classifications and legislative goals. Such classifications were also upheld if the Court found a conceivable basis upon which to support the reasoning of the legislature in

---

[11]See selections 64–66 for contrasting views of Supreme Court justices on the abortion issue.

[12]An important exception to the rigid application of equal protection standards to racial classification was the holding of the Supreme Court in *Korematsu v. United States,* 323 U.S. 214 (1944), which upheld a racial classification that treated Japanese Americans differently than other citizens. The Court found that the federal government could exclude Japanese Americans from military zones on the West Coast on the ground of national security, a holding that in effect supported the establishment of relocation centers for Japanese American citizens during World War II.

creating classifications. These equal protection standards are referred to as the "old equal protection."

The Warren court inaugurated the "new equal protection" standards to apply to legislative classifications based on race or other "suspect" group classifications. For example, gender classifications were regarded by the Burger court as at least partly suspect.[13]

The new equal protection standards required the demonstration of a "compelling" governmental interest to uphold the legislative classifications under review. The new equal protection standards also required the demonstration of a compelling governmental interest to sustain legislative classifications that burdened fundamental rights. For example, in *Shapiro v. Thompson*, 394 U.S. 618 (1969), the Warren court reviewed challenges to state and District of Columbia laws denying welfare assistance to persons who had not resided within their jurisdictions for at least one year immediately prior to applying for assistance. The Court found that the laws burdened the fundamental right to travel, and therefore could be sustained only upon the demonstration of a compelling governmental interest. The Court found no such compelling interest present and held the laws to be unconstitutional. The application of the new equal protection standard is called strict judicial scrutiny. When the Court employs this strict judicial scrutiny, the invariable effect is to declare unconstitutional the classification in the law under review.

In the *Bakke* case, presented below, the opinions of Justices Powell and Brennan discuss the circumstances under which strict judicial scrutiny is required by the equal protection clause of the Fourteenth Amendment. This case arose out of a complex set of circumstances. Title VI of the Civil Rights Act of 1964 provided that no person was to be "subjected to discrimination under any program or activity receiving federal financial assistance." The Department of Health, Education, and Welfare found this section to require affirmative action programs by private institutions receiving federal aid, to achieve a racial balance among employees and, in institutions of higher learning, within their student bodies as well. Throughout the country, pressure from civil rights groups, women, and other minorities prompted the adoption of affirmative action plans that contained racial classifications providing for the favored treatment of racial minorities in school admissions and private employment.

The *Bakke* case was initiated by Allan Bakke, a 36-year-old white engineer who decided that he wanted to become a doctor. In 1973 and 1974 he applied, unsuccessfully, for admission to the University of California Medical School at Davis. The school informed Bakke that there were too many qualified applicants and that it could admit only 1 out of 26 in 1973, and 1 out of 37 in 1974. However, 16 of the 100 openings in the Davis medical school were set aside for minority applicants. Bakke's objective qualifications, such as his Medical College Admission Test scores and his undergraduate grades, were better than those of some of the minority applicants who were accepted during the years when he was rejected. The minority applicants competed among themselves for the 16 places reserved for them, making it possible to admit minority students with different qualifications than were required of nonminority applicants. Bakke claimed that the admissions procedures violated the equal protection clause and Title VI of the Civil Rights Act of 1964.

---

[13]See, for example, *Frontiero v. Richardson*, 411 U.S. 677 (1973).

The trial court in the *Bakke* case held that the admissions program established racial quotas in violation of the equal protection clause and Title VI. However, the court refused to order the admission of Bakke to the medical school because of his failure to prove that he would have been admitted in the absence of the special program for minorities. The California Supreme Court sustained the trial court's finding that the program violated the equal protection clause and the Civil Rights Act but overruled the trial court's denial of an order that Bakke be admitted. The United States Supreme Court granted certiorari to the California Supreme Court to review the case.

The California Supreme Court, by a 5–4 vote, ruled that Bakke should be admitted to the Davis medical school. The majority on the issue of admittance agreed that the racial quota system at the school was not an acceptable means to decide who should be admitted. The majority justices favoring admission and a ban on quotas were Powell, Burger, Stevens, Rehnquist, and Stewart. Brennan, White, Marshall, and Blackmun dissented on these issues, arguing that "Davis's special admissions program cannot be said to violate the Constitution simply because it has set aside a predetermined number of places for qualified minority applicants. . . ."

Justice Louis F. Powell, who was in the majority favoring admission and a ban on quotas, joined with the four justices who dissented from the Court's decision and opinion on those issues to form another majority that held that an applicant's race can be considered in deciding who should be admitted to a university program.

After the Bakke case affirmative action took many twists and turns. The courts continued to be a forum for the resolution of political conflict as proponents and opponents of national and state affirmative action legislation took their cases to court. Nowhere was litigation as a political process more evident than in the affirmative action area.

For their part, Supreme Court justices could not agree upon constitutional standards for affirmative action. The split among the justices that had occurred in the Bakke case, and the resulting confusion in affirmative action jurisprudence, continued throughout the 1980s and into the 1990s. The Supreme Court, as the body of final appeal, confronted the question of whether or not the racial classifications used in affirmative action programs at all governmental levels were, in judicial terms, "suspect" and therefore subject to "strict judicial scrutiny." Such scrutiny required the demonstration of a compelling governmental interest, where the burden of proof was placed upon the governmental body that had created an affirmative action program.

During the 1980s the Supreme Court appeared to apply different constitutional standards to national and state and local affirmative action programs. Essentially, a close majority and sometimes plurality of the Court held that Congress has broad remedial power under the Fourteenth Amendment's Section 5 to remedy the effects of past societal discrimination by passing affirmative action programs, such as minority set-aside programs for small businesses receiving federal funds. At the same time, Supreme Court conservatives were able to marshall a majority or plurality that applied stricter constitutional standards to state and local programs. In the latter area the Court sometimes overturned state and local affirmative action programs as unjustified racial discrimination in violation of the equal protection clause of the Fourteenth Amendment. Only if the states or localities could prove that their affirmative action programs were designed to remedy the effects of past discrimination would the Supreme Court uphold them. The result of these Supreme Court opinions was that Congress had far more leeway to pass affirmative action legislation than did the states or local governments.[14]

The Supreme Court, in a 5–4 decision, finally moved to end the constitutional confusion over the different treatment of national and state affirmative action in the following case.

--- **25** ---

ADARAND CONSTRUCTORS, INC. V. PENA

515 U.S. 200 (1995)

Justice Sandra Day O'Connor announced the judgment of the Court:

Petitioner Adarand Constructors, Inc., claims that the Federal Government's practice of giving general contractors on government projects a financial incentive to hire subcontractors controlled by "socially and economically disadvantaged individuals," and in particular, the Government's use of race-based presumptions in identifying such individuals, violates the equal protection component of the Fifth Amendment's Due Process Clause. The Court of Appeals rejected Adarand's claim. We conclude, however, that courts should analyze cases of this kind under a different standard of review than the one the Court of Appeals applied. We therefore vacate the Court of Appeals' judgment and remand the case for further proceedings.

In 1989, the Central Federal Lands Highway Division (CFLHD), which is part of the United States Department of Transportation (DOT), awarded the prime contract for a highway construction project in Colorado to Mountain Gravel & Construction Company. Mountain Gravel then solicited bids from subcontractors for the guardrail portion of the contract. Adarand, a Colorado-based highway construction company specializing in guardrail work, submitted the low bid. Gonzales Construction Company also submitted a bid.

---

[14]Major cases concerning congressional authority in affirmative action include *Fullilove v. Klutznick*, 448 U.S. 448 (1980); *Metro Broadcasting. Inc. v. Federal Communications Commission*, 497 U.S. 547 (1990). For state and local affirmative action authority see, for example, *Wygant v. Jackson Board of Education*, 476 U.S. 267 (1986); *United States v. Paradise*, 480 U.S. 149 (1987); *City of Richmond v. J. A. Croson Co.*, 488 U.S. 469 (1989).

The prime contract's terms provide that Mountain Gravel would receive additional compensation if it hired subcontractors certified as small businesses controlled by "socially and economically disadvantaged individuals," App. 24. Gonzales is certified as such a business; Adarand is not. Mountain Gravel awarded the subcontract to Gonzales, despite Adarand's low bid, and Mountain Gravel's Chief Estimator has submitted an affidavit stating that Mountain Gravel would have accepted Adarand's bid, had it not been for the additional payment it received by hiring Gonzales instead. Id., at 28–31. Federal law requires that a subcontracting clause similar to the one used here must appear in most federal agency contracts, and it also requires the clause to state that "[t]he contractor shall presume that socially and economically disadvantaged individuals include Black Americans, Hispanic Americans, Native Americans, Asian Pacific Americans, and other minorities, or any other individual found to be disadvantaged by the [Small Business] Administration pursuant to section 8(a) of the Small Business Act." 15 U.S.C. §§ 637(d)(2), (3). Adarand claims that the presumption set forth in that statute discriminates on the basis of race in violation of the Federal Government's Fifth Amendment obligation not to deny anyone equal protection of the laws. . . .

The Government urges that "[t]he Subcontracting Compensation Clause program is . . . a program based on disadvantage, not on race," and thus that it is subject only to "the most relaxed judicial scrutiny." To the extent that the statutes and regulations involved in this case are race neutral, we agree. The Government concedes, however, that "the race-based rebuttable presumption used in some certification determinations under the Subcontracting Compensation Clause" is subject to some heightened level of scrutiny. The parties disagree as to what that level should be. . . .

Adarand's claim arises under the Fifth Amendment to the Constitution, which provides that "No person shall . . . be deprived of life, liberty, or property, without due process of law." Although this Court has always understood that Clause to provide some measure of protection against arbitrary treatment by the Federal Government, it is not as explicit a guarantee of equal treatment as the Fourteenth Amendment, which provides that "No State shall . . . deny to any person within its jurisdiction the equal protection of the laws. . . ."

[Case law, however, has treated] the equal protection obligations imposed by the Fifth and the Fourteenth Amendments as indistinguishable. . . .

Most . . . cases [have] involved classifications burdening groups that have suffered discrimination in our society. In 1978, the Court confronted the question whether race-based governmental action designed to benefit such groups should also be subject to "the most rigid scrutiny." *Regents of Univ. of California v. Bakke*, 438 U.S. 265, involved an equal protection challenge to a state run medical school's practice of reserving a number of spaces in its entering class for minority students. The petitioners argued that "strict scrutiny" should apply only to "classifications that disadvantage 'discrete and insular minorities.' " . . . *Bakke* did not produce an opinion for the Court, but Justice Powell's opinion announcing the Court's judgment rejected the argument. In a passage joined by Justice White, Justice Powell wrote that "[t]he guarantee of equal protection cannot mean one thing when applied to one individual and something else when applied to a person of another color." 438 U.S., at 289–290. He concluded that "[r]acial and ethnic distinctions of any sort are inherently suspect and thus call for the most exacting judicial examination." . . . On the other hand, four Justices in *Bakke* would have applied a less stringent standard of review to racial classifications "designed to further remedial purposes," . . . (Brennan, White, Marshall, and Blackmun, JJ., concurring in judgment in part and dissenting in part). And four Justices thought the case should be decided on statutory grounds. . . . (Stevens, J., joined by Burger, C. J., Stewart, and Rehnquist, JJ., concurring in judgment in part and dissenting in part). . . .

Despite lingering uncertainty in the details, however, the Court's cases . . . established three general propositions with respect to governmental racial classifications. First, skepticism: " '[a]ny preference based on racial or ethnic criteria must necessarily receive a most searching examination.' " Second, consistency: "the standard of review under the Equal Protection Clause is not dependent on the race of those burdened or benefited by a particular classification." . . . And third, congruence: "[e]qual protection analysis in the Fifth Amendment area is the same as that under the Fourteenth Amendment." . . .

The three propositions . . . all derive from the basic principle that the Fifth and Fourteenth Amendments to the Constitution protect persons, not groups. It follows from that principle that all governmental action based on race . . . should be subjected to detailed judicial inquiry to ensure that the personal right to equal protection of the laws has not been infringed. These ideas have long been central to this Court's understanding of equal protection, and holding "benign" state and federal racial classifications to different standards does not square with them. "[A] free people whose institutions are founded upon the doctrine of equality," should tolerate no retreat from the principle that government may treat people differently because of their race only for the most compelling reasons. Accordingly, we hold today that all racial classifications, imposed by whatever federal, state, or local governmental actor, must be analyzed by a reviewing court under strict scrutiny. In other words, such classifications are constitutional only if they are narrowly tailored measures that further compelling governmental interests. . . .

Justice Stevens, with whom Justice Ginsburg joins, dissenting.

Instead of deciding this case in accordance with controlling precedent, the Court today delivers a disconcerting lecture about the evils of governmental racial classifications. For its text the Court has selected three propositions, represented by the bywords "skepticism," "consistency," and "congruence." . . .

The Court's concept of skepticism is, at least in principle, a good statement of law and of common sense. Undoubtedly, a court should be wary of a governmental decision that relies upon a racial classification. . . .

The Court's concept of "consistency" assumes that there is no significant difference between a decision by the majority to impose a special burden on the members of a minority race and a decision by the majority to provide a benefit to certain members of that minority notwithstanding its incidental burden on some members of the majority. In my opinion that assumption is untenable. . . .

The consistency that the Court espouses would disregard the difference between a "No Trespassing" sign and a welcome mat. It would treat a Dixiecrat Senator's decision to vote against Thurgood Marshall's confirmation in order to keep African Americans off the Supreme Court as on a par with President Johnson's evaluation of his nominee's race as a positive factor. It would equate a law that made black citizens ineligible for military service with a program aimed at recruiting black soldiers. An attempt by the majority to exclude members of a minority race from a regulated market is fundamentally different from a subsidy that enables a relatively small group of newcomers to enter that market. An interest in "consistency" does not justify treating differences as though they were similarities. . . .

My skeptical scrutiny of the Court's opinion leaves me in dissent. The majority's concept of "consistency" ignores a difference, fundamental to the idea of equal protection, between oppression and assistance. The majority's concept of "congruence" ignores a difference, fundamental to our constitutional system, between the Federal Government and the States. And the majority's concept of stare decisis ignores the force of binding precedent.

Justice Ginsburg, with whom Justice Breyer joins, dissenting.

. . . [I]n view of the attention the political branches are currently giving the matter of affirmative action, I see no compelling cause for the intervention the Court has made in this case. I further agree with Justice Stevens that, in this area, large deference is owed by the Judiciary to "Congress' institutional competence and constitutional authority to overcome historic racial subjugation." . . .

The statutes and regulations at issue, as the Court indicates, were adopted by the political branches in response to an "unfortunate reality": "[t]he unhappy persistence of both the practice and the lingering effects of racial discrimination against minority groups in this country." . . . For generations, our lawmakers and judges were unprepared to say that there is in this land no superior race, no race inferior to any other. In *Plessy v. Ferguson,* 163 U.S. 537 (1896), not only did this Court endorse the oppressive practice

> The white race deems itself to be the dominant race in this country. And so it is, in prestige, in achievements, in education, in wealth and in power. So, I doubt not, it will continue to be for all time, if it remains true to its great heritage and holds fast to the principles of constitutional liberty. (Harlan, J., dissenting).

Not until *Loving v. Virginia,* 388 U.S. 1 (1967), which held unconstitutional Virginia's ban on interracial marriages, could one say with security that the Constitution and this Court would abide no measure "designed to maintain White Supremacy." . . .

The divisions in this difficult case should not obscure the Court's recognition of the persistence of racial inequality and a majority's acknowledgement of Congress' authority to act affirmatively, not only to end discrimination, but also to counteract discrimination's lingering effects. . . . Those effects, reflective of a system of racial caste only recently ended, are evident in our workplaces, markets, and neighborhoods. Job applicants with identical resumes, qualifications, and interview styles still experience different receptions, depending on their race. White and African American consumers still encounter different deals. People of color looking for housing still face discriminatory treatment by landlords, real estate agents, and mortgage lenders. Minority entrepreneurs sometimes fail to gain contracts though they are the low bidders, and they are sometimes refused work even after winning contracts. Bias both conscious and unconscious, reflecting traditional and unexamined habits of thought, keeps up barriers that must come down if equal opportunity and nondiscrimination are ever genuinely to become this country's law and practice.

Given this history and its practical consequences, Congress surely can conclude that a carefully designed affirmative action program may help to realize, finally, the "equal protection of the laws" the Fourteenth Amendment has promised since 1868. . . .

The Death Penalty

The death penalty is a front burner political issue particularly at the state level. The Supreme Court's death penalty decisions are among the most controversial it has made. Liberal and conservative Justices have split sharply over how the Constitution applies to death penalty laws. The following threshold case set the stage for future death penalty litigation. In the process of discussing constitutional standards that may or may not govern the death penalty the case also addressed, inappropriately in the views of the dissenters, political concerns about death penality laws and their implementation through the criminal process.

26

FURMAN V. GEORGIA

408 U.S. 238 (1972)

Per Curiam.

Petitioner in No. 69-5003 was convicted of murder in Georgia and was sentenced to death. . . . Petitioner in No. 69-5030 was convicted of rape in Georgia and was sentenced to death. . . . Petitioner in No. 69-5031 was convicted of rape in Texas and was sentenced to death. . . . Certiorari was granted limited to the following question: "Does the imposition and carrying out of the death penalty in [these cases] constitute cruel and unusual punishment in violation of the Eighth and Fourteenth Amendments?"

The Court holds that the imposition and carrying out of the death penalty in these cases constitute cruel and unusual punishment in violation of the Eighth and

Fourteenth Amendments. The judgment in each case is therefore reversed insofar as it leaves undisturbed the death sentence imposed, and the cases are remanded for further proceedings.

So ordered.

Mr. Justice Douglas, Mr. Justice Brennan, Mr. Justice Stewart, Mr. Justice White, and Mr. Justice Marshall have filed separate opinions in support of the judgments. The Chief Justice, Mr. Justice Blackmun, Mr. Justice Powell, and Mr. Justice Rehnquist have filed separate dissenting opinions.

Mr. Justice Douglas, concurring.

In these three cases the death penalty was imposed, one of them for murder, and two for rape. In each the determination of whether the penalty should be death or a lighter punishment was left by the State to the discretion of the judge or of the jury. In each of the three cases the trial was to a jury. They are here on petitions for certiorari which we granted limited to the question whether the imposition and execution of the death penalty constitute "cruel and unusual punishment" within the meaning of the Eighth Amendment as applied to the States by the Fourteenth.

I vote to vacate each judgment, believing that the exaction of the death penalty does violate the Eighth and Fourteenth Amendments. . . .

We cannot say from facts disclosed in these records that these defendants were sentenced to death because they were black. Yet our task is not restricted to an effort to divine what motives impelled these death penalties. Rather, we deal with a system of law and of justice that leaves to the uncontrolled discretion of judges or juries the determination whether defendants committing these crimes should die or be imprisoned. Under these laws no standards govern the selection of the penalty. People live or die, dependent on the whim of one man or of 12. . . .

Those who wrote the Eighth Amendment knew what price their forebears had paid for a system based, not on equal justice, but on discrimination. In those days the target was not the blacks or the poor, but the dissenters, those who opposed absolutism in government, who struggled for a parliamentary regime, and who opposed governments' recurring efforts to foist a particular religion on the people. . . . But the tool of capital punishment was used with vengeance against the opposition and those unpopular with the regime. One cannot read this history without realizing that the desire for equality was reflected in the ban against "cruel and unusual punishments" contained in the Eighth Amendment.

In a Nation committed to equal protection of the laws there is no permissible "caste" aspect of law enforcement. Yet we know that the discretion of judges and juries in imposing the death penalty enables the penalty to be selectively applied, feeding prejudices against the accused if he is poor and despised, and lacking political clout, or if he is a member of a suspect or unpopular minority, and saving those who by social position may be in a more protected position. In ancient Hindu law a Brahman was exempt from capital punishment, and under that law, "[g]enerally, in the law books, punishment increased in severity as social status diminished." We have, I fear, taken in practice the same position, partially as a result of making the death penalty discretionary and partially as a result of the ability of the rich to purchase the services of the most respected and most resourceful legal talent in the Nation. . . .

Thus, these discretionary statutes are unconstitutional in their operation. They are pregnant with discrimination and discrimination is an ingredient not compatible with the idea of equal protection of the laws that is implicit in the ban on "cruel and unusual" punishments.

Any law which is nondiscriminatory on its face may be applied in such a way as to violate the Equal Protection Clause of the Fourteenth Amendment. *Yick Wo v. Hopkins*, 118 U.S. 356. . . . Such conceivably might be the fate of a mandatory death penalty, where equal or lesser sentences were imposed on the elite, a harsher one on the minorities or members of the lower castes. Whether a mandatory death penalty would otherwise be constitutional is a question I do not reach.

I concur in the judgments of the Court.

Mr. Justice Stewart, concurring.

The penalty of death differs from all other forms of criminal punishment, not in degree but in kind. It is unique in its total irrevocability. It is unique in its rejection of rehabilitation of the convict as a basic purpose of criminal justice. And it is unique, finally, in its absolute renunciation of all that is embodied in our concept of humanity. . . .

These death sentences are cruel and unusual in the same way that being struck by lightning is cruel and unusual. For, of all the people convicted of rapes and murders in 1967 and 1968, many just as reprehensible as these, the petitioners are among a capriciously selected random handful upon whom the sentence of death has in fact been imposed.

My concurring Brothers have demonstrated that, if any basis can be discerned for the selection of these few to be sentenced to die, it is the constitutionally impermissible basis of race. . . . But racial discrimination has not been proved, and I put it to one side. I simply conclude that the Eighth and Fourteenth Amendments cannot tolerate the infliction of a sentence of death under legal systems that permit this unique penalty to be so wantonly and so freakishly imposed.

For these reasons I concur in the judgments of the Court.

Mr. Justice White, concurring.

The facial constitutionality of statutes requiring the imposition of the death penalty for first-degree murder, for more narrowly defined categories of murder, or for rape would present quite different issues under the Eighth Amendment than are posed by the cases before us. In joining the Court's judgments, therefore, I do not at all intimate that the death penalty is unconstitutional per se or that there is no system of capital punishment that would comport with the Eighth Amendment. That question, ably argued by several of my Brethren, is not presented by these cases and need not be decided.

The narrower question to which I address myself concerns the constitutionality of capital punishment statutes under which (1) the legislature authorizes the imposition of the death penalty for murder or rape; (2) the legislature does not itself mandate the penalty in any particular class or kind of case (that is, legislative will is not frustrated if the penalty is never imposed), but delegates to judges or juries the decisions as to those cases, if any, in which the penalty will be utilized; and (3) judges and juries have ordered the death penalty with such infrequency that the odds are now very much against imposition and execution of the penalty with respect to any convicted murderer or rapist. It is in this context that we must consider whether the execution of these petitioners would violate the Eighth Amendment. . . .

. . . [T]he death penalty is exacted with great infrequency even for the most atrocious crimes and . . . there is no meaningful basis for distinguishing the few cases in which it is imposed from the many cases in which it is not. The short of it is that the policy of vesting sentencing authority primarily in juries—a decision largely motivated by the desire to mitigate the harshness of the law and to bring community judgment to bear on the sentence as well as guilt or innocence—has so effectively achieved its aims that capital punishment within the confines of the statutes now before us has for all practical purposes run its course. . . .

In this respect, I add only that past and present legislative judgment with respect to the death penalty loses much of its force when viewed in light of the recurring practice of delegating sentencing authority to the jury and the fact that a jury, in its own discretion and without violating its trust or any statutory policy, may refuse to impose the death penalty no matter what the circumstances of the crime. Legislative "policy" is thus necessarily defined not by what is legislatively authorized but by what juries and judges do in exercising the discretion so regularly conferred upon them. In my judgment what was done in these cases violated the Eighth Amendment.

I concur in the judgments of the Court.

Mr. Chief Justice Burger, with whom Mr. Justice Blackmun, Mr. Justice Powell, and Mr. Justice Rehnquist join, dissenting.

At the outset it is important to note that only two members of the Court, Mr. Justice Brennan and Mr. Justice Marshall, have concluded that the Eighth Amendment prohibits capital punishment for all crimes and under all circumstances. Mr. Justice Douglas has also determined that the death penalty contravenes the Eighth Amendment, although I do not read his opinion as necessarily requiring final abolition of the penalty.

. . . I conclude that the constitutional prohibition against "cruel and unusual punishments" cannot be construed to bar the imposition of the punishment of death.

Mr. Justice Stewart and Mr. Justice White have concluded that petitioners' death sentences must be set aside because prevailing sentencing practices do not comply with the Eighth Amendment. . . . I believe this approach fundamentally misconceives the nature of the Eighth Amendment guarantee and flies directly in the face of controlling authority of extremely recent vintage.

I

If we were possessed of legislative power, I would either join with Mr. Justice Brennan and Mr. Justice Marshall or, at the very least, restrict the use of capital punishment to a small category of the most heinous crimes. Our constitutional inquiry, however, must be divorced from personal feelings as to the morality and efficacy of the death penalty, and be confined to the meaning and applicability of the uncertain language of the Eighth Amendment. There is no novelty in being called upon to interpret a constitutional provision that is less than self-defining, but, of all our fundamental guarantees, the ban on "cruel and unusual punishments" is one of the most difficult to translate into judicially manageable terms. The widely divergent views of the Amendment expressed in today's opinions reveal the haze that surrounds this constitutional command. Yet it is essential to our role as a court that we not seize upon the enigmatic character of the guarantee as an invitation to enact our personal predilections into law. . . .

Mr. Justice Powell, with whom The Chief Justice, Mr. Justice Blackmun, and Mr. Justice Rehnquist join, dissenting.

The Court granted certiorari in these cases to consider whether the death penalty is any longer a permissible form of punishment. . . .

It is the judgment of five Justices that the death penalty, as customarily prescribed and implemented in this country today, offends the constitutional prohibition against cruel and unusual punishments. The reasons for that judgment are stated in five separate opinions, expressing as many separate rationales. In my view, none of these opinions provides a constitutionally adequate foundation for the Court's decision.

Mr. Justice Douglas concludes that capital punishment is incompatible with notions of "equal protection" that he finds to be "implicit" in the Eighth Amendment. Mr. Justice Brennan bases his judgment primarily on the thesis that the penalty "does not comport with human dignity." Mr. Justice Stewart concludes that the penalty is applied in a "wanton" and "freakish" manner. For Mr. Justice White it is the "infrequency" with which the penalty is imposed that renders its use unconstitutional. And Mr. Justice Marshall finds that capital punishment is an impermissible form of punishment because it is "morally unacceptable" and "excessive." . . .

In terms of the constitutional role of this Court, the impact of the majority's ruling is all the greater because the decision encroaches upon an area squarely within the historic prerogative of the legislative branch—both state and federal—to protect the citizenry through the designation of penalties for prohibitable conduct. It is the very sort of judgment that the legislative branch is competent to make and for which the judiciary is ill-equipped. Throughout our history, Justices of this Court have emphasized the gravity of decisions invalidating legislative judgments, admonishing the nine men who sit on this bench of the duty of self-restraint, especially when called upon to apply the expansive due process and cruel and unusual punishment rubrics. I can recall no case in which, in the name of deciding constitutional questions, this Court has subordinated national and local democratic processes to such an extent. . . .

. . . [T]he overriding question in these cases [is] whether this Court, acting in conformity with the Constitution, can justify its judgment to abolish capital punishment as heretofore known in this country. It is important to keep in focus the enormity of the step undertaken by the Court today. Not only does it invalidate hundreds of state and federal laws, it deprives those jurisdictions of the power to legislate with respect to capital punishment in the future, except in a manner consistent with the cloudily outlined views of those Justices who do not purport to undertake total abolition. Nothing short of an amendment to the United States Constitution can reverse the Court's judgments. Meanwhile, all flexibility is foreclosed. The normal democratic process, as well as the opportunities for the several States to respond to the will of their people expressed through ballot referenda (as in Massachusetts, Illinois, and Colorado), is now shut off. . . .

With deference and respect for the views of the Justices who differ, it seems to me that all these studies—both in this country and elsewhere—suggest that, as a matter of policy and precedent, this is a classic case for the exercise of our oft-announced allegiance to judicial restraint. I know of no case in which greater gravity and delicacy have attached to the duty that this Court is called on to perform whenever legislation—state or federal—is challenged on constitutional grounds.

It seems to me that the sweeping judicial action undertaken today reflects a basic lack of faith and confidence in the democratic process. Many may regret, as I do, the failure of some legislative bodies to address the capital punishment issue with greater frankness or effectiveness. Many might decry their failure either to abolish the penalty entirely or selectively, or to establish standards for its enforcement. But impatience with the slowness, and even the unresponsiveness, of legislatures is no justification for judicial intrusion upon their historic powers. . . .

After the *Furman* case state death penality laws were temporarily suspended as state legislatures attempted to find a way around the confusing and conflicting reasoning of the Court's majority. The *Furman* majority seemed to reason that it was the arbitrariness of the imposition of the death penality that made it unconstitutional or inappropriate. State legislatures answered the Court by severely reducing jury discretion in imposing the death penalty which was gradually reinstated in 23 states. The Court in the following case upheld the constitutionality of a death penalty law that addressed and answered the *Furman* majority's concerns that death penalty laws were implemented arbitrarily or capriciously. The law imposed sufficient standards to eliminate excessive jury discretion to impose the death penalty.

27

GREGG V. GEORGIA

428 U.S. 153 (1976)

Judgment of the Court, and opinion of Mr. Justice Stewart, Mr. Justice Powell, and Mr. Justice Stevens, announced by Mr. Justice Stewart.

The issue in this case is whether the imposition of the sentence of death for the crime of murder under the law of Georgia violates the Eighth and Fourteenth Amendments.

I

The petitioner, Troy Gregg, was charged with committing armed robbery and murder. In accordance with Georgia procedure in capital cases, the trial was in two stages, a guilt stage and a sentencing stage. The evidence at the guilt trial established that on November 21, 1973, the petitioner and a traveling companion, Floyd Allen, while hitchhiking north in Florida were picked up by Fred Simmons and Bob Moore. Their car broke down, but they continued north after Simmons purchased another vehicle with some of the cash he was carrying. While still in Florida, they picked up another hitchhiker, Dennis Weaver, who rode with them to Atlanta, where he was let out about 11 P.M. [428 U.S. 153, 159]. A short time later the four men interrupted their journey for a rest stop along the highway. The next morning the bodies of Simmons and Moore were discovered in a ditch nearby.

On November 23, after reading about the shootings in an Atlanta newspaper, Weaver communicated with the Gwinnett County police and related information concerning the journey with the victims, including a description of the car. The next afternoon, the petitioner and Allen, while in Simmons' car, were arrested in Asheville, N.C. In the search incident to the arrest a .25-caliber pistol, later shown to be that used to kill Simmons and Moore, was found in the petitioner's pocket. After receiving the warnings required by *Miranda v. Arizona*, 384 U.S. 436 (1966), and signing a written waiver of his rights, the petitioner signed a statement in which he admitted shooting, then robbing Simmons and Moore. He justified the slayings on grounds of self-defense. The next day, while being transferred to Lawrenceville, Ga., the petitioner and Allen were taken to the scene of the shootings. Upon arriving there, Allen recounted the events leading to the slayings. His version of these events was as follows: After Simmons and Moore left the car, the petitioner stated that he intended to rob them. The petitioner then took his pistol in hand and positioned himself on the car to improve his aim. As Simmons and Moore came up an embankment toward the car, the petitioner fired three shots and the two men fell near a ditch. The petitioner, at close range, then fired a shot into the head of each. He robbed them of valuables and drove away with Allen.

A medical examiner testified that Simmons died from a bullet wound in the eye and that Moore died from bullet wounds in the cheek and in the back of the head. He further testified that both men had several bruises [428 U.S. 153, 160] and abrasions about the face and head which probably were sustained either from the fall into the ditch or from being dragged or pushed along the embankment. Although Allen did not testify, a police detective recounted the substance of Allen's statements about the slayings and indicated that directly after Allen had made these statements the petitioner had admitted that Allen's account was accurate. The petitioner testified in his own defense. He confirmed that Allen had made the statements described by the detective, but denied their truth or ever having admitted to their accuracy. He indicated that he had shot Simmons and Moore because of fear and in self-defense, testifying they had attacked Allen and him, one wielding a pipe and the other a knife.

The trial judge submitted the murder charges to the jury on both felony-murder and nonfelony-murder theories. He also instructed on the issue of self-defense but declined to instruct on manslaughter. He submitted the robbery case to the jury on both an armed-robbery theory and on the lesser included offense of robbery by intimidation. The jury found the petitioner guilty of two counts of armed robbery and two counts of murder.

At the penalty stage, which took place before the same jury, neither the prosecutor nor the petitioner's lawyer offered any additional evidence. Both counsel, however, made lengthy arguments dealing generally with the propriety of capital punishment under the circumstances and with the weight of the evidence of guilt. The trial judge instructed the jury that it could recommend either a death sentence or a life prison sentence on each count. [428 U.S. 153, 161]. The judge further charged the jury that in determining what sentence was appropriate the jury was free to consider the facts and circumstances, if any, presented by the parties in mitigation or aggravation.

Finally, the judge instructed the jury that it "would not be authorized to consider [imposing] the penalty of death" unless it first found beyond a reasonable doubt one of these aggravating circumstances:

> "One—That the offense of murder was committed while the offender was engaged in the commission of two other capital felonies, to-wit the armed robbery of [Simmons and Moore].

> "Two—That the offender committed the offense of murder for the purpose of receiving money and the automobile described in the indictment.

> "Three—The offense of murder was outrageously and wantonly vile, horrible and inhuman, in that they [sic] involved the depravity of [the] mind of the defendant."

Finding the first and second of these circumstances, the jury returned verdicts of death on each count.

The Supreme Court of Georgia affirmed the convictions and the imposition of the death sentences for murder. 233 Ga. 117, 210 S. E. 2d 659 (1974). After reviewing the trial transcript and the record, including the evidence, and comparing the evidence and sentence in similar cases in accordance with the requirements of Georgia law, the court concluded that, considering the nature of the crime and the defendant, the sentences of death had not resulted from prejudice or any other arbitrary factor and were not excessive or disproportionate to the penalty applied in similar cases. . . .

IV

We now consider whether Georgia may impose the death penalty on the petitioner in this case. . . .

   . . . [T]he concerns expressed in *Furman* that the penalty of death not be imposed in an arbitrary or capricious manner can be met by a carefully drafted statute that ensures that the sentencing authority is given adequate information and guidance. As a general proposition these concerns are best met by a system that provides for a bifurcated proceeding at which the sentencing authority is apprised of the information relevant to the imposition of sentence and provided with standards to guide its use of the information.

We do not intend to suggest that only the above-described procedures would be permissible under *Furman* or that any sentencing system constructed along these general lines would inevitably satisfy the concerns of *Furman*, for each distinct system must be examined on an individual basis. Rather, we have embarked upon this general exposition to make clear that it is possible to construct capital-sentencing systems capable of meeting *Furman*'s constitutional concerns. . . .

V

The basic concern of *Furman* centered on those defendants who were being condemned to death capriciously and arbitrarily. Under the procedures before the Court in that case, sentencing authorities were not directed to give attention to the nature or circumstances of the crime committed or to the character or record of the defendant. Left unguided, juries imposed the death sentence in a way that could only be called freakish. The new Georgia sentencing procedures, by contrast, focus the jury's attention on the particularized nature of the crime and the particularized characteristics of the individual defendant. While the jury is permitted to consider any aggravating or mitigating circumstances, it must find and identify at least one statutory aggravating factor before it may impose a penalty of death. In this way the jury's discretion is channeled. No longer can a jury wantonly and freakishly impose the death sentence; it is always circumscribed by the legislative guidelines. In addition, the review function of the Supreme Court of Georgia affords additional assurance that the concerns that prompted our decision in *Furman* are not present to any significant degree in the Georgia procedure applied here.

For the reasons expressed in this opinion, we hold that the statutory system under which Gregg was sentenced to death does not violate the Constitution. Accordingly, the judgment of the Georgia Supreme Court is affirmed.

It is so ordered.

PART TWO

∽

POLITICAL PARTIES, ELECTORAL BEHAVIOR, AND INTEREST GROUPS

CHAPTER 4

POLITICAL PARTIES AND THE ELECTORATE

Constitutional Background

Political parties and interest groups have developed outside of the original constitutional framework to channel political power in the community, and for this reason they deserve special consideration from students of American government. The Constitution was designed to structure power relationships in such a way that the arbitrary exercise of political power by any one group or individual would be prevented. One important concept held by the framers of the Constitution was that faction, that is, parties and interest groups, is inherently dangerous to political freedom and stable government. This is evident from *Federalist 10.*

28

FEDERALIST 10

James Madison

Among the numerous advantages promised by a well constructed Union, none deserves to be more accurately developed than its tendency to break and control the violence of faction. The friend of popular governments never finds himself so much alarmed for their character and fate as when he contemplates their propensity to this dangerous vice. He will not fail, therefore, to set a due value on any plan which, without violating the principles to which he is attached, provides a proper cure for it. The instability, injustice, and confusion, introduced into the public councils, have, in truth been the mortal diseases under which popular governments have everywhere perished; as they continue to be the favorite and fruitful topics from which the adversaries to liberty derive their most specious declamations. The valuable improvements made by the American constitutions on the popular models, both ancient and modern, cannot certainly be too much admired; but it would be an unwarrantable partiality, to contend that they have as effectually obviated the danger on this side, as was wished and expected. Complaints are everywhere heard from our most considerate and virtuous citizens, equally the friends of public and private faith, and of public and personal liberty, that our governments are too unstable; that the public good is disregarded in the conflicts of rival parties; and that measures are too often decided, not according to the rules of justice, and the rights of the minor party, but by the superior force of an interested and overbearing majority. However anxiously we may wish that these complaints had no foundation, the evidence of known facts will not permit us to deny that they are in some degree true. It will be found, indeed, on a candid review of our situation, that some of the distresses under which we labor, have been erroneously charged on the operation of our governments; but it will be found, at the same time, that other causes will not alone account for many of our heaviest misfortunes; and, particularly, for the prevailing and increasing distrust of public engagements, and alarm for private rights, which are echoed from one end of the continent to the other. These must be chiefly, if not wholly, effects of the unsteadiness and injustice, with which a factious spirit has tainted our public administrations.

By a faction, I understand a number of citizens, whether amounting to a majority or minority of the whole, who are united and actuated by some common impulse of passion, or of interest, adverse to the rights of other citizens, or to the permanent and aggregate interest of the community.

There are two methods of curing the mischiefs of faction: the one, by removing its causes; the other, by controlling its effects.

There are again two methods of removing the causes of faction: the one, by destroying the liberty which is essential to its existence; the other, by giving to every citizen the same opinions, the same passions, and the same interests.

It could never be more truly said, than of the first remedy, that it was worse than the disease. Liberty is to faction what air is to fire, an ailment, without which it instantly expires. But it could not be a less folly to abolish liberty, which is essential to political life because it nourishes faction, than it would be to wish the annihilation of air, which is essential to animal life, because it imparts to fire its destructive agency.

The second expedient is as impracticable, as the first would be unwise. As long as the reason of man continues fallible, and he is at liberty to exercise it, different opinions will be formed. As long as the connection subsists between his reason and his self-love, his opinions and his passions will have a reciprocal influence on each other; and the former will be objects to which the latter will attach themselves. The diversity in the faculties of men, from which the rights of property originate, is not less an insuperable obstacle to a uniformity of interests. The protection of those faculties is the first object of government. From the protection of different and unequal faculties of acquiring property, the possession of different degrees and kinds of property immediately results; and from the influence of these on the sentiments and views of the respective proprietors, ensues a division of the society into different interests and parties.

The latent causes of faction are thus sown in the nature of man; and we see them everywhere brought into different degrees of activity, according to the different circumstances of civil society. A zeal for different opinions concerning religion, concerning government, and many other points, as well of speculation as of practice; an attachment to different leaders, ambitiously contending for preeminence and power; or to persons of other descriptions, whose fortunes have been interesting to the human passions, have, in turn, divided mankind into parties, inflamed them with mutual animosity, and rendered them much more disposed to vex and oppress each other, than to cooperate for their common good. So strong is this propensity of mankind, to fall into mutual animosities, that where no substantial occasion presents itself, the most frivolous and fanciful distinctions have been sufficient to kindle their unfriendly passions, and excite their most violent conflicts. But the most common and durable source of factions has been the various and unequal distribution of property. Those who hold, and those who are without property, have even formed distinct interests in society. Those who are creditors, and those who are debtors, fall under a like discrimination. A landed interest, a manufacturing interest, a mercantile interest, a moneyed interest, with many lesser interests, grow up of necessity in civilized nations, and divide them into different classes, actuated by different sentiments and views. The regulation of these various and interfering interests forms the principal task of modern legislation, and involves the spirit of party and faction in the necessary and ordinary operations of government.

No man is allowed to be a judge in his own cause; because his interest will certainly bias his judgment, and, not improbably, corrupt his integrity. With equal, nay, with greater reason, a body of men are unfit to be both judges and parties at the same time; yet what are many of the most important acts of legislation, but so many judicial determinations, not indeed concerning the rights of single persons, but concerning the rights of large bodies of citizens? And what are the different classes of legislators, but advocates and parties to the cause which they determine? Is a law proposed concerning private debts? It is a question to which the creditors are parties on one side, and the debtors on the other. Justice ought to hold the balance between them. Yet the parties are, and must be, themselves the judges; and the most numerous party, or, in other words, the most powerful faction, must be expected to prevail. Shall domestic manufactures be encouraged, and in what degree, by restrictions on foreign manufactures are questions which would be differently decided by the landed and the manufacturing classes; and probably by neither with a sole regard to justice and the public good. . . .

It is vain to say, that enlightened statesmen will be able to adjust these clashing interests, and render them all subservient to the public good. Enlightened statesmen will not always be at the helm; nor, in many cases, can such an adjustment be made at all, without taking into view indirect and remote considerations, which will rarely prevail over the immediate interest which one party may find in disregarding the rights of another, or the good of the whole.

The inference to which we are brought is, that the *causes* of faction cannot be removed; and that relief is only to be sought in the means of controlling its effects.

If a faction consists of less than a majority, relief is supplied by the republican principle, which enables the majority to defeat its sinister views, by regular vote. It may clog the administration, it may convulse the society; but it will be unable to execute and mask its violence under the forms of the constitution. When a majority is included in a faction, the form of popular government, on the other hand, enables it to sacrifice to its ruling passion or interest, both the public good and the rights of other citizens. To secure the public good, and private rights, against the danger of such a faction, and at the same time to preserve the spirit and the form of popular government, is then the great object to which our inquiries are directed. Let me add, that it is the great desideratum, by which alone this form of government can be rescued from the opprobrium under which it has so long labored, and be recommended to the esteem and adoption of mankind.

By what means is this object attainable? Evidently by one of two only. Either the existence of the same passion or interest in a majority, at the same time must be prevented; or the majority, having such coexistent passion or interest, must be rendered, by their number and local situation, unable to concert and carry into effect schemes of oppression. If the impulse and the opportunity be suffered to coincide, we well know, that neither moral nor religious motives can be relied on as an adequate control. They are not found to be such on the injustice and violence of individuals, and lose their efficacy in proportion to the number combined together; that is, in proportion as their efficacy becomes needful.

From this view of the subject, it may be concluded, that a pure democracy, by which I mean a society consisting of a small number of citizens, who assemble and administer the government in person, can admit of no cure from the mischiefs of faction. A common passion or interest will, in almost every case, be felt by a majority of the whole; a communication and concert, results from the form of government itself; and there is nothing to check the inducements to sacrifice the weaker party, or an obnoxious individual. Hence it is, that such democracies have ever been spectacles of turbulence and contention; have ever been found incompatible with personal security, or the rights of property; and have, in general, been as short in their lives, as they have been violent in their deaths. Theoretic politicians, who have patronized this species of government, have erroneously supposed that by reducing mankind to a perfect equality in their political rights, they would, at the same time, be perfectly equalized and assimilated in their possessions, their opinions, and their passions.

A republic, by which I mean a government in which the scheme of representation takes place, opens a different prospect, and promises the cure for which we are seeking. Let us examine the points in which it varies from pure democracy, and we shall comprehend both the nature of the cure and the efficacy which it must derive from the union.

The two great points of difference, between a democracy and a republic, are, first, the delegation of the government, in the latter, to a small number of citizens elected by the rest; secondly, the greater number of citizens, and greater sphere of country, over which the latter may be extended.

The effect of the first difference is on the one hand, to refine and enlarge the public views, by passing them through the medium of a chosen body of citizens, whose wisdom may best discern the true interest in their country, and whose patriotism and love of justice, will be least likely to sacrifice it to temporary or partial considerations. Under such a regulation, it may well happen, that the public voice, pronounced by the representatives of the people, will be more consonant to the public good, than if pronounced by the people themselves, convened for the purpose. On the other hand, the effect may be inverted. Men of factious tempers, of local prejudices, or of sinister designs, may by intrigue, by corruption, or by other means, first obtain the suffrages, and then betray the interest of the people. The question resulting is, whether small or extensive republics are most favorable to the election of proper guardians of the public weal; and it is clearly decided in favor of the latter by two obvious considerations.

In the first place, it is to be remarked, that however small the republic may be, the representatives must be raised to a certain number, in order to guard against the cabals of a few; and that however large it may be, they must be limited to a certain number, in order to guard against the confusion of a multitude. Hence, the number of representatives in the two cases not being in proportion to that of the constituents, and being proportionally greatest in the small republic, it follows that if the proportion of fit characters be not less in the large than in the small republic, the former will present a greater option, and consequently a greater probability of a fit choice.

In the next place, as each representative will be chosen by a greater number of citizens in the large than in the small republic, it will be more difficult for unworthy candidates to practice with success the vicious arts, by which elections are too often carried; and the suffrages of the people being more free, will be more likely to center in men who possess the most attractive merit, and the most diffusive and established characters. . . .

The other point of difference is, the greater number of citizens, and extent of territory, which may be brought within the compass of republican, than of democratic government; and it is this circumstance principally which renders factious combinations less to be dreaded in the former, than in the latter. The smaller the society, the fewer probably will be the distinct parties and interests composing it; the fewer the distinct parties and interests, the more frequently will a majority be found of the same party; and the smaller the number of individuals composing a majority, and the smaller the compass within which they are placed, the more easily they will concert and execute their plans of oppression. Extend the sphere, and you take in a greater variety of parties and interests; you make it less probable that a majority of the whole will have a common motive to invade the rights of other citizens; or if such a common motive exists, it will be more difficult for all who feel it to discover their own strength, and to act in unison with each other. . . .

Hence, it clearly appears, that the same advantage, which a republic has over a democracy, in controlling the effects of faction, is enjoyed by a large over a small republic—is enjoyed by the union over the states composing it. Does this advantage consist in the substitution of representatives, whose enlightened views and virtuous sentiments render them superior to local prejudices, and to schemes of injustice? It will not be denied, that the representation of the union will be most likely to pos-sess these requisite endowments. Does it consist in the greater security afforded by a greater variety of parties, against the event of any one party being able to outnum-ber and oppress the rest? In an equal degree does the increased variety of parties, comprised within the union, increase this security? Does it, in fine, consist in the greater obstacles opposed to the concert and accomplishment of the secret wishes of an unjust and interested majority? Here, again, the extent of the union gives it the most palpable advantage.

The influence of factious leaders may kindle a flame within their particular states, but will be unable to spread a general conflagration through the other states; a religious sect may degenerate into a political faction in a part of the confederacy; but the variety of sects dispersed over the entire face of it, must secure the national councils against any danger from the source; a rage for paper money, for an aboli-tion of debts, for an equal division of property, or for any other improper or wicked project, will be less apt to pervade the whole body of the union, than a particular member of it; in the same proportion as such a malady is more likely to taint a par-ticular county or district, than an entire state.

In the extent and proper structure of the union, therefore, we behold a republi-can remedy for the diseases most incident to republican government. And accord-ing to the degree of pleasure and pride we feel in being republicans, ought to be our zeal in cherishing the spirit, and supporting the character of Federalists.

The following selection is taken from E. E. Schattschneider's classic treatise, *Party Government*. In this material he examines both the implications of *Federalist 10* and coun-terarguments to the propositions stated by Madison with regard to political parties and interest groups.

29

Party Government

E. E. Schattschneider

∽

The Convention at Philadelphia provided a constitution with a dual attitude: it was proparty in one sense and antiparty in another. The authors of the Constitution refused to suppress the parties by destroying the fundamental liberties in which parties originate. They or their immediate successors accepted amendments that guaranteed civil rights and thus established a system of party tolerance, i.e., the right to agitate and to organize. This is the proparty aspect of the system. On the other hand, the authors of the Constitution set up an elaborate division and balance of powers within an intricate governmental structure designed to make parties ineffective. It was hoped that the parties would lose and exhaust themselves in futile attempts to fight their way through the labyrinthine framework of the government, much as an attacking army is expected to spend itself against the defensive works of a fortress. This is the antiparty part of the Constitution scheme. To quote Madison, the "great object" of the Constitution was "to preserve the public good and private right against the danger of such a faction [party] and at the same time to preserve the spirit and form of popular government."

In Madison's mind the difference between an autocracy and a free republic seems to have been largely a matter of the precise point at which parties are stopped by the government. In an autocracy parties are controlled (suppressed) at the source; in a republic parties are tolerated but are invited to strangle themselves in the machinery of government. The result in either case is much the same, sooner or later the government checks the parties but *never do the parties control the government*. Madison was perfectly definite and unmistakable in his disapproval of party government as distinguished from party tolerance. In the opinion of Madison, parties were intrinsically bad, and the sole issue for discussion was the means by which bad parties might be prevented from becoming dangerous. What never seems to have occurred to the authors of the Constitution, however, is that parties might be *used* as beneficent instruments of popular government. It is at this point that the distinction between the modern and the antique attitude is made.

The offspring of this combination of ideas was a constitutional system having conflicting tendencies. The Constitution made the rise of parties inevitable yet was incompatible with party government. This scheme, in spite of its subtlety, involved a miscalculation. Political parties refused to be content with the role assigned to them. The vigor and enterprise of the parties have therefore made American political

history the story of the unhappy marriage of the parties and the Constitution, a remarkable variation of the case of the irresistible force and the immovable object, which in
this instance have been compelled to live together in a permanent partnership. . . .

The Raw Materials of Politics

People who write about interests sometimes seem to assume that all interests are special and exclusive, setting up as a result of this assumption a dichotomy in which the
interests on the one side are perpetually opposed to the public welfare on the other
side. But there are common interests as well as special interests, and common interests resemble special interests in that they are apt to influence political behavior.
The raw materials of politics are not all antisocial. Alongside of Madison's statement
that differences in wealth are the most durable causes of faction there should be
placed a corollary that the common possessions of the people are the most durable
cause of unity. To assume that people have merely conflicting interests and nothing
else is to invent a political nightmare that has only a superficial relation to reality.
The body of agreement underlying the conflicts of a modern society ought to be sufficient to sustain the social order provided only that the common interests supporting this unity are mobilized. Moreover, not all differences of interest are durable
causes of conflict. Nothing is apt to be more perishable than a political issue. In the
democratic process, the nation moves from controversy to agreement to forgetful-
ness; politics is not a futile exercise like football, forever played back and forth over
the same ground. The government creates and destroys interests at every turn.

There are, in addition, powerful factors inhibiting the unlimited pursuit of special aims by an organized minority. To assume that minorities will stop at nothing to
get what they want is to postulate a degree of unanimity and concentration within
these groups that does not often exist in real life. If every individual were capable of
having only one interest to the exclusion of all others, it might be possible to form
dangerous unions of monomaniacs who would go to great extremes to attain their
objectives. In fact, however, people have many interests leading to a dispersion of
drives certain to destroy some of the unanimity and concentration of any group.
How many interests can an individual have? Enough to make it extremely unlikely
that any two individuals will have the same combination of interests. Anyone who
has ever tried to promote an association of people having some special interest in
common will realize, first, that there are marked differences of enthusiasm within
the group and, second, that interests compete with interests for the attention and
enthusiasm of every individual. Every organized special interest consists of a group
of busy, distracted individuals held together by the efforts of a handful of specialists
and enthusiasts who sacrifice other matters in order to concentrate on one. The notion of resolute and unanimous minorities on the point of violence is largely the invention of paid lobbyists and press agents.

The result of the fact that every individual is torn by the diversity of his own
interests, the fact that he is a member of many groups, is *the law of the imperfect political mobilization of interests*. That is, it has never been possible to mobilize any interest 100 percent. . . .

It is only another way of saying the same thing to state that conflicts of interests are not cumulative. If it were true that the dividing line in every conflict (or in all major conflicts) split the community identically in each case so that individuals who are opposed on one issue would be opposed to each other on all other issues also, while individuals who joined hands on one occasion would find themselves on the same side on all issues, always opposed to the same combination of antagonists, the cleavage created by the cumulative effect of these divisions would be fatal. But actually conflicts are not cumulative in this way. In real life the divisions are not so clearly marked, and the alignment of people according to interests requires an enormous shuffling back and forth from one side to the other, tending to dissipate the tensions created.

In view of the fact, therefore, (1) that there are many interests, including a great body of common interests, (2) that the government pursues a multiplicity of policies and creates and destroys interests in the process, (3) that each individual is capable of having many interests, (4) that interests cannot be mobilized perfectly, and (5) that conflicts among interests are not cumulative, it seems reasonable to suppose that the government is not the captive of blind forces from which there is no escape. There is nothing wrong about the raw materials of politics.

Constitutional Protection of Parties

Madison recognized in *Federalist 10* that a natural right to liberty protects factions. Factions are evil but they cannot be eliminated without destroying the liberty that we all cherish. Schattschneider highlights the way in which the Constitution is pro and anti-party at the same time. The First Amendment protects the right of parties to organize and the freedom to express their ideas. The separation of powers and checks and balances systems puts a major roadblock in the path of party rule by dividing government. Madison in *Federalist 10* adds federalism to the constitutional limits on parties. He argues that factions are diluted in large republics with representative government.

Political parties nominate candidates in several ways, the most common now being primaries. To maintain some degree of cohesiveness and responsibility, parties want their primaries to be "closed" to non-party voters by requiring participants to be registered party members. In this way nominees represent the majority of party members. "Open" primaries on the other hand allow voters who are not registered in a party to participate in its primary. If a sufficient number of crossover voters enter a party's primary they can sabotage the party by shifting the primary vote to a candidate who does not represent the majority of registered party members. Blanket primaries are the most open of all in which party primaries are combined. Each voter's ballot lists all candidates regardless of party affiliation and allows voters to choose whomever they want.

A California citizens' initiative, Proposition 198, changed the state's closed primaries to a blanket primary system in 1996. The California Democratic, Republican, Libertarian, and Freedom parties had closed primaries prior to 1996. They sued in the following case to overturn the blanket primary law alleging that it violated their First Amendment rights of association. The federal district court sustained the law and the circuit court affirmed, finding that California had substantial interests that justified the law. The parties appealed to the Supreme Court.

———————— 30 ————————

CALIFORNIA DEMOCRATIC PARTY ET AL. V. JONES, SECRETARY OF STATE OF CALIFORNIA, ET AL.

Supreme Court of the United States (2000)

Justice Scalia delivered the opinion of the Court.

This case presents the question whether the State of California may, consistent with the First Amendment to the United States Constitution, use a so-called "blanket" primary to determine a political party's nominee for the general election. . . .

[The state of California and Californians for an Open Primary defend] . . . the blanket primary upon the proposition that primaries play an integral role in citizens' selection of public officials. As a consequence, they contend, primaries are public rather than private proceedings, and the States may and must play a role in ensuring that they serve the public interest. Proposition 198 [that established the blanket primary], respondents conclude, is simply a rather pedestrian example of a State's regulating its system of elections.

We have recognized, of course, that States have a major role to play in structuring and monitoring the election process, including primaries. . . .

What we have not held, however, is that the processes by which political parties select their nominees are, as respondents would have it, wholly public affairs that States may regulate freely. To the contrary, we have continually stressed that when States regulate parties' internal processes they must act within limits imposed by the Constitution. . . .

Representative democracy in any populous unit of governance is unimaginable without the ability of citizens to band together in promoting among the electorate candidates who espouse their political views. The formation of national political parties was almost concurrent with the formation of the Republic itself. . . . Consistent with this tradition, the Court has recognized that the First Amendment protects "the freedom to join together in furtherance of common political beliefs," . . . which "necessarily presupposes the freedom to identify the people who constitute the association, and to limit the association to those people only." . . . That is to say, a corollary of the right to associate is the right not to associate. " 'Freedom of association would prove an empty guarantee if associations could not limit control over their decisions to those who share the interests and persuasions that underlie the association's being.' " . . .

In no area is the political association's right to exclude more important than in the process of selecting its nominee. That process often determines the party's positions on the most significant public policy issues of the day, and even when those positions are predetermined it is the nominee who becomes the party's ambassador to the general electorate in winning it over to the party's views. . . .

California's blanket primary violates the principles set forth in [our prior] cases. Proposition 198 forces political parties to associate with—to have their nominees, and hence their positions, determined by—those who, at best, have refused to affiliate with the party, and, at worst, have expressly affiliated with a rival. In this respect, it is qualitatively different from a closed primary. Under that system, even when it is made quite easy for a voter to change his party affiliation the day of the primary, and thus, in some sense, to "cross over," at least he must formally become a member of the party; and once he does so, he is limited to voting for candidates of that party. . . .

Respondents' legitimate state interests and petitioners' First Amendment rights are not inherently incompatible. To the extent they are in this case, the State of California has made them so by forcing political parties to associate with those who do not share their beliefs. And it has done this at the "crucial juncture" at which party members traditionally find their collective voice and select their spokesman. . . . The burden Proposition 198 places on petitioners' rights of political association is both severe and unnecessary. The judgment for the Court of Appeals for the Ninth Circuit is reversed.

It is so ordered.

The Party Model of Government

The framers of the constitution believed in *mixed* government and at every point stressed the importance of limiting majority rule, which they essentially relegated to the House of Representatives. The "evil" factions of *Federalist 10* included, in modern terms, parties as well as interest groups. The framers' goal was deliberative, not democratic, government. Ultimately, the consent of the people, in Lockean terms, checked government, but popular consent was different than participation. A balanced and deliberative government would be more capable of acting in the national interest, thereby more likely to achieve the consent of all of the people, than would a process controlled by a popular majority or dominated by special interests.

Mixed government is the eighteenth-century model, while the idea of democratic government became ascendant in the nineteenth century. Madison and Hamilton in *The Federalist* admired and cited the mixed government of Rome as their paradigm. By the middle of the nineteenth century Athenian democracy supported the emerging nineteenth-century democratic and party model of government. Gary Wills has pointed out in his brilliant treatise, *Lincoln at Gettysburg,* that "America as a second Athens was an idea whose moment had come in the nineteenth century. This nation's founders first looked to Rome, not to Greece, for their model. Like most men of the eighteenth century, they thought of Athens as ruled by mobs. . . . The 'mixed government' of Rome—not Athens' direct democracy—was the model invoked in debates over the proper constitution for the United States."[1]

The party model of government transforms the consent of the people into the rule of the majority. Majority rule can only be accomplished through *aggregative* parties. Party as well as balanced government is a deliberative process, but, in eighteenth-century terms, party deliberations are aimed at achieving not the national interest but the selfish or factional interests of the party organization and its members. Electoral victory by whatever means becomes the primary goal of parties.

Proponents of party government push aside eighteenth-century skepticism of faction and democracy. The only politically viable way to define the national interest, party proponents argue, is through aggregative parties that give the electorate a choice between programs that will determine what the government will do.

In contrast to the eighteenth-century, democratic and party government is based upon a belief in the rationality of man, and therefore the viability of a "government by discussion" through the mechanisms of political parties.[2] The framers were skeptical of raw politics and political incentives, which they viewed as more likely to be selfish than altruistic.

Woodrow Wilson expressed the ideas of the nineteenth century in his classic work, *Congressional Government,* written when he was a graduate student at Johns Hopkins University and published in 1885. He observed, "Whatever intention may have controlled the compromises of constitution-making in 1787, their result was to give us, not government by discussion, which is the only tolerable sort of government for a people which tries to do its own governing, but only legislation by discussion, which is no more than a small part of government by discussion."[3] Wilson admired the party government of Great Britain and he bemoaned the lack of leadership and discipline in American political parties. Lack of leadership, he wrote, "gives to our national parties their curious, conglomerate character. It would seem to be scarcely an exaggeration to say that they are homogeneous only in name. Neither of the two principal parties is of one mind with itself. Each tolerates all sorts of difference of creed and variety of aim within its own ranks. Each pretends to the same purposes and permits among its partisans the same contradictions to those purposes."[4]

Proponents of party government echoed Woodrow Wilson's views on many occasions long after he wrote. During much of the twentieth century political scientists and pundits have called for stronger political parties, arguing that our weak party system is a major deficiency and barrier to effective democratic leadership. The American Political Science Association formed a committee on political parties that wrote a widely circulated report in 1950

---

[1]Gary Wills, *Lincoln at Gettysburg* (Touchstone: 1992), p. 42.

[2]See Sir Ernst Barker, *Reflections on Government* (London: Oxford University Press, 1942).

[3]Woodrow Wilson, *Congressional Government* (New York: Meridian Books, Inc., 1956, from the original edition published in 1885), pp. 197–198.

[4]Ibid, p. 210.

which supported stronger political parties. The report, excerpted in the following selection, became a lasting rallying point for those favoring party government to the present day.

—————————— **31** ——————————

TOWARD A MORE RESPONSIBLE TWO-PARTY SYSTEM

❧

Report of the Committee of Political Parties, American Political Science Association

Part I. The Need for Greater Party Responsibility

1. The Role of the Political Parties

1. *The Parties and Public Policy.* Throughout this report political parties are treated as indispensable instruments of government. That is to say, we proceed on the proposition *that popular government in a nation of more than 150 million people requires political parties which provide the electorate with a proper range of choice between alternatives of action.* The party system thus serves as the main device for bringing into continuing relationship those ideas about liberty, majority rule and leadership which Americans are largely taking for granted.

For the great majority of Americans, the most valuable opportunity to influence the course of public affairs is the choice they are able to make between the parties in the principal elections. While in an election the party alternative necessarily takes the form of a choice between candidates, putting a particular candidate into office is not an end in itself. The concern of the parties with candidates, elections and appointments is misunderstood if it is assumed that parties can afford to bring forth aspirants for office without regard to the views of those so selected. Actually, the party struggle is concerned with the direction of public affairs. Party nominations are no more than a means to this end. In short, party politics inevitably involves public policy in one way or another. *In order to keep the parties apart, one must consider the relations between each and public policy.*

This is not to ignore that in the past the American two-party system has shown little propensity for evolving original or creative ideas about public policy; that it has even been rather sluggish in responding to such ideas in the public interest; that it reflects in an enlarged way those differences throughout the country which are expressed in the operation of the federal structure of government; and that in all political organizations a considerable measure of irrationality manifests itself.

Giving due weight to each of these factors, we are nevertheless led to conclude that the choices provided by the two-party system are valuable to the American people in proportion to their definition in terms of public policy. *The reasons for the growing emphasis on public policy in party politics are to be found, above all, in the very operations of modern government.* With the extraordinary growth of the responsibilities of government, the discussion of public affairs for the most part makes sense only in terms of public policy.

2. *The New Importance of Program.* One of the most pressing requirements of contemporary politics is for the party in power to furnish a general kind of direction over the government as a whole. *The crux of public affairs lies in the necessity for more effective formulation of general policies and programs and for better integration of all of the far-flung activities of modern government.*

Only large-scale and representative political organizations possess the qualifications needed for these tasks. The ascendancy of national issues in an industrial society, the impact of the widening concern of government with problems of the general welfare, the entrance into the realm of politics of millions of new voters— all of these factors have tended to broaden the base of the parties as the largest political organizations in the country. *It is in terms of party programs that political leaders can attempt to consolidate public attitudes toward the work plans of government.*

Modern public policy, therefore, accentuates the importance of the parties, not as mere brokers between different groups and interests, but as agencies of the electorate. Because it affects unprecedented numbers of people and because it depends for its execution on extensive and widespread public support, modern public policy requires a broad political base. That base can be provided only by the parties, which reach people touched by no other political organization. . . .

In brief, our view is this: *The party system that is needed must be democratic, responsible and effective—*a system that is accountable to the public, respects and expresses differences of opinion, and is able to cope with the great problems of modern government. . . .

1. *An effective party system requires, first, that the parties are able to bring forth programs to which they commit themselves and, second, that the parties possess sufficient internal cohesion to carry out these programs.* . . .

Clearly *such a degree of unity within the parties cannot be brought about without party procedures that give a large body of people an opportunity to share in the development of the party program.* . . .

2. *The Need for an Effective Opposition Party.* The argument for a stronger party system cannot be divorced from measures designed to make the parties more fully accountable to the public. *The fundamental requirement of such accountability is a two-party system in which the opposition party acts as the critic of the party in power, developing, defining and presenting the policy alternatives which are necessary for a true choice in reaching public decisions.* . . .

Anything as close to the vital process of representative government as the party system is bound to affect the nation's political life in more than one way. Whatever impairs the essential operation of the party system also produces serious difficulties in other spheres of national existence. Inaction in the face of needed change in this central area therefore increases the dangers which may be present.

Four of these *dangers warrant special emphasis. The first danger is that the inadequacy of the party system in sustaining well-considered programs and providing broad public support for them may lead to grave consequences in an explosive era. The second danger is that the American people may go too far for the safety of constitutional government in compensating for this inadequacy by shifting excessive responsibility to the President. The third danger is that with growing public cynicism and continuing proof of the ineffectiveness of the party system the nation may eventually witness the disintegration of the two major parties. The fourth danger is that the incapacity of the two parties for consistent action based on meaningful programs may rally support for extremist parties poles apart, each fanatically bent on imposing on the country its particular panacea. . . .*

3. *The Danger of Overextending the Presidency.* The presidency is the greatest political office in this country. There is no other republic, in fact, that entrusts to its President as much constitutional responsibility as Americans have entrusted to the President of the United States.

He is the Chief Executive, and as such in command not only of the civilian departments of the Federal Government but also of the whole military establishment. His executive authority puts at his disposal all the administrative resources—in management, fact-finding, analysis and planning—that are available in the departmental system. By making authoritative legislative proposals and exercising his veto power, the President under the Constitution has a significant share in the work of Congress. In addition, he is the central figure in the leadership of his party, in and out of Congress.

It is still more important, perhaps, that the President is the only politically responsible organ of government that has the whole nation as constituency. Elected by the people at large, the President must look upon himself as its spokesman. In him alone all Americans find a single voice in national affairs.

It is therefore a natural tendency that time and again governmental responsibility for formulation of coherent programs and unity of action has been placed upon the President. He has been charged with the preparation of the annual budget—the work plan of the Federal Government that goes to Congress for review and final determination. He has also been charged with the presentation of the government's economic program, submitted to Congress in the periodic economic reports of the President. He cannot relinquish the burden of establishing the general lines of American foreign policy. He has been charged with the development of coordinated policies to safeguard the country's national security.

In each of these large areas, the President is called upon to prepare the ground, to initiate the process of program formulation, to come forth with proposed programs for which he is prepared to assume political responsibility. As a result, Congress has the benefit of prior effort and concrete recommendations. This division of functions reflects a sound formula, evolved in practical experience. But to apply it effectively, somewhere *dependable political support has to be built up for the governmental program* as finally adopted. *When there is no other place to get that done, when the political parties fail to do it, it is tempting once more to turn to the President.*

But the President has no magic wand. If he acts in pursuit of a broad program that has been democratically formulated in his party, nearly all of his party is likely to put itself behind the measures called for by the program. Then the question of political support presents no difficulties, which is the solution suggested in this report. Lacking his party's support for a broad program, the President is left with only one course. He can attempt to fill the void caused by the absence of an effective party program by working up a broad political program of his own.

If he does, however, he has to go out and build the necessary support for that program through his personal effort without benefit of party. There are people who say that this is a realistic way of getting somewhere with good political ideas, especially ideas bound to leave cool both Congress and the larger part of the President's party. Some others say that the scheme is not the happiest thing but the only one practically available under presidential-congressional government.

Yet can there be much doubt about the ultimate implications? *When the President's program actually is the sole program in this sense, either his party becomes a flock of sheep or the party falls apart. In effect this concept of the presidency disposes of the party system by making the President reach directly for the support of a majority of the voters. It* favors a President who exploits skillfully the arts of demagoguery, who uses the whole country as his political backyard, and who does not mind turning into the embodiment of personal government. . . .

4. *The Danger of Disintegration of the Two Parties.* It is a thing both familiar and deeply disturbing that many Americans have only caustic words or disdainful shrugs of the shoulder for the party system as it operates today. . . .

A chance that the electorate will turn its back upon the two parties is by no means academic. As a matter of fact, this development has already occurred in considerable part, and it is still going on. Present conditions are a great incentive for the voters to dispose of the parties as intermediaries between themselves and the government. In a way, a sizable body of the electorate has shifted from hopeful interest in the parties to the opposite attitude. This mass of voters sees itself as the President's or his opponent's direct electoral support.

Continued alienation between increasing numbers of voters and both major parties is an ominous tendency. It has a splintering effect and may lead to a system of several smaller parties. *American political institutions are too firmly grounded upon the two-party system to make its collapse a small matter.*

Orientation of the American two-party system along the lines of meaningful national programs . . . is a way of keeping differences within bounds. It is a way of reinforcing the constitutional framework within which the voter may without peril exercise his freedom of political choice.

The author of the following selection points out that parties can be viewed from various perspectives. Parties perform important roles in government, but also within the electorate by encouraging and reflecting partisanship. The role of parties in government and within the electorate is inextricably linked, requiring party effectiveness in each area if parties are to do their job.

32

PERSPECTIVES ON AMERICAN POLITICAL PARTIES

Martin P. Wattenberg

Political parties have been accorded a preeminent position in the study of American politics. For nearly a century political scientists have written of the potential of political parties to establish effective popular control over the government. In a system designed to fragment political power, parties have been held to be the one institution capable of providing a unifying centripetal force. The functions that parties have been said to perform in American society are impressive and diverse. These include:

1. Generating symbols of identification and loyalty.
2. Aggregating and articulating political interests.
3. Mobilizing majorities in the electorate and in government.
4. Socializing voters and maintaining a popular following.
5. Organizing dissent and opposition.
6. Recruiting political leadership and seeking governmental offices.
7. Institutionalizing, channeling, and socializing conflict.
8. Overriding the dangers of sectionalism and promoting the national interest.
9. Implementing policy objectives.
10. Legitimizing decisions of government.
11. Fostering stability in government.

Given all of these functions, many political scientists have accepted E. E. Schattschneider's famous assertion that modern democracy is unthinkable save in terms of parties. Not surprisingly, then, the various indications that political parties have weakened in recent years have been met with a great deal of alarm among commentators on American politics. David Broder, for example, has stated flatly, "The governmental system is not working because the political parties are not working." Although most experts would not go so far, few would deny that the decline of American political parties has had a significant impact on the character of politics in this country.

Perhaps the most frequently cited consequences of the decline of parties are the growing importance of special interest groups and the dwindling of the principles of collective responsibility. The result, as Morris Fiorina has written, is that we now have "a system that articulates interests superbly but aggregates them poorly." The making of public policy has thus become a more conflictual process with far less central direction and coherence. Individual policy decisions are increasingly made by ad hoc coalitions without relation to other policies. As Jimmy Carter found out during his four years in office, governing without the continuous support of a political party is an extremely difficult task.

Yet the question of party decline is a complex one, for political parties are complex, multifaceted institutions. While most of the attention has been focused on the aspects of parties that have been weakened, there is evidence suggesting that in certain aspects parties have been strengthened. According to Malcolm Jewell and David Olson, for example, state political party organizations have been revitalized with the result being a more active role for state parties. And on the national level, Cornelius Cotter and John Bibby have concluded from their extensive study of the history of national party organizations that there has been a growth in terms of institutionalization and nationalization of the parties in recent years.

Thus, although most of the evidence does point toward party decline, to make global statements about the decay, decomposition, disappearance, or end of parties (as many have) may lead us to overlook the aspects of parties that have not been weakened. In order to get beyond the "sky-is-falling" stage in the discussion of parties, it must be recognized that not all the trends match and that evidence about one particular aspect is not necessarily generalizable to the condition of parties as a whole. As Austin Ranney has noted, those who have written about changes in the strength of parties all have something in mind, but the "something" differs from one observer to another.

Political scientists who write about political parties fall into two main types, according to the noted British author S. E. Finer—"those who think of parties as things that *do,* and those who think of them as things that *are.*" The former primarily concern themselves with how well parties as organizations perform functions related to the machinery of government and the contesting of elections. Those among this school who are most empirically oriented study party activists and what they do; others study the various structures of the parties and how they operate. In contrast, writers who concern themselves with what parties are focused mainly on partisan attitudes among the mass public. Authors of this school address questions of alignment and dealignment in the party system, largely based on micro-level survey data on party identification and voting patterns. . . .

[The study of political partisanship] belongs in the latter category, but what political parties do . . . [is related.] If it were not for the crucial role that parties play in the operation of American government, the study of partisanship in the electorate would be far less important. Furthermore, one can reasonably infer that what parties are from the perspective of the mass electorate will have a major impact on what parties do in the political system. For example, if members of the electorate cast their ballots on the basis of factors other than partisanship, then those public officials who are elected can be expected to act more as individuals and less as members of a collective body committed to common goals. Similarly, if the mass public conceptualizes issues in terms of candidates rather than in terms of parties, then the direction of public policy can be expected to be hardly any more stable than the names on the ballot from year to year.

Of course, the flow of causality is by no means a unidirectional one from the state of parties in the electorate to the state of parties in government. If parties in government are weakened, the public will naturally have less of a stimulus to think of themselves politically in partisan terms. In fact, it will be argued here that one of the major factors behind the decline of partisanship in the electorate is that parties have become less integral in the processes of governing and campaigning, thereby resulting in the mass public's more neutral attitudes toward them. However, these altered public attitudes have themselves become a major reason why it will be very difficult to go back and reinstitutionalize political parties. Political behavior has a distinct habitual flavor to it—conceptualizing politics in a nonpartisan and candidate-centered fashion may well become a behavior pattern that could be difficult to alter. . . .

—————————————————— ✑ ——————————————————

Political Parties in Divided Government

A recurring and important theme of commentators on the American political system is that the separation of powers between the president and Congress produces a deadlock of democracy. Major constitutional change to unify the president and Congress by creating a parliamentary system is unrealistic and completely out of the question. Critics of divided government have proposed more disciplined political parties to unify the president and Congress, thereby helping to overcome the effects of the separation of powers. Putting aside the fact that the separation of powers itself makes party government difficult if not impossible, in theory would disciplined political parties that unified the executive and legislative branches make an important difference? In the following selection political scientist David Mayhew presents the provocative and important thesis that the divided government, which the separation of powers produces, works as well as the unified government that party discipline would create.

—————————————— **33** ——————————————

DIVIDED WE GOVERN

David R. Mayhew

✑

Introduction

Since World War II, divided party control of the American national government has come to seem normal. Between the 1946 and 1990 elections, one of the two parties held the presidency, the Senate, and the House simultaneously for eighteen of those years. But control was divided for twenty-six years, it is divided right now, and we may see more such splits. Some opinion studies suggest that today's voters prefer divided control on principle: Parties jointly in power are seen to perform a service by checking each other.

Of course, divided control is not a new phenomenon. During a twenty-two-year stretch between 1874 and 1896, to take the extreme case, the two parties shared control of the government for sixteen years. But after that, the country settled into a half-century habit of unified control broken only by two-year transitions from one party's monopoly to the other's that closed out the Taft, Wilson, and Hoover administrations. It is against this immediate background that the post–World War II experience stands out.

Should we care whether party control is unified or divided? That depends on whether having one state of affairs rather than the other makes any important difference. Does it? Much received thinking says yes. The political party, according to one of political science's best-known axioms about the American system, is "the indispensable instrument that [brings] cohesion and unity, and hence effectiveness, to the government as a whole by linking the executive and legislative branches in a bond of common interest." In the words of Woodrow Wilson, "You cannot compound a successful government out of antagonisms."

At a concrete level, this means at least that significant lawmaking can be expected to fall off when party control is divided. "Deadlock" or "stalemate" will set in. Variants of this familiar claim could be cited endlessly. Randall B. Ripley argued in a 1969 study, for example: "To have a productive majority in the American system of government the President and a majority of both houses must be from the same party. Such a condition does not guarantee legislative success but is necessary for it." V. O. Key, Jr., wrote: "Common partisan control of executive and legislature does not assure energetic government, but division of party control precludes it." . . . These authors do not argue that unified party control always generates large collections of notable legislation. But they can be read to predict that it should generate, over a long period of time when contrasted with divided control, considerably more such legislation.

Another familiar claim has to do with congressional oversight. It is that Congress acting as an investigative body will give more trouble to the executive branch when a president of the opposite party holds power. That propensity can be viewed as bad or good. Woodrow Wilson might say that accelerated probing of the executive provides just another kind of unfortunate "antagonism." From another perspective, it can be expected to keep presidents and bureaucrats in line better. Either way, what causes the effect is a predicted difference between unified and divided control. Morris S. Ogul has written, "A congressman of the president's party is less likely to be concerned with oversight than a member of the opposition party." . . .

I . . . argue . . . that the above claims are wrong, or at least mostly or probably wrong. . . . But are there not . . . ways in which unified as opposed to divided party control might make a significant difference?

There are. In closing, five such ways will be introduced here by posing questions and speculating briefly about what their answers might be. In all instances the speculation ends in skepticism: Unified versus divided control has probably not made a notable difference during the postwar era. . . .

The first question is: Even if important laws win enactment just as often under conditions of divided party control, might they not be *worse* laws? Isn't "seriously defective legislation" a likelier result? That is sometimes alleged, and if true it would obviously count heavily. The subject is murky, even if kept free of ideological tests of "worseness," but the case seems to have a two-pronged logic. First, enacting coalitions under divided control, being composed of elements not "naturally" united on policy goals, might be less apt to write either clear ends or efficient means into their statutes. Second, such coalitions, absolved from unambiguous "party government" checks by the electorate down the line, might worry less about the actual effects of laws.

These are reasonable enough logics and instances, but the overall case is dubious. . . .

The second question is: Even if important individual statutes can win enactment regardless of conditions of party control, how about programmatic "coherence" across statutes? Isn't that a likelier outcome under unified party control? The argument is sometimes made. Confronted by this claim, one's first response is to note that "coherence" exists in the eyes of beholders, that beholders differ in what they see, and in any event, why is "coherence" necessary or desirable? Democracy, according to some leading models, can function well enough as an assortment of decentralized, unconnected incursions into public affairs. . . .

Still, widespread agreement does exist about the features and importance of at least two patterns of coherence across statutes, and those should be considered. One is *ideological coherence,* for which an argument might go as follows. To permit broad-ranging change of the sort recommended by ideologies that arise now and then, and to provide a graspable politics to sectors of the public who might be interested in such change, a system needs to allow ideological packaging. That is, it needs to allow, at least sometimes, the enactment of rather large collections of laws thrusting in the same ideological direction. But such packaging has already been discussed. The postwar American system has accommodated it under circumstances of both unified and divided party control—notably in the successfully enacted presidential programs of Johnson (UNI) and Reagan (DIV), and in the liberal legislative surge of 1963 through 1975–76 (UNI then DIV). Presidential programs, given their properties as drama, can probably reach the general public more effectively, but ideological surges arising from "moods" can unquestionably engage appreciable sectors of the public.

Then there is *budgetary coherence*—that is, a match between revenue and expenditure across all government programs. Whether such a match occurs is of course ultimately a matter of statutes, including appropriations bills. It goes without saying that the federal government's immense deficits have daunted and preoccupied the country's political elite as much as anything during the last decade. For some observers, the deficits have also posed a clear test of divided party control, which it has flunked. A single ruling party would have done better, the argument goes, for reasons either of ideological uniformity or electoral accountability. Lloyd N. Cutler made the latter argument in 1988: "If one party was responsible for all three power centers [House, Senate, and presidency] and produced deficits of the magnitude in which they have been produced in recent years, there would be no question of the accountability and the responsibility of that party and its elected public officials for what had happened."

Is this a valid case, finally, against divided party control? That has to remain an open question, since not much scholarship has yet appeared about the history of budgeting as it may have been affected by conditions of party control; also, highly relevant events will no doubt continue to take place. But the case is considerably less compelling than it may first look. For one thing, there is evidently no statistical relation between divided party control and deficit financing over the two centuries of American national history, or more specifically since World War II. That recent period includes the 1950s, it is useful to remember, when Eisenhower, who faced Democratic Congresses for six years, fought major political battles and drew much criticism from liberal intellectuals because he would not accept unbalanced budgets. Taking into account size of deficit or surplus, what the postwar pattern does show is a "sudden break" under Reagan. Deficits "blossomed suddenly in 1981." A time series of federal debt as a percentage of gross national product falls almost monotonically from 1946 through 1974, holds more or less steady until 1981, and then surges. The 1980s are the problem.

An explanation that seems to fit this pre-1980 versus post-1980 experience involves not conditions of party control but rather individual presidents' policies. At least since World War II, according to Paul E. Peterson, Congress "has generally followed the presidential lead on broad fiscal policies." Overall congressional appropriations—that is, for each year the total across all programs—have ordinarily come quite close to overall presidential spending requests. Changes in total revenue generated by congressional tax enactments have ordinarily approximated those proposed by presidents. . . .

The third question is: Doesn't government administration suffer as a result of divided party control? Doesn't exaggerated pulling and hauling between president and Congress undermine the implementation of laws and, in general, the functioning of agencies and the administration of programs? High-publicity Capitol Hill investigations, which have been discussed, are relevant to an answer, but the subject is broader than that. It is also vaguer and quite difficult to address. The strategy here will be to present a plausible case *for* an instance of such undermining of administration and then draw a historical comparison. This will scarcely exhaust the topic, but the instances to be compared are important in their own right as well as suggestive about conditions of party control in general.

The plausible instance is Congress's thrust toward "micro-managing" the executive branch in recent decades. That is, Congress has greatly increased its staff who monitor the administration, multiplied its days of oversight hearings, greatly expanded its use of the legislative veto (until a federal court ruled that device unconstitutional in 1983), taken to writing exceptionally detailed statutes that limit bureaucratic discretion (notably in environmental law), and tried to trim presidential power through such measures as the War Powers Act of 1973 and the Budget and Impoundment Act of 1974. Whether these moves have helped or harmed the system can be argued either way, but let us stipulate for the moment that they have undermined administration.

Has "micro-management" resulted, at least partly, from divided party control of the government? That too can be argued either way. An abundant list of alternative causes includes public and congressional reaction to the Vietnam war (as conducted by both Johnson and Nixon) and the public's rising distrust of bureaucracy. But let us hypothesize that divided party control is at least partly the cause. Here is the argument. Rather than appearing gradually, "micro-management" came into its own rather quickly under Nixon and Ford in the 1970s—especially during the Nixon-Ford term of 1973–76. To cite some quantitative evidence, days spent per year on congressional oversight hearings, and average number of pages per enacted law (an indicator of statutory detail), achieved *most* of the considerable increase they showed from 1961 through 1984 during just the four years of 1973–76.

That was during a period of divided party control. Obviously, micro-management has not flashed on whenever party control became divided (as under Eisenhower) or flashed off whenever it became unified (as under Carter). Much of it, at least, came in under Nixon-Ford and stayed. One might say that those years saw the initiation of a "regime" of micro-management—that is, a durable set of views and institutionally located practices could survive the transition to Carter and then to Reagan. Their origin is what counts. To implicate divided party control plausibly, one has to argue that two conditions were necessary for this "micro-management regime" to come into existence. First, party control had to be divided: Congress would not have inaugurated such a regime otherwise. Second, there had to occur some unusual shock to the system such as Watergate, Nixon's conduct of the war, or simply Nixon's aggressive presidency: Divided control would not have engendered such a regime otherwise. Divided control, that is, was a necessary *part* of the causal structure that triggered the regime.

That is a plausible, particular argument. Can it be generalized? The broader case would be that members of a relevant class of congressional regimes that includes the micro-management one—that is, regimes that can reasonably be alleged to undermine administration—can be expected to arise under the same circumstances. That is, they require some similar shock to the system plus a background of divided party control.

Has any other such regime ever existed? As it happens, what looks like a particularly good instance of one originated in 1938 and led a vibrant life through 1954. It was that era's "loyalty regime"—the brilliant innovation of Democratic Congressman Martin Dies of Texas, founder of the House Un-American Activities Committee. Dies pioneered a formula that carried through the Hiss, McCarran, Army-McCarthy and other investigations after the war. It was a low-cost, high-publicity, committee-centered way of waging a congressional opposition against the New Deal, the Truman administration, and then Eisenhower. Its chief technique was the hearing where someone could accuse members of the executive branch of being disloyal to the United States. No one should be surprised that that evidently had a pronounced effect on administration. Beyond its effects on the targeted personnel, it could demoralize agencies, preoccupy the White House, put a chill on unorthodox policy options, and even exile whole schools of thought from the government (as with China specialists after 1949).

It seems a good bet that this loyalty regime made as much of a mark on administration—to be sure, its own kind of mark—as has Congress's more recent micromanagement regime. . . .

The fourth question is: Does the conduct of foreign policy suffer under divided party control? That might be a special concern, since "coordination" is often held to be central to effective foreign policymaking. Perhaps an excess of "deadlock" or "non-coordination" occurs under conditions of divided control. But of course such disorderliness, looked at from the other side as by opponents of Truman's China policy or Reagan's Central America policy, figures as a healthy exercise of checks and balances. Foreign policy is often a fighting matter at home. There does not seem to be any way around this. "Coordination," however much sense it may seem to make, does not and cannot dominate every other value.

Yet once past that realization, it is not clear what standards to apply. None will be proposed here. But let the reader try the following thought experiment. Choose any plausible set of standards and, using them, scan through the history of American foreign policymaking since World War II. Here is a prediction of what most readers will conclude: In general, the record was no worse when the two parties shared power. Any appraisal has to accommodate or steer around, for example, the Marshall Plan, which owed to bipartisan cooperation during a time of divided control; the Kennedy-Johnson intervention in Indochina, which, whatever else may be said about it, scarcely took its shape because of a lack of coordination; Nixon's openings to China and the Soviet Union, which were maneuvered with little Capitol Hill dissent during a time of divided control; and Bush's liberation of Kuwait in 1990–91. Given just these items, many readers may agree, considerable ingenuity would be needed to concoct a verdict spanning the four and a half decades that favors unified party control. . . .

The fifth question: Are the country's lower-income strata served less well under divided party control? One can assemble a theory that they might be, assuming for a moment that "serve" refers to direct government action rather than, say, encouragement of long-term economic growth. Separation of powers biases the American regime toward the rich, Progressive theorists used to argue at the outset of the twentieth century. The rich profit when the government does nothing, whereas the non-rich require concerted public action that can all too easily be blocked somewhere in the system's ample array of veto-points. An obvious remedy would be a constitution allowing strict majority rule. But lacking that, according to a conventional argument of political science, much depends on political parties. Their distinctive role is to impose on the country's collection of government institutions a kind of order that serves majority interests. In principle, that might be done by one party embodying the views and experiences of the non-rich (a socialist sort of argument) or by two parties bidding for the votes of the non-rich (a Downsian sort of argument). Either way, unified control is needed to deliver the goods. It allows action, rules out buck-passing, fixes responsibility, permits accountability.

That is a plausible line of argument, and the Great Society as well as the New Deal might be said to bear it out. But altogether too much of the record since World War II does not. What were the origins of the "social safety net" that the Reagan administration—during a time of divided control, for what that is worth—

succeeded in widening the holes of? In fact, that net owed much of its weaving to the Nixon and Ford years—also a time of divided control. That period was the source of EEA and CETA jobs, expanded unemployment insurance, low-income energy assistance, post–1974 housing allowances, Pell grants for lower-income college students, greatly multiplied food-stamps assistance, a notable progressivizing of tax incidence, Supplementary Security Income for the aged, blind, and disabled, and Social Security increases that cut the proportion of aged below the poverty line from 25 percent in 1970 to 16 percent in 1974. The laws just kept getting passed. The Reaganite assault against both the Great Society and the 1970s pitted era against era and mood against mood. But it did not pit divided party control against unified party control or even all that clearly Republicans against Democrats.

These five questions are not the only additional ones that might be asked about unified as opposed to divided party control. This work skirts, moreover, the separate and obviously important question of whether the American system of government, with its separation-of-powers features, has been functioning adequately in recent times. Some analysts, for example John E. Chubb and Paul E. Peterson, say no: "When governments of quite different political combinations [that is, unified as well as divided control] all fail to perform effectively, it is worth considering whether the problem is the government itself and not the people or parties that run it." Energy and budgetary policies have been creaking. Each of the last two decades has ended with a riveting spectacle of government inefficacy or disorder—Carter's "malaise" crisis in 1979 and Bush's budget wrangle in 1990. Otherwise, the country is faced with declining voter turnout as well as a rise in election technologies and incumbent-serving practices that seem to be delegitimizing elected officials.

There is no end of taking steps to reform American political institutions, or of good reasons for it. But short of jettisoning the separation-of-powers core of the Constitution—an unlikely event—it would probably be a mistake to channel such concern into "party government" schemes. This work has tried to show that, surprisingly, it does not seem to make all that much difference whether party control of the American government happens to be unified or divided. One reason we assume it does is that "party government" plays a role in political science somewhere between a Platonic form and a grail. When we reach for it as a standard, we draw on abstract models, presumed European practice, and well-airbrushed American experience, but we seldom take a cold look at real American experience. We forget about Franklin Roosevelt's troubles with HUAC and the Rules Committee, Truman's and Kennedy's domestic policy defeats, McCarthy's square-off against Eisenhower, Johnson versus Fulbright on Vietnam, and Carter's energy program and "malaise."

Political parties can be powerful instruments, but in the United States they seem to play more of a role as "policy factions" than as, in the British case, governing instruments. A party as policy faction can often get its way even in circumstances of divided control: Witness the Taftite Republicans in 1947, congressional Democrats under Nixon, or the Reaganites in 1981. How, one might ask, were these temporary policy ascendancies greatly different from that of the Great Society Democrats in 1964–66?

To demand more of American parties—to ask that they become governing instruments—is to run them up against components of the American regime as fundamental as the party system itself. There is a strong pluralist component, for example, as evidenced in the way politicians respond to cross-cutting issue cleavages. There is a public-opinion component that political science's modern technologies do not seem to reach very well. The government floats in public opinion; it goes up and down on great long waves of it that often have little to do with parties. There is the obvious structural component—separation of powers—that brings on deadlock and chronic conflict, but also nudges officials toward deliberation, compromise, and super-majority outcomes. And there is a component of deep-seated individualism among American politicians, who build and tend their own electoral bases and maintain their own relations of responsibility with electorates. This seems to be a matter of political culture—perhaps a survival of republicanism—that goes way back. Unlike most politicians elsewhere, American ones at both legislative and executive levels have managed to navigate the last two centuries of history without becoming minions of party leaders. In this complicated, multi-component setting, British-style governing by party majorities does not have much of a chance.

Functions and Types of Elections

Most people transmit their political desires to government through elections. Elections are a critical part of the democratic process, and the existence of *free* elections is a major difference between democracies and totalitarian or authoritarian forms of government. Because elections reflect popular attitudes toward governmental parties, policies, and personalities, it is useful to attempt to classify different types of elections on the basis of changes and trends that take place within the electorate. Every election is not the same. For example, the election of 1932 with the resulting Democratic landslide was profoundly different from the election of 1960, in which Kennedy won by less than one percent of the popular vote.

Members of the Center for Political Studies at the University of Michigan, as well as V. O. Key, Jr., have developed a typology of elections that is useful in analyzing the electoral system. The most prevalent type of election can be classified as a "maintaining election," "one in which the pattern of partisan attachments prevailing in the preceding period persists and is the primary influence on the forces governing the vote,"[5] Most elections fall into the maintaining category, a fact significant for the political system because such elections result in

---

[5]Angus Campbell, Philip E. Converse, Warren E. Miller, and Donald E. Stokes, *The American Voter* (New York: John Wiley & Sons, 1960), chap. 19.

political continuity and reflect a lack of serious upheavals within the electorate and government. Maintaining elections result in the continuation of the majority political party.

At certain times in American history, what V. O. Key, Jr., has called "critical elections" take place. He discusses this type of election, which results in permanent realignment of the electorate and reflects basic changes in political attitudes.

Apart from maintaining and critical elections, a third type, in which only temporary shifts take place within the electorate, occurs, which can be called "deviating elections." For example, the Eisenhower victories of 1952 and 1956 were deviating elections for several reasons, including the personality of Eisenhower and the fact that voters could register their choice for president without changing their basic partisan loyalties at congressional and state levels. Deviating elections, with reference to the office of president, are probable when popular figures are running for the office.

In "reinstating elections," a final category that can be added to a typology of elections, there is a return to normal voting patterns. Reinstating elections take place after deviating elections as a result of the demise of the temporary forces that caused the transitory shift in partisan choice. The election of 1960, in which most of the Democratic majority in the electorate returned to the fold and voted for John F. Kennedy,[6] has been classified as a reinstating election.

------------------------------ **34** ------------------------------

A THEORY OF CRITICAL ELECTIONS

V. O. Key, Jr.

Perhaps the basic differentiating characteristic of democratic order consists in the expression of effective choice by the mass of the people in elections. The electorate occupies, at least in the mystique of such orders, the position of the principal organ of governance; it acts through elections. An election itself is a formal act of collective decision that occurs in a stream of connected antecedent and subsequent behavior. Among democratic orders elections, so broadly defined, differ enormously in their nature, their meaning, and their consequences. Even within a single nation the reality of election differs greatly from time to time. A systematic comparative

------

[6]See Philip E. Converse, Angus Campbell, Warren E. Miller, and Donald E. Stokes, "Stability and Change in 1960: A Reinstating Election," *The American Political Science Review* 55 (June 1961): 269–280.

approach, with a focus on variations in the nature of elections would doubtless be fruitful in advancing the understanding of the democratic governing process. In behavior antecedent to voting, elections differ in the proportions of the electorate psychologically involved, in the intensity of attitudes associated with campaign cleavages, in the nature of expectations about the consequences of the voting, in the impact of objective events relevant to individual political choice, in individual sense of effective connection with community decision, and in other ways. These and other antecedent variations affect the act of voting itself as well as subsequent behavior. An understanding of elections and, in turn, of the democratic process as a whole must rest partially on broad differentiations of the complexes of behavior that we call elections.

While this is not the occasion to develop a comprehensive typology of elections, the foregoing remarks provide an orientation for an attempt to formulate a concept of one type of election—based on American experience—which might be built into a more general theory of elections. Even the most fleeting inspection of American elections suggests the existence of a category of elections in which voters are, at least from impressionistic evidence, unusually deeply concerned, in which the extent of electoral involvement is relatively quite high, and in which the decisive results of the voting reveal a sharp alteration of the preexisting cleavage within the electorate. Moreover, and perhaps this is the truly differentiating characteristic of this sort of election, the realignment made manifest in the voting in such elections seems to persist for several succeeding elections. All these characteristics cumulate to the conception of an election type in which the depth and intensity of electoral involvement are high, in which more or less profound readjustments occur in the relations of power within the community, and in which new and durable electoral groupings are formed. These comments suppose, of course, the existence of other types of complexes of behavior centering about formal elections, the systematic isolation and identification of which, fortunately, are not essential for the present discussion.

I

The presidential election of 1928 in the New England states provides a specific case of the type of critical election that has been described in general terms. In that year Alfred E. Smith, the Democratic presidential candidate, made gains in all the New England states. The rise in Democratic strength was especially notable in Massachusetts and Rhode Island. When one probes below the surface of the gross election figures it becomes apparent that a sharp and durable realignment also occurred within the electorate, a fact reflective of the activation by the Democratic candidate of low-income, Catholic, urban voters of recent immigrant stock. In New England, at least, the Roosevelt revolution of 1932 was in large measure an Al Smith revolution of 1928, a characterization less applicable to the remainder of the country.

The intensity and extent of electoral concern before the voting of 1928 can only be surmised, but the durability of the realignment formed at the election can be determined by simple analyses of election statistics. An illustration of the new division thrust through the electorate by the campaign of 1928 is provided by the graphs in Figure A, which show the Democratic percentages of the presidential vote from 1916 through 1952 for the city of Somerville and the town of Ashfield in Massachusetts. Somerville, adjacent to Boston, had a population in 1930 of 104,000 of which 28 percent was foreign born and 41 percent was of foreign born or mixed parentage. Roman Catholics constituted a large proportion of its relatively low-income population. Ashfield, a farming community in western Massachusetts with a 1930 population of 860, was predominantly native born (8.6 percent foreign born), chiefly rural-farm (66 percent), and principally Protestant.

The impressiveness of the differential impact of the election of 1928 on Somerville and Ashfield may be read from the graphs in Figure A. From 1920 the Democratic percentage in Somerville ascended steeply while the Democrats in Ashfield, few in 1920, became even less numerous in 1928. Inspection of graphs also suggests that the great reshuffling of voters that occurred in 1928 was perhaps the final and decisive stage in a process that had been under way for some time. That antecedent process involved a relatively heavy support in 1924 for La Follette in those towns in which Smith was subsequently to find special favor. Hence, in Figure A, as in all the other charts, the 1924 figure is the percentage of the total ac-counted for by the votes of both the Democratic and Progressive candidates rather than the Democratic percentage of the two-party vote. This usage conveys a mini-mum impression of the size of the 1924–1928 Democratic gain but probably depicts the nature of the 1920–1928 trend.

For present purposes, the voting behavior of the two communities shown in Figure A after 1928 is of central relevance. The differences established between them in 1928 persisted even through 1952, although the two series fluctuated slightly in response to the particular influences of individual campaigns. The nature of the process of maintenance of the cleavage is, of course, not manifest from these

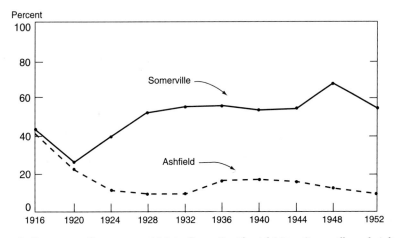

Figure A *Democratic Percentages of Major-Party Presidential Vote, Somerville and Ashfield, Massachusetts, 1916–1952*

data. Conceivably the impress of the events of 1928 on individual attitudes and loyalties formed partisan attachments of lasting nature. Yet it is doubtful that the new crystallization of 1928 projected itself through a quarter of a century solely from the momentum given it by such factors. More probably subsequent events operated to reenforce and to maintain the 1928 cleavage. Whatever the mechanism of its maintenance, the durability of the realignment is impressive.

Somerville and Ashfield may be regarded more or less as samples of major population groups within the electorate of Massachusetts. Since no sample survey data are available for 1928, about the only analysis feasible is inspection of election returns for geographic units contrasting in their population composition. Lest it be supposed, however, that the good citizens of Somerville and Ashfield were aberrants simply unlike the remainder of the people of the Commonwealth, examination of a large number of towns and cities is in order. In the interest of both compression and comprehensibility, a mass of data is telescoped into Figure B. The graphs in that figure compare over the period 1916–1952 the voting behavior of the 29 Massachusetts towns and cities having the sharpest Democratic increases, 1920–1928, with that of the 30 towns and cities having the most marked Democratic loss, 1920–1928. In other words, the figure averages out a great many Ashfields and Somervilles. The data of Figure B confirm the expectation that the pattern exhibited by the pair of voting units in Figure A represented only a single case of a much more general phenomenon. Yet by virtue of the coverage of the data in the figure, one gains a stronger impression of the difference in the character of the election of 1928 and the other elections recorded there. The cleavage confirmed by the 1928 returns persisted. At subsequent elections the voters shifted to and fro within the outlines of the broad division fixed in 1928.

Examination of the characteristics of the two groups of cities and towns of Figure B—those with the most marked Democratic gains, 1920–1928, and those with

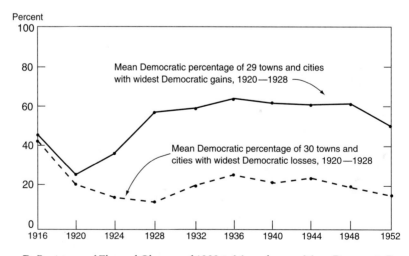

Figure B *Persistence of Electoral Cleavage of 1928 in Massachusetts: Mean Democratic Percentage of Presidential Vote in Towns with Sharpest Democratic Gains, 1920–1928, and in Towns of Widest Democratic Losses, 1920–1928*

the widest movement in the opposite direction—reveals the expected sorts of differences. Urban, industrial, foreign-born, Catholic areas made up the bulk of the
first group of towns, although an occasional rural Catholic community increased its
Democratic vote markedly. The towns with a contrary movement tended to be
rural, Protestant, native born. The new Democratic vote correlated quite closely
with a 1930 vote on state enforcement of the national prohibition law.

Melancholy experience with the eccentricities of data, be they quantitative or
otherwise, suggests the prudence of a check on the interpretation of 1928. Would
the same method applied to any other election yield a similar result, i.e., the appearance of a more or less durable realignment? Perhaps there can be no doubt that
the impact of the events of any election on many individuals forms lasting party
loyalties; yet not often is the number so affected so great as to create sharp realignment. On the other hand, some elections are characterized by a large-scale transfer
of party affection that is quite short-term, a different sort of phenomenon from that
which occurs in elections marked by broad and durable shifts in party strength. The
difference is illustrated by the data on the election of 1932 in New Hampshire in
Figure C. The voting records of the 25 towns with the widest Democratic gains
from 1928 to 1932 are there traced from 1916 to 1952. Observe that Democratic
strength in these towns shot up in 1932 but fairly quickly resumed about the same
position in relation to other towns that it had occupied in 1928. It is also evident
from the graph that this group of towns has on the whole been especially strongly
repelled by the Democratic appeal of 1928. Probably the depression drove an appreciable number of hardened Republicans of these towns to vote for a change in 1932,
but they gradually found their way back to the party of their fathers. In any case, the
figure reflects a type of behavior differing markedly from that of 1928. To the extent
that 1932 resembled 1928 in the recrystallization of party lines, the proportions of
new Democrats did not differ significantly among the groups of towns examined. In

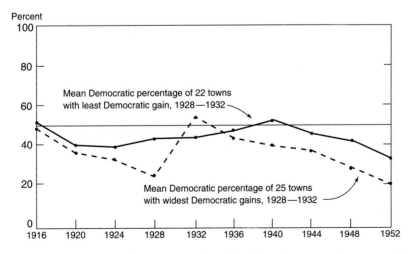

Figure C *Impact of Election of 1932 in New Hampshire: Mean Democratic Percentage of Presidential Vote of Towns with Sharpest Democratic Gain, 1928–1932, Compared with Mean Vote of
Towns at Opposite Extreme of 1928–1932 Change*

fact, what probably happened to a considerable extent in New England was that the 1928 election broke the electorate into two new groups that would have been formed in 1932 had there been no realignment in 1928.

The Massachusetts material has served both to explain the method of analysis and to present the case of a single state. Examinations of the election of 1928 in other New England states indicate that in each a pattern prevailed similar to that of Massachusetts. The total effect of the realignment differed, of course, from state to state. In Massachusetts and Rhode Island the number of people affected by the up-heaval of 1928 was sufficient to form a new majority coalition. In Maine, New Hampshire, and Vermont the same sort of reshuffling of electors occurred, but the proportions affected were not sufficient to overturn the Republican combination, although the basis was laid in Maine and New Hampshire for later limited Democ-ratic success. To underpin these remarks the materials on Connecticut, Maine, New Hampshire, and Rhode Island are presented in Figure D. The data on Vermont, ex-cluded for lack of space, form a pattern similar to that emerging from the analysis of the other states.

In the interpretation of all these 1928 analyses certain limitations of the tech-nique need to be kept in mind. The data and the technique most clearly reveal a shift when voters of different areas move in opposite directions. From 1928 to 1936 apparently a good deal of Democratic growth occurred in virtually all geographic units, a shift not shown up sharply by the technique. Hence, the discussion may fail adequately to indicate the place of 1928 as the crucial stage in a process of electoral change that began before and concluded after that year.

II

One of the difficulties with an ideal type is that no single actual case fits exactly its specifications. Moreover, in any system of categorization the greater the number of differentiating criteria for classes, the more nearly one tends to create a separate class for each instance. If taxonomic systems are to be of analytical utility, they must almost inevitably group together instances that are unlike at least in periph-eral characteristics irrelevant to the purpose of the system. All of which serves to warn that an election is about to be classified as critical even though in some re-spects the behavior involved differed from that of the 1928 polling.

Central to our concept of critical elections is a realignment within the elec-torate both sharp and durable. With respect to these basic criteria the election of 1896 falls within the same category as that of 1928, although it differed in other re-spects. The persistence of the new division of 1896 was perhaps not so notable as that of 1928; yet the Democratic defeat was so demoralizing and so thorough that the party could make little headway in regrouping its forces until 1916. Perhaps the significant feature of the 1896 contest was that, at least in New England, it did not form a new division in which partisan lines became more nearly congruent with lines separating classes, religions, or other such social groups. Instead, the Republi-cans succeeded in drawing new support, in about the same degree, from all sorts of economic and social classes. The result was an electoral coalition formidable in

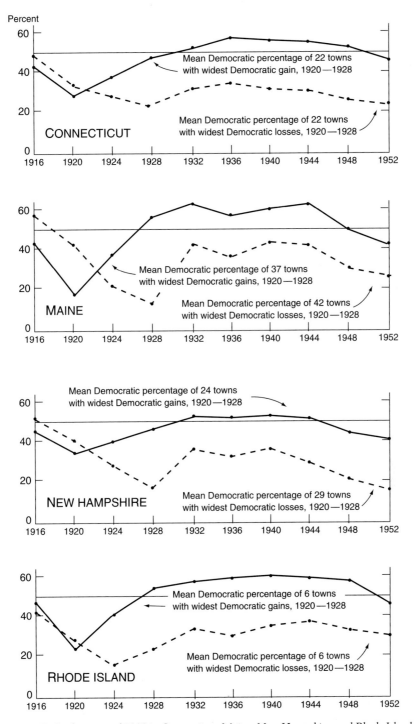

Figure D *Realignment of 1928 in Connecticut, Maine, New Hampshire, and Rhode Island*

mass but which required both good fortune and skill in political management for its maintenance, given its latent internal contradictions.

If the 1896 election is described in our terms as a complex of behavior preceding and following the formal voting, an account of the action must include the panic of 1893. Bank failures, railroad receiverships, unemployment, strikes, Democratic championship of deflation and of the gold standard, and related matters created the setting for a Democratic setback in 1894. Only one of the eight New England Democratic Representatives survived the elections of 1894. The two 1892 Democratic governors fell by the wayside and in all the states the Democratic share of the gubernatorial vote fell sharply in 1894. The luckless William Jennings Bryan and the free-silver heresy perhaps did not contribute as much as is generally supposed to the 1892–1896 decline in New England Democratic strength; New England Democrats moved in large numbers over to the Republican ranks in 1894.

The character of the 1892–1896 electoral shift is suggested by the data of Figure E, which presents an analysis of Connecticut and New Hampshire made by the technique used earlier in examining the election of 1928. The graphs make plain that in these states (and the other New England states show the same pat-

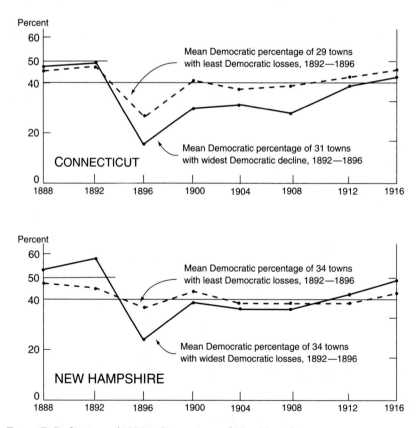

Figure E *Realignment of 1896 in Connecticut and New Hampshire*

tern) the rout of 1896 produced a basic realignment that persisted at least until 1916. The graphs in Figure E also make equally plain that the 1892–1896 realignment differed radically from that of 1928 in certain respects. In 1896 the net movement in all sorts of geographic units was toward the Republicans; towns differed not in the direction of their movement but only in the extent. Moreover, the persistence of the realignment of 1896 was about the same in those towns with the least Democratic loss from 1892 to 1896 as it was in those with the most marked decline in Democratic strength. Hence, the graphs differ from those on 1928 which took the form of opening scissors. Instead, the 1896 realignment appears as a parallel movement of both groups to a lower plateau of Democratic strength.

If the election of 1896 had had a notable differential impact on geographically segregated social groups, the graphs in Figure E of towns at the extremes of the greatest and least 1892–1896 change would have taken the form of opening scissors as they did in 1928. While the election of 1896 is often pictured as a last-ditch fight between the haves and the have-nots, that understanding of the contest was, at least in New England, evidently restricted to planes of leadership and oratory. It did not extend to the voting actions of the electorate. These observations merit some buttressing, although the inference emerges clearly enough from Figure E.

Unfortunately the census authorities have ignored the opportunity to advance demographic inquiry by publishing data of consequence about New England towns. Not much information is available on the characteristics of the populations of these small geographic areas. Nevertheless, size of total population alone is a fair separator of towns according to politically significant characteristics. Classification of towns according to that criterion groups them roughly according to industrialization and probably generally also according to religion and national origin. Hence, with size of population of towns and cities as a basis, Table 1 contrasts the elections of 1896 and 1928 for different types of towns. Observe from the table that the mean shift between 1892 and 1896 was about the same for varying size groups of towns. Contrast this lack of association between size and political movement with the radically different 1920–1928 pattern which also appears in the table.

Table 1 Contrasts Between Elections of 1896 and 1928 in Massachusetts: Shifts in Democratic Strength, 1892–1896 and 1920–1928, in Relation to Population Size of Towns

Population size group	Mean Democratic percentage		Mean change	Mean Democratic percentage		Mean change
	1892	1896	1892–96	1920	1928	1920–28
1–999	34.0	14.7	−19.3	16.5	18.6	+2.1
2000–2999	38.8	18.3	−20.5	21.0	33.1	+12.1
10,000–14,999	46.7	26.9	−19.8	25.8	43.7	+17.9
50,000+	47.7	30.1	−17.6	29.5	55.7	+26.2

Table 1 makes clear that in 1896 the industrial cities, in their aggregate vote at least, moved toward the Republicans in about the same degree as did the rural farming communities. Some of the misinterpretations of the election of 1896 flow from a focus on that election in isolation rather than in comparison with the preceding election. In 1896, even in New England cities, the Democrats tended to be strongest in the poor, working-class, immigrant sections. Yet the same relation had existed, in a sharper form, in 1892. In 1896 the Republicans gained in the working-class wards, just as they did in the silk-stocking wards, over their 1892 vote. They were able to place the blame for unemployment upon the Democrats and to propagate successfully the doctrine that the Republican Party was the party of prosperity and the "full dinner pail." On the whole, the effect apparently was to reduce the degree of coincidence of class affiliation and partisan inclination. Nor was the election of 1896, in New England at least, a matter of heightened tension between city and country. Both city and country voters shifted in the same direction. Neither urban employers nor industrial workers could generate much enthusiasm for inflation and free trade; rather they joined in common cause. Instead of a sharpening of class cleavages within New England the voting apparently reflected more a sectional antagonism and anxiety, shared by all classes, expressed in opposition to the dangers supposed to be threatening from the West.

Other contrasts between the patterns of electoral behavior of 1896 and 1928 could be cited but in terms of sharpness and durability of realignment both elections were of roughly the same type, at least in New England. In these respects they seem to differ from most other elections over a period of a half century, although it may well be that each round at the ballot boxes involves realignment within the electorate similar in kind but radically different in extent.

III

The discussion points toward the analytical utility of a system for the differentiation of elections. A concept of critical elections has been developed to cover a type of election in which there occurs a sharp and durable electoral realignment between parties, although the techniques employed do not yield any information of consequence about the mechanisms for the maintenance of a new alignment, once it is formed. Obviously any sort of system for the gross characterization of elections presents difficulties in application. The actual election rarely presents in pure form a case fitting completely any particular concept. Especially in a large and diverse electorate a single polling may encompass radically varying types of behavior among different categories of voters; yet a dominant characteristic often makes itself apparent. Despite such difficulties, the attempt to move toward a better understanding of elections in the terms here employed could provide a means for better integrating the study of electoral behavior with the analysis of political systems. In truth, a considerable proportion of the study of electoral behavior has only a tenuous relation to politics.

The sorts of questions here raised, when applied sufficiently broadly on a comparative basis and carried far enough, could lead to a consideration of basic problems of the nature of democratic orders. A question occurs, for example, about the character of the consequences for the political system of the temporal frequency of critical elections. What are the consequences for public administration, for the legislative process, for the operation of the economy of frequent serious upheavals within the electorate? What are the correlates of that pattern of behavior? And, for those disposed to raise such questions, what underlying changes might alter the situation? Or, when viewed from the contrary position, what consequences flow from an electorate which is disposed, in effect, to remain largely quiescent over considerable periods? Does a state of moving equilibrium reflect a pervasive satisfaction with the course of public policy? An indifference about matters political? In any case, what are the consequences for the public order? Further, what are the consequences when an electorate builds up habits and attachments, or faces situations, that make it impossible for it to render a decisive and clear-cut popular verdict that promises not to be upset by caprice at the next round of polling? What are the consequences of a situation that creates recurring, evenly balanced conflict over long periods? On the other hand, what characteristics of an electorate or what conditions permit sharp and decisive changes in the power structure from time to time? Such directions of speculation are suggested by a single criterion for the differentiation of elections. Further development of an electoral topology would probably point to useful speculation in a variety of directions.

Party Decline and Electoral Decay

Political parties and elections play a central role in democratic theory. Parties aggregate political and economic interests, and party competition, particularly in a two-party system, gives the electorate a choice in determining the course of government. But the American political system is not based solely on democratic theory or party government. On the contrary, the Constitution discourages political parties through the separation of powers, and dampens direct democracy through a number of devices, including the separation of powers, bicameralism, and provisions requiring extraordinary majorities to make treaties, amend the Constitution, and impeach the president. Political parties have nevertheless played a central role in the political process since the adoption of the Constitution. The authors of the following selection suggest that not only may political parties be declining in importance but politics is increasingly carried out by other means.

—————————— **35** ——————————

POLITICS BY OTHER MEANS

Benjamin Ginsberg and Martin Shefter

❡

Electoral Decay and Institutional Conflict

For much of America's history, elections have been central arenas of popular choice and political combat. In recent years, however, elections have become less decisive as mechanisms for resolving conflicts and constituting governments in the United States. As a result of party decline and deadlock in the electoral arena, political struggles have come more frequently to be waged elsewhere and crucial choices more often made outside the electoral realm. Rather than engage voters directly, contending political forces have come to rely upon such weapons of institutional combat as congressional investigations, media revelations, judicial proceedings, and alliances with foreign governments. In contemporary America, electoral success often fails to confer the capacity to govern; and political forces have been able to exercise considerable power even if they lose at the polls or, indeed, do not compete in the electoral arena. As the twentieth century draws to a close, America is entering what might be called a *postelectoral era*.

The use of institutional weapons of political combat is not without precedent in American history; but over the past two decades, the importance of these weapons has increased while the significance and decisiveness of elections has diminished. This development has profound consequences for the nation's domestic affairs and international economic and political standing. Because contemporary elections fail to establish conclusively who will—or will not—exercise power, conflict over this question continues to rage throughout the political system. This exacerbates the historic fragmentation of government in the United States, further weakening the American state and making it difficult to achieve collective national purposes. Contending political groups are increasingly able to seize portions of the state apparatus and pursue divergent and often contradictory goals even in the face of serious domestic problems and international challenges. In short, a good deal of the difficulty America has recently faced in maintaining its position in the world is attributable to its politics.

From Electoral
to Institutional Combat

Several trends in contemporary American political life bring into focus the declining significance of the electoral arena and the growing importance of other forms of political conflict. American elections in recent decades have been characterized by strikingly low levels of voter turnout and the disappearance of meaningful competition in an increasing number of races. . . .

The extent to which genuine competition takes place in the electoral arena has also declined sharply in recent decades—especially in congressional races, which have come to be dominated by incumbents who are able to use the resources of their office to overwhelm any opponents who might present themselves. . . .

As competition in the electoral arena has declined, the significance of other forms of political combat has increased. One indication of this displacement of conflict from the electoral arena is the growing use of a powerful nonelectoral weapon—the criminal justice system. Between the early 1970s and the late 1980s, there has been more than a tenfold increase in the number of indictments brought by federal prosecutors against national, state, and local officials. . . . Many of those indicted are lower-level civil servants, but large numbers have been prominent political figures—among them more than a dozen members of Congress, several federal judges, and numerous state and local officials. Many of these indictments have been initiated by Republican administrations, and their targets have been primarily Democrats. But a substantial number of high-ranking Republicans in the executive branch—including presidential aides Michael Deaver and Lyn Nofziger, and National Security official Oliver North—have also been the targets of criminal prosecutions stemming from allegations or investigations initiated by Democrats. . . .

There is no reason to believe that the level of political corruption in the United States has actually increased tenfold over the past decade and a half; but it could be argued that this sharp rise in the number of criminal indictments of government officials reflects a heightened level of public concern with governmental misconduct. However, both the issue of government ethics and the growing use of criminal sanctions against public officials have been closely linked to struggles for political power in the United States. In the aftermath of Watergate, institutions were established and processes created to investigate allegations of unethical conduct on the part of public figures. Increasingly, political forces have sought to make use of these mechanisms to discredit their opponents. When scores of investigators, accountants, and lawyers are deployed to scrutinize the conduct of a John Tower or Jim Wright, it is all but certain that something questionable will be found. The creation of these processes, more than changes in the public's moral standards, explains why public officials are increasingly being charged with ethical and criminal violations.

The number of major issues that are fought in the courts has also sharply increased in recent decades, further revealing the importance of nonelectoral conflict in America's current political system. The federal judiciary has become the central institution for resolving struggles over such issues as race relations and abortion and has also come to play a more significant part in deciding questions of social welfare and economic policy. The suits brought by civil rights, environmental, feminist, and other liberal groups seeking to advance their policy goals increased dramatically during the seventies and eighties—reflecting the willingness and ability of these groups to fight their battles in the judicial arena. . . . After the emergence of a conservative majority on the Supreme Court in 1989, forces on the political right formulated plans to use litigation to implement their own policy agenda.

Finally, the national security apparatus has been used as a political weapon in recent decades. One of the best-documented examples of this phenomenon is the substantial expansion that took place during the 1960s and early 1970s in the number of domestic counterintelligence operations directed against groups opposed to the policies of the executive branch. Such activities included wiretaps, surveillance, and efforts to disrupt the activities of these groups. During the 1970s, congressional opposition brought a halt to this particular set of counterintelligence efforts; however, recent revelations have indicated that in the 1980s the FBI placed under surveillance groups opposing the Reagan administration's policies in Central America. The administration also came to rely upon the national security apparatus to circumvent and undercut congressional resistance to its policies.

Party Decline and Electoral Deadlock

Most analyses of American politics assume the primacy of elections. But elections are political institutions, and their significance cannot be taken for granted. The role played by elections has varied over time, and these shifts must be understood in the same terms as changes in the role and power of other institutions. Over the course of American history, political actors have undertaken to transfer decision making on a number of major issues from the electoral to other arenas, such as administrative agencies, the courts, and, in the Civil War, the battlefield. Indeed, forces defeated at the polls have not been averse to using other institutions they control to nullify electoral results. For example, during the late nineteenth and early twentieth centuries, middle- and upper-class "reformers" in American cities were at times able to use state legislative investigations, newspaper exposés, and judicial proceedings to drive from office the machine politicians whom they were unable to defeat through the ballot box.

The declining significance of elections in contemporary America is a product of the electoral deadlock that has developed in the United States over the past quarter century. The duration and scope of this deadlock are without precedent in American history. For eighteen of the twenty-two years between 1968 and 1990, neither the Republican nor the Democratic party was able simultaneously to control the presidency and both houses of Congress. Moreover, for twelve of the eighteen years that the Republicans controlled the White House during this period, the Democrats held majorities in both the House and the Senate.

This deadlock is linked to the decay of America's traditional partisan and electoral institutions. That decay began in the Progressive era, accelerated with the events surrounding the presidencies of Franklin D. Roosevelt and Lyndon Johnson, and has resulted in the virtual destruction of local party organizations and a sharp decline in voting turnout rates. Of course, the Democratic and Republican parties still exist. But they have essentially become coalitions of public officials, office seekers, and political activists; they lack the direct organizational ties to rank-and-file voters that had formerly permitted parties to shape all aspects of politics and government in the United States.

The decay of party organization is a major theme in analyses of contemporary American politics. Political scientists have attributed to it declines in voter turnout, increased electoral volatility, and a diminution in the accountability of public officials to voters. But in focusing on the effects of the decline of party within the electoral arena, analysts have paid insufficient heed to its implications for the relationship between elections and other political institutions.

Generally speaking, strong party organizations enhance the significance of elections, while declines in party strength reduce the importance of electoral processes. Inasmuch as their influence derives from the electoral arena, political parties are the institutions with the largest stake in upholding the principle that power should be allocated through elections. Thus, a diminution of party influence and an increase in the power of other political agencies is likely not only to reduce the relevance of elections for governmental programs and policies but also to allow electoral results themselves to be circumvented, resisted, or even reversed by forces that control powerful institutions outside the electoral realm.

In contemporary American politics, party decline has fostered a stalemate in the national electoral arena and encouraged contenders for power to look elsewhere for weapons to use against their political foes. . . .

. . . In effect, the decay of America's traditional electoral structures has permitted each of the major contenders for power to establish an institutional stronghold from which it cannot easily be dislodged through electoral means.

Institutional Combat

Party decline and electoral stalemate have had critically important consequences for the locus of political combat in the United States. Of course, the Democrats and Republicans continue to contest elections. But rather than pin all its hopes on defeating its foes in the electoral arena, each party has begun to strengthen the institutions it commands and to use them to weaken its foe's governmental and political base.

President and Congress

The Republicans continue to enter candidates in most congressional races but have reacted to their inability to win control of Congress by seeking to enhance the powers of the White House relative to the legislative branch. Thus, President Nixon impounded billions of dollars appropriated by Congress and sought, through various reorganization schemes, to bring executive agencies under closer White House control while severing their ties to the House and Senate. Presidents Reagan and Bush tolerated budget deficits of unprecedented magnitude in part because these precluded new congressional spending; they also sought to increase presidential authority over executive agencies and diminish that of Congress by centralizing control over administrative rule making in the Office of Management and Budget. In addition, Reagan undertook to circumvent the legislative restrictions on presidential conduct embodied in the War Powers Act.

The Democrats, for their part, compete vigorously in presidential elections but have responded to the Republican presidential advantage by seeking to strengthen the Congress while reducing the powers and prerogatives of the presidency—a sharp contrast to Democratic behavior from the 1930s to the 1960s, when that party enjoyed an advantage in presidential elections. In the 1970s, Congress greatly expanded the size of its committee and subcommittee staffs, thus enabling the House and Senate to monitor and supervise closely the activities of executive agencies. Through the 1974 Budget and Impoundment Act, Congress has sought to increase its control over fiscal policy. Congress has also enacted a number of statutory restrictions on presidential authority in the realm of foreign policy, including the Foreign Commitments Resolution and the Arms Export Control Act.

Finally, congressional investigations, often conducted in conjunction with media exposés and judicial proceedings, have been effective in constraining executive power. Ironically, the techniques that have contributed to the Republican dominance of presidential elections have left them vulnerable to these tactics. The GOP's effective use of television has helped it win presidential elections without engaging in the long and arduous task of building up grass-roots electoral organizations. If it possessed strong organizational ties to its supporters, the GOP would not be so vulnerable to investigations and allegations aired through the media.

Institutional combat of the sort that has characterized American politics in recent years is most likely to occur when the major branches of government are controlled by hostile political forces. . . .

Deadlock in the electoral arena has encouraged contending political forces to attempt to use not only Congress and the presidency but also the federal judiciary, the national security apparatus, and the mass media as instruments of political combat. These institutions, in turn, have been able to ally with such forces and to bolster their own autonomy and power. Through this process, institutions that are not directly subject to the control of the electorate have become major players in contemporary American politics. . . .

Postelectoral Politics
and Governmental Disarray

America has now entered an era in which institutional combat has increased in importance relative to electoral competition. This is not to say that electoral outcomes can make no difference. If the Republicans were able to break the Democratic stranglehold on Congress or the Democrats were able more than occasionally to overcome the GOP's advantage in the presidential arena, the stalemate that has characterized American electoral politics for the past quarter century would be broken and the patterns of institutional combat we describe would become less prominent. . . .

Governmental Disarray

The postelectoral political order that has emerged in the United States has three consequences that, taken together, contribute to the disarray of American government and pose problems for the nation's place in the world. First, as each party has strengthened the institutions it commands, the constitutional separation of powers has been transformed into a system of dual sovereignty. The Democrats have undertaken to endow Congress and allied institutions with administrative and coercive capacities that give them the power to govern without controlling the executive branch. In a parallel fashion, the Republicans have worked to make the presidency an institution capable of governing on its own. As a result, the United States often pursues two divergent and contradictory policy agendas. . . .

Second, the American governmental system is increasingly characterized by the absence of political closure. Electoral stalemate and the enhanced political power of non-electoral institutions means that the question of who will govern—and, equally important, who will not govern—is less likely to be resolved in the electoral arena. Because the "winners" in the electoral process do not acquire firm control of the government and the "losers" are not deprived of power, governments are characteristically too weak to implement policies that impose costs upon powerful political interests. . . .

Third, the political patterns emerging in the United States are undermining the administrative capabilities of the American state. As Congress and the president struggle to gain control of segments of the state apparatus, administrative agencies become battlegrounds and can be rendered incapable of carrying out their governmental tasks. . . .

Struggles between Congress and the president also provide subordinate officials in the executive branch with the opportunity to increase their autonomy. Officials seeking to pursue an independent course can use the media to generate support in Congress, thereby preventing their superiors from reining them in. . . .

Underlying America's current governmental disarray is the decay of electoral democracy in the United States. The electoral deadlock which helped to produce contemporary patterns of political struggle, as we have noted, emerged from the destruction of the nation's traditional electoral institutions, in particular from the collapse of political party organizations and the concomitant erosion of voter turnout to the point where, at most, 50 percent of the eligible electorate goes to the polls. Today, rather than focus on outmobilizing their opponents in the electoral arena, political leaders increasingly employ institutional weapons of political struggle that neither require nor encourage popular mobilization. Through such techniques as RIP, political actors with a narrow base of popular support (e.g., journalists, federal prosecutors, and public-interest groups) can end the careers of politicians such as presidents and big-city mayors, who enjoy a broader popular base. And when political struggle takes this form, voters are given little reason to participate. Thus the contemporary system of institutional combat emerged from and helps to perpetuate a political order characterized by remarkably limited popular mobilization.

This postelectoral pattern has become increasingly entrenched in recent years because it serves the interests of major political actors. Political forces lacking a broad popular base obviously benefit from forms of competition that do not allocate power in proportion to mass support. Elected officials and party politicians also have reason to be satisfied with the present state of affairs. The constricted electorate helps to maintain the Republicans' hold on the presidency. The Democrats have established an even firmer grip on Congress and have been able to strengthen it as an instrument of both governance and political combat.

Neither party is prepared to assume the risks that seeking to change the present system would entail. To break the electoral deadlock underlying this system, large numbers of new voters would have to be brought into the electorate—and each party fears that a significant expansion of the electorate would threaten its hold on the institution it currently controls. Postelectoral political patterns and the governmental consequences that flow from them have thus become deeply entrenched features of the contemporary American political order.

Voting Behavior: Rational or Irrational?

Parties are supposed to bridge the gap between the people and their government. Theoretically they are the primary vehicles for translating the wishes of the electorate into public policy, sharing this role with interest groups and other governmental instrumentalities in varying degrees. If parties are to perform this aspect of their job properly, the party system must be conducive to securing meaningful debate and action. Party organization and procedure profoundly affect the ability of parties to act in a democratically responsible manner. It should also be pointed out, however, that the electorate has a responsibility in the political process—the responsibility to act rationally, debate the issues of importance, and record a vote for one party or the other at election time. These, at least, are electoral norms traditionally discussed. But does the electorate act in this manner? Is it desirable to have 100 percent electoral participation considering the characteristics of voting behavior? What are the determinants of electoral behavior? These questions are discussed in the following selection.

——— 36 ———

DEMOCRATIC PRACTICE
AND DEMOCRATIC THEORY

Bernard R. Berelson, Paul F. Lazarsfeld, and William N. McPhee

⤬

Requirements for the Individual

Perhaps the main impact of realistic research on contemporary politics has been to temper some of the requirements set by our traditional normative theory for the typical citizen. "Out of all this literature of political observation and analysis, which is relatively new," says Max Beloff, "there has come to exist a picture in our minds of the political scene which differs very considerably from that familiar to us from the classical texts of democratic politics."

Experienced observers have long known, of course, that the individual voter was not all that the theory of democracy requires of him. As [British Lord James] Bryce put it [in his 1888 treatise, *The American Commonwealth*]:

> How little solidity and substance there is in the political or social beliefs of nineteen persons out of every twenty. These beliefs, when examined, mostly resolve themselves into two or three prejudices and aversions, two or three prepossessions for a particular party or section of a party, two or three phrases or catch-words suggesting or embodying arguments which the man who repeats them has not analyzed.

While our data do not support such an extreme statement, they do reveal that certain requirements commonly assumed for the successful operation of democracy are not met by the behavior of the "average" citizen. The requirements, and our conclusions concerning them, are quickly reviewed.

Interest, Discussion, Motivation

The democratic citizen is expected to be interested and to participate in political affairs. His interest and participation can take such various forms as reading and listening to campaign materials, working for the candidate or the party, arguing politics, donating money, and voting. . . . Many vote without real involvement in the election, and even the party workers are not typically motivated by ideological concerns or plain civic duty.

If there is one characteristic for a democratic system (besides the ballot itself) that is theoretically required, it is the capacity for and the practice of discussion. "It is as true of the large as of the small society," says [A.D.] Lindsay, "that its health depends on the mutual understanding which discussion makes possible; and that discussion is the only possible instrument of its democratic government." How much participation in political discussion there is in the community, what it is, and among whom—these questions have been given answers . . . earlier. . . . In this instance there was little true discussion between the candidates, little in the newspaper commentary, little between the voters and the official party representatives, some within the electorate. On the grass roots level there was more talk than debate, and, at least inferentially, the talk had important effects upon voting, in reinforcing or activating the partisans if not in converting the opposition.

An assumption underlying the theory of democracy is that the citizenry has a strong motivation for participation in political life. But it is a curious quality of voting behavior that for large numbers of people motivation is weak if not almost absent. It is assumed that this motivation would gain its strength from the citizen's perception of the difference that alternative decisions made to him. Now when a person buys something or makes other decisions of daily life, there are direct and immediate consequences for him. But for the bulk of the American people the voting decision is not followed by any direct, immediate, visible personal consequences. Most voters, organized or unorganized, are not in a position to foresee the distant and indirect consequences for themselves, let alone the society. The ballot is cast, and for most people that is the end of it. If their side is defeated, "it doesn't really matter."

Knowledge

The democratic citizen is expected to be well informed about political affairs. He is supposed to know what the issues are, what their history is, what the relevant facts are, what alternatives are proposed, what the party stands for, what the likely consequences are. By such standards the voter falls short. Even when he has the motivation, he finds it difficult to make decisions on the basis of full information when the subject is relatively simple and proximate; how can he do so when it is complex and remote? The citizen is not highly informed on details of the campaign, nor does he avoid a certain misperception of the political situation when it is to his psychological advantage to do so. The electorate's perception of what goes on in the campaign is colored by emotional feeling toward one or the other issue, candidate, party, or social group.

Principle

The democratic citizen is supposed to cast his vote on the basis of principle—not fortuitously or frivolously or impulsively or habitually, but with reference to standards not only of his own interest but of the common good as well. Here, again, if this requirement is pushed at all strongly, it becomes an impossible demand on the democratic electorate.

Many voters vote not for principle in the usual sense but "for" a group to which they are attached—their group. The Catholic vote or the hereditary vote is explainable less as principle than as a traditional social allegiance. The ordinary voter, bewildered by the complexity of modern political problems, unable to determine clearly what the consequences are of alternative lines of action, remote from the arena, and incapable of bringing information to bear on principle, votes the way trusted people around him are voting. . . .

On the issues of the campaign there is a considerable amount of "don't know"—sometimes reflecting genuine indecision, more often meaning "don't care." Among those with opinions the partisans agree on most issues, criteria, expectations, and rules of the game. The supporters of the different sides disagree on only a few issues. Not, for that matter, do the candidates themselves always join the issue sharply and clearly. The partisans do not agree overwhelmingly with their own party's position, or, rather, only the small minority of highly partisan do; the rest take a rather moderate position on the political consideration involved in an election.

Rationality

The democratic citizen is expected to exercise rational judgment in coming to his voting decision. He is expected to have arrived at his principles by reason and to have considered rationally the implications and alleged consequences of the alternative proposals of the contending parties. Political theorists and commentators have always exclaimed over the seeming contrast here between requirement and fulfillment. . . . The upshot of this is that the usual analogy between the voting "decision" and the more or less carefully calculated decisions of consumers or businessmen or courts, incidentally, may be quite incorrect. For many voters political preferences may better be considered analogous to cultural tastes—in music, literature, recreational activities, dress, ethics, speech, social behavior. Consider the parallels between political preferences and general cultural tastes. Both have their origin in ethnic, sectional, class, and family traditions. Both exhibit stability and resistance to change for individuals but flexibility and adjustment over generations for the society as a whole. Both seem to be matters of sentiment and disposition rather than "reasoned preferences." While both are responsive to changed conditions and unusual stimuli, they are relatively invulnerable to direct argumentation and vulnerable to indirect social influences. Both are characterized more by faith than by conviction and by wishful expectation rather than careful prediction or consequences. The preference for one party rather than another must be highly similar to the preference for one kind of literature or music rather than another, and the choice of the same political party every four years may be parallel to the choice of the same old standards of conduct in new social situations. In short, it appears that a sense of fitness is a more striking feature of political preference than reason and calculation.

Requirements for the System

If the democratic system depended solely on the qualifications of the individual voter, then it seems remarkable that democracies have survived through the centuries. After examining the detailed data on how individuals misperceive political reality or respond to irrelevant social influences, one wonders how a democracy ever solves its political problems. But when one considers the data in a broader perspective—how huge segments of the society adapt to political conditions affecting them or how the political system adjusts itself to changing conditions over long periods of time—he cannot fail to be impressed with the total result. Where the rational citizen seems to abdicate, nevertheless angels seem to tread. . . .

That is the paradox. *Individual voters* today seem unable to satisfy the requirements for a democratic system of government outlined by political theorists. But *the system of democracy* does meet certain requirements for a going political organization. The individual members may not meet all the standards, but the whole nevertheless survives and grows. This suggests that where the classic theory is defective is in its concentration on the *individual citizen*. What are undervalued are certain collective properties that reside in the electorate as a whole and in the political and social system in which it functions.

The political philosophy we have inherited, then, has given more consideration to the virtues of the typical citizen of the democracy than to the working of the system as a whole. Moreover, when it dealt with the system, it mainly considered the single constitutive institutions of the system, not those general features necessary if the institutions are to work as required. For example, the rule of law, representative government, periodic elections, the party system, and the several freedoms of discussion, press, association, and assembly have all been examined by political philosophers seeking to clarify and to justify the idea of political democracy. But liberal democracy is more than a political system in which individual voters and political institutions operate. For political democracy to survive, other features are required: the intensity of conflict must be limited, the rate of change must be restrained, stability in the social and economic structure must be maintained, a pluralistic social organization must exist, and a basic consensus must bind together the contending parties.

Such features of the system of political democracy belong neither to the constitutive institutions nor to the individual voter. It might be said that they form the atmosphere or the environment in which both operate. In any case, such features have not been carefully considered by political philosophers, and it is on these broader properties of the democratic political system that more reflection and study by political theory is called for. In the most tentative fashion let us explore the values of the political system, as they involve the electorate, in the light of the foregoing considerations.

Underlying the paradox is an assumption that the population is homogeneous socially and should be homogeneous politically: that everybody is about the same in relevant social characteristics; that, if something is a political virtue (like interest in the election), then everyone should have it; that there is such a thing as "the" typical citizen on whom uniform requirements can be imposed.

The tendency of classic democratic literature to work with an image of "the" voter was never justified. For, as we will attempt to illustrate here, some of the most important requirements that democratic values impose on a system require a voting population that is not homogeneous but heterogeneous in its political qualities.

The need for heterogeneity arises from the contradictory functions we expect our voting system to serve. We expect the political system to adjust itself and our affairs to changing conditions; yet we demand too that it display a high degree of stability. We expect the contending interests and parties to pursue their ends vigorously and the voters to care; yet, after the election is over, we expect reconciliation. We expect the voting outcome to serve what is best for the community; yet we do not want disinterested voting unattached to the purposes and interests of different segments of that community. We want voters to express their own free and self-determined choices; yet, for the good of the community, we would like voters to avail themselves of the best information and guidance available from the groups and leaders around them. We expect a high degree of rationality to prevail in the decision; but were all irrationality and mythology absent, and all ends pursued by the most coldly rational selection of political means, it is doubtful if the system would hold together.

In short, our electoral system calls for apparently incompatible properties—which, although they cannot all reside in each individual voter, can (and do) reside in a heterogeneous electorate. What seems to be required of the electorate as a whole is a *distribution* of qualities along important dimensions. We need some people who are active in a certain respect, others in the middle, and still others passive. The contradictory things we want from the total require that the parts be different. This can be illustrated by taking up a number of important dimensions by which an electorate might be characterized.

Involvement and Indifference

How could a mass democracy work if all the people were deeply involved in politics? Lack of interest by some people is not without its benefits, too. True, the highly interested voters vote more, and know more about the campaign, and read and listen more, and participate more; however, they are also less open to persuasion and less likely to change. Extreme interest goes with extreme partisanship and might culminate in rigid fanaticism that could destroy democratic processes if generalized throughout the community. Low affect toward the election—not caring much—underlies the resolution of many political problems; votes can be resolved into a two-party split instead of fragmented into many parties (the splinter parties of the left, for example, splinter because their advocates are too interested in politics). Low interest provides maneuvering room for political shifts necessary for a complex society in a period of rapid change. Compromise might be based upon sophisticated awareness of costs and returns—perhaps impossible to demand of a mass society—but it is more often induced by indifference. Some people are and should be highly interested in politics, but not everyone is or needs to be. Only the doctrinaire would deprecate the moderate indifference that facilitates compromise.

Hence, an important balance between action motivated by strong sentiments and action with little passion behind it is obtained by heterogeneity within the electorate. Balance of this sort is, in practice, met by a distribution of voters rather than by a homogeneous collection of "ideal" citizens.

Stability and Flexibility

A similar dimension along which an electorate might be characterized is stability-flexibility. The need for change and adaptation is clear, and the need for stability ought equally to be (especially from observation of current democratic practice in, say, certain Latin American countries). . . . [I]t may be that the very people who are most sensitive to changing social conditions are those most susceptible to political change. For, in either case, the people exposed to membership in overlapping strata, those whose former life-patterns are being broken up, those who are moving about socially or physically, those who are forming new families and new friendships—it is they who are open to adjustments of attitudes and tastes. They may be the least partisan and the least interested voters, but they perform a valuable function for the entire system. Here again is an instance in which an individual "inadequacy" provides a positive service for society: The campaign can be a reaffirming force for the settled majority and a creative force for the unsettled minority. There is stability on both sides and flexibility in the middle.

Progress and Conservation

Closely related to the question of stability is the question of past versus future orientation of the system. In America a progressive outlook is highly valued, but, at the same time, so is a conservative one. Here a balance between the two is easily found in the party system and in the distribution of voters themselves from extreme conservatives to extreme liberals. But a balance between the two is also achieved by a distribution of political dispositions through time. There are periods of great political agitation (i.e., campaigns) alternating with periods of political dormancy. Paradoxically, the former—the campaign period—is likely to be an instrument of conservatism, often even of historical regression. . . .

Again, then, a balance (between preservation of the past and receptivity to the future) seems to be required of a democratic electorate. The heterogeneous electorate in itself provides a balance between liberalism and conservatism; and so does the sequence of political events from periods of drifting change to abrupt rallies back to the loyalties of earlier years.

Consensus and Cleavage . . .

[T]here are required *social* consensus and cleavage—in effect pluralism—in politics. Such pluralism makes for enough consensus to hold the system together and enough cleavage to make it move. Too much consensus would be deadening and restrictive of liberty; too much cleavage would be destructive of the society as a whole. . . . Thus again a requirement we might place on an electoral system—

balance between total political war between segments of the society and total political indifference to group interests of that society—translates into varied requirements for different individuals. With respect to group or bloc voting, as with other aspects of political behavior, it is perhaps not unfortunate that "some do and some do not."

Individualism and Collectivism

Lord Bryce pointed out the difficulties in a theory of democracy that assumes that each citizen must himself be capable of voting intelligently:

> Orthodox democratic theory assumes that every citizen has, or ought to have, thought out for himself certain opinions, i.e., ought to have a definite view, defensible by argument, of what the country needs, of what principles ought to be applied in governing it, of the man to whose hands the government ought to be entrusted. There are persons who talk, though certainly very few who act, as if they believed this theory, which may be compared to the theory of some ultra-Protestants that every good Christian has or ought to have . . . worked out for himself from the Bible a system of theology.

In the first place, however, the information available to the individual voter is not limited to that directly possessed by him. True, the individual casts his own personal ballot. But, as we have tried to indicate . . . that is perhaps the most individualized action he takes in an election. His vote is formed in the midst of his fellows in a sort of group decision—if, indeed, it may be called a decision at all—and the total information and knowledge possessed in the group's present and past generations can be made available for the group's choice. Here is where opinion-leading relationships, for example, play an active role.

Second, and probably more important, the individual voter may not have a great deal of detailed information, but he usually has picked up the crucial general information as part of his social learning itself. He may not know the parties' position on the tariff, or who is for reciprocal trade treaties, or what are the differences on Asiatic policy, or how the parties split on civil rights, or how many security risks were exposed by whom. But he cannot live in an American community without knowing broadly where the parties stand. He has learned that the Republicans are more conservative and the Democrats more liberal—and he can locate his own sentiments and case his vote accordingly. After all, he must vote for one or the other party, and, if he knows the big thing about the parties, he does not need to know all the little things. The basic role a party plays as an institution in American life is more important to his voting than a particular stand on a particular issue.

It would be unthinkable to try to maintain our present economic style of life without a complex system of delegating to others what we are not competent to do ourselves, without accepting and giving training to each other about what each is expected to do, without accepting our dependence on others in many spheres and taking responsibility for their dependence on us in some spheres. And, like it or not, to maintain our present political style of life, we may have to accept much the same interdependence with others in collective behavior. We have learned slowly in economic life that it is useful not to have everyone a butcher or a baker, any more than it is useful to have no one skilled in such activities. The same kind of division of labor—as repugnant as it may be in some respects to our individualistic tradition—is serving us well today in mass politics. There is an implicit division of political labor within the electorate.

$\mathcal{CSD}$

Political Campaigns and the Electorate

The voice of the people is always heard in the electoral process, but it is not always clear exactly what the people have chosen. The candidates and their political consultants concentrate upon the projection of images rather than on the serious discussion of public issues. The media, interested in gaining as wide an audience as possible, encourage candidates to be brief in the presentation of their programs and to act with an eye to what is newsworthy in the view of television producers and newspaper editors. A maze confronts the electorate, which must be able to peer through the smoke screen of electoral politics in order to be able to vote intelligently. The following selection, from Key's oft-quoted book, *The Responsible Electorate,* argues that voters are not the fools that many politicians and their advisers often take them to be. The electorate, concludes the author, "behaves about as rationally and responsibly as we should expect, given the clarity of the alternatives presented to it and the character of the information available to it."

37

THE RESPONSIBLE ELECTORATE

V. O. Key, Jr.

$\mathcal{CSD}$

In his reflective moments even the most experienced politician senses a nagging curiosity about why people vote as they do. His power and his position depend upon the outcome of the mysterious rites we perform as opposing candidates harangue the multitudes who finally march to the polls to prolong the rule of their champion, to thrust him, ungratefully, back into the void of private life, or to raise to eminence a new tribune of the people. What kinds of appeals enable a candidate to win the favor of the great god, The People? What circumstances move voters to shift their preferences in this direction or that? What clever propaganda tactic or slogan led to this result? What mannerism of oratory or style of rhetoric produced another outcome? What band of electors rallied to this candidate to save the day for him? What policy of state attracted the devotion of another bloc of voters? What action repelled a third sector of the electorate?

The victorious candidate may claim with assurance that he has the answers to all such questions. He may regard his success as vindication of his beliefs about why voters vote as they do. And he may regard the swing of the vote to him as indubitably a response to the campaign positions he took, as an indication of the acuteness of his intuitive estimates of the mood of the people, and as a ringing manifestation of the esteem in which he is held by a discriminating public. This narcissism assumes its most repulsive form among election winners who have championed intolerance, who have stirred the passions and hatreds of people, or who have advocated causes known by decent men to be outrageous or dangerous in their long-run consequences. No functionary is more repugnant or more arrogant than the unjust man who asserts, with a color of truth, that he speaks from a pedestal of popular approbation.

It thus can be a mischievous error to assume, because a candidate wins, that a majority of the electorate shares his views on public questions, approves his past actions, or has specific expectations about his future conduct. Nor does victory establish that the candidate's campaign strategy, his image, his television style, or his fearless stand against cancer and polio turned the trick. The election returns establish only that a winner attracted a majority of votes—assuming the existence of a modicum of rectitude in election administration. They tell us precious little about why the plurality was his.

For a glaringly obvious reason, electoral victory cannot be regarded as necessarily a popular ratification of a candidate's outlook. The voice of the people is but an echo. The output of an echo chamber bears an inevitable and invariable relation to the input. As candidates and parties clamor for attention and vie for popular support, the people's verdict can be no more than a selective reflection from among the alternatives and outlooks presented to them. Even the most discriminating popular judgment can reflect only ambiguity, uncertainty, or even foolishness if those are the qualities of the input into the echo chamber. A candidate may win despite his tactics and appeals rather than because of them. If the people can choose only from among rascals, they are certain to choose a rascal.

Scholars, though they have less at stake than do politicians, also have an abiding curiosity about why voters act as they do. In the past quarter of a century they have vastly enlarged their capacity to check the hunches born of their curiosities. The invention of the sample survey—the most widely known example of which is the Gallup poll—enabled them to make fairly trustworthy estimates of the characteristics and behaviors of large human populations. This method of mass observation revolutionized the study of politics—as well as the management of political campaigns. The new technique permitted large-scale tests to check the validity of old psychological and sociological theories of human behavior. These tests led to new hunches and new theories about voting behavior, which could in turn, be checked and which thereby contributed to the extraordinary ferment in the social sciences during recent decades.

The studies of electoral behavior by survey methods cumulate into an imposing body of knowledge which conveys a vivid impression of the variety and subtlety of factors that enter into individual voting decisions. In their first stages in the 1930s the new electoral studies chiefly lent precision and verification to the working maxims of practicing politicians and to some of the crude theories of political speculators. Thus, sample surveys established that people did, indeed, appear to vote their pocketbooks. Yet the demonstration created its embarrassments because it also established that exceptions to the rule were numerous. Not all factory workers, for example, voted alike. How was the behavior of the deviants from "group interest" to be explained? Refinement after refinement of theory and analysis added complexity to the original simple explanation. By introducing a bit of psychological theory it could be demonstrated that factory workers with optimistic expectations tended less to be governed by pocketbook considerations than did those whose outlook was gloomy. When a little social psychology was stirred into the analysis, it could be established that identifications formed early in life, such as attachments to political parties, also reinforced or resisted the pull of the interest of the moment. A sociologist, bringing to play the conceptual tools of his trade, then could show that those factory workers who associate intimately with like-minded persons on the average vote with greater solidarity than do social isolates. Inquiries conducted with great ingenuity along many such lines have enormously broadened our knowledge of the factors associated with the responses of people to the stimuli presented to them by political campaigns.

Yet, by and large, the picture of the voter that emerges from a combination of the folklore of practical politics and the findings of the new electoral studies is not a pretty one. It is not a portrait of citizens moving to considered decision as they play their solemn role of making and unmaking governments. The older tradition from practical politics may regard the voter as an erratic and irrational fellow susceptible to manipulation by skilled humbugs. One need not live through many campaigns to observe politicians, even successful politicians, who act as though they regarded the people as manageable fools. Nor does a heroic conception of the voter emerge from the new analyses of electoral behavior. They can be added up to a conception of voting not as a civic decision but as an almost purely deterministic act. Given knowledge of certain characteristics of a voter—his occupation, his residence, his religion, his national origin, and perhaps certain of his attributes—one can predict with a high probability the direction of his vote. The actions of persons are made to appear to be only predictable and automatic responses to campaign stimuli.

Most findings of the analysts of voting never travel beyond the circle of the technicians; the popularizers, though, give wide currency to the most bizarre—and most dubious—theories of electoral behavior. Public-relations experts share in the process of dissemination as they sell their services to politicians (and succeed in establishing that politicians are sometimes as gullible as businessmen). Reporters pick up the latest psychological secret from campaign managers and spread it through a larger public. Thus, at one time a goodly proportion of the literate population must have placed some store in the theory that the electorate was a pushover for a candidate who projected an appropriate "father image." At another stage, the "sincere" candidate supposedly had an overwhelming advantage. And even so kindly a gentleman as General Eisenhower was said to have an especial attractiveness to those of authoritarian personality within the electorate.

Conceptions and theories of the way voters behave do not raise solely arcane problems to be disputed among the democratic and antidemocratic theorists or questions to be settled by the elegant techniques of the analysts of electoral behavior. Rather, they touch upon profound issues at the heart of the problem of the nature and workability of systems of popular government. Obviously the perceptions of the behavior of the electorate held by political leaders, agitators, and activists condition if they do not fix, the types of appeals politicians employ as they seek popular support. These perceptions—or theories—affect the nature of the input to the echo chamber, if we may revert to our earlier figure, and thereby control its output. They may govern, too, the kinds of actions that governments take as they look forward to the next election. If politicians perceive the electorate as responsive to father images, they will give it father images. If they see voters as most certainly responsive to nonsense, they will give them nonsense. If they see voters as susceptible to delusion, they will delude them. If they see an electorate receptive to the cold, hard realities, they will give it the cold, hard realities.

In short, theories of how voters behave acquire importance not because of their effects on voters, who may proceed blithely unaware of them. They gain significance because of their effects, both potentially and in reality, on candidates and other political leaders. If leaders believe the route to victory is by projection of images and cultivation of styles rather than by advocacy of policies to cope with the problems of the country, they will project images and cultivate styles to the neglect of the substance of politics. They will abdicate their prime function in a democratic system, which amounts, in essence, to the assumption of the risk of trying to persuade us to lift ourselves by our bootstraps.

Among the literary experts on politics there are those who contend that, because of the development of tricks of the manipulation of the masses, practices of political leadership in the management of voters have moved far toward the conversion of election campaigns into obscene parodies of the models set up by democratic idealists. They point to the good old days when politicians were deep thinkers, eloquent orators, and farsighted statesmen. Such estimates of the course of change in social institutions must be regarded with reserve. They may be only manifestations of the inverted optimism of aged and melancholy men who, estopped from hope for the future, see in the past a satisfaction of their yearning for greatness in our political life.

Whatever the trends may have been, the perceptions that leadership elements of democracies hold of the modes of response of the electorate must always be a matter of fundamental significance. Those perceptions determine the nature of the voice of the people, for they determine the character of the input into the echo chamber. While the output may be governed by the nature of the input, over the longer run the properties of the echo chamber may themselves be altered. Fed a steady diet of buncombe, the people may come to expect and to respond with highest predictability to buncombe. And those leaders most skilled in the propagation of buncombe may gain lasting advantage in the recurring struggles for popular favor.

[My] perverse and unorthodox argument . . . is that voters are not fools. To be sure, many individual voters act in odd ways indeed; yet in the large the electorate behaves about as rationally and responsibly as we should expect, given the clarity of the alternatives presented to it and the character of the information available to it. In American presidential campaigns of recent decades the portrait of the American electorate that develops from the data is not one of an electorate straitjacketed by social determinants or moved by subconscious urges triggered by devilishly skillful propagandists. It is rather one of an electorate moved by concern about central and relevant questions of public policy, of governmental performance, and of executive personality. Propositions so uncompromisingly stated inevitably represent overstatements. Yet to the extent that they can be shown to resemble the reality, they are propositions of basic importance for both the theory and the practice of democracy. . . .

The Role of Political Parties in Campaign Finance

Political parties have assumed a new and important role as campaign funders. Because parties are broader representatives of the electorate than are interest groups it can be argued that they should be freer than PACs to raise and distribute money for their candidates.

The following selection describes the importance of parties, particularly their legislative campaign Committees (LCCs), in the ever-growing and controversial arena of campaign finance.

— 38 —

POLITICAL PARTIES AND CAMPAIGN FINANCE

Frank J. Sorauf

Consequences and Scenarios

At both the state and national levels, the growth of the parties' role as campaign funders moved at an accelerated pace in 1995–1996. The money raised and spent, especially by the national party committees, increased dramatically. The almost threefold increase in their receipts from 1992 to 1996, from one presidential cycle to the next, greatly altered the curve of growth. At the same time, the 1990s saw the maturing of a new form of party organization, the legislative campaign committee, that bore much of the responsibility for that growth, even usurping much of the funding that had been done earlier by the regular hierarchy of party organizations.

Moreover, there is no sign that the flood of party money has even crested. Reform of the FECA [Federal Election Campaign Act] appears stalled in the Congress in early 1997, and while reform goes on in some of the states, the parties are not its chief targets. In fact, since PACs and affluent individual contributors are the targets, the parties' funding role advances simply if their committees' spending is unaffected. It is often the case, too, that majorities for reform are built within the legislature by protecting or even expanding the spending authority of the parties particularly of party caucuses or legislative campaign committees. To protect them is to protect the collective interests of legislators.

As for the new opportunities opened up by the courts the party independent spending and the unrestricted use of issue ads there is no sign that the Supreme Court is reconsidering its applications of the First Amendment to them. The nascent movements to bring test cases seeking the Court's reconsideration of *Buckley v. Valeo* and its applications are in their very early stages. Moreover, a modest constitutional amendment to permit the Congress to legislate spending limits for its elections was soundly defeated in the Senate iri March 1996. Only an unlikely congressional decision to curb soft money receipts would threaten party spending, and then only for issue advocacy. For the short run, therefore, party expenditures at the national level would seem likely to expand, and in the states they will probably gain their first footholds.

In short, efforts to reform campaign finance in most instances do not threaten the parties' new role as financial patron to America's campaigns. Their newly strengthened legislative campaign committees are in that enviable position described in the sports idiom as "win-win." So, it remains only to try to assess the consequences of the new party role in the campaigns the consequences both for campaign finance and for the parties. First, does the new party role promise to be good for campaign finance? Is party money a better source of candidate money than PACs and individual contributors? And, second, is the role good for the parties? Is it an adaptation that will foster the health of the political parties in a healthy mass, popular democracy?

First, to the effect on campaign finance: Conventional wisdom has long had it that money from a party committee is more likely than individual or PAC money to promote the competitiveness of elections. The parties do give more money than the other two sources to candidates other than incumbents, and they do put more of their money behind challengers than other contributors do. They do not, however, set out to raise the competitiveness of elections, and their decisions, for example, to help incumbents turn a competitive seat into a safe one work in quite the opposite direction. Party committees, especially the legislative campaign committees, seek to maximize the number of party victories, not to elevate electoral competitiveness.

Party money, to be sure, enables some challengers to mount competitive races, and for that reason it moves more elections to competitiveness than do the other sources of money. But the basic problem of competitiveness lies in the unwillingness of all contributors to give money to candidates who, even early in the campaign, appear not to have a 'reasonable chance of winning. Parties make that same calculation, even if somewhat more adventuresomely than other contributors. Only a source of funds that goes to the candidate regardless of chances of winning will greatly alter the aggregate competitiveness of elections. For now, only some programs of public funding meet that test.

The same conventional wisdom claims that party money also cleanses funds of the interests and demands of its origins. If a PAC contributes to a party, then, the interests of the PAC somehow disappear from the money before it is transmitted to a candidate or spent on behalf of one. In the words of a group of political scientists in their brief of amicus curiae on the side of the Colorado Republicans in their case [*Colorado Republican Federal Campaign Committee v. FEC* (1996)] against the FEC:

As a source of campaign funds, American parties probably constitute the cleanest money in politics. Recognizing that political parties are large aggregators of many contributions [sic] diffuses any real or perceived undue influence that might arise from a financial contribution. . . . Parties are too large and too diverse to be controlled by any special interest. The old rule of sanitary engineers applies: the solution to pollution is dilution. . . . That argument requires a number of leaps of faith. It assumes that the identity of the original sources is not transmitted to the candidate and vice versa. It assumes that the policy interests of the original source will not be incorporated into the party program. And it also assumes that the interests of the party are more benign or less insistent, or both, than those of the original source.

If, however, party leaders do respond to the claims of large nonparty contributors, their agenda for the legislative party will incorporate those claims. And in many American legislatures, party leadership has points of leverage on the individual legislator that lobbyists and PACs can only dream of. That must certainly be among the reasons that PACs in Illinois prefer to contribute to party leaders rather than directly to candidates.

Finally, what are the implications of the new financial role for the parties themselves? That role is, first, a great force for centralization. National party committees assume the spending authority of state committees via agency agreements, and the party committees in Congress replace the local parties as the "party" that incumbents and candidates deal with. And national party committees, and their growing field staffs, take over what had been the local party's main role in nominations: the recruitment of candidates. Within the states, similarly, the LCCs [Legislative Campaign Committees] in the state legislature displace the local party units as the part of the party holding legislators accountable.

To put the matter another way, as the units of the party closer to the grass roots begin to atrophy, those in capital cities thrive. When the prime resources for the parties and election campaigns were volunteer activism and patronage-fed workers, the resource was local. The money for today's candidate centered campaigns is more easily raised at state and national levels. Major contributors seek the major political players, the big and visible political stages, even the celebrities of government and politics. All politics, or even some politics, may be local, but political money is not, and that has cost the local party committees dearly.

Furthermore, the role of party funder strengthens the independence of the legislative party. Until the rise of the [Legislative Campaign Committees], state and national party committees had been executive parties, controlled by presidents and govemors and working closely with their personnel campaign committees to elect and reelect them. The LCCs, however, buttress the agenda and political power of the legislative party. They work to strengthen it against executive policy pressures and the dominance of the party. Thus, they import the separation of powers into the political party. At the least, they make it more difficult for the executive to use the political party to bridge the gulf between the two branches and unite them behind policy initiatives.

The rise of the [Legislative Campaign Committees], moreover, has brought them into conflict with local units of the parties. The LCCs have organized electoral influence around an agenda of issues and a set of interests that are limited and even provincial those of the legislative party as the legislative party defines them. They disconnect the political power of their part of the party from the rest of the party, whether it be the party of mass loyalties, of the activists who tend what remains of the grass roots, or of visible executives and the majoritarian interests of executive party. . . .

. . . [T]he [Legislative Campaign Committees] contribute to the disuniting, even the disintegration, of the mass political party by fragmenting party interests and restricting party committees to championing only some of them.

Ironically, there is a good deal of scattered evidence that the LCCs promote party cohesion in American legislatures. The combination of gratitude and fear they generate as their role in campaign funding grows unquestionably leads to a heightened deference to the legislative party and its leaders. But loyalty so "purchased" is in the interests of the legislative party and its leaders and, above all, works toward the prime goal of reaching and enhancing a legislative majority and the perquisites and power that flow from it.

Once again, assessment comes down to the kind of parties one wants. The most durable American model of the reformed party is, of course, the "responsible political party" (American Political Science Association, 1950). It is the integrated party that unites candidates, public officials, party organization, and loyal party voters in order to enact party programs into public policy. It is the party of "party government." Program or ideology binds the party together, and that bound and integrated party in turn can bind the disparate institutions together and enable them to write the party program into policy.

Whatever the merits of that vision, it is not the vision fostered by the party as campaign funder. Maximizing seats in a legislature is a strategy for holding power; it fails to address the question of program, of "power for what." Indeed, the party as funder rarely, if ever, asks questions of program or issue commitment of those it helps; the question is electability—not loyalty to party programs or issues positions. Whatever programmatic commitments it has are commitments, not of a mass based party but of the legislative cohort. The Republicans' Contract with America in 1994 was written by House Republicans for House Republicans.

Rather, the new funding role pushes the parties additional steps into their development as service vendor parties. . . . It advances the parties' accommodation to the realities of candidate-centered electoral politics and declining local activism and party organizations, but it also advances them by staying well within the limits of the immediately possible. Above all, it does not challenge the dominance of electoral politics by the candidates, and thus it does not aspire to recapture, even in part, past forms, past glories, or past visions.

As the almost uninhibited party fund-raising of 1996 demonstrates, the parties have learned how to master one of the major resources of electoril politics in an era in which the political grass roots wither and media spending escalates. They have learned to exploit their advantages in both raising and spending money. As the federal courts increasingly free them from statutory constraints in spending it, their favored position is increasingly favored. The directions of party adaptation easily follow the widening paths of opportunity.

In our system of politics by other means virtually no political process or policy is immune from challenges through litigation. In *Buckley v. Valeo* (1976), Chapter 5, *selection no. 45*, the Supreme Court held that the First Amendment forbids limits on political candidates' expenditures of their own money to get elected. The decision also held unconstitutional limits on "indirect" expenditures in behalf of issues or candidates. But the Court held that Congress could regulate both PAC and party contributions to candidates. The *Buckley* opinion did not spell out in detail how far Congress could go in regulating campaign finance without breaching the First Amendment. The decision left the Federal Election Commission with the responsibility of deciding in concrete cases how the Campaign Finance laws would apply to both interest groups and political parties.

The Supreme Court revisited the *Buckley* opinion and First Amendment protections of party fund-raising in the following case.

39

COLORADO REPUBLICAN FEDERAL CAMPAIGN COMMITTEE V. FEDERAL ELECTION COMMISSION

518 U.S. 604 (1996)

Justice Breyer announced the judgment of the Court and delivered an opinion, in which Justice O'Connor and Justice Souter join.

In April 1986, before the Colorado Republican Party had selected its senatorial candidate for the fall's election, that Party's Federal Campaign Committee bought radio advertisements attacking Timothy Wirth, the Democratic Party's likely candidate. The Federal Election Commission (FEC) charged that this "expenditure" exceeded the dollar limits that a provision of the Federal Election Campaign Act of 1971 (FECA) imposes upon political party "expenditure[s] in connection with" a "general election campaign" for congressional office. 90 Stat. 486, as amended, 2 U.S.C. Section(s) 441a(d)(3). This case focuses upon the constitutionality of those limits as applied to this case. We conclude that the First Amendment prohibits the application of this provision to the kind of expenditure at issue here—an expenditure that the political party has made independently, without coordination with any candidate.

I

To understand the issues and our holding, one must begin with FECA as it emerged from Congress in 1974. That Act sought both to remedy the appearance of a "corrupt" political process (one in which large contributions seem to buy legislative votes) and to level the electoral playing field by reducing campaign costs. It consequently imposed limits upon the amounts that individuals, corporations, "political committees" (such as political action committees, or PAC's), and political parties could contribute to candidates for federal office, and it also imposed limits upon the amounts that candidates, corporations, labor unions, political committees, and political parties could spend, even on their own, to help a candidate win election. . . .

[The] FECA's special provision, which we shall call the "Party Expenditure Provision," creates a general exception from [the law's] contribution limitation, and from any other limitation on expenditures. It says: "Notwithstanding any other provision of law with respect to limitations on expenditures or limitations on contributions, . . . political party [committees] . . . may make expenditures in connection with the general election campaign of candidates for Federal office . . ."

. . . [W]e . . . treat [this] expenditure, for constitutional purposes, as an "independent" expenditure, not an indirect campaign contribution.

So treated, the expenditure falls within the scope of the Court's precedents that extend First Amendment protection to independent expenditures. Beginning with *Buckley*, the Court's cases have found a "fundamental constitutional difference between money spent to advertise one's views independently of the candidate's campaign and money contributed to the candidate to be spent on his campaign." . . . This difference has been grounded in the observation that restrictions on contributions impose "only a marginal restriction upon the contributor's ability to engage in free communication," because the symbolic communicative value of a contribution bears little relation to its size, and because such limits leave "persons free to engage in independent political expression, to associate actively through volunteering their services, and to assist to a limited but nonetheless substantial extent in supporting candidates and committees with financial resources." . . . At the same time, reasonable contribution limits directly and materially advance the Government's interest in preventing exchanges of large financial contributions for political favors. . . .

In contrast, the Court has said that restrictions on independent expenditures significantly impair the ability of individuals and groups to engage in direct political advocacy and "represent substantial . . . restraints on the quantity and diversity of political speech." . . . And at the same time, the Court has concluded that limitations on independent expenditures are less directly related to preventing corruption, since "[t]he absence of prearrangement and coordination of an expenditure with the candidate . . . not only undermines the value of the expenditure to the candidate, but also alleviates the danger that expenditures will be given as a quid pro quo for improper commitments from the candidate." . . .

Given these established principles, we do not see how a provision that limits a political party's independent expenditures can escape their controlling effect. A political party's independent expression not only reflects its members' views about the philosophical and governmental matters that bind them together, it also seeks to convince others to join those members in a practical democratic task, the task of creating a government that voters can instruct and hold responsible for subsequent success or failure. The independent expression of a political party's views is "core" First Amendment activity no less than is the independent expression of individuals, candidates, or other political committees. . . .

We therefore believe that this Court's prior case law controls the outcome here. We do not see how a Constitution that grants to individuals, candidates, and ordinary political committees the right to make unlimited independent expenditures could deny the same right to political parties. . . .

For these reasons, the judgment of the Court of Appeals is vacated, and the case is remanded for further proceedings.

It is so ordered.

Justice Kennedy, with whom The Chief Justice and Justice Scalia join, concurring in the judgment and dissenting in part.

In agreement with Justice Thomas. . . . I would hold that the Colorado Republican Party, in its pleadings in the District Court and throughout this litigation, has preserved its claim that the constraints imposed by the Federal Election Campaign Act of 1971 (FECA), both on its face and as interpreted by the Federal Elections Commission (FEC), violate the First Amendment. . . .

The central holding in *Buckley v. Valeo* . . . that spending money on one's own speech must be permitted, and this is what political parties do when they make the expenditures FECA restricts. FECA calls spending of this nature a "contribution," and it is true that contributions can be restricted consistent with *Buckley*. As the plurality acknowledges, however, and as our cases hold, we cannot allow the Government's suggested labels to control our First Amendment analysis. . . .

The First Amendment embodies a "profound national commitment to the principle that debate on public issues should be uninhibited, robust, and wide-open." *New York Times Co. v. Sullivan*, 376 U.S. 254, 270 (1964). Political parties have a unique role in serving this principle; they exist to advance their members' shared political beliefs. . . . A party performs this function, in part, by "identify[ing] the people who constitute the association, and . . . limit[ing] the association to those people only." . . . Having identified its members, however, a party can give effect to their views only by selecting and supporting candidates. A political party has its own traditions and principles that transcend the interests of individual candidates and campaigns; but in the context of particular elections, candidates are necessary to make the party's message known and effective, and vice versa. . . .

We have a constitutional tradition of political parties and their candidates engaging in joint First Amendment activity; we also have a practical identity of interests between the two entities during an election. Party spending "in cooperation, consultation, or concert with" a candidate therefore is indistinguishable in substance from expenditures by the candidate or his campaign committee. . . .

I would resolve the Party's First Amendment claim in accord with these principles rather than remit the Party to further protracted proceedings. Because the plurality would do otherwise, I concur only in the judgment.

CHAPTER 5

⨎

INTEREST GROUPS

Interest groups are vital cogs in the wheels of the democratic process. Although *Federalist 10* suggests that one major purpose of the separation-of-powers system is to break and control the "evil effects" of faction, modern political theorists take a much more sanguine view of the role that political interest groups as well as parties play in government. No longer are interest groups defined as being opposed to the "public interest." They are vital channels through which particular publics participate in the governmental process. But the Madisonian theme of *Federalist 10* that attacks "factions" continues in our political rhetoric and influences our politics. In sharp contrast to Madison and the traditional view of interest groups, group theory, as we will see in this chapter, defines democratic politics in terms of specialized interests. Interest groups are not a necessary evil but the core of democratic politics.

Constitutional Background

Interest groups challenge Madison's carefully laid plans for limited and deliberative government in the national interest. Interest groups, or as Madison called them, factions, elevate special interests over the national interest. Madison designed the Constitution to filter factions through a process of balanced powers and representative government, which he explained in *The Federalist* papers 10, 47, 48, and 51, all of which are given in previous selections. The following selection discusses interest groups politics in our Madisonian system.

40

MADISON'S DILEMMA

Jeffrey M. Berry

A troubling dilemma lies at the core of the American political system. In an open and free society in which people have the right to express their political views, petition their government, and organize on behalf of causes, some segments of the population are likely to pursue their own selfish interests. Dairy farmers will push Congress to adopt price subsidies even though it means families will have to pay more at the grocery store. Manufacturers and labor unions will press for tariffs and other trade barriers to protect profits and jobs. Consumers, however, will be saddled with higher prices as a result. Environmentalists will fight for increasing the number of parks and wilderness preserves, though development of those lands might provide jobs for some who are out of work. In short, people will pursue their self-interest even though the policies they advocate may hurt others and may not be in the best interest of the nation.

The dilemma is this: If the government does not allow people to pursue their self-interest, it takes away their political freedom. When we took at the nations of the world in which people are forbidden to organize and to freely express their political views, we find that there the dilemma has been solved by authoritarianism. Although the alternative permitting people to advocate whatever they want is far more preferable, it carries dangers. In a system such as ours, interest groups constantly push government to enact policies that benefit small constituencies at the expense of the general public. This dilemma is as old as the country itself, yet never more relevant than today. As lobbying has grown in recent years, anxiety has mounted over the consequences of interest group politics. Political action committees (PACs) threaten the integrity of congressional elections. Liberal citizen groups are blamed for slowing economic development with the regulatory policies they have fought for. Labor unions are held responsible because America fails to compete effectively in many world markets, while tax cuts granted to businesses seem to increase their profits at the expense of huge federal budget deficits. Beyond the sins allegedly committed by sectors of the interest group community is a broader worry. Are the sheer number of interest groups and their collective power undermining American democracy?

Many agree that interest groups are an increasingly troublesome part of American politics, yet there is little consensus on what, if anything, ought to be done about it. The dilemma remains: Interest groups are no less a threat than they are an expression of freedom.

Curing the Mischiefs of Faction

Is there no middle ground between these two alternatives? Must a government accept one or the other? Contemporary discussions of this question inevitably turn to *The Federalist*, for James Madison's analysis in essay No. 10 remains the foundation of American political theory on interest groups.

With great foresight, Madison recognized the problem that the fragile new nation would face. Although at the time he was writing the country had no political parties or lobbies as we know them, Madison correctly perceived that people would organize in some way to further their common interests. Furthermore, these groupings, or "factions" as he called them, were a potential threat to popular government. Factions were not anomalies, nor would they be occasional problems. Rather, as Madison saw it, the propensity to pursue self-interest was innate. The "causes of faction," he concluded, are "sown in the nature of man."

As any society develops, it is inevitable that different social classes will emerge, that competing interests based on differing occupations will arise, and that clashing political philosophies will take hold among the populace. This tendency was strong in Madison's eyes: He warned that free men are more likely to try to oppress each other than they are to "co-operate for their common good."

Madison worried that a powerful faction could eventually come to tyrannize others in society. What, then, was the solution for "curing the mischiefs of faction"? He rejected out of hand any restrictions on the freedoms that permitted people to pursue their own selfish interests, remarking that the remedy would be "worse than the disease." Instead, he reasoned that the effects of faction must be controlled rather than eliminating factions themselves. This control could be accomplished by setting into place the structure of government proposed in the Constitution.

In Madison's mind, a republican form of government, as designed by the framers, would provide the necessary checks on the worst impulses of factions. A republican form of government gives responsibility for decisions to a small number of representatives who are elected by the larger citizenry. Furthermore, for a government whose authority extends over a large and dispersed population, the effects of faction would be diluted by the clash of many competing interests across the country. Thus, Madison believed that in a land as large as the United States, so many interests would arise that a representative government with its own checks and balances would not become dominated by any faction. Instead, government could deal with the views of all, producing policies that would be in the common good.

Madison's cure for the mischiefs of faction was something of a leap of faith.

The structure of American government has not, by itself, prevented some interests from gaining great advantage at the expense of others. Those with large resources have always been better represented by interest groups, and the least wealthy in society have suffered because of their failure to organize. Still, even though the republican form of government envisioned by Madison has not always been strong enough to prevent abuse by factions, the beliefs underlying *Federalist No. 10* have endured.

This view that the natural diversity of interests would prevent particular groups from dominating politics found a later incarnation in American social science of the 1950s and 1960s. Pluralist scholars argued that the many (that is, plural) interests in society found representation in the policymaking process through lobbying by organizations.

The bargaining that went on between such groups and government led to policies produced by compromise and consensus. Interest groups were seen as more beneficial to the system than Madison's factions, with emphasis placed on the positive contributions made by groups in speaking for their constituents before government. Although the pluralist school was later discredited for a number of reasons (these will be outlined shortly), it furthered the Madisonian ideal: groups freely participating in the policymaking process, none becoming too powerful because of the natural conflict of interests, and government acting as a synthesizer of competing interests. This ideal remains contemporary America's hope for making interest group politics compatible with democratic values.

Interest Groups and Their Functions

One purpose in this [reading] is to reexamine the fundamental questions raised by *Federalist No. 10.* Can an acceptable balance be struck between the right of people to pursue their own interests and the need to protect society from being dominated by one or more interests? Can we achieve true pluralism, or is a severe imbalance of interest group power a chronic condition in a free and open society?

Our means of answering this question will be to look broadly at behavior among contemporary interest groups. We will often follow research questions that political scientists have asked about the internal and external operations of lobbying organizations. Data for this study come not only from the literature on interest groups, but also from interviews with Washington lobbyists. Although the topics addressed are varied, one argument runs throughout: Important changes have taken place in interest group politics in recent years, because of which renewed thought must be given to controlling the effects of faction. . . .

Understanding Interest Groups

. . . [I]nterest groups remain misunderstood and maligned organizations. Americans distrust interest groups in general but value the organizations that represent them. People join an interest group not simply because they agree with its views but because they equate those views with the "public interest." Groups that stand on opposite sides of the same issues are regarded with disdain. Intellectually we accept the legitimacy of all interest groups; emotionally we separate them into those we support and those we must view with suspicion.

The basis of any reasoned judgment about interest groups is a factual understanding of how they operate. This is not easy, for though interest groups all have the same goal to influence government, organizationally and politically they seem endlessly diverse. Yet patterns are recognizable, and . . . such factors as size, type of membership, and resources are used to distinguish basic forms of interest group behavior.

To place this analysis in perspective, we must step back to see how perceptions and attitudes of political scientists toward interest groups have changed in the latter part of the twentieth century. This is more than an interesting piece of intellectual history: A critical change in the thinking of political scientists helped broaden acceptance of the role of interest groups in public policymaking. That change, in turn, helped spur the growth of interest groups.

The Rise and Fall of Pluralism

The early forerunner of pluralism in political science was known as "group theory," most widely associated with David Truman's *The Governmental Process*, published in 1951. Truman makes a simple assertion: Politics can be understood only by looking at the interaction of groups. He casts his lot with Madison, agreeing that "tendencies toward such groupings are 'sown in the nature of man.' " He also draws on cultural anthropology and social psychology to prove his case that political man is a product of group influences. "In all societies of any degree of complexity the individual is less affected directly by the society as a whole than differentially through various of its subdivisions, or groups.' "

The pluralist influence in political science reached its zenith a decade later when Robert Dahl published *Who Governs?*, a study of local politics in New Haven, Connecticut. Dahl examined three areas of local politics to see just who influenced policy outcomes. His crucial finding was that in the three areas—political party nominations, urban redevelopment, and public education—different groups of people were active and influential. New Haven did not have a small, closed circle of important people who together decided all the important issues in town politics.

Dahl found policymaking in New Haven to be a process by which loose coalitions of groups and politicians would become active on issues they cared about. Although most citizens might be apathetic about most issues, many do get interested in the issues that directly affect them. Businessmen were very active in urban redevelopment; teachers, school administrators, and the Parent Teacher Association (PTA) were involved in school politics. Politicians, always on the lookout for supporters, would court groups, hoping to build their own resources. Consequently, groups representing different interests were not only active, but their support was sought and their views carried weight.

Dahl argued that a realistic definition of democracy was not 50 percent plus one getting their way on each and every issue. Rather, as he wrote in an earlier work, the " 'normal' American political process [is] one in which there is a high probability that an active and legitimate group in the population can make itself heard effectively at some crucial stage in the process of decision."

Through bargaining and compromise between affected groups and political elites, democratic decisions are reached, with no one group consistently dominating. The influence of pluralist thought, and Dahl's writings in particular, was enormous. He had gone a step further than Truman by putting his findings in such an approving light. That is, he not only seemed to be saying this is the way things are, but this is the way things should be.

Policymaking through group interaction is a positive virtue, not a threat to democracy. Placing interest groups at the center of policymaking revived democratic theory by offering an explicit defense of the American political process.

Elegantly and systematically, pluralism made sense of the bargaining between interest groups and government officials. There was a reason to it beyond the selfishness of individual groups. To most social scientists who stood in the ideological mainstream of their disciplines, pluralism was an attractive counterpoint to radical critiques of American society. Books like C. Wright Mills's *The Power Elite* (1956) had gained a good deal of attention with the claim that America was ruled by a small stratum of wealthy and powerful individuals. Members of this power elite were said to be the true decision makers in society, "democracy" being an effective illusion perpetrated on the masses. But if the power elite thesis was false, as most social scientists believed it was, what was the counter theory?

Pluralism thus became the refutation of this damning interpretation of American politics. *Who Governs?* acknowledged that political elites had disproportionate amounts of resources but said that the use of these resources in ways inimical to the system was reasonably well countered by the natural working of interest group politics. Elected officials responded to different groups on different issues, seeking out groups to enhance their own power. Group politics forced elites to be responsive to a broad range of constituencies rather than to a small group of powerful individuals. . . .

Conclusion

The events of the 1960s led many Americans to question the way their democratic system was operating. For their part, American political scientists were more and more disillusioned with the dominant theory in their discipline that purported to explain how that democracy worked. Both alienation from American government and scholarly rejection of pluralism contributed to a powerful new idea: Increased participation was needed to balance a system of interest groups that skewed policymaking toward organizations unrepresentative of the American people.

Although no new theory as such came along to replace pluralism, the idea of expanded interest group participation by the chronically underrepresented was at least a first step toward finding a new solution to the dilemma of *Federalist No. 10*. Real world events and the philosophical musings of scholars that contributed to the movement toward increased participation by interest groups could not be selective in their influence. The new interest group politics went far beyond citizen participation programs and public interest groups for those traditionally unrepresented in the governmental process. Rather, extraordinary growth in all types of lobbying organizations raised anew questions about curing the mischiefs of faction.

The Nature and Functions of Interest Groups

Group theory is an important component of democratic political theory. The essence of group theory is that in the democratic process interest groups interact naturally and properly to produce public policy. In American political thought, the origins of this theory can be found in the theory of concurrent majority in John C. Calhoun's *Disquisition on Government*.

It is very useful to discuss the operation of interest groups within the framework of what can best be described as a *concurrent majority system*. In contemporary usage the phrase *concurrent majority* means a system in which major government policy decisions must be approved by the dominant interest groups directly affected. The word *concurrent* suggests that each group involved must give its consent before policy can be enacted. Thus a concurrent majority is a majority of each group considered separately. If we take as an example an area such as agricultural policy, in which three or four major private interest groups can be identified, we can say that the concurrent majority is reached when each group affected gives its approval before agricultural policy is passed. The extent to which such a system of concurrent majority is actually functioning is a matter that has not been fully clarified by empirical research. Nevertheless, it does seem tenable to conclude that in many major areas of public policy, it is necessary at least to achieve a concurrent majority of the *major* or *dominant* interests affected.

The *theory* of concurrent majority originated with John C. Calhoun. Calhoun, born in 1781, had a distinguished career in public service at both the national and state levels. The idea of concurrent majority evolved from the concept of state nullification of federal law. Under this states' rights doctrine, states would be able to veto any national action. The purpose of this procedure, theoretically, was to protect states in a minority from encroachment by a national majority that could act through Congress, the president, and even the Supreme Court. Those who favored this procedure had little faith in the separation-of-powers doctrine as an effective device to prevent the arbitrary exercise of national power. At the end of his career Calhoun decided to incorporate his earlier views on state nullification into a more substantial theoretical treatise in political science; thus he wrote his famous *Disquisition on Government* (New York: D. Appleton & Co., 1853) in the decade between 1840 and 1850. He attempted to develop a general theory of constitutional (limited) government, the primary mechanism of which would be the ability of the major interest groups (states in Calhoun's time) to veto legislation adverse to their interests. Students should overlook some of the theoretical inconsistencies in Calhoun and concentrate upon the basic justification he advances for substituting his system of concurrent majority for the separation-of-powers device. Under the latter, group interests are not necessarily taken into account, for national laws can be passed on the basis of a numerical majority. And even though this majority may reflect the interests of some groups, it will not necessarily reflect the interests of all groups affected. Calhoun argued that a system in which the major interest groups can dominate the policy process is really more in accord with constitutional democracy than the system established in our Constitution and supported in *Federalist 10*.

The group theory of John C. Calhoun has been updated and carried over into modern political science by several writers, one of the most important being David B. Truman. David Truman's selection, taken from The Governmental Process (1951), contains (1) a definition of the term interest group and (2) a brief outline of the frame of reference within which the operations of interest groups should be considered. A fairly articulate interest group theory of the governmental process is sketched by Truman. It will become evident to the student of American government that interest groups, like political parties, form an integral part of our political system. Further, interest group theory suggests an entirely new way of looking at government.

— 41 —

THE GOVERNMENTAL PROCESS

David B. Truman

༄

Interest Groups

Interest group refers to any group that, on the basis of one or more shared attitudes, makes certain claims upon other groups in the society for the establishment, maintenance, or enhancement of forms of behavior that are implied by the shared attitudes. . . . [F]rom interaction in groups arise certain common habits of response, which may be called norms, or shared attitudes. These afford the participants frames of reference for interpreting and evaluating events and behaviors. In this respect all groups are interest groups because they are shared-attitude groups. In some groups at various points in time, however, a second kind of common response emerges, in addition to the frame of reference. These are shared attitudes toward what is needed or wanted in a given situation, as demands or claims upon other groups in the society. The term "interest group" will be reserved here for those groups that exhibit both aspects of the shared attitudes. . . .

Definition of the interest group in this fashion . . . permits the identification of various potential as well as existing interest groups. That is, it invites examination of an interest whether or not it is found at the moment as one of the characteristics of a particular organized group. Although no group that makes claims upon other groups in society will be found without an interest or interests, it is possible to examine interests that are not at a particular point in time the basis of interactions among individuals, but that may become such. . . .

Groups and Government: Difficulties in a Group Interpretation of Politics

Since we are engaged in an effort to develop a conception of the political process in the United States that will account adequately for the role of groups, particularly interest groups, it will be appropriate to take account of some of the factors that have been regarded as obstacles to such a conception and that have caused such groups to be neglected in many explanations of the dynamics of government. Perhaps the most important practical reason for this neglect is that the significance of groups has only fairly recently been forced to the attention of political scientists by the tremendous growth in the number of formally organized groups in the United States within the last few decades. It is difficult and unnecessary to attempt to date the beginning of such attention, but Herring in 1929, in his groundbreaking book, *Group Representation Before Congress*, testified to the novelty of the observations he reported when he stated: "There has developed in this government an extra-legal machinery of as integral and of as influential a nature as the system of party government that has long been an essential part of the government. . . . " Some implications of this development are not wholly compatible with some of the proverbial notions about representative government held by specialists as well as laymen. . . . This apparent incompatibility has obstructed the inclusion of group behaviors in an objective description of the governmental process.

More specifically, it is usually argued that any attempt at the interpretation of politics in terms of group patterns inevitably "leaves something out" or "destroys something essential" about the processes of "our" government. On closer examination, we find this argument suggesting that two "things" are certain to be ignored: the individual, and a sort of totally inclusive unity designated by such terms as "society" and "the state."

The argument that the individual is ignored in any interpretation of politics as based upon groups seems to assume a differentiation or conflict between "the individual" and some such collectivity as the group. . . .

Such assumptions need not present any difficulties in the development of a group interpretation of politics, because they are essentially unwarranted. They simply do not square with . . . evidence concerning group affiliations and individual behavior. . . . We do not, in fact, find individuals otherwise than in groups; complete isolation in space and time is so rare as to be an almost hypothetical situation. It is equally demonstrable that the characteristics of any interest group, including the activities by which we identify it, are governed by the attitudes and the circumstances that gave rise to the interactions of which it consists. There are variable factors, and, although the role played by a particular individual may be quite different in a lynch mob from that of the same individual in a meeting of the church deacons, the attitudes and behaviors involved in both are as much a part of his personality as is his treatment of his family. "The individual" and "the group" are at most merely convenient ways of classifying behavior, two ways of approaching the same phenomena, not different things.

The persistence among nonspecialists of the notion of an inherent conflict between "the individual" and "the group" or "society" is understandable in view of the doctrines of individualism that have underlain various political and economic conflicts over the past three centuries. The notion persists also because it harmonizes with a view of the isolated and independent individual as the "cause" of complicated human events. The personification of events, quite apart from any ethical considerations, is a kind of shorthand convenient in everyday speech and, like supernatural explanations of natural phenomena, has a comforting simplicity. Explanations that take into account multiple causes, including group affiliations, are difficult. The "explanation" of a national complex like the Soviet Union wholly in terms of a Stalin or the "description" of the intricacies of the American government entirely in terms of a Roosevelt is quick and easy. . . .

The second major difficulty allegedly inherent in any attempt at a group interpretation of the political process is that such an explanation inevitably must ignore some greater unity designated as society or the state. . . .

Many of those who place particular emphasis upon this difficulty assume explicitly or implicitly that there is an interest of the nation as a whole, universally and invariably held and standing apart from and superior to those of the various groups included within it. This assumption is close to the popular dogmas of democratic government based on the familiar notion that if only people are free and have access to "the facts," they will all want the same thing in any political situation. It is no derogation of democratic preferences to state that such an assertion flies in the face of all that we know of the behavior of men in a complex society. Were it in fact true, not only the interest group but even the political party should properly be viewed as an abnormality. The differing experiences and perceptions of men not only encourage individuality but also . . . inevitably result in differing attitudes and conflicting group affiliations. "There are," says Bentley in his discussion of this error of the social whole, "always some parts of the nation to be found arrayed against other parts." [From *The Process of Government* (1908).] Even in war, when a totally inclusive interest should be apparent if it is ever going to be, we always find pacifists, conscientious objectors, spies, and subversives, who reflect interests opposed to those of "the nation as a whole."

There is a political significance in assertions of a totally inclusive interest within a nation. Particularly in times of crisis, such as an international war, such claims are a tremendously useful promotional device by means of which a particularly extensive group or league of groups tries to reduce or eliminate opposing interests. Such is the pain attendant upon not "belonging" to one's "own" group that if a normal person can be convinced that he is the lone dissenter to an otherwise universally accepted agreement, he usually will conform. This pressure accounts at least in part for the number of prewar pacifists who, when the United States entered World War II, accepted the draft or volunteered. Assertion of an inclusive "national" or "public interest" is an effective device in many less critical situations as well. In themselves, these claims are part of the data of politics. However, they do not describe any actual or possible political situation within a complex modern nation. In developing a group interpretation of politics, therefore, we do not need to account for a totally inclusive interest, because one does not exist.

Denying the existence of an interest of the nation as a whole does not completely dispose of the difficulty raised by those who insist that a group interpretation must omit "the state." We cannot deny the obvious fact that we are examining a going political system that is supported or at least accepted by a large proportion of the society. We cannot account for such a system by adding up in some fashion the National Association of Manufacturers, the Congress of Industrial Organizations, the American Farm Bureau Federation, the American Legion, and other groups that come to mind when "lobbies" and "pressure groups" are mentioned. Even if the political parties are added to the list, the result could properly be designated as "a view which seems hardly compatible with the relative stability of the political system. . . ." Were such the exclusive ingredients of the political process in the United States, the entire system would have torn itself apart long since.

If these various organized interest groups more or less consistently reconcile their differences, adjust, and accept compromises, we must acknowledge that we are dealing with a system that is not accounted for by the "sum" of the organized interest groups in the society. We must go further to explain the operation of such ideals or traditions as constitutionalism, civil liberties, representative responsibility, and the like. These are not, however, a sort of disembodied metaphysical influence, like Mr. Justice Holmes's "brooding omnipresence." We know of the existence of such factors only from the behavior and the habitual interactions of men. If they exist in this fashion, they are interests. We can account for their operation and for the system by recognizing such interests as representing what . . . we called potential interest groups in the "becoming" stage of activity. "It is certainly true," as Bentley has made clear, "that we must accept a . . . group of this kind as an interest group itself." It makes no difference that we cannot find the home office and the executive secretary of such a group. Organization in this formal sense, as we have seen, represents merely a stage or degree of interaction that may or may not be significant at any particular point in time. Its absence does not mean that these interests do not exist, that the familiar "pressure groups" do not operate as if such potential groups were organized and active, or that these interests may not move from the potential to the organized stage of activity.

It thus appears that the two major difficulties supposedly obstacles to a group interpretation of the political process are not insuperable. We can employ the fact of individuality and we can account for the existence of the state without doing violence to the evidence available from the observed behaviors of men and groups. . . .

Interest Groups and the Nature of the State

Men, wherever they are observed, are creatures participating in those established patterns of interaction that we call groups. Excepting perhaps the most casual and transitory, these continuing interactions, like all such interpersonal relationships, involve power. This power is exhibited in two closely interdependent ways. In the first place, the group exerts power over its members; an individual's group affiliations largely determine his attitudes, values, and the frames of reference in terms of which he interprets his experiences. For a measure of conformity to the norms of the group is the price of acceptance within it. . . . In the second place, the group, if it is or becomes an interest group, which any group in society may be, exerts power over other groups in the society when it successfully imposes claims upon them.

Many interest groups, probably an increasing proportion in the United States, are politicized. That is, either from the outset or from time to time in the course of their development they make their claims through or upon the institutions of government. Both the forms and functions of government in turn are a reflection of the activities and claims of such groups. . . .

The institutions of government are centers of interest-based power; their connections with interest groups may be latent or overt and their activities range in political character from the routinized and widely accepted to the unstable and highly controversial. In order to make claims, political interest groups will seek access to the key points of decision within these institutions. Such points are scattered throughout the structure, including not only the formally established branches of government but also the political parties in their various forms and the relationships between governmental units and other interest groups. The extent to which a group achieves effective access to the institutions of government is the resultant of a complex of interdependent factors. For the sake of simplicity these may be classified in three somewhat overlapping categories: (1) factors relating to a group's strategic position in the society; (2) factors associated with the internal characteristics of the group; and (3) factors peculiar to the governmental institutions themselves. In the first category are: the group's status or prestige in the society, affecting the ease with which it commands deference from those outside its bounds; the standing it and its activities have when measured against the widely held but largely unorganized interests or "rules of the game"; the extent to which government officials are formally or informally "members" of the group; and the usefulness of the group as a source of technical and political knowledge. The second category includes: the degree of appropriateness of the group's organization; the degree of cohesion it can achieve in a given situation, especially in the light of competing group demands upon its membership; the skills of the leadership; and the group's resources in numbers and money. In the third category are: the operating structure of the government institutions, since such established features involve relatively fixed advantages and handicaps; and the effects of the group life of particular units or branches of the government. . . .

A characteristic feature of the governmental system in the United States is that it contains a multiplicity of points of access. The federal system establishes decentralized and more or less independent centers of power, vantage points from which to secure privileged access to the national government. Both a sign and a cause of the strength of the constituent units in the federal scheme is the peculiar character of our party system, which has strengthened parochial relationships, especially those of national legislators. National parties, and to a lesser degree those in the states, tend to be poorly cohesive leagues of locally based organizations rather than unified and inclusive structures. Staggered terms for executive officials and various types of legislators accentuate differences in the effective electorates that participate in choosing these officers. Each of these different, often opposite, localized patterns (constituencies) is a channel of independent access to the larger party aggregation and to the formal government. Thus, especially at the national level, the party is an electing-device and only in limited measure an integrated means of policy determination. Within the Congress, furthermore, controls are diffused among committee chairmen and other leaders in both chambers. The variety of these points of access is further supported by relationships stemming from the constitutional doctrine of separation of powers, from related checks and balances, and at the state and local level from the common practice of choosing an array of executive officials by popular election. At the federal level the formal simplicity of the executive branch has been complicated by a Supreme Court decision that has placed a number of administrative agencies beyond the removal power of the President. The position of these units, however, differs only in degree from that of many that are constitutionally within the Executive Branch. In consequence of alternative lines of access available through the legislature and the Executive and of divided channels for the control of administrative policy, many nominally executive agencies are at various times virtually independent of the Chief Executive.

 . . . Within limits, therefore, organized interest groups, gravitating toward responsive points of decision, may play one segment of the structure against another as circumstances and strategic considerations permit. The total pattern of government over a period of time thus presents a protean complex of crisscrossing relationships that change in strength and direction with alterations in the power and standing of interests, organized and unorganized.

From Truman's definition any group, organized or unorganized, that has a shared attitude toward goals and methods for achieving them should be classified as an interest group. Truman is essentially saying that, since people generally function as members of groups, it is more useful and accurate for the political observer to view the governmental process as the interaction of political interest groups. If one accepts the sociologist's assumption that people act and interact only as members of groups, then it is imperative that the governmental process be viewed as one of interest group interaction.

Within the framework of Truman's definition it is possible to identify both *public* and *private* interest groups. In the political process, governmental groups sometimes act as interest groups in the same sense as private organizations. In many public policies, governmental groups may have more at stake than private organizations. Thus administrative agencies, for example, may lobby as vigorously as their private counterparts to advance their own interests.

Theodore Lowi refers to group theory as "interest-group liberalism." The following selection is taken from his well-known book *The End of Liberalism* (1969), in which he severely criticizes group theory and its pervasive influence upon governmental decision makers. In reading the following selection, remember that the author does not use the term *liberal* in its ordinary sense. The political "liberal" in Lowi's terminology is much like the "economic Liberal" of the early nineteenth century. Just as economic liberalism preached that the public good emerged automatically from the free clash of private interests, the political liberal (in Lowi's terms) supports group theory, which holds that the public interest in government is automatically achieved through the interaction of pressure groups.

42

THE END OF LIBERALISM: THE INDICTMENT

Theodore J. Lowi

The corruption of modern democratic government began with the emergence of interest-group liberalism as the public philosophy. Its corrupting influence takes at least four important forms, four counts, therefore, of an indictment. . . . Also to be indicted, on at least three counts, is the philosophic component of the ideology, pluralism.

Summation 1: Four Counts Against the Ideology

1. Interest-group liberalism as public philosophy corrupts democratic government because it deranges and confuses expectations about democratic institutions. Liberalism promotes popular decision-making but derogates from the decisions so made by misapplying the notion to the implementation as well as the formulation of policy. It derogates from the processes by treating all values in the process as equivalent interests. It derogates from democratic rights by allowing their exercise in foreign policy, and by assuming they are being exercised when access is provided. Liberal practices reveal a basic disrespect for democracy. Liberal leaders do not wield the authority of democratic government with the resoluteness of men certain of the legitimacy of their positions, the integrity of their institutions, or the justness of the programs they serve.

2. Interest-group liberalism renders government impotent. Liberal governments cannot plan. Liberals are copious in plans but irresolute in planning. Nineteenth-century liberalism was standard without plans. This was an anachronism in the modern state. But twentieth-century liberalism turned out to be plans without standards. As an anachronism it, too, ought to pass. But doctrines are not organisms. They die only in combat over the minds of men, and no doctrine yet exists capable of doing the job. All the popular alternatives are so very irrelevant, helping to explain the longevity of interest-group liberalism. Barry Goldwater most recently proved the irrelevance of one. The embourgeoisement of American unions suggests the irrelevance of others.

The Departments of Agriculture, Commerce, and Labor provide illustrations, but hardly exhaust illustrations, of such impotence. Here clearly one sees how liberalism has become a doctrine whose means are its ends, whose combatants are its clientele, whose standards are not even those of the mob but worse, are those the bargainers can fashion to fit the bargain. Delegation of power has become alienation of public domain—the gift of sovereignty to private satrapies. The political barriers to withdrawal of delegation are high enough. But liberalism reinforces these through the rhetoric of justification and often even permanent legal reinforcement: Public corporations—justified, oddly, as efficient planning instruments—permanently alienate rights of central coordination to the directors and to those who own the corporation bonds. Or, as Walter Adams finds, the "most pervasive method . . . for alienating public domain is the certificate of convenience and necessity, or some variation thereof in the form of an exclusive franchise, license or permit. . . . Government has become increasingly careless and subservient in issuing them. The net result is a general legalization of private monopoly. . . ." While the best examples still are probably the 10 self-governing systems of agriculture policy, these are obviously only a small proportion of all the barriers the interest-group liberal ideology has erected to democratic use of government.

3. Interest-group liberalism demoralizes government, because liberal governments cannot achieve justice. The question of justice has engaged the best minds for almost as long as there have been notions of state and politics, certainly ever since Plato defined the ideal as one in which republic and justice were synonymous. And since that time philosophers have been unable to agree on what justice is. But outside the ideal, in the realms of actual government and citizenship, the problem is much simpler. We do not have to define justice at all in order to weight and assess justice in government, because in the case of liberal policies we are prevented by what the law would call a "jurisdictional fact." In the famous jurisdictional case of *Marbury v. Madison* Chief Justice Marshall held that even if all the Justices hated President Jefferson for refusing to accept Marbury and the other "midnight judges" appointed by Adams, there was nothing they could do. They had no authority to judge President Jefferson's action one way or another because the Supreme Court did not possess such jurisdiction over the President. In much the same way, there is something about liberalism that prevents us from raising the question of justice at all, no matter what definition of justice is used.

Liberal governments cannot achieve justice because their policies lack the sine qua non of justice—that quality without which a consideration of justice cannot even be initiated. Considerations of the justice in or achieved by an action cannot be made unless a deliberate and conscious attempt was made by the actor to derive his action from a general rule or moral principle governing such a class of acts. One can speak personally of good rules and bad rules, but a homily or a sentiment, like liberal legislation, is not a rule at all. The best rule is one which is relevant to the decision or action in question and is general in the sense that those involved with it have no direct control over its operation. A general rule is, hence, a priori. Any governing regime that makes a virtue of avoiding such rules puts itself totally outside the context of justice.

Take the homely example of the bull and the china shop. Suppose it was an op art shop and that we consider op worthy only of the junk pile. That being the case, the bull did us a great service, the more so because it was something we always dreamed of doing but were prevented by law from entering and breaking. But however much we may be pleased, we cannot judge the act. We can only like or dislike the consequences. The consequences are haphazard; the bull cannot have intended them. The act was a thoughtless, animal act which bears absolutely no relation to any aesthetic principle. We don't judge the bull. We only celebrate our good fortune. Without the general rule, the bull can reenact his scenes of creative destruction daily and still not be capable of achieving, in this case, aesthetic justice. The whole idea of justice is absurd.

The general rule ought to be a legislative rule because the United States espouses the ideal of representative democracy. However, that is merely an extrinsic feature of the rule. All that counts is the character of the rule itself. Without the rule we can only like or dislike the consequences of the governmental action. In the question of whether justice is achieved, a government without good rules, and without acts carefully derived therefrom, is merely a big bull in an immense china shop.

4. Finally, interest-group liberalism corrupts democratic government in the degree to which it weakens the capacity of governments to live by democratic formalisms. Liberalism weakens democratic institutions by opposing formal procedure with informal bargaining. Liberalism derogates from democracy by derogating from all formality in favor of informality. Formalism is constraining; playing it "by the book" is a role often unpopular in American war films and sports films precisely because it can dramatize personal rigidity and the plight of the individual in collective situations. Because of the impersonality of formal procedures, there is inevitably a separation in the real world between the forms and the realities, and this kind of separation gives rise to cynicism, for informality means that some will escape their collective fate better than others. There has as a consequence always been a certain amount of cynicism toward public objects in the United States, and this may be to the good, since a little cynicism is the father of healthy sophistication. However, when the informal is elevated to a positive virtue, and hard-won access becomes a share of official authority, cynicism becomes distrust. It ends in reluctance to submit one's fate to the governmental process under any condition, as is the case in the United States in the mid-1960s.

Public officials more and more frequently find their fates paradoxical and their treatment at the hands of the public fickle and unjust when in fact they are only reaping the results of their own behavior, including their direct and informal treatment of the public and the institutions through which they serve the public. The more government operates by the spreading of access, the more public order seems to suffer. The more public men pursue their constituencies, the more they seem to find their constituencies alienated. Liberalism has promoted concentration of democratic authority but deconcentration of democratic power. Liberalism has opposed privilege in policy formulation only to foster it, quite systematically, in the implementation of policy. Liberalism has consistently failed to recognize, in short, that in a democracy forms are important. In a medieval monarchy all formalisms were at court. Democracy proves, for better or worse, that the masses like that sort of thing too.

Another homely parable may help. In the good old days, everyone in the big city knew that traffic tickets could be fixed. Not everyone could get his ticket fixed, but nonetheless a man who honestly paid his ticket suffered in some degree a dual loss: his money, and his self-esteem for having so little access. Cynicism was widespread, violations were many, but perhaps it did not matter, for there were so few automobiles. Suppose, however, that as the automobile population increased a certain city faced a traffic crisis and the system of ticket fixing came into ill repute. Suppose a mayor, victorious on the Traffic Ticket, decided that, rather than eliminate fixing by universalizing enforcement, he would instead reform the system by universalizing the privileges of ticket fixing. One can imagine how the system would work. One can imagine that some sense of equality would prevail, because everyone could be made almost equally free to bargain with the ticket administrators. But one would find it difficult to imagine how this would make the total city government more legitimate. Meanwhile, the purpose of the ticket would soon have been destroyed.

Traffic regulation, fortunately, was not so reformed. But many other government activities were. The operative principles of interest-group liberalism possess the mentality of a world of universalized ticket fixing: Destroy privilege by universalizing it. Reduce conflict by yielding to it. Redistribute power by the maxim of each according to his claim. Reserve an official place for every major structure of power. Achieve order by worshipping the processes (as distinguished from the forms and the procedures) by which order is presumed to be established.

If these operative principles will achieve equilibrium—and such is far from proven—that is all they will achieve. Democracy will have disappeared, because all of these maxims are founded upon profound lack of confidence in democracy. Democracy fails when it lacks confidence in its own authority.

Democratic forms were supposed to precede and accompany the formulation of politics so that policies could be implemented authoritatively and firmly. Democracy is indeed a form of absolutism, but ours was fairly well contrived to be an absolutist government under the strong control of consent-building prior to taking authoritative action in law. Interest-group liberalism fights the absolutism of democracy but succeeds only in taking away its authoritativeness. Whether it is called "creative federalism" by President Johnson, "cooperation" by the farmers, "local autonomy" by the Republicans, or "participatory democracy" by the New Left, the interest-group liberal effort does not create democratic power but rather negates it.

***

How American Government and Politics Enhance Interest Group Power

The unique characteristics of our Madisonian government and our political process contribute to interest group power as the following selection describes.

43

INTEREST GROUPS AND THE AMERICAN POLITICAL SYSTEM

Mark J. Rozell and Clyde Wilcox

Interest groups' high level of involvement in American elections stems, in part, from distinctive characteristics of American government, political parties, and elections. First, governmental decision making offers multiple incentives and opportunities for influencing policy. Second, the major U.S. parties are permeable to outside interests, enabling interest group activists to obtain powerful positions within local, state, and national party organizations. Third, American elections are unique: they are much more frequent than those of most other Western democracies, and far smaller percentages of citizens vote. Moreover, American elections are candidate centered: candidates must decide to run, raise their own funds, assemble their own coalitions, and reach voters with carefully targeted messages—all of which occurs outside the formal party structure.

Characteristics of American Government

At the saine time that our federal system creates incentives for interest group involvement, it also places demands on interest groups, which must work within the system in order to successfully influence policy. First, because policy can be made at the national, state, and local levels, interest groups are generally called upon to be active at all three levels. . . .

Second, interest groups are well aware that local councils and state legislatures constitute a "pipeline" of potential candidates for the House of Representatives. Thus, they often participate in state and local races with the intention of cultivating arid training potential candidates for national office.

Third, the division of powers between the executive and legislative branches means that interest groups must try to cultivate access to both the president and Congress. Given that the executive and legislative branches have different constituencies, timetables, and interests, this is a difficult enough task, but it has been made even more complex during the past forty years because the two branches have often been under the control of different parties. . . .

Fourth, because members of Congress are not bound to vote for the policies of party leaders but are independent actors, even those of the minority party are in a position to help or hurt an interest group's policy agenda. Any member of the House or Senate can introduce a bill drafted in consultation with an interest group and offer amendments in committee or on the floor to make the bill more palatable to interest groups. When a bill is up for a vote, members of Congress may vote however they choose. In the Senate, any member can put a "hold" on a bill, delaying a vote perhaps indefinitely.

[I]nterest groups often bolster their lobbying efforts by engaging in electoral activities. By helping members of Congress win elections, interest groups hope to establish relationships with senators and representatives and to get some return on their investment in the form of public policy actions. On occasion, relationships cultivated through electoral activity enable interest groups to build coalitions in support of their policy positions, even over the objections of party leaders.

Finally, the U.S. government is perhaps more willing than that of many other countries to distribute particularistic economic benefits to interest groups. Appropriations, tax, and even substantive bills such as highway bills are generally filled with specific language benefiting one or more companies or interest groups. Corporations get government contracts, special tax provisions, and exemptions from regulations (or, more commonly, delays in implementing regulations), all of which can affect their profits. In addition, members of Congress and occasionally even presidents intercede with the bureaucracy in an attempt to win favorable treatment for particular groups. The opportunity to obtain specific economic benefits is yet another incentive for interest groups to develop close relationships with policy makers—and one important way to do so is through electoral politics.

Characteristics of American Parties

Like the American government, American political parties differ from their counterparts in other democracies. In many countries, parties are closely linked with one or a few interests that they can be said to represent. In Europe, labor unions are represented by labor or social democratic parties, the Catholic Church speaks through Christian democratic parties, environmentalists have formed "green" parties, and very conservative citizens are represented by "new radical right" parties. In Israel, orthodox religious groups have their own political parties. In some countries, interest groups are represented by distinct sectors of a party. In Mexico, for example, the Partido Revolucionario Institucionalizado (PRI) has separate sectors representing agriculture, workers, and students.

In the United States, however, the parties have established relationships with a variety of interest groups that make up their core constituencies, but they also interact with groups that are nonpartisan or that are willing to back candidates of either party. . . .

Because interest groups have resources—mailing lists, newsletters, conventions, and volunteers—that can help political parties reach out to group members and other voters, parties often rely on interest groups to help them communicate with voters, often working closely with particular groups to develop and distribute distinctive messages targeting group members. When GOP leaders want to get the word out to white evangelical voters that theirs is the party of moral conservatism, they ask the Christian Coalition to carry the message in its publications, to distribute voters' guides in conservative churches, and to allow party leaders to speak at the organization's annual convention. Similarly, Democratic officials rely on unions to reach workers, on feminist organizations to reach working women, and on environmental groups to reach voters who are concerned about pollution.

Perhaps the most distinctive feature of American parties and elections is that party leaders play only a small role in selecting candidates. Through party primaries, caucuses, and conventions, interest groups can help to determine which candidates win nomination and can even work to nominate activists and members from their own groups. Although party officials are usually neutral in intraparty contests, interest groups both individually and in coalition with others are extremely active in aiding one candidate over another. . . .

Finally, unlike many European parties, which receive most or all of their campaign money from the government, American parties must raise their own money from individual and group contributions. Interest groups provide much of the money for parties through a variety of legal mechanisms. Money from interest groups helps fund party electoral activities, as well as buildings, computers, and party workers' salaries. Interest groups also contribute to party foundations and think tanks that develop policy proposals for party leaders.

Characteristics of American Elections

Elections are a necessary component of democracy, but democracies implement elections in very different ways. In most countries, elections are held at regular intervals and generally occur at the same time, both for national executive and legislative offices and for regional and local government posts. Moreover, campaigns in most countries are relatively short: in Britain, for example, the 1996 campaign lasted six weeks and included all the seats in the national legislature and most local races.

In the United States, in contrast, elections are held almost continuously. . . . .

Because members of the House of Representatives stand for election every two years, representatives are constantly running for reelection—raising money, addressing voters, refining their images and their messages. And their challengers sometimes begin campaigning more than a year before the election. Senators, who are elected for six-year terms, generally campaign for at least two years, and some focus on fund raising throughout their terms. Even before a new president is sworn into office, prospective candidates from the other major party may drop in on the early presidential caucus and primary states of Iowa and New Hampshire to "test the political waters."

Another distinctive characteristic of American elections is that they are candidate centered. . . .

The difficulties of running a candidate-centered campaign render interest groups obvious allies. Interest groups can recruit candidates and encourge them to run, help finance their campaigns, and assist them in selecting campaign themes. By providing access to special communication channels such as newsletters and group gatherings, interest groups can also help candidates reach interest group members effectively and inexpensively. . . .

A third unique characteristic of American elections is the low rate of voter turnout. . . .

Low levels of voter turnout create opportunities for organized groups to greatly influence election outcomes. . . .

Finally, American elections are nearly always winner-take-all contests in single-member districts. To see why this creates an incentive for interest groups to participate in elections, consider the consequences of a 2 percent shift under two different systems: if German labor unions succeeded in increasing by 2 percent the vote share of the German Social Democratic Party, that party would gain approximately 2 percent of the seats in the Bundestag, the German parliament, because a party's share of seats in the legislature is proportional to its percentage of the popular vote. In the United States, where representation is not proportional but is based on single-member districts, a 2 percent increase in the Democratic Party's share of the vote for the U.S. House would likely enable Democrats to regain control of that body, because the increase would allow a number of Democratic candidates in close races to win the seats. Thus, a modest aggregate swing in votes may allow one party to capture most of the close contests in the United States, resulting in a much larger swing in seats. In 1994, the Republicans won control of the House by a net swing of less than 2 percent of the popular vote. . . .

Taken together, the distinctive features of American government, parties, and elections give interest groups many opportunities and incentives to participate in election campaigns. . . .

Money, PACS, and Elections

Political campaigning has become increasingly expensive at all levels of government. Only presidential campaigns are publicly funded, although candidates in presidential primaries have to garner a certain amount of private contributions to qualify for federal matching funds. The rise of political action committees, which the campaign finance laws of the 1970s recognized as legitimate, has enhanced the influence of private money and interest group power in the political process. Money and politics go together in the contemporary political environment, and political action committees are a major source of campaign funds. While PACs are perfectly legitimate organizations, authorized and even encouraged by the campaign finance laws of the 1970s, they are often portrayed as the bad guys of American politics. They are the modern-day "factions" of the James Madison attack in *Federalist 10*. The author of the following selection suggests that PAC-bashing is overdone.

44

THE MISPLACED OBSESSION WITH PACS

Larry J. Sabato

The disturbing statistics and the horror stories about political action committees seem to flow like a swollen river, week after week, year in and year out. Outrage extends across the ideological spectrum: the liberal interest group Common Cause has called the system "scandalous," while conservative former senator Barry Goldwater (R–Ariz.) has bluntly declared, "PAC money is destroying the election process. . . ."

In more and more recent campaigns, political action committees have been portrayed as the central corrupting evil in American politics. In Massachusetts in 1984, for example, all the major contenders for the U.S. Senate in both parties refused to take PAC money, and one candidate even got his Democratic opponent to sign a statement pledging to resign his seat in Congress should he "ever knowingly accept and keep a campaign contribution from a political action committee."

Candidates from Maine to California have scored points by for-swearing the acceptance of PAC gifts earlier and more fervently than their opponents. The Democratic party included in its 1984 national platform a call for banning PAC funds from all federal elections, despite its aggressiveness in attracting PAC money to itself and its candidates.

PAC-bashing is undeniably a popular campaign sport, but the "big PAC attack" is an opiate that obscures the more vital concerns and problems in campaign finance. PAC excesses are merely a symptom of other serious maladies in the area of political money, but the near-obsessive focus by public interest groups and the news media on the PAC evils has diverted attention from more fundamental matters. The PAC controversy, including the charges most frequently made against them, can help explain why PACs are best described as agents of pseudo corruption.

The PAC Era

While a good number of PACs of all political persuasions existed prior to the 1970s, it was during that decade of campaign reform that the modern PAC era began. Spawned by the Watergate-inspired revisions of the campaign finance laws, PACs grew in number from 113 in 1972 to 4,196 by 1988, and their contributions to congressional candidates multiplied more than fifteenfold, from $8.5 million in 1971–72 to $130.3 million in 1985–86.

The rapid rise of PACs has engendered much criticism, yet many of the charges made against political action committees are exaggerated and dubious. While the widespread use of the PAC structure is new, special interest money of all types has always found its way into politics. Before the 1970s it simply did so in less traceable and far more disturbing and unsavory ways. And while, in absolute terms, PACs contribute a massive sum to candidates, it is not clear that there is proportionately more interest-group money in the system than before. As political scientist Michael Malbin has argued, we will never know the truth because the earlier record is so incomplete.

The proportion of House and Senate campaign funds provided by PACs has certainly increased since the early 1970s, but individuals, most of whom are unaffiliated with PACs, together with the political parties, still supply about three-fifths of all the money spent by or on behalf of House candidates and three-quarters of the campaign expenditures for Senate contenders. So while the importance of PAC spending has grown, PACs clearly remain secondary as a source of election funding. PACs, then, seem rather less awesome when considered within the entire spectrum of campaign finance.

Apart from the argument over the relative weight of PAC funds, PAC critics claim that political action committees are making it more expensive to run for office. There is some validity to this assertion. Money provided to one candidate funds the purchase of campaign tools that the other candidate must match in order to stay competitive.

In the aggregate, American campaign expenditures seem huge. In 1988, the total amount spent by all U.S. House of Representatives candidates taken together was about $256 million, and the campaign cost of the winning House nominee averaged over $392,000. Will Rogers's 1931 remark has never been more true: "Politics has got so expensive that it takes lots of money to even get beat with."

Yet $256 million is far less than the annual advertising budgets of many individual commercial enterprises. These days it is expensive to communicate, whether the message is political or commercial. Television time, polling costs, consultants' fees, direct-mail investment, and other standard campaign expenditures have been soaring in price, over and above inflation. PACs have been fueling the use of new campaign techniques, but a reasonable case can be made that such expenses are necessary, and that more and better communication is required between candidates and an electorate that often appears woefully uninformed about politics. PACs therefore may be making a positive contribution by providing the means to increase the flow of information during elections.

PACs are also accused of being biased toward the incumbent, and except for the ideological committees, they do display a clear and overwhelming preference for those already in office. But the same bias is apparent in contributions from individuals, who ask the same reasonable, perhaps decisive, economic question: Why waste money on contenders if incumbents almost always win? On the other hand, the best challengers—those perceived as having fair-to-good chances to win—are usually generously funded by PACs. Well-targeted PAC challenger money clearly helped the GOP win a majority in the U.S. Senate in 1980, for instance, and in turn aided the Democrats in their 1986 Senate takeover.

The charge that PACs limit the number of strong challengers is true, because by giving so much money so early in the race to incumbents, they deter potential opponents from declaring their candidacies. On the other hand, the money that PACs channel to competitive challengers late in the election season may actually help increase the turnover of officeholders on election day. PAC money also tends to invigorate competitiveness in open-seat congressional races where there is no incumbent.

One line of attack on PACs that seems fairly justified is the feeling that these important components of our democratic political system are themselves undemocratic in some respects. For example, in some cases their candidate selection process completely severs the connecting link between contributor and candidate. As political scientist David Adamany has noted, this condition is most apparent in many of the politically ideological nonconnected PACs, whose lack of a parent body and whose freestyle organization make them accountable to no one and responsive mainly to their own whims. Leaders of ideological PACs, however, insist that their committees are still democratic, since contributors will simply stop giving if dissatisfied with the PACs' candidate choices.

But ideological PACs raise most of their money by direct mail, which means that the average donor's only source of information about the PAC's activities is their own communication, which, not surprisingly, tends to be upbeat and selective in reporting the committee's work. Moreover, as political scientist Frank Sorauf has stressed, since direct mail can succeed with only a 2 to 5 percent response rate, and since prospecting for new donors is continuous, decisions by even a large number of givers to drop out will have little impact on PAC fundraising.

Ideological PACs are not alone in following undemocratic practices. When the AFL-CIO overwhelmingly endorsed Democrat Walter Mondale for president in 1983, thereby making available to him the invaluable resources of most labor PACs, a CBS News/*New York Times* poll showed that less than a quarter of the union members interviewed had their presidential preferences solicited in any fashion. If a representative sampling had taken place, the AFL-CIO might not have been so pro-Mondale, since the CBS/*Times* poll indicated that Mondale was not favored by a majority of the respondents and was in fact in a statistical dead heat with Senator John Glenn (D–Ohio) for a plurality edge.

Nor can many corporate PACs be considered showcases of democracy. In a few PACs the chief executive officers completely rule the roost, and in many the CEOs have inordinate influence on PAC decisions.

PAC Money and Congressional "Corruption"

The most serious charge leveled at PACs is that they succeed in buying the votes of legislators on issues important to their individual constituencies. It seems hardly worth arguing that many PACs are shopping for congressional votes and that PAC money buys access, or opens doors, to congressmen. But the "vote-buying" allegation is generally not supported by a careful examination of the facts. PAC contributions do make a difference, at least on some occasions, in securing access and influencing the course of events, but those occasions are not nearly as frequent as anti-PAC spokesmen, even congressmen themselves, often suggest.

PACs affect legislative proceedings to a decisive degree only when certain conditions prevail. First, the less visible the issue, the more likely that PAC funds can change or influence congressional votes. A corollary is that PAC money has more effect in the early stages of the legislative process, such as agenda setting and votes in subcommittee meetings, than in later and more public floor deliberations. Press, public, and even "watchdog" groups are not nearly as attentive to initial legislative proceedings.

PAC contributions are also more likely to influence the legislature when the issue is specialized and narrow, or unopposed by other organized interests. PAC gifts are less likely to be decisive on broad national issues such as American policy in Nicaragua or the adoption of a Star Wars missile defense system. But the more technical measures seem tailor-made for the special interests. Additionally, PAC influence in Congress is greater when large PACs or groups of PACs (such as business and labor PACs) are allied. In recent years, despite their natural enmity, business and labor have lobbied together on a number of issues, including defense spending, trade policy, environmental regulation, maritime legislation, trucking legislation, and nuclear power. The combination is a weighty one, checked in many instances only by a tendency for business and labor in one industry (say, the railroads) to combine and oppose their cooperating counterparts in another industry (perhaps the truckers and teamsters).

It is worth stressing, however, that most congressmen are not unduly influenced by PAC money on most votes. The special conditions simply do not apply to most legislative issues, and the overriding factors in determining a legislator's votes include party affiliation, ideology, and constituents' needs and desires. Much has been made of the passage of large tax cuts for oil and business interests in the 1981 omnibus tax package. The journalist Elizabeth Drew said there was a "bidding war" to trade campaign contributions for tax breaks benefiting independent oil producers. Ralph Nader's Public Citizen group charged that the $280,000 in corporate PAC money accepted by members of the House Ways and Means Committee helped to produce a bill that "contained everything business ever dared to ask for, and more." Yet as Robert Samuelson has convincingly argued, the "bidding war" between Democrats and Republicans was waged not for PAC money but for control of a House of Representatives sharply divided between Reaganite Republicans and liberal Democrats, with conservative "boll weevil" Democrats from the southern oil states as the crucial swing votes. The Ways and Means Committee actions cited by Nader were also more correctly explained in partisan terms. After all, if these special interests were so influential in writing the 1981 omnibus tax package, how could they fail so completely to derail the much more important (and, for them, threatening) tax reform legislation of 1986?

If party loyalty can have a stronger pull than PAC contributions, then surely the views of a congressman's constituents can also take precedence over those of political action committees. If an incumbent is faced with choice of either voting for a PAC-backed bill that is very unpopular in his district or forgoing the PAC's money, the odds are that any politician who depends on a majority of votes to remain in office is going to side with his constituency and vote against the PAC's interest. PAC gifts are merely a means to an end: reelection. If accepting money will cause a candidate embarrassment, then even a maximum donation will likely be rejected. The flip side of this proposition makes sense as well: if a PAC's parent organization has many members or a major financial stake in the congressman's home district, he is much more likely to vote the PAC's way—not so much because he receives PAC money but because the group accounts for an important part of his electorate. Does a U.S. senator from a dairy state vote for dairy price supports because he received a significant percentage of his PAC contributions from agriculture, or because the farm population of his state is relatively large and politically active? When congressmen vote the National Rifle Association's preferences is it because of the money the NRA's PAC distributes, or because the NRA, unlike gun-control advocates, has repeatedly demonstrated the ability to produce a sizable number of votes in many legislative districts?

If PACs have appeared more influential than they actually are, it is partly because many people believe legislators are looking for opportunities to exclaim (as one did during the Abscam scandal) "I've got larceny in my blood!" It is certainly disturbing that the National Republican Congressional Committee believed it necessary to warn its PAC-soliciting candidates: "Don't ever suggest to the PAC that it is 'buying' your vote, should you get elected." Yet knowledgeable Capitol Hill observers agree that there are few truly corrupt congressmen. Simple correlations notwithstanding, when most legislators vote for a PAC-supported bill, it is because of the merits of the case, or the entreaties of their party leaders, peers, or constituents, and not because of PAC money.

When the PAC phenomenon is viewed in the broad perspective of issues, party allegiance, and constituent interests, it is clear that merit matters most in the votes most congressmen cast. It is naive to contend that PAC money never influences decisions, but it is unjustifiably cynical to believe that PACs always, or even usually, push the voting buttons in Congress.

PACs in Perspective

As the largely unsubstantiated "vote-buying" controversy suggests, PACs are often misrepresented and unfairly maligned as the embodiment of corrupt special interests. Political action committees are a contemporary manifestation of what James Madison called "factions." In his *Federalist, No. 10*, Madison wrote that through the flourishing of these competing interest groups, or factions, liberty would be preserved.

In any democracy, and particularly in one as pluralistic as the United States, it is essential that groups be relatively unrestricted in advocating their interests and positions. Not only is that the mark of a free society, it also provides a safety valve for the competitive pressures that build on all fronts in a capitalistic democracy. And it provides another means to keep representatives responsive to legitimate needs.

This is not to say that all groups pursue legitimate interests, or that vigorously competing interests ensure that the public good prevails. The press, the public, and valuable watchdog groups such as Common Cause must always be alert to instances in which narrow private interests prevail over the commonwealth—occurrences that generally happen when no one is looking.

Besides the press and various public interest organizations, there are two major institutional checks on the potential abuses wrought by factions, associations, and now PACs. The most fundamental of these is regular free elections with general suffrage. As Tocqueville commented:

> Perhaps the most powerful of the causes which tend to mitigate the excesses of political association in the United States is Universal Suffrage. In countries in which universal suffrage exists, the majority is never doubtful, because neither party can pretend to represent that portion of the community which has not voted.
>
> The associations which are formed are aware, as well as the nation at large, that they do not represent the majority: this is, indeed, a condition inseparable from their existence; for if they did represent the prepondering power, they would change the law instead of soliciting its reform.

Senator Robert Dole (R–Kan.) has said, "There aren't any poor PACs or Food Stamp PACs or Nutrition PACs or Medicare PACs," and PAC critics frequently make the point that certain segments of the electorate are underrepresented in the PAC community. Yet without much support from PACs, there are food stamps, poverty and nutrition programs, and Medicare. Why? Because the recipients of governmental assistance constitute a hefty slice of the electorate, and votes matter more than dollars to politicians. Furthermore, many citizens outside the affected groups have also made known their support of aid to the poor and elderly—making yet a stronger electoral case for these PAC-less programs.

The other major institution that checks PAC influence is the two-party system. While PACs represent particular interests, the political parties build coalitions of groups and attempt to represent a national interest. They arbitrate among competing claims, and they seek to reach a consensus on matters of overriding importance to the nation. The parties are one of the few unifying forces in an exceptionally diverse country.

If interest groups and their PACs are useful to a functioning democracy, then political parties are essential. Yet just as PACs began gathering strength in the 1970s, the parties began a steady decline in power. In the past decade the rehabilitation of the party system has begun, but there is a long way to go. A central goal of the campaign financing reform agenda should be to strengthen the political parties, and to grant them a kind of "most favored nation" preferential status in the machinery of elections and campaign finance. Reforms to bolster the parties will also serve to temper the excesses of PACs by reducing their proportional impact on the election of public officials.

However limited and checkmated by political realities PACs may be, they are still regarded by a skeptical public as thoroughly unsavory. PACs have become the embodiment of greedy special interest politics, rising campaign costs, and corruption. It does not seem to matter that most experts in the field of campaign finance take considerable exception to the prevailing characterization of political action committees. PACs have become, in the public's mind, a powerful symbol of much that is wrong with America's campaign process, and candidates for public office naturally manipulate this symbol as well as others for their own ends. It is a circumstance as old as the Republic.

PACs, however, have done little to change their image for the better. Other than the business-oriented Public Affairs Council, few groups or committees have moved to correct one-sided press coverage or educate the public on campaign financing's fundamentals. In fact, many PACs fuel the fires of discontent by refusing to defend themselves while not seeming to care about appearances. Giving to both candidates in the same race, for example—an all-too-common practice—may be justifiable in theory, but it strikes most people as unprincipled, rank influence purchasing. Even worse, perhaps, are PACs that "correct their mistakes" soon after an election by sending a donation to the winning, but not originally PAC-supported, candidate. In the seven 1986 U.S. Senate races where a Democratic challenger defeated a Republican incumbent, there were 150 instances in which a PAC gave to the GOP candidate before the election and to the victorious Democrat once the votes were counted. These practices PACs themselves should stop. Every PAC should internally ban double giving, and there should be a moratorium on gifts to previously opposed candidates until at least the halfway point of the officeholder's term.

Whether PACs undertake some necessary rehabilitative steps or not, any fair appraisal of their role in American elections must be balanced. PACs are neither political innocents nor selfless civic boosters. But, neither are they cesspools of corruption and greed, nor modern-day versions of Tammany Hall.

PACs will never be popular with idealistic reformers because they represent the rough, cutting edge of a democracy teeming with different peoples and conflicting interests. Indeed, PACs may never be hailed even by natural allies; it was the business-oriented *Wall Street Journal*, after all, that editorially referred to Washington, D.C., as "a place where politicians, PACs, lawyers, and lobbyists for unions, business or you-name-it shake each other down full time for political money and political support."

Viewed in perspective, the root of the problem in campaign finance is not PACs; it is money. Americans have an enduring mistrust of the mix of money (particularly business money) and politics, as Finley Peter Dunne's Mr. Dooley revealed:

> I niver knew a pollytician to go wrong ontil he'd been contaminated be contact with a business man. . . . It seems to me that th' only thing to do is to keep pollyticians an' business men apart. They seem to have a bad infloonce on each other. Whiniver I see an alderman an' a banker walkin' down th' street together I know th' Recordin' Angel will have to ordher another bottle iv ink.

As a result of the new campaign finance rules of the 1970s, political action committees superceded the "fat cats" of old as the public focus and symbol of the role of money in politics, and PACs inherited the suspicions that go with the territory. Those suspicions are valuable because they keep the spotlight on PACs and guard against undue influence. It may be regrettable that such supervision is required, but human nature—not PACs—demands it.

Regulating Political Campaigns

First Amendment Barriers to the Regulation of Interest Groups and Political Parties

James Madison pointed out in *Federalist 10* that in a free society factions, although "evil," cannot be eliminated without destroying liberty at the same time. He wrote, "Liberty is to faction what air is to fire, an ailment, without which it instantly expires. But it could not be a less folly to abolish liberty, which is essential to political life because it nourishes faction, than it would be to wish the annihilation of air, which is essential to animal life, because it imparts to fire its destructive agency."

The liberty Madison referred to in *Federalist 10* was an eighteenth-century natural right, which became explicit in the First Amendment's list of freedoms of expression. The First Amendment's freedoms of speech, press, assembly, and its right to petition government for a redress of grievances protect political parties and interest groups from governmental intrusion. Neither these nor other freedoms and rights listed in the Bill of Rights are, however, absolute.

Congress as well as state legislatures have perennially attempted to regulate interest groups and, especially in the 1970s, political parties in various ways. Proponents of interest group regulation accept one prong of Madison's *Federalist 10* argument but ignore his caveat. They view interest groups as "evil" factions, but then propose a cure that invariably treads upon the liberty of groups under the First Amendment.

The following case involves a constitutional challenge on First Amendment grounds to a major congressional attempt to regulate interest groups and parties in the campaign finance legislation of the 1970s. The Federal Election Campaign Act of 1971, amended in 1974, limited individual and political action committee (PAC) contributions to political candidates and parties, and also imposed limits upon spending in behalf of and by political candidates. The law created the Federal Election Commission (FEC), a regulatory body to oversee the complex provisions of the laws. Political candidates and PACs had to register with the Commission and file a detailed report on their contributions and spending.

In the following opinion the Supreme Court held that political spending is protected speech under the First Amendment that Congress cannot burden. However, there is sufficient public interest in establishing a level political playing field to justify limits upon political contributions and their disclosure.

45

Buckley v. Valeo

424 U.S. 1 (1976)

Per Curiam

I. Contribution and Expenditure Limitations

The intricate statutory scheme adopted by Congress to regulate federal election campaigns includes restrictions on political contributions and expenditures that apply broadly to all phases of and all participants in the election process. The major contribution and expenditure limitations in the Act prohibit individuals from contributing more than $25,000 in a single year or more than $1,000 to any single candidate for an election campaign and from spending more than $1,000 a year "relative to a clearly identified candidate." Other provisions restrict a candidate's use of personal and family resources in his campaign and limit the overall amount that can be spent by a candidate in campaigning for federal office.

. . .

A. General Principles

The Act's contribution and expenditure limitations operate in an area of the most fundamental First Amendment activities. Discussion of public issues and debate on the qualifications of candidates are integral to the operation of the system of government established by our Constitution. . . .

The First Amendment protects political association as well as political expression. . . .

It is with these principles in mind that we consider the primary contentions of the parties with respect to the Act's limitations upon the giving and spending of money in political campaigns. Those conflicting contentions could not more sharply define the basic issues before us. Appellees contend that what the Act regulates is conduct, and that its effect on speech and association is incidental at most. Appellants respond that contributions and expenditures are at the very core of political speech, and that the Act's limitations thus constitute restraints on First Amendment liberty that are both gross and direct. . . .

A restriction on the amount of money a person or group can spend on political communication during a campaign necessarily reduces the quantity of expression by restricting the number of issues discussed, the depth of their exploration, and the size of the audience reached. This is because virtually every means of communicating ideas in today's mass society requires the expenditure of money. . . .

The expenditure limitations contained in the Act represent substantial rather than merely theoretical restraints on the quantity and diversity of political speech. The $1,000 ceiling on spending "relative to a clearly identified candidate," 18 U.S.C. § 608(e)(1) . . . would appear to exclude all citizens and groups except candidates, political parties and the institutional press from any significant use of the most effective modes of communication. Although the Act's limitations on expenditures by campaign organizations and political parties provide substantially greater room for discussion and debate, they would have required restrictions in the scope of a number of past congressional and Presidential campaigns and would operate to constrain campaigning by candidates who raise sums in excess of the spending ceiling.

By contrast with a limitation upon expenditures for political expression, a limitation upon the amount that any one person or group may contribute to a candidate or political committee entails only a marginal restriction upon the contributor's ability to engage in free communication. A contribution serves as a general expression of support for the candidate and his views, but does not communicate the underlying basis for the support. . . . While contributions may result in political expression if spent by a candidate or an association to present views to the voters, the transformation of contributions into political debate involves speech by someone other than the contributor.

Given the important role of contributions in financing political campaigns, contribution restrictions could have a severe impact on political dialogue if the limitations prevented candidates and political committees from amassing the resources necessary for effective advocacy. There is no indication, however, that the contribution limitations imposed by the Act would have any dramatic adverse effect on the funding of campaigns and political associations. The overall effect of the Act's contribution ceilings is merely to require candidates and political committees to raise funds from a greater number of persons and to compel people who would otherwise contribute amounts greater than the statutory limits to expend such funds on direct political expression, rather than to reduce the total amount of money potentially available to promote political expression.

The Act's contribution and expenditure limitations also impinge on protected associational freedoms. Making a contribution, like joining a political party, serves to affiliate a person with a candidate. In addition, it enables like-minded persons to pool their resources in furtherance of common political goals. The Act's contribution ceilings thus limit one important means of associating with a candidate or committee, but leave the contributor free to become a member of any political association and to assist personally in the association's efforts on behalf of candidates. And the Act's contribution limitations permit associations and candidates to aggregate large sums of money to promote effective advocacy. By contrast, the Act's $1,000 limitation on independent expenditures "relative to a clearly identified candidate" precludes most associations from effectively amplifying the voice of their adherents, the original basis for the recognition of First Amendment protection of the freedom of association. . . .

In sum, although the Act's contribution and expenditure limitations both implicate fundamental First Amendment interests, its expenditure ceilings impose significantly more severe restrictions on protected freedoms of political expression and association than do its limitations on financial contributions.

B. Contribution Limitations

. . . We find that, under the rigorous standard of review established by our prior decisions, the weighty interests served by restricting the size of financial contributions to political candidates are sufficient to justify the limited effect upon First Amendment freedoms caused by the $1,000 contribution ceiling.

. . .

C. Expenditure Limitations

The Act's expenditure ceilings impose direct and substantial restraints on the quantity of political speech. . . . It is clear that a primary effect of these expenditure limitations is to restrict the quantity of campaign speech by individuals, groups, and candidates. The restrictions, while neutral as to the ideas expressed, limit political expression "at the core of our electoral process and of the First Amendment freedoms." . . .

1. The $1,000 Limitation on Expenditures "Relative to a Clearly Identified Candidate"

. . .

. . . [T]he constitutionality of § 608(e)(1) turns on whether the governmental interests advanced in its support satisfy the exacting scrutiny applicable to limitations on core First Amendment rights of political expression.

We find that the governmental interest in preventing corruption and the appearance of corruption is inadequate to justify § 608(e)(1)'s ceiling on independent expenditures. . . .

. . .

It is argued, however, that the ancillary governmental interest in equalizing the relative ability of individuals and groups to influence the outcome of elections serves to justify the limitation on express advocacy of the election or defeat of candidates imposed by § 608(e)(1)'s expenditure ceiling. But the concept that government may restrict the speech of some elements of our society in order to enhance the relative voice of others is wholly foreign to the First Amendment . . . The First Amendment's protection against governmental abridgment of free expression cannot properly be made to depend on a person's financial ability to engage in public discussion. . . .

. . .

For the reasons stated, we conclude that § 608(e)(1)'s independent expenditure limitation is unconstitutional under the First Amendment.

2. Limitation on Expenditures by Candidates from Personal or Family Resources
. . .

The ceiling on personal expenditures by candidates on their own behalf, like the limitations on independent expenditures contained in § 608(e)(1), imposes a substantial restraint on the ability of persons to engage in protected First Amendment expression. . . .

The ancillary interest in equalizing the relative financial resources of candidates competing for elective office, therefore, provides the sole relevant rationale for § 608(a)'s expenditure ceiling. That interest is clearly not sufficient to justify the provision's infringement of fundamental First Amendment rights. . . .

3. Limitations on Campaign Expenditures

Section 608(c) places limitations on overall campaign expenditures by candidates seeking nomination for election and election to federal office. . . .

No governmental interest that has been suggested is sufficient to justify the restriction on the quantity of political expression imposed by § 608(c)'s campaign expenditure limitations. The major evil associated with rapidly increasing campaign expenditures is the danger of candidate dependence on large contributions. The interest in alleviating the corrupting influence of large contributions is served by the Act's contribution limitations and disclosure provisions rather than by § 608(c)'s campaign expenditure ceilings. . . .

The interest in equalizing the financial resources of candidates competing for federal office is no more convincing a justification for restricting the scope of federal election campaigns. . . .

The campaign expenditure ceilings appear to be designed primarily to serve the governmental interests in reducing the allegedly skyrocketing costs of political campaigns. . . . The First Amendment denies government the power to determine that spending to promote one's political views is wasteful, excessive, or unwise. In the free society ordained by our Constitution it is not the government but the people—individually as citizens and candidates and collectively as associations and political committees—who must retain control over the quantity and range of debate on public issues in a political campaign.

For these reasons we hold that § 608(c) is constitutionally invalid. . . .

II. Reporting and Disclosure Requirements

. . . Each political committee is required to register with the Commission, § 433, and to keep detailed records of both contributions and expenditures, §§ 432(c), (d). . . .

Each committee and each candidate also is required to file quarterly reports. . . . The reports are to contain detailed financial information. . . .

Every individual or group, other than a political committee or candidate, who makes "contributions" or "expenditures" of over $100 in a calendar year "other than by contribution to a political committee or a candidate" is required to file a statement with the Commission. . . .

A. General Principles

Unlike the overall limitations on contributions and expenditures, the disclosure requirements impose no ceiling on campaign-related activities. But we have repeatedly found that compelled disclosure, in itself, can seriously infringe on privacy of association and belief guaranteed by the First Amendment. . . .

We long have recognized that significant encroachments on First Amendment rights of the sort that compelled disclosure imposes cannot be justified by a mere showing of some legitimate governmental interest. Since *NAACP v. Alabama* [1958] we have required that the subordinating interests of the State must survive exacting scrutiny. . . .

The strict test established by *NAACP v. Alabama* is necessary because compelled disclosure has the potential for substantially infringing the exercise of First Amendment rights. But we have acknowledged that there are governmental interests sufficiently important to outweigh the possibility of infringement, particularly when the "free functioning of our national institutions" is involved. . . .

The governmental interests sought to be vindicated by the disclosure requirements are of this magnitude. They fall into three categories. First, disclosure provides the electorate with information "as to where political campaign money comes from and how it is spent by the candidate" in order to aid the voters in evaluating those who seek federal office. It allows voters to place each candidate in the political spectrum more precisely than is often possible solely on the basis of party labels and campaign speeches. The sources of a candidate's financial support also alert the voter to the interests to which a candidate is most likely to be responsive and thus facilitate predictions of future performance in office.

Second, disclosure requirements deter actual corruption and avoid the appearance of corruption by exposing large contributions and expenditures to the light of publicity. . . .

. . .

Third, and not least significant, record keeping, reporting, and disclosure requirements are an essential means of gathering the data necessary to detect violations of the contribution limitations described above.

The disclosure requirements, as a general matter, directly serve substantial governmental interests. In determining whether these interests are sufficient to justify the requirements we must look to the extent of the burden that they place on individual rights. . . .

—————————————— *CA* ——————————————

The Supreme Court made it clear in *Buckley v. Valeo* (1976) that the Constitution permits only limited government regulation of interest groups and political parties. But political corruption remains a persistent phenomenon. Corruption is a relative term, and disagreement is widespread on what actually "corrupts" a political system. Societal definitions of political corruption vary greatly over time and from one political system to another.

For example, both common (judge-made) and statutory law have long defined bribery as a corrupt act. The term corruption is normative, that is, subjective to the user. What is corrupt or not must be defined in the law. As *Black's Law Dictionary* states, corruption is "a vicious and fraudulent intention to evade the prohibitions of the law; something against or forbidden by the law; moral turpitude or exactly opposite of honesty involving intentional disregard of law from improper motives." Bribery is defined as the "offering, giving, receiving, or soliciting of anything of value to influence action as official or in disregard of legal or public duty."[1]

Congress, then, at the federal level defines and forbids political corruption. The Supreme Court determines how far the First Amendment permits Congress to regulate interest groups and parties.

The campaign finance laws of the 1970s that regulated political contributions were premised on the idea that excessive amounts of money from any given source corrupts the political process. The Federal Election Commission is the body that administers the campaign finance laws through a complicated process of rule making and adjudication. Campaign law is an ever-expanding field that burdens political candidates and requires them constantly to seek legal advice.

The following selection focuses on problems in campaign finance and calls for the deregulation of political campaigns accompanied by full disclosure of political contributions.

— 46 —

CAMPAIGN FINANCE REFORM

Larry J. Sabato and Glenn R. Simpson

❦

Campaign Finance Reform

One of the broad problems with our campaign financing system . . . is that our complex campaign regulatory structure—administered by the Federal Election Commission—has become catastrophically overburdened. That is why we see declining compliance with the law and the opening of ever-wider loopholes. Regulators are simply unable to keep up. As one knowledgeable critic of the current system has noted, the current state of affairs is corrosive:

> The FEC's weak enforcement has made the campaign finance laws a fraud on the public. Such sham reform not only breeds contempt for those laws among the lawmakers themselves, but also produces in turn contempt among the voters for politi-

---

[1] *Blacks Law Dictionary*, 4th ed., rev. (St. Paul, MN: 1968).

cians and the political process. This should not be surprising, since even the most honest candidates, seeing violations by their opponents going unpunished, feel tremendous pressure to cheat. This leads to a competitive cycle in which a loophole opened by one side is widened by the other, so that eventually there is little left of the original intent of the law.

Undoubtedly, part of the situation has been a willful effort on the part of Congress to hamstring the Federal Election Commission, starve it of resources, and block any statutory improvements in the Federal Election Campaign Act. Yet a powerful new agency equipped with vast new funds administering a slew of new legal provisions might not make things any better. The system is already monstrously complex. As House Speaker Newt Gingrich fairly observed, "We've created all sorts of Mickey Mouse rules." The 1995 edition of the Federal Election Commission's code of regulations stretches to 264 pages of dense legalese, virtually indecipherable to the layman. It makes sense to ask whether we really want to complicate the law further and vest greater powers in a political regulatory agency.

There is a good argument to be made that in many respects, the FEC should be a weak agency. As the veteran election attorney Jan Baran suggests, it is perhaps too idealistic and naive to suppose that the FEC can be "the first benign political police in the history of mankind." The United States has thrived on unfettered political activity; it is a core national value. Practically speaking, it may also be unrealistic to think that political participants—and the courts—will ever abide the draconian new restrictions on political activity contemplated by some reformers. Finally, there is a simple question of efficacy. The last two decades have produced greater regulation of politics than occurred in all of the preceding two centuries, and yet many critics contend that the problems are worse now than they have ever been. Is the logical step really more regulation?

The Real Ills

A critical symptom (and disturbing product) of the system's ills has been the growth of shadow campaign organizations allegedly outside the purview of the campaign laws, such as the Christian Coalition and GOPAC. . . . Anyone who visits the Federal Election Commission to learn more about the groups that were among the most important in the 1994 elections—the Christian Coalition, the term limit advocates, GOPAC—will be sorely disappointed. The Christian Coalition and term limit groups have not registered at all, while GOPAC discloses only about 10 percent of its activity. . . .

A similar and related problem at the federal level is the blurring of distinctions between the relatively unrestricted funds known as "soft" money (used to finance a party's general overhead and generic "get out the vote" appeals) and the tightly limited "hard" money (direct contributions to individual candidates). All hard money counts against the federal contribution limits (for example, $1,000 per candidate per election for an individual citizen), whereas only a portion of the soft money gifts do so. Yet the distinction between hard and soft money is increasingly artificial. . . . Political operatives believe soft money can affect election outcomes just as directly as hard money, and they do not hesitate to use it in this manner. . . .

The final major defect of the American system of campaign finance is its potent pro-incumbent bias. Since the 1970s, a declining sense of ideological and party loyalty has generally led political action committees and other special-interest contributors to gravitate with abandon toward incumbents of all persuasions, a trend that congressional Democrats both encouraged and exploited to maintain themselves in power for decades. Since the 1994 election, Republican legislators have done much the same, with the new majority party continuing the PAC shakedown. This practice reeks of cynical, principle-free influence-peddling, where lobbyists unashamedly try to secure access to powerful legislators with whom they usually disagree.

Phony Cures Versus a Workable Solution: Deregulation Plus

The system's problems, then, are vexing. Indeed, is it possible to fashion a solution to all of them simultaneously? Over the years, the reformers' panacea has been taxpayer financing of elections and limits on how much candidates can spend. Public financing is a seductively simple proposition: if there is no private money, presumably there will be none of the difficulties associated with private money. But in a country such as ours, which places great emphasis on the freedoms of speech and association, it is unrealistic to expect that the populace at large or even many of the elite activists will come to support greater federal subsidization of our election system at the cost of their individual and group political involvements. Spending limits are also enticing. Are politicians raising and spending too much money? Let's pass a law against it! Yet such a statute may be difficult to enforce in an era when politicians and the public seek less regulation, not more—not to mention the serious, maybe fatal, problem of plugging all the money loopholes (the C(4)s; Supreme Court–sanctioned, unlimited "independent expenditures" by groups and individuals unconnected to a campaign, and so on). Once again, the biggest, the original, and the unpluggable loophole is the First Amendment.

Public financing and spending limits are both also objectionable on the basic merits: the right to organize and attempt to influence politics is a fundamental constitutional guarantee, derived from the same First Amendment protections that need to be forcefully protected. To place draconian limits on political speech is simply a bad idea. (The call for a ban on political action committees suffers from the same defect.)

Once again, even if candidates could be persuaded to comply voluntarily with a *public financing and spending limits* scheme such a solution would fail to take into consideration the many ways that interest groups such as the Christian Coalition and labor unions can influence elections without making direct contributions to candidates. Even if we passed laws that appeared to be taking private money out, we would not really be doing so. This is a recipe for deception, and consequently—once the truth becomes apparent—for still greater cynicism.

In our opinion, there is another way, one that takes advantage of both current realities and the remarkable self-regulating tendencies of a free-market democracy, not to mention the spirit of the age. Consider the American stock markets. Most government oversight of them simply makes sure that publicly traded companies accurately disclose vital information about their finances. The philosophy here is that buyers, given the information they need, are intelligent enough to look out for themselves. There will be winners and losers, of course, both among companies and the consumers of their securities, but it is not the government's role to guarantee anyone's success (indeed, the idea is abhorrent). The notion that people are smart enough, and indeed have the duty, to think and choose for themselves, also underlies our basic democratic arrangement. There is no reason why the same principle cannot be successfully applied to a free market for campaign finance. In this scenario, disclosure laws would be broadened and strengthened, and penalties for failure to disclose would be ratcheted up, while rules on other aspects—such as sources of funds and sizes of contributions—could be greatly loosened or even abandoned altogether.

Call it *Deregulation Plus*. Let a well-informed marketplace, rather than a committee of federal bureaucrats, be the judge of whether someone has accepted too much money from a particular interest group or spent too much to win an election. Reformers who object to money in politics would lose little under such a scheme, since the current system—itself a product of reform—has already utterly failed to inhibit special-interest influence. (Plus, the reformers' new plans will fail spectacularly, as we have already argued.) On the other hand, reform advocates might gain substantially by bringing all financial activity out into the open where the public can see for itself the truth about how our campaigns are conducted. If the facts are really as awful as reformers contend (and as close observers of the system, much of what we see is appalling), then the public will be moved to demand change.

Moreover, a new disclosure regime might just prove to be the solution in itself. It is worth noting that the stock-buying public, by and large, is happy with the relatively liberal manner by which the Securities and Exchange Commission regulates stock markets. Companies and brokers (the candidates and consultants of the financial world) actually *appreciate* the SEC's efforts to enforce vigorously what regulations it does have, since such enforcement maintains public confidence in the system and encourages honest, ethical behavior, without unnecessarily impinging on the freedom of market players. Again, the key is to ensure the availability of the requisite information for people to make intelligent decisions. . . .

A new disclosure-based regime, to be successful, would obviously require more stringent reporting rules. Most important, new reporting rules would require groups such as organized labor and the Christian Coalition to disclose the complete extent of their involvement in campaigns. . . .

For political parties, there seems little alternative to simply legitimizing what has already happened de facto: the abolition of all limits. When the chairman of a national political party bluntly admits that millions of dollars in "soft money" receipts mean that the committee will be able to spend millions of dollars in "hard money," it is time for everyone to acknowledge reality. . . . Moreover, such an outcome is not to be lamented. Political parties deserve more fundraising freedom, which would give these critical institutions a more substantial role in elections.

How would the new disclosure regime work? While the FEC has already moved to impose some tighter disclosure requirements, it lacks the resources as currently constituted to enforce the new rules across the board. However, the solution does not necessarily require a massive increase in funding. Under a disclosure regime, the agency could reduce efforts to police excessive contributions and other infractions, devoting itself primarily to providing information to the public. . . .

PART THREE

❧

NATIONAL
GOVERNMENT
INSTITUTIONS

CHAPTER 6

THE PRESIDENCY

The American presidency is the only unique political institution that the United States has contributed to the world. It developed first in this country and later was imitated, usually unsuccessfully, in many nations. In no country and at no time has the institution of the presidency achieved the status and power that it possesses in the United States. This chapter will analyze the basis, nature, and implications of the power of this great American institution.

Constitutional Background: Single Versus Plural Executive

The change that has taken place in the presidency since the office was established in 1789 is dramatic and significant. The framers of the Constitution were primarily concerned with the control of the arbitrary exercise of power by the legislature; thus they were willing to give the president broad power since he was not to be popularly elected and would be constantly under attack by the coordinate legislative branch. Although the framers were not afraid of establishing a vigorous presidency, there was a great deal of opposition to a potentially strong executive at the time the Constitution was drafted. In *Federalist 70* Alexander Hamilton attempts to persuade the people of the desirability of a strong presidential office, and while persuading, he sets forth the essential constitutional basis of the office.

47

Federalist 70

Alexander Hamilton

There is an idea, which is not without its advocates, that a vigorous executive is inconsistent with the genius of republican government. The enlightened well-wishers to this species of government must at least hope that the supposition is destitute of foundation; since they can never admit its truth, without, at the same time, admitting the condemnation of their own principles. Energy in the executive is a leading character in the definition of good government. It is essential to the protection of the community against foreign attacks; it is not less essential to the steady administration of the laws, to the protection of property against those irregular and high-handed combinations, which sometimes interrupt the ordinary course of justice, to the security of liberty against the enterprises and assaults of ambition, of faction, and of anarchy. Every man, the least conversant in Roman story, knows how often that republic was obliged to take refuge in the absolute power of a single man, under the formidable title of dictator, as well as against the intrigues of ambitious individuals, who aspired to the tyranny, and the seditions of whole classes of the community, whose conduct threatened the existence of all government, as against the invasions of external enemies, who menaced the conquest and destruction of Rome.

There can be no need, however, to multiply arguments or examples on this head. A feeble executive implies a feeble execution of the government. A feeble execution is but another phrase for a bad execution; and government ill executed, whatever it may be in theory, must be, in practice, a bad government.

Taking it for granted, therefore, that all men of sense will agree in the necessity of an energetic executive, it will only remain to inquire, what are the ingredients which constitute this energy? How far can they be combined with those other ingredients, which constitute safety in the republican sense? And how far does this combination characterize the plan which has been reported by the convention?

The ingredients which constitute energy in the executive are: unity; duration; and adequate provision for its support; competent powers.

The ingredients which constitute safety in the republican sense are: a due dependence on the people; a due responsibility.

Those politicians and statesmen, who have been the most celebrated for the soundness of their principles, and for the justness of their views, have declared in favor of a single executive, and a numerous legislature. They have, with great propriety, considered energy as the most necessary qualification of the former, and have regarded this as most applicable to power in a single hand; while they have, with equal propriety, considered the latter as the best adapted to deliberation and wisdom, and best calculated to conciliate the confidence of the people, and to secure their privileges and interests.

That unity is conducive to energy will not be disputed. Decision, activity, secrecy, and dispatch, will generally characterize the proceedings of one man, in a much more eminent degree than the proceedings of any greater number; and in proportion as the number is increased, these qualities will be diminished.

This unity may be destroyed in two ways; either by vesting the power in two or more magistrates, of equal dignity and authority; or by vesting it ostensibly in one man, subject, in whole or in part, to the control and cooperation of others, in the capacity of counsellors to him. . . .

The experience of other nations will afford little instruction on this head. As far, however, as it teaches anything, it teaches us not to be enamored of plurality in the executive. . . .

Wherever two or more persons are engaged in any common enterprise or pursuit, there is always danger of difference of opinion. If it be a public trust of office, in which they are clothed with equal dignity and authority, there is peculiar danger of personal emulation and even animosity. From either, and especially from all these causes, the most bitter dissensions are apt to spring. Whenever these happen, they lessen the respectability, weaken the authority, and distract the plans and operations of those whom they divide. If they should unfortunately assail the supreme executive magistracy of a country, consisting of a plurality of persons, they might impede or frustrate the most important measures of the government, in the most critical emergencies of state. And what is still worse, they might split the community into violent and irreconcilable factions, adhering differently to the different individuals who composed the magistracy. . . .

Upon the principles of a free government, inconveniences from the source just mentioned, must necessarily be submitted to in the formation of the legislature; but it is unnecessary, and therefore unwise, to introduce them into the constitution of the executive. It is here, too, that they may be most pernicious. In the legislature, promptitude of decision is oftener an evil than a benefit. The differences of opinion, and the jarrings of parties in that department of the government, though they may sometimes obstruct salutary plans, yet often promote deliberation and circumspection; and serve to check excesses in the majority. When a resolution, too, is once taken, the opposition must be at an end. That resolution is a law, and resistance to it punishable. But no favorable circumstances palliate, or atone for the disadvantages of dissention in the executive department. Here they are pure and unmixed. There is no point at which they cease to operate. They serve to embarrass and weaken the execution of the plan or measure to which they relate, from the first step to the final conclusion of it. They constantly counteract those qualities in the executive, which are the most necessary ingredients in its composition—vigor and expedition; and this without any counterbalancing good. In the conduct of war, in which the energy of the executive is the bulwark of the national security, everything would be to be apprehended from its plurality.

It must be confessed, that these observations apply with principal weight to the first case supposed, that is, to a plurality of magistrates of equal dignity and authority, a scheme, the advocates for which are not likely to form a numerous sect; but they apply, though not with equal, yet with considerable weight, to the project of a council, whose concurrence is made constitutionally necessary to the operations of the ostensible executive. An artful cabal in that council would be able to distract and to enervate the whole system of administration. If no such cabal should exist, the mere diversity of views and opinions would alone be sufficient to tincture the exercise of the executive authority with the spirit of habitual feebleness and dilatoriness.

But one of the weightiest objections to a plurality in the executive, and which lies as much against the last as the first plan, is, that it tends to conceal faults, and destroy responsibility. . . . It often becomes impossible, amidst mutual accusations, to determine on whom the blame or the punishment of a pernicious measure . . . ought really to fall. It is shifted from one to another with so much dexterity, and under such plausible appearances, that the public opinion is left in suspense about the real author. . . .

A little consideration will satisfy us, that the species of security sought for in the multiplication of the executive, is unattainable. Numbers must be so great as to render combination difficult; or they are rather a source of danger than security. The united credit and influence of several individuals must be more formidable to liberty than the credit and influence of either of them separately. When power, therefore, is placed in the hands of so small a number of men, as to admit of their interests and views being easily combined in a common enterprise, by an artful leader, it becomes more liable to abuse, and more dangerous when abused, than if it be lodged in the hands of one man; who, from the very circumstances of his being alone, will be more narrowly watched and more readily suspected, and who cannot unite so great a mass of influence as when he is associated with others. . . .

I will only add, that prior to the appearance of the constitution, I rarely met with an intelligent man from any of the states, who did not admit as the result of experience, that the unity of the executive of this state was one of the best of the distinguishing features of our constitution.

The Nature of the Presidency: Power, Persuasion, and Paradoxes

What is the position of the presidential office today? There is little doubt that it has expanded far beyond the expectations of the framers of the Constitution. The presidency is the only governmental branch with the necessary unity and energy to meet many of the most crucial problems of twentieth-century government in the United States; people have turned to the president in times of crisis to supply the central direction necessary for survival. In the next selection Clinton Rossiter, one of the leading American scholars of the presidency, gives his view of the role of the office.

— 48 —

The Presidency—Focus of Leadership

Clinton Rossiter

No American can contemplate the presidency . . . without a feeling of solemnity and humility—solemnity in the face of a historically unique concentration of power and prestige, humility in the thought that he has had a part in the choice of a man to wield the power and enjoy the prestige.

Perhaps the most rewarding way to grasp the significance of this great office is to consider it as a focus of democratic leadership. Free men, too, have need of leaders. Indeed, it may be argued that one of the decisive forces in the shaping of American democracy has been the extraordinary capacity of the presidency for strong, able, popular leadership. If this has been true of our past, it will certainly be true of our future, and we should therefore do our best to grasp the quality of this leadership. Let us do this by answering the essential question: For what men and groups does the president provide leadership?

First, the president is *leader of the Executive Branch*. To the extent that our federal civil servants have need of common guidance, he alone is in a position to provide it. We cannot savor the fullness of the president's duties unless we recall that he is held primarily accountable for the ethics, loyalty, efficiency, frugality, and responsiveness to the public's wishes of the two and one-third million Americans in the national administration.

Both the Constitution and Congress have recognized his power to guide the day-to-day activities of the Executive Branch, strained and restrained though his leadership may often be in practice. From the Constitution, explicitly or implicitly, he receives the twin powers of appointment and removal, as well as the primary duty, which no law or plan or circumstances can ever take away from him, to "take care that the laws be faithfully executed."

From Congress, through such legislative mandates as the Budget and Accounting Act of 1921 and the succession of Reorganization Acts, the president has received further acknowledgment of his administrative leadership. Although independent agencies such as the Interstate Commerce Commission and the National Labor Relations Board operate by design outside his immediate area of responsibility, most of the government's administrative tasks are still carried on within the fuzzy-edged pyramid that has the president at its lonely peak; the laws that are executed daily in his name and under his general supervision are numbered in the hundreds.

Many observers, to be sure, have argued strenuously that we should not ask too much of the president as administrative leader, lest we burden him with impossible detail, or give too much to him, lest we inject political considerations too forcefully into the steady business of the civil service. Still, he cannot ignore the blunt mandate of the Constitution, and we should not forget the wisdom that lies behind it. The president has no more important tasks than to set a high personal example of integrity and industry for all who serve the nation, and to transmit a clear lead downward through his chief lieutenants to all who help shape the policies by which we live.

Next, the president is *leader of the forces of peace and war.* Although authority in the field of foreign relations is shared constitutionally among three organs—president, Congress, and for two special purposes, the Senate—his position is paramount, if not indeed dominant. Constitution, laws, customs, the practice of other nations, and the logic of history have combined to place the president in a dominant position. Secrecy, dispatch, unity, continuity, and access to information—the ingredients of successful diplomacy—are properties of his office, and Congress, needless to add, possesses none of them. Leadership in foreign affairs flows today from the president—or it does not flow at all.

The Constitution designates him specifically as "Commander in Chief of the Army and Navy of the United States." In peace and war he is the supreme commander of the armed forces, the living guarantee of the American belief in "the supremacy of the civil over military authority."

In time of peace he raises, trains, supervises, and deploys the forces that Congress is willing to maintain. With the aid of the Secretary of Defense, the Joint Chiefs of Staff, and the National Security Council—all of whom are his personal choices—he looks constantly to the state of the nation's defenses. He is never for one day allowed to forget that he will be held accountable by the people, Congress, and history for the nation's readiness to meet an enemy assault.

In time of war his power to command the forces swells out of all proportion to his other powers. All major decisions of strategy, and many of tactics as well, are his alone to make or to approve. Lincoln and Franklin Roosevelt, each in his own way and time, showed how far the power of military command can be driven by a president anxious to have his generals and admirals get on with the war.

But this, the power of command, is only a fraction of the vast responsibility the modern president draws from the Commander in Chief clause. We need only think back to three of Franklin D. Roosevelt's actions in World War II—the creation and staffing of a whole array of emergency boards and offices, the seizure and operation of more than sixty strike-bound or strike-threatened plants and industries, and the forced evacuation of 70,000 American citizens of Japanese descent from the West

Coast—to understand how deeply the president's authority can cut into the lives and liberties of the American people in time of war. We may well tremble in contemplation of the kind of leadership he would be forced to exert in a total war with the absolute weapon.

The president's duties are not all purely executive in nature. He is also intimately associated, by Constitution and custom, with the legislative process, and we may therefore consider him as *leader of Congress*. Congress has its full share of strong men, but the complexity of the problems it is asked to solve by a people who still assume that all problems are solvable has made external leadership a requisite of effective operation.

The president alone is in a political, constitutional, and practical position to provide such leadership, and he is therefore expected, within the limits of propriety, to guide Congress in much of its lawmaking activity. Indeed, since Congress is no longer minded or organized to guide itself, the refusal or inability of the president to serve as a kind of prime minister results in weak and disorganized government. His tasks as leader of Congress are difficult and delicate, yet he must bend to them steadily or be judged a failure. The president who will not give his best thoughts to leading Congress, more so the president who is temperamentally or politically unfitted to "get along with Congress," is now rightly considered a national liability.

The lives of Jackson, Lincoln, Wilson, and the two Roosevelts should be enough to remind us that the president draws much of his real power from his position as *leader of his party*. By playing the grand politician with unashamed zest, the first of these men gave his epic administration a unique sense of cohesion, the second rallied doubting Republican leaders and their followings to the cause of the Union, and the other three achieved genuine triumphs as catalysts of Congressional action. That gifted amateur, Dwight D. Eisenhower, has also played the role for every drop of drama and power in it. He has demonstrated repeatedly what close observers of the presidency know well: that its incumbent must devote an hour or two of every working day to the profession of Chief Democrat or Chief Republican.

It troubles many good people, not entirely without reason, to watch the president dabbling in politics, distributing loaves and fishes, smiling on party hacks, and endorsing candidates he knows to be unfit for anything but immediate delivery to the county jail. Yet if he is to persuade Congress, if he is to achieve a loyal and cohesive administration, if he is to be elected in the first place (and reelected in the second), he must put his hand firmly to the plow of politics. The president is inevitably the nation's No. 1 political boss.

Yet he is, at the same time, if not in the same breath, *leader of public opinion*. While he acts as political chieftain of some, he serves as moral spokesman for all. It took the line of presidents some time to sense the nation's need for a clear voice, but since the day when Andrew Jackson thundered against the Nullifiers of South Carolina, no effective president has doubted his prerogative to speak the people's mind on the great issues of his time, to serve, in Wilson's words, as "the spokesman for the real sentiment and purpose of the country."

Sometimes, of course, it is no easy thing, even for the most sensitive and large-minded presidents, to know the real sentiment of the people or to be bold enough to state it in defiance of loudly voiced contrary opinion. Yet the president who senses the popular mood and spots new tides even before they start to run, who practices shrewd economy in his appearances as spokesman for the nation, who is conscious of his unique power to compel discussion on his own terms and who talks the language of Christian morality and the American tradition, can shout down any other voice or chorus of voices in the land. The president is the American people's one authentic trumpet, and he has no higher duty than to give a clear and certain sound.

The president is easily the most influential leader of opinion in this country principally because he is, among all his other jobs, our Chief of State. He is, that is to say, the ceremonial head of the government of the United States, the *leader of the rituals of American democracy*. The long catalogue of public duties that the Queen discharges in England and the Governor General in Canada is the President's responsibility in this country, and the catalogue is even longer because he is not a king, or even the agent of one, and is therefore expected to go through of some rather undignified paces by a people who think of him as a combination of scout-master, Delphic oracle, hero of the silver screen, and father of the multitudes.

The role of Chief of State may often seem trivial, yet it cannot be neglected by a president who proposes to stay in favor and, more to the point, in touch with the people, the ultimate support of all his claims to leadership. And whether or not he enjoys this role, no president can fail to realize that his many powers are invigorated, indeed are given a new dimension of authority, because he is the symbol of our sovereignty, continuity, and grandeur as a people.

When he asks a senator to lunch in order to enlist his support for a pet project, when he thumps his desk and reminds the antagonists in a labor dispute of the larger interests of the American people, when he orders a general to cease caviling or else be removed from his command, the senator and the disputants and the general are well aware—especially if the scene is laid in the White House—that they are dealing with no ordinary head of government. The framers of the Constitution took a momentous step when they fused the dignity of a king and the power of a prime minister in one elective office—when they made the president a national leader in the mystical as well as the practical sense.

Finally, the president has been endowed—whether we or our friends abroad like it or not—with a global role as a leader of the free nations. His leadership in this area is not that of a dominant executive. The power he exercises is in a way comparable to that which he holds as a leader of Congress. Senators and congressmen can, if they choose, ignore the president's leadership with relative impunity. So, too, can our friends abroad; the action of Britain and France in the Middle East is a case in point. But so long as the United States remains the richest and most powerful member of any coalition it may enter, then its president's words and deeds will have a direct bearing on the freedom and stability of a great many other countries.

Having engaged in this piecemeal analysis of the categories of presidential leadership, we must now fit the pieces back together into a seamless unity. For that, after all, is what the presidency is, and I hope this exercise in political taxonomy has not obscured the paramount fact that this focus of democratic leadership is a single office filled by a single man.

The president is not one kind of leader one part of the day, another kind in another part—leader of the bureaucracy in the morning, of the armed forces at lunch, of Congress in the afternoon, of the people in the evening. He exerts every kind of leadership every moment of the day, and every kind feeds upon and into all the others. He is a more exalted leader of ritual because he can guide opinion, a more forceful leader in diplomacy because he commands the armed forces personally, a more effective leader of Congress because he sits at the top of his party. The conflicting demands of these categories of leadership give him trouble at times, but in the end all unite to make him a leader without any equal in the history of democracy.

I think it important to note the qualification: "the history of democracy." For what I have been talking about here is not the Fuehrerprinzip of Hitler or the "cult of personality," but the leadership of free men. The presidency, like every other instrument of power we have created for our use, operates within a grand and durable pattern of private liberty and public morality, which means that the president can lead successfully only when he honors the pattern—by working towards ends to which a "persistent and undoubted majority of people has given support, and by selecting means that are fair, dignified, and familiar.

The president, that is to say, can lead us only in the direction we are accustomed to travel. He cannot lead the gentlemen of Congress to abdicate their functions; he cannot order our civil servants to be corrupt and slothful; he cannot even command our generals to bring off a coup d'état. And surely he cannot lead public opinion in a direction for which public opinion is not prepared—a truth to which our strongest presidents would make the most convincing witnesses. The leadership of free men must honor their freedom. The power of the presidency can move as a mighty host only with the grain of liberty and morality.

The president, then, must provide a steady focus of leadership—of administrators, ambassadors, generals, congressmen, party chieftains, people, and men of good will everywhere. In a constitutional system compounded of diversity and antagonism, the presidency looms up as the countervailing force of unity and harmony. In a society ridden by centrifugal forces, it is the only point of reference we all have in common. The relentless progress of this continental republic has made the presidency our truly national political institution.

There are those, to be sure, who would reserve this role to Congress, but, as the least aggressive of our presidents, Calvin Coolidge, once testified, "It is because in their hours of timidity the Congress becomes subservient to the importunities of organized minorities that the president comes more and more to stand as the champion of the rights of the whole country." The more Congress becomes, in Burke's phrase, "a confused and scuffling bustle of local agency," the more the presidency must become a clear beacon of national purpose.

It has been such a beacon at most great moments in our history. In this great moment, too, we may be confident it will burn brightly.

The constitutional and statutory *authority* of the president is indeed extraordinary. However, it is more important to point out that the actual power of the president depends upon his political abilities. The president must act within the framework of a complex and diversified political constituency. He can use the authority of his office to buttress his strength, but this alone is not sufficient. Somehow he must be able to persuade those with whom he deals to follow him; otherwise, he will be weak and ineffective.

— 49 —

PRESIDENTIAL POWER

Richard E. Neustadt

In the United States we like to "rate" a president. We measure him as "weak" or "strong" and call what we are measuring his "leadership." We do not wait until a man is dead; we rate him from the moment he takes office. We are quite right to do so. His office has become the focal point of politics and policy in our political system. Our commentators and our politicians make a specialty of taking the man's measurements. The rest of us join in when we feel "government" impinging on our private lives. In the third quarter of the twentieth century millions of us have that feeling often.

. . . Although we all make judgments about presidential leadership, we often base our judgments upon images of office that are far removed from the reality. We also use those images when we tell one another whom to choose as president. But it is risky to appraise a man in office or to choose a man for office on false premises about the nature of his job. When the job is the presidency of the United States the risk becomes excessive. . . .

We deal here with the president himself and with his influence on governmental action. In institutional terms the presidency now includes 2,000 men and women. The president is only one of them. But *his* performance scarcely can be measured without focusing on *him*. In terms of party, or of country, or the West, so-called, his leadership involves far more than governmental action. But the sharpening of spirit and of values and of purposes is not done in a vacuum. Although governmental action may not be the whole of leadership, all else is nurtured by it and gains meaning from it. Yet if we treat the presidency as the president, we cannot measure him as though he were the government. Not action as an outcome but his impact on the outcome is the measure of the man. His strength or weakness, then, turns on his personal capacity to influence the conduct of the men who make up government. His influence becomes the mark of leadership. To rate a president according to these rules, one looks into the man's own capabilities as seeker and as wielder of effective influence upon the other men involved in governing the country. . . .

"Presidential" . . . means nothing but the president. "Power" means *his* influence. It helps to have these meanings settled at the start.

There are two ways to study "presidential power." One way is to focus on the tactics, so to speak, of influencing certain men in given situations: how to get a bill through Congress, how to settle strikes, how to quiet Cabinet feuds, or how to stop a Suez. The other way is to step back from tactics on those "givens" and to deal with influence in more strategic terms: what is its nature and what are its sources? What can *this* man accomplish to improve the prospect that he will have influence when he wants it? Strategically, the question is not how he masters Congress in a peculiar instance, but what he does to boost his chance for mastery in any instance, looking toward tomorrow from today. The second of these two ways has been chosen for this [selection]. . . .

In form all presidents are leaders, nowadays. In fact this guarantees no more than that they will be clerks. Everybody now expects the man inside the White House to do something about everything. Laws and customs now reflect acceptance of him as the Great Initiator, an acceptance quite as widespread at the Capitol as at his end of Pennsylvania Avenue. But such acceptance does not signify that all the rest of government is at his feet. It merely signifies that other men have found it practically impossible to do *their* jobs without assurance of initiatives from him. Service for themselves, not power for the president, has brought them to accept his leadership in form. They find his actions useful in their business. The transformation of his routine obligations testifies to their dependence on an active White House. A president, these days, is an invaluable clerk. His services are in demand all over Washington. His influence, however, is a very different matter. Laws and customs tell us little about leadership in fact.

Why have our presidents been honored with this clerkship? The answer is that no one else's services suffice. Our Constitution, our traditions, and our politics provide no better source for the initiatives a president can take. Executive officials need decisions, and political protection, and a referee for fights. Where are these to come from but the White House? Congressmen need an agenda from outside, something with high status to respond to or react against. What provides it better than the program of the president? Party politicians need a record to defend in the next national campaign. How can it be made except by "their" Administration? Private persons with a public ax to grind may need a helping hand or they may need a grinding stone. In either case who gives more satisfaction than a president? And outside the United States, in every country where our policies and postures influence home politics, there will be people needing just the "right" thing said and done or just the "wrong" thing stopped in *Washington*. What symbolizes Washington more nearly than the White House?

A modern president is bound to face demands for aid and service from five more or less distinguishable sources: the Executive officialdom, from Congress, from his partisans, from citizens at large, and from abroad. The presidency's clerkship is expressive of these pressures. In effect they are constituency pressures and each president has five sets of constituents. The five are not distinguished by their membership; membership is obviously an overlapping matter. And taken one by one they do not match the man's electorate; one of them, indeed, is outside his electorate. They are distinguished, rather, by their different claims upon him. Initiatives are what they want, for five distinctive reasons. Since government and politics have offered no alternative, our laws and customs turn those wants into his obligations.

Why, then, is the president not guaranteed an influence commensurate with services performed? Constituent relations are relations of dependence. Everyone with any share in governing this country will belong to one (or two, or three) of his "constituencies." Since everyone depends on him why is he not assured of everyone's support? The answer is that no one else sits where he sits, or sees quite as he sees; no one else feels the full weight of his obligations. Those obligations are a tribute to his unique place in our political system. But just because it is unique they fall on him alone. *The same conditions that promote his leadership in form preclude a guarantee of leadership in fact.* No man or group at either end of Pennsylvania Avenue shares his peculiar status in our government and politics. That is why his services are in demand. By the same token, though, the obligations of all other men are different from his own. His Cabinet officers have departmental duties and constituents. His legislative leaders head *Congressional* parties, one in either House. His national party organization stands apart from his official family. His political allies in the states need not face Washington, or one another. The private groups that seek him out are not compelled to govern. And friends abroad are not compelled to run in our elections. Lacking his position and prerogatives, these men cannot regard his obligations as his own. They have their jobs to do; none is the same as his. As they perceive their duty they may find it right to follow him, in fact, or they may not. Whether they will feel obliged *on their responsibility* to do what he wants done remains an open question. . . .

There is reason to suppose that in the years immediately ahead the power problems of a president will remain what they have been in the decades just behind us. If so there will be equal need for presidential expertise of the peculiar sort . . . that has [been] stressed [i.e., political skill]. Indeed, the need is likely to be greater. The president himself and with him the whole government are likely to be more than ever at the mercy of his personal approach.

What may the sixties do to politics and policy and to the place of presidents in our political system? The sixties may destroy them as we know them; that goes without saying. But barring deep depression or unlimited war, a total transformation is the least of likelihoods. Without catastrophes of those dimensions nothing in our past experience suggests that we shall see either consensus of the sort available to F.D.R. in 1933 and 1942, or popular demand for institutional adjustments likely to assist a president. Lacking popular demand, the natural conservatism of established institutions will keep Congress and the party organizations quite resistant to reforms that could give him a clear advantage over them. Four-year terms for congressmen and senators might do it, if the new terms ran with his. What will occasion a demand for that? As for crisis consensus it is probably beyond the reach of the next president. We may have priced ourselves out of the market for "productive" crises on the pattern Roosevelt knew—productive in the sense of strengthening his chances for sustained support *within* the system. Judging from the fifties, neither limited war nor limited depression is productive in those terms. Anything unlimited will probably break the system.

In the absence of productive crises, and assuming that we manage to avoid destructive ones, nothing now foreseeable suggests that our next president will have assured support from any quarter. There is no use expecting it from the bureaucracy unless it is displayed on Capitol Hill. Assured support will not be found in Congress unless contemplation of their own electorates keeps a majority of members constantly aligned with him. In the sixties it is to be doubted . . . that pressure from electors will move the same majority of men in either House toward consistent backing for the president. Instead the chances are that he will gain majorities, when and if he does so, by ad hoc coalition-building, issue after issue. In that respect the sixties will be reminiscent of the fifties; indeed, a closer parallel may well be in the late forties. As for "party discipline" in English terms—the favorite cure-all of political scientists since Woodrow Wilson was a youth—the first preliminary is a party link between the White House and the leadership on both sides of the Capitol. But even this preliminary has been lacking in eight of the fifteen years since the Second World War. If ballot-splitting should continue through the sixties it will soon be "un-American" for president and Congress to belong to the same party.

Even if the trend were now reversed, there is no short-run prospect that behind each party label we would find assembled a sufficiently like-minded bloc of voters, similarly aligned in states and districts all across the country, to negate the massive barriers our institutions and traditions have erected against "discipline" on anything like the British scale. This does not mean that a reversal of the ballot-splitting trend would be without significance. If the White House and the legislative leadership were linked by party ties again, a real advantage would accrue to both. Their opportunities for mutually productive bargaining would be enhanced. The policy results might surprise critics of our system. Bargaining "within the family" has a rather different quality than bargaining with members of the rival clan. But we would still be a long way from "party government." Bargaining, not "discipline," would still remain the key to Congressional action on a president's behalf. The crucial distinctions between presidential party and Congressional party are not likely to be lost in the term of the next president.

Johson

⌒⌒

50

PRESIDENTIAL PARADOXES

Thomas E. Cronin and Michael A. Genovese

⌒⌒

He must have "common opinions." But it is equally imperative that he be an "uncommon man." The public must see themselves in him, but they must, at the same time, be confident that he is something bigger than themselves.

  Harold J. Laski, *The American Presidency: An Interpretation* (Harper & Brothers, 1940), p. 38

To become president, Lincoln had to talk more radically on occasion than he actually felt; to be an effective president he was compelled to act more conservatively than he wanted.

Richard Hofstadler, *The American Political Tradition* (Vintage, 1948), p. 128

A law of opposites frequently influences the American Presidency. Once in office, Presidents are seen to do things least expected of them, often things they had explicitly promised not to do. Previous commitments or perceived inclinations act as a kind of insurance that protects against any great loss if a President behaves contrary to expectation.

Daniel P. Moynihan, *The New Republic*, December 31, 1983, p. 18

The mind searches for answers to the complexities of life. We often gravitate toward simple explanations for the world's mysteries. This is a natural way to try and make sense out of a world that seems to defy understanding. We are uncomfortable with contradictions so we reduce reality to understandable simplifications. And yet, contradictions and clashing expectations are part of life. "No aspect of society, no habit, custom, movement, development, is without cross-currents," says historian Barbara Tuchman. "Starving peasants in hovels live alongside prosperous landlords in featherbeds. Children are neglected and children are loved." In life we are confronted with paradoxes for which we seek meaning. The same is true for the American presidency. We admire presidential power, yet fear it. We yearn for the heroic, yet are also inherently suspicious of it. We demand dynamic leadership, yet grant only limited powers to the president. We want presidents to be dispassionate analysts and listeners, yet they must also be decisive. We are impressed with presidents who have great self-confidence, yet we dislike arrogance and respect those who express reasonable self-doubt.

How then are we to make sense of the presidency? This complex, multidimensional, even contradictory institution is vital to the American system of government. The physical and political laws that seem to constrain one president, liberate another. What proves successful in one, leads to failure in another. Rather than seeking one unifying theory of presidential politics that answers all our questions, we believe that the American presidency might be better understood as a series of paradoxes, clashing expectations and contradictions.

Leaders live with contradictions. Presidents, more than most people, learn to take advantage of contrary or divergent forces. Leadership situations commonly require successive displays of contrasting characteristics. Living with, even embracing, contradictions is a sign of political and personal maturity.

The effective leader understands the presence of opposites. The aware leader, much like a first-rate conductor, knows when to bring in various sections, knows when and how to turn the volume up and down, and learns how to balance opposing sections to achieve desired results. Effective presidents learn how to manage these contradictions and give meaning and purpose to confusing and often clashing expectations. The novelist F. Scott Fitzgerald once suggested that, "The test of a first-rate intelligence is the ability to hold two opposed ideas in the mind at the same time." Casey Stengel, long-time New York Yankee manager and occasional (if accidental) Zen philosopher, captured the essence of the paradox when he noted, "Good pitching will always stop good hitting, and vice versa."

Our expectations of, and demands on, the president are frequently so contradictory as to invite two-faced behavior by our presidents. Presidential powers are often not as great as many of us believe, and the president gets unjustly condemned as ineffective. Or a president will overreach or resort to unfair play while trying to live up to our demands.

The Constitution is of little help. The founders purposely left the presidency imprecisely defined. This was due in part to their fears of both the monarchy and the masses, and in part to their hopes that future presidents would create a more powerful office than the framers were able to do at the time. They knew that at times the president would have to move swiftly and effectively, yet they went to considerable lengths to avoid enumerating specific powers and duties in order to calm the then widespread fear of monarchy. After all, the nation had just fought a war against executive tyranny. Thus the paradox of the invention of the presidency: To get the presidency approved in 1787 and 1788, the framers had to leave several silences and ambiguities for fear of portraying the office as an overly centralized leadership institution. Yet when we need central leadership we turn to the president and read into Article II of the Constitution various prerogatives or inherent powers that allow the president to perform as an effective national leader.

Today the informal and symbolic powers of the presidency account for as much as the formal, stated ones. Presidential powers expand and contract in response to varying situational and technological changes. The powers of the presidency are thus interpreted so differently that they sometimes seem to be those of different offices. In some ways the modem presidency has virtually unlimited authority for almost anything its occupant chooses to do with it. In other ways, a president seems hopelessly ensnarled in a web of checks and balances.

Presidents and presidential candidates must constantly balance conflicting demands, cross pressures, and contradictions. It is characteristic of the American mind to hold contradictory ideas without bothering to resolve the conflicts between them. Perhaps some contradictions are best left unresolved, especially as ours is an imperfect world and our political system is a complicated one, held together by countless compromises. We may not be able to resolve many of these clashing expectations. Some of the inconsistencies in our judgments about presidents doubtless stem from the many ironies and paradoxes of the human condition. While difficult, at the least we should develop a better understanding of what it is we ask of our presidents, thereby increasing our sensitivity to the limits and possibilities of what a president can achieve. This might free presidents to lead and administer more effectively in those critical times when the nation has no choice but to turn to them. Whether we like it or not, the vitality of our democracy depends in large measure upon the sensitive interaction of presidential leadership with an understanding public willing to listen and willing to provide support. Carefully planned innovation is nearly impossible without the kind of leadership a competent and fair-minded president can provide.

The following are some of the paradoxes of the presidency. Some are cases of confused expectations. Some are cases of wanting one kind of presidential behavior at one time, and another kind later. Still others stem from the contradiction inherent in the concept of democratic leadership, which on the surface at least, appears to set up "democratic" and "leadership" as warring concepts. Whatever the source, each has implications for presidential performance and for how Americans judge presidential success and failure.

Paradox #1. Americans demand powerful, popular presidential leadership that solves the nation's problems. Yet we are inherently suspicious of strong centralized leadership and the abuse of power. Thus we place significant limits on the president's powers.

Paradox #2. We yearn for the democratic "common person" and simultaneously a leader who is uncommon, charismatic, heroic, and visionary.

Paradox #3. We want a decent, just, caring, and compassionate president, yet we also admire a cunning, guileful, and, on occasions that warrant it, even a ruthless, manipulative president.

Paradox #4. We admire the "above politics" nonpartisan or bipartisan approach, and yet the presidency is perhaps the most political office in the American system, which requires a creative entrepreneurial master politician.

Paradox #5. We want a president who can unify diverse people and interests; however, the job requires taking firm stands, making unpopular or controversial decisions that necessarily upset and divide.

Paradox #6. We expect our presidents to provide bold, visionary, innovative, programmatic leadership, and at the same time to respond pragmatically to the will of public opinion majorities. That is to say, we expect presidents to lead and to follow, and to exercise "democratic leadership."

Paradox #7. Americans want powerful, self-confident presidential leadership. Yet we are inherently suspicious of leaders who view themselves as infallible and above criticism.

Paradox #8. What it takes to become president may not be what is needed to govern the nation.

Paradox #9. The presidency is sometimes too strong yet at other times too weak.

To govern successfully, presidents must manage these paradoxes, and must balance a variety of competing demands and expectations.

Presidential Politics

Whether the Founding Fathers intended that the president would be a king or a clerk, they clearly did not foresee the deep involvement of the presidency in *partisan* politics. All presidents after George Washington were party chiefs, a role that grew more important as national parties expanded their electoral bases and began to act in a more disciplined fashion to facilitate their control of government. American parties have never been disciplined in the European sense, but they have managed to achieve sufficient organizational unity at both national and more importantly state and local levels to affect and sometimes determine the course of government.

Presidential parties help to identify and translate the political demands of popular majorities into government action. Theoretically at least, presidents should be able to use their role as party chief to bridge the constitutional gap between the presidency and Congress that the separation of powers created. Before becoming party chief, politicians must capture their party's presidential nomination. Whether or not parties should choose their nominees through "brokered" conventions, in which party power brokers and "bosses" dominate, or through a grass roots process controlled by rank-and-file party members, continues to be hotly debated. Proponents of brokered conventions argue that party leaders tend to choose "better" candidates, those more representative of broad party interests and more likely to appeal to a national electorate, than candidates nominated by a grass roots process that reflects the views of a relatively narrow party electorate.

Presidential Character and Style

The preceding selections in this chapter have focused upon the institutional aspects of the presidency and the constitutional and political responsibilities of the office. Richard Neustadt does focus upon certain personal dimensions of the power equation, the ability to persuade, but he does not deal with presidential character outside the power context. The following selection is taken from one of the most important and innovative of the recent books dealing with the presidency, in which the author, James David Barber, presents the thesis that it is the *total character* of the person who occupies the White House that is the determinant of presidential performance. As he states, "The presidency is much more than an institution." It is not only the focus of the emotional involvement of most people in politics, but also occupied by an emotional person. How that person is able to come to grips with his feelings and emotions often shapes his orientation toward issues and the way in which he makes decisions. From the very beginning the office was thought of in highly personal terms, for the framers of the Constitution, in part at least, built the office around the character of George Washington, who virtually everyone at the time thought would be the first occupant of the office. And evolution of the office since 1787 has added to its personal quotient. James David Barber provides a framework for the analysis of presidential character and its effect upon performance in the White House.

—— 51 ——

THE PRESIDENTIAL CHARACTER

James David Barber

When a citizen votes for a presidential candidate he makes, in effect, a prediction. He chooses from among the contenders the one he thinks (or feels, or guesses) would be the best president. He operates in a situation of immense uncertainty. If he has a long voting history, he can recall time and time again when he guessed wrong. He listens to the commentators, the politicians, and his friends, then adds it all up in some rough way to produce his prediction and his vote. Earlier in the game, his anticipations have been taken into account, either directly in the polls and primaries or indirectly in the minds of politicians who want to nominate someone he will like. But he must choose in the midst of a cloud of confusion, a rain of phony advertising, a storm of sermons, a hail of complex issues, a fog of charisma and boredom, and a thunder of accusation and defense. In the face of this chaos, a great many citizens fall back on the past, vote their old allegiances, and let it go at that. Nevertheless, the citizen's vote says that on balance he expects Mr. X would outshine Mr. Y in the presidency.

This [book] is meant to help citizens and those who advise them cut through the confusion and get at some clear criteria for choosing presidents. To understand what actual presidents do and what potential presidents might do, the first need is to see the man whole—not as some abstract embodiment of civic virtue, some scorecard of issue stands, or some reflection of a faction, but as a human being like the rest of us, a person trying to cope with a difficult environment. To that task he brings his own character, his own view of the world, his own political style. None of that is new for him. If we can see the pattern he has set for his political life we can, I contend, estimate much better his pattern as he confronts the stresses and chances of the presidency.

The presidency is a peculiar office. The founding fathers left it extraordinarily loose in definition, partly because they trusted George Washington to invest a tradition as he went along. It is an institution made a piece at a time by successive men in the White House. Jefferson reached out to Congress to put together the beginnings of political parties; Jackson's dramatic force extended electoral partisanship to its mass base; Lincoln vastly expanded the administrative reach of the office; Wilson and the Roosevelts showed its rhetorical possibilities—in fact, every President's mind and demeanor has left its mark on a heritage still in lively development.

But the presidency is much more than an institution. It is a focus of feelings. In general, popular feelings about politics are low-key, shallow, casual. For example, the vast majority of Americans knows virtually nothing of what Congress is doing and cares less. The presidency is different. The presidency is the focus for the most intense and persistent emotions in the American polity. The president is a symbolic leader, the one figure who draws together the people's hopes and fears for the political future. On top of all his routine duties, he has to carry that off—or fail.

Our emotional attachment to presidents shows up when one dies in office. People were not just disappointed or worried when President Kennedy was killed; people wept at the loss of a man most had never even met. Kennedy was young and charismatic—but history shows that whenever a president dies in office, heroic Lincoln or debased Harding, McKinley or Garfield, the same wave of deep emotion sweeps across the country. On the other hand, the death of an ex-president brings forth no such intense emotional reaction.

The president is the first political figure children are aware of (later they add Congress, the Court, and others, as "helpers" of the president). With some exceptions among children in deprived circumstances, the president is seen as a "benevolent leader," one who nurtures, sustains, and inspires the citizenry. Presidents regularly show up among "most admired" contemporaries and forebears, and the president is the "best known" (in the sense of sheer name recognition) person in the country. At inauguration time, even presidents elected by close margins are supported by much larger majorities than the election returns show, for people rally round as he actually assumes office. There is a similar reaction when the people see their president threatened by crisis: if he takes action, there is a favorable spurt in the Gallup poll whether he succeeds or fails.

Obviously the president gets more attention in schoolbooks, press, and television than any other politician. He is one of very few who can make news by doing good things. His emotional state is a matter of continual public commentary, as is the manner in which his personal and official families conduct themselves. The media bring across the president not as some neutral administrator or corporate executive to be assessed by his production, but as a special being with mysterious dimensions.

We have no king. The sentiments English children—and adults—direct to the Queen have no place to go in our system but to the president. Whatever his talents—Coolidge-type or Roosevelt-type—the president is the only available object for such national-religious-monarchical sentiments as Americans possess.

The president helps people make sense of politics. Congress is a tangle of committees, the bureaucracy is a maze of agencies. The president is one man trying to do a job—a picture much more understandable to the mass of people who find themselves in the same boat. Furthermore, he is the top man. He ought to know what is going on and set it right. So when the economy goes sour, or war drags on, or domestic violence erupts, the president is available to take the blame. Then when things go right, it seems the president must have had a hand in it. Indeed, the flow of political life is marked off by presidents: the "Eisenhower Era," the "Kennedy Years."

What all this means is that the president's main responsibilities reach far beyond administering the Executive Branch or commanding the armed forces. The White House is first and foremost a place of public leadership. That inevitably brings to bear on the president intense moral, sentimental, and quasi-religious pressures which can, if he lets them, distort his own thinking and feeling. If there is such a thing as extraordinary sanity, it is needed nowhere so much as in the White House.

Who the president is at a given time can make a profound difference in the whole thrust and direction of national politics. Since we have only one president at a time, we can never prove this by comparison, but even the most superficial speculation confirms the commonsense view that the man himself weighs heavily among other historical factors. A Wilson reelected in 1920, a Hoover in 1932, a John F. Kennedy in 1964 would, it seems very likely, have guided the body politic along rather different paths from those their actual successors chose. Or try to imagine a Theodore Roosevelt ensconced behind today's "bully pulpit" of a presidency, or Lyndon Johnson as president in the age of McKinley. Only someone mesmerized by the lures of historical inevitability can suppose that it would have made little or no difference to government policy had Alf Landon replaced FDR in 1936, had Dewey beaten Truman in 1948, or Adlai Stevenson reigned through the 1950s. Not only would these alternative presidents have advocated different policies—they would have approached the office from very different psychological angles. It stretches credibility to think that Eugene McCarthy would have run the institution the way Lyndon Johnson did.

The burden of this [argument] is that the crucial differences can be anticipated by an understanding of a potential president's character, his world view, and his style. This kind of prediction is not easy; well-informed observers often have guessed wrong as they watched a man step toward the White House. One thinks of Woodrow Wilson, the scholar who would bring reason to politics; of Herbert Hoover, the Great Engineer who would organize chaos into progress; of Franklin D. Roosevelt, that champion of the balanced budget; of Harry Truman, whom the office would surely overwhelm; of Dwight D. Eisenhower, militant crusader; of John F. Kennedy, who would lead beyond moralisms to achievements; of Lyndon B. Johnson, the Southern conservative; and of Richard M. Nixon, conciliator. Spotting the errors is easy. Predicting with even approximate accuracy is going to require some sharp tools and close attention in their use. But the experiment is worth it because the question is critical and because it lends itself to correction by evidence.

My argument comes in layers.

First, a president's personality is an important shaper of his presidential behavior on nontrivial matters.

Second, presidential personality is patterned. His character, world view, and style fit together in a dynamic package understandable in psychological terms.

Third, a president's personality interacts with the power situation he faces and the national "climate of expectations" dominant at the time he serves. The tuning, the resonance—or lack of it—between these external factors and his personality sets in motion the dynamics of his presidency.

Fourth, the best way to predict a president's character, world view, and style is to see how they were put together in the first place. That happened in his early life, culminating in his first independent political success.

But the core of the argument . . . is that presidential character—the basic stance a man takes toward his presidential experience—comes in four varieties. The most important thing to know about a president or candidate is where he fits among these types, defined according to (a) how active he is and (b) whether or not he gives the impression he enjoys his political life.

Let me spell out these concepts briefly before getting down to cases.

Personality Shapes Performance

I am not about to argue that once you know a president's personality you know everything. But as the cases will demonstrate, the degree and quality of a president's emotional involvement in an issue are powerful influences on how he defines the issue itself, how much attention he pays to it, which facts and persons he sees as relevant to its resolution, and finally, what principles and purposes he associates with the issue. Every story of presidential decision-making is really two stories: an outer one in which a rational man calculates and an inner one in which an emotional man feels. The two are forever connected. Any real president is one whole man and his deeds reflect his wholeness.

As for personality, it is a matter of tendencies. It is not that one president "has" some basic characteristic that another president does not "have." That old way of treating a trait as a possession, like a rock in a basket, ignores the universality of aggressiveness, compliancy, detachment, and other human drives. We all have all of them, but in different amounts and in different combinations.

The Pattern of Character, World View, and Style

The most visible part of the pattern is style. *Style is the president's habitual way of performing his three political roles: rhetoric, personal relations, and homework.* Not to be confused with "stylishness," charisma, or appearance, style is how the president goes about doing what the office requires him to do—to speak, directly or through media, to large audiences; to deal face to face with other politicians, individually and in small, relatively private groups; and to read, write, and calculate by himself in order to manage the endless flow of details that stream onto his desk. No president can escape doing at least some of each. But there are marked differences in stylistic emphasis from president to president. The *balance* among the three style elements varies; one president may put most of himself into rhetoric, another may stress close, informal dealing, while still another may devote his energies mainly to study and cogitation. Beyond the balance, we want to see each president's peculiar habits of style, his mode of coping with and adapting to these presidential demands. For example, I think both Calvin Coolidge and John F. Kennedy were primarily rhetoricians, but they went about it in contrasting ways.

A president's *world view consists of his primary, politically relevant beliefs, particularly his conceptions of social causality, human nature, and the central moral conflicts of the time.* This is how he sees the world and his lasting opinions about what he sees. Style is his way of acting; world view is his way of seeing. Like the rest of us, a president develops over a lifetime certain conceptions of reality—how things work in politics, what people are like, what the main purposes are. These assumptions or conceptions help him make sense of his world, give some semblance of order to the chaos of existence. Perhaps most important: a man's world view affects what he pays attention to, and a great deal of politics is about paying attention. The name of the game for many politicians is not so much "Do this, do that" as it is "Look here!"

"Character" comes from the Greek word for engraving; in one sense it is what life has marked into a man's being. As used here, *character is the way the president orients himself toward life*—not for the moment, but enduringly. Character is the person's stance as he confronts experience. And at the core of character, a man confronts himself. The president's fundamental self-esteem is his prime personal resource; to defend and advance that, he will sacrifice much else he values. Down there in the privacy of his heart, does he find himself superb, or ordinary, or debased, or in some intermediate range? No president has been utterly paralyzed by self-doubt and none has been utterly free of midnight self-mockery. In between, the real presidents move out on life from positions of relative strength or weakness. Equally important are the criteria by which they judge themselves. A president who rates himself by the standard of achievement, for instance, may be little affected by losses of affection.

Character, world view, and style are abstractions from the reality of the whole individual. In every case they form an integrated pattern: the man develops a combination which makes psychological sense for him, a dynamic arrangement of motives, beliefs, and habits in the service of his need for self-esteem.

The Power Situation
and "Climate of Expectations"

Presidential character resonates with the political situation the president faces. It adapts him as he tries to adapt it. The support he has from the public and interest groups, the party balance in Congress, the thrust of Supreme Court opinion together set the basic power situation he must deal with. An activist president may run smack into a brick wall of resistance, then pull back and wait for a better moment. On the other hand, a president who sees himself as a quiet caretaker may not try to exploit even the most favorable power situation. So it is the relationship between president and the political configuration that makes the system tick.

Even before public opinion polls, the president's real or supposed popularity was a large factor in his performance. Besides the power mix in Washington, the president has to deal with a national climate of expectations, the predominant needs thrust up to him by the people. There are at least three recurrent themes around which these needs are focused.

People look to the president for *reassurance*, a feeling that things will be all right, that the president will take care of his people. The psychological request is for a surcease of anxiety. Obviously, modern life in America involves considerable doses of fear, tension, anxiety, worry; from time to time, the public mood calls for a rest, a time of peace, a breathing space, a "return to normalcy."

Another theme is the demand for a sense of *progress and action*. The president ought to do something to direct the nation's course—or at least be in there pitching for the people. The president is looked to as a take-charge man, a doer, a turner of the wheels, a producer of progress—even if that means some sacrifice of serenity.

A third type of climate of expectations is the public need for a sense of *legitimacy* from, and in, the presidency. The president should be a master politician who is above politics. He should have a right to his place and a rightful way of acting in it. The respectability—even religiosity—of the office has to be protected by a man who presents himself as defender of the faith. There is more to this than dignity, more than propriety. The president is expected to personify our betterness in an inspiring way, to express in what he does and is (not just in what he says) a moral idealism which, in much of the public mind, is the very opposite of "politics."

Over time the climate of expectations shifts and changes. Wars, depressions, and other national events contribute to that change, but there also is a rough cycle, from an emphasis on action (which begins to look too "political") to an emphasis on legitimacy (the moral uplift of which creates its own strains) to an emphasis on reassurance and rest (which comes to seem like drift) and back to action again. One need not be astrological about it. The point is that the climate of expectations at any given time is the political air the president has to breathe. Relating to this climate is a large part of his task.

Johnson
Reagan
Clinton

Predicting Presidents

The best way to predict a president's character, world view, and style is to see how he constructed them in the first place. Especially in the early stages, life is experimental; consciously or not, a person tries out various ways of defining and maintaining and raising self-esteem. He looks to his environment for clues as to who he is and how well he is doing. These lessons of life slowly sink in: certain self-images and evaluations, certain ways of looking at the world, certain styles of action get confirmed by his experience and he gradually adopts them as his own. If we can see that process of development, we can understand the product. The features to note are those bearing on presidential performance.

Experimental development continues all the way to death; we will not blind ourselves to midlife changes, particularly in the full-scale prediction case, that of Richard Nixon. But it is often much easier to see the basic patterns in early life histories. Later on a whole host of distractions—especially the image-making all politicians learn to practice—clouds the picture.

In general, character has its main development in childhood, world view in adolescence, style in early adulthood. The stance toward life I call character grows out of the child's experiments in relating to parents, brothers and sisters, and peers at play and in school, as well as to his own body and the objects around it. Slowly the child defines an orientation toward experience; once established, that tends to last despite much subsequent contradiction. By adolescence, the child has been hearing and seeing how people make their worlds meaningful, and now he is moved to relate himself—his own meanings—to those around him. His focus of attention shifts toward the future; he senses that decisions about his fate are coming and he looks into the premises for those decisions. Thoughts about the way the world works and how one might work in it, about what people are like and how one might be like them or not, and about the values people share and how one might share in them too—these are typical concerns for the post-child, pre-adult mind of the adolescent.

These themes come together strongly in early adulthood, when the person moves from contemplation to responsible action and adopts a style. In most biographical accounts this period stands out in stark clarity—the time of emergence, the time the young man found himself. I call it his first independent political success. It was then he moved beyond the detailed guidance of his family; then his self-esteem was dramatically boosted; then he came forth as a person to be reckoned with by other people. The way he did that is profoundly important to him. Typically he grasps that style and hangs onto it. Much later, coming into the presidency, something in him remembers this earlier victory and reemphasizes the style that made it happen.

Character provides the main thrust and broad direction—but it does not *determine*, in any fixed sense, world view and style. The story of development does not end with the end of childhood. Thereafter, the culture one grows in and the ways that culture is translated by parents and peers shape the meanings one makes of his character. The going world view gets learned and that learning helps channel character forces. Thus it will not necessarily be true that compulsive characters have reactionary beliefs, or that compliant characters believe in compromise. Similarly for style: historical accidents play a large part in furnishing special opportunities for action—and in blocking off alternatives. For example, however much anger a young man may feel, that anger will not be expressed in rhetoric unless and until his life situation provides a platform and an audience. Style thus has a stature and independence of its own. Those who would reduce all explanation to character neglect these highly significant later channelings. For beyond the root is the branch, above the foundation the superstructure, and starts do not prescribe finishes.

Four Types of Presidential Character

The five concepts—character, world view, style, power situation, and climate of expectations—run through the accounts of presidents in [later chapters of Barber's book], which cluster the presidents since Theodore Roosevelt into four types. This is the fundamental scheme of the study. It offers a way to move past the complexities to the main contrasts and comparisons.

The first baseline in defining presidential types is *activity-passivity*. How much energy does the man invest in his presidency? Lyndon Johnson went at his day like a human cyclone, coming to rest long after the sun went down. Calvin Coolidge often slept eleven hours a night and still needed a nap in the middle of the day. In between the presidents array themselves on the high or low side of the activity line.

The second baseline is *positive-negative affect* toward one's activity—this is, how he feels about what he does. Relatively speaking, does he seem to experience his political life as happy or sad, enjoyable or discouraging, positive or negative in its main effect? The feeling I am after here is not grim satisfaction in a job well done, not some philosophical conclusion. The idea is this: is he someone who, on the surfaces we can see, gives forth the feeling that he has *fun in political* life? Franklin Roosevelt's Secretary of War, Henry L. Stimson, wrote that the Roosevelts "not only understood the *use* of power, they knew the *enjoyment* of power, too. . . . Whether a man is burdened by power or enjoys power; whether he is trapped by responsibility or made free by it; whether he is moved by other people and outer forces or moves them—that is the essence of leadership."

The positive-negative baseline, then, is a general symptom of the fit between the man and his experience, a kind of register of *felt* satisfaction.

Why might we expect these two simple dimensions to outline the main character types? Because they stand for two central features of anyone's orientation toward life. In nearly every study of personality, some form of the active-passive contrast is critical; the general tendency to act or be acted upon is evident in such concepts as dominance-submission, extraversion-introversion, aggression-timidity, attack-defense, fight-flight, engagement-withdrawal, approach-avoidance. In everyday life we sense quickly the general energy output of the people we deal with. Similarly we catch on fairly quickly to the affect dimension—whether the person seems to be optimistic or pessimistic, hopeful or skeptical, happy or sad. The two baselines are clear and they are also independent of one another: all of us know people who are very active but seem discouraged, others who are quite passive but seem happy, and so forth. The activity baseline refers to what one does, the affect baseline to how one feels about what he does.

Both are crude clues to character. They are leads into four basic character patterns long familiar in psychological research. In summary form, these are the main configurations:

Active-Positive. There is a congruence, a consistency, between much activity and the enjoyment of it, indicating relatively high self-esteem and relative success in relating to the environment. The man shows an orientation toward productiveness as a value and an ability to use his styles flexibly, adaptively, suiting the dance to the music. He sees himself as developing over time toward relatively well defined personal goals—growing toward his image of himself as he might yet be. There is an emphasis on rational mastery, on using the brain to move the feet. This may get him into trouble; he may fail to take account of the irrational in politics. Not everyone he deals with sees things his way and he may find it hard to understand why.

Active-Negative. The contradiction here is between relatively intense effort and relatively low emotional reward for that effort. The activity has a compulsive quality, as if the man were trying to make up for something or to escape from anxiety into hard work. He seems ambitious, striving upward, power-seeking. His stance toward the environment is aggressive and he has a persistent problem in managing his aggressive feelings. His self-image is vague and discontinuous. Life is a hard struggle to achieve and hold power, hampered by the condemnations of a perfectionistic conscience. Active-negative types pour energy into the political system, but it is an energy distorted from within.

Passive-Positive. This is the receptive, compliant, other-directed character whose life is a search for affection as a reward for being agreeable and cooperative rather than personally assertive. The contradiction is between low self-esteem (on grounds of being unlovable, unattractive) and a superficial optimism. A hopeful attitude helps dispel doubt and elicits encouragement from others. Passive-positive types help soften the harsh edges of politics. But their dependence and the fragility of their hopes and enjoyments make disappointment in politics likely.

Passive-Negative. The factors are consistent—but how are we to account for the man's *political* role-taking? Why is someone who does little in politics and enjoys it less there at all? The answer lies in the passive-negative's character-rooted orientation toward doing dutiful service; this compensates for low self-esteem based on a sense of uselessness. Passive-negative types are in politics because they think they ought to be. They may be well adapted to certain nonpolitical roles, but they lack the experience and flexibility to perform effectively as political leaders. Their tendency is to withdraw, to escape from the conflict and uncertainty of politics by emphasizing vague principles (especially prohibitions) and procedural arrangements. They become guardians of the right and proper way, above the sordid politicking of lesser men. Active-positive presidents want most to achieve results. Active-negatives aim to get and keep power. Passive-positives are after love. Passive-negatives emphasize their civic virtue. The relation of activity to enjoyment in a president thus tends to outline a cluster of characteristics, to set apart the adapted from the compulsive, compliant, and withdrawn types.

The first four presidents of the United States, conveniently, ran through this gamut of character types. (Remember, we are talking about tendencies, broad directions; no individual man exactly fits a category.) George Washington—clearly the most important president in the pantheon—established the fundamental legitimacy of an American government at a time when this was a matter in considerable question. Washington's dignity, judiciousness, his aloof air of reserve and dedication to duty fit the passive-negative or withdrawing type best. Washington did not seek innovation, he sought stability. He longed to retire to Mount Vernon, but fortunately was persuaded to stay on through a second term, in which, by rising above the political conflict between Hamilton and Jefferson and inspiring confidence in his own integrity, he gave the nation time to develop the organized means for peaceful change.

John Adams followed, a dour New England Puritan, much given to work and worry, an impatient and irascible man—an active-negative president, a compulsive type. Adams was far more partisan than Washington; the survival of the system through his presidency demonstrated that the nation could tolerate, for a time, domination by one of its nascent political parties. As president, an angry Adams brought the United States to the brink of war with France, and presided over the new nation's first experiment in political representation: the Alien and Sedition Acts, forbidding, among other things, unlawful combinations "with intent to oppose any measure or measures of the government of the United States," or "any false, scandalous, and malicious writing or writings against the United States, or the president of the United States, with intent to defame . . . or to bring them or either of them, into contempt or disrepute."

Then came Jefferson. He too had his troubles and failures—in the design of national defense, for example. As for his presidential character (only one element in success or failure), Jefferson was clearly active-positive. A child of the Enlightenment, he applied his reason to organizing connections with Congress aimed at strengthening the more popular forces. A man of catholic interests and delightful humor, Jefferson combined a clear and open vision of what the country could be with a profound political sense, expressed in his famous phrase, "Every difference of opinion is not a difference of principle."

The fourth president was James Madison, "Little Jemmy," the constitutional philosopher thrown into the White House at a time of great international turmoil. Madison comes closest to the passive-positive, or compliant, type; he suffered from irresolution, tried to compromise his way out, and gave in too readily to the "warhawks" urging combat with Britain. The nation drifted into war, and Madison wound up ineptly commanding his collection of amateur generals in the streets of Washington. General Jackson's victory at New Orleans saved the Madison administration's historical reputation; but he left the presidency with the United States close to bankruptcy and secession.

These four presidents—like all presidents—were persons trying to cope with the roles they had won by using the equipment they had built over a lifetime. The president is not some shapeless organism in a flood of novelties, but a man with a memory in a system with a history. Like all of us, he draws on his past to shape his future. The pathetic hope that the White House will turn a Caligula into a Marcus Aurelius is as naive as the fear that ultimate power inevitably corrupts. The problem is to understand—and to state understandably—what in the personal past foreshadows the presidential future. . . .

——————————————— ✑ ———————————————

The following selection assesses President Clinton's presidential style and how it defined his leadership.

52

CAMPAIGNING IS NOT GOVERNING: BILL CLINTON'S RHETORICAL PRESIDENCY

George C. Edwards III

James David Barber has identified three political roles that all presidents must perform: rhetoric, personal relations, and homework. The habitual way of performing these roles is what he terms presidential style. The relative emphases in a president's style reflect not only the president's strengths but also his perceptions about the requirements of effective leadership.

The Clinton presidency is the ultimate example of the rhetorical presidency, a presidency based on a perpetual campaign to obtain the public's support and fed by public opinion polls, focus groups, and public relations memos. No president ever invested more in measuring, and attempting to mold, public opinion. The White House even polled voters on where it was best for the First Family to vacation. This is an administration that spent $18 million on ads in 1995—a nonelection year! And this is an administration that repeatedly interpreted its setbacks, whether in elections or on health care reform, in terms of its failure to communicate rather than in terms of the quality of its initiatives or the strategy for governing. Reflecting his orientation in the White House, Bill Clinton declared that "the role of the President of the United States is message."

To understand the . . . Clinton presidency, we must explore the president's leadership style and ask whether it was effective for advancing his views. The focus on governing to accomplish goals requires us to answer two central questions about the Clinton administation. First, did the president accurately identify the possibilities in his environment for accomplishing his goals and, more specifically, the potential of his governing style? Second, was the president's strategy of emphasizing rhetoric an effective one for accomplishing his goals? These questions tap the essential aspects of the leadership challenges faced by all presidents, independent of their ideologies.

Implicit in the first question is an appreciation for the importance of the context in which the president operates. It makes little sense to fault presidents for not passing a great deal of legislation if their parties had only a modest number of seats in Congress, for example. Similarly, it is much easier to win support for bold initiatives when budgetary resources are available (as in the mid-1960s) than when they are scarce (as in the 1990s).

The first question is also premised on the view that presidents will not be able to change their environments very much. . . . [T]here is little evidence that presidents can restructure the political landscape to pave the way for change. Although not prisoners of their environment, they are likely to be highly constrained by it.

A critical aspect of presidential leadership, then, is understanding the constraints and possibilities in the environment so as to exploit them most effectively. Once having evaluated the environment, an effective president must fashion a strategy to work within it to accomplish his goals. . . .

Understanding His Strategic Position

At the core of successful political leadership in America is the ability to understand the political system in general and one's strategic position in it at any point in time so as to assess accurately the potential for policy change. A critical aspect of understanding the political environment is understanding the potential of various sources of influence.

In his first two years in office, President Clinton accentuated a problem inherent in our separation of powers system by overreaching—overestimating the extent of change that a president elected with a minority of the vote could make. Any president elected with only 43 percent of the vote should not expect to pass far-reaching social legislation without involving the other party, especially when the public is dubious and well-organized interest groups are fervently opposed. So, a partisan, unitarian approach was unlikely to succeed; yet this is exactly the strategy the president adopted. For example, the "us against them" approach to policy-making encouraged the president to develop his health care plan in Democrats-only secrecy and to pursue a left-in coalition-building strategy instead of a center-out one. Failure was inevitable.

Moreover, the greater the breadth and complexity of the policy change a president proposes, the more opposition it is likely to engender. In an era when a few opponents can effectively tie up bills, the odds are clearly against the White House. Yet when it came to health care reform, the president proposed perhaps the most sweeping, complex prescriptions to control the conduct of state governments, employers, drug manufacturers, doctors, hospitals, and individuals in American history. . . .

In the end, the president was not able to cut taxes for the middle class or substantially increase spending on education, job training, public works, and health care. Nor was he able to obtain welfare reform on his terms. He could not devise strategies for moving in the context in which he found himself, partly because he misread his political environment.

Many of his most notable successes, including the North American Free Trade Agreement (NAFTA), family leave, and motor voter registration had substantial support in Congress before he arrived in Washington. In the case of NAFTA, he was able to rely on Republican support for George Bush's policy initiative. He understood that he needed to engage in a bipartisan strategy that had the additional advantage of entailing no direct budgetary implications. In the latter two cases, the bills had passed before (and been vetoed by Bush) and little leadership was required. . . .

The Limits of the
Rhetorical Presidency

The belief in the importance of rhetoric is not surprising for presidents elected in the age of mass communications or for White House political advisers who employed public relations techniques adeptly during a successful presidential campaign. Yet there are important differences between campaigning and governing, and the president must adjust if he is to succeed.

The transition is rarely smooth. As Charles O. Jones put it, "After heading a temporary, highly convergent, and concentrated organization" in a presidential campaign, the winner moves into the White House and becomes the "central figure in a permanent, divergent, and dispersed structure." As we have seen, communication becomes more difficult as the president loses control of his agenda and has to convince people not that he is superior to his opponent(s)—a relatively simple comparative judgment—but that his calls for specific change deserve support. At the same time, his opponents need only to cast doubt on the president's proposals to kill them.

In such an environment, it is important for the White House to have a clear understanding of the potential of governing through the rhetorical presidency. To start, there are very real limits to what public support can do for the president. The impact of public approval or disapproval on the support the president receives in Congress occurs at the margins of the effort to build coalitions behind proposed policies. No matter how low presidential standing dips, the president still receives support from a substantial number of senators and representatives. Similarly, no matter how high approval levels climb, a significant portion of the Congress will still oppose certain presidential policies. Members of Congress are unlikely to vote against the clear interests of their constituencies or the firm tenets of their ideology out of deference to a widely supported chief executive. Public approval gives the president leverage, not control.

Yet despite the history of failures and frustrations of the emphasis on rhetoric, the Clinton White House continued to assign strategic primacy to communications. In a discussion of his problems in his first year in office, the president declared that he needed to do a better job of communicating: "There have been times when I've been surprised by my inability to shape the agenda on a daily basis or to shape the message that's going out to the folks. . . . It's always frustrating to feel that you're misunderstood. . . . And you can't quite get through." A year later the president sounded the same theme as the solution to his political problems: "What I've got to do is to spend more time communicating with the American people about what we've done and where we're going." Four years later things had not changed. The president's legislative program was largely dead, and the White House was embattled, fighting charges that the president had committed impeachable offenses. Once again, the White House employed the rhetoric of campaigning in the hopes of surviving to govern for two more years. The question remains whether the president can successfully employ his leadership style to leave his mark on public policy.

———————————————— ℘ ————————————————

The President and the Media

The media spotlight is on the presidency more than on other governmental institutions. Theodore Roosevelt was the first president to undertake a major effort to co-opt the press, giving Washington reporters space in the White House in order to facilitate his use of them as much as to accommodate the growing presidential press corps. Teddy Roosevelt knew that the press could be an important ally of government, that publicity for presidential policies and actions could help to build public support and ease the job of his administration.

Teddy Roosevelt set a precedent for twentieth-century presidents in recognizing the power of the press and the importance of turning the political reporters' craft to the advantage of the White House by managing the news. Teddy Roosevelt's cousin, Franklin D. Roosevelt, held regular informal press conferences with reporters in the Oval Office, knowing that if he kept them informed of his programs and progress the nation would learn about and, he hoped, support the New Deal.

From the vantage point of the White House, the press, while potentially a useful conduit of managed news, is seen more as a critic than an ally. Presidents tend to view the press as the enemy with which they have to deal. Charged with the responsibility of coping with the press is the presidential press secretary, who conducts daily briefings apprising White House reporters of the president's actions and plans.

A former White House press corps insider, George E. Reedy, portrays the world of the White House reporter and the way in which presidents view and treat the press.

——————————————— **53** ———————————————

FEEDING THE BEAST

Kenneth T. Walsh

℘

Maureen Dowd was shell-shocked. The normally glib and irreverent *New York Times* correspondent could barely manage a coherent sentence as she sat forlornly on a folding metal chair. Her eyes were swollen with fatigue, and she rested her chin awkardly on the palm of her hand.

Dowd was among sixteen reporters and eight White House staffers who were stranded in Cambridge, England, on President Bill Clinton's June 1994 trip to commemorate the fiftieth anniversary of D day. White House logistics had broken down completely. The helicopter that was to have transported the group a hundred miles to Portsmouth, England, could not fly because of bad weather. Worse, the buses that were supposed to serve as backups were out of service; the drivers had already been on the job for ten hours, the maximum workday, according to their contracts, and they refused to make the long drive to the coast. The increasingly frantic reporters had no idea what kind of news Clinton was making in Portsmouth, where he was scheduled to meet the queen of England that evening. They could be missing one of the biggest stories of the trip. Dowd begged Jeremy Games, a peach-fuzed White House aide who found himself in charge, to get a message to her bureau chief, R. W. "Johnny" Apple: She doubted that she could file a story before her deadline, because she would miss the meeting with the queen and whatever else was going on in Portsmouth. "Johnny," Dowd moaned, "is gonna be pissed."

It was one of the low points on the most badly organized trip I had ever seen in nearly a decade of covering the presidency. As is customary, the White House had agreed to provide transportation, at media expense, for the small army of reporters, editors, and photographers. No one, however, had made adequate contingency plans for bad weather, even though storms are common in Britain and Normandy every June, as anyone familiar with the D day landing would have known.

In the end, a rump group of half a dozen radio correspondents, fed up with White House incompetency, took a British Rail line to London and connected to a train to Portsmouth. They arrived twelve hours late. Most of us in the "Cambridge 24" waited it out and finally boarded a bus driven by a chap hastily recruited by the local transportation company. We rolled into Portsmouth eleven hours behind schedule, just after a fireworks display to commemorate D day that caused a horrendous traffic jam. At a standstill, our weary group decided to file off the bus, toting our carry-on bags and laptop computers, in an attempt to make our way to the media center where we could file our stories. At various points as we trudged along the seawall in the dark, young Jeremy would flash his White House identification pin to puzzled tourists and ask them how to get to the media center. No one knew, so we kept shuffling toward some lights in the distance.

After two miles, we reached a chain-link fence where a kindly guard took pity on us and let us through the gate. More than twelve hours late, we had finally arrived at the Portsmouth filing center, long after Clinton had gone to bed. Everyone was fuming.

This episode was only a skirmish in the war between the press corps and the White House, but it gave reporters more evidence that either the Clintonites didn't respect journalists enough to treat them decently or that they weren't competent enough to make their own helicopters and buses run on time. Even the big media stars were treated with surprising ineptitude. Army helicopters transporting network television hotshots—Tom Brokaw of NBC, Sam Donaldson of ABC, and Harry Smith of CBS—got lost trying to find the USS George Washington, the aircraft carrier on which President Clinton was to spend the night.

Maureen Dowd, for one, got her revenge in a piece for *The New York Times Magazine* on June 19. "With the exception of the First Lady, a tidy traveler, the presidential operation has the smell of a dormitory about it, with everyone crashing for exams," Dowd wrote. "Each White House reflects the personality of its leader, and this President, immune to punctuality and discipline, will always have a Pigpen cloud of chaos around him."

There was a final insult. A few days after the trip, the executive officer of the aircraft carrier billed the White House $562 for sixty-eight towels and sixteen bathrobes that had disappeared from the staterooms being used by forty White House staffers and twenty-three journalists. White House press secretary Dee Dee Myers was quick to point fingers at the reporters, even though we journalists didn't have any bathrobes in our rooms and our towels were of the threadbare white institutional variety that no one would want to take home. It was the White House staffers who had fluffy blue robes and towels bearing the insignia of the USS George Washington. The President made matters worse on June 24 when he exploded in anger during an interview with KMOX radio in St. Louis. Not only did Clinton suggest that "press people" stole those robes and towels, but he went on to deliver a diatribe against the mainstream media, the Christian conservative movement, and right-wing radio pundits such as Rush Limbaugh. All of them, the President complained, were out to get him.

Even Clinton's critics were embarrassed by his foolishness. Sheila Tate, the former press secretary for First Lady Nancy Reagan and later for presidential candidate George Bush, saw the trouble that the President and his staff were causing for themselves. "You can't have that kind of belligerent, in-your face message all the time," Tate said. "The press corps is writing about you every day. If you treat them like garbage collectors, they will reflect it in their coverage. They're human beings." A senior Clinton adviser, who was appalled at the growing animosity between the two sides, put it more succinctly. "It goes to show you," he said. "When the White House treats the media like shit, the media will treat the White House like shit."

Too often, this is exactly what happens.

The sad fact is that the White House and the news media have entered an era in which neither side trusts or understands the other, and the American public is getting shortchanged in the process. Whoever wins the 1996 presidential election will have to cope with this harmful legacy.

First, some misconceptions about the White House and the Clinton administration need clearing up. There has never been any media conspiracy to destroy Bill and Hillary Rodham Clinton, as many Democrats around the country and people in the Clinton White House have believed. Nor was there a media conspiracy to protect and promote them, as Republicans have charged. The two thousand members of the accredited White House press corps—and certainly the sixty or seventy reporters who are full-time White House regulars—are too competitive, independent, and frazzled by deadline pressures for any of that.

Yet, conspiracy theories aside, there is ample reason for concern about the relationship between the presidency and the news media. Logistics have improved in the Clinton administration since the June 1994 trip, but there is still an unprecedented mutual cynicism between the two institutions.

Many veteran reporters say the worst relationship between a President and a White House press corps occurred during Richard Nixon's administration. Nixon kept an "enemies list" that included a variety of journalists, he had a deep hatred of the Washington media, and he authorized his Vice-President, Spiro Agnew, to re-peatedly berate the fourth estate for unfairness and vindictiveness.

But what has happened in recent years is in some ways worse. Today, in late 1995, it is not solely Republicans who have contempt for the media; now the De-mocrats agree with them, and a significant portion of the public is heading in that direction. Virtually all Washington politicians say that the mainstream media are too eager to expose the character flaws of the nation's leaders and the failures of public policy rather than to inform the country about the positive side of govern-ment and the people who run it.

To some extent . . . the politicians are correct. We in the news media are too cynical and have lost touch in some important ways with our readers, viewers, and listeners. Part of the reason is cultural. At the upper levels of the media establish-ment in Washington, journalists don't live like ordinary middleclass Americans. They make far more money than average citizens and operate in a world that is dominated by politics and government. Too often Washington journalists—includ-ing members of the White House press corps—think that by talking to one another they are really talking to America. Of course they aren't.

One fundamental fact affecting the relationship between the media and the presidency is that both institutions are changing so drastically that we will hardly recognize either of them within a generation. The media are more competitive than ever, and reporters are trying to set themselves apart by adding opinion or "edge"—often in the form of a derisive tone or smart-ass attitude—to their stories or by rush-ing to judgment about the people and events they cover. Adding to the problem is that today's news cycle never ends. The traditional morning-and afternoon-edition newspaper and evening-news-show deadlines have been supplanted by round-the-clock televised news capability and coverage: Anything that happens around the world can be shown on America's television screens instantaneously, at any time of day or night. This means the mainstream media are constantly groping for ways to move a breaking story forward rather than cover it in depth, and too often the re-sult is sensational, superficial, or negative coverage. Just as important, television has greatly accelerated the velocity of White House decision-making and increased the difficulty of governing.

The presidency has always been what political scientist Thomas Cronin calls "a very elastic institution," able to accommodate great change. But for good or ill, the presidency has been diminished as one of the central institutions in our national life and, with it, the White House press corps. Yet the news media and the White House are behaving as if the notion of the magisterial executive branch were still in full bloom. Neither the Clinton administration nor the news media has come to terms with what is gradually becoming a marginalized presidency.

For six decades, Americans looked to the White House for their national salva-tion first from the Great Depression and then from the evils of fascism during World War II. During the Cold War, the country—indeed much of the world—looked to the President of the United States as the ultimate protector against what Ronald Reagan so dramatically called "the Evil Empire" of Communism. Every President during that period had the fate of the world in his hands, and a misstep could have resulted in a nuclear holocaust. Under such conditions, it was natural that the White House became the most important, most glamorous, and most exciting beat in the world. Over the years, the best reporters in the business made it their career objective to reach 1600 Pennsylvania Avenue. Once these journalists reached the pinnacle, they could count on a steady diet of stories virtually guaranteed to lead the nightly news or page one. When the Cold War ended, however, the presidency deflated like a red, white, and blue balloon.

Another factor in the marginalization of the presidency and the White House press corps was cynicism about Washington and centralized political power. The desire to devolve power to the states and municipalities was an underlying theme in the midterm elections of 1994, in which Bill Clinton and big-government Democrats were repudiated as the Republicans took over Congress for the first time in a generation. It is clear that the days of increasing power in Washington are over, at least for the foreseeable future.

For their part, the Clintonites made some basic errors as they ascended to power—errors that amount to case studies in how not to handle the press. They neglected to forge relationships with the journalists covering them. Instead, they started off by treating the mainstream media with distrust, condescension, and disrespect, and tried—with pathetic results—to go over the heads of the press corps via "new media" techniques such as television and radio talk shows, electronic mail, local cable stations, town meetings, and satellite interviews with local reporters. The Clintonites made little or no effort to understand the folkways of the fourth estate, let alone the needs and personalities of individual journalists. . . .

One of the Clintonites' biggest problems was their failure to "feed the beast," as the media are called by Washington insiders. The White House would have been well advised to listen to Jack DeVore, the longtime press secretary to former senator and Treasury secretary Lloyd Bentsen, who said that a press secretary's job was to manufacture a constant supply of doggie biscuits for the press. Reporters would gleefully lick the hand that fed them, but if you ran out of treats or news, DeVore said, the press would devour your arm and try for more.

Complaints from the press corps were unusually intense and bitter. Not only were logistics a mess, suggesting a broader incompetence in the administration, but the Clinton White House seemed to disdain journalism as a profession and journalists as individuals. Phone calls were not returned by the press staff. Appointments were made and not kept by nearly everyone from press secretary Myers to communications director George Stephanopoulos. "They've been contempuous of the way we do things," fumed Gene Gibbons, chief White House correspondent for the Reuters news agency. This view was widely shared in the press corps during President Clinton's first two years. "On the simple, really ordinary stuff," said Bill Plante, who covers the White House for CBS News, "they paid very little attention to filing time and deadline concerns at first, because they thought they didn't have to. 'You don't have time to file? Well, too bad. Make the best of it. We have to leave at six.' Stupid stuff like that, where it's not worth the antagonism that it causes you. . . . They not only didn't get it right, but they often seemed not to care that they didn't get it right."

Day after day, the press corps felt humiliated and frustrated. A report by Freedom Forum Media Studies Center at Columbia University summarized the problem in late 1994 by suggesting that White House reporters suffered from a painful conflict: "At the pinnacle of their craft, working some of the highest profile and most prestigious jobs in journalism, their day-to-day job is excruciatingly dull and demeaning. And now they are assigned to cover a President who seems to dislike them, would prefer not to have to deal with them and has available to him a variety of alternate means for getting his message out to the public without enduring the media filter."

Stan Greenberg, a White House pollster, admits that there was never any press strategy at the beginning of the Clinton administration. That was the first mistake. It was always assumed that the effective campaign plan of going around the mainstream national media would simply continue once the candidate was in the White House. Further aggravating this blunder, the Clintonites had no qualms about boasting of their intentions publicly, which seemed to be an insult to mainstream journalists.

A key misstep was naming Stephanopoulos to be Clinton's chief spokesman in the first place. Stephanopoulos was a policy specialist and congressional strategist, not a press expert. He had no real philosophy for dealing with the media other than acting as if the White House press corps were irrelevant and as if he had no obligation to convey information. The atmosphere at Stephanopoulos's press conferences was angry and confrontational. He lorded over journalists his intent to keep secrets from them, and refused to tell them even the smallest details about Clinton's activities at the White House, as if his number-one mission was to show the press corps how inconsequential and powerless it was.

The White House staff, and the Clintons in private, began whining about their press coverage instead of doing something to improve it. Bill Clinton always thought of himself as a political empath[izer], telling Americans, "I feel your pain." Yet the voters increasingly saw him as precisely the reverse, a public figure on whom Americans would project their fears, angers, doubts, and concerns. America didn't know him. He never explained what he stood for, and the media never knew what to believe about him. In large part because he would not reveal himself to the country or the press corps, Clinton became a caricature—an overeating, indecisive, womanizing, waffling adolescent commander-in-chief. Many of his . . . image problems [could] he traced to those early days in the White House. . . .

When Clinton could not meet the expectations he had raised about new, bold leadership, the media and the voters turned on him. As he broke some of his key campaign promises to grant a middle-class tax cut, to revolutionize government in his first one hundred days, to reverse George Bush's foreign policy in Haiti, Cuba, and China—he was derided in the press as a phony. At that point—less than six months into his presidency—Clinton had generated so little goodwill among journalists that he had few allies willing to defend him.

Clinton has also had to deal with a relatively new dynamic in the mainstream media: A President's character has become, for both the press and the public, the single most important measure of his fitness for office. After a string of lies, deceits, and betrayals that included the Vietnam War and the Watergate scandal, reporters were no longer willing to give a President the benefit of the doubt, and many were always ready to assume the worst.

"As many people have observed," says ABC White House correspondent Brit Hume, "it grew out of Vietnam and Watergate, because of two lessons coming out of those two stories. One of them was that the government could and would lie, and that extraordinarily crummy and dishonorable things were engaged in at a higher level than we might once have thought possible. The second thing was that those times when these things were happening may have been difficult times for the country, but they were absolutely wonderful times to be a journalist in Washington, particularly one who had a piece of the story. It helped to promote a certain romance about the news media and its role in American life, and it also enhanced the prestige of the news media generally, and made news media personalities, print and broadcast alike, into much bigger players on the national scene than they had ever previously been. And there was a tendency then by everybody from the generals down to the buck privates in our trade to fight that last war over and over again, and to look for entry points into what might be the great new scandals of the day."

As a group, White House reporters are the most privileged and prosperous journalists covering any beat in the nation and are among the most hard-working, self-disciplined, and careful in the world. Yet they often work under humiliating and exhausting conditions. They are lied to and dismissed as untrustworthy or ignorant. They are cooped up in an area of tiny work spaces and cubicles, penned behind rope lines, or herded about in large groups—conditions that would make most American workers chafe. No wonder these reporters often get cantankerous, rude, and angry.

More troubling are the profound changes affecting the news business as a whole. Recent surveys indicate that journalists are distrusted by increasing numbers of Americans, who consider the national news media isolated, out of touch, and arrogant—and often inaccurate. It has not helped the media that the distinction is so often blurred between real journalists, politicians, commentators, lobbyists, and public-relations specialists, all of whom appear regularly on the same television talk shows. Even the nightly network news shows often feature journalists and beat reporters as "experts" giving their opinions willy-nilly. Increasingly, local and cable news shows imitate the national shows.

As a result of all this, journalism's credibility is in tatters.

Presidential Power in Foreign and Domestic Affairs

President George Bush's decision in 1991 to go to war against Iraq to free Kuwait illustrated once again the presidential dominance in military and foreign policy making that has existed since World War II. Presidents have always put their stamp upon foreign policy, but during the nineteenth and early twentieth centuries Congress, particularly the Senate, was more often than not an equal partner with the president in foreign affairs as the Constitution intended.

Franklin D. Roosevelt's administration marked the modern presidency and presidential ascendancy in foreign and military policy making. At the end of FDR's first term in 1936 the Supreme Court acknowledged presidential supremacy in foreign affairs in *United States v. Curtiss-Wright*.[1] Writing for the Court's majority, conservative Justice Sutherland referred to "the very delicate, plenary and exclusive power of the president

---

[1] *United States v. Curtiss-Wright*, 299 U.S. 304 (1936).

as the sole organ of the federal government in the field of international relations—a power which does not require as a basis for its exercise an act of Congress. . . . It is quite apparent that if, in the maintenance of our international relations, embarrassment—perhaps serious embarrassment—is to be avoided and success for our aims achieved, congressional legislation which is to be made effective through negotiation and inquiry within the international field must often accord to the president a degree of discretion and freedom from statutory restriction which would not be admissible were domestic affairs alone involved."

During World War II the president unilaterally conducted foreign and military affairs, and presidents after FDR followed his example although not always with the same success. Truman did not hesitate to proclaim, "I make foreign policy." President Truman alone essentially made the decision to make war in Korea, although he did symbolically consult Congress and involve the United Nations. Presidential, not congressional, initiatives brought about the Bay of Pigs fiasco during John F. Kennedy's administration, which also saw the president along with a small group of advisers negotiate the Cuban missile crisis. Lyndon B. Johnson and Richard M. Nixon, the latter acting secretly, escalated the Vietnam war.

Congress passed the War Powers Act in 1973, requiring the president to consult with Congress before involving troops in military action abroad beyond 90 days. The act was one of many attempts made by the resurgent Congress of the 1970s to restrict presidential power in foreign affairs. But the Reagan and Bush presidencies illustrated that regardless of what Congress does presidents will continue to make important foreign policy decisions, even deceiving Congress as in the Iran-Contra affair during the Reagan presidency.

The following selection contrasts presidential power in foreign and domestic affairs, concluding that we have not one but two presidencies. Although the author wrote his classic piece in 1966, his thesis remains valid. The complexities of foreign policy and the recognized need for unity and dispatch in decision making support continued presidential control over foreign affairs.

54

THE TWO PRESIDENCIES

Aaron Wildavsky

The United States has one president, but it has two presidencies; one presidency is for domestic affairs, and the other is concerned with defense and foreign policy. Since World War II, presidents have had much greater success in controlling the nation's defense and foreign policies than in dominating its domestic policies. Even

Lyndon Johnson has seen his early record of victories in domestic legislation diminish as his concern with foreign affairs grows.

What powers does the president have to control defense and foreign policies and so completely overwhelm those who might wish to thwart him?

The president's normal problem with domestic policy is to get congressional support for the programs he prefers. In foreign affairs, in contrast, he can almost always get support for policies that he believes will protect the nation—but his problem is to find a viable policy.

Whoever they are, whether they begin by caring about foreign policy like Eisenhower and Kennedy or about domestic policies like Truman and Johnson, presidents soon discover they have more policy preferences in domestic matters than in foreign policy. The Republican and Democratic parties possess a traditional roster of policies, which can easily be adopted by a new president—for example, he can be either for or against Medicare and aid to education. Since existing domestic policy usually changes in only small steps, presidents find it relatively simple to make minor adjustments. However, although any president knows he supports foreign aid and NATO, the world outside changes much more rapidly than the nation inside—presidents and their parties have no prior policies on Argentina and the Congo. The world has become a highly intractable place with a whirl of forces we cannot or do not know how to alter.

The Record of Presidential Control

It takes great crises, such as Roosevelt's hundred days in the midst of the depression, or the extraordinary majorities that Barry Goldwater's candidacy willed to Lyndon Johnson, for presidents to succeed in controlling domestic policy. From the end of the 1930s to the present (what may roughly be called the modern era), presidents have often been frustrated in their domestic programs. From 1938, when conservatives regrouped their forces, to the time of his death, Franklin Roosevelt did not get a single piece of significant domestic legislation passed. Truman lost out on most of his intense domestic preferences, except perhaps for housing. Since Eisenhower did not ask for much domestic legislation, he did not meet consistent defeat, yet he failed in his general policy of curtailing governmental commitments. Kennedy, of course, faced great difficulties with domestic legislation.

In the realm of foreign policy there has not been a single major issue on which presidents, when they were serious and determined, have failed. The list of their victories is impressive: entry into the United Nations, the Marshall Plan, NATO, the Truman Doctrine, the decisions to stay out of Indochina in 1954 and to intervene in Vietnam in the 1960s, aid to Poland and Yugoslavia, the test-ban treaty, and many more. Serious setbacks to the president in controlling foreign policy are extraordinary and unusual.

. . . [P]residents have significantly better records in foreign and defense matters than in domestic policies. When refugees and immigration—which Congress considers primarily a domestic concern—are removed from the general foreign policy area, it is clear that presidents prevail about 70 percent of the time in defense and foreign policy, compared with 40 percent in the domestic sphere.

World Events and
Presidential Resources

Power in politics is control over governmental decisions. How does the president manage his control of foreign and defense policy? The answer does not reside in the greater constitutional power in foreign affairs that presidents have possessed since the founding of the Republic. The answer lies in the changes that have taken place since 1945.

The number of nations with which the United States has diplomatic relations has increased from 53 in 1939 to 113 in 1966. But sheer numbers do not tell enough; the world has also become a much more dangerous place. However remote it may seem at times, our government must always be aware of the possibility of nuclear war.

Yet the mere existence of great powers with effective thermonuclear weapons would not, in and of itself, vastly increase our rate of interaction with most other nations. We see [all foreign] events as important because they are also part of a larger worldwide contest, called the cold war, in which great powers are rivals for the control or support of other nations. Moreover, the reaction against the blatant isolationism of the 1930s has led to a concern with foreign policy that is worldwide in scope. We are interested in what happens everywhere because we see these events as connected with larger interests. involving, at the worst, the possibility of ultimate destruction.

Given the overriding fact that the world is dangerous and that small causes are perceived to have potentially great effects in an unstable world, it follows that presidents must be interested in relatively "small" matters. So they give Azerbaijan or Lebanon or Vietnam huge amounts of their time. Arthur Schlesinger, Jr., wrote of Kennedy that "in the first two months of his administration he probably spent more time on Laos than on anything else." Few failures in domestic policy, presidents soon realize, could have as disastrous consequences as any one of dozens of mistakes in the international arena.

The result is that foreign policy concerns tend to drive out domestic policy. Except for occasional questions of domestic prosperity and for civil rights, foreign affairs have consistently higher priority for presidents. Once, when trying to talk to President Kennedy about natural resources, Secretary of the Interior Stewart Udall remarked, "He's imprisoned by Berlin."

The importance of foreign affairs to presidents is intensified by the increasing speed of events in the international arena. The event and its consequences follow closely on top of one another. The blunder at the Bay of Pigs is swiftly followed by the near catastrophe of the Cuban missile crisis. Presidents can no longer count on passing along their most difficult problems to their successors. They must expect to face the consequences of their actions—or failure to act—while still in office.

Domestic policy making is usually based on experimental adjustments to an existing situation. Only a few decisions, such as those involving large dams, irretrievably commit future generations. Decisions in foreign affairs, however, are often perceived to be irreversible. This is expressed, for example, in the fear of escalation or the various "spiral" or "domino" theories of international conflict.

If decisions are perceived to be both important and irreversible, there is every reason for presidents to devote a great deal of resources to them. Presidents have to be oriented toward the future in the use of their resources. They serve a fixed term in office, and they cannot automatically count on support from the populace, Congress, or the administrative apparatus. They have to be careful, therefore, to husband their resources for pressing future needs. But because the consequences of events in foreign affairs are potentially more grave, faster to manifest themselves, and less easily reversible than in domestic affairs, presidents are more willing to use up their resources.

The Power to Act

Their formal powers to commit resources in foreign affairs and defense are vast. Particularly important is their power as commander-in-chief to move troops. Faced with situations like the invasion of South Korea or the emplacement of missiles in Cuba, fast action is required. Presidents possess both the formal power to act and the knowledge that elites and the general public expect them to act. Once they have committed American forces, it is difficult for Congress or anyone else to alter the course of events. The Dominican venture is a . . . case in point.

Presidential discretion in foreign affairs also makes it difficult (though not impossible) for Congress to restrict their actions. Presidents can use executive agreements instead of treaties, enter into tacit agreements instead of written ones, and otherwise help create *de facto* situations not easily reversed. Presidents also have far greater ability than anyone else to obtain information on developments abroad through the Departments of State and Defense. The need for secrecy in some aspects of foreign and defense policy further restricts the ability of others to compete with presidents. These things are all well known. What is not so generally appreciated is the growing presidential ability to *use* information to achieve goals.

In the past presidents were amateurs in military strategy. They could not even get much useful advice outside of the military. As late as the 1930s the number of people outside the military establishment who were professionally engaged in the study of defense policy could be numbered on the fingers. Today there are hundreds of such men. The rise of the defense intellectuals has given the president of the United States enhanced ability to control defense policy. He is no longer dependent on the military for advice. He can choose among defense intellectuals from the research corporations and the academies for alternative sources of advice. He can install these men in his own office. He can play them off against each other or use them to extend spheres of coordination.

Even with these advisers, however, presidents and secretaries of defense might still be too bewildered by the complexity of nuclear situations to take action—unless they had an understanding of the doctrine and concepts of deterrence. But knowledge of doctrine about deterrence has been widely diffused; it can be picked up by any intelligent person who will read books or listen to enough hours of conversation. Whether or not the doctrine is good is a separate question; the point is that civilians can feel they understand what is going on in defense policy. Perhaps the most extraordinary feature of presidential action during the Cuban missile crisis was the degree to which the Commander-in-Chief of the Armed Forces insisted on controlling even the smallest moves. From the positioning of ships to the methods of boarding, to the precise words and actions to be taken by individual soldiers and sailors, the president and his civilian advisers were in control.

Although presidents have rivals for power in foreign affairs, the rivals do not usually succeed. Presidents prevail not only because they may have superior resources but because their potential opponents are weak, divided, or believe that they should not control foreign policy. Let us consider the potential rivals—the general citizenry, special interest groups, the Congress, the military, the so-called military-industrial complex, and the State Department.

Competitors for Control of Policy

The Public

The general public is much more dependent on presidents in foreign affairs than in domestic matters. While many people know about the impact of social security and Medicare, few know about politics in Malawi. So it is not surprising that people expect the president to act in foreign affairs and reward him with their confidence. . . .

Although presidents lead opinion in foreign affairs, they know they will be held accountable for the consequences of their actions. . . . We will support your initiatives, the people seem to say, but we will reserve the right to punish you (or your party) if we do not like the results.

Special Interest Groups

Opinions are easier to gauge in domestic affairs because, for one thing, there is a stable structure of interest groups that covers virtually all matters of concern. The farm, labor, business, conservation, veteran, civil rights, and other interest groups provide cues when a proposed policy affects them. Thus people who identify with these groups may adopt their views. But in foreign policy matters the interest group structure is weak, unstable, and thin rather than dense. In many matters affecting Africa and Asia, for example, it is hard to think of well-known interest groups. While ephemeral groups arise from time to time to support or protest particular policies, they usually disappear when the immediate problem is resolved. In contrast, longer lasting elite groups like the Foreign Policy Association and Council on Foreign Relations are composed of people of diverse views; refusal to take strong positions on controversial matters is a condition of their continued viability.

The strongest interest groups are probably the ethnic associations whose members have strong ties with a homeland, as in Poland or Cuba, so they are rarely activated simultaneously on any specific issue. They are most effective when most narrowly and intensely focused—as in the fierce pressure from Jews to recognize the state of Israel. But their relatively small numbers limits their significance to presidents in the vastly more important general foreign policy picture—as continued aid to the Arab countries shows. . . .

The Congress

Congressmen also exercise power in foreign affairs. Yet they are ordinarily not serious competitors with the president because they follow a self-denying ordinance. They do not think it is their job to determine the nation's defense policies. . . .

The Military

The outstanding feature of the military's participation in making defense policy is their amazing weakness. Whether the policy decisions involve the size of the armed forces, the choice of weapons systems, the total defense budget, or its division into components, the military have not prevailed. Let us take budgetary decisions as representative of the key choices to be made in defense policy. Since the end of World War II the military has not been able to achieve significant (billion dollar) increases in appropriations by their own efforts. . . .   *WHAT? NSC GD?*

Military Industrial

But what about the fabled military-industrial complex? If the military alone is divided and weak, perhaps the giant industrial firms that are so dependent on defense contracts play a large part in making policy.

First, there is an important distinction between the questions "Who will get a given contract?" and "What will our defense policy be?" It is apparent that different answers may be given to these quite different questions. There are literally tens of thousands of defense contractors. They may compete vigorously for business. In the course of this competition, they may wine and dine military officers, use retired generals, seek intervention by their congressmen, place ads in trade journals, and even contribute to political campaigns. The famous TFX controversy—should General Dynamics or Boeing get the expensive contract?—is a larger than life example of the pressures brought to bear in search of lucrative contracts.

But neither the TFX case nor the usual vigorous competition for contracts is involved with the making of substantive defense policy. Vital questions like the size of the defense budget, the choice of strategic programs, massive retaliation vs. a counter-[insurgency] strategy, and the like were far beyond the policy aims of any company. Industrial firms, then, do not control such decisions, nor is there much evidence that they actually try. No doubt a precipitous and drastic rush to disarmament would meet with opposition from industrial firms among other interests. However, there has never been a time when any significant element in the government considered a disarmament policy to be feasible.

. . .

The State Department

Modern presidents expect the State Department to carry out their policies. John F. Kennedy felt that State was "in some particular sense 'his' department." If a secretary of state forgets this, as was apparently the case with James Byrnes under Truman, a president may find another man. But the State Department, especially the

Foreign Service, is also a highly professional organization with a life and momentum of its own. If a president does not push hard, he may find his preferences somehow dissipated in time. Arthur Schlesinger fills his book on Kennedy [A *Thousand Days*] with laments about the bureaucratic inertia and recalcitrance of the State Department.

. . .

[But] Schlesinger comes closest to the truth when he writes that "the White House could always win any battle it chose over the [Foreign] Service; but the prestige and proficiency of the Service limited the number of battles any White House would find it profitable to fight." When the president knew what he wanted, he got it. . . .

The growth of a special White House staff to help presidents in foreign affairs expresses their need for assistance, their refusal to rely completely on the regular executive agencies, and their ability to find competent men. The deployment of this staff must remain a presidential prerogative, however, if its members are to serve presidents and not their opponents. . . . But presidents resolutely refuse to become prisoners of their advisers by using them as other people would like. Presidents remain in control of their staff as well as of major foreign policy decisions.

How Complete Is the Control?

. . .

Are there significant historical examples which might refute the thesis of presidential control of foreign policy? Foreign aid may be a case in point. For many years, presidents have struggled to get foreign aid appropriations because of hostility from public and congressional opinion. Yet several billion dollars a year are appropriated regularly despite the evident unpopularity of the program. . . .

The World Influence

The forces impelling presidents to be concerned with the widest range of foreign and defense policies also affect the ways in which they calculate their power stakes. As Kennedy used to say, "Domestic policy . . . can only defeat us; foreign policy can kill us."

It no longer makes sense for presidents to "play politics" with foreign and defense policies. In the past, presidents might have thought that they could gain by prolonged delay or by not acting at all. The problem might disappear or be passed on to their successors. Presidents must now expect to pay the high costs themselves if the world situation deteriorates. The advantages of pursuing a policy that is viable in the world, that will not blow up on presidents or their fellow citizens, far outweigh any temporary political disadvantages accrued in supporting an initially unpopular policy. Compared with domestic affairs, presidents engaged in world politics are immensely more concerned with meeting problems on their own terms. Who supports and opposes a policy, though a matter of considerable interest, does not assume the crucial importance that it does in domestic affairs. The best policy presidents can find is also the best politics.

The fact that there are numerous foreign and defense policy situations competing for a president's attention means that it is worthwhile to organize political activity in order to affect his agenda. For if a president pays more attention to certain problems he may develop different preferences; he may seek and receive different advice; his new calculations may lead him to devote greater resources to seeking a solution. Interested congressmen may exert influence not by directly determining a presidential decision, but indirectly by making it costly for a president to avoid reconsidering the basis for his action. For example, citizen groups, such as those concerned with a change in China policy, may have an impact simply by keeping their proposals on the public agenda. A president may be compelled to reconsider a problem even though he could not overtly be forced to alter the prevailing policy.

In foreign affairs we may be approaching the stage where knowledge is power. There is a tremendous receptivity to good ideas in Washington. Most anyone who can present a convincing rationale for dealing with a hard world finds a ready audience. The best way to convince presidents to follow a desired policy is to show that it might work. . . . It is, to be sure, extremely difficult to devise good policies or to predict their consequences accurately. Nor is it easy to convince others that a given policy is superior to other alternatives. But it is the way to influence with presidents. For if they are convinced that the current policy is best, the likelihood of gaining sufficient force to compel a change is quite small. The man who can build better foreign policies will find presidents beating a path to his door.

Presidential Leadership and Political Parties

Our eighteenth-century constitutional system of divided government weakens political parties. The Founding Fathers did not intend for either the president or Congress to govern through parties. As the following selection reveals, modern presidents have taken a leaf from the founders' notebook by relying more on administrative than party government.

55

THE PRESIDENCY AND POLITICAL PARTIES

Sidney M. Milkis

The relationship between the presidency and the American party system has always been difficult. The architects of the Constitution established a nonpartisan president who, with the support of the judiciary, was intended to play the leading institutional role in checking and controlling the "violence of faction" that the framers feared would rend the fabric of representative democracy. Even after the presidency became a more partisan office during the early part of the nineteenth century, its authority continued to depend on an ability to transcend party politics. The president is nominated by a party but, unlike the British prime minister, is not elected by it.

The inherent tension between the presidency and the party system reached a critical point during the 1930s. The institutionalization of the modern presidency, arguably the most significant constitutional legacy of Franklin D. Roosevelt's New Deal, ruptured severely the limited, albeit significant, bond that linked presidents to their parties. In fact, the modern presidency was crafted with the intention of reducing the influence of the party system on American politics. In this sense Roosevelt's extraordinary party leadership contributed to the decline of the American party system. This decline continued—even accelerated—under the administrations of subsequent presidents, notably Lyndon B. Johnson and Richard M. Nixon. Under Ronald Reagan, however, the party system showed at least some signs of transformation and renewal. Reagan and his successor, George Bush, supported efforts by Republicans in the national committee and congressional campaign organizations to restore some of the importance of political parties by refashioning them into highly untraditional but politically potent national organizations. Yet the 1992 election and its aftermath raised serious doubts about the capacity of these emergent national parties to build popular support for political principles and programs.

New Deal Party Politics, Presidential Reform, and the Decline of the American Party System

The New Deal seriously questioned the adequacy of the traditional natural rights liberalism of John Locke and the framers, which emphasized the need to limit constitutionally the scope of government's responsibilities. The modern liberalism that became the public philosophy of the New Deal entailed a fundamental reappraisal of the concept of rights. As Roosevelt first indicated in his 1932 campaign speech at the Commonwealth Club in San Francisco, effective political reform would require, at a minimum, the development of "an economic declaration of rights, an economic constitutional order," grounded in a commitment to guarantee a decent level of economic well-being for the American people. Although equality of opportunity had traditionally been promoted by limited government interference in society, recent economic and social changes, such as the closing of the frontiers and the growth of industrial combinations, demanded that America now recognize "the new terms of the old social contract."

The establishment of a new constitutional order would require a reordering of the political process. The traditional patterns of American politics, characterized by constitutional mechanisms that impeded collective action, would have to give way to a more centralized and administrative government. As Roosevelt put it, "The day of enlightened administration has come."

The concerns Roosevelt expressed in the Commonwealth Club speech are an important guide to understanding the New Deal and its effects on the party system. The pursuit of an economic constitutional order presupposed a fundamental change in the relationship between the presidency and the party system. In Roosevelt's view, the party system, which was essentially based on state and local organizations and interests and was thus suited to congressional primacy, would have to be transformed into a national, executive-oriented system organized on the basis of public issues.

In this understanding, Roosevelt was no doubt influenced by the thought of Woodrow Wilson. The reform of parties, Wilson believed, depended on extending the influence of the presidency. The limits on partisanship inherent in American constitutional government notwithstanding, the president represented his party's "vital link of connection" with the nation: "He can dominate his party by being spokesman for the real sentiment and purpose of the country, by giving the country at once the information and statements of policy which will enable it to form its judgments alike of parties and men."

. . .

In the final analysis, the "benign dictatorship" that Roosevelt sought to impose on the Democratic party was more conducive to corroding the American party system than to reforming it. His prescription for party reform—extraordinary presidential leadership—posed a serious, if not intractable, dilemma: on the one hand, the decentralized character of politics in the United States can be modified only by strong presidential leadership; on the other, a president determined to alter fundamentally the connection between the executive and the party eventually will shatter party unity.

. . .

The most significant institutional reforms of the New Deal did not promote party government but fostered instead a program that would help the president to govern in the absence of party government. This program, as embodied in the 1937 executive reorganization bill, would have greatly extended presidential authority over the executive branch, including the independent regulatory commissions. The president and the executive agencies would also be delegated extensive authority to govern, making unnecessary the constant cooperation of party members in Congress. As the Report of the President's Committee on Administrative Management put it, with administrative reform the "brief exultant commitment" to progressive government that was expressed in the elections of 1932 and, especially, 1936 would now be more firmly established in "persistent, determined, competent, day by day administration of what the Nation has decided to do."

. . .

Interestingly, the administrative reform bill, which was directed to making politics less necessary, became, at Roosevelt's urging, a party government-style "vote of confidence" for the administration in Congress. Roosevelt initially lost this vote in 1938, when the reorganization bill was defeated in the House of Representatives, but he did manage, through the purge campaign and other partisan actions, to keep administrative reform sufficiently prominent in party councils that a compromise version passed in 1939. Although considerably weaker than Roosevelt's original proposal, the 1939 Executive Reorganization Act was a significant measure. It not only provided authority for the creation of the Executive Office of the President, which included the newly formed White House Office and a strengthened and refurbished Bureau of the Budget, but also enhanced the president's control of the expanding activities of the executive branch. As such, this legislation represents the genesis of the institutional presidency, which was equipped to govern independently of the constraints imposed by the regular political process.

The civil service reform carried out by the Roosevelt administration was another important part of the effort to replace partisan politics with executive administration. The original reorganization proposals of 1937 had contained provisions to make the administration of the civil service more effective and to expand the merit system. The reorganization bill passed in 1939 was shorn of this controversial feature; but Roosevelt found it possible to accomplish extensive civil service reform through executive action. He did so by extending merit protection to personnel appointed by the administration during its first term, four-fifths of whom had been brought into government outside of merit channels. Patronage appointments had traditionally been used to nourish the party system; the New Deal celebrated an administrative politics that fed instead an executive department oriented to expanding liberal programs. As the administrative historian Paul Van Riper has noted, the new practices created a new kind of patronage, "a sort of intellectual and ideological patronage rather than the more traditional partisan type."

Roosevelt's leadership transformed the Democratic party into a way station on the road to administrative government. As the presidency developed into an elaborate and ubiquitous institution, it preempted party leaders in many of their limited, but significant, duties: providing a link from government to interest groups, staffing the executive department, contributing to policy development, and organizing election campaigns. Moreover, New Deal administrative reform was directed not just to creating presidential government but to embedding progressive principles (considered tantamount to political rights) in a bureaucratic structure that would insulate reform and reformers from electoral change.

Lyndon Johnson's Great Society and the Transcendence of Partisan Politics

Presidential leadership during the New Deal prepared the executive branch to be a government unto itself and established the presidency rather than the party as the locus of political responsibility. But the modern presidency was created to chart the course for, and direct the voyage to, a more liberal America. Roosevelt's pronouncement of a "second bill of rights" proclaimed and began this task, but it fell to Johnson, as one journalist noted, to "codify the New Deal vision of a good society."

Johnson's attempt to create the Great Society marked a significant extension of programmatic liberalism and accelerated the effort to transcend partisan politics. Roosevelt's ill-fated efforts to guide the affairs of his party were well remembered by Johnson, who came to Congress in 1937 in a special House election as an enthusiastic supporter of the New Deal. He took Roosevelt's experience to be the best example of the generally ephemeral nature of party government in the United States, and he fully expected the cohesive Democratic support he received from Congress after the 1964 election to be temporary. Thus Johnson, like Roosevelt, looked beyond the party system toward the politics of "enlightened administration."

. . .

Richard Nixon, Nonpartisanship, and the Demise of the Modern Presidency

Considering that the New Deal and Great Society were established by replacing traditional party politics with administration, it is not surprising that when a conservative challenge to liberal reform emerged, it entailed the creation of a conservative "administrative presidency." This development further contributed to the decline of partisan politics.

Until the 1960s, opponents of the welfare state were generally opposed to the modern presidency, which had served as the fulcrum of liberal reform. Nevertheless, by the end of the Johnson administration, it became clear that a strong conservative movement would require an activist program of retrenchment in order to counteract the enduring effects of the New Deal and Great Society. Once the opponents of liberal public policy, primarily housed in the Republican party, recognized this, they looked to the possibility that, ideologically, the modern presidency could be a two-edged sword.

The administrative actions of the Nixon presidency were a logical extension of the practices of Roosevelt and Johnson. The centralization of authority in the White House and the reduction of the regular Republican organization to perfunctory status during the Nixon years was hardly new. The complete autonomy of the Committee for the Re-Election of the President (CREEP) from the regular Republican organization in the 1972 campaign was but the final stage of a long process of White House preemption of the national committee's political responsibilities. And the administrative reform program that was pursued after Nixon's reelection, in which executive authority was concentrated in the hands of White House operatives and four cabinet "supersecretaries," was the culmination of a long-standing tendency in the modern presidency to reconstitute the executive branch as a formidable and independent instrument of government.

Thus, just as Roosevelt's presidency anticipated the Great Society, Johnson's presidency anticipated the administrative presidency of Richard Nixon. Indeed, the strategy of pursuing policy goals through administrative capacities that had been created for the most part by Democratic presidents was considered especially suitable by a minority Republican president who faced a hostile Congress and bureaucracy intent on preserving those presidents' programs. Nixon actually surpassed previous modern presidents in viewing the party system as an obstacle to effective governance.

Yet, mainly because of the Watergate scandal, Nixon's presidency had the effect of strengthening opposition to the unilateral use of presidential power, even as it further attenuated the bonds that linked presidents to the party system. The evolution of the modern presidency now left the office in complete institutional isolation. This isolation continued during the Ford and Carter years, so much so that by the end of the 1970s scholars were lamenting the demise of the presidency as well as of the party system.

The Reagan Presidency and the Revitalization of Party Politics

The development of the modern presidency fostered a serious decline in the traditional local and patronage-based parties. Yet some developments during the Reagan presidency suggested that a phoenix had emerged from the ashes. The erosion of old-style partisan politics had allowed a more national and issue-oriented party system to develop, forging new links between presidents and their parties.

The Republican party in particular developed a formidable organizational apparatus, which displayed unprecedented strength at the national level. . . .

The revival of the Republican party as a force against government by administration seemed to complete the development of a new American party system. The nomination and election of Ronald Reagan, a far more ideological conservative than Nixon, galvanized the Republican commitment to programs, such as "regulatory relief" and "new federalism," that severely challenged the institutional legacy of the New Deal. Had such a trend continued, the circumvention of the regular political process by administrative action may well have been displaced by the sort of full-scale debate about political questions usually associated with critical realignments.

Significantly, it was Reagan who broke with the tradition of the modern presidency and identified closely with his party. The president worked hard to strengthen the Republicans' organizational and popular base, surprising his own political director with his "total readiness" to shoulder such partisan responsibilities as making numerous fund-raising appearances for the party and its candidates. Apparently, after having spent the first fifty years of his life as a Democrat, Reagan brought the enthusiasm of a convert to Republican activities.

The experience of the Reagan administration suggests how the relationship between the president and the party can be mutually beneficial. Republican party strength provided Reagan with the support of a formidable institution, solidifying his personal popularity and facilitating the support of his program in Congress. As a result, the Reagan presidency was able to suspend the paralysis that seemed to afflict American government in the 1970s, even though the Republicans never attained control of the House of Representatives. In turn, Reagan's popularity served the party by strengthening its fund-raising efforts and promoting a shift in voters' party loyalties, placing the Republicans by 1985 in a position of virtual parity with the Democrats for the first time since the 1940s. It may be, then, that the 1980s marked the watershed both for a new political era and for a renewed link between presidents and the party system.

Nevertheless, the separation of political institutions in the United States provides a precarious setting for comprehensive party programs. It is unlikely that the emergence of strong national party organizations will fundamentally alter the limited possibilities for party government under the American Constitution, a fact that will continue to encourage modern presidents, particularly those intent on ambitious policy reform, to emphasize popular appeal and administrative action rather than "collective responsibility." It is not surprising, therefore, that the Reagan presidency frequently pursued its program with acts of administrative discretion that short-circuited the legislative process and weakened efforts to carry out broad-based party policies. The Iran-contra scandal, for example, was not simply a matter of the president's being asleep on his watch. Rather, it revealed the Reagan administration's determination to assume a more forceful anti-communist posture in Central America in the face of a recalcitrant Congress and bureaucracy.

. . .

As such, Reagan did not transform Washington completely. Rather, he strengthened the Republican beachhead in the nation's capital, solidifying his party's recent dominance of the presidency and providing better opportunities for conservatives in the Washington community. Reagan's landslide reelection in 1984 did not prevent the Democrats from maintaining control of the House of Representatives; nor did his plea to the voters during the 1986 congressional campaign to elect Republican majorities prevent the Democrats from recapturing control of the Senate.

Concomitantly, Reagan's two terms witnessed a revitalization of the struggle between the executive and legislative branches; indeed, his conservative program became the foundation for more fundamental philosophical and policy differences between them than in the past. The Iran-contra affair and the battles to control regulatory policy were marked not just by differences between the president and Congress about policy, but by each branch's efforts to weaken the other. The efforts of Republicans to compensate for their inability to control Congress by seeking to circumvent legislative restrictions on presidential conduct were matched by Democratic initiatives to burden the executive with smothering legislative oversight. The opposition to liberal reform, then, did not end in a challenge to national administrative power but in a raw and disruptive battle to control its services.

Reagan's Legacy and the Accession of George Bush

The 1988 election seemed to indicate that divided government had become an enduring characteristic of American politics. The Bush campaign took its shape from the Reagan legacy: in the final analysis, Bush's nomination by the Republican party and his victory by a substantial margin against his Democratic opponent, Gov. Michael Dukakis of Massachusetts, were expressions of the voters' approval of the

Reagan administration. Yet the 1988 election also revealed the limits of the Reagan revolution, reflecting in its outcome the underlying pattern that had characterized American politics since 1968: Republican dominance in the White House, Democratic ascendancy almost everywhere else. In fact, the 1988 election represented an extreme manifestation of this pattern. Never before had a president been elected while the other party gained ground in the House, Senate, the state legislatures, and the state governorships. Never before had voters given a newly elected president fewer fellow partisans in Congress than they gave Bush.

. . .

In sum, the closer ties that Reagan and Bush tried to forge between the modern presidency and the Republican party did not alter the unprecedented partisan and electoral divisions that characterized the era of divided government. Indeed, the persistence of divided government itself retarded the restoration of partisanship to the presidency. During the early days of his presidency, Bush attempted to reach out to Democrats in Congress in order to restore the badly frayed consensus in American politics. But he gave no reasonable defense of his pragmatism. Thus, once he abandoned his antitax pledge and lost his top political strategist to illness, Bush's presidency floated adrift. His search for agreement with Congress in the absence of any clear principles threatened the modern presidency with the same sort of isolation and weakness that had characterized the Ford and Carter years.

. . .

Bill Clinton and the Politics of Divided Democracy

The Bush presidency was a painful reminder of the modern executive's "extraordinary isolation." Since FDR, the president had been freed from the constraints of party, only to be enslaved by a volatile political environment that often would rapidly undercut popular support. In 1991, Bush basked in the triumphs of the Gulf and cold wars, his popularity rating at a historic high of about 90 percent; in 1992, he was soundly defeated in his bid for reelection by the governor of Arkansas, William "Bill" Clinton. The Democrats not only captured the presidency but also preserved their majorities in the House and the Senate, ending twelve years of divided rule in American politics. Indeed, Clinton's victory seemed to represent more than a rejection of the incumbent president; in part, it expressed the voters' hope that the institutional conflict they had witnessed during the era of divided government would now come to an end. This hope was urged on by Clinton's promise to govern as a "new Democrat," an "agent of change" who would restore political consensus in American politics.

In truth, the 1992 election contained both optimistic and pessimistic portents for the modern presidency. Although the Democrats ran an effective campaign and Clinton skillfully, if not always boldly, addressed his party's liabilities, the election results showed that fundamental conflicts continued to divide Americans, even as they seemed united in their dissatisfaction with the way government worked. Clinton won only 43 percent of the popular vote, roughly the same percentage that losing Democratic candidates had received in the previous three elections. The strong support for the independent candidate H. Ross Perot reflected the continuing erosion of partisan loyalties in the electorate.

. . .

Clinton pledged to dedicate his party to the new concept of justice he espoused. But his commitment to control government spending and recast the welfare state was obscured during the early days of his presidency by many traditional liberal actions. No sooner had he been inaugurated than Clinton announced his intention to issue executive orders to reverse the policy of Reagan and Bush of forbidding abortion counseling at federally funded clinics (the so-called "gag rule")—and to lift the long-standing ban on homosexuals in the military. These policies could be carried out "with a stroke of the pen," Clinton believed, leaving him free, as he promised during his quest for the presidency, to focus "like a laser" on the economy.

There was no prospect, however, that such divisive social issues could be resolved through executive orders. To be sure, the development of the administrative presidency gave presidents more power to exercise domestic policy autonomously. Yet with the expansion of national administration to issues that shaped the direction and character of American public life, this power proved to be illusory. . . .

The apologetic stance that Clinton displayed in the face of traditional liberal causes was, to a point, understandable; it was a logical response to the modern institutional separation between the presidency and the party. . . . The moderate wing of the Democratic party that he represented—including the Democratic Leadership Council—was a minority wing. The majority of liberal interest group activists and Democratic members of Congress still preferred entitlements to obligations and regulations to responsibilities. The media-driven caucuses and primaries . . . had given him the opportunity to seize the Democratic label as an outsider candidate but offered no means to effect a transformation of his party when he took office. To bring about the new mission of progressivism that he advocated during the election, Clinton would have to risk a brutal confrontation with the major powers in the Democratic party.

Yet no president had risked such a confrontation with his party since Roosevelt's failed purge campaign. It is not surprising, therefore, that Clinton's allies in the Democratic Leadership Council urged him to renew his "credentials as an outsider" by going over the heads of the party leadership in Congress and taking his message directly to the people. The new president could "break gridlock," they argued, only by appealing to the large number of independents in the electorate who had voted for Perot—that is, by "forging new and sometimes bipartisan coalitions around an agenda that moves beyond the polarized left-right debate."

In the fall of 1993, Clinton took a page from his former political associates in his successful campaign to secure congressional approval of the North American Free Trade Agreement (NAFTA) with Canada and Mexico. The fight for NAFTA caused Clinton to defend free enterprise ardently and to oppose the protectionism of labor unions, which still represented one of the most important constituencies in the national Democratic party. . . .

With the successful fight over NAFTA, moderate Democrats began to hope that Clinton had finally begun the task of dedicating his party to the principles and policies he had espoused during the campaign. But the next major legislative battle was over the administration's health care program, which promised to "guarantee all Americans a comprehensive package of benefits over the course of an entire lifetime." . . . In the end, this proved impractical. The health care bill died in the 103rd Congress. . . .

By proposing such an ambitious health care reform bill, Clinton angered conservatives. By failing to deliver on his promise to provide a major overhaul of the health care system, he dismayed the ardent liberals of his party. Most significant, the defeat of the president's health care program created the overwhelming impression that he had not lived up to his campaign promise to transcend the bitter philosophical and partisan battles of the Reagan and Bush years.

The president and his party paid dearly for this failure in the 1994 election. . . .

The dramatic Republican triumph in the 1994 midterm election led scholars and pundits to suggest that the nation might be on the threshold of a critical partisan realignment. But the American people had become alienated from both the Republican and Democratic parties by the 1990s, so much so that the renewal of partisan loyalties, let alone a full-scale partisan transformation, seemed unlikely. . . .

. . . Clinton held firmly to the centrist ground he had staked out after the 1994 election, campaigning on the same "New" Democratic themes of "opportunity, responsibility, and community" that had served him well during his first run for the White House. He won 49 percent of the popular vote to Dole's 41 percent and Perot's 8 percent, along with 379 electoral votes to Dole's 159.

Clinton thus became the first Democratic president to be elected to a second term since FDR. But his candidate-centered campaign, abetted by a strong economy, did little to help his party. The Democrats lost two seats in the Senate, and gained but a modest nine seats in the House, thus failing to gain control of either legislative body. In truth, Clinton's campaign testified to the fragility of the nationalized party system that arose during the 1980s. The president's remarkable political comeback in 1995 was supported by so-called "soft" money that was designated for party building activities and thus not covered by campaign finance laws. But these expenditures were used overwhelmingly to mount television advertising campaigns, such as the media blast of the Republicans during the 1995 budget battles, that championed the president's independence from partisan squabbles. Indeed, Clinton scarcely endorsed the election of a Democratic Congress; moreover, his fund-raising efforts for the party supported Congressional candidates only late in the campaign. Adding insult to injury, the administration's questionable fund-raising methods led to revelations during the final days of the election that might have reduced Clinton's margin of victory and, thereby, undermined the Democrats' effort to retake the House.

If the recent past is prologue, the relationship between the Clinton White House and the Republican Congress during the president's second term will not be friendly. To be sure, the president and Congress have principled and strategic reasons to cooperate; indeed, in May, 1997, the White House and Republican leadership reached a compromise on a tentative plan to balance the budget by 2002. But this uneasy agreement was made possible by a revenue windfall caused by the robust economy, thus enabling Clinton and GOP leaders to avoid the sort of hard choices over program cuts and taxes that animated the bitter struggles of the 104th Congress. Even so, this rapprochement might prove difficult to maintain once Congress moves from generalities to specific decisions about such controversial matters as entitlement spending and tax relief. Moreover, Clinton's command eventually might be jeopardized not only by his lame-duck status, but also by mounting accusations of improper campaign fund-raising for the 1996 election. Not surprisingly, Democratic members of Congress, still smarting from the president's seeming indifference to their programmatic commitments and election prospects, maintained a deafening silence as the Republicans sought to exploit the White House's campaign peccadillos. Thus, even after his triumphant re-election, Clinton still faced the profound challenge of establishing the boundaries in which his party and domestic policy could be reformed.

Yet it might be unreasonable, indeed, dangerous, to rely so heavily on presidents to determine the contours of political action. The modern presidency operates in a political arena that is seldom congenial to meaningful political debate and that all too often is guilty of deflecting attention from the painful struggles about the appropriate meaning of liberalism or the relative merits of contemporary liberalism and conservatism. With the liberation of the executive from many of the constraints of party leadership and the rise of the mass media, presidents have resorted to rhetoric and administration, tools with which they have sought to forge new, more personal ties with the public. But, as the nation has witnessed all too clearly during the past twenty-five years, this form of "populist" presidential politics can all too readily degenerate into rank opportunism. Moreover, it risks exposing the people to the kind of public figures who will exploit citizens' impatience with the difficult tasks involved in sustaining a healthy constitutional democracy.

Presidents who enjoy prominent places in history have justified their reform programs in constitutional terms, claiming to restore the proper understanding of first principles, even as they have attempted to transfuse the Declaration and Constitution with new meaning. But they have done so as great party leaders, in the midst of major partisan realignments. Critical partisan elections have enabled each generation to claim its right to redefine the Constitution's principles and reorganize its institutions. The New Deal continued this unending task to ensure that each generation could affirm its attachment to constitutional government. The burden of this generation is to hold the modern presidency to account, to recapture the understanding of democracy that has made such momentous deliberation and choice so central to the pursuit of America's political destiny.

CHAPTER 7

❧

THE BUREAUCRACY

American bureaucracy today is an important fourth branch of the government. Too frequently the administrative branch is lumped under the heading of "the Executive" and is considered to be subordinate to the president. But the following selections will reveal that the bureaucracy is often autonomous, acting outside of the control of Congress, the president, and even the judiciary. This fact raises an important problem for our constitutional democracy: How can the bureaucracy be kept responsible if it does not fit into the constitutional framework that was designed to guarantee limited and responsible government?

Constitutional Background

While the Constitution carefully outlined the responsibilities and powers of the president, Congress, and to a lesser extent the Supreme Court, it did not mention the bureaucracy. The position of the bureaucracy in the separation-of-powers scheme developed by custom and statutory law rather than by explicit constitutional provisions. The following selection makes it clear that, although the Constitution did not provide for an administrative branch, it did have a bearing upon the development of the bureaucracy. Perhaps the most important result of constitutional democracy is that the administrative agencies have become pawns in the constant power struggle between the president and Congress.

— 56 —

CONSTITUTIONAL DEMOCRACY AND BUREAUCRATIC POWER

Peter Woll

The administrative branch today stands at the very center of our governmental process; it is the keystone of the structure. And administrative agencies exercise legislative and judicial as well as executive functions—a fact that is often overlooked. . . .

How should we view American bureaucracy? Ultimately, the power of government comes to rest in the administrative branch. Agencies are given the responsibility of making concrete decisions carrying out vague policy initiated in Congress or by the president. The agencies can offer expert advice, closely attuned to the most interested pressure groups, and they often not only determine the policies that the legislature and executive recommend in the first place, but also decisively affect the policy-making process. Usually it is felt that the bureaucracy is politically "neutral," completely under the domination of the president, Congress, or the courts. We will see that this is not entirely the case, and that the president and Congress have only sporadic control over the administrative process.

The bureaucracy is a semi-autonomous branch of the government, often dominating Congress, exercising strong influence on the president, and only infrequently subject to review by the courts. If our constitutional democracy is to be fully analyzed, we must focus attention upon the administrative branch. What is the nature of public administration? How are administration and politics intertwined? How are administrative constituencies determined? What is the relationship between agencies and their constituencies? What role should the president assume in relation to the administrative branch? How far should Congress go in controlling agencies which in fact tend to dominate the legislative process? Should judicial review be expanded? What are the conditions of judicial review? How do administrative agencies perform judicial functions, and how do these activities affect the ability of courts to oversee their actions? These questions confront us with what is called the problem of administrative responsibility: that is, how can we control the activities of the administrative branch? In order to approach an understanding of this difficult problem, it is necessary to appreciate the nature of the administrative process and how it interacts with other branches of the government and with the general public. It is also important to understand the nature of our constitutional system, and the political context within which agencies function.

We operate within the framework of a constitutional democracy. This means, first, that the government is to be limited by the separation of powers and Bill of Rights. Another component of the system, federalism, is designed in theory to provide states with a certain amount of authority when it is not implied at the national level. Our separation of powers, the system of checks and balances, and the federal system help to explain some of the differences between administrative organization here and in other countries. But the Constitution does not explicitly provide for the administrative branch, which has become a new fourth branch of government. This raises the question of how to control the bureaucracy when there are no clear constitutional limits upon it. The second aspect of our system, democracy, is of course implied in the Constitution itself, but has expanded greatly since it was adopted. We are confronted, very broadly speaking, first with the problem of constitutional limitation, and secondly with the problem of democratic participation in the activities of the bureaucracy. The bureaucracy must be accommodated within the framework of our system of constitutional democracy. This is the crux of the problem of administrative responsibility.

Even though the Constitution does not explicitly provide for the bureaucracy, it has had a profound impact upon the structure, functions, and general place that the bureaucracy occupies in government. The administrative process was incorporated into the constitutional system under the heading of "The Executive Branch." But the concept of "administration" at the time of the adoption of the Constitution was a very simple one, involving the "mere execution" of "executive details," to use the phrases of Hamilton in *The Federalist*. The idea, at that time, was simply that the president as Chief Executive would be able to control the Executive Branch in carrying out the mandates of Congress. In *Federalist 72*, after defining administration in this very narrow way, Hamilton stated:

> . . . The persons, therefore, to whose immediate management the different administrative matters are committed ought to be considered as Assistants or Deputies of the Chief Magistrate, and on this account, they ought to derive their offices from his appointment, at least from his nomination, and ought to be subject to his superintendence.

It was clear that Hamilton felt the president would be responsible for administrative action as long as he was in office. This fact later turned up in what can be called the "presidential supremacy" school of thought, which held and still holds that the president is *constitutionally* responsible for the administrative branch, and that Congress should delegate to him all necessary authority for this purpose. Nevertheless, whatever the framers of the Constitution might have planned if they could have foreseen the nature of bureaucratic development, the fact is that the system they constructed in many ways supported bureaucratic organization and functions independent of the president. The role they assigned to Congress in relation to administration assured this result, as did the general position of Congress in the governmental system as a check or balance to the power of the president. Congress has a great deal of authority over the administrative process.

If we compare the power of Congress and the president over the bureaucracy it becomes clear that they both have important constitutional responsibility. Congress retains primary control over the organization of the bureaucracy. It alone creates and destroys agencies, and determines whether they are to be located within the executive branch or outside it. This has enabled Congress to create a large number of *independent* agencies beyond presidential control. Congress has the authority to control appropriations and may thus exercise a great deal of power over the administrative arm, although increasingly the Bureau of the Budget and the president have the initial, and more often than not the final, say over the budget. Congress also has the authority to define the jurisdiction of agencies. Finally, the Constitution gives to the legislature the power to interfere in high-level presidential appointments, which must be "by and with the advice and consent of the Senate."

Congress may extend the sharing of the appointive power when it sets up new agencies. It may delegate to the president pervasive authority to control the bureaucracy. But one of the most important elements of the separation of power is the electoral system, which gives to Congress a constituency which is different from and even conflicting with that of the president. This means that Congress often decides to set up agencies beyond presidential purview. Only rarely will it grant the president any kind of final authority to structure the bureaucracy. During World War II, on the basis of the War Powers Act, the president had the authority to reorganize the administrative branch. Today he has the same authority, provided that Congress does not veto presidential proposals within a certain time limit. In refusing to give the president permanent reorganization authority, Congress is jealously guarding one of its important prerogatives.

Turning to the constitutional authority of the president over the bureaucracy, it is somewhat puzzling to see that it gives him a relatively small role. He appoints certain officials by and with the advice and consent of the Senate. He has directive power over agencies that are placed within his jurisdiction by Congress. His control over patronage, once so important, has diminished sharply under the merit system. The president is Commander-in-Chief of all military forces, which puts him in a controlling position over the Defense Department and agencies involved in military matters. In the area of international relations, the president is by constitutional authority the "Chief Diplomat," to use [presidential scholar Clinton] Rossiter's phrase. This means that he appoints Ambassadors (by and with the advice and consent of the Senate), and generally directs national activities in the international arena—a crucially important executive function. But regardless of the apparent intentions of some of the framers of the Constitution as expressed by Hamilton in *The Federalist*, and in spite of the predominance of the presidency in military and foreign affairs, the fact remains that we seek in vain for explicit constitutional authorization for the president to be "Chief Administrator."

This is not to say that the president does not have an important responsibility to act as chief of the bureaucracy, merely that there is no constitutional mandate for this. As our system evolved, the president was given more and more responsibility until he became, in practice, Chief Administrator. At the same time the constitutional system has often impeded progress in this direction. The president's Committee on Administrative Management in 1937, and later the Hoover Commissions of

1949 and 1955, called upon Congress to initiate a series of reforms increasing presidential authority over the administrative branch. It was felt that this was necessary to make democracy work. The president is the only official elected nationally, and if the administration is to be held democratically accountable, he alone can stand as its representative. But meaningful control from the White House requires that the president have a comprehensive program which encompasses the activities of the bureaucracy. He must be informed as to what they are doing, and be able to control them. He must understand the complex responsibilities of the bureaucracy. Moreover, he must be able to call on sufficient political support to balance the support which the agencies draw from private clientele groups and congressional committees. This has frequently proven a difficult and often impossible task for the president. He may have the *authority* to control the bureaucracy in many areas, but not enough power.

On the basis of the Constitution, Congress feels it quite proper that when it delegates legislative authority to administrative agencies it can relatively often place these groups outside the control of the president. For example, in the case of the Interstate Commerce Commission . . . Congress has delegated final authority to that agency to control railroad mergers and other aspects of transportation activity, without giving the president the right to veto. The president may feel that a particular merger is undesirable because it is in violation of the antitrust laws, but the Interstate Commerce Commission is likely to feel differently. In such a situation, the president can do nothing because he does not have the *legal authority* to take any action. If he could muster enough political support to exercise influence over the ICC, he would be able to control it, but the absence of legal authority is an important factor in such cases and diminishes presidential power. Moreover, the ICC draws strong support from the railroad industry, which has been able to counterbalance the political support possessed by the president and other groups that have wished to control it. Analogous situations exist with respect to other regulatory agencies.

Besides the problem of congressional and presidential control over the bureaucracy, there is the question of judicial review of administrative decisions. The rule of law is a central element in our Constitution. The rule of law means that decisions judicial in nature should be handled by common law courts, because of their expertise in rendering due process of law. When administrative agencies engage in adjudication their decisions should be subject to judicial review—at least, they should if one supports the idea of the supremacy of law. Judicial decisions are supposed to be rendered on an independent and impartial basis, through the use of tested procedures, in order to arrive at the accurate determination of the truth. Administrative adjudication should not be subject to presidential or congressional control, which would mean political determination of decisions that should be rendered in an objective manner. The idea of the rule of law, derived from the common law and adopted within the framework of our constitutional system, in theory limits legislative and executive control over the bureaucracy.

The nature of our constitutional system poses very serious difficulties to the development of a system of administrative responsibility. The Constitution postulates that the functions of government must be separated into different branches with differing constituencies and separate authority. The idea is that the departments should oppose each other, thereby preventing the arbitrary exercise of political power. Any combination of functions was considered to lead inevitably to arbitrary government. This is a debatable point, but the result of the Constitution is quite clear. The administrative process, on the other hand, often combines various functions of government in the same hands. Attempts are made, of course, to separate those who exercise the judicial functions from those in the prosecuting arms of the agencies. But the fact remains that there is a far greater combination of functions in the administrative process than can be accommodated by strict adherence to the Constitution.

It has often been proposed, as a means of alleviating what may be considered the bad effects of combined powers in administrative agencies, to draw a line of control from the original branches of the government to those parts of the bureaucracy exercising similar functions. Congress would control the legislative activities of the agencies, the president the executive aspects, and the courts the judicial functions. This would maintain the symmetry of the constitutional system. But this solution is not feasible, because other parts of the Constitution, giving different authority to these three branches, make symmetrical control of this kind almost impossible. The three branches of the government are not willing to give up whatever powers they may have over administrative agencies. For example, Congress is not willing to give the president complete control over all executive functions, nor to give the courts the authority to review all the decisions of the agencies. At present, judicial review takes place only if Congress authorizes it, except in those rare instances where constitutional issues are involved.

Another aspect of the problem of control is reflected in the apparent paradox that the three branches do not always use to the fullest extent their authority to regulate the bureaucracy, even though they wish to retain their power to do so. The courts, for example, have exercised considerable self-restraint in their review of administrative decisions. They are not willing to use all their power over the bureaucracy. Similarly, both Congress and the president will often limit their dealings with the administrative branch for political and practical reasons.

In the final analysis, we are left with a bureaucratic system that has been fragmented by the Constitution, and in which administrative discretion is inevitable. The bureaucracy reflects the general fragmentation of our political system. It is often the battleground for the three branches of government, and for outside pressure groups which seek to control it for their own purposes.

The Political Roots and Consequences
of Bureaucracy

With the exception of those executive departments that all governments need, such as State, Treasury, and Defense, *private*-sector political demands have led to the creation of American bureaucracy. In response to those demands, Congress has over the years created more and more executive departments and agencies to solve economic, political, and social problems. It is important to realize that the bureaucracy is not, as many of its critics have suggested, a conspiracy by government officials to increase their power. The following selection traces the rise of the administrative state and particularly notes how political pluralism has affected the character of the bureaucracy by dividing it into clientele sectors.

—————————— **57** ——————————

THE RISE OF THE BUREAUCRATIC STATE

James Q. Wilson

During its first 150 years, the American republic was not thought to have "bureaucracy," and thus it would have been meaningless to refer to the "problems" of a "bureaucratic state." There were, of course, appointed civilian officials: Though only about 3,000 at the end of the Federalist period, there were about 95,000 by the time Grover Cleveland assumed office in 1881, and nearly half a million by 1925. Some aspects of these numerous officials were regarded as problems—notably, the standard by which they were appointed and the political loyalties to which they were held—but these were thought to be matters of proper character and good management. The great political and constitutional struggles were not over the power of the administrative apparatus, but over the power of the President, of Congress, and of the states.

The Founding Fathers had little to say about the nature or function of the executive branch of the new government. The Constitution is virtually silent on the subject and the debates in the Constitutional Convention are almost devoid of reference to an administrative apparatus. This reflected no lack of concern about the matter, however. Indeed, it was in part because of the Founders' depressing experience with chaotic and inefficient management under the Continental Congress and the Articles of Confederation that they had assembled in Philadelphia. Management by committees composed of part-time amateurs had cost the colonies dearly in the War of Independence and few, if any, of the Founders wished to return to that system. The argument was only over how the heads of the necessary departments of government were to be selected, and whether these heads should be wholly subordinate to the President or whether instead they should form some sort of council that would advise the President and perhaps share in his authority. In the end, the Founders left it up to Congress to decide the matter.

There was no dispute in Congress that there should be executive departments, headed by single appointed officials, and, of course, the Constitution specified that these would be appointed by the President with the advice and consent of the Senate. The only issue was how such officials might be removed. After prolonged debate and by the narrowest of majorities, Congress agreed that the President should have the sole right of removal, thus confirming that the infant administrative system would be wholly subordinate—in law at least—to the President. Had not Vice-President John Adams, presiding over a Senate equally divided on the issue, cast the deciding vote in favor of presidential removal, the administrative departments might conceivably have become legal dependencies of the legislature, with incalculable consequences for the development of the embryonic government.

The "Bureaucracy Problem"

The original departments were small and had limited duties. The State Department, the first to be created, had but nine employees in addition to the Secretary. The War Department did not reach 80 civilian employees until 1801; it commanded only a few thousand soldiers. Only the Treasury Department had substantial powers—it collected taxes, managed the public debt, ran the national bank, conducted land surveys, and purchased military supplies. Because of this, Congress gave the closest scrutiny to its structure and its activities.

The number of administrative agencies and employees grew slowly but steadily during the 19th and early 20th centuries and then increased explosively on the occasion of World War I, the Depression, and World War II. It is difficult to say at what point in this process the administrative system became a distinct locus of power or an independent source of political initiatives and problems. What is clear is that the emphasis on the sheer size of the administrative establishment—conventional in many treatments of the subject—is misleading.

The government can spend vast sums of money—wisely or unwisely—without creating that set of conditions we ordinarily associate with the bureaucratic state. For example, there could be massive transfer payments made under government auspices from person to person or from state to state, all managed by a comparatively small staff of officials and a few large computers. In 1971, the federal government paid out $54 billion under various social insurance programs, yet the Social Security Administration employs only 73,000 persons, many of whom perform purely routine jobs.

And though it may be harder to believe, the government could in principle employ an army of civilian personnel without giving rise to those organizational patterns that we call bureaucratic. Suppose, for instance, that we as a nation should decide to have in the public schools at least one teacher for every two students.

This would require a vast increase in the number of teachers and schoolrooms, but almost all of the persons added would be performing more or less identical tasks, and they could be organized into very small units (e.g., neighborhood schools). Though there would be significant overhead costs, most citizens would not be aware of any increase in the "bureaucratic" aspects of education—indeed, owing to the much greater time each teacher would have to devote to each pupil and his or her parents, the citizenry might well conclude that there actually had been a substantial reduction in the amount of "bureaucracy."

To the reader predisposed to believe that we have a "bureaucracy problem," these hypothetical cases may seem farfetched. Max Weber, after all, warned us that in capitalist and socialist societies alike, bureaucracy was likely to acquire an "overtowering" power position. Conservatives have always feared bureaucracy, save perhaps the police. Humane socialists have frequently been embarrassed by their inability to reconcile a desire for public control of the economy with the suspicion that a public bureaucracy may be as immune to democratic control as a private one. Liberals have equivocated, either dismissing any concern for bureaucracy as reactionary quibbling about social progress or embracing that concern when obviously nonreactionary persons (welfare recipients, for example) express a view toward the Department of Health and Human Services indistinguishable from the view businessmen take of the Internal Revenue Service.

Political Authority

There are at least three ways in which political power may be gathered undesirably into bureaucratic hands: by the growth of an administrative apparatus so large as to be immune from popular control, by placing power over a governmental bureaucracy of any size in private rather than public hands, or by vesting discretionary authority in the hands of a public agency so that the exercise of that power is not responsive to the public good. These are not the only problems that arise because of bureaucratic organization. From the point of view of their members, bureaucracies are sometimes uncaring, ponderous, or unfair; from the point of view of their political superiors, they are sometimes unimaginative or inefficient; from the point of view of their clients, they are sometimes slow or unjust. No single account can possibly treat of all that is problematic in bureaucracy; even the part I discuss here—the extent to which political authority has been transferred undesirably to an unaccountable administrative realm—is itself too large for a single essay. But it is, if not the most important problem, then surely the one that would most have troubled our Revolutionary leaders, especially those that went on to produce the Constitution. It was, after all, the question of power that chiefly concerned them, both in redefining our relationship with England and in finding a new basis for political authority in the Colonies.

To some, following in the tradition of [Max] Weber, bureaucracy is the inevitable consequence and perhaps necessary concomitant of modernity. A money economy, the division of labor, and the evolution of legal-rational norms to justify organizational authority require the efficient adaptation of means to ends and a high degree of predictability in the behavior of rulers. To this, Georg Simmel added the view that organizations tend to acquire the characteristics of those institutions with which they are in conflict, so that as government becomes more bureaucratic, private organizations—political parties, trade unions, voluntary associations—will have an additional reason to become bureaucratic as well.

By viewing bureaucracy as an inevitable (or, as some would put it, "functional") aspect of society, we find ourselves attracted to theories that explain the growth of bureaucracy in terms of some inner dynamic to which all agencies respond and which makes all barely governable and scarcely tolerable. Bureaucracies grow, we are told, because of Parkinson's Law: Work and personnel expand to consume the available resources. Bureaucracies behave, we believe, in accord with various other maxims, such as the Peter Principle: In hierarchical organizations, personnel are promoted up to that point at which their incompetence becomes manifest—hence, all important positions are held by incompetents. More elegant, if not essentially different, theories have been propounded by scholars. The tendency of all bureaus to expand is explained by William A. Niskanen by the assumption, derived from the theory of the firm, that "bureaucrats maximize the total budget of their bureau during their tenure"—hence, "all bureaus are too large." What keeps them from being not merely too large but all-consuming is that fact that a bureau must deliver to some degree on its promised output, and if it consistently underdelivers, its budget will be cut by unhappy legislators. But since measuring the output of a bureau is often difficult—indeed, even *conceptualizing* the output of the State Department is mind-boggling—the bureau has a great deal of freedom within which to seek the largest possible budget.

Such theories, both the popular and the scholarly, assign little importance to the nature of the tasks an agency performs, the constitutional framework in which it is embedded, or the preferences and attitudes of citizens and legislators. Our approach will be quite different: Different agencies will be examined in historical perspective to discover the kinds of problems—if any, to which their operations give rise, and how those problems were affected—perhaps determined—by the tasks which they were assigned, the political system in which they operated, and the preferences they were required to consult. What follows will be far from a systematic treatment of such matters, and even farther from a rigorous testing of any theory of bureaucratization. Our knowledge of agency history and behavior is too sketchy to permit that.

Bureaucracy and Size

During the first half of the 19th century, the growth in the size of the federal bureaucracy can be explained, not by the assumption of new tasks by the government or by the imperialistic designs of the managers of existing tasks, but by the addition to existing bureaus of personnel performing essentially routine, repetitive tasks for which the public demand was great and unavoidable. The principal problem facing a bureaucracy thus enlarged was how best to coordinate its activities toward given and noncontroversial ends.

The increase in the size of the executive branch of the federal government at this time was almost entirely the result of the increase in the size of the Post Office. From 1816 to 1861, federal civilian employment in the executive branch increased nearly eightfold (from 4,837 to 36,672), but 86 percent of this growth was the result of additions to the postal service. The Post Office Department was expanding as population and commerce expanded. By 1869 there were 27,000 post offices scattered around the nation; by 1901, nearly 77,000. In New York alone, by 1894 there were nearly 3,000 postal employees, the same number required to run the entire federal government at the beginning of that century. . . .

The Military Establishment

Not all large bureaucracies grow in response to demands for service. The Department of Defense, since 1941 the largest employer of federal civilian officials, has become, as the governmental keystone of the "military-industrial complex," the very archetype of an administrative entity that is thought to be so vast and so well-entrenched that it can virtually ignore the political branches of government, growing and even acting on the basis of its own inner imperatives. . . .

A "Military-Industrial Complex"?

The argument for the existence of an autonomous, bureaucratically led military-industrial complex is supported primarily by events since 1950. Not only has the United States assumed during this period worldwide commitments that necessitate a larger military establishment, but the advent of new, high-technology weapons has created a vast industrial machine with an interest in sustaining a high level of military expenditures, especially on weapons research, development, and acquisition. This machine, so the argument goes, is allied with the Pentagon in ways that dominate the political officials nominally in charge of the armed forces. There is some truth in all this. We have become a world military force, though that decision was made by elected officials in 1949–1950 and not dictated by a (then nonexistent) military-industrial complex. High-cost, high-technology weapons have become important and a number of industrial concerns will prosper or perish depending on how contracts for those weapons are let. The development and purchase of weapons is sometimes made in a wasteful, even irrational, manner. And the allocation of funds among the several armed services is often dictated as much by inter-service rivalry as by strategic or political decisions. . . .

Bureaucracy and Clientelism

After 1861, the growth in the federal administrative system could no longer be explained primarily by an expansion of the postal service and other traditional bureaus. Though these continued to expand, new departments were added that reflected a new (or at least greater) emphasis on the enlargement of the scope of government. Between 1861 and 1901, over 200,000 civilian employees were added to the federal service, only 52 percent of whom were postal workers. Some of these, of course, staffed a larger military and naval establishment stimulated by the Civil War and the Spanish-American War. By 1901 there were over 44,000 civilian defense employees, mostly workers in government-owned arsenals and shipyards. But even those could account for less than one fourth of the increase in employment during the preceding 40 years.

What was striking about the period after 1861 was that the government began to give formal, bureaucratic recognition to the emergence of distinctive interest in a diversifying economy. As Richard L. Schott has written, "whereas earlier federal departments had been formed around specialized governmental functions (foreign affairs, war, finance, and the like), the new departments of this period—Agriculture, Labor, and Commerce—were devoted to the interests and aspirations of particular economic groups."

The original purpose behind these clientele-oriented departments was neither to subsidize nor to regulate, but to promote, chiefly by gathering and publishing statistics and (especially in the case of agriculture) by research. . . .

Public Power and Private Interests

. . . The New Deal was perhaps the high water mark of at least the theory of bureaucratic clientelism. Not only did various sectors of society, notably agriculture, begin receiving massive subsidies, but the government proposed, through the National Industry Recovery Act (NRA), to cloak with public power a vast number of industrial groupings and trade associations so that they might control production and prices in ways that would end the depression. The NRA's Blue Eagle fell before the Supreme Court—the wholesale delegation of public power to private interests was declared unconstitutional. But the piecemeal delegation was not, as the continued growth of specialized promotional agencies attests. The Civil Aeronautics Board, for example, erroneously thought to be exclusively a regulatory agency, was formed in 1938 "to promote" as well as regulate civil aviation and it has done so by restricting entry and maintaining above-market rate fares.

Agriculture, of course, provides the leading case of clientelism. Theodore J. Lowi finds "at least 10 separate, autonomous, local self-governing systems" located in or closely associated with the Department of Agriculture that control to some significant degree the flow of billions of dollars in expenditures and loans. Local committees of farmers, private farm organizations, agency heads, and committee chairmen in Congress dominate policymaking in this area—not, perhaps, to the exclusion of the concerns of other publics, but certainly in ways not powerfully constrained by them.

"Cooperative Federalism"

The growing edge of client-oriented bureaucracy can be found, however, not in government relations with private groups, but in the relations among governmental units. In dollar volume, the chief clients of federal domestic expenditures are state and local government agencies. . . .

The degree to which such grants, and the federal agencies that administer them, constrain or even direct state and local bureaucracies is a matter of dispute. No general answer can be given—federal support of welfare programs has left considerable discretion in the hands of the states over the size of benefits and some discretion over eligibility rules, whereas federal support of highway construction carries with it specific requirements as to design, safety, and (since 1968) environmental and social impact.

A few generalizations are possible, however. The first is that the states and not the cities have been from the first, and remain today, the principal client group for grants-in-aid. It was not until the Housing Act of 1937 that money was given in any substantial amount directly to local governments and though many additional programs of this kind were later added, as late as 1970 less than 12 percent of all federal aid went directly to cities and towns. The second general observation is that the 1960s mark a major watershed in the way in which the purposes of federal aid are determined. Before that time, most grants were for purposes initially defined by states—to build highways and airports, to fund unemployment insurance programs, and the like. Beginning in the 1960s, the federal government, at the initiative of the President and his advisors, increasingly came to define the purposes of these grants—not necessarily over the objection of the states, but often without any initiative from them. Federal money was to be spent on poverty, ecology, planning, and other "national" goals for which, until the laws were passed, there were few, if any, well-organized and influential constituencies. Whereas federal money was once spent in response to the claims of distinct and organized clients, public or private, in the contemporary period federal money has increasingly been spent in ways that have created such clients.

And once rewarded or created, they are rarely penalized or abolished. . . .

Self-Perpetuating Agencies

If the Founding Fathers were to return to examine bureaucratic clientelism, they would, I suspect, be deeply discouraged. James Madison clearly foresaw that American society would be "broken into many parts, interests and classes of citizens" and that this "multiplicity of interest" would help ensure against "the tyranny of the majority," especially in a federal regime with separate branches of government. Positive action would require a "coalition of a majority"; in the process of forming this coalition, the rights of all would be protected, not merely by self-interested bargains, but because in a free society such a coalition "could seldom take place on any other principles than those of justice and the general good." To those who wrongly believed that Madison thought of men as acting only out of base motives, the phrase is instructive: Persuading men who disagree to compromise their differences can rarely be achieved solely by the parceling out of relative advantage; the belief is also required that what is being agreed to is right, proper, and defensible before public opinion.

Most of the major new social programs of the United States, whether for the good of the few or the many, were initially adopted by broad coalitions appealing to general standards of justice or to conceptions of the public weal. This is certainly the case with most of the New Deal legislation—notably such programs as Social Security—and with most Great Society legislation—notably Medicare and aid to education; it was also conspicuously the case with respect to post–Great Society legislation pertaining to consumer and environmental concerns. State occupational licensing laws were supported by majorities instead in, among other things, the contribution of these statutes to public safety and health.

But when a program supplies particular benefits to an existing or newly created interest, public or private, it creates a set of political relationships that make exceptionally difficult further alteration of that program by coalitions of the majority. What was created in the name of the common good is sustained in the name of the particular interest. Bureaucratic clientelism becomes self-perpetuating, in the absence of some crisis or scandal, because a single interest group to which the program matters greatly is highly motivated and well-situated to ward off the criticisms of other groups that have a broad but weak interest in the policy.

In short, a regime of separated powers makes it difficult to overcome objections and contrary interests sufficiently to permit the enactment of a new program or the creation of a new agency. Unless the legislation can be made to pass either with little notice or at a time of crisis or extraordinary majorities—and sometimes even then—the initiation of new programs requires public interest arguments. But the same regime works to protect agencies, once created, from unwelcome change because a major change is, in effect, new legislation that must overcome the same hurdles as the original law, but this time with one of the hurdles—the wishes of the agency and its client—raised much higher. As a result, the Madisonian system makes it relatively easy for the delegation of public power to private groups to go unchallenged and, therefore, for factional interests that have acquired a supportive public bureaucracy to rule without submitting their interests to the effective scrutiny and modification of other interests. . . .

CHAPTER 8

❦

CONGRESS

The United States Congress, exercising supreme legislative power, was at the beginning of the nineteenth century the most powerful political institution in the national government. It was feared by the framers of the Constitution, who felt that unless it was closely guarded and limited it would easily dominate both the presidency and the Supreme Court. Its powers were carefully enumerated, and it was made a bicameral body. This latter provision not only secured representation of different interests but also limited the power of the legislature which, when hobbled by two houses often working against each other, could not act as swiftly and forcefully as a single body could. Although still important, the power and prestige of Congress have declined while the powers of the president and the Supreme Court, not to mention those of the vast governmental bureaucracy, have increased. Congressional power, its basis, and the factors influencing the current position of Congress vis-à-vis coordinate governmental departments are discussed in this chapter.

Constitutional Background: Representation of Popular, Group, and National Interests

Article I, Section 1 of the Constitution states that "all legislative powers herein granted shall be vested in a Congress of the United States, which shall consist of a Senate and House of Representatives." Section 8 specifically enumerates congressional powers, and provides that Congress shall have power "to make all laws which shall be necessary and proper for carrying into execution the foregoing powers, and all other powers vested by this Constitution in the government of the United States, or in any department or officer thereof."

Apart from delineating the powers of Congress, Article I provides that the House shall represent the people, and the Senate the states through appointment of members by the state legislatures. The representative function of Congress is written into the Constitution, and at the time of the framing of the Constitution much discussion centered on the nature of representation and what constituted adequate representation in a national legislative body. Further, relating in part to the question of representation, the framers of the Constitution had to determine what the appropriate tasks for each branch of the legislature were and to what extent certain legislative activities should be within the exclusive or initial jurisdiction of the House or the Senate. All these questions depended to some extent upon the conceptualization the framers had of the House as representative of popular interests on a short-term basis and the Senate as a reflection of conservative interests on a long-term basis. These selections from *The Federalist* indicate the thinking of the framers about the House of Representatives and the Senate.

58

FEDERALIST 53

James Madison

. . . No man can be a competent legislator who does not add to an upright intention and a sound judgment a certain degree of knowledge of the subjects on which he is to legislate. A part of this knowledge may be acquired by means of information, which lie within the compass of men in private, as well as public stations. Another part can only be attained, or at least thoroughly attained, by actual experience in the station which requires the use of it. The period of service ought, therefore, in all such cases, to bear some proportion to the extent of practical knowledge requisite to the due performance of the service. . . .

In a single state the requisite knowledge relates to the existing laws, which are uniform throughout the state, and with which all the citizens are more or less conversant. . . . The great theater of the United States presents a very different scene. The laws are so far from being uniform that they vary in every state; whilst the public affairs of the union are spread throughout a very extensive region, and are extremely diversified by the local affairs connected with them, and can with difficulty be correctly learnt in any other place than in the central councils, to which a knowledge of them will be brought by representatives of every part of the empire. Yet some knowledge of the affairs, and even of the laws of all the states, ought to be possessed by the members from each of the states. . . .

A branch of knowledge which belongs to the acquirements of a federal representative, and which has not been mentioned, is that of foreign affairs. In regulating our own commerce he ought to be not only acquainted with the treaties between the United States and other nations, but also with the commercial policy and laws of other nations. He ought not to be altogether ignorant of the law of nations; for that, as far as it is a proper object of municipal legislation, is submitted to the federal government. And although the House of Representatives is not immediately to participate in foreign negotiations and arrangements, yet from the necessary connection between the several branches of public affairs, those particular subjects will frequently deserve attention in the ordinary course of legislation, and will sometimes demand particular legislative sanction and cooperation. Some portion of this knowledge may, no doubt, be acquired in a man's closet; but some of it also can only be acquired to best effect, by a practical attention to the subject, during the period of actual service in the legislature. . . .

FEDERALIST 56

The . . . charge against the House of Representatives is, that it will be too small to possess a due knowledge of the interests of its constituents.

As this objection evidently proceeds from a comparison of the proposed number of representatives, with the great extent of the United States, the number of their inhabitants, and the diversity of their interests, without taking into view, at the same time, the circumstances which will distinguish the Congress from other legislative bodies, the best answer that can be given to it, will be a brief explanation of these peculiarities.

It is a sound and important principle that the representative ought to be acquainted with the interests and circumstances of his constituents. But this principle can extend no farther than to those circumstances and interests to which the authority and care of the representative relate. An ignorance of a variety of minute and particular objects, which do not lie within the compass of legislation, is consistent with every attribute necessary to a due performance of the legislative trust. In determining the extent of information required in the exercise of a particular authority, recourse then must be had to the objects within the purview of that authority.

What are to be the objects of federal legislation? Those which are of most importance, and which seem most to require knowledge, are commerce, taxation, and the militia.

A proper regulation of commerce requires much information, as has been elsewhere remarked; but as far as this information relates to the laws, and local situation of each individual state, a very few representatives would be sufficient vehicles of it to the federal councils.

Taxation will consist, in great measure, of duties which will be involved in the regulation of commerce. So far the preceding remark is applicable to this object. As far as it may consist of internal collections, a more diffusive knowledge of the circumstances of the state may be necessary. But will not this also be possessed in sufficient degree by a very few intelligent men, diffusively elected within the state? . . .

With regard to the regulation of the militia there are scarcely any circumstances in reference to which local knowledge can be said to be necessary. . . . The art of war teaches general principles of organization, movement, and discipline, which apply universally.

The attentive reader will discern that the reasoning here used, to prove the sufficiency of a moderate number of representatives, does not, in any respect, contradict what was urged on another occasion, with regard to the extensive information which the representatives ought to possess, and the time that might be necessary for acquiring it. . . .

FEDERALIST 57

. . . The House of Representatives is so constituted as to support in the members an habitual recollection of their dependence on the people. Before the sentiments impressed on their minds by the mode of their elevation, can be effaced by the exercise of power, they will be compelled to anticipate the moment when their power is to cease, when their exercise of it is to be reviewed, and when they must descend to the level from which they were raised; there for ever to remain unless a faithful discharge of their trust shall have established their title to a renewal of it.

I will add, as a . . . circumstance in the situation of the House of Representatives, restraining them from oppressive measures, that they can make no law which will not have its full operation on themselves and their friends, as well as on the great mass of the society. This has always been deemed one of the strongest bonds by which human policy can connect the rulers and the people together. It creates between them that communion of interest, and sympathy of sentiments, of which few governments have furnished examples; but without which every government degenerates into tyranny. If it be asked, what is to restrain the House of Representatives from making legal discriminations in favor of themselves, and a particular class of the society? I answer, the genius of the whole system; the nature of just and constitutional laws; and, above all, the vigilant and manly spirit which actuates the people of America; a spirit which nourishes freedom, and in return is nourished by it.

If this spirit shall ever be so far debased as to tolerate a law not obligatory on the legislature, as well as on the people, the people will be prepared to tolerate anything but liberty.

Such will be the relation between the House of Representatives and their constituents. Duty, gratitude, interest, ambition itself, are the cords by which they will be bound to fidelity and sympathy with the great mass of the people. It is possible that these may all be insufficient to control the caprice and wickedness of men. But are they not all that government will admit, and that human prudence can devise?

Are they not the genuine, and the characteristic means, by which republican government provides for the liberty and happiness of the people? . . .

FEDERALIST 58

. . . In this review of the constitution of the House of Representatives . . . one observation . . . I must be permitted to add . . . as claiming, in my judgment, a very serious attention. It is, that in all legislative assemblies, the greater the number composing them may be, the fewer will be the men who will in fact direct their proceedings. In the first place, the more numerous any assembly may be, of whatever characters composed, the greater is known to be the ascendancy of passion over reason. In the next place, the larger the number, the greater will be the proportion of members of limited information and of weak capacities. Now it is precisely on characters of this description that the eloquence and address of the few are known to act with all their force. In the ancient republics, where the whole body of the people assembled in person, a single orator, or an artful statesman, was generally seen to rule with as complete a sway as if a sceptre had been placed in his single hands. On the same principle, the more multitudinous a representative assembly may be rendered, the more it will partake of the infirmities incident to collective meetings of the people. Ignorance will be the dupe of cunning; and passion the slave of sophistry and declamation. The people can never err more than in supposing, that by multiplying their representatives beyond a certain list, they strengthen the barrier against the government of a few. Experience will for ever admonish them, that, on the contrary, after securing a sufficient number for the purposes of safety, of local information, and of diffusive sympathy with the whole society, they will counteract their own views by every addition to their representatives. The countenance of the government may become more democratic; but the soul that animates it will be more oligarchic. The machine will be enlarged, but the fewer, and often the more secret, will be the springs by which its motions are directed. . . .

FEDERALIST 62

Having examined the constitution of the House of Representatives . . . I enter next on the examination of the Senate.

The heads under which this member of the government may be considered are—I. The qualifications of senators; II. The appointment of them by the state legislatures; III. The equality of representation in the Senate; IV. The number of senators, and the term for which they are to be elected; V. The powers vested in the Senate.

I

The qualifications proposed for senators, as distinguished from those of representatives, consist in a more advanced age and a longer period of citizenship. A senator must be thirty years of age at least; as a representative must be twenty-five. And the former must have been a citizen nine years; as seven years are required for the latter. The propriety of these distinctions is explained by the nature of the senatorial trust; which, requiring greater extent of information and stability of character, requires at the same time, that the senator should have reached a period of life most likely to supply these advantages. . . .

II

It is equally unnecessary to dilate on the appointment of senators by the state legislators. Among the various modes which might have been devised for constituting this branch of the government, that which has been proposed by the convention is probably the most congenial with the public opinion. It is recommended by the double advantage of favoring a select appointment, and of giving to the state governments such an agency in the formation of the federal government, as must secure the authority of the former, and may form a convenient link between the two systems.

III

The equality of representation in the Senate is another point, which, being evidently the result of compromise between the opposite pretensions of the large and the small states, does not call for much discussion. If indeed it be right, that among a people thoroughly incorporated into one nation, every district ought to have a proportional share in the government: and that among independent and sovereign states bound together by a simple league, the parties, however unequal in size, ought to have an equal share in the common councils, it does not appear to be without some reason, that in a compound republic, partaking both of the national and federal character, the government ought to be founded on a mixture of the principles of proportional [as found in the House of Representatives] and equal representation [in the Senate]. . . .

. . . The equal vote allowed to each state, is at once a constitutional recognition of the portion of sovereignty remaining in the individual states, and an instrument for preserving that residuary sovereignty. So far the equality ought to be no less acceptable to the large than to the small states; since they are not less solicitous to guard by every possible expedient against an improper consolidation of the states into one simple republic.

Another advantage accruing from this ingredient in the constitution of the senate is, the additional impediment it must prove against improper acts of legislation. No law or resolution can now be passed without the concurrence, first, of a majority of the people, and then, of a majority of the states. It must be acknowledged that this complicated check on legislation may, in some instances, be injurious as well as beneficial; and that the peculiar defense which it involves in favor of the smaller states, would be more rational, if any interests common to them, and distinct from those of the other states, would otherwise be exposed to peculiar danger. But as the larger states will always be able, by their power over the supplies, to defeat unreasonable exertions of this prerogative of the lesser states; and as the facility and excess of law-making seem to be the diseases to which our governments are most liable, it is not impossible, that this part of the constitution may be more convenient in practice than it appears to many in contemplation.

IV

The number of senators, and the duration of their appointment, come next to be considered. In order to form an accurate judgment on both these points, it will be proper to inquire into the purposes which are to be answered by the Senate; and, in order to ascertain these, it will be necessary to review the inconveniences which a republic must suffer from the want of such an institution.

First

It is a misfortune incident to republican government, though in a lesser degree than to other governments, that those who administer it may forget their obligations to their constituents, and prove unfaithful to their important trust. In this point of view, a senate, as a second branch of the legislative assembly, distinct from, and dividing the power with, a first, must be in all cases a salutary check on the government. It doubles the security to the people by requiring the concurrence of two distinct bodies in schemes of usurpation or perfidy, where the ambition or corruption of one would otherwise be sufficient. . . . [A]s the improbability of sinister combinations will be in proportion to the dissimilarity in the genius of the two bodies, it must be politic to distinguish them from each other by every circumstance which will consist with a due harmony in all proper measures, and with the genuine principles of republican government.

Second

The necessity of a senate is not less indicated by the propensity of all single and numerous assemblies, to yield to the impulse of sudden and violent passions, and to be seduced by factious leaders into intemperate and pernicious resolutions. Examples on this subject might be cited without number; and from proceedings within the United States, as well as from the history of other nations. But a position that will not be contradicted need not be proved. All that need be remarked is that a body which is to correct this infirmity ought itself to be free from it, and consequently ought to be less numerous. It ought, moreover, to possess great firmness, and consequently ought to hold its authority by a tenure of considerable duration.

Third

Another defect to be supplied by a senate lies in a want of due acquaintance with objects and principles of legislation. It is not possible that an assembly of men, called, for the most part, from pursuits of a private nature, continued in appointments for a short time, and led by no permanent motive to devote the intervals of public occupation to a study of the laws, the affairs, and the comprehensive interests of their country, should, if left wholly to themselves, escape a variety of important errors in the exercise of their legislative trust. . . .

Fourth

The mutability in the public councils, arising from a rapid succession of new members, however qualified they may be, points out, in the strongest manner, the necessity of some stable institution in the government. Every new election in the states is found to change one-half of the representatives. From this change of men must proceed a change of opinions; and from a change of opinions, a change of measures. But a continued change even of good measures is inconsistent with every rule of prudence, and every prospect of success. . . .

FEDERALIST 63

A fifth desideratum, illustrating the utility of a senate, is the want of a due sense of national character. Without a select and stable member of the government, the esteem of foreign powers will not only be forfeited by an unenlightened and variable policy . . .; but the national councils will not possess that sensibility to the opinion of the world, which is perhaps not less necessary in order to merit, than it is to obtain, its respect and confidence. . . .

I add, as a sixth defect, the want in some important cases of a due responsibility in the government to the people, arising from that frequency of elections, which in other cases produces this responsibility. . . .

Responsibility, in order to be reasonable, must be limited to objects within the power of the responsible party, and in order to be effectual, must relate to operations of that power, of which a ready and proper judgment can be formed by the constituents. The objects of government may be divided into two general classes; the one depending on measures, which have singly an immediate and sensible operation; the other depending on a succession of well chosen and well connected measures, which have a gradual and perhaps unobserved operation. The importance of the latter description to the collective and permanent welfare of every country, needs no explanation. And yet it is evident that an assembly elected for so short a term as to be unable to provide more than one or two links in a chain of measures, on which the general welfare may essentially depend, ought not to be answerable for the final result, any more than a steward or tenant, engaged for one year, could be justly made to answer for plans or improvements, which could not be accomplished in less than half a dozen years. Nor is it possible for the people to estimate the share of influence, which their annual assemblies may respectively have on events resulting from the mixed transactions of several years. It is sufficiently difficult, at any rate, to preserve a personal responsibility in the members of a numerous body, for such acts of the body as have an immediate, detached, and palpable operation on its constituents.

The proper remedy for this defect must be an additional body in the legislative department, which, having sufficient permanency to provide for such objects as require a continued attention, and a train of measures, may be justly and effectually answerable for the attainment of those objects.

Thus far I have considered the circumstances, which point out the necessity of a well constructed senate, only as they relate to the representatives of the people. To a people as little blinded by prejudice, or corrupted by flattery, as those whom I address, I shall not scruple to add, that such an institution may be sometimes necessary, as a defense to the people against their own temporary errors and delusions. As the cool and deliberate sense of the community ought, in all governments, and actually will, in all free governments, ultimately prevail over the views of its rulers; so there are particular moments in public affairs, when the people, stimulated by some irregular passion, or some illicit advantage, or misled by the artful misrepresentations of interested men, may call for measures which they themselves will afterwards be the most ready to lament and condemn. In these critical moments, how salutary will be the interference of some temperate and respectable body of citizens, in order to check the misguided career, and to suspend the blow meditated by the people against themselves, until reason, justice and truth can regain their authority over the public mind? What bitter anguish would not the people of Athens have often avoided, if their government had contained so provident a safeguard against the tyranny of their own passions? Popular liberty might then have escaped the indelible reproach of decreeing to the same citizens the hemlock on one day, and statues on the next.

It may be suggested that a people spread over an extensive region cannot, like the crowded inhabitants of a small district, be subject to the infection of violent passions; or to the danger of combining in the pursuit of unjust measures. I am far from denying that this is a distinction of peculiar importance. I have, on the contrary, endeavored in a former paper to show that it is one of the principal recommendations of a confederated republic. At the same time this advantage ought not to be considered as superseding the use of auxiliary precautions. It may even be remarked that the same extended situation, which will exempt the people of America from some of the dangers incident to lesser republics, will expose them to the inconveniency of remaining for a longer time under the influence of those misrepresentations which the combined industry of interested men may succeed in distributing among them. . . .

❧

Congress and the Washington Political Establishment

The author of the following selection agrees with David Mayhew (see selection 65) that the principal goal of members of Congress is reelection. That incentive, the author suggests, has led Congress to create a vast federal bureaucracy to implement programs that ostensibly benefit constituents. Congress has delegated substantial authority to administrative departments and agencies to carry out programs, inevitably resulting in administrative decisions that frequently step on constituents' toes. Congress, which has gained credit for establishing the programs in the first place, steps in once again to receive credit for handling constituent complaints against the bureaucracy. The author's provocative thesis is that both the establishment and maintenance of a vast federal bureaucracy is explained by the congressional reelection incentive.

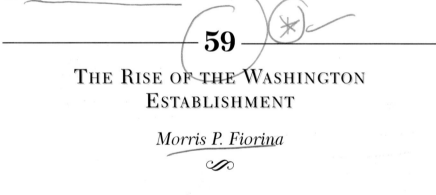

— 59 —

THE RISE OF THE WASHINGTON ESTABLISHMENT

Morris P. Fiorina

❧

Dramatis Personae

In this [selection] I will set out a theory of the Washington establishment(s). The theory is quite plausible from a common-sense standpoint, and it is consistent with the specialized literature of academic political science. Nevertheless, it is still a theory, not proven fact. Before plunging in let me bring out in the open the basic axiom on which the theory rests: the self-interest axiom.

I assume that most people most of the time act in their own self-interest. This is not to say that human beings seek only to amass tangible wealth but rather to say that human beings seek to achieve their own ends—tangible and intangible—rather than the ends of their fellow men. I do not condemn such behavior nor do I condone it (although I rather sympathize with Thoreau's comment that "if I knew for a certainty that a man was coming to my house with the conscious design of doing me good, I should run for my life."). I only claim that political and economic theories which presume self-interested behavior will prove to be more widely applicable than those which build on more altruistic assumptions.

What does the axiom imply when used in the specific context of this [selection], a context peopled by congressmen, bureaucrats, and voters? I assume that the primary goal of the typical congressman is reelection. Over and above the [six-figure] salary plus "perks" and outside money, the office of congressman carries with it prestige, excitement, and power. It is a seat in the cockpit of government. But in order to retain the status, excitement, and power (not to mention more tangible things) of office, the congressman must win reelection every two years. Even those congressmen genuinely concerned with good public policy must achieve reelection in order to continue their work. Whether narrowly self-serving or more publicly oriented, the individual congressman finds reelection to be at least a necessary condition for the achievement of his goals.

Moreover, there is a kind of natural selection process at work in the electoral arena. On average, those congressmen who are not primarily interested in reelection will not achieve reelection as often as those who are interested. We, the people, help to weed out congressmen whose primary motivation is not reelection. We admire politicians who courageously adopt the aloof role of the disinterested statesman, but we vote for those politicians who follow our wishes and do us favors.

What about the bureaucrats? A specification of their goals is somewhat more controversial—those who speak of appointed officials as public servants obviously take a more benign view than those who speak of them as bureaucrats. The literature provides ample justification for asserting that most bureaucrats wish to protect and nurture their agencies. The typical bureaucrat can be expected to seek to expand his agency in terms of personnel, budget, and mission. One's status in Washington (again, not to mention more tangible things) is roughly proportional to the importance of the operation one oversees. And the sheer size of the operation is taken to be a measure of importance. As with congressmen, the specified goals apply even to those bureaucrats who genuinely believe in their agency's mission. If they believe in the efficacy of their programs, they naturally wish to expand them and add new ones. All of this requires more money and more people. The genuinely committed bureaucrat is just as likely to seek to expand his agency as the proverbial empire-builder.

And what of the third element in the equation, us? What do we, the voters who support the Washington system, strive for? Each of us wishes to receive a maximum of benefits from government for the minimum cost. This goal suggests maximum government efficiency, on the one hand, but it also suggests mutual exploitation on the other. Each of us favors an arrangement in which our fellow citizens pay for our benefits!

With these brief descriptions of the cast of characters in hand, let us proceed.

Tammany Hall Goes to Washington

What should we expect from a legislative body composed of individuals whose first priority is their continued tenure in office? We should expect, first, that the normal activities of its members are those calculated to enhance their chances of reelection. And we should expect, second, that the members would devise and maintain institutional arrangements which facilitate their electoral activities. . . .

For most of the twentieth century, congressmen have engaged in a mix of three kinds of activities: lawmaking, pork barreling, and casework. Congress is first and foremost a lawmaking body, at least according to constitutional theory. In every postwar session Congress "considers" thousands of bills and resolutions, many hundreds of which are brought to a record vote. . . . Naturally the critical consideration in taking a position for the record is the maximization of approval in the home district. If the district is unaffected by and unconcerned with the matter at hand, the congressman may then take into account the general welfare of the country. (This sounds cynical, but remember that "profiles in courage" are sufficiently rare that their occurrence inspires books and articles.) Abetted by political scientists of the pluralist school, politicians have propounded an ideology which maintains that the good of the country on any given issue is simply what is best for a majority of congressional districts. This ideology provides a philosophical justification for what congressmen do while acting in their own self-interest.

A second activity favored by congressmen consists of efforts to bring home the bacon to their districts. Many popular articles have been written about the pork barrel, a term originally applied to rivers and harbors legislation but now generalized to cover all manner of federal largesse. Congressmen consider new dams, federal buildings, sewage treatment plants, urban renewal projects, etc. as sweet plums to be plucked. Federal projects are highly visible, their economic impact is easily detected by constituents, and sometimes they even produce something of value to the district. The average constituent may have some trouble translating his congressman's vote on some civil rights issue into a change in his personal welfare. But the workers hired and supplies purchased in connection with a big federal project provide benefits that are widely appreciated. The historical importance congressmen attach to the pork barrel is reflected in the rules of the House. That body accords certain classes of legislation "privileged" status: they may come directly to the floor without passing through the Rules Committee, a traditional graveyard for legislation. What kinds of legislation are privileged? Taxing and spending bills, for one: the government's power to raise and spend money must be kept relatively unfettered. But in addition, the omnibus rivers and harbors bills of the Public Works Committee and public lands bills from the Interior Committee share privileged status. The House will allow a civil rights or defense procurement or environmental bill to languish in the Rules Committee, but it takes special precautions to insure that nothing slows down the approval of dams and irrigation projects.

A third major activity takes up perhaps as much time as the other two combined. Traditionally, constituents appeal to their congressman for myriad favors and services. Sometimes only information is needed, but often constituents request that their congressman intervene in the internal workings of federal agencies to affect a decision in a favorable way, to reverse an adverse decision, or simply to speed up the glacial bureaucratic process. On the basis of extensive personal interviews with congressmen, Charles Clapp writes:

> Denied a favorable ruling by the bureaucracy on a matter of direct concern to him, puzzled or irked by delays in obtaining a decision, confused by the administrative

Casework

maze through which he is directed to proceed, or ignorant of whom to write, a constituent may turn to his congressman for help. These letters offer great potential for political benefit to the congressman since they affect the constituent personally. If the legislator can be of assistance, he may gain a firm ally; if he is indifferent, he may even lose votes.

Actually congressmen are in an almost unique position in our system, a position shared only with high-level members of the executive branch. Congressmen possess the power to expedite and influence bureaucratic decisions. This capability flows directly from congressional control over what bureaucrats value most: higher budgets and new program authorizations. In a very real sense each congressman is a monopoly supplier of bureaucratic unsticking services for his district.

Every year the federal budget passes through the appropriations committees of Congress. Generally these committees make perfunctory cuts. But on occasion they vent displeasure on an agency and leave it bleeding all over the Capitol. The most extreme case of which I am aware came when the House committee took away the entire budget of the Division of Labor Standards in 1947 (some of the budget was restored elsewhere in the appropriations process). Deep and serious cuts are made occasionally, and the threat of such cuts keeps most agencies attentive to congressional wishes. Professors Richard Fenno and Aaron Wildavsky have provided extensive documentary and interview evidence of the great respect (and even terror) federal bureaucrats show for the House Appropriations Committee. Moreover, the bureaucracy must keep coming back to Congress to have its old programs reauthorized and new ones added. Again, most such decisions are perfunctory, but exceptions are sufficiently frequent that bureaucrats do not forget the basis of their agencies' existence. . . . The bureaucracy needs congressional approval in order to survive, let alone expand. Thus, when a congressman calls about some minor bureaucratic decision or regulation, the bureaucracy considers his accommodation a small price to pay for the goodwill its cooperation will produce, particularly if he has any connection to the substantive committee or the appropriations subcommittee to which it reports.

From the standpoint of capturing voters, the congressman's lawmaking activities differ in two important respects from his pork-barrel and casework activities. First, programmatic actions are inherently controversial. Unless his district is homogeneous, a congressman will find his district divided on many major issues. Thus when he casts a vote, introduces a piece of nontrivial legislation, or makes a speech with policy content he will displease some elements of his district. Some constituents may applaud the congressman's civil rights record, but others believe integration is going too fast. Some support foreign aid, while others believe it's money poured down a rathole. Some advocate economic equality, others stew over welfare cheaters. On such policy matters the congressman can expect to make friends as well as enemies. Presumably he will behave so as to maximize the excess of the former over the latter, but nevertheless a policy stand will generally make some enemies.

In contrast, the pork barrel and casework are relatively less controversial. New federal projects bring jobs, shiny new facilities, and general economic prosperity, or so people believe. Snipping ribbons at the dedication of a new post office or dam is a much more pleasant pursuit than disposing of a constitutional amendment on

abortion. Republicans and Democrats, conservatives and liberals, all generally prefer a richer district to a poorer one. Of course, in recent years the river damming
and stream-bed straightening activities of the Army Corps of Engineers have
aroused some opposition among environmentalists. Congressmen happily reacted
by absorbing the opposition and adding environmentalism to the pork barrel: water
treatment plants are currently a hot congressional item.

Casework is even less controversial. Some poor, aggrieved constituent becomes
enmeshed in the tentacles of an evil bureaucracy and calls upon Congressman
St. George to do battle with the dragon. Again Clapp writes:

> A person who has a reasonable complaint or query is regarded as providing an op
> portunity rather than as adding an extra burden to an already busy office. The party
> affiliation of the individual even when known to be different from that of the con
> gressman does not normally act as a deterrent to action. Some legislators have built
> their reputations and their majorities on a program of service to all constituents ir
> respective of party. Regularly, voters affiliated with the opposition in other contests
> lend strong support to the lawmaker whose intervention has helped them in their
> struggle with the bureaucracy.

Even following the revelation of sexual improprieties, Wayne Hays won his Ohio
Democratic primary by a two-to-one margin. According to a *Los Angeles Times* feature story, Hay's constituency base was built on a foundation of personal service to
constituents:

> They receive help in speeding up bureaucratic action on various kinds of federal as
> sistance—black lung benefits to disabled miners and their families, Social Security
> payments, veterans' benefits and passports.
>   Some constituents still tell with pleasure of how Hays stormed clear to the
> seventh floor of the State Department and into Secretary of State Dean Rusk's of
> fice to demand, successfully, the quick issuance of a passport to an Ohioan.

Practicing politicians will tell you that word of mouth is still the most effective
mode of communication. News of favors to constituents gets around and no doubt
is embellished in the process.

In sum, when considering the benefits of his programmatic activities, the congressman must tote up gains and losses to arrive at a net profit. Pork barreling and
casework, however, are basically pure profit.

A second way in which programmatic activities differ from casework and the
pork barrel is the difficulty of assigning responsibility to the former as compared
with the latter. No congressman can seriously claim that he is responsible for the
1964 Civil Rights Act, the ABM, or the 1972 Revenue Sharing Act. Most constituents do have some vague notion that their congressman is only one of hundreds
and their senator one of an even hundred. Even committee chairmen may have a
difficult time claiming credit for a piece of major legislation, let alone a rank-and-
file congressman. Ah, but casework, and the pork barrel. In dealing with the bureaucracy, the congressman is not merely one vote of 435. Rather, he is a
nonpartisan power, someone whose phone calls snap an office to attention. He is
not kept on hold. The constituent who receives aid believes that his congressman
and his congressman alone got results. Similarly, congressmen find it easy to claim

credit for federal projects awarded their districts. The congressman may have instigated the proposal for the project in the first place, issued regular progress reports,
and ultimately announced the award through his office. Maybe he can't claim
credit for the 1965 Voting Rights Act, but he can take credit for Littletown's spank-
ing new sewage treatment plant.

Overall then, programmatic activities are dangerous (controversial), on the
one hand, and programmatic accomplishments are difficult to claim credit for, on
the other. While less exciting, casework and pork barreling are both safe and profitable. For a reelection-oriented congressman the choice is obvious.

The key to the rise of the Washington establishment (and the vanishing marginals) is the following observation: the growth of an activist federal government
has stimulated a change in the mix of congressional activities. Specifically, a lesser
proportion of congressional effort is now going into programmatic activities and a
greater proportion into pork-barrel and casework activities. As a result, today's congressmen make relatively fewer enemies and relatively more friends among the people of their districts.

To elaborate, a basic fact of life in twentieth-century America is the growth of
the federal role and its attendant bureaucracy. Bureaucracy is the characteristic
mode of delivering public goods and services. Ceteris paribus, the more government
attempts to do for people, the more extensive a bureaucracy it creates. As the scope
of government expands, more and more citizens find themselves in direct contact
with the federal government. Consider the rise in such contacts upon passage of the
Social Security Act, work relief projects and other New Deal programs. Consider
the millions of additional citizens touched by the veterans' programs of the postwar
period. Consider the untold numbers whom the Great Society and its aftermath
brought face to face with the federal government. In 1930 the federal bureaucracy
was small and rather distant from the everyday concerns of Americans. By 1975 it
was neither small nor distant.

As the years have passed, more and more citizens and groups have found themselves dealing with the federal bureaucracy. They may be seeking positive actions—
eligibility for various benefits and awards of government grants. Or they may be
seeking relief from the costs imposed by bureaucratic regulations—on working conditions, racial and sexual quotas, market restrictions, and numerous other subjects.
While not malevolent, bureaucracies make mistakes, both of commission and omission, and normal attempts at redress often meet with unresponsiveness and inflexi-
bility and sometimes seeming incorrigibility. Whatever the problem, the citizen's
congressman is a source of succor. The greater the scope of government activity, the
greater the demand for his services.

Private monopolists can regulate the demand for their product by raising or
lowering the price. Congressmen have no such (legal) option. When the demand
for their services rises, they have no real choice except to meet that demand—to
supply more bureaucratic unsticking services—so long as they would rather be
elected than unelected. This vulnerability to escalating constituency demands is
largely academic, though. I seriously doubt that congressmen resist their gradual
transformation from national legislators to errand boy-ombudsmen. As we have
noted, casework is all profit. Congressmen have buried proposals to relieve the case-

work burden by establishing a national ombudsman or Congressman Reuss's proposed Administrative Counsel of the Congress. One of the congressmen interviewed by Clapp stated:

> Before I came to Washington I used to think that it might be nice if the individual states had administrative arms here that would take care of necessary liaison between citizens and the national government. But a congressman running for reelection is interested in building fences by providing personal services. The system is set to reelect incumbents regardless of party, and incumbents wouldn't dream of giving any of this service function away to any subagency. As an elected member I feel the same way.

In fact, it is probable that at least some congressmen deliberately stimulate the demand for their bureaucratic fixit services. (See [Figure A].) Recall that the new Republican in district A travels about his district saying:

> I'm your man in Washington. What are your problems? How can I help you?

And in district B, did the demand for the congressman's services rise so much between 1962 and 1964 that a "regiment" of constituency staff became necessary? Or, having access to the regiment, did the new Democrat stimulate the demand to which he would apply his regiment?

In addition to greatly increased casework, let us not forget that the growth of the federal role has also greatly expanded the federal pork barrel. The creative pork barreler need not limit himself to dams and post offices—rather old-fashioned interests. Today, creative congressmen can cadge LEAA money for the local police,

NEED HELP WITH A FEDERAL PROBLEM?

Please feel free to communicate with me in person by phone or by mail Daily from 9 a m until 5 p m my Congressional District office in Fullerton is open to serve you and your family The staff will be able to help you with information or assistance on proposed Federal legislation and procedures of Federal agencies If you are experiencing a problem with Social Security educational assistance Veterans Administration, Immigration Internal Revenue Service Postal Service Environmental Protection Agency, Federal Energy Office or any other Federal agency please contact me through this office If you decide to write to me please provide a telephone number as many times I can call you with information within a day or two

CONGRESSMAN CHARLES E. WIGGINS
Brashears Center, Suite 103
1400 N. Harbor Boulevard
Fullerton, Ca 92635 (714) 870-7266

My Washington address is
Room 2445 Rayburn Building, Washington, D.C.
20515. Telephone (202) 225-4111.

U S House of Representatives
WASHINGTON D C 20515
PUBLIC DOCUMENT
OFFICIAL BUSINESS

Charles E. Wiggins
M C

POSTAL CUSTOMER-LOCAL
39th District

CALIFORNIA

Figure A *How the Congressman-as-Ombudsman Drums Up Business*

urban renewal and housing money for local politicians, educational program grants for the local education bureaucracy. And there are sewage treatment plants, worker training and retraining programs, health services, and programs for the elderly. The pork barrel is full to overflowing. The conscientious congressman can stimulate applications for federal assistance (the sheer number of programs makes it difficult for local officials to stay current with the possibilities), put in a good word during consideration, and announce favorable decisions amid great fanfare.

In sum, everyday decisions by a large and growing federal bureaucracy bestow significant tangible benefits and impose significant tangible costs. Congressmen can affect these decisions. Ergo, the more decisions the bureaucracy has the opportunity to make, the more opportunities there are for the congressman to build up credits.

The nature of the Washington system is . . . quite clear. Congressmen (typically the majority Democrats) earn electoral credits by establishing various federal programs (the minority Republicans typically earn credits by fighting the good fight). The legislation is drafted in very general terms, so some agency, existing or newly established, must translate a vague policy mandate into a functioning program, a process that necessitates the promulgation of numerous rules and regulations and, incidentally, the trampling of numerous toes. At the next stage, aggrieved and/or hopeful constituents petition their congressman to intervene in the complex (or at least obscure) decision processes of the bureaucracy. The cycle closes when the congressman lends a sympathetic ear, piously denounces the evils of bureaucracy, intervenes in the latter's decisions, and rides a grateful electorate to ever more impressive electoral showings. Congressmen take credit coming and going. They are the alpha and the omega.

The popular frustration with the permanent government in Washington is partly justified, but to a considerable degree it is misplaced resentment. Congress is the linchpin of the Washington establishment. The bureaucracy serves as a convenient lightning rod for public frustration and a convenient whipping boy for congressmen. But so long as the bureaucracy accommodates congressmen, the latter will oblige with ever larger budgets and grants of authority. Congress does not just react to big government—it creates it. All of Washington prospers. More and more bureaucrats promulgate more and more regulations and dispense more and more money. Fewer and fewer congressmen suffer electoral defeat. Elements of the electorate benefit from government programs, and all of the electorate is eligible for ombudsman services. But the general, long-term welfare of the United States is no more than an incidental by-product of the system.

Committee Chairmen as Political Entrepreneurs

The preceding selection pointed out how the personal power incentive on Capitol Hill supports and expands committee government. Congressional committees became a dominant force in the legislative process toward the end of the nineteenth century. In 1885 Woodrow Wilson was able to state categorically in his famous work, Congressional Government:

The leaders of the House are the chairmen of the principal Standing Committees. Indeed, to be exactly accurate, the House has as many leaders as there are subjects of legislation; for there are as many Standing Committees as there are leading classes of legislation, and in the consideration of every topic of business the House is guided by a special leader in the person of the chairman of the Standing Committee, charged with the superintendence of measures of the particular class to which that topic belongs. It is this multiplicity of leaders, this many-headed leadership, which makes the organization of the House too complex to afford uninformed people and unskilled observers any easy clue to its methods of rule. For the chairmen of the Standing Committees do not constitute a cooperative body like a ministry. They do not consult and concur in the adoption of homogeneous and mutually helpful measures; there is no thought of acting in concert. Each Committee goes its own way at its own pace. It is impossible to discover any unity or method in the disconnected and therefore unsystematic, confused, and desultory action of the House, or any common purpose in the measures which its Committees from time to time recommend.

With regard to the Senate he noted:

It has those same radical defects of organization which weaken the House. Its functions also, like those of the House, are segregated in the prerogatives of numerous Standing Committees. In this regard Congress is all of a piece. There is in the Senate no more opportunity than exists in the House for gaining such recognized party leadership as would be likely to enlarge a man by giving him a sense of power, and to steady and sober him by filling him with a grave sense of responsibility. So far as its organization controls it, the Senate . . . proceedings bear most of the characteristic features of committee rule.

The Legislative Reorganization Act of 1946 was designed to streamline congressional committee structure and provide committees and individual members of Congress with increased expert staff; however, although the number of standing committees was reduced, subcommittees have increased so that the net numerical reduction is not as great as was originally intended. Further, because Congress still conducts its business through committees, (1) the senior members of the party with the majority in Congress dominate the formulation of public policy through the seniority rule; (2) policy formulation is fragmented, with each committee maintaining relative dominance over policy areas within its jurisdiction; and (3) stemming from this fragmentation, party control is weakened, especially when the president attempts to assume legislative dominance.

Although Congress is often pictured as powerless in confrontation with the executive branch, the fact is that the chairmen of powerful congressional committees often dominate administrative agencies over which they have jurisdiction. They are an important part of the broad Washington establishment. This is particularly true of the chairmen of appropriations committees and subcommittees; because of their control of the purse strings, they are able to wield far more influence over the bureaucracy than are the chairmen of other committees. The appropriations committees have a direct weapon—money—that they can wield against administrative adversaries. And, the chairmen of all committees have seniority that often exceeds that of the bureaucrats with whom they are dealing. The secretaries and assistant secretaries of executive departments are political appointees who rarely stay in government more than two years, whereas powerful members of Congress have been around for one or more decades. This gives the latter expertise that the political levels of the bureaucracy often lack. Political appointees in the bureaucracy must rely upon their professional staff in order to match the expertise of senior members of Congress. The power of the chairmen of the appropriations committees often leads them to interfere directly in administrative operations. They become, in effect, part of the bureaucracy, often dominating it and determining what programs it will implement. The constant interaction between committee chairs and agencies results in "government without passing laws," to use the phrase of Michael W. Kirst. (See Michael W. Kirst, *Government Without Passing Laws*, Chapel Hill: University of North Carolina Press, 1969.)

While committees remain an important part of the Washington power establishment, their chairmen often becoming informal "prime ministers" dominating the policy arenas their committees control, though the chairmen are no longer the feudal barons Woodrow Wilson portrayed. But congressional committees, more than political parties, continue to define the legislative process. The dispersion of committee power adds new dimensions to divided government. As the president confronts Congress he must deal with multiple power centers, making presidential leadership more complex and difficult.

60

CONGRESS AND THE QUEST FOR POWER*

Lawrence C. Dodd

The postwar years have taught students of Congress a very fundamental lesson: Congress is a dynamic institution. The recent congressional changes picture an institution that is much like a kaleidoscope. At first glance the visual images and structural patterns appear frozen in a simple and comprehensive mosaic. Upon closer and longer inspection the realization dawns that the picture is subject to constant transformations. These transformations seem to flow naturally from the prior observations, yet the resulting mosaic is quite different and is not ordered by the same static principles used to interpret and understand the earlier one. The appreciation and understanding of the moving image requires not only comprehending the role of each colorful geometric object in a specific picture, not developing a satis-

---

*Author's Note: For critical assistance at various stages in the writing of this essay, I would like to thank Arnold Fleischmann, Michael N. Green, Bruce I. Oppenheimer, Diana Phillips, Russ Renka, Terry Sullivan, and numerous graduate and undergraduate students who shared with me their questions and insights.

factory interpretation of the principles underlying a specific picture or change in specific aspects of the picture, but grasping the dynamics underlying the structural transformations themselves. So it is with Congress. To understand and appreciate it as an institution we must focus not only on particular aspects of internal congressional structure and process, nor on changes in particular patterns. We must seek to understand the more fundamental dynamics that produce the transformations in the congressional mosaic. This essay represents an attempt to explain the dynamics of congressional structure. . . .

I

As with politicians generally, members of Congress enter politics in a quest for personal power. This quest may derive from any number of deeper motives: a desire for ego gratification or for prestige, a search for personal salvation through good works, a hope to construct a better world or to dominate the present one, or a preoccupation with status and self-love. Whatever the source, most members of Congress seek to attain the power to control policy decisions that impose the authority of the state on the citizenry at large.

The most basic lesson that any member of Congress learns on entering the institution is that the quest for power by service within Congress requires reelection. First, reelection is necessary in order to remain in the struggle within Congress for "power positions." Staying in the struggle is important not only in that it provides the formal status as an elected representative without which an individual's influence on national legislative policy lacks legal authority; the quest for power through election and reelection also signals one's acceptance of the myth of democratic rule and thus one's acceptability as a power seeker who honors the society's traditional values. Second, reelection, particularly by large margins, helps create an aura of personal legitimacy. It indicates that one has a special mandate from the people, that one's position is fairly secure, that one will have to be "reckoned with." Third, long-term electoral success bestows on a member of Congress the opportunity to gain the experience and expertise, and to demonstrate the legislative skill and political prescience, that can serve to justify the exercise of power.

Because reelection is so important, and because it may be so difficult to ensure, its pursuit can become all-consuming. The constitutional system, electoral laws, and social system together have created political parties that are weak coalitions. A candidate for Congress normally must create a personal organization rather than rely on her or his political party. The "electoral connection" that intervenes between the desire for power and the realization of power may lead members to emphasize form over substance, position taking, advertising, and credit claiming rather than problem solving. In an effort to sustain electoral success, members of Congress may fail to take controversial and clear positions, fail to make hard choices, fail to exercise power itself. Yet members of Congress generally are not solely preoccupied with reelection. Most members have relatively secure electoral margins. This security stems partially from the fact that members of Congress are independent of political parties and are independent from responsibility for selecting the executive, and thus can be judged more on personal qualities than on partisan or executive affiliations. Electoral security is further reinforced because members of Congress personally control financial and casework resources that can help them build a loyalty from their constituents independent of policy or ideological considerations. The existence of secure electoral margins thus allows members to devote considerable effort toward capturing a "power position" within Congress and generating a mystique of special authority that is necessary to legitimize a select decision-making role for them in the eyes of their nominal peers.

The concern of members of Congress with gaining congressional power, rather than just securing reelection, has had a considerable influence on the structure and life of Congress. Were members solely preoccupied with reelection, we would expect them to spend little time in Washington and devote their personal efforts to constituent speeches and district casework. One would expect Congress to be run by a centralized, efficient staff who, in league with policy-oriented interest groups, would draft legislation, investigate the issues, frame palatable solutions, and present the members with the least controversial bills possible. Members of Congress would give little attention to committee work, and then only to committees that clearly served reelection interests. The primary activity of congresspeople in Congress, rather, would be extended, televised floor debates and symbolic roll call votes, all for show. Such a system would allow the appearance of work while providing ample opportunity for the mending of home fences. Alternatively, were only a few members of Congress concerned about power, with others concerned with reelection, personal finances, or private lives, one might expect a centralized system with a few leaders exercising power and all others spending their time on personal or electoral matters.

Virtually all members of the U.S. Congress are preoccupied with power considerations. They are unwilling—unless forced by external events—to leave the major decisions in either a centralized, autonomous staff system or a central leadership. Each member wants to exercise power—to make the key policy decisions. This motive places every member in a personal conflict with every other member: to the extent that one member realizes her or his goal personally to control all key decisions, all others must lose. Given this widespread power motive, an obvious way to resolve the conflict is to disperse power—or at least power positions—as widely as possible. One logical solution, in other words, is to place basic policy-making responsibility in a series of discrete and relatively autonomous committees and subcommittees, each having control over the decisions in a specified jurisdictional area. Each member can belong to a small number of committees and, within them, have a significant and perhaps dominant influence on policy. Although such a system denies every member the opportunity to control all policy decisions, it ensures that most members, particularly if they stay in Congress long enough to obtain a subcommittee or committee chair, and if they generate the mystique of special authority necessary to allow them to activate the power potential of their select position, can satisfy a portion of their power drive.

Within Congress, as one would expect in light of the power motive, the fundamental structure of organization is a committee system. Most members spend most of their time not in their district but in Washington, and most of their Washington time not on the floor in symbolic televised debate but rather in the committee or subcommittee rooms, in caucus meetings, or in office work devoted to legislation. While the staff, particularly the personal staff, may be relegated to casework for constituents, the members of Congress sit through hearing after hearing, debate after debate, vote after vote seeking to shape in subcommittee, committee, and floor votes the contours of legislation. This is not to suggest, of course, that members of Congress do not engage in symbolic action or personal casework and do not spend much time in the home district; they do, in their effort at reelection. Likewise, staff do draft legislation, play a strong role in committee investigations, and influence the direction of public policy; they do this, however, largely because members of Congress just do not have enough time in the day to fulfill their numerous obligations. Seen in this perspective, Congress is not solely, simply, or primarily a stage on which individuals intentionally and exclusively engage in meaningless charades. Whatever the end product of their effort may be, members of Congress have actively sought to design a congressional structure and process that would maximize their ability to exercise personal power within Congress and, through Congress, within the nation at large.

The congressional committee structure reflects rather naturally the various dimensions that characterize the making of public policy. There are authorization committees that create policies and programs, specify their duties and powers, and establish absolute funding levels. There are appropriations committees that specify the actual funding level for a particular fiscal year. There are revenue committees that raise the funds to pay for the appropriations necessary to sustain the authorized programs. In addition, since Congress itself is an elaborate institution that must be serviced, there are housekeeping committees—those that provide for the day-to-day operation of Congress. In the House of Representatives there is also an internal regulation committee, the House Rules Committee, that schedules debate and specifies the rules for deliberation on specific bills.

These committees vary greatly in the nature and comprehensiveness of their impact on national policy making. The housekeeping committees tend to be service committees and carry little national weight except through indirect influence obtained from manipulating office and staff resources that other members may want so desperately as to modify their policy stances on other committees. A second set of committees, authorization committees such as Interior or Post Office, have jurisdictions that limit them to the concerns of fairly narrow constituencies; these are "reelection committees that allow members to serve their constituencies' parochial interests but offer only limited potential to effect broad-scale public policy. A third group of committees are policy committees, such as Education and Labor or International Relations, that consider fairly broad policy questions, though questions that have fairly clear and circumscribed jurisdictional limits. A fourth set of committees are the "power" committees, which make decisions on issues such as the scheduling of rules (the House Rules Committee), appropriations (House and Senate Appropriations committees), or revenues (House Ways and Means or Senate Finance) that allow them to affect most or all policy areas. Within a pure system of committee government, power committees are limited in the comprehensiveness of their control over the general policy-making process. No overarching control committee exists to coordinate the authorization, appropriations, or revenue process.

Because an essential type of legislative authority is associated with each congressional committee, members find that service on any committee can offer some satisfaction of their power drive. There are, nevertheless, inherent differences in the power potential associated with committees, differences that are tied to the variation in legislative function and in the comprehensiveness of a committee's decisional jurisdiction. This variation between committees is sufficient to make some committees more attractive as a place to gain power. Because members are in a quest for power, not simply reelection, they generally will seek to serve on committees whose function and policy focus allow the broadest personal impact on policy.

Maneuvering for membership on the more attractive committees is constrained by two fundamental factors. First, there are a limited number of attractive committee slots, and much competition will exist for these vacancies. Most members cannot realize their goal to serve on and gain control of these committees. For this reason, much pressure exists to establish norms by which members "prove" themselves deserving of membership on an attractive committee. Such norms include courtesy to fellow members, specialization in limited areas of public policy, a willingness to work hard on legislation, a commitment to the institution, adherence to the general policy parameters seen as desirable by senior members of Congress who will dominate the committee nominations process, and a willingness to reciprocate favors and abide by the division of policy domains into the set of relatively independent policy-making entities. Members who observe these norms faithfully will advance to the more desirable committees because they will have shown themselves worthy of special privilege, particularly if they also possess sufficient congressional seniority.

Seniority is particularly important because of the second constraint on the process—the fact that service on the more powerful committees may limit one's ability to mend electoral fences. On the more comprehensive committees, issues often can be more complex and difficult to understand, necessitating much time and concentration on committee work; members may not be able to get home as often or as easily. Issues will be more controversial and will face members with difficult and often unpopular policy choices; members will be less able to engage in the politics of form over substance. The national visibility of the members will be greater, transforming them into public figures whose personal lives may receive considerable attention. Indiscretions that normally might go unreported will become open game for the press and can destroy careers. Thus, although it is undoubtedly true that service on the more comprehensive committees may bring with it certain attributes that can help reelection (campaign contributions from interest groups, name identification and status, a reputation for power that may convince constituents that "our member can deliver"), service on the more attractive committees does thrust members into a more unpredictable world. Although members generally will want to serve on the most powerful committees, it will normally be best for them to put off such service until they have a secure electoral base and to approach their quest for power in sequential steps.

Because of the constraints operating within a system of committee government, congressional careers reflect a set of stages. The first stage entails an emphasis on shoring up the electoral base through casework, service on constituent-oriented reelection committees, and gaining favor within Congress by serving on the house-keeping committees. Of course, the first stage is never fully "completed": there is never a time at which a member of Congress is "guaranteed" long-term reelection or total acceptance within Congress, so both constituent and congressional service are a recurring necessity. But a point is normally reached—a point defined by the circumstances of the member's constituency, the opportunities present in Congress, and the personality and competence of the member—when he or she will feel secure enough, or perhaps unhappy enough, to attempt a move to a second stage. In the second stage members broaden their horizons and seek service on key policy committees that draft important legislation regulating such national policy dimensions as interstate commerce, education, or labor. In this stage, representatives begin to be "legislators," to preoccupy themselves with national policy matters. Because of the limited number of positions on power committees, many members will spend most, perhaps the rest, of their career in this stage, moving up by committee seniority to subcommittee and committee chairs on the policy committees. As they gain expertise in the specific policy area, and create a myth of special personal authority, they will gain power in some important but circumscribed area of national policy. For members who persist, however, and/or possess the right attributes of electoral security and personal attributes, a third stage exists: service on a power committee—Rules, Ways and Means, or Finance, Appropriations, and, in the Senate, Foreign Relations. Service on these committees is superseded, if at all, only by involvement in a fourth stage: service in the party leadership as a floor leader or Speaker. Few individuals ever have the opportunity to realize this fourth and climactic step; in a system of committee government, in fact, this step will be less sought and the battles less bitter than one might expect, considering the status associated with them, because power will rest primarily in committees rather than in the party. Although party leadership positions in a system of committee government do carry with them a degree of responsibility, particularly the obligation to mediate conflicts between committees and to influence the success of marginal legislation on the house floor, members will generally be content to stay on a power committee and advance to subcommittee and committee chair positions rather than engage in an all-out effort to attain party leadership positions.

This career path, presented here in an idealized and simplified fashion, is a general "power ladder" that members attempt to climb in their quest for power within Congress. Some members leave the path voluntarily to run for the Senate (if in the House), to run for governor, to serve as a judge, or to serve as president. Some for special reasons bypass one or another stage, choose to stay at a lower rung, are defeated, or retire. Despite exceptions, the set of stages is a very real guide to the long-term career path that members seek to follow. Implicit within this pattern is the very real dilemma discussed earlier: progress up the career ladder brings with it a greater opportunity for significant personal power, but also greater responsibility. As members move up the power ladder, they move away from a secure world in which reelection interest can be their dominant concern and into a world in which concerns with power and public policy predominate. They take their chance and leave the security of the reelection stage because of their personal quest for power, without which reelection is a largely meaningless victory.

The attempt to prove oneself and move up the career ladder requires enormous effort. Even after one succeeds and gains a power position, this attainment is not in itself sufficient to guarantee the personal exercise of power. To utilize fully the power prerogatives that are implicit in specific power positions, a member must maintain the respect, awe, trust, and confidence of committee and house colleagues; he or she must sustain the aura of personal authority that is necessary to legitimize the exercise of power. Although the norm of seniority under a system of pure committee government will protect a member's possession of a power position, seniority is not sufficient to guard personal authority. In order to pass legislation and dominate policy decisions in a committee's jurisdictional area, a committee chair must radiate an appearance of special authority. The member must abide by the norms of the house and the committee, demonstrate legislative competence, and generate policy decisions that appear to stay within the general policy parameters recognized as acceptable by the member's colleagues. Among reelection efforts, efforts to advance in Congress to power positions, efforts to sustain and nurture personal authority, and efforts to exercise power, the members of Congress confront an incredible array of crosscutting pressures and internal dilemmas—decisions about how to balance external reelection interests with the internal institutional career, how to maximize the possibility of power within Congress by service on particular committees, how to gain and nurture authority within committees by specific legislative actions. The world of the congressman or congresswoman is complicated further, however, by a very special irony.

II

As a form of institutional organization, committee government possesses certain attributes that recommend it. By dividing policy concerns among a variety of committees it allows members to specialize in particular policy areas; this division provides a congressional structure through which the members can be their own expert advisers and maintain a degree of independence from lobbyists or outside specialists. Specialization also provides a procedure whereby members can become acquainted with particular programs and agencies and follow their behavior over a period of years, thus allowing informed oversight of the implementation of public policy. The dispersion of power implicit in committee government is important, furthermore, because it brings a greater number of individuals into the policy-making process and thus allows a greater range of policy innovation. In addition, as stressed above, committee government also serves the immediate power motive of congresspeople by creating so many power positions that all members can seek to gain power in particular policy domains.

Despite its assets, committee government does have severe liabilities, flaws that undermine the ability of Congress to fulfill its constitutional responsibilities to make legislative policy and oversee the implementation of that policy. First, committee government by its very nature lacks strong, centralized leadership, thereby undermining its internal decision-making capacity and external authority. Internally, Congress needs central leadership because most major questions of public policy (such as economic or energy policy) cut across individual committee jurisdictions. Since each committee and subcommittee may differ in its policy orientation from all others, and since the support of all relevant committees will be essential to an overall program, it is difficult, if not impossible, to enact a coherent general approach to broad policy questions. A central party leader or central congressional steering committee with extensive control over the standing committees could provide the leadership necessary to assist the development and passage of a coherent policy across the various committees, but committee government rejects the existence of strong centralized power. The resulting dispersion of power within Congress, and the refusal to allow strong centralized leadership, ensures that congressional decisions on major policy matters (unless aided and pushed by an outside leader) will be incremental at best, immobilized and incoherent as a norm. And to the extent that a Congress governed by committees can generate public policy, it faces the external problem of leadership, the inability of outside political actors, the press, or the public to identify a legitimate spokesperson for Congress on any general policy question. The wide dispersion of power positions allows numerous members to gain a degree of dominance over specific dimensions of a policy domain; all of these members can speak with some authority on a policy question, presenting conflicting and confusing approaches and interpretations. In cases where Congress does attempt to act, Congress lacks a viable mechanism through which to publicize and justify its position in an authoritative manner. Should Congress be in a conflict with the president, who can more easily present a straightforward and publicized position, Congress almost certainly will lose out in the eyes of public opinion. Lacking a clearly identifiable legislative leader in its midst, Congress is unable to provide the nation with unified, comprehensible, or persuasive policy leadership.

Closely related to the lack of leadership is a lack of fiscal coordination. Nowhere within a system of committee government is there a mechanism to ensure that the decisions of authorization, appropriations, and revenue committees have some reasonable relationship to one another. The authorization committees make their decisions about the programs to authorize largely independent of appropriations committee decisions about how much money the government will spend. The appropriations committees decide on spending levels largely independent of revenue committee decisions on taxation. Since it is always easier to promise (or authorize) than to deliver (or spend), program goals invariably exceed the actual financial outlays and thus the actual delivery of service. And since it is easier to spend money than to make or tax money, particularly for politicians, expenditures will exceed the revenues to pay the bills. Moves to coordinate the authorization, appropriations, and revenue processes are inconsistent with committee government, since such an effort would necessarily create a central mechanism with considerable say over all public policy and thus centralize power in a relatively small number of individuals. Committee government thus by its very nature is consigned to frustration: the policies that it does produce will invariably produce higher expectations than they can deliver; its budgets, particularly in periods of liberal, activist Congresses, will produce sizable and unplanned deficits in which expenditures far exceed revenues. The inability of committee government to provide realistic program goals and fiscal discipline will invite the executive to intervene in the budget process in order to provide fiscal responsibility and coordination. The result, of course, will be a concomitant loss of the congressional control over the nation's purse strings.

A third detriment associated with committee government, and one that is exacerbated by the absence of leadership and committee coordination, is the lack of accountability and responsibility. A fundamental justification of congressional government is that it allows political decision making to be responsive to the will of a national majority. Committee government distributes this decision-making authority among a largely autonomous set of committees. Since seniority protects each committee's membership from removal and determines who will chair each committee, a committee's members can feel free to follow their personal policy predilections and stop any legislation they wish that falls within their committee's jurisdiction, or propose any that they wish. Within a system of committee government, resting as it does on the norm of seniority, no serious way exists to hold a specific committee or committee chair accountable to the majority views of Congress or the American people, should those views differ from the views held within a particular committee. Because of the process whereby members are selected to serve on major committees—a process that emphasizes not their compatibility with the majority's policy sentiment but rather their adherence to congressional norms, general agreement with the policy views of senior congresspeople, and possession of seniority—the top committees (especially at the senior ranks) are quite likely to be out of step with a congressional or national majority. This lack of representativeness is particularly likely if patterns of electoral security nationwide provide safe seats (and thus seniority) to regions or localities that are unrepresentative of the dominant policy perspectives of the country. Responsiveness is further undermined because the absence of strong central leaders, and a widespread desire among members for procedural protection of their personal prerogatives, require reliance on rigid rules and regulations to govern the flow of legislation and debate, rules such as the Senate's cloture rule that allows the existence of filibusters. Under a system of party government, where limiting rules may exist on the books, strong party leaders can mitigate their effects. In a system of committee government, rules become serious hurdles that can block the easy flow of legislation, particularly major, controversial legislation, thereby decreasing the ability of Congress to respond rapidly to national problems. Committee government thus undermines the justification of Congress as an institution that provides responsive, representative government. Since institutions derive their power not solely from constitutional legalisms but from their own mystique of special authority that comes from their legitimizing myths, committee government undercuts not only Congress's ability to exercise power but also the popular support that is necessary to maintain its power potential.

The lack of accountability and the damage to Congress's popular support are augmented by a fourth characteristic of committee government—a tendency toward insulation of congressional decision making. This insulation derives from three factors. First, members of committees naturally try to close committee sessions from public purview, limiting thereby the intrusion of external actors such as interest groups or executive agencies and thus protecting committee members' independent exercise of power within committees. Second, the creation of a multiplicity of committees makes it difficult for the public or the press to follow policy deliberations even if they are open. Third, it is difficult if not impossible to create clear jurisdictional boundaries between committees. The consequent ambiguity that exists between jurisdictional boundaries will often involve committees themselves in extensive disputes over the control of particular policy domains, further confusing observers who are concerned with policy deliberations. By closing its committee doors, creating a multiplicity of committees, and allowing jurisdictional ambiguities, a system of committee government isolates Congress from the nation at large. Out of sight and out of mind, Congress loses the attention, respect, and understanding of the nation and becomes an object of scorn and derision, thus further undermining the authority or legitimacy of its pronouncements and itself as an institution.

Finally, committee government undermines the ability of Congress to perform that one function for which committee government would seem most suited—aggressive oversight of administration. According to the classic argument, the saving grace of committee government is that the dispersion of power and the creation of numerous policy experts ensure congressional surveillance of the bureaucracy. Unfortunately, this argument ignores the fact that the individuals on the committees that pass legislation will be the very people least likely to investigate policy implementation. They will be committed to the program, as its authors or most visible supporters, and will not want to take actions that might lead to a destruction of the program. The impact of publicity and a disclosure of agency or program shortcomings, after all, is very unpredictable and difficult to control and may create a public furor against the program. The better part of discretion is to leave the agency largely to its own devices and rely on informal contacts and special personal arrangements, lest the glare of publicity and the discovery of shortcomings force Congress to deauthorize a pet program, casting aspersions on those who originally drafted the legislation. Members of Congress are unwilling to resolve this problem by creating permanent and powerful oversight committees because such committees, by their ability to focus attention on problems of specific agencies and programs, would threaten the authority of legislative committees to control and direct policy in their allotted policy area. Committee government thus allows a failure of executive oversight.

In the light of these five problems, the irony of committee government is that it attempts to satisfy members' individual desires for personal power by dispersing internal congressional authority so widely that the resulting institutional impotence cripples the ability of Congress to perform its constitutional roles, thereby dissipating the value of internal congressional power. Members of Congress thus are not only faced with the daily dilemma of balancing reelection interests with their efforts at upward power mobility within Congress; their lives are also complicated by a cruel paradox, the ultimate incompatibility of widely dispersed power within Congress, on the one hand, and a strong role for Congress in national decision making, on the other. This inherent tension generates an explosive dynamic within Congress as an organization and between Congress and the executive.

In the short run, as members of Congress follow the immediate dictates of the personal power motive, they are unaware of, or at least unconcerned with, the long-term consequences of decentralized power; they support the creation of committee government. The longer committee government operates, the more unhappy political analysts and the people generally become with the inability of Congress to make national policy or ensure policy implementation. With Congress deadlocked by immobilism, political activists within Congress and the nation at large turn to the president (as the one alternative political figure who is popularly elected and thus should be responsive to popular sentiments) and encourage him (or her, if we ever break the sex barrier) to provide policy leadership and fiscal coordination, to open up congressional decision making to national political forces and ensure congressional responsiveness, and to oversee the bureaucracy. Presidents, particularly those committed to activist legislation, welcome the calls for intervention and will see their forthright role as an absolute necessity to the well-being of the Republic. Slowly at first, presidents take over the roles of chief legislator, chief budgetary officer, overseer of the bureaucracy, chief tribune, and protector of the people. Eventually the president's role in these regards becomes so central that he feels free to ignore the wishes of members of Congress, even those who chair very important committees, and impose presidential policy on Congress and the nation at large.

The coming of a strong, domineering, imperial president who ignores Congress mobilizes its members into action. They see that their individual positions of power within Congress are meaningless unless the institution can impose its legislative will on the nation. They search for ways to regain legislative preeminence and constrain the executive. Not being fools, members identify part of the problem as an internal institutional one and seek to reform Congress. Such reform efforts come during or immediately following crises in which presidents clearly and visibly threaten fundamental power prerogatives of Congress. The reforms will include attempts to provide for more centralized congressional leadership, fiscal coordination, congressional openness, better oversight mechanisms, clarification of committee jurisdictions, procedures for policy coordination, and procedures to encourage committee accountability. Because the quest for personal power continues as the underlying motivation of individual members, the reforms are basically attempts to strengthen the value of internal congressional power by increasing the power of Congress vis-à-vis the executive. The reform efforts, however, are constrained by consideration of personal power prerogatives of members of Congress. The attempt to protect personal prerogatives while centralizing power builds structural flaws into the centralization mechanisms, flaws that would not be present were the significance of congressional structure for the national power of Congress itself the only motive. The existence of these flaws provides the openings through which centralization procedures are destroyed when institutional crises pass and members again feel free to emphasize personal power and personal careers. In addition, because policy inaction within Congress often will be identified as the immediate cause of presidential power aggrandizement, and because policy immobilism may become identified with key individuals or committees that have obstructed particular legislation, reform efforts also may be directed toward breaking up the authority of these individuals or committees and dispersing it among individuals and committees who seem more amenable to activist policies. This short-term dispersal of power, designed to break a legislative logjam (and, simultaneously, to give power to additional individuals), will serve to exacerbate immobilism in the long run when the new mechanisms of centralization are destroyed.

Viewed in a broad historical perspective, organizational dynamics within Congress, and external relations of Congress to the president, have a "cyclical" pattern. At the outset, when politicians in a quest for national power first enter Congress, they decentralize power and create committee government. Decentralization is followed by severe problems of congressional decision making, presidential assumption of legislative prerogatives, and an eventual presidential assault on Congress itself. Congress reacts by reforming its internal structure: some reform efforts will involve legislation that attempts to circumscribe presidential action; other reforms will attempt to break specific points of deadlock by further decentralization and dispersal of congressional authority; eventually, however, problems of internal congressional leadership and coordination will become so severe that Congress will be forced to undertake centralizing reforms. As Congress moves to resolve internal structural problems and circumscribe presidential power, presidents begin to cooperate so as to defuse the congressional counterattack; to do otherwise would open a president to serious personal attack as anticongressional and thus anti-democratic, destroying the presidency's legitimizing myth as a democratic institution and identifying presidential motivations as power aggrandizement rather than protection of the Republic. As the immediate threat to congressional prerogatives recedes, members of Congress (many of whom will not have served in Congress during the era of institutional crisis) become preoccupied with their immediate careers and press once again for greater power dispersal within Congress and removal of centralizing mechanisms that inhibit committee and subcommittee autonomy. Decentralization reasserts itself and Congress becomes increasingly leaderless, uncoordinated, insulated, unresponsive, unable to control executive agencies. Tempted by congressional weakness and hounded by cries to "get the country moving," the executive again reasserts itself and a new institutional crisis eventually arises. A review of American history demonstrates the existence of this cycle rather clearly, particularly during the twentieth century. . . .

Congress and the Media

Television has transformed politics in many ways. Perhaps most importantly, because of television images have become as important as—and in some cases more important than—issues in political campaigns. On Capitol Hill members of Congress, as the following selection illustrates, spend as much time on the media as they do on their legislative work. The press has always followed members of Congress, but television has changed the rules of the game. Legislators have found that more than in the past media exposure is essential not only to reelection but to a successful Capitol Hill career.

— 61 —

MEDIA POWER AND CONGRESSIONAL POWER

Timothy E. Cook

⁓

The House of Representatives has long witnessed the chaotic comings and goings of its 435 members—from offices to committee rooms to the floor and back again while lobbyists and constituents try to get in a word or two on the run. But increasingly relations with the news media seem to take up legislators' time and effort. Dressed in telegenic blue shirts and red neckties, they stand before television cameras in the swamp, the section of the Capitol lawn set aside for interviews. Inside the Capitol, too, floor debates are often aimed at the discreetly placed cameras that broadcast the proceedings to members' offices, the press galleries, and homes across the country. Staffers and interns dash from one gallery to the next with stacks of press releases to be distributed. Reporters crowd outside hearing rooms to receive a committee report or corner a witness. In short, much of the hubbub of Capitol Hill today is contributed by the press and their would-be subjects. Making laws is far from the only business of the House. It has been supplemented by making news.

Making news was not always so important. Reporters have been present on Capitol Hill for nearly two centuries, but rarely before has seeking publicity been such a significant part of every House member's job. For most of the twentieth century the way to get things done and to advance a career in Washington was to play an inside game, building relationships with colleagues, deferring to senior members, and bargaining, while slowly building up the legislative longevity necessary to achieve a position of power. Legislators paid little attention to reporters except those from the press back home, and they severely restricted the access of radio and television to the House. The House was governed by party leaders and committee chairs who preferred to stay out of the spotlight whenever possible.

Now all that has changed. The media are useful to members for publicity to help them get reelected, of course, but increasingly also in policymaking, wielding influence in Congress and in Washington, and pursuing their personal ambitions. Making news has frequently become integral to the legislative process. Reporters for all kinds of news outlets can now be present at any stage of the legislative process and can be instrumental in shaping the results. Sophisticated House press operations try to create national constituencies for issues on which members can serve as authoritative sources and build reputations. At the very least, legislators who wish to be considered influential experts have to ensure that their media image fits their chosen self-portrait, so few of them, inside or outside leadership circles, can pass up opportunities to be newsworthy. Making news, in short, has become a crucial component of making laws.

This reliance shows few signs of abating, even after the departure of Ronald Reagan, whose presidency has thus far been the high-water mark of going public. His successor, George Bush, has carefully crafted a media strategy, but it has shown him off as more a manager than a great communicator. However, Bush's recent choice of the Iwo Jima Memorial as the backdrop for introducing a constitutional amendment to ban flag burning shows that the adept use of sound bites and visual imagery that marked his presidential campaign could easily turn into a strategy of governing by campaigning. On Capitol Hill the Senate in 1986 finally followed the House's lead in broadcasting floor proceedings, further cementing the conjuncture of making laws and making news. And Tip O'Neill, the self-confessed backroom politician who brought the House into the television age, was succeeded first in 1987 by Jim Wright, whose aggressive, policy-oriented loner style was well-suited for the press, and in 1989 by Thomas Foley, perhaps "the first House Speaker whom most colleagues feel comfortable putting in front of television cameras" and whose tenure as majority leader had been marked by unprecedented attention to publicity.

The conditions that made it not only possible but necessary to use the media to get legislative business accomplished also show few signs of abating. The expansion of congressional staffs in the 1970s will not be reversed; and each new Congress will see members naming more full-time press secretaries. Likewise, the number of Washington reporters should continue to grow steadily. News organizations may be tightening their belts, but the rise of newspaper chains, the abundance of stringers, and the creation of groups such as Conus that contract out television news services mean that virtually any news outlet can have a relatively inexpensive link to Washington. Such easy hookups allow members to add their comments to stories that are bouncing among various newsbeats in the capital. Above all, the news media help House members set the legislative agenda, define the alternatives, influence public moods, and affect outcomes at a time when the political process is confused and unpredictable.

Yet if legislators need reporters, reporters also need legislators to create the events or provide the observations that can become the basis of a story. Even though the needs of the two are rarely identical, they can work in a symbiosis. House members, even at high levels of power, cannot automatically make news. Instead, they must ensure that their information and stories meet journalistic standards of timeliness, pertinence, and interest. Reporters' dependence on authoritative sources to suggest news means that journalism tends to reflect the perspectives of the more powerful. But such power is not absolute, because while politicians control definitions of importance, journalists still decide what is interesting. So House members and reporters negotiate and renegotiate newsworthiness. The question should not then be what the news media have done to the House, or what the House has done to the news media, but what these two institutions have done with one another. What is the effect of this negotiation on policymaking and on representative democracy? The answers must be speculative, but they are well worth contemplating.

Policymaking Processes and the Media

The power of the press often buttresses established power and procedures in the House. Hill traditions of pursuing expertise and influence dovetail with reporters' search for sources who are in a position to know. Reporters accord a reassuring coherence to the legislative process by focusing on "particularly and peculiarly congressional actions," stressing the gradual, orderly nature of the way bills are passed rather than the chaos or stasis that characterizes much of congressional life.

But the priorities of journalists and politicians are not always so synchronized. Reporters have less leeway in whom to report about or when to report it than in the issues that will receive coverage. Some of the coverage of Congress is a by-product of the coverage of issues. Issues most likely to make news are easily described, have clearly characterized sides, affect a large part of the audience, and come with straightforward reform remedies. Journalists tend to pass up matters that are complex, unfamiliar, specialized, or not apparently easily addressed.

If members want news coverage, they must choose clear-cut issues or try to present the complex as simple. But such choices invite distortion or omission of complicating factors. . . .

Setting the agenda is only the first step in the journey of legislation; press attention affects later stages, too. Bargaining among members, once the hallmark of a legislative institution, becomes more difficult when reporters are watching—not so much because members act differently in public than in private but because reporters' dislike for noncommittal stances tends to discourage the fluidity and maneuverability necessary to resolve differences on the fine points and to enact legislation.

Legislators who wish to get something done must be both outside and inside players. Press coverage can enhance their reputations and direct colleagues' attention toward them as people to listen to. Inside strategies can lead to the influential post that can be used to gain the media's attention. Using them together can be synergistic, accomplishing more than using either one on its own. . . .

To the extent that the press spotlights problems and helps set the legislative agenda, an additional complication arises: the clock of Congress will resemble that of the news. The media have a limited attention span. They discover problems suddenly, but their interest rapidly wanes, whether or not the problems have been solved. As entrepreneurial politicians take advantage of the brief window of opportunity to get something done, agenda items can rise and fall in importance with dizzying rapidity. . . .

Yet for all these drawbacks, the conjunction of media strategies and legislative strategies can aid policymaking, particularly in surmounting entrenched interests and facilitating large-scale legislative initiatives. The news suggests problems or alternatives that Congress has bypassed. It helps inform and mobilize public opinion.

At the very least it forces legislators to look beyond the interests of organized groups with the most immediate stakes and perhaps toward the larger public interest. When members would prefer to do nothing, publicity can increase the risks of inaction. In short, members in the spotlight are pressured to deal with problems in a way that corresponds to their readings of public opinion.

Congress and
Mass-Mediated Democracy

To evaluate more fully the implications of the media's role in the House, though, one must set forth standards for the roles of legislators and legislatures in representative democracy. After all, the Constitution assigned the House in particular to represent the people. At its most basic, political representation means that officials are elected to act on behalf of their constituents' interests. . . .

At the local level the relationship of House member and constituency would initially seem to be working wonderfully. If, as in 1988, nearly 99 percent of the House incumbents standing for reelection are returned for another term, what could possibly be wrong? But as Hanna Pitkin has pointed out, a legislator's reelection "is not absolute proof that he is a good representative; it proves at most that the voters think so." And when reasons for that approval are examined, optimism about the idealness of the relationship must be tempered. Incumbents win reelection more or less by default against invisible opposition. To be sure, even under these circumstances members are constrained by the realization that they might have to account for their actions. To compile a record that can be easily explained back home, when they present themselves in person to as many constituents as possible, they end up anticipating their constituents' will and responding to it. Their accessibility can result in dialogue. But when legislators rely on explaining through the media rather than explaining in person, dialogue is replaced by one-way rhetoric.

The ascendancy of rhetoric might not be a problem if it were informative and balanced, but it is not. Even local news outlets rarely report House elections with the same effort and initiative they devote to statewide or presidential elections. This neglect works to the incumbents' advantage, because in effect they can shape the timing, content, and tone of their own coverage. All of this means that the voters lack enough information and tilt toward incumbents because they have no reason to be against them. Far from being watchdogs, the local media usually reinforce an incumbent's advantage by benign neglect.

What can be done? Cutting back on the incumbent's franking privilege or other perquisites of office is no answer: it can be valuable in a democracy to have legislators communicate with their constituents or travel home. And regulating perks does little to right the balance. Banning mass mailings within sixty days of an election simply moved them from November to September. Regulating the content of postal patron newsletters has created a Franking Commission that diligently counts the number of times a personal pronoun is used but that has little say over substance.

To ensure dialogue and choice, more information must be available. For all the criticism of television advertisements, their content is sometimes more substantive than that allowed by the horse-race mentality of election coverage, and voters may actually learn as much from them. But though campaign managers have considered television the most crucial medium, they rarely buy television time. Airing ads, even those lasting no more than thirty seconds, is so prohibitively expensive that by themselves they are responsible for spiraling campaign expenditures. Reforms must control the expense at its root, or else such proposals as publicly financing congressional elections or placing limits on fundraising (as by restricting the contributions of political action committees) would not improve the quality of information and the quality of voters' decisionmaking.

One answer: since television and radio are regulated by the government, they could be required to broadcast a certain number of messages from the major candidates of each district in the media market, much as stations are already obliged to carry a certain number of public service announcements. Naturally, incumbents are not keen on this idea; in a 1986 survey, 61 percent of the challengers endorsed the idea but only 30 percent of the incumbents. Similar provisions could allow an equal number of campaign mailings sent at government expense by challengers opposing representatives who have sent out newsletters. Members may think twice about blanketing the district with self-serving propaganda if they know their challengers will receive equal treatment. Without some such reforms, elections will remain trials that are all defense and no prosecution.

Of course, providing candidates with free air time does not preclude them from using it to obscure or distort—witness the number of liberal Democrats who used television ads to portray themselves as fiscal conservatives in the Reaganite year of 1984. And reforms aimed at television or at newsletters only indirectly affect newspapers. To answer these concerns, news about House members and House campaigns must be made easier to report. A barrier to providing enough information to the voters is the nature of district boundaries. The few districts that receive complete coverage of House elections correspond closely to television media markets or newspaper circulation areas. The less overlap, the less coverage and the less information about the candidates, especially the challenger. House districts, assembled to meet court standards of population equality, are gerrymandered to protect partisans or incumbents. Their boundaries do not match those of existing political communities or, more importantly, media markets. In 1986 the Supreme Court ruled that political gerrymandering is a justiciable issue, so plans may now be tossed out for favoring particular political outcomes, including protection of incumbents. If state legislatures considered media market boundaries in carving up districts, or if, perhaps more likely, courts took them into account when reviewing redistricting plans, there would be fewer election contests for each news organization to try to cover and probably more information about both incumbent and challenger.

Redrawing district lines would make House races easier to cover, but for reelection to be less routine, journalistic definitions of newsworthiness, balance, and completeness must change. If news organizations are not to give incumbents a boost for reelection, there must be stories other than those instigated by the members themselves. Instead of waiting for legislators to provide a peg for news, local outlets could easily come up with stories out of the public record such as analyses of what the members did in committee or on the floor and how they voted. During the campaign itself, editors and publishers should take care to identify both the incumbent and the challenger as serious candidates, perhaps even assigning different reporters to each one to ensure treatment that is as even-handed as possible. Until this is done, local news organizations, if only by overlooking the House campaigns, will end up being on the incumbent's side, and accountability will be poorly overseen.

At the national level, too, the increasing presence of the media may have some unfavorable effects for representative democracy. Outside strategies tend to converge on only some issues—those that fit the media's preferences. How closely are these issues connected to the people's concerns and preferences? Do media strategies help to open the legislative process to public scrutiny and encourage informed democracy or do they reinforce inequities of access and of power?

To answer these questions, perhaps it would be wise to ask to whom the media themselves are responsive. Though national journalists operate outside of Congress, they are inside the Washington beltway, routinely involved with elected officials, congressional staff, interest-group representatives, bureaucrats, and think-tank scholars. By facilitating communication within Washington, news organizations tend to represent the views of organized groups or otherwise already prominent actors, not only to each other but to the rest of the nation. The debates that Washington reporters discuss are those among organized political and economic groups, and if there is no debate, they do not rush in to fill the void.

Often, the media's role in the political process is akin to recirculating air in a building with no windows. The unexpected becomes so routinized that news itself is almost predictable. Freshness is only occasionally brought in by unanticipated dramatic events: the death of a basketball star from cocaine poisoning, an accident at a Soviet nuclear power plant, hospital waste washing up on New Jersey beaches, a massacre of schoolchildren by a gunman carrying an AK-47. Such disruptions of routine provide an opportunity for sources outside governmental and corporate hierarchies to be heard. But the sources are usually insufficiently organized, and by the time they are ready the spotlight is back to the existing agenda and the usual authoritative sources. "Washington news gathering, in other words, is an interaction among elites," Stephen Hess has written. "One elite reports on another elite." An advertisement in the *New York Times* business section even encouraged this interaction.

> If the news were about you, you'd read it, wouldn't you?
>   So Washington reads Washington Talk in the New York Times. It's where corporate messages will be seen and read by government leaders.
>   Reserve the Washington Talk ad corner for your important corporate ad.
>   Just call (212) 556-1446.
>   The New York Times.

Elites partly adopt and incorporate the concerns of other elites, an interaction only somewhat mitigated by the connections that each has with the people. But if representatives can become detached from constituents, journalists have even fewer direct connections with their readers or viewers, except for fellow reporters, superiors, and sources. Far from giving the public just what it wants, they prefer to avoid information about their mass audiences. Anticipating the latter's needs and reactions adds a potentially paralyzing complication, not to mention a threat to journalists' control of choosing and presenting news. They may ask people outside positions of power for opinions in person-in-the-street interviews or polls, but they choose the subject, which usually reflects issues that are hot in Washington. The result may be top-down policymaking: instead of bringing public opinion to official Washington, the news disseminates the views of Washington across the country.

None of this is the fault of reporters in general or of politicians in general. The Hill reporters I have met are exceedingly conscientious about standards of objectivity and excellence. And even though House press secretaries may present one-sided accounts, their reports are seldom fabrications or distortions of their bosses' records. But these people work within news organizations or political institutions that define what is worth attending to and what may be neglected, and reward workers accordingly. As Warren Breed noted, "Newsmen define their job as producing a certain quantity of what is called ` news' every 24 hours. . . . They are not rewarded for analyzing the social structure, but for getting news." Or in the words of Todd Gitlin, "Political news is like crime news; it's about what went wrong today, not what goes wrong every day."

As House members and their staffs decide what course to pursue and increasingly incorporate a definition of news as something that happened since yesterday, they become directed toward problems that are quickly fixed and away from chronic conditions that find a news peg only with difficulty. Political debate under the spotlight is directed to more technical, less politicized questions of governance instead of essential social concerns that the news rarely directly addresses and that thus remain rarely discussed.

Turning to the news media to help the process of governance is a reasonable option that House members and their staffs may profitably adopt. But merely linking media and legislative strategies, although it could well be a precondition for democratic decisionmaking, is insufficient. Legislating in the spotlight can move politicians away from the influence of organized groups, encourage them to take account of the public interest, and allow them to build coalitions on complex issues. The paradox of the 1980s, however, has been that such results have often occurred without the full-scale public mobilization that marked Reagan's 1981 campaign to cut taxes and spending. Just as theater critics can shut down a play even if the public likes it, so the involvement of the media can turn legislators toward or away from particular issues and particular options whether or not public opinion is on one side or the other.

If representative democracy is to work well, there must be more participation not merely by news organizations on behalf of the people but by the people themselves in shaping the options and decisions of government. Bringing the republic back into politics, of course, entails many possible steps not connected with either Congress or the media. Reforms in House election campaigns to cut down the inherent advantage of the incumbent could help, as would more general reforms, such as easing voter registration requirements. But the democratization of political news to include perspectives besides those provided by Washington is also necessary. It has been suggested that "multiperspectival" news is needed—news that would include opinions of the public as well as those of officials, news about programs as they actually operate rather than as they are intended to work, and news that reflects a much greater variety of sources. None of this need necessarily change how

Washington reporters go about their work; but it does require that officials' views be supplemented by others so that news organizations do not become unwitting adjuncts to the already powerful.

Of course, this very willingness on the part of the media to negotiate a relationship favorable to politicians enables House members to use publicity and to craft media strategies in pursuit of legislative goals. By taking advantage of news routines that emphasize a scripted process with authoritative sources, by working to manage journalists' access both formally and informally, by building a professionalized press operation with a full-time press secretary, House members today are adroitly pursuing and using the opportunities presented to them. Media strategies in the House have become valuable, not merely to take positions or gratify egos; they are now crucial ways to attain, maintain, and exert power in Washington.

Congress and the Electoral Connection

Edmund Burke was a quintessential eighteen-century statesman and political philosopher. He served in the House of Commons during the 1760s, representing a county that was essentially "owned" by a wealthy peer. After the King dissolved Parliament in 1774 Burke was invited to stand for election in the thriving commercial city of Bristol, known as the "capital of Western England." Wealthy merchants controlled the city politically, and sought in their representative in Parliament a person who would open the trade with America that had been lost as a result of the American Revolution.

Following his electoral victory in October of 1774 Burke delivered to his constituents the following speech, which became a political classic. His speech perfectly reflects the underlying philosophy of the framers of the Constitution that government should be *deliberative* and carried out in the *national interest*.

62

SPEECH TO THE ELECTORS OF BRISTOL

Edmund Burke

. . . I owe myself, in all things, to all the freemen of this city. My particular friends have a demand on me that I should not deceive their expectations. Never was cause or man supported with more constancy, more activity, more spirit. I have been supported with a zeal, indeed, and heartiness in my friends, which (if their object had

been at all proportioned to their endeavors) could never be sufficiently com-
mended. They supported me upon the most liberal principles. They wished that the
members for Bristol should be chosen for the city, and for their country at large, and
not for themselves.

So far they are not disappointed. If I possess nothing else, I am sure I possess
the temper that is fit for your service. . . .

I shall ever retain, what I now feel, the most perfect and grateful attachment to
my friends—and I have no enmities, no resentments. I never can consider fidelity
to engagements and constancy in friendships but with the highest approbation,
even when those noble qualities are employed against my own pretensions. The
gentleman who is not so fortunate as I have been in this contest enjoys, in this respect, a consolation full of honor both to himself and to his friends. They have certainly left nothing undone for his service. . . .

I am sorry I cannot conclude without saying a word on a topic touched upon by
my worthy colleague.[1] I wish that topic had been passed by at a time when I have so
little leisure to discuss it. But since he has thought proper to throw it out, I owe you
a clear explanation of my poor sentiments on that subject.

He tells you that "the topic of instructions has occasioned much altercation
and uneasiness in this city"; and he expresses himself (if I understand him rightly)
in favor of the coercive authority of such instructions.

Certainly, Gentlemen, it ought to be the happiness and glory of a representative to live in the strictest union, the closest correspondence, and the most unre-
served communication with his constituents. Their wishes ought to have great
weight with him; their opinions high respect; their business unremitted attention.
It is his duty to sacrifice his repose, his pleasure, his satisfactions, to theirs—and
above all, ever, and in all cases, to prefer their interest to his own.

But his unbiased opinion, his mature judgment, his enlightened conscience, he
ought not to sacrifice to you, to any man, or to any set of men living. These he does
not derive from your pleasure—no, nor from the law and the constitution. They are
a trust from Providence, for the abuse of which he is deeply answerable. Your representative owes you, not his industry only, but his judgment; and he betrays, instead
of serving you, if he sacrifices it to your opinion.

My worthy colleague says his will ought to be subservient to yours. If that be
all, the thing is innocent. If government were a matter of will upon any side, yours,
without question, ought to be superior. But government and legislation are matters
of reason and judgment, and not of inclination; and what sort of reason is that in
which the determination precedes the discussion, in which one set of men deliberate and another decide, and where those who form the conclusion are perhaps three
hundred miles distant from those who hear the arguments?

To deliver an opinion is the right of all men; that of constituents is a weighty
and respectable opinion, which a representative ought always to rejoice to hear, and
which he ought always most seriously to consider. But *authoritative* instructions,
mandates issued, which a member is bound blindly and implicitly to obey, to vote,

---

[1]Henry Cruger, also elected for Bristol.

and to argue for, though contrary to the clearest conviction of his judgment and conscience; these are things utterly unknown to the laws of this land, and which arise from a fundamental mistake of the whole order and tenor of our constitution.

Parliament is not a congress of ambassadors from different and hostile interests, which interests each must maintain, as an agent and advocate, against other agents and advocates; but Parliament is a *deliberative* assembly of one nation, with one interest, that of the whole—where not local purposes, not local prejudices, ought to guide, but the general good, resulting from the general reason of the whole. You choose a member, indeed; but when you have chosen him he is not a member of Bristol, but he is a member of *Parliament*. If the local constituent should have an interest or should form a hasty opinion evidently opposite to the real good of the rest of the community, the member for that place ought to be as far as any other from any endeavor to give it effect. . . . Your faithful friend, your devoted servant, I shall be to the end of my life: a flatterer you do not wish for. . . .

From the first hour I was encouraged to court your favor, to this happy day of obtaining it, I have never promised you anything but humble and persevering endeavors to do my duty. The weight of that duty, I confess, makes me tremble; and whoever well considers what it is, of all things in the world, will fly from what has the least likeness to a positive and precipitate engagement. To be a good member of Parliament is, let me tell you, no easy task—especially at this time, when there is so strong a disposition to run into the perilous extremes of servile compliance or wild popularity. To unite circumspection with vigor is absolutely necessary, but it is extremely difficult. We are now members for a rich commercial city; this city, however, is but a part of a rich commercial nation, the interests of which are various, multiform, and intricate. We are members for that great nation, which, however, is itself but part of a great *empire*, extended by our virtue and our fortune to the farthest limits of the East and of the West. All these wide-spread interests must be considered—must be compared—must be reconciled, if possible. We are members for a *free* country; and surely we all know that the machine of a free constitution is no simple thing, but as intricate and as delicate as it is valuable. We are members in a great and ancient *monarchy*; and we must preserve religiously the true, legal rights of the sovereign, which form the keystone that binds together the noble and well-constructed arch of our empire and our constitution. A constitution made up of balanced powers must ever be a critical thing. As such I mean to touch that part of it which comes within my reach. . . .

Throughout the 1970s public opinion polls consistently revealed that Congress was held in low esteem by the American people. The book *Who Runs Congress?*, published by the Ralph Nader Congress Project, reflected and at the same time helped to crystallize public disenchantment with Capitol Hill.[1] The book emphasized the need for citizens to take on

---

[1] Mark J. Green et al., eds., *Who Runs Congress?* (New York: Bantam/Grossman, 1972).

Congress to prevent a further flagging of the institution. In his introduction, Ralph Nader summarized the contents of the book by stating that "the people have indeed abdicated their power, their money, and their democratic birthright to Congress. As a result, without the participation of the people, Congress has surrendered its enormous authority and resources to special interest groups, waste, insensitivity, ignorance, and bureaucracy."[2] The 1972 theme of the Nader project that Congress was in crisis continues to be accepted by the vast majority of people.

While Ralph Nader and his colleagues feel that the major cause of the demise of Congress is its detachment from the people, Richard Fenno in the following selection adopts a different viewpoint. He feels that people fault the *institution* of Congress, not their individual representatives on Capitol Hill. In fact, he points out that there is a close connection between legislators and constituents, and often, a feeling of affection by voters for their representatives. Fenno feels that we apply different standards in judging individual members of Congress than we do in assessing the institution, being far more lenient in the former than the latter case. The individual is judged for his or her personality, style, and representativeness, while the institution is judged by its ability to recognize and solve the nation's problems. But the institution cannot be thought of apart from the members that compose it. It is they who have given it its unique character. It is the individual member who, more often than not, has supported a decentralized and fragmented legislature because of the members' incentive to achieve personal power and status on Capitol Hill.

63

IF, AS RALPH NADER SAYS, CONGRESS IS "THE BROKEN BRANCH," HOW COME WE LOVE OUR CONGRESSMEN SO MUCH?

Richard F. Fenno, Jr.

Off and on during the past two years, I accompanied ten members of the House of Representatives as they traveled around in their home districts. In every one of those districts I heard a common theme, one that I had not expected. Invariably, the representative I was with—young or old, liberal or conservative, Northerner, Southerner, Easterner, or Westerner, Democrat or Republican—was described as

---

[2]Ibid., p. 1.

"the best congressman in the United States." Having heard it so often, I now accept the description as fact. I am even prepared to believe the same thing (though I cannot claim to have heard it with my own ears) of the members of the Senate. Each of our 435 representatives and 100 senators is, indeed, "the best congressman in the United States." Which is to say that each enjoys a great deal of support and approbation among his or her constituents. Judging by the election returns, this isn't much of an exaggeration. In [recent elections], 96 percent of all House incumbents who ran were reelected; and 85 percent of all Senate incumbents who ran were reelected. These convincing figures are close to the average reelection rates of incumbents for the past ten elections. We do, it appears, love our congressmen.

On the other hand, it seems equally clear that we do not love our Congress. Louis Harris reported in 1970 that only one-quarter of the electorate gave Congress a positive rating on its job performance—while nearly two-thirds expressed themselves negatively on the subject. . . . There [is] considerable concern—dramatized recently by the critical Nader project—for the performance of Congress as an institution. On the evidence, we seem to approve of our legislators a good deal more than we do our legislature. And therein hangs something of a puzzle. If our congressmen are so good, how can our Congress be so bad? If it is the individuals that make up the institution, why should there be such a disparity in our judgments? What follows are a few reflections on this puzzle.

A first answer is that we apply different standards of judgment, those that we apply to the individual being less demanding than those we apply to the institution. For the individual, our standard is one of representativeness—of personal style and policy views. Stylistically, we ask that our legislator display a sense of identity with us so that we, in turn, can identify with him or her—via personal visits to the district, concern for local projects and individual "cases," and media contact of all sorts, for example. On the policy side, we ask only that his general policy stance does not get too frequently out of line with ours. And, if he should become a national leader in some policy area of interest to us, so much the better. These standards are admittedly vague. But because they are locally defined and locally applied, they are consistent and manageable enough so that legislators can devise rules of thumb to meet them. What is more, by their performance they help shape the standards, thereby making them easier to meet. Thus they win constituent recognition as "the best in the United States." And thus they establish the core relationship for a representative democracy.

For the institution, however, our standards emphasize efforts to solve national problems—a far less tractable task than the one we (and he) set for the individual. Given the inevitable existence of unsolved problems, we are destined to be unhappy with congressional performance. The individual legislator knows when he has met our standards of representativeness; he is reelected. But no such definitive measure of legislative success exists. And, precisely because Congress is the most familiar and most human of our national institutions, lacking the distant majesty of the Presidency and the Court, it is the easy and natural target of our criticism. We have met our problem solvers, and they are us.

Furthermore, such standards as we do use for judging the institutional performance of Congress are applied inconsistently. In 1963, when public dissatisfaction was as great as in 1970, Congress was criticized for being obstructionist, dilatory and insufficiently cooperative with regard to the Kennedy programs. Two years later, Congress got its highest performance rating of the decade when it cooperated completely with the executive in rushing the Great Society program into law. But by the late 1960s and early 1970s the standard of judgment had changed radically—from cooperation to counterbalance in Congressional relations with the Executive. Whereas, in 1963, Harris had found "little in the way of public response to the time-honored claim that the Legislative Branch is . . . the guardian against excessive Executive power," by 1968 he found that three-quarters of the electorate wanted Congress to act as the watchdog of the Executive and not to cooperate so readily with it. The easy passage of the Tonkin Resolution reflects the cooperative standards set in the earlier period; its repeal reflects the counterbalancing standards of the recent period. Today we are concerned about Ralph Nader's "broken branch" which, we hear, has lost—and must reclaim from the Executive—its prerogatives in areas such as war-making and spending control. To some degree, then, our judgments on Congress are negative because we change our minds frequently concerning the kind of Congress we want. A Congress whose main job is to cooperate with the Executive would look quite different from one whose main job is to counterbalance the Executive.

Beneath the differences in our standards of judgment, however, lies a deeper dynamic of the political system. Senators and representatives, for their own reasons, spend a good deal more of their time and energy polishing and worrying about their individual performance than they do working at the institution's performance. Though it is, of course, true that their individual activity is related to institutional activity, their first-order concerns are individual, not institutional. Foremost is their desire for reelection. Most members of Congress like their job, want to keep it, and know that there are people back home who want to take it away from them. So they work long and hard at winning reelection. Even those who are safest want election margins large enough to discourage opposition back home and/or to help them float further political ambitions. No matter what other personal goals representatives and senators wish to accomplish—increased influence in Washington and helping to make good public policy are the most common—reelection is a necessary means to those ends.

We cannot criticize these priorities—not in a representative system. If we believe the representative should mirror constituency opinion, we must acknowledge that it requires considerable effort for him to find out what should be mirrored. If we believe a representative should be free to vote his judgment, he will have to cultivate his constituents assiduously before they will trust him with such freedom. Either way we will look favorably on his efforts. We come to love our legislators, in the *second* place, because they so ardently sue for our affections.

As a courtship technique, moreover, they re-enforce our unfavorable judgments about the institution. Every representative with whom I traveled criticized the Congress and portrayed himself, by contrast, as a fighter against its manifest evils. Members run *for* Congress by running *against* Congress. They refurbish their individual reputations as "the best congressman in the United States" by attacking the collective reputation of the Congress of the United States. Small wonder the voters feel so much more warmly disposed and so much less fickle toward the individuals than toward the institution. One case in point: the House decision to grant President Nixon a spending ceiling plus authority to cut previously appropriated funds to maintain that ceiling. One-half the representatives I was with blasted the House for being so spineless that it gave away its power of the purse to the President. The other half blasted the House for being so spineless in exercising its power of the purse that the President had been forced to act. Both groups spoke to supportive audiences; and each man enhanced his individual reputation by attacking the institution. Only by raising both questions, however, could one see the whole picture. Once the President forced the issue, how come the House didn't stand up to him and protect its crucial institutional power over the purse strings? On the other hand, if economic experts agreed that a spending ceiling was called for, how come the House didn't enact it and make the necessary budget cuts in the first place? The answer to the first question lies in the proximity of their reelection battles, which re-enforced the tendency of all representatives to think in individualistic rather than institutional terms. The answer to the second question lies in the total absence of institutional machinery whereby the House (or, indeed, Congress) can make overall spending decisions.

Mention of the institutional mechanisms of Congress leads us to a *third* explanation for our prevailing pattern of judgments. When members of Congress think institutionally—as, of course they must—they think in terms of a structure that will be most congenial to the pursuit of their individual concerns—for reelection, for influence, or for policy. Since each individual has been independently designated "the best in the United States," each has an equal status and an equal claim to influence within the structure. For these reasons, the members naturally think in terms of a very fragmented, decentralized institution, providing a maximum of opportunity for individual performance, individual influence, and individual credit.

The 100-member Senate more completely fits this description than the 435-member House. The smaller body permits a more freewheeling and creative individualism. But both chambers tend strongly in this direction, and representatives as well as senators chafe against centralizing mechanisms. Neither body is organized in hierarchical—or even in well-coordinated—patterns of decision-making. Agreements are reached by some fairly subtle forms of mutual adjustment—by negotiation, bargaining, and compromise. And interpersonal relations—of respect, confidence, trust—are crucial building blocks. The members of Congress, in pursuit of their individual desires, have thus created an institution that is internally quite complex. Its structure and processes are, therefore, very difficult to grasp from the outside.

In order to play out some aspects of the original puzzle, however, we must make the effort. And the committee system, the epitome of fragmentation and decentralization, is a good place to start. The performance of Congress as an institution is very largely the performance of its committees. The Nader project's "broken branch" description is mostly a committee-centered description because that is where the countervailing combination of congressional expertise and political skill resides. To strengthen Congress means to strengthen its committees. To love Congress means to love its committees. Certainly when we have not loved our Congress, we have heaped our displeasure upon its committees. The major legislative reorganizations, of 1946 and 1970, were committee-centered reforms—centering on committee jurisdictions, committee democracy, and committee staff support. Other continuing criticisms—of the seniority rule for selecting committee chairmen, for example—have centered on the committees.

Like Congress as a whole, committees must be understood first in terms of what they do for the individual member. To begin with, committees are relatively more important to the individual House member than to the individual senator. The representative's career inside Congress is very closely tied to his committee. For the only way such a large body can function is to divide into highly specialized and independent committees. Policy-making activity funnels through these committees; so does the legislative activity and influence of the individual legislator. While the Senate has a set of committees paralleling those of the House, a committee assignment is nowhere near as constraining for the career of the individual senator. The Senate is more loosely organized, senators sit on many more committees and subcommittees than representatives, and they have easy access to the work of committees of which they are not members. Senators, too, can command and utilize national publicity to gain influence beyond the confines of their committee. Whereas House committees act as funnels for individual activity, Senate committees act as facilitators of individual activity. The difference in functions is considerable—which is why committee chairmen are a good deal more important in the House than in the Senate and why the first modifications of the seniority rule should have come in the House rather than the Senate. My examples will come from the House.

Given the great importance of his committee to the career of the House member, it follows that we will want to know how each committee can affect such careers. . . .

Where a committee's members are especially interested in pyramiding their individual influence, they will act so as to maintain the influence of their committee (and, hence, their personal influence) within the House. They will adopt procedures that enhance the operating independence of the committee. They will work hard to remain relatively independent of the Executive Branch. And they will try to underpin that independence with such resources as specialized expertise, internal cohesion, and the respect of their House colleagues. Ways and Means and Appropriations are committees of this sort. By contrast, where a committee's members are especially interested in getting in on nationally controversial policy action, they will not be much concerned about the independent influence of their committee. They will want to ally themselves closely with any and all groups outside the committee who share their policy views. They want to help enact what they individually regard as good public policy; and if that means ratifying policies shaped elsewhere—in the Executive Branch particularly—so be it. And, since their institutional independence is not a value for them, they make no special effort to acquire such underpinnings as expertise, cohesion, or chamber respect. Education and Labor and Foreign Affairs are committees of this sort.

These two types of committees display quite different strengths in their performance. Those of the first type are especially influential. Ways and Means probably makes a greater independent contribution to policy making than any other House committee. Appropriations probably exerts a more influential overview of executive branch activities than any other House committee. The price they pay, however, is a certain decrease in their responsiveness to noncommittee forces—as complaints about the closed rule on tax bills and executive hearings on appropriations bills will attest. Committees of the second type are especially responsive to noncommittee forces and provide easy conduits for outside influence in policy making. Education and Labor was probably more receptive to President Johnson's Great Society policies than any other House committee; it successfully passed the largest part of the program. Foreign Affairs has probably remained as thoroughly responsive to Executive Branch policies, in foreign aid for instance, as any House committee. The price they pay, however, is a certain decrease in their influence—as complaints about the rubber-stamp Education and Labor Committee and about the impotent Foreign Affairs Committee will attest. In terms of the earlier discussions of institutional performance standards, our hopes for a cooperative Congress lie more with the latter type of committee; our hopes for a counterbalancing Congress lie more with the former.

So, committees differ. And they differ to an important degree according to the desires of their members. This ought to make us wary of blanket descriptions. Within the House, Foreign Affairs may look like a broken branch, but Ways and Means does not. And, across chambers, Senate Foreign Relations (where member incentives are stronger) is a good deal more potent than House Foreign Affairs. With the two Appropriations committees, the reverse is the case. It is not just that "the broken branch" is an undiscriminating, hence inaccurate, description. It is also that blanket descriptions lead to blanket prescriptions. And it just might be that the wisest course of congressional reform would be to identify existing nodes of committee strength and nourish them rather than to prescribe, as we usually do, reforms in equal dosages for all committees.

One lesson of the analysis should be that member incentives must exist to support any kind of committee activity. Where incentives vary, it may be silly to prescribe the same functions and resources for all committees. The Reorganization Act of 1946 mandated all committees to exercise "continuous watchfulness" over the executive branch—in the absence of any supporting incentive system. We have gotten overview activity only where random individuals have found an incentive for doing so—not by most committees and certainly not continuously. Similarly, I suspect that our current interest in exhorting all committees to acquire more information with which to combat the executive may be misplaced. Information is relatively easy to come by—and some committees have a lot of it. What is hard to come by is the incentive to use it, not to mention the time and the trust necessary to make it useful. I am not suggesting a set of reforms but rather a somewhat different strategy of committee reforms—less wholesale, more retail.

Since, the best-known target of wholesale committee reform is the seniority rule, it deserves special comment. If our attacks on the rule have any substance to them, if they are anything other than symbolic, the complaint must be that some or all committee chairmen are not doing a good job. But we can only find out whether this is so by conducting a committee-by-committee examination. Paradoxically, our discussions of the seniority rule tend to steer us away from such a retail examination by mounting very broad, across-the-board kinds of arguments against chairmen as a class—arguments about their old age, their conservatism, their national unrepresentativeness. Such arguments produce great cartoon copy, easy editorial broadsides, and sitting-duck targets for our congressmen on the stump. But we ought not to let the arguments themselves, nor the Pavlovian public reactions induced by our cartoonists, editorial writers, and representatives, pass for good institutional analysis. Rather, they have diverted us from that task.

More crucial to a committee's performance than the selection of its chairman is his working relationship with the other committee members. Does he agree with his members on the functions of the committee? Does he act to facilitate the achievement of their individual concerns? Do they approve of his performance as chairman? Where there is real disagreement between chairman and members, close analysis may lead us to fault the members and not the chairman. If so, we should be focusing our criticisms on the members. If the fault lies with the chairman, a majority of the members have the power to bring him to heel. They need not kill the king; they can constitutionalize the monarchy. While outsiders have been crying "off with his head," the members of several committees have been quietly and effectively constitutionalizing the monarchy. Education and Labor, Post Office, and Interior are recent examples where dissatisfied committee majorities have subjected their chairmen to majority control. Where this has not been done, it is probably due to member satisfaction, member timidity, member disinterest, or member incompetence. And the time we spend railing against the seniority rule might be better spent finding out, for each congressional committee, just which of these is the case. If, as a final possibility, a chairman and his members are united in opposition to the majority part or to the rest of us, the seniority rule is not the problem. More to the point, as I suspect is usually the case, the reasons and the ways individual members get sorted onto the various committees is the critical factor. In sum, I am not saying that the seniority rule is a good thing, I am saying that, for committee performance, it is not a very important thing.

What has all this got to do with the original puzzle—that we love our congressmen so much more than our Congress? We began with a few explanatory guesses. Our standards of judgment for individual performance are more easily met: the individual member works harder winning approval for himself than for his institution; and Congress is a complex institution, difficult for us to understand. The more we try to understand Congress—as we did briefly with the committee system—the more we are forced to peel back the institutional layers until we reach the individual member. At that point, it becomes hard to separate, as we normally do, our judgments about congressmen and Congress. The more we come to see institutional performance as influenced by the desires of the individual member, the more the original puzzle ought to resolve itself. For as the independence of our judgments decreases, the disparity between them ought to grow smaller. But if we are to hold this perspective on Congress, we shall need to understand the close individual-institution relationship—chamber by chamber, party by party, committee by committee, legislator by legislator.

This is not a counsel of despair. It is a counsel of sharper focus and a more discriminating eye. It counsels the mass media, for example, to forego "broken branch" type generalizations about Congress in favor of examining a committee in depth, or to forego broad criticism of the seniority rule for a close look at a committee chairman. It counsels the rest of us to focus more on the individual member and to fix the terms of our dialogue with him more aggressively. It counsels us to fix terms that will force him to think more institutionally and which will hold him more accountable for the performance of the institution. "Who Runs Congress," asks the title of the Nader report, "the President, Big Business or You?" From the perspective of this paper, it is none of these. It is the members who run Congress. And we get pretty much the kind of Congress they want. We shall get a different kind of Congress when we elect different kinds of congressmen or when we start applying different standards of judgment to old congressmen. Whether or not we ought to have a different kind of Congress is still another, much larger, puzzle.

Richard F. Fenno, Jr., explains in selection 63 that the public holds Congress and its members to different standards. *Congress-bashing*, to use the author's colorful term in the following selection, is popular not only with the public but, more importantly, with those who shape public opinion, including political journalists and pundits, network news anchors and television commentators, self-proclaimed public interest representatives, and, perhaps most importantly of all, members of Congress themselves who have found that running against Congress is a successful campaign tactic.

The author of the following selection, a prominent congressional scholar, describes the popular support of Congress-bashing and concludes that criticism of Congress has gone too far.

64

CONGRESS-BASHING FOR BEGINNERS

Nelson W. Polsby

On a shelf not far from where I am writing these words sit a half a dozen or so books disparaging Congress and complaining about the congressional role in the constitutional separation of powers. These books date mostly from the late 1940s and the early 1960s, and typically their authors are liberal Democrats. In those years, Congress was unresponsive to liberal Democrats and, naturally enough, aggrieved members of that articulate tribe sought solutions in structural reform.

In fact, instead of reforms weakening Congress what they—and we—got was a considerably strengthened presidency. This was mostly a product of World War II and not the result of liberal complaints. Before World War II Congress would not enact even the modest recommendations of the Brownlow Commission to give the president a handful of assistants with "a passion for anonymity," and it killed the National Resources Planning Board outright. After World War II everything changed: Congress gave the president responsibility for smoothing the effects of the business cycle, created a Defense Department and two presidential agencies—the NSC and the CIA—that enhanced the potential for presidential dominance of national security affairs, and laid the groundwork for the growth of a presidential branch, politically responsive to both Democratic and Republican presidents.

Congress and the Goring of Oxen

Though it took time for the presidential branch to grow into its potential, the growth of this branch, separate and at arm's length from the executive branch that it runs in the president's behalf, is the big news of the postwar era—indeed, of the last half-century in American government. It is customary today to acknowledge that Harry Truman's primary agenda, in the field of foreign affairs, was quite successfully enacted even though Congress was dominated by a conservative coalition, and what Truman wanted in the way of peacetime international involvement was for the United States quite unprecedented. Dwight Eisenhower's agenda was also largely international in its impact. Looking back, it seems that almost all Eisenhower really cared about was protecting the international position of the United States from diminution by Republican isolationists. Everything else was expendable.

Congress responded sluggishly and in its customary piecemeal fashion. It was right around John Kennedy's first year in office that liberals rediscovered that old roadblock in Congress, a "deadlock of democracy," as one of them put it. It was Congress that had thwarted the second New Deal after 1937, the packing of the Supreme Court, and Harry Truman's domestic program; it was Congress that had stalled civil rights and buried Medicare; it was Congress that had sponsored the Bricker Amendment to limit the president's power to make treaties. Are memories so short that we do not recall these dear, departed days when Congress was the graveyard of the forward-looking proposals of liberal presidents? Then, Congress was a creaky eighteenth-century machine unsuited to the modern age, and Congress-bashers were liberal Democrats.

To be sure, Congress had a few defenders, mostly Republicans and Dixiecrats, who found in its musty cloakrooms and windy debates a citadel (as one of them said) of old-time legislative virtues, where the historic functions of oversight and scrutiny were performed, where the run-away proposals of the presidency could be subjected to the sober second thoughts of the people's own elected representatives, and so on.

Why rehash all this? In part, it is to try to make the perfectly obvious point that Congress-bashing then was what people did when they controlled the presidency but didn't control Congress. And that, in part, is what Congress-bashing is about now. Today, Republicans and conservatives are doing most (although not all) of the complaining. It is worth a small bet that a fair number of editorial pages claimed that the separation of powers made a lot of sense during the Kennedy-Johnson years—but no longer say the same today. On the other side, backers of FDR's scheme to pack the Court have turned into vigorous defenders of the judicial status quo since Earl Warren's time.

There is nothing wrong with letting the goring of oxen determine what side we take in a political argument. In a civilized country, however, it makes sense to keep political arguments civil, and not to let push come to shove too often. There is something uncivil, in my view, about insisting upon constitutional reforms to cure political ailments. What liberal critics of Congress needed was not constitutional reform. What they needed was the 89th Congress, which, in due course, enacted much of the agenda that the Democratic party had built up over the previous two decades. History didn't stop with the rise of the presidential branch and the enactment of the second New Deal/New Frontier/Great Society. President Johnson overreached. He concealed from Congress the costs of the Vietnam War. He created a credibility gap.

This, among other things, began to change Congress. The legislative branch no longer was altogether comfortable relying on the massaged numbers and other unreliable information coming over from the presidential branch. They began to create a legislative bureaucracy to cope with this challenge. They beefed up the General Accounting Office and the Congressional Research Service. They created an Office of Technology Assessment and a Congressional Budget Office. They doubled and redoubled their personal staffs and committee staffs.

Sentiments supporting this expansion began, oddly enough, after a landslide election in which the Democratic party swept the presidency and both houses of Congress. So mistrust between the branches in recent history has by no means been entirely a partisan matter. Nevertheless, Richard Nixon's presidency, conducted entirely in unhappy harness with a Democratic Congress, did not improve relations between the two branches of government. Johnson may have been deceitful, but Nixon, especially after his reelection in 1972, was positively confrontational.

It was Nixon's policy to disregard comity between the branches. This, and not merely his commission of impeachable offenses, fueled the impeachment effort in Congress. That effort was never wholly partisan. Republicans as well as Democrats voted articles of impeachment that included complaints specifically related to obstruction of the discharge of congressional responsibilities.

It is necessary to understand this recent history of the relations between Congress and the president in order to understand the provenance of the War Powers Act, the Boland Amendment, numerous other instances of congressional micromanagement, the unprecedented involvement of the NSC in the Iran-contra affair, and like manifestations of tension and mistrust between Congress and the president. These tensions are, to a certain degree, now embedded in law and in the routines of responsible public officials; they cannot be made to disappear with a wave of a magic wand. They are, for the most part, regrettable in the consequences they have had for congressional-presidential relations, but they reflect real responses to real problems in these relations. Congressional responses, so far as I can see, have been completely legal, constitutional, and—in the light of historical circumstances—understandable. The best way to turn the relations between the legislative and the presidential branches around would be for the presidential side to take vigorous initiatives to restore comity. As head of the branch far more capable of taking initiatives, and the branch far more responsible for the underlying problem, this effort at restoration is in the first instance up to the President.

President Bush and the Item Veto

In this respect, President Bush is doing a decent job, giving evidence of reaching out constructively. It is not my impression that the Bush administration has done a lot of Congress-bashing. After all, what Bush needs isn't a weakened Congress so much as a Republican Congress. Over the long run (though probably not in time to do Bush much good) Republicans are bound to regret despairing of the latter and therefore seeking the former. We have seen enough turns of the wheel over the last half-century to be reasonably confident that sooner or later Republicans will start to do better in congressional elections. The presidential item veto, the Administration's main Congress-bashing proposal, won't help Republicans in Congress deal with a Democratic president when the time comes, as sooner or later it will, for a Democrat to be elected president.

The item veto would effectively take congressional politics out of the legislative process, and would weaken Congress a lot. It would encourage members of Congress, majority and minority alike, to be irresponsible and to stick the president with embarrassing public choices. It would reduce the incentives for members to acquire knowledge about public policy or indeed to serve.

By allocating legislative responsibilities to Congress, the Constitution as originally (and currently) designed forces representatives of diverse interest to cooperate. Because what Congress does as a collectivity matters, legislative work elicits the committed participation of members. The item veto would greatly trivialize the work product of Congress by requiring the president's acquiescence on each detail of legislation. Members would lose their independent capacity to craft legislation. Their individual views and knowledge would dwindle in importance; only the marshalling of a herd capable of overturning a veto would matter in Congress.

The item veto is, in short, a truly radical idea. It is also almost certainly unconstitutional. To espouse it requires a readiness to give up entirely on the separation of powers and on the constitutional design of the American government. There are plenty of people, some of them well-meaning, who are ready to do that. I am not, nor should people who identify themselves as conservatives or liberals or anywhere in the political mainstream.

The separation of powers is actually a good idea. It gives a necessary weight to the great heterogeneity of our nation—by far the largest and most heterogeneous nation unequivocally to have succeeded at democratic self-government in world history. It would take a medium-sized book to make all the qualifications and all the connections that would do justice to this argument. The conclusion is worth restating anyway: the item veto is a root-and-branch attack on the separation of powers; it is a very radical and a very bad idea.

Term Limitations

Less serious in its impact, but still destructive, is the proposal to limit the terms of members of Congress. This proposal relies heavily for its appeal upon ignorance in the population at large about what members of Congress actually do. For in order to take seriously the idea of limiting congressional terms, one must believe that the job of a representative in Congress is relatively simple, and quickly and easily mastered. It is not.

The job of a member of Congress is varied and complex. It includes: (1) Managing a small group of offices that attempt on request to assist distressed constituents, state and local governments, and enterprises in the home district that may have business with the federal government. This ombudsman function gives members an opportunity to monitor the performance of the government in its dealings with citizens and can serve to identify areas of general need. (2) Serving on committees that oversee executive-branch activity on a broad spectrum of subjects (such as immigration, copyright protection, telecommunications, or health policy) and that undertake to frame issues of national scope for legislative action. This entails mastering complicated subject matter; working with staff members, expert outsiders, and colleagues to build coalitions; understanding justifications; and answering objections. (3) Participating in general legislative work. Members have to vote on everything, not merely on the work of their own committees. They have to inform themselves of the merits of bills, and stand ready to cooperate with colleagues whose support they will need to advance their own proposals. (4) Keeping track of their own political business. This means watching over and occasionally participating in the politics of their own states and localities, and mending fences with interest groups, friends and neighbors, backers, political rivals, and allies. (5) Educating all the varied people with whom they come in contact about issues that are high on the agenda and about reasonable expectations of performance. This includes the performance of the government, the Congress, and the member.

Plenty of members never try to master the job, or try and fail, and these members would be expendable. The objection might still be raised that constituents, not an excess of constitutional limitations, ought to decide who represents whom in Congress. But that aside, what about the rather substantial minority of members who learn their jobs, do their homework, strive to make an impact on public policy, and—through long experience and application to work—actually make a difference? Can we, or should we, dispense with them as well?

It is a delusion to think that good public servants are a dime a dozen in each congressional district, and that only the good ones would queue up to take their twelve-year fling at congressional office. But suppose they did. In case they acquired expertise, what would they do next? Make money, I suppose. Just about the time that their constituents and the American people at large could begin to expect a payoff because of the knowledge and experience that these able members had acquired at our expense, off they would go to some Washington law firm.

And what about their usefulness in the meantime? It would be limited, I'm afraid, by the greater expertise and better command of the territory by lobbyists, congressional staff, and downtown bureaucrats—career people one and all. So this is, once again, a proposal merely to weaken the fabric of Congress in the political system at large, and thereby to limit the effectiveness of the one set of actors most accessible to ordinary citizens.

The standard objection to this last statement is that members of Congress aren't all that accessible. Well, neither is Ralph Nader, who has long overstayed the dozen years that contemporary Congress-bashers wish to allocate to members. Neither is the author of *Wall Street Journal* editorials in praise of limitations. And it must be said that a very large number of members take their representational and ombudsman duties very seriously indeed. This includes holders of safe seats, some of whom fear primary-election opposition, some of whom are simply conscientious. A great many of them do pay attention—close attention—to their constituents. That is one of the reasons—maybe the most important reason—that so many of them are reelected. Much Congress-bashing these days actually complains about high reelection rates, as though a large population of ill-served constituents would be preferable.

Congressional Salaries

While we have Ralph Nader on our minds, it is certainly appropriate to pay our disrespects to his completely off-the-wall effort, temporarily successful, at the head of a crazed phalanx of self-righteous disk jockeys and radio talk-show hosts, to deprive members of Congress of a salary increase. The issue of congressional salaries is a straightforward one. Many members, being well-to-do, don't need one. But some do. The expenses of maintaining two places of residence—in Washington and at home—make membership in Congress nearly unique and singularly expensive among upper-middle-class American jobs. Here is the point once more: it is a job, requiring skill and dedication to be done properly. Moreover, membership in Congress brings responsibilities. National policy of the scope and scale now encompassed by acts of the federal government requires responsible, dedicated legislators. People with far less serious responsibilities in the private sector are ordinarily paid considerably better than members of Congress. Think, for example, how far down the organizational chart at General Motors or at CBS or at some other large corporation one would have to go before reaching executives making what members of Congress do, and compare their responsibilities with those of Congress and its members. Actually, most corporations won't say what their compensation packages are like. But at a major auto company, people who make around $100,000 a year are no higher than upper middle management, and certainly don't have responsibilities remotely comparable to those of members of Congress.

There is a case for decent congressional salaries to be made on at least two grounds: one is the rough equity or opportunity-cost ground that we ought not financially to penalize people who serve, and the second is the ground of need for those members who have the expense of families or college educations to think of, and who have no extraordinary private means. The long-run national disadvantage of failing to recognize the justice of these claims is of course a Congress deprived of people for whom these claims are exigent, normal middle-class people with family responsibilities and without money of their own. These are not the sorts of people a sane electorate should wish to prevent from serving.

Members of Congress, knowing very well of the irrational hostilities that the proposal of a congressional pay raise can stir up, have taken the unfortunate precaution of holding hostage the salaries of federal judges, who are now ludicrously underpaid by the admittedly opulent standards of the legal profession, and senior civil servants. An unhealthy impasse has been created owing, at bottom, to Congress-bashing of the most unattractive kind, which exploits the ignorance of ordinary citizens of the dimensions of the members' working lives, and incites citizens to a mindless social envy, in which it is assumed that paying a decent professional salary to professional officeholders is automatically some sort of rip-off.

Members of Congress now make about $98,000. The bottom salary for major-league baseball players is $100,000. Some law firms in New York start new graduates of good law schools at $90,000 or more. How can we argue that members of Congress and others at the top of the federal government should not be paid at least a modest premium above these beginners' wages? There is, evidently, no talking sense to the American people on this subject.

I believe we can dismiss out of hand the charge that large numbers of members individually, or Congress collectively, live in a world all their own, divorced from realities of everyday life. The sophomores who have written attacks of this sort in recent years in the *Atlantic, Newsweek,* and elsewhere simply don't know what they are talking about. They abuse their access to large audiences by neglecting to explain the real conditions that govern the lives of members, conditions that provide ample doses of everyday life.

No doubt scandals involving various members have in recent times made Congress as an institution vulnerable to criticism. But much of this criticism is irresponsible and irrelevant. Suppose we were to discover instances of cupidity, unusual sexual activity, and abuses of power among the rather sizable staff of an important daily newspaper? Or a symphony orchestra? Or, God forbid, a university? I suppose that would shake our confidence in at least part of the collective output, but one would hope for relevant discriminations. One might distrust the ticket office, perhaps, but not the symphony's performance of Mozart; the stock tips, perhaps, but not the Washington page; the basketball program, but not the classics department. I do not think that the existence of scandal excuses us from attempting to draw sensible conclusions about institutions and their performance.

This sort of balanced and discriminating analysis isn't what proposals for item vetoes, limitations on terms of service, or depressed rates of pay are all about. They are about the ancient but now slightly shopworn American custom of Congress-bashing.

A commonly held assumption about members of Congress is that their primary incentive is to engage in activities that strengthen their prospects for reelection. David Mayhew, one proponent of this theory, argues in his book *Congress: The Electoral Connection* that both the formal and informal organizations of Congress are oriented principally toward the reelection of its members. For example, the dispersion of committees, which number close to three hundred, maximizes the opportunities of committee chairs to use their power to distribute benefits directly to their districts and states and to take positions on issues that will be appealing to their constituents. Moreover, the weak party structure of Capitol Hill allows individual members to go their own ways in dealing with their diverse constituencies. Unified congressional parties, argues Mayhew, would not allow Congress the necessary flexibility to advertise, claim credit, and take positions to gain electoral support. In the following selection Mayhew illustrates the kinds of activities Senate and House members engage in to maximize their electoral support.

65

CONGRESS: THE ELECTORAL CONNECTION

David R. Mayhew

Whether they are safe or marginal, cautious or audacious, congressmen must constantly engage in activities related to reelection. There will be differences in emphasis, but all members share the root need to do things—indeed, to do things day in and day out during their terms. The next step here is to present a typology, a short list of the *kinds* of activities congressmen find it electorally useful to engage in. The case will be that there are three basic kinds of activities. It will be important to lay them out with some care. . . .

One activity is *advertising*, defined here as any effort to disseminate one's name among constituents in such a fashion as to create a favorable image but in messages having little or no issue content. A successful congressman builds what amounts to a brand name, which may have a generalized electoral value for other politicians in the same family. The personal qualities to emphasize are experience, knowledge, responsiveness, concern, sincerity, independence, and the like. Just getting one's name across is difficult enough; only about half the electorate, if asked, can supply their House members' names. It helps a congressman to be known. "In the main, recognition carries a positive valence; to be perceived at all is to be perceived favorably." A vital advantage enjoyed by House incumbents is that they are much better known among voters than their November challengers. They are better known because they spend a great deal of time, energy, and money trying to make themselves better known. There are standard routines—frequent visits to the constituency, nonpolitical speeches to home audiences, the sending out of infant care booklets and letters of condolence and congratulations. Of 158 House members questioned. . . . 121 said that they regularly sent newsletters to their constituents; 48 wrote separate news or opinion columns for newspapers; 82 regularly reported to their constituencies by radio or television; 89 regularly sent out mail questionnaires. Some routines are less standard. Congressman George E. Shipley (D., Ill.) claims to have met personally about half his constituents (i.e., some 200,000 people). For over twenty years Congressman Charles C. Diggs, Jr. (D., Mich.) has run a radio program featuring himself as a "combination disc jockey–commentator and minister." Congressman Daniel J. Flood (D., Pa.) is "famous for appearing unannounced and often uninvited at wedding anniversaries and other events." Anniversaries and other events aside, congressional advertising is done largely at public expense. Use of the franking privilege has mushroomed in recent years; in early 1973 one estimate predicted that House and Senate members would send out about 476 million pieces of mail in the year 1974, at a public cost of $38.1 million—or about 900,000 pieces per member with a subsidy of $70,000 per member. By far the heaviest mailroom traffic comes in Octobers of even-numbered years. There are some differences between House and Senate members in the ways they go about getting their names across. House members are free to blanket their constituencies with mailings for all boxholders; senators are not. But senators find it easier to appear on national television—for example, in short reaction statements on the nightly news shows. Advertising is a staple congressional activity, and there is no end to it. For each member there are always new voters to be apprised of his worthiness and old voters to be reminded of it.

A second activity may be called *credit claiming,* defined here as acting so as to generate a belief in a relevant political actor (or actors) that one is personally responsible for causing the government, or some unit thereof, to do something that the actor (or actors) considers desirable. The political logic of this, from the congressman's point of view, is that an actor who believes that a member can make pleasing things happen will no doubt wish to keep him in office so that he can make pleasing things happen in the future. The emphasis here is on individual accomplishment (rather than, say, party or governmental accomplishment) and on the congressman as doer (rather than as, say, expounder of constituency views). Credit claiming is highly important to congressmen, with the consequence that much of congressional life is a relentless search for opportunities to engage in it.

Where can credit be found? If there were only one congressman rather than 535, the answer would in principle be simple enough. Credit (or blame) would attach in Downsian fashion to the doing of the government as a whole. But there are 535. Hence it becomes necessary for each congressman to try to peel off pieces of governmental accomplishment for which he can believably generate a sense of responsibility. For the average congressman the staple way of doing this is to traffic in what may be called "particularized benefits." Particularized governmental benefits, as the term will be used here, have two properties: (1) Each benefit is given out to a specific individual, group, or geographical constituency, the recipient unit being of a scale that allows a single congressman to be recognized (by relevant political actors and other congressmen) as the claimant for the benefit (other congressmen being perceived as indifferent or hostile). (2) Each benefit is given out in apparently ad hoc fashion (unlike, say, social security checks) with a congressman apparently having a hand in the allocation. A particularized benefit can normally be regarded as a member of a class. That is, a benefit given out to an individual, group, or constituency can normally be looked upon by congressmen as one of a class of similar benefits given out to sizable numbers of individuals, groups, or constituencies. Hence the impression can arise that a congressman is getting "his share" of whatever it is the government is offering. (The classes may be vaguely defined. Some state legislatures deal in what their members call "local legislation.")

In sheer volume the bulk of particularized benefits come under the heading of "casework"—the thousands of favors congressional offices perform for supplicants in ways that normally do not require legislative action. High school students ask for essay materials, soldiers for emergency leaves, pensioners for location of missing checks, local governments for grant information, and on and on. Each office has skilled professionals who can play the bureaucracy like an organ—pushing the right pedals to produce the desired effects. But many benefits require new legislation, or at least they require important allocative decisions on matters covered by existent legislation. Here the congressman fills the traditional role of supplier of goods to the home district. It is a believable role; when a member claims credit for a benefit on the order of a dam, he may well receive it. Shiny construction projects seem especially useful. . . .

The third activity congressmen engage in may be called *position taking*, defined here as the public enunciation of a judgmental statement on anything likely to be of interest to political actors. The statement may take the form of a roll call vote. The most important classes of judgmental statements are those prescribing American governmental ends (a vote cast against the war; a statement that "the war should be ended immediately") or governmental means (a statement that "the way to end the war is to take it to the United Nations"). The judgments may be implicit rather than explicit, as in: "I will support the president on this matter." But judgments may range far beyond these classes to take in implicit or explicit statements on what almost anybody should do or how he should do it: "The great Polish scientist Copernicus has been unjustly neglected" "The way for Israel to achieve peace is to give up the Sinai." The congressman as position taker is a speaker rather than a doer. The electoral requirement is not that he make pleasing things happen but that he make pleasing judgmental statements. The position itself is the political commodity. Especially on matters where governmental responsibility is widely diffused it is not surprising that political actors should fall back on positions as tests of incumbent virtue. For voters ignorant of congressional processes the recourse is an easy one. The following comment [by a Congressman] is highly revealing: "Recently, I went home and began to talk about the——act. I was pleased to have sponsored that bill, but it soon dawned on me that the point wasn't getting through at all. What was getting through was that the act might be a help to people. I changed the emphasis: I didn't mention my role particularly, but stressed my support of the legislation."

The ways in which positions can be registered are numerous and often imaginative. There are floor addresses ranging from weighty orations to mass-produced "nationality day statements." There are speeches before home groups, television appearances, letters, newsletters, press releases, ghostwritten books, *Playboy* articles, even interviews with political scientists. On occasion congressmen generate what amount to petitions; whether or not to sign the 1956 Southern Manifesto defying school desegregation rulings was an important decision for southern members. Outside the roll call process the congressman is usually able to tailor his positions to suit his audiences. A solid consensus in the constituency calls for ringing declarations. . . .   *All Politics Is Local!*

Probably the best position-taking strategy for most congressmen at most times is to be conservative—to cling to their own positions of the past where possible and to reach for new ones with great caution where necessary. Yet in an earlier discussion of strategy the suggestion was made that it might be rational for members in electoral danger to resort to innovation. The form of innovation available is entrepreneurial position taking, its logic being that for a member facing defeat with his old array of positions it makes good sense to gamble on some new ones. It may be that congressional marginals fulfill an important function here as issue pioneers—experimenters who test out new issues and thereby show other politicians which ones are usable. An example of such a pioneer is Senator Warren Magnuson (D., Wash.), who responded to a surprisingly narrow victory in 1962 by reaching for a reputation in the area of consumer affairs. Another example is Senator Ernest Hollings (D., S.C.), a servant of a shaky and racially heterogeneous southern constituency who launched "hunger" as an issue in 1969—at once pointing to a problem and giving it a useful nonracial definition. One of the most successful issue entrepreneurs of recent decades was the late Senator Joseph McCarthy (R., Wis.); it was all there—the close primary in 1946, the fear of defeat in 1952, the desperate casting about for an issue, the famous 1950 dinner at the Colony Restaurant where suggestions were tendered, the decision that "Communism" might just do the trick.

The effect of position taking on electoral behavior is about as hard to measure as the effect of credit claiming. Once again there is a variance problem; congressmen do not differ very much among themselves in the methods they use or the skills they display in attuning themselves to their diverse constituencies. All of them, after all, are professional politicians. . . .

There can be no doubt that congressmen believe positions make a difference. An important consequence of this belief is their custom of watching each other's elections to try to figure out what positions are salable. Nothing is more important in Capitol Hill politics than the shared conviction that election returns have proven a point. . . .

These, then, are the three kinds of electorally oriented activities congressmen engage in—advertising, credit claiming, and position taking. . . .

David Mayhew's thesis, part of which is presented in the preceding selection, is that the Washington activities of members of Congress are, with few exceptions, geared toward reelection. In contrast, Richard Fenno argues that the Washington careers of members of Congress may or may not be related to reelection. In his early work on Congress, Fenno pointed out that the *incentives* of members of Congress fall generally into three categories: (1) reelection, (2) internal power and influence on Capitol Hill, and (3) good public policy. While the incentives of House and Senate members cannot always be placed neatly into one of these categories, Fenno's research suggested that the behavior of members in *Congress* tends to be dominated by one of these incentives.[3]

Committee selection, in particular, is made to advance reelection, increase power and status on Capitol Hill, or make a good public policy. For example, such committees as Interior and Insular Affairs in the House serve the reelection incentives of their members by channeling specific benefits, such as water and conservation projects, into their districts. Members seeking influence in the House prefer such committees as Ways and Means and Appropriations, both of which reflect the role of the House in the constitutional system and represent it in the outside world. Representatives on the Ways and Means and the Appropriations committees, particularly the chairs and ranking minority members, can use their positions effectively to bolster their reputations for power in the House. "Good public policy" committees are those that are used to reflect ideological viewpoints, such as the House Education and Labor Committee, rather than to give particular benefits to constituents or to augment internal influence.

While members of Congress have varying degrees of success in their pursuit of internal power and good public policy, they are overwhelmingly successful in achieving reelection. The power of incumbency is truly formidable. Over 95 percent of House incumbents are regularly reelected, usually by margins in excess of 55 percent and frequently without opposition. Senators are somewhat more vulnerable than representatives, for Senate seats are attractive targets of opportunity for political parties, interest groups, and ambitious politicians. Nevertheless, Senate incumbents, too, have great advantages over challengers, and normally well over 80 percent of them are easily reelected. Certainly, as David Mayhew points out in selection 65, members of Congress have shaped the legislative environment to enhance their reelection prospects.

Generally, as members of Congress gain seniority, their Washington careers become separated from their constituency activities. The incumbency effect, buttressed by an effective organization within their constituency, leaves them free to pursue goals on Capitol Hill that are not specifically for the purpose of gaining votes. In the following selection Richard Fenno discusses the linkage between the constituency and Washington activities of House and Senate members.

---

[3]Richard F. Fenno, Jr., *Congressmen in Committees* (Boston: Little, Brown and Co., 1973).

66

HOME STYLE AND WASHINGTON CAREER

Richard F. Fenno, Jr.

∾

. . . When we speak of constituency careers, we speak primarily of the pursuit of the goal of reelection. When we speak of Washington careers, we speak primarily of the pursuit of the goals of influence in the House and the making of good public policy. Thus the intertwining of careers is, at bottom, an intertwining of member goals.

So long as they are in the expansionist stage of their constituency careers, House members will be especially attentive to their home base. They will pursue the goal of reelection with single-minded intensity and will allocate their resources disproportionately to that end. . . . [F]irst-term members go home more frequently, place a larger proportion of their staff in the district, and more often leave their families at home than do their senior colleagues. Building a reelection constituency at home and providing continuous access to as much of that constituency as possible requires time and energy. Inevitably, these are resources that might otherwise be allocated to efforts in Washington. "The trouble is," said one member near the end of his second term,

> I haven't been a congressman yet. The first two years, I spent all of my time getting myself reelected. The last two years, I spent getting myself a district so that I could get reelected. So I won't be a congressman until next year.

By being "a congressman" he means pursuing goals above and beyond that of reelection (i.e., power in the House and good public policy).

In a House member's first years, the opportunities for gaining inside power and policy influence are limited. Time and energy and staff can be allocated to home without an acute sense of conflict. At rates that vary from congressman to congressman, however, the chances to have some institutional or legislative effect improve. As members stretch to avail themselves of the opportunity, they may begin to experience some allocative strain. It requires time and energy to develop a successful career in Washington just as it does to develop a successful career in the district. Because it may not be possible to allocate these resources to House and home, each to an optimal degree, members may have to make allocative and goal choices.

A four-term congressman with a person-to-person home style described the dilemma of choice:

> I'm beginning to be a little concerned about my political future. I can feel myself getting into what I guess is a natural and inevitable condition—the gradual erosion of my local orientation. I'm not as enthused about tending my constituency relations as I used to be and I'm not paying them the attention I should be. There's a natural tension between being a good representative and taking an interest in government. I'm getting into some heady things in Washington, and I want to make an input into the government. It's making me a poorer representative than I was. I find myself avoiding the personal collisions that arise in the constituency—turning away from that one last handshake, not bothering to go to that one last meeting. I find myself forgetting people's names. And I find myself caring less about it than I used to. Right now, it's just a feeling I have. In eight years I have still to come home less than forty weekends a year. This is my thirty-sixth trip this year. What was it Arthur Rubinstein said? "If I miss one practice, I notice it. If I miss two practices, my teacher notices it. If I miss a week of practice, my audience notices it." I'm at stage one right now—or maybe stage one and stage two. But I'm beginning to feel that I could be defeated before long. And I'm not going to change. I don't want the status. I want to contribute to government.

The onset of a Washington career is altering his personal goals and his established home style. He is worried about the costs of the change; but he is willing to accept some loss of reelection support in exchange for his increased influence in Congress.

The dilemma faces every member of Congress. It is built into the twin requirements that Congress be a representative and a legislative institution. Some members believe they can achieve reelection at home together with influence or policy in Washington without sacrificing either. During Congressman O's first year as a subcommittee chairman, I asked him whether his new position would make it more difficult to tend to district matters. He replied,

> If you mean, am I getting Potomac fever, the answer is, no. If you mean, has the change in my official duties here made me a better congressman, the answer is, yes. If you mean has it taken away from my activity in the constituency, the answer is no.

Congressman O, we recall, has been going home less; but he has been increasing the number and the activity of his district staff. Although he speaks confidently of his allocative solution, he is not unaware of potential problems. "My staff operation runs by itself. They don't need me. Maybe I should worry about that. You aren't going back and say I'm ripe for the plucking are you? I don't think I am."

A three-term member responded very positively when I paraphrased the worries of the congressman friend of his who had quoted Arthur Rubinstein:

> You can do your job in Washington and in your district if you know how. My quarrel with [the people like him] of this world is that they don't learn to be good politicians before they get to Congress. They get there because some people are sitting around the table one day and ask them to do it. They're smart, but they don't

learn to organize a district. Once you learn to do that, it's much easier to do your job in Washington.

This member, however, has not yet tasted the inside influence of his friend. Moreover, he does not always talk with such assurance. His district is not so well organized that he has reduced his personal attentiveness to it.

> Ralph Krug [the congressman in the adjacent district] tells me I spoil my constituents. He says, "You've been elected twice, you know your district; once a month is enough to come home." But that's not my philosophy. Maybe it will be someday. . . . My lack of confidence is still a pressure which brings me home. This is my political base. Washington is not my political base. I feel I have to come home to get nourished, to see for myself what's going on. It's my security blanket—coming home.

For now, he feels no competing pulls; but he is not unaware of his friend's dilemma.

Members pose the dilemma with varying degrees of immediacy. No matter how confident members may be of their ability to pursue their Washington and their constituency careers simultaneously, however, they all recognize the potentiality of conflict and worry about coping with it. It is our guess that the conflict between the reelection goal on the one hand and the power or policy goals on the other hand becomes most acute for members as they near the peak of influence internally. For, at this stage of their Washington career, the resource requirements of the Washington job make it nearly impossible to meet established expectations of attentiveness at home. Individuals who want nothing from their Washington careers except the status of being a member of Congress will never pursue any other goal except reelection. For these people, the dilemma of which we speak is minimal. Our concern is with those individuals who find, sooner or later, that they wish to pursue a mix of goals in which reelection must be weighed along with power or policy.

One formula for managing a mix of goals that gives heavy weight to a Washington career is to make one's influence in Washington the centerpiece of home style. The member says, in effect, "I can't come home to present myself in person as much as I once did, because I'm so busy tending to the nation's business; but my seniority, my influence, my effectiveness in Washington is of great benefit to you." He asks his supportive constituents to adopt a new set of expectations, one that would put less of a premium on access. Furthermore, he asks these constituents to remain sufficiently intense in their support to discourage challengers—especially those who will promise access. All members do some of this when they explain their Washington activity—especially in connection with "explaining power." And, where possible, they quote from favorable national commentary in their campaign literature. But [very few Congressmen] have made Washington influence the central element of [their] home style.

One difficulty of completely adopting such a home style is that the powerful Washington legislator can actually get pretty far out of touch with his supportive constituents back home. One of the more senior members of [Congress], and a leader of his committee, recounted the case when his preoccupation with an internal legislative impasse affecting Israel caused him to neglect the crucial Jewish element of his primary constituency—a group "who contribute two-thirds of my money." A member of the committee staff had devised an amendment to break the deadlock.

> Peter Tompkins looked at it and said to me, "Why don't we sponsor it?" So we put it forward, and it became known as the Crowder-Tompkins Amendment. I did it because I respected the staff man who suggested it and because I wanted to get something through that was reasonable. Well, a member of the committee called people back home and said, "Crowder is selling out." All hell broke loose. I started getting calls at two and three in the morning from my friends asking me what I was doing. So I went back home and discussed the issue with them. When I walked into the room, it made me feel sad and shocked to feel their hostility. They wanted me to know that they would clobber me if they thought I was selling out. Two hours later, we walked out friends again. I dropped the Crowder-Tompkins Amendment. That's the only little flare up I've ever had with the Jewish community. But it reminded me of their sensitivity to anything that smacks of discrimination.

The congressman survived. But he would not have needed so forceful a reminder of his strongest supporters' concerns were he nearer the beginning of his constituency career. But, of course, neither would he have been a committee leader, and neither would the imperatives of a House career bulked so large in his mix of goals.

Another way to manage conflicting reelection and Washington career goals might be to use one's Washington influence to alter support patterns at home. That is, instead of acting—as is the normal case—to reenforce home support, to keep what he had "last time," the congressman might act to displace that old support with compensating new support. He might even accomplish this inadvertently, should his pursuit of power or policy attract, willy-nilly, constituents who welcome his new mix of goals. The very Washington activity that left him out of touch with previously supportive constituents might put him in touch with newly supportive ones. A newly acquired position of influence in a particular policy area or a new reputation as an effective legislator might produce such a feedback effect. . . .

. . . [There is] a tendency for successful home styles to harden over time and to place stylistic constraints on the congressman's subsequent behavior. The pursuit of a Washington career helps us explain this constituency phenomenon. That is, to the degree that a congressman pursues power or policy goals in the House, he will have that much less time or energy to devote to the consideration of alternative home styles. His predisposition to "do what we did last time" at home will be further strengthened by his growing preoccupation with Washington matters. Indeed, the speed with which a congressman begins to develop a Washington career will affect the speed with which his home style solidifies. . . .

In all of this speculation about career linkages, we have assumed that most members of Congress develop, over time, a mix of personal goals. We particularly assume that most members will trade off some of their personal commitment to reelection in order to satisfy a personal desire for institutional or policy influence. It is our observation . . . that House members do, in fact, exhibit varying degrees of commitment to reelection. All want reelection in the abstract, but not all will pay any price to achieve it; nor will all pay the same price. . . .

One senior member contemplated retirement in the face of an adverse redistricting but, because he had the prospect of a committee chairmanship, he decided to run and hope for the best. He wanted reelection because he wanted continued influence; but he was unwilling to put his present influence in jeopardy by pursuing reelection with the same intensity that marked his earlier constituency career. As he put it,

> Ten years ago, I whipped another redistricting. And I did it by neglecting my congressional duties. . . . Today I don't have the time, and I'm not going to neglect my duties. . . . If I do what is necessary to get reelected and thus become chairman of the committee, I will lose the respect and confidence of my fellow committee members because of being absent from the hearings and, occasionally, the votes.

He did not work hard at reelection, and he won by his narrowest margin ever. But he succeeded in sustaining a mix of personal goals very different from an earlier one. . . .

The congressman's home activities are more difficult and taxing than we have previously recognized. Under the best of circumstances, the tension involved in maintaining constituency contact and achieving legislative competence is considerable. Members cannot be in two places at once, and the growth of a Washington career exacerbates the problem. But, more than that, the demands in both places have grown recently. The legislative workload and the demand for legislative expertise are steadily increasing. So is the problem of maintaining meaningful contact with their several constituencies. Years ago, House members returned home for months at a time to live among their supportive constituencies, soak up the home atmosphere, absorb local problems at first hand. Today, they race home for a day, a weekend, a week at a time. [Few] maintain a family home in their district. [Many] stay with relatives or friends or in barely furnished rooms when they are at home. The citizen demand for access, for communication, and for the establishment of trust is as great as ever. So members go home. But the quality of their contact has suffered. "It's like a one-night stand in a singles bar." It is harder to sustain a genuine two-way communication than it once was. House member worries about the home relationship—great under any circumstances, but greater now—contribute to the strain and frustration of the job. Some cope; but others retire. It may be those members who cannot stand the heat of the home relationship who are getting out of the House kitchen. If so, people prepared to be more attentive to home . . . are likely to replace them.

The interplay between home careers and Washington careers continues even as House members leave Congress. For, in retirement or in defeat, they still face a choice—to return home or to remain in Washington. The subject of post-congressional careers is too vast to be treated here. But students of home politics can find, in these choices, indications of the depth and durability of home attachments in the face of influential Washington careers. It is conventional wisdom in the nation's capital that senators and representatives "get Potomac fever" and that "they don't go back to Pocatello" when their legislative careers end. Having pursued the goals of power and policy in Washington with increasing success, they prefer, it is said, to continue their Washington career in some nonlegislative job rather than to go back home. In such a choice, perhaps, we might find the ultimate displacement of the constituency career with the Washington career.

An examination of the place of residence of 370 individuals who left the House between 1954 and 1974, and who were alive in 1974, sheds considerable doubt on this Washington wisdom. It appears that most House members do, indeed, "go back to Pocatello." Of the 370 former members studied, 253 (68 percent) resided in their home states in 1974; 91 lived in the Washington, D.C., area; and 26 resided someplace else. Of those 344 who chose either Washington or home, therefore, nearly three-quarters chose home. This simple fact underscores the very great strength of the home attachments we have described in this [selection].

No cross section of living former members will tell us for sure how many members lingered in Washington for a while before eventually returning home. Only a careful tracing of all individual cases, therefore, will give us a full and accurate description of the Washington-home choice. Even so, among the former members most likely to be attracted to Washington—those who left Congress from 1970 to 1974—only 37 percent have chosen to remain there. A cursory glance at all those who have chosen to prolong their Washington careers, however, tell us what we might expect—that they have already had longer congressional careers than those who returned home. Our data also tell us that these members are younger than those who choose to return home. Thus, we speculate, the success of a member's previous career in Congress and the prospect that he or she still has time to capitalize on that success in the Washington community are positive inducements to stay. And these inducements seem unaffected by the manner of his or her leaving Congress—whether by electoral defeat (for renomination or reelection) or retirement. Those who were defeated, however, had shorter congressional careers and were younger than those who had voluntarily retired.

Congress and Interest Groups

The Madisonian model designed a bicameral Congress to represent the people in the House and the states in the Senate. Checks and balances between the two congressional branches balance popular and group interests as the House and the Senate must work together to make laws. The following selection analyzes interest group power on Capitol Hill and concludes that a decentralized Congress characterized by weak congressional parties, committee dominance, and reliance on staff gives interest groups direct access to legislative power.

—— 67 ——

CONGRESS AND ORGANIZED INTERESTS

Roger H. Davidson and Walter J. Oleszek

A subcommittee markup of the House Banking Committee attracted scores of lobbyists representing Wall Street and other interests. Early each morning before a scheduled markup session, people formed long lines outside the meeting room for the limited number of seats. "Places on the line [were] being held for lobbyists by some people being paid almost $20 an hour."

Capitol Hill lobbyists regularly fill committee hearings and markups, jam into conference committee rooms, and pack House and Senate galleries. These emissaries of organized interests do more than observe congressional events. They wield their vast resources money, personnel, information, and organization—to win passage of legislation they favor and to reward the politicians who help them. Practically every major corporation, trade association, and professional group has Washington lobbyists. They even have their own associations: the American Society of Association Executives and the American League of Lobbyists. Like many other groups, both are based in Washington, D.C., where more national associations are located than in any other city

Looking in the Washington telephone directory under "associations" reveals as much about what moves Congress as the Constitution does. More than 80,000 employees work for various associations. Numerous law firms have moved to the District of Columbia, and growing cadres of consultants and lawyers represent diverse clients, including foreign governments. In the decade from 1973 to 1993 membership in the District of Columbia Bar Association soared from 11,000 to more than 59,000.

A Nation of Joiners

The American penchant for joining groups was observed long ago by the French chronicler Alexis de Tocqueville. Americans of all "conditions, minds, and ages, daily acquire a general taste for association and grow accustomed to the use of it," he wrote in 1825. During the 1990s about 65 percent of the population belonged to at least one organization. There are scholars, however, who worry about the apparent decline of people's "civic engagement" and point to signs of slumping memberships

Table 12.1 Membership in Various Groups, 1980–1994

Percentage of population who belong Organization	1980	1984	1988	1991	1994
Church affiliated groups	30.0	33.3	34.3	33.2	33.3
Sports groups	17.0	21.1	19.5	17.5	21.5
Labor unions	13.0	14.1	12.8	9.6	11.7
Professional or academic societies	12.8	15.3	13.5	16.3	18.6
Fraternal groups	10.4	9.1	8.4	9.0	10.0
School service groups	9.9	12.2	12.4	14.3	16.0
Service clubs	8.9	10.4	11.0	8.9	10.0
Hobby or garden clubs	8.4	8.8	10.3	10.8	9.2
Literary, art, discussion or study groups	8.4	8.7	8.5	9.2	9.8
Youth groups	8.0	9.4	10.7	8.6	10.4
Veterans groups	7.4	6.9	8.4	7.0	7.8
School fraternities or sororities	4.2	5.8	4.3	4.7	5.7
Farm organizations	4.0	4.2	3.4	3.2	3.7
Political clubs	3.1	3.9	4.4	3.7	4.7
Nationality organizations	2.5	3.3	2.2	4.5	3.5

Source: National Opinion Research Center, General Social Surveys, 1972–1994: Cumulative Codebook, November 1994, 299—302. Data compiled by Royce Crocker, Congressional Research Service.

in "all sorts of groups." Table 12.1 lists some of the more popular types of groups that people join, such as church, sports, or service organizations.

Not all groups seek to influence congressional policy making, but each has the right to do so. The First Amendment protects the people's right to "petition the Government for a redress of grievances." Throughout American history groups speaking for different subsets of "the people" have swayed

In 1994 only half the sample was asked the questions about membership. In other years the full sample was asked the questions. . . .

A free society nurtures politically active groups. "Liberty is to faction what air is to fire," wrote James Madison in *The Federalist, Number 10*. Until recent years national policy making was dominated by a few well-organized, well-financed groups: farm, labor, business, veterans, and medical interests. The current era has seen an explosion in the growth and diversity of interest groups, including narrow based groups that focus on single issues such as abortion or gun control.

Many factors account for the proliferation of interest groups: social and economic complexity, the surge in scientific and technological developments, the government's regulatory role, the competition for scarce federal dollars, and the diffusion of power in Congress and throughout the government, which enhances access for outside interests. Not long ago, for instance, the American Medical Association dominated health lobbying. Today, with health care reform high on the national agenda, hundreds of health advocacy groups woo lawmakers and orchestrate grassroots efforts. In 1975 there were about 90 health groups; today there are nearly 750. "You name a disease, there's probably a Washington lobby for it," said an official of the American Heart Association.

Pressure Group Methods

Groups have influenced congressional decisions from the beginning. During the nation's early technological and industrial expansion, railroad interests lobbied for federal funds and land grants to build their routes. Some of the lobbyists' tactics—offering bribes, for example—helped foster the traditional public suspicion of pressure tactics. In 1874 Sen. Simon Cameron, R-Pa., described an honest politician as one who "when he is bought, stays bought" (or stays "rented" with a long lease). Samuel Ward, the "king of the lobby" for fifteen years after the Civil War, once wrote to his friend Henry Wadsworth Longfellow:

> When I see you again I will tell you how a client, eager to prevent the arrival at a committee of a certain member before it should adjourn, offered me $5,000 to accomplish this purpose, which I did, by having [the congressman's] boots mislaid while I smoked a cigar and condoled with him until they could be found at 11:45. I had the satisfaction of a good laugh [and] a good fee in my pocket.

Lobbying methods during the twentieth century became more varied, urbane, and subtle. But the move from limited government to big government deepened the mutual dependence of legislators and lobbyists. . . .

Groups' modern-day methods vary according to the nature and visibility of the issue and the groups' resources. As Table 12.2 reveals, there is no dearth of techniques by which groups can influence Congress. Among the most important practices are direct and social lobbying, group alliances, and grassroots support.

These diverse techniques typically overlap. For example, a small group of business lobbyists meet privately every Thursday (the "Thursday Group") with House Republican Conference chairman John Boehner of Ohio to formulate strategy to advance GOP issues and goals. The lobbyists then work to mobilize grassroots support for the GOP initiatives.

Direct Lobbying

In the traditional method of direct lobbying, lobbyists present their client's case directly to members and congressional staff. (This method is likely to become less prevalent than it used to be: in 1995 the House and Senate banned members from accepting most gifts including meals—except in specific circumstances.) An aide to former Speaker Thomas P. "Tip" O'Neill, Jr., explained the importance of the personal touch:

> (Lobbyists] know members of Congress are here three nights a week, alone, without their families. So they say, "Let's have dinner. Let's go see a ballgame." Schmooze with them. Make friends. And they don't lean on it all the time. Every once in a while, they call up maybe once or twice a year, ask a few questions. . . . Anne Wexler [a former official in the Carter White House, now a lobbyist] will call up and spend half an hour talking about . . . politics, and suddenly she'll pop a question, pick up something. They want that little bit of access.

Table 12.2 Lobbying Techniques Used by 174 Sampled Interest Groups

Technique	Percentage of groups that use technique
Testify at hearings	99
Contact government officials directly to present your point of view	98
Engage in informal contacts with officials at conventions, over lunch, etc.	95
Present research results or technical information	92
Send letters to members of your organization to inform them about your activities	92
Enter into coalitions with other organizations	90
Attempt to shape the implementation of policies	89
Talk with people from the press and the media	86
Consult with government officials to plan legislative strategy	85
Help to draft legislation	85
Inspire letter-writing or telegram campaigns	84
Shape the government's agenda by raising new issues and calling attention to previously ignored problems	84
Mount grassroots lobbying efforts	80
Have influential constituents contact their congressman's office	80
Help to draft regulations, rules, or guidelines	78
Serve on advisory commissions and boards	76
Alert congressmen to the effects of a bill on their districts	75
File suit or otherwise engage in litigation	72
Make financial contributions to electoral campaigns	58
Do favors for officials who need assistance	56
Attempt to influence appointments to public office	53
Publicize candidates' voting records	44
Engage in direct-mail fund raising for your organization	44
Run advertisements in the media about your position on issues	31
Contribute work or personnel to electoral campaigns	24
Make public endorsements of candidates for office	22
Engage in protests or demonstrations	20

Source: Kay Lehman Schlozman and John I. Tierney, *Organized Interests and American Democracy* (New York: Harper and Row, 1986), 150.

> That's what does it. You can hear it. It clicks home. They'll call their chief executive officer, and they've delivered. That's how it works. It's not illegal. They work on a personal basis.

Hollywood movie stars, the sons and daughters of powerful members, former staff aides, and some former members of Congress are particularly effective at direct lobbying. "Since I will continue to be active in the Congressional Prayer Breakfast Group, in the House gym, the members' Dining Room and on the House Floor, I will maintain contact with my good friends who affect legislation," a just-retired representative of twenty years wrote in a letter to prospective clients. He promised to "unravel red tape, open doors, make appointments, work with the Administration or government agencies, influence legislation, and assist in any other service required.

Member-to-member lobbying can be uniquely effective: no outsider has the same access to lawmakers (or to certain areas of Congress) that other colleagues have. But some members are offended by the entree that former legislators who are lobbyists have to the floor and to other Capitol Hill locations not generally open to the public. Since 1991 former lawmakers are prohibited for one year from lobbying members of Congress directly, although they may plan strategy and advise others who do lobby members.

Direct lobbying takes many forms. Lobbyists monitor committees and testify at hearings; interpret Hill decisions to clients and clients' interests to legislators; perform services, such as writing speeches for members; and give campaign assistance. The House offers more occasions for contacting members directly than does the Senate, where lobbyists are more likely to target the staff who surround each member. "Essentially, we operate as an extension of congressmen's staff," explained one lobbyist. "Occasionally we come up with the legislation, or speeches and questions [for lawmakers to ask at hearings] all the time. We look at it as providing staff work for allies." Or, as one of Washington's premier lobbyists, Thomas Hale Boggs, Jr. (son of former House majority leader Hale Boggs, D-La., and former representative Lindy Boggs, D-La.), explained, "Congressional staffs are overworked and underpaid. Lobbyists help fill the information vacuum."

The direct approach has limitations, however. From the client's perspective, rapid turnover in Congress weakens a lobbyist's personal rapport with members. From the legislator's perspective, it is sometimes unclear whether a lobbyist actually "speaks" for an organization. A classic example is illustrated by the Medicare Catastrophic Coverage Act of 1988. The legislation, designed to defray certain medical costs for the elderly, was strongly endorsed by lobbyists for the American Association of Retired Persons (AARP). A year after passing the law, however, Congress was compelled to repeal it when a grassroots rebellion was waged by many elderly people who opposed paying higher Medicare premiums.

Nonetheless, lobbyists are major players in congressional policymaking. "Lobbyists contribute a lot to democracy," stated Rep. James F. Moran, D-Va. "They provide continuity and institutional memory. Most of them have been around longer than members."

Social Lobbying

Although the Washington social circuit is vastly overrated, some lobbyists gain access to members at dinner parties or receptions. "When you want to make an end run, meet someone at a party," explained an experienced power dealer. "Another option is for lobbyists to play cards with lawmakers who sit on committees with jurisdiction over issues important to their clients."

Because of the public's clamor and members' concern about free gifts, meals, and trips from lobbyists, the House and Senate in 1995 imposed tighter restrictions on gift giving. "By themselves, gifts and meals are not sufficient to corrupt the whole System," remarked Sen. Russell Feingold, D-Wis. "But they create a psychological feeling that you are obliged. Somebody might not be aware of it, but I think it does have that effect."

Under the amended House rules, virtually all gifts—free meals, free trips, and free presents—are banned. Only six representatives voted against the gift ban, in part because they believed it was unnecessary. "If people think their representatives are so easily corruptible [by accepting a free lunch or dinner from lobbyists], they shouldn't elect them," said Rep. Chaka Fattah, D-Pa. "I think this [gift ban] is incriminating to our integrity." The Senate's new rules include a number of exceptions for meals and gifts.

A variation on social lobbying is offering legislators speaking fees (honoraria). Although lawmakers are now banned by law from pocketing honoraria, they still may accept speaking fees that they donate to charities. . . .

Regulation of Lobbying

For more than 100 years Congress intermittently considered ways to regulate lobbying, a right, as noted earlier, protected by the First Amendment: "the right of the people . . . to petition the Government for a redress of grievances." Not until 1946, however, did Congress enact its first comprehensive lobbying law: the Federal Regulation of Lobbying Act (Title III of the Legislative Reorganization Act of that year). This law's ineffectiveness finally led to passage of the Lobby Disclosure Act of 1995.

The 1946 Lobbying Law

The main objective of the 1946 act was to disclose lobbying activities to the public. Persons trying to influence Congress were required to register with the clerk of the House or the secretary of the Senate and to report quarterly on the amount of money received and spent for lobbying. The law's authors, although loath to propose direct control of lobbying, believed that "professionally inspired efforts to put pressure upon Congress cannot be conducive to well-considered legislation." Hence the law stressed registration and reporting. . . .

The lobby law soon proved ineffective, however. In 1954 the Supreme Court upheld its constitutionality, but the decision (*United States v. Harriss*) significantly weakened the law. First, the Court said that only lobbyists paid to represent someone else must register, exempting lobbyists who spent their own money. Second, the Court held that registration applied only to persons whose "principal purpose" was to influence legislation. As a result, many trade associations, labor unions, professional organizations, Consumer groups, and Washington lawyers avoided registering because lobbying was not their principal purpose. Some lobbyists even claimed immunity from the law on the pretext that their job was to inform—not influence—legislators. Finally, the Court held that the act applied only to lobbyists who contacted members directly. This interpretation excluded lobbying activities that generated grassroots pressure on Congress.

Lawmakers tried repeatedly to plug the loopholes of the 1946 law. These attempts foundered largely because it was difficult to regulate lobbying without trespassing on citizens' rights to contact their elected representatives. Practical and political obstacles also hampered revision of the law. For example, there was no consensus on a threshold to trigger stricter registration and reporting requirements, such as the number of hours or days spent lobbying or the amount of money expended during a quarter.

Finally, after repeated efforts to "change the way Washington does business," a campaign theme advocated by many members, including the assertive GOP freshmen in the 104th Congress, the two parties came together to enact the first major overhaul of the 1946 act. Speaker Gingrich and President Clinton, at a June 11, 1995, rally in New Hampshire, had shaken hands and promised to propose campaign finance and lobby reforms. The latter, but not the former, was enacted into law.

The Lobby Disclosure Act of 1995

Under the Lobby Disclosure Act of 1995, which took effect in 1996, new rules apply to lobbyists. . . . Significantly, the law broadened the definition of people who must register as lobbyists (anyone who spends one-fifth of his or her time trying to influence lawmakers, their aides, or high executive officials). Lobbyists are required to "provide semiannual disclosures showing who their clients are, what policies they are trying to influence and roughly how much money they are spending for lobbying. Civil fines of up to $50,000 could be imposed on those who fail to comply. Grassroots lobbying is exempt from the law as are lobbyists paid $5,000 or less semiannually and organizations that use their own employees to lobby.

The new law also prohibits lobbying by certain nonprofit groups that receive federal contracts. . . .

The 1995 law also amended the Foreign Agents Registration Act of 1938. The 1938 law requires those who lobby on behalf of foreign governments or political parties to register with the Department of Justice. . . .

With the ink hardly dry on the 1995 law, some members began proposing even tougher disclosure requirements for lobbyists. One measure would prohibit lawmakers and high federal officials from representing foreign entities after they leave office. It also would impose penalties on interest groups that falsify names on letters and telegrams to members. "We will look at the main issue areas," Rep. Charles Canady, R-Fla., said: "Representing foreign interests, revolving door, astroturf lobbying—the misrepresentation of the identification of a person communicating with members."

Conclusion

From the nation's beginning, lobbying and lawmaking have been twin phenomena. Lobbying "has been so deeply woven into the American political fabric that one could, with considerable justice, assert that the history of lobbying comes close to being the history of American legislation."

Recent years have witnessed an explosion in the number and types of groups organized to pursue their ends on Capitol Hill. Compared with a decade ago, there are more industry associations, public affairs lobbies (such as Common Cause), single-issue groups, political action committees, and agents representing foreign governments. Some of these groups employ new grassroots lobbying techniques. Many victories today are won in Washington because of sophisticated lobbying campaigns back in home states or districts.

No one questions that groups and lobbyists have a rightful public role, but some aspects of lobbying warrant concern. Groups push Congress to pass laws that benefit the few and not the many. They exaggerate their members' views and hinder compromise. They frequently misrepresent members' voting records in their rating schemes and pour money into campaigns of their allies (mainly incumbents). Lawmakers who defy single issue groups find at election time that these organizations pull out all the stops to defeat them.

Built-in checks constrain group pressures, however. First, there often are competing groups on any issue, and legislators can play one off against the other. Second, knowledgeable staff aides can forearm members to counter the lobbyists' arguments. Lawmakers' own expertise is still another informal check on lobbyists. Finally, there are self-imposed constraints. Lobbyists who misrepresent issues or mislead members soon find their access permanently closed off.

The political atmosphere also constrains the influence of groups. When the GOP controlled Congress launched efforts to slash or eliminate federal social programs, there was initially relatively little response from liberal advocacy groups. "Fifteen years ago, if there was a proposal to take $40 out of some demonstration project here on the Senate floor, there would be 40 representatives of various advocacy groups outside," charged Sen. Daniel Patrick Moynihan, D-N.Y. Now "there are very few advocacy groups outside" protecting the interests of children or the helpless."

Stung by Senator Moynihan's challenge, many liberal groups found their voices and mounted a counteroffensive to the GOP assault on the welfare state. External threats, after all, are a powerful stimulus for group formation and mobilization as David B. Truman taught us more than forty years ago. Still, the politics of the moment presented many obstacles to groups associated with "liberal" government programs. Some maintain that conservative groups have the offensive momentum while liberal groups are forced to play defense. Others say there are so many legislative battles to fight on Capitol Hill that liberal groups cannot muster forceful opposition. Still others suggest that it is difficult to arouse public support for many of these programs when citizens have little faith in the national government's capacity to perform either efficiently or in a cost effective manner. "The larger story is that this is a time when Americans doubt the ability of the government to do anything, so it's hard to rally public support," said John Rolher, legislative director of the American Association of Retired Persons.

Many interest groups are especially active when government funding for their programs is under review. During the struggle between Congress and the White House to reach a balanced-budget accord in late 1995 and early 1996, lawmakers and the president mobilized supporters to convince the public that their fiscal approach represented the best choice for the nation.

CHAPTER 9

THE JUDICIARY

An independent judicial system is an important part of constitutional government. The United States Supreme Court was created with this view, and its members were given life tenure and guaranteed compensation to maintain their independence. However, Congress was given power to structure the entire subordinate judicial system, including control over the appellate jurisdiction of the Supreme Court. Regardless of any initial lack of power and various attempts made by and through Congress to curb its power, the Supreme Court today occupies a predominant position in the governmental system. The evolution of the Court, its present powers, and their implications are analyzed in this chapter.

Constitutional Background: Judicial Independence and Judicial Review

The Supreme Court and the judicial system play important roles in the intricate separation-of-powers scheme. Through judicial review, both legislative and executive decisions may be overruled by the courts for a number of reasons. To some extent, then, the judiciary acts as a check upon arbitrary action by governmental departments and agencies. The intent of the framers of the Constitution regarding the role of the judiciary, particularly the Supreme Court, in our governmental system is examined in *Federalist 78*.

68

FEDERALIST 78

Alexander Hamilton

We proceed now to an examination of the judiciary department of the proposed government.

In unfolding the defects of the existing confederation, the utility and necessity of a federal judicature have been clearly pointed out. It is the less necessary to recapitulate the considerations there urged; as the propriety of the institution in the abstract is not disputed; the only questions which have been raised being relative to the manner of constituting it, and to its extent. To these points, therefore, our observations shall be confined.

The manner of constituting it seems to embrace these several objects: 1st. The mode of appointing the judges; 2nd. The tenure by which they are to hold their places; 3rd. The partition of the judiciary authority between different courts, and their relations to each other.

First

As to the mode of appointing the judges: This is the same with that of appointing the officers of the union in general, and has been so fully discussed . . . that nothing can be said here which would not be useless repetition.

Second

As to the tenure by which the judges are to hold their places: This chiefly concerns their duration in office; the provisions for their support; the precautions for their responsibility.

According to the plan of the convention, all the judges who may be appointed by the United States are to hold their offices *during good behavior*; which is conformable to the most approved of the state constitutions. . . . The standard of good behavior for the continuance in office of the judicial magistracy is certainly one of the most valuable of the modern improvements in the practice of government. In a monarchy, it is an excellent barrier to the despotism of the prince; in a republic, it is a no less excellent barrier to the encroachments and oppressions of the representative body. And it is the best expedient which can be devised in any government, to secure a steady, upright, and impartial administration of the laws.

Whoever attentively considers the different departments of power must perceive, that, in a government in which they are separated from each other, the judiciary, from the nature of its functions, will always be the least dangerous to the political rights of the constitution; because it will be least in a capacity to annoy or injure them. The executive not only dispenses the honors, but holds the sword of the community. The legislature not only commands the purse, but prescribes the rules by which the duties and rights of every citizen are to be regulated. The judiciary, on the contrary, has no influence over either the sword or the purse; no direction either of the strength or of the wealth of the society; and can take no active resolution whatever. It may truly be said to have neither FORCE NOR WILL, but merely judgment; and must ultimately depend upon the aid of the executive arm for the efficacious exercise even of this faculty.

This simple view of the matter suggests several important consequences: It proves incontestably, that the judiciary is beyond comparison, the weakest of the three departments of power, that it can never attack with success either of the other two; and that all possible care is requisite to enable it to defend itself against their attacks. It equally proves, that, though individual oppression may now and then proceed from the courts of justice, the general liberty of the people can never be endangered from that quarter; I mean so long as the judiciary remains truly distinct from both the legislature and executive. For I agree, that "there is no liberty, if the power of judging be not separated from the legislative and executive powers." It proves, in the last place, that as liberty can have nothing to fear from the judiciary alone, but would have everything to fear from its union with either of the other departments; that, as all the effects of such a union must ensue from a dependence of the former on the latter, notwithstanding a nominal and apparent separation; that as, from the natural feebleness of the judiciary, it is in continual jeopardy of being overpowered, awed or influenced by its coordinate branches; that, as nothing can contribute so much to its firmness and independence as PERMANENCY IN OFFICE, this quality may therefore be justly regarded as an indispensable ingredient in its constitution; and, in a great measure, as the CITADEL of the public justice and the public security.

The complete independence of the courts of justice is peculiarly essential in a limited constitution. By a limited constitution, I understand one which contains certain specified exceptions to the legislative no ex post facto laws, and the like. Limitations of this kind can be preserved in practice no other way than through the medium of the courts of justice, whose duty it must be to declare all acts contrary to the manifest tenor of the constitution void. Without this, all the reservations of particular rights or privileges would amount to nothing.

Some perplexity respecting the right of the courts to pronounce legislative acts void, because contrary to the constitution, has arisen from an imagination that the doctrine would imply a superiority of the judiciary to the legislative power. It is urged that the authority which can declare the acts of another void, must necessarily be superior to the one whose acts may be declared void. As this doctrine is of great important in all the American constitutions, a brief discussion of the grounds on which it rests cannot be unacceptable.

There is no position which depends on clearer principles than that every act of a delegated authority, contrary to the tenor of the commission under which it is exercised, is void. No legislative act, therefore, contrary to the constitution, can be valid. To deny this would be to affirm, that the deputy is greater than his principal; that the servant is above his master; that the representatives of the people are superior to the people themselves; that men, acting by virtue of powers, may do not only what their powers do not authorize, but what they forbid.

If it be said that the legislative body are themselves the constitutional judges of their powers, and that the construction they put upon them is conclusive upon the other departments, it may be answered, that this cannot be the natural presumption, where it is not to be collected from any particular provisions in the constitution. It is not otherwise to be supposed that the constitution could intend to enable the representatives of the people to substitute their will to that of their constituents. It is far more rational to suppose that the courts were designed to be an intermediate body between the people and the legislature, in order, among other things, to keep the latter within the limits assigned to their authority. The interpretation of the laws is the proper and peculiar province of the courts. A constitution is, in fact, and must be, regarded by the judges as a fundamental law. It must therefore belong to them to ascertain its meaning, as well as the meaning of any particular act proceeding from the legislative body. If there should happen to be an irreconcilable variance between the two, that which has the superior obligation and validity ought, of course, to be preferred; in other words, the constitution ought to be preferred to the statute, the intention of the people to the intention of their agents.

Nor does this conclusion by any means suppose a superiority of the judicial to the legislative power. It only supposes that the power of the people is superior to both; and that where the will of the legislature declared in its statutes, stands in opposition to that of the people declared in the constitution, the judges ought to be governed by the latter, rather than the former. They ought to regulate their decisions by the fundamental laws, rather than by those which are not fundamental. . . .

It can be no weight to say, that the courts, on the pretense of a repugnancy, may substitute their own pleasure to the constitutional intentions of the legislature. This might as well happen in the case of two contradictory statutes; or it might as well happen in every adjudication upon any single statute. The courts must declare the sense of the law; and if they should be disposed to exercise WILL instead of JUDGMENT, the consequence would equally be the substitution of their pleasure to that of the legislative body. The observation, if it proved anything, would prove that there ought to be no judges distinct from the body.

If then the courts of justice are to be considered as the bulwarks of a limited constitution, against legislative encroachments, this consideration will afford a strong argument for the permanent tenure of judicial officers, since nothing will contribute so much as this to that independent spirit in the judges, which must be essential to the faithful performance of so arduous a duty.

This independence of the judges is equally requisite to guard the constitution and the rights of individuals, from the effects of those ill-humors which the arts of designing men, or the influence of particular conjunctures, sometimes disseminate among the people themselves, and which, though they speedily give place to better information, and more deliberate reflection, have a tendency, in the meantime, to occasion dangerous innovations in the government, and serious oppression of the minor party in the community. . . . Until the people have, by some solemn and authoritative act, annulled or changed the established form, it is binding upon themselves collectively, as well as individually; and no presumption, or even knowledge of their sentiments, can warrant their representatives in a departure from it, prior to such an act. But it is easy to see, that it would require an uncommon portion of fortitude in the judges to do their duty as faithful guardians of the constitution, where legislative invasions of it had been instigated by the major voice of the community.

But it is not with a view to infractions of the constitution only, that the independence of the judges may be an essential safeguard against the effects of occasional ill-humors in the society. These sometimes extend no farther than to the injury of the private rights of particular classes of citizens, by unjust and partial laws. Here also the firmness of the judicial magistracy is of vast importance in mitigating the severity, and confining the operation of such laws. It not only serves to moderate the immediate mischiefs of those which may have been passed, but it operates as a check upon the legislative body in passing them; who, perceiving that obstacles to the success of an iniquitous intention are to be expected from the scruples of the courts, are in a manner compelled by the very motives of the injustice they mediate, to quality their attempts. . . .

That inflexible and uniform adherence to the rights of the constitution, and of individuals, which we perceive to be indispensable in the courts of justice, can certainly not be expected from judges who hold their offices by a temporary commission. Periodical appointments, however regulated, or by whomsoever made, would, in some way or other, be fatal to their necessary independence. If the power of making them was committed either to the executive or legislature, there would be danger of an improper compliance to the branch which possessed it; if to both, there would be an unwillingness to hazard the displeasure of either; if to the people, or to persons chosen by them for the special purpose, there would be too great a disposition to consult popularity to justify a reliance that nothing would be consulted but the constitution and the laws.

There is yet a further and a weighty reason for the permanency of judicial offices, which is deducible from the nature of the qualifications they require. It has been frequently remarked, with great propriety, that a voluminous code of laws is one of the inconveniences necessarily connected with the advantages of a free government. To avoid an arbitrary discretion in the courts, it is indispensable that they should be bound down by strict rules and precedents, which serve to define and point out their duty in every particular case that comes before them; and it will readily be conceived, from the variety of controversies which grow out of the folly and wickedness of mankind, that the records of those precedents must unavoidably swell to a very considerable bulk, and must demand long and laborious study to acquire a competent knowledge of them. Hence it is, that there can be but few men in the society, who will have sufficient skill in the laws to qualify them for the stations of judges. And making the proper deductions for the ordinary depravity of human nature, the number must be still smaller, of those who unite the requisite integrity with the requisite knowledge. . . .

From *Federalist 78* students can observe that the intent of the framers of the Constitution, at least as expressed and represented by Hamilton, was to give to the courts the power of judicial review over legislative acts. Students should note that this concept was not explicitly written into the Constitution. Although the cause of this omission is not known, it is reasonable to assume that the framers felt that judicial power implied judicial review. Further, it is possible that the framers did not expressly mention judicial review because they had to rely on the states for adoption of the Constitution; judicial power would extend to the states as well as to the coordinate departments of the national government.

The power of the Supreme Court to invalidate an act of Congress was stated by John Marshall in *Marbury v. Madison,* 1 Cranch 137 (1803). At issue was a provision in the Judiciary Act of 1789 which extended the *original jurisdiction* of the Supreme Court by authorizing it to issue writs of mandamus in cases involving public officers of the United States and private persons, a power not conferred upon the Court in the Constitution. Marbury had been appointed a justice of the peace by President John Adams under the Judiciary Act of 1801, passed by the Federalists after Jefferson and the Republican party won the elections in the fall of 1800 so that President Adams could fill various newly created judicial posts with Federalists before he left office in March 1801. Marbury was scheduled to receive one of these commissions, but when Jefferson took office on March 4, with Madison as his secretary of state, it had not been delivered. Marbury filed a suit with the Supreme Court requesting it to exercise its original jurisdiction and issue a writ of mandamus (a writ to compel an official to perform his or her duty) to force Madison to deliver the commission, an act which both Jefferson and Madison were opposed to doing. In his decision, Marshall, a prominent Federalist, stated that although Marbury had a legal right to his commission, and although mandamus was the proper remedy, the Supreme Court could not extend its original jurisdiction beyond the limits specified in the Constitution; therefore, that section of the Judiciary Act of 1789 permitting the court to issue such writs to public officers was unconstitutional. Incidentally, the Republicans were so outraged at Adams's last-minute appointments that there were threats that Marshall would be impeached if he issued a writ of mandamus directing Madison to deliver the commission. This is not to suggest that Marshall let such considerations influence him; however, politically his decision was thought to be a masterpiece of reconciling his position as a Federalist with the political tenor of the times.

69

MARBURY V. MADISON

⚜

1 Cranch 137 (1803)

Mr. Chief Justice Marshall delivered the opinion of the Court, saying in part:

. . . The authority, therefore, given to the Supreme Court, by the [Judiciary Act of 1789] . . . establishing the judicial courts of the United States, to issue writs of mandamus to public officers, appears not to be warranted by the Constitution [because it adds to the original jurisdiction of the Court delineated by the framers of the Constitution in Article III; had they wished this power to be conferred upon the Court it would be so stated, in the same manner that the other parts of the Court's original jurisdiction are stated]; . . . it becomes necessary to inquire whether a jurisdiction so conferred can be exercised.

The question whether an act repugnant to the Constitution can become the law of the land, is a question deeply interesting to the United States; but, happily, not of an intricacy proportioned to its interests. It seems only necessary to recognize certain principles supposed to have been long and well established, to decide it.

That the people have an original right to establish, for their future government, such principles as, in their opinion, shall most conduce to their own happiness, is the basis on which the whole American fabric has been erected. The exercise of this original right is a very great exertion; nor can it nor ought it to be frequently repeated. The principles, therefore, so established, are deemed fundamental. And as the authority from which they proceed is supreme, and can seldom act, they are designed to be permanent.

This original and supreme will organizes the government, and assigns to different departments their respective powers. It may either stop here, or establish certain limits not to be transcended by those departments.

The government of the United States is of the latter description. The powers of the legislature are defined and limited; and that those limits may not be mistaken, or forgotten, the Constitution is written. To what purpose are powers limited, and to what purpose is that limitation committed to writing, if these limits may, at any time, be passed by those intended to be restrained? The distinction between a government with limited powers is abolished, if those limits do not confine the persons on whom they are imposed, and if acts prohibited and acts allowed, are of equal obligation. It is a proposition too plain to be contested, that the Constitution controls any legislative act repugnant to it; or, that the legislature may alter the Constitution by an ordinary act.

Between these alternatives there is no middle ground. The Constitution is either a superior paramount law, unchangeable by ordinary means, or it is on a level with ordinary legislative acts, and, like other acts, is alterable when the legislature shall please to alter it.

If the former part of the alternative be true, then a legislative act contrary to the Constitution, is not law; if the latter part be true, then written constitutions are absurd attempts, on the part of the people, to limit a power in its own nature illimitable.

Certainly all those who have framed written constitutions contemplate them as forming the fundamental and paramount law of the nation, and, consequently, the theory of every such government must be, that an act of the legislature, repugnant to the constitution, is void.

This theory is essentially attached to a written constitution, and is consequently to be considered, by this court, as one of the fundamental principles of our society. It is not, therefore, to be lost sight of in the further consideration of this subject.

If an act of the legislature, repugnant to the Constitution, is void, does it, notwithstanding its invalidity, bind the courts, and oblige them to give it effect? Or, in other words, though it be not law, does it constitute a rule as operative as if it was a law? This would be to overthrow in fact what was established in theory; and would seem, at first view, an absurdity too gross to be insisted on. It shall, however, receive a more attentive consideration.

It is emphatically the province and duty of the judicial department to say what the law is. Those who apply the rule to particular cases, must of necessity expound and interpret that rule. If two laws conflict with each other, the courts must decide on the operation of each.

So if the law be in opposition to the Constitution; if both the law and the Constitution apply to a particular case, so that the court must either decide that case conformably to the law, disregarding the Constitution, or conformably to the Constitution, disregarding the law, the court must determine which of these conflicting rules governs the case. This is of the very essence of judicial duty.

If, then, the courts are to regard the Constitution, and the Constitution is superior to any ordinary act of the legislature, the Constitution, and not such ordinary act, must govern the case to which they both apply.

Those, then, who controvert the principle that the Constitution is to be considered, in court, as a paramount law, are reduced to the necessity of maintaining that courts must close their eyes on the Constitution, and see only the law.

This doctrine would subvert the very foundation of all written constitutions. It would declare that an act which, according to the principles and theory of our government, is entirely void, is yet, in practice, completely obligatory. It would declare that if the legislature shall do what is expressly forbidden, such act, notwithstanding the express prohibition, is in reality effectual. It would be giving to the legislature a practical and real omnipotence, with the same breath which professes to restrict their powers within narrow limits. It is prescribing limits, and declaring that those limits may be passed at pleasure.

That it thus reduces to nothing what we have deemed the greatest improvement on political institutions, a written constitution, would of itself be sufficient, in America, where written constitutions have been viewed with so much reverence, for rejecting the construction. But the peculiar expressions of the Constitution of the United States furnish additional arguments in favor of its rejection.

The judicial power of the United States is extended to all cases arising under the Constitution.

Could it be the intention of those who gave this power, to say that in using it the Constitution should not be looked into? That a case arising under the Constitution should be decided without examining the instrument under which it arises?

This is too extravagant to be maintained.

In some cases, then, the Constitution must be looked into by the judges. And if they can open it at all, what part of it are they forbidden to read or obey?

There are many other parts of the Constitution which serve to illustrate this subject.

It is declared that "no tax or duty shall be laid on articles exported from any State." Suppose a duty on the export of cotton, of tobacco, or of flour; and a suit instituted to recover it. Ought judgment to be rendered in such a case? Ought the judges to close their eyes on the Constitution, and only see the law?

The Constitution declares "that no bill of attainder or ex post facto law shall be passed."

If, however, such a bill should be passed, and a person should be prosecuted under it, must the court condemn to death those victims whom the Constitution endeavors to preserve?

"No person," says the Constitution, "shall be convicted of treason unless on the testimony of two witnesses to the same overt act, or on confession in open court."

Here the language of the Constitution is addressed especially to the courts. It prescribes, directly for them, a rule of evidence not to be departed from. If the legislature should change that rule, and declare one witness, or a confession out of court, sufficient for conviction, must the constitutional principle yield to the legislative act?

From these, and many other selections which might be made, it is apparent that the framers of the Constitution contemplated that instrument as a rule for the government of courts, as well as of the legislature.

Why otherwise does it direct the judges to take an oath to support it? This oath certainly applies in an especial manner to this conduct in their official character. How immoral to impose it on them, if they were to be used as the instruments, and the knowing instruments, for violating what they swear to support!

The oath of office, too, imposed by the legislature, is completely demonstrative of the legislative opinion on this subject. It is in these words: "I do solemnly swear that I will administer justice without respect to persons, and do equal right to the poor and to the rich; and that I will faithfully and impartially discharge all the duties incumbent on me as ———————, according to the best of my abilities and understanding, agreeably to the Constitution and laws of the United States."

Why does a judge swear to discharge his duties agreeably to the Constitution of the United States, if that Constitution forms no rule for his government—if it is closed upon him, and cannot be inspected by him?

If such be the real state of things, this is worse than solemn mockery. To prescribe, or to take this oath, becomes equally a crime.

It is also not entirely unworthy of observation, that in declaring what shall be the supreme law of the land, the Constitution itself is first mentioned; and not the laws of the United States generally, but those only which shall be made in pursuance of the Constitution, have that rank.

Thus, the particular phraseology of the Constitution of the United States confirms and strengthens the principle, supposed to be essential to all written constitutions, that a law repugnant to the Constitution is void; and that courts, as well as other departments, are bound by that instrument.

The rule must be discharged.

Marbury v. Madison unequivocally established the Supreme Court's supremacy over Congress. But the history of the Supreme Court is not one of activism in overruling congressional laws. Judicial review has been most significant and controversial in overturning state actions.

While the Court rarely tangled with Congress over its first two hundred years, Chief Justice Rehnquist's Court took on Congress in a series of important cases as the twentieth century ended and the twenty-first century began. It resurrected a dormant commerce clause to limit congressional power to enact gun control legislation (*Lopez*, 1995) and the regulation of violence against women (*Morrison*, 2000). It overturned the Religious Freedom Restoration Act of 1993 in which Congress attempted to overrule a Supreme Court decision (*City of Boerne*, 1997). The Supreme Court also limited congressional authority to enact affirmative action programs (*Adarand*, 1995).[1]

In the following case the Supreme Court continued its activism over Congress and overturned yet another law that overturned the landmark *Miranda* opinion. That opinion required what became widely known as the Miranda warning before the police could take statements or confessions from criminal suspects.

---

[1]Chapter 2 discusses the *Lopez* case and has an excerpt from *United States v. Morrison* (Reading 10). Chapter 3 discusses the Boerne case and has an excerpt from *Adarand Constructors v. Pena* (Reading 25).

70

DICKERSON V. UNITED STATES

⊗

United States Supreme Court (2000)

Chief Justice Rehnquist delivered the opinion of the Court.

In *Miranda v. Arizona*, 384 U.S. 436 (1966), we held that certain warnings must be given before a suspect's statement made during custodial interrogation could be admitted in evidence. In the wake of that decision, Congress enacted 18 U.S.C. §3501, which in essence laid down a rule that the admissibility of such statements should turn only on whether or not they were voluntarily made. We hold that *Miranda*, being a constitutional decision of this Court, may not be in effect overruled by an Act of Congress, and we decline to overrule *Miranda* ourselves. We therefore hold that *Miranda* and its progeny in this Court govern the admissibility of statements made during custodial interrogation in both state and federal courts. . . .

The law in this area is clear. This Court has supervisory authority over the federal courts, and we may use that authority to prescribe rules of evidence and procedure that are binding in those tribunals. . . . However, the power to judicially create and enforce nonconstitutional "rules of procedure and evidence for the federal courts exists only in the absence of a relevant Act of Congress." . . . Congress retains the ultimate authority to modify or set aside any judicially created rules of evidence and procedure that are not required by the Constitution.

But Congress may not legislatively supersede our decisions interpreting and applying the Constitution. See, e.g., *City of Boerne v. Flores,* 521 U.S. 507, 517–521 (1997). This case therefore turns on whether the Miranda Court announced a constitutional rule or merely exercised its supervisory authority to regulate evidence in the absence of congressional direction. Recognizing this point, the Court of Appeals surveyed *Miranda* and its progeny to determine the constitutional status of the *Miranda* decision. . . . Relying on the fact that we have created several exceptions to *Miranda's* warnings requirement and that we have repeatedly referred to the *Miranda* warnings as "prophylactic," . . . and "not themselves rights protected by the Constitution," the Court of Appeals concluded that the protections announced in Miranda are not constitutionally required. . . .

We disagree with the Court of Appeals' conclusion, although we concede that there is language in some of our opinions that supports the view taken by that court. But first and foremost of the factors on the other side—that *Miranda* is a constitutional decision—is that both *Miranda* and two of its companion cases applied the rule to proceedings in state courts—to wit, Arizona, California, and New York. . . . Since that time, we have consistently applied *Miranda's* rule to prosecutions arising in state courts. . . . It is beyond dispute that we do not hold a supervisory power over the courts of the several States. . . . With respect to proceedings in state courts, our "authority is limited to enforcing the commands of the United States Constitution." . . .

The *Miranda* . . . majority opinion is replete with statements indicating that the majority thought it was announcing a constitutional rule.

Indeed, the Court's ultimate conclusion was that the unwarned confessions obtained in the four cases before the Court in *Miranda* "were obtained from the defendant under circumstances that did not meet constitutional standards for protection of the privilege." . . .

Whether or not we would agree with *Miranda*'s reasoning and its resulting rule, were we addressing the issue in the first instance, the principles of stare decisis weigh heavily against overruling it now. . . .

We do not think there is . . . justification for overruling *Miranda*. *Miranda* has become embedded in routine police practice to the point where the warnings have become part of our national culture. . . .

In sum, we conclude that *Miranda* announced a constitutional rule that Congress may not supersede legislatively. Following the rule of stare decisis, we decline to overrule *Miranda* ourselves.

The judgment of the Court of Appeals is therefore Reversed.

Justice Scalia, with whom Justice Thomas joins, dissenting.

Those to whom judicial decisions are an unconnected series of judgments that produce either favored or disfavored results will doubtless greet today's decision as a paragon of moderation, since it declines to overrule *Miranda v. Arizona*. . . . Those who understand the judicial process will appreciate that today's decision is not a reaffirmation of *Miranda*, but a radical revision of the most significant element of *Miranda* (as of all cases): the rationale that gives it a permanent place in our jurisprudence.

Marbury v. Madison . . . held that an Act of Congress will not be enforced by the courts if what it prescribes violates the Constitution of the United States. That was the basis on which *Miranda* was decided. One will search today's opinion in vain, however, for a statement (surely simple enough to make) that what 18 U.S.C. §3501 prescribes—the use at trial of a voluntary confession, even when a *Miranda* warning or its equivalent has failed to be given—violates the Constitution. The reason the statement does not appear is not only (and perhaps not so much) that it would be absurd, inasmuch as §3501 excludes from trial precisely what the Constitution excludes from trial, viz., compelled confessions; but also that Justices whose votes are needed to compose today's majority are on record as believing that a violation of *Miranda* is not a violation of the Constitution. . . . And so, to justify today's agreed-upon result, the Court must adopt a significant new, if not entirely comprehensible, principle of constitutional law. As the Court chooses to describe that principle, statutes of Congress can be disregarded, not only when what they prescribe violates the Constitution, but when what they prescribe contradicts a decision of this Court that "announced a constitutional rule,". . . . As I shall discuss in some detail, the only thing that can possibly mean in the context of this case is that this Court has the power, not merely to apply the Constitution but to expand it, imposing what it regards as useful "prophylactic" restrictions upon Congress and the States. That is an immense and frightening antidemocratic power, and it does not exist. . . .

The Court therefore acts in plain violation of the Constitution when it denies effect to this Act of Congress.

I

Early in this Nation's history, this Court established the sound proposition that constitutional government in a system of separated powers requires judges to regard as inoperative any legislative act, even of Congress itself, that is "repugnant to the Constitution."

"So if a law be in opposition to the constitution; if both the law and the constitution apply to a particular case, so that the court must either decide that case conformably to the law, disregarding the constitution; or conformably to the constitution, disregarding the law; the court must determine which of these conflicting rules governs the case." *Marbury* [*v. Madison*].

The power we recognized in *Marbury* will thus permit us, indeed require us, to "disregar[d]" §3501, a duly enacted statute governing the admissibility of evidence in the federal courts, only if it "be in opposition to the constitution"—here, assertedly, the dictates of the Fifth Amendment.

It was once possible to characterize the so-called *Miranda* rule as resting (however implausibly) upon the proposition that what the statute here before us permits—the admission at trial of un-Mirandized confessions—violates the Constitution. That is the fairest reading of the *Miranda* case itself. . . .

. . . [A]ny conclusion that a violation of the *Miranda* rules necessarily amounts to a violation of the privilege against compelled self-incrimination can claim no support in history, precedent, or common sense, and as a result would at least presumptively be worth reconsidering even at this late date. But that is unnecessary, since the Court has (thankfully) long since abandoned the notion that failure to comply with *Miranda*'s rules is itself a violation of the Constitution.

II

As the Court today acknowledges, since *Miranda* we have explicitly, and repeatedly, interpreted that decision as having announced, not the circumstances in which custodial interrogation runs afoul of the Fifth or Fourteenth Amendment, but rather only "prophylactic" rules that go beyond the right against compelled self-incrimination. . . .

Today's judgment converts *Miranda* from a milestone of judicial overreaching into the very Cheops' Pyramid (or perhaps the Sphinx would be a better analogue) of judicial arrogance. In imposing its Court-made code upon the States, the original opinion at least asserted that it was demanded by the Constitution. Today's decision does not pretend that it is—and yet still asserts the right to impose it against the will of the people's representatives in Congress. Far from believing that stare decisis compels this result, I believe we cannot allow to remain on the books even a celebrated decision—especially a celebrated decision—that has come to stand for the proposition that the Supreme Court has power to impose extraconstitutional constraints upon Congress and the States. This is not the system that was established by the Framers, or that would be established by any sane supporter of government by the people.

I dissent from today's decision, and, until §3501 is repealed, will continue to apply it in all cases where there has been a sustainable finding that the defendant's confession was voluntary.

Powers and Limitations
of the Supreme Court

Paul A. Freund, in his book *On Understanding the Supreme Court* (1949), notes that the Supreme Court has a definite political role. He asks:

> Is the law of the Supreme Court a reflection of the notions of "policy" held by its members? The question recalls the controversy over whether judges "make" or "find" the law. A generation or two ago it was thought rather daring to insist that judges make law. Old Jeremiah Smith, who began the teaching of law at Harvard after a career on the New Hampshire Supreme Court, properly deflated the issue. "Do judges make law?" he repeated. "Course they do. Made some myself." Of course Supreme Court Justices decide cases on the basis of their ideas of policy.

To emphasize this point today is to repeat the familiar. The Court makes policy. It would be difficult to conceive how a Court having the power to interpret the Constitution could fail to make policy, that is, could fail to make rulings that have general impact upon the community as a whole. The essential distinction between policymaking and adjudication is that the former has a general effect while the latter touches only a specifically designated person or group.

If the Supreme Court has this power of constitutional interpretation, how is it controlled by the other governmental departments and the community? Is it, as some have claimed, completely arbitrary in rendering many of its decisions? Is it potentially a dictatorial body? The Supreme Court and lower courts are limited to the consideration of cases and controversies brought before them by outside parties. Courts cannot initiate law. Moreover, all courts, and the Supreme Court in particular, exercise judicial self-restraint in certain cases to avoid difficult and controversial issues and to avoid outside pressure to limit the powers of the judiciary. John P. Roche, in the next selection, deals with the background, the nature, and the implications of judicial doctrines of self-restraint.

71

Judicial Self-Restraint

John P. Roche

Every society, sociological research suggests, has its set of myths which incorporate and symbolize its political, economic, and social aspirations. Thus, as medieval society had the Quest for the Holy Grail and the cult of numerology, we, in our enlightened epoch, have as significant manifestations of our collective hopes the dream of impartial decision-making and the cult of "behavioral science." While in my view these latter two are but different facets of the same fundamental drive, namely, the age-old effort to exorcise human variables from human action, our concern here is with the first of them, the pervasive tendency in the American political and constitutional tradition directed toward taking the politics out of politics, and substituting some set of Platonic guardians for fallible politicians.

While this dream of objectivizing political Truth is in no sense a unique American phenomenon, it is surely true to say that in no other democratic nation has the effort been carried so far and with such persistence. Everywhere one turns in the United States, he finds institutionalized attempts to narrow the political sector and to substitute allegedly "independent" and "impartial" bodies for elected decisionmakers. The so-called "independent regulatory commissions" are a classic example of this tendency in the area of administration, but unquestionably the greatest hopes for injecting pure Truth-serum into the body politic have been traditionally reserved for the federal judiciary, and particularly for the Supreme Court. The rationale for this viewpoint is simple: "The people must be protected from themselves, and no institution is better fitted for the role of chaperone than the federal judiciary, dedicated as it is to the supremacy of the rule of law."

Patently central to this function of social chaperonage is the right of the judiciary to review legislative and executive actions and nullify those measures which derogate from eternal principles of truth and justice as incarnated in the Constitution. Some authorities, enraged at what the Supreme Court has found the Constitution to mean, have essayed to demonstrate that the framers did not intend the Court to exercise this function, to have, as they put it, "the last word." I find no merit in this contention; indeed, it seems to me undeniable not only that the authors of the Constitution intended to create a federal government, but also that they assumed *sub silentio* that the Supreme Court would have the power to review both national and state legislation.

However, since the intention of the framers is essentially irrelevant except to antiquarians and polemicists, it is unnecessary to examine further the matter of

Review

origins. The fact is that the United States Supreme Court, and the inferior federal courts under the oversight of the high Court, have enormous policy-making functions. Unlike their British and French counterparts, federal judges are not merely technicians who live in the shadow of a supreme legislature, but are fully equipped to intervene in the process of political decision making. In theory, they are limited by the Constitution and the jurisdiction it confers, but, in practice, it would be a clumsy judge indeed who could not, by a little skillful exegesis, adapt the Constitution to a necessary end. This statement is in no sense intended as a condemnation; on the contrary, it has been this perpetual reinvigoration by reinterpretation, in which the legislature and the executive as well as the courts play a part, that has given the Constitution its survival power. Applying a Constitution which contains at key points inspired ambiguity, the courts have been able to pour the new wine in the old bottle. Note that the point at issue is not the legitimacy or wisdom of judicial legislation; it is simply the enormous scope that this prerogative gives to judges to substitute their views for those of past generations, or, more controversially, for those of a contemporary Congress and President.

Thus it is naive to assert that the Supreme Court is limited by the Constitution, and we must turn elsewhere for the sources of judicial restraint. The great power exercised by the Court has carried with it great risks, so it is not surprising that American political history has been sprinkled with demands that the judiciary be emasculated. The really startling thing is that, with the notable exception of the McCardle incident in 1869, the Supreme Court has emerged intact from each of these encounters. Despite the plenary power that Congress, under Article III of the Constitution, can exercise over the appellate jurisdiction of the high Court, the national legislature has never taken sustained and effective action against its House of Lords. It is beyond the purview of this analysis to examine the reasons for Congressional inaction; suffice it here to say that the most significant form of judicial limitation has remained self-limitation. This is not to suggest that such a development as statutory codification has not cut down the area of interpretive discretion, for it obviously has. It is rather to maintain that when the justices have held back from assaults on legislative or executive actions, they have done so on the basis of self-established rationalizations. . . .

The remainder of this paper is therefore concerned with two aspects of this auto-limitation: first, the techniques by which it is put into practice; and, second, the conditions under which it is exercised. . . .

Techniques of Judicial Self-Restraint

The major techniques of judicial self-restraint appear to fall under the two familiar rubrics: procedural and substantive. Under the former fall the various techniques by which the Court can avoid coming to grips with substantive issues, while under the latter would fall those methods by which the Court, in a substantive holding, finds that the matter at issue in the litigation is not properly one for judicial settlement. Let us examine these two categories in some detail.

Procedural + Substantive

Procedural Self-Restraint

Since the passage of the Judiciary Act of 1925, the Supreme Court has had almost complete control over its business. United States Supreme Court *Rule 38*, which governs the certiorari policy, states, (§ 5) that discretionary review will be granted only "where there are special and important reasons therefor." Professor Fowler Harper has suggested in a series of detailed and persuasive articles on the application of this discretion [*University of Pennsylvania Law Review*, vols. 99–101; 103] that the Court has used it in such a fashion as to duck certain significant but controversial problems. While one must be extremely careful about generalizing in this area, since the reasons for denying certiorari are many and complex, Harper's evidence does suggest that the Court in the period since 1949 has refused to review cases involving important civil liberties problems which on their merits appeared to warrant adjudication. As he states at one point: "It is disconcerting when the Court will review a controversy over a patent on a pin ball machine while one man is deprived of his citizenship and another of his liberty without Supreme Court review of a plausible challenge to the validity of government action." . . .

Furthermore, the Supreme Court can issue certiorari on its own terms. Thus in *Dennis v. United States*, appealing the Smith Act convictions of the American communist leadership, the Court accepted the evidential findings of the Second Circuit as final and limited its review to two narrow constitutional issues. This, in effect, burked the basic problem: whether the evidence was sufficient to demonstrate that the Communist Party, U.S.A., was *in fact* clear and present danger to the security of the nation, or whether the communists were merely shouting "Fire!" in an empty theater.

Other related procedural techniques are applicable in some situations. Simple delay can be employed, perhaps in the spirit of the Croatian proverb that "delay is the handmaiden of justice." . . . However, the technique of procedural self-restraint is founded on the essentially simple gadget of refusing jurisdiction, or of procrastinating the acceptance of jurisdiction, and need not concern us further here.

Substantive Self-Restraint

Once a case has come before the Court on its merits, the justices are forced to give some explanation for whatever action they may take. Here self-restraint can take many forms, notably, the doctrine of political questions, the operation of judicial parsimony, and—particularly with respect to the actions of administrative officers of agencies—the theory of judicial inexpertise.

The doctrine of political questions is too familiar to require much elaboration here. Suffice it to say that if the Court feels that a question before it, e.g., the legitimacy of a state government, the validity of a legislative apportionment, or the correctness of executive action in the field of foreign relations, is one that is not properly amenable to judicial settlement, it will refer the plaintiff to the "political" organs of government for any possible relief. The extent to which this doctrine is applied seems to be a direct coefficient of judicial egotism, for the definition of a political question can be expanded or contracted in accordian-like fashion to meet the exigencies of the times. A juridical definition of the term is impossible, for at root the logic that supports it is circular: political questions are matters not soluble by the judicial process; matters not soluble by the judicial process are political questions. As an early dictionary explained, violins are small cellos, and cellos are large violins.

Nor do examples help much in definition. While it is certainly true that the Court cannot mandamus a legislature to apportion a state in equitable fashion, it seems equally true that the Court is without the authority to force state legislators to implement unsegregated public education. Yet in the former instance the Court genuflected to the "political" organs and took no action, while in the latter it struck down segregation as violative of the Constitution.

Judicial parsimony is another major technique of substantive self-restraint. In what is essentially a legal application of Occam's razor, the court has held that it will not apply any more principles to the settlement of a case than are absolutely necessary, e.g., it will not discuss the constitutionality of a law if it can settle the instant case by statutory construction. Furthermore, if an action is found to rest on erroneous statutory construction, the review terminates at that point: the Court will not go on to discuss whether the statute, properly construed, would be constitutional. A variant form of this doctrine, and a most important one, employs the "case of controversy" approach, to wit, the Court, admitting the importance of the issue, inquires as to whether the litigant actually has standing to bring the matter up. . . .

A classic use of parsimony to escape from a dangerous situation occurred in connection with the evacuation of the Nisei from the West Coast in 1942. Gordon Hirabayashi, in an attempt to test the validity of the regulations clamped on the American-Japanese by the military, violated the *curfew* and refused to report to an evacuation center. He was convicted on both counts by the district court and sentenced to three months for each offense, the sentences to run concurrently. When the case came before the Supreme Court, the justices sustained his conviction for violating the curfew, but refused to examine the validity of the evacuation order on the ground that it would not make any difference to Hirabayashi anyway; he was in for ninety days no matter what the Court did with evacuation.

A third method of utilizing substantive self-restraint is particularly useful in connection with the activities of executive departments or regulatory agencies, both state and federal. I have entitled it the doctrine of judicial *inexpertise,* for it is founded on the unwillingness of the Court to revise the findings of experts. The earmarks of this form of restraint are great deference to the holdings of the expert agency usually coupled with such a statement as "It is not for the federal courts to supplant the [Texas Railroad] Commission's judgment even in the face of convincing proof that a different result would have been better." In this tradition, the Court has refused to question *some* exercises of discretion by the National Labor Relations Board, the Federal Trade Commission, and other federal and state agencies. But the emphasis on *some* gives the point away; in other cases, apparently on all fours with those in which it pleads its technical *inexpertise,* the Court feels free to assess evidence de novo and reach independent judgment on the technical issues involved. . . .

In short, with respect to expert agencies, the Court is equipped with both offensive and defensive gambits. It if chooses to intervene, one set of precedents is brought out, while if it decides to hold back, another set of equal validity is invoked. Perhaps the best summary of this point was made by Justice Harlan in 1910, when he stated bluntly that "the Courts have rarely, if ever, felt themselves so restrained by technical rules that they could not find some remedy, consistent with the law, for acts . . . that violated natural justice or were hostile to the fundamental principles devised for the protection of the essential rights of property."

This does not pretend to be an exhaustive analysis of the techniques of judicial self-restraint; on the contrary, others will probably find many which are not given adequate discussion here. The remainder of this paper, however, is devoted to the second area of concern: the conditions under which the Court refrains from acting.

The Conditions
of Judicial Self-Restraint

The conditions which lead the Supreme Court to exercise auto-limitation are many and varied. In the great bulk of cases, this restraint is an outgrowth of sound and quasi-automatic legal maxims which defy teleological interpretation. It would take a master of the conspiracy theory of history to assign meaning, for example, to the great majority of certiorari denials; the simple fact is that these cases do not merit review. However, in a small proportion of cases, purpose does appear to enter the picture, sometimes with a vengeance. It is perhaps unjust to the Court to center our attention on this small proportion, but it should be said in extenuation that these cases often involve extremely significant political and social issues. In the broad picture, the refusal to grant certiorari in 1943 to the Minneapolis Trotskyites convicted under the Smith Act is far more meaningful than the similar refusal to grant five hundred petitions to prison "lawyers" who have suddenly discovered the writ of habeas corpus. Likewise, the holding that the legality of Congressional apportionment is a "political question" vitally affects the operation of the whole democratic process.

What we must therefore seek are the conditions under which the Court holds back in this *designated category of cases*. Furthermore, it is important to realize that there are positive consequences of negative action; as Charles Warren has implied, the post–Civil War Court's emphasis on self-restraint was a judicial concomitant of the resurgence of states' rights. Thus self-restraint may, as in wartime, be an outgrowth of judicial caution, or it may be part of a purposeful pattern of abdicating national power to the states.

Ever since the first political scientist discovered Mr. Dooley, the changes have been run on the aphorism that the Supreme Court "follows the election returns," and I see no particular point in ringing my variation on this theme through again. Therefore, referring those who would like a more detailed explanation to earlier analyses, the discussion here will be confined to the bare bones of my hypothesis.

The power of the Supreme Court to invade the decision-making arena, I submit, is a consequence of that fragmentation of political power which is normal in the United States. No cohesive majority, such as normally exists in Britain, would permit a politically irresponsible judiciary to usurp decision-making functions, but, for complex social and institutional reasons, there are few issues in the United States on which cohesive majorities exist. The guerrilla warfare which usually rages between Congress and the President, as well as the internal civil wars which are endemic in both the legislature and the administration, give the judiciary considerable room for maneuver. If, for example, the Court strikes down a controversial decision of the Federal Power Commission, it will be supported by a substantial bloc of congressmen; if it supports the FPC's decision, it will also receive considerable congressional support. But the important point is that either way it decides the case, there is no possibility that Congress will exact any vengeance on the Court for its action. A disciplined majority would be necessary to clip the judicial wings, and such a majority does not exist on this issue.

On the other hand, when monolithic majorities do exist on issues, the Court is likely to resort to judicial self-restraint. A good case here is the current tidal wave of anti-communist legislation and administrative action, the latter particularly with regard to aliens, which the Court has treated most gingerly. About the only issues on which there can be found cohesive majorities are those relating to national defense, and the Court has, as Clinton Rossiter demonstrated in an incisive analysis [*The Supreme Court and the Commander-in-Chief*, Ithaca, 1951], traditionally avoided problems arising in this area irrespective of their constitutional merits. Like the slave who accompanied a Roman consul on his triumph whispering "You too are mortal," the shade of Thad Stevens haunts the Supreme Court chamber to remind the justices what an angry Congress can do.

To state the proposition in this brief compass is to oversimplify it considerably. I have, for instance, ignored the crucial question of how the Court knows when a majority *does* exist, and I recognize that certain aspects of judicial behavior cannot be jammed into my hypothesis without creating essentially spurious epicycles. However, I am not trying to establish a monistic theory of judicial action; group action, like that of individuals, is motivated by many factors, some often contradictory, and my objective is to elucidate what seems to be one tradition of judicial motivation. In short, judicial self-restraint and judicial power seem to be opposite sides of the same coin: it has been by judicious application of the former that the latter has been maintained. A tradition beginning with Marshall's *coup* in *Marbury v. Madison* and running through *Mississippi v. Johnson* and *Ex Parte Vallandigham* to *Dennis v. United States* suggests that the Court's power has been maintained by a wise refusal to employ it in unequal combat.

�⌐

Judicial Decision Making

Judicial decision making is not quasi-scientific, always based clearly upon legal principles and precedent, with the judges set apart from the political process. The interpretation of law, whether constitutional or statutory, involves a large amount of discretion. The majority of the Court can always read its opinion into law if it so chooses.

Justice William J. Brennan, Jr., a former member of the Supreme Court, discusses below the general role of the Court and the procedures it follows in decision making.

———————— **72** ————————

HOW THE SUPREME COURT ARRIVES
AT DECISIONS

William J. Brennan, Jr.

Throughout its history the Supreme Court has been called upon to face many of the dominant social, political, economic and even philosophical issues that confront the nation. But Solicitor General Cox only recently reminded us that this does not mean that the Court is charged with making social, political, economic or philosophical decisions.

Quite the contrary, the Court is not a council of Platonic guardians for deciding our most difficult and emotional questions according to the Justices' own notions of what is just or wise or politic. To the extent that this is a government function at all, it is the function of the people's elected representatives.

The Justices are charged with deciding according to law. Because the issues arise in the framework of concrete litigation they must be decided on facts embalmed in a record made by some lower court or administrative agency. And while the Justices may and do consult history and the other disciplines as aids to constitutional decisions, the text of the Constitution and relevant precedents dealing with that text are their primary tools.

It is indeed true, as Judge Learned Hand once said, that the judge's authority

> depends upon the assumption that he speaks with the mouth of others: the momentum of his utterances must be greater than any which his personal reputation and character can command; if it is to do the work assigned to it—if it is to stand against the passionate resentments arising out of the interests he must frustrate—he must preserve his authority by cloaking himself in the majesty of an over-shadowing past, but he must discover some composition with the dominant trends of his times.

Answers Unclear

However, we must keep in mind that, while the words of the Constitution are binding, their application to specific problems is not often easy. The Founding Fathers knew better than to pin down their descendants too closely.

Enduring principles rather than petty details were what they sought.

Thus the Constitution does not take the form of a litany of specifics. There are, therefore, very few cases where the constitutional answers are clear, all one way or all the other, and this is also true of the current cases raising conflicts between the individual and governmental power—an area increasingly requiring the Court's attention.

Ultimately, of course, the Court must resolve the conflicts of competing interests in these cases, but all Americans should keep in mind how intense and troubling these conflicts can be.

Where one man claims a right to speak and the other man claims the right to be protected from abusive or dangerously provocative remarks the conflict is inescapable.

Where the police have ample external evidence of a man's guilt, but to be sure of their case put into evidence a confession obtained through coercion, the conflict arises between his right to a fair prosecution and society's right to protection against his depravity.

Where the orthodox Jew wishes to open his shop and do business on the day which non-Jews have chosen, and the Legislature has sanctioned, as a day of rest, the Court cannot escape a difficult problem of reconciling opposed interests.

Finally, the claims of the Negro citizen, to borrow Solicitor General Cox's words, present a "conflict between the ideal of liberty and equality expressed in the Declaration of Independence, on the one hand, and, on the other hand, a way of life rooted in the customs of many of our people."

Society Is Disturbed

If all segments of our society can be made to appreciate that there are such conflicts, and that cases which involve constitutional rights often require difficult choices, if this alone is accomplished, we will have immeasurably enriched our common understanding of the meaning and significance of our freedoms. And we will have a better appreciation of the Court's function and its difficulties.

How conflicts such as these ought to be resolved constantly troubles our whole society. There should be no surprise, then, that how properly to resolve them often produces sharp division within the Court itself. When problems are so fundamental, the claims of the competing interests are often nicely balanced, and close divisions are almost inevitable.

Supreme Court cases are usually one of three kinds: the "original" action brought directly in the Court by one state against another state or states, or between a state or states and the federal government. Only a handful of such cases arise each year, but they are an important handful.

A recent example was the contest between Arizona and California over the waters of the lower basin of the Colorado River. Another was the contest between the federal government and the newest state of Hawaii over the ownership of lands in Hawaii.

The second kind of case seeks review of the decisions of a federal Court of Appeals—there are eleven such courts—or of a decision of a federal District Court—there is a federal District Court in each of the fifty states.

The third kind of case comes from a state court—the Court may review a state court judgment by the highest court of any of the fifty states, if the judgment rests on the decision of a federal question.

When I came to the Court seven years ago the aggregate of the cases in the three classes was 1,600. In the term just completed there were 2,800, an increase of 75 percent in seven years. Obviously, the volume will have doubled before I complete ten years of service.

How is it possible to manage such a huge volume of cases? The answer is that we have the authority to screen them and select for argument and decision only those which, in our judgment, guided by pertinent criteria, raise the most important and far-reaching questions. By that device we select annually around 6 percent—between 150 and 170 cases—for decision.

Petition and Response

That screening process works like this: when nine Justices sit, it takes five to decide a case on the merits. But it takes only the votes of four of the nine to put a case on the argument calendar for argument and decision. Those four voters are hard to come by—only an exceptional case raising a significant federal question commands them.

Each application for review is usually in the form of a short petition, attached to which are any opinions of the lower courts in the case. The adversary may file a response—also, in practice usually short. Both the petition and response identify the federal questions allegedly involved, argue their substantiality, and whether they were properly raised in the lower courts.

Each Justice receives copies of the petition and response and such parts of the record as the parties may submit. Each Justice then, without any consultation at this stage with the others, reaches his own tentative conclusion whether the application should be granted or denied.

The first consultation about the case comes at the Court conference at which the case is listed on the agenda for discussion. We sit in conference almost every Friday during the term. Conferences begin at ten in the morning and often continue until six, except for a half-hour recess for lunch.

Only the Justices are present. There are no law clerks, no stenographers, no secretaries, no pages—just the nine of us. The junior Justice acts as guardian of the door, receiving and delivering any messages that come in or go from the conference.

Order of Seating

The conference room is a beautifully oak-paneled chamber with one side lined with books from floor to ceiling. Over the mantel of the exquisite marble fireplace at one end hangs the only adornment in the chamber—a portrait of Chief Justice John Marshall. In the middle of the room stands a rectangular table, not too large but large enough for the nine of us comfortably to gather around it.

The Chief Justice sits at the south end and Mr. Justice Black, the senior Associate Justice, at the north end. Along the side to the left of the Chief Justice sit Justices Stewart, Goldberg, White and Harlan. On the right side sit Justice Clark, myself and Justice Douglas in that order.

We are summoned to conference by a buzzer which rings in our several chambers five minutes before the hour. Upon entering the conference room each of us shakes hands with his colleagues. The handshake tradition originated when Chief Justice Fuller presided many decades ago. It is a symbol that harmony of aims if not of views is the Court's guiding principle.

Each of us has his copy of the agenda of the day's cases before him. The agenda lists the cases applying for review. Each of us before coming to the conference has noted on his copy his tentative view whether or not review should be granted in each case.

The Chief Justice begins the discussion of each case. He then yields to the senior Associate Justice and discussion proceeds down the line in order of seniority until each Justice has spoken.

Voting goes the other way. The junior Justice votes first and voting then proceeds up the line to the Chief Justice, who votes last.

Each of us has a docket containing a sheet for each case with appropriate places for recording the votes. When any case receives four votes for review, that case is transferred to the oral argument list. Applications in which none of us sees merits may be passed over without discussion.

Now how do we process the decisions we agree to review?

There are rare occasions when the question is so clearly controlled by an earlier decision of the Court that a reversal of the lower court judgment is inevitable. In these rare instances we may summarily reverse without oral argument.

Each Side Gets Hour

The case must very clearly justify summary disposition, however, because our ordinary practice is not to reverse a decision without oral argument. Indeed, oral argument of cases taken for review, whether from the state or federal courts, is the usual practice. We rarely accept submissions of cases on briefs.

Oral argument ordinarily occurs about four months after the application for review is granted. Each party is usually allowed one hour, but in recent years we have limited oral argument to a half-hour in cases thought to involve issues not requiring longer arguments.

Counsel submit their briefs and record in sufficient time for the distribution of one set to each Justice two or three weeks before the oral argument. Most of the members of the present Court follow the practice of reading the briefs before the argument. Some of us often have a bench memorandum prepared before the argument. This memorandum digests the facts and the arguments of both sides, highlighting the matters about which we may want to question counsel at the argument.

Often I have independent research done in advance of argument and incorporate the results in the bench memorandum.

We follow a schedule of two weeks of argument from Monday through Thursday, followed by two weeks of recess for opinion writing and the study of petitions for review. The argued cases are listed on the conference agenda on the Friday following argument. Conference discussions follow the same procedure I have described for the discussions of certiorari petitions.

Opinion Assigned

Of course, it is much more extended. Not infrequently discussion of particular cases may be spread over two or more conferences.

Not until the discussion is completed and a vote taken is the opinion assigned. The assignment is not made at the conference but formally in writing some few days after the conference.

The Chief Justice assigns the opinions in those cases in which he has voted with the majority. The senior Associate Justice voting with the majority assigns the opinion in the other cases. The dissenters agree among themselves who shall write the dissenting opinion. Of course, each Justice is free to write his own opinion, concurring or dissenting.

The writing of an opinion always takes weeks and sometimes months. The most painstaking research and care are involved.

Research, of course, concentrates on relevant legal materials—precedents particularly. But Supreme Court cases often require some familiarity with history, economics, the social and other sciences, and authorities in these areas, too, are consulted when necessary.

When the author of an opinion feels he has an unanswerable document he sends it to a print shop, which we maintain in our building. The printed draft may be revised several times before his proposed opinion is circulated among the other Justices. Copies are sent to each member of the Court, those in the dissent as well as those in the majority.

Some Change Minds

Now the author often discovers that his work has only begun. He receives a return, ordinarily in writing, from each Justice who voted with him and sometimes also from the Justices who voted the other way. He learns who will write the dissent if one is to be written. But his particular concern is whether those who voted with him are still of his view and what they have to say about his proposed opinion.

Often some who voted with him at conference will advise that they reserve final judgment pending the circulation of the dissent. It is a common experience that dissents change votes, even enough votes to become the majority.

I have had to convert more than one of my proposed majority opinions into a dissent before the final decision was announced. I have also, however, had the more satisfying experience of rewriting a dissent as a majority opinion for the Court.

Before everyone has finally made up his mind a constant interchange by memoranda, by telephone, at the lunch table continues while we hammer out the final form of the opinion. I had one case during the past term in which I circulated ten printed drafts before one was approved as the Court opinion.

Uniform Rule

The point of this procedure is that each Justice, unless he disqualifies himself in a particular case, passes on every piece of business coming to the Court. The Court does not function by means of committees or panels. Each Justice passes on each petition, each time, no matter how drawn, in long hand, by typewriter, or on a press. Our Constitution vests the judicial power in only one Supreme Court. This does not permit Supreme Court action by committees, panels, or sections.

The method that the Justices use in meeting an enormous caseload varies. There is one uniform rule: Judging is not delegated. Each Justice studies each case in sufficient detail to resolve the question for himself. In a very real sense, each decision is an individual decision of every Justice.

The process can be a lonely, troubling experience for fallible human beings conscious that their best may not be adequate to the challenge.

"We are not unaware," the late Justice Jackson said, "that we are not final because we are infallible; we know that we are infallible only because we are final."

One does not forget how much may depend on his decision. He knows that usually more than the litigants may be affected, that the course of vital social, economic and political currents may be directed.

This then is the decisional process in the Supreme Court. It is not without its tensions, of course—indeed, quite agonizing tensions at times.

I would particularly emphasize that, unlike the case of a Congressional or White House decision, Americans demand of their Supreme Court judges that they produce a written opinion, the collective expression of the judges subscribing to it, setting forth the reason which led them to the decision.

These opinions are the exposition, not just to lawyers, legal scholars and other judges, but to our whole society, of the bases upon which a particular result rests—why a problem, looked at as disinterestedly and dispassionately as nine human beings trained in a tradition of the disinterested and dispassionate approach can look at it, is answered as it is.

It is inevitable, however, that Supreme Court decisions—and the Justices themselves—should be caught up in public debate and be the subjects of bitter controversy.

An editorial in *The Washington Post* did not miss the mark by much in saying that this was so because

> one of the primary functions of the Supreme Court is to keep the people of the country from doing what they would like to do—at times when what they would like to do runs counter to the Constitution. . . . The function of the Supreme Court is not to count constituents; it is to interpret a fundamental charter which imposes restraints on constituents. Independence and integrity, not popularity, must be its standards.

Freund's View

Certainly controversy over its work has attended the Court throughout its history. As Professor Paul A. Freund of Harvard remarked, this has been true almost since the Court's first decision:

> When the Court held, in 1793, that the state of Georgia could be sued on a contract in the federal courts, the outraged Assembly of that state passed a bill declaring that any federal marshal who should try to collect the judgment would be guilty of a felony and would suffer death, without benefit of clergy, by being hanged. When the Court decided that state criminal convictions could be reviewed in the Supreme Court, Chief Justice Roane of Virginia exploded, calling it a "most monstrous and unexampled decision. It can only be accounted for by that love of power which history informs us infects and corrupts all who possess it, and from which even the eminent and upright judges are not exempt."

But public understanding has not always been lacking in the past. Perhaps it exists today. But surely a more informed knowledge of the decisional process should aid a better understanding.

It is not agreement with the court's decisions that I urge. Our law is the richer and the wiser because academic and informed lay criticism is part of the stream of development.

Consensus Needed

It is only a greater awareness of the nature and limits of the Supreme Court's function that I seek.

The ultimate resolution of questions fundamental to the whole community must be based on a common consensus of understanding of the unique responsibility assigned to the Supreme Court in our society.

The lack of that understanding led Mr. Justice Holmes to say fifty years ago:

> We are very quiet there, but it is the quiet of a storm center, as we all know. Science has taught the world skepticism and has made it legitimate to put everything to the test of proof. Many beautiful and noble reverences are impaired, but in these days no one can complain if any institution, system, or belief is called on to justify its continuance in life. Of course we are not excepted and have not escaped.

Painful Accusation

Doubts are expressed that go to our very being. Not only are we told that when Marshall pronounced an Act of Congress unconstitutional he usurped a power that the Constitution did not give, but we are told that we are the representatives of a class—a tool of the money power.

I get letters, not always anonymous, intimating that we are corrupt. Well, gentlemen, I admit that it makes my heart ache. It is very painful, when one spends all the energies of one's soul in trying to do good work, with no thought but that of solving a problem according to the rules by which one is bound, to know that many see sinister motives and would be glad of evidence that one was consciously bad.

But we must take such things philosophically and try to see what we can learn from hatred and distrust and whether behind them there may not be a germ of inarticulate truth. The attacks upon the Court are merely an expression of the unrest that seems to wonder vaguely whether law and order pay. When the ignorant are taught to doubt they do not know what they safely may believe. And it seems to me that at this time we need education in the obvious more than investigation of the obscure.

Interpreting the Constitution

Justice William J. Brennan, Jr., in his discussion of how the Supreme Court arrives at decisions in the preceding selection, points out that inevitably Supreme Court decisions and the justices are the subjects of public debate and often bitter controversy. It is not surprising that when Supreme Court justices and lower-court judges as well follow the early dictum of Chief Justice John Marshall, which he stated in *Marbury v. Madison* in 1803, that "It is emphatically the province and duty of the judicial department to say what the law is," they will become the center of political storms stirred up by those who feel the Court has overstepped its bounds.

While the Supreme Court may not enter unequal political combat, as John Roche contends in selection 71, it has made many highly controversial decisions since Roche wrote his article in 1955. (For example, see selections 22–27.) One conservative law scholar has gone so far as to state, "In the years since *Brown v. Board of Education* (1954) nearly every fundamental change in domestic social policy has been brought about not by the decentralized democratic (or, more accurately, republican) process contemplated by the Constitution, but simply by the Court's decree."[1]

Conservatives, clearly unhappy with the trend in Supreme Court decision making not only during the Warren era (1953–1969) but under the chief justiceship of Warren Burger (1969–1986), charged that the Court's "loose" constitutional interpretations have been contrary to the wishes of the majority of the people and have made a mockery of the Constitution itself. Responding to their conservative constituencies, Republican presidential candidates Richard M. Nixon in 1968 and Ronald Reagan in 1980 promised to take action to reverse the Supreme Court's alleged liberalism by appointing conservative justices.

Ironically, one of Nixon's appointees, Harry Blackmun, authored the Court's controversial abortion decision in 1973 (see selection 24). Another Nixon appointee, Lewis Powell, joined the more liberal justices in the *Bakke* case to allow universities and the colleges to take race into account in their admissions processes, a tacit although far from direct support for the affirmative action programs conservatives so strongly opposed. Nixon found, as had Dwight D. Eisenhower who appointed Earl Warren to be chief justice in 1953, that presidents have no control over their appointees once they are on the Court.

---

[1]Lino A. Graglia, "How the Constitution Disappeared," *Commentary*, February 1986, p. 19.

For his part in the conservative cause, President Ronald Reagan, while choosing Sandra Day O'Connor as the first woman Supreme Court justice, tried to make certain before-
hand that she would support conservative positions on such issues as abortion. Reagan
added three conservative Supreme Court justices and had an even greater impact upon the
lower federal judiciary, which he "stacked" with conservative judges.

Debate over the role of the Supreme Court intensified during Reagan's second term.
His attorney general, Edwin Meese, in a speech given before the American Bar Association,
attacked the Supreme Court for interpreting the Constitution according to its own values
rather than the intent of the Founding Fathers. In response, Associate Justice William J.
Brennan, speaking to a Georgetown University audience, called the attorney general "arrogant" and "doctrinaire," stating that it is impossible to "gauge accurately the intent of the
framers on the application of principle to specific, contemporary questions." Another
Supreme Court justice, John Paul Stevens, joined the attack on Meese.

The arguments in the 1980s over the proper role of the Supreme Court recalled the debate in the early days of the Republic between proponents of "strict" construction of the
Constitution on the one hand and "loose" construction on the other. No less an intellectual
and political giant than Thomas Jefferson favored the former approach, arguing that judges
should not interpret the Constitution to reflect their own political values. He particularly opposed Chief Justice John Marshall's "loose" construction of congressional authority under
Article I and the implied powers clause, which supported an expansion of national power
over the states. Prior to Marshall's historic decisions in *McCulloch v. Maryland* (1819) and
Gibbons v. Ogden that flexibly interpreted the Constitution to support broad congressional
powers over the states (see selection 9), Alexander Hamilton had provided the rationale for
loose construction in *The Federalist.* He suggested that Congress should be able to carry out
its enumerated powers by whatever means it considered to be necessary and proper.

An old adage states that where one stands on political issues depends upon whose ox is
being gored. Liberal supporters of Franklin D. Roosevelt attacked the conservative Supreme
Court during the early New Deal when it was systematically declaring the core of FDR's program to be unconstitutional. After his overwhelming 1936 electoral victory Roosevelt attempted to "pack" the Court by seeking congressional approval of legislation that would give
him the authority to appoint one new justice for each justice over 70 years of age. The legislation would have given him at the time the authority to appoint a Supreme Court majority because there were seven septuagenarian justices on the Court. Conservatives attacked
Roosevelt's plan, charging that it was an unconstitutional and even un-American attempt to
undermine the Supreme Court's independence. They wanted the Court to continue acting as
a superlegislature as long as it advocated conservative views. However, when the tables
were turned, and the Court became the advocate of "liberal" views during the Warren era,
conservatives were quick to attack it for acting as a superlegislature against the will of the
majority, which was the same argument liberals had used against the Court in the 1930s.

The Contemporary Debate over
Constitutional Interpretation

Debate over constitutional interpretation arises because the Constitution itself is, in the
words of Chief Justice John Marshall in *McCulloch v. Maryland,* one of enumerated, not defined, powers. "A Constitution," Marshall wrote, "to contain an accurate detail of all the

subdivisions of which its great powers will admit, and of all the means of which they may be carried into execution, would partake of the prolixity of a legal code, and could scarcely be embraced by the human mind. It would probably never be understood by the public. Its nature, therefore, requires, that only its great outlines should be marked. . . ."

Ultimately, the Supreme Court defines the Constitution. Ironically, the Supreme Court's authority to be the final arbiter of constitutional issues is nowhere explicitly defined in the Constitution. But, as previous selections have pointed out, eighteenth-century American jurisprudence and political philosophy supported the concept of a higher law and the authority of courts to apply it to legislative actions.

In the following selections, excerpted from the abortion case, *Planned Parenthood of Southeastern Pennsylvania v. Casey* (1992), Supreme Court justices give contrasting opinions on how the Court should interpret the Constitution and its own constitutional precedents. The justices address the question of whether or not the original abortion decision, *Roe v. Wade* (1973), should be modified or overruled. The constitutional provision being interpreted is the "liberty" of the due process clause of the Fourteenth Amendment. As the different justices grapple with the question of how liberty should be defined in the Constitution, students will become aware of the highly subjective character of constitutional interpretation.

73

CONSTITUTIONAL LIBERTY
AND THE RIGHT TO ABORTION

Justice Sandra Day O'Connor

I

Liberty finds no refuge in a jurisprudence of doubt. Yet 19 years after our holding that the Constitution protects a woman's right to terminate her pregnancy in its early stages, *Roe v. Wade*, that definition of liberty is still questioned. Joining the respondents as *amicus curiae*, the United States, as it has done in five other cases in the last decade, again asks us to overrule *Roe*.

At issue in these cases are five provisions of the Pennsylvania Abortion Control Act of 1982 as amended in 1988 and 1989. . . . The Act requires that a woman seeking an abortion give her informed consent prior to the abortion procedure, and specifies that she be provided with certain information at least 24 hours before the abortion is performed. For a minor to obtain an abortion, the Act requires the informed consent of one of her parents, but provides for a judicial bypass option if the minor does not wish to or cannot obtain a parent's consent. Another provision of the Act requires that, unless certain exceptions apply, a married woman seeking an abortion must sign a statement indicating that she has notified her husband of her intended abortion. The Act exempts compliance with these three requirements in the event of a "medical emergency," which is defined in § 3203 of the Act. In addition to the above provisions regulating the performance of abortions, the Act imposes certain reporting requirements on facilities that provide abortion services.

. . .

After considering the fundamental constitutional questions resolved by *Roe*, principles of institutional integrity, and the rule of *stare decisis*, we are led to conclude this: the essential holding of *Roe v. Wade* should be retained and once again reaffirmed.

It must be stated at the outset and with clarity that *Roe*'s essential holding, the holding we reaffirm, has three parts. First is a recognition of the right of the woman to choose to have an abortion before viability and to obtain it without undue interference from the State. Before viability, the State's interests are not strong enough to support a prohibition of abortion or the imposition of a substantial obstacle to the woman's effective right to elect the procedure. Second is a confirmation of the State's power to restrict abortions after fetal viability, if the law contains exceptions for pregnancies which endanger a woman's life or health. And third is the principle that the State has legitimate interests from the outset of the pregnancy in protecting the health of the woman and the life of the fetus that may become a child. These principles do not contradict one another; and we adhere to each.

II

Constitutional protection of the woman's decision to terminate her pregnancy derives from the Due Process Clause of the Fourteenth Amendment. It declares that no State shall "deprive any person of life, liberty, or property, without due process of law." The controlling word in the case before us is "liberty." Although a literal reading of the Clause might suggest that it governs only the procedures by which a State may deprive persons of liberty, for at least 105 years . . . the Clause has been understood to contain a substantive component as well, one "barring certain government actions regardless of the fairness of the procedures used to implement them." . . . "[T]he guaranties of due process, though having their roots in Magna Carta's '*per legem terrae*' and considered as procedural safeguards 'against executive usurpation and tyranny,' have in this country 'become bulwarks also against arbitrary legislation.' " . . .

The most familiar of the substantive liberties protected by the Fourteenth Amendment are those recognized by the Bill of Rights. We have held that the Due Process Clause of the Fourteenth Amendment incorporates most of the Bill of Rights against the States. It is tempting, as a means of curbing the discretion of federal judges, to suppose that liberty encompasses no more than those rights already guaranteed to the individual against federal interference by the express provisions of the first eight amendments to the Constitution. But of course this Court has never accepted that view.

It is also tempting, for the same reason, to suppose that the Due Process Clause protects only those practices, defined at the most specific level, that were protected against government interference by other rules of law when the Fourteenth Amendment was ratified. . . . But such a view would be inconsistent with our law. It is a premise of the Constitution that there is a realm of personal liberty which the government may not enter. We have vindicated this principle before. Marriage is mentioned nowhere in the Bill of Rights and interracial marriage was illegal in most States in the 19th century, but the Court was no doubt correct in finding it to be an aspect of liberty protected against state interference by the substantive component of the Due Process Clause in *Loving*. . . .

Neither the Bill of Rights nor the specific practices of States at the time of the adoption of the Fourteenth Amendment marks the outer limits of the substantive sphere of liberty which the Fourteenth Amendment protects. See U.S. Const., Amend. 9. As the second Justice Harlan recognized in [*Poe v. Ullman*]:

> [T]he full scope of the liberty guaranteed by the Due Process Clause cannot be found in or limited by the precise terms of the specific guarantees elsewhere provided in the Constitution. This ` liberty' is not a series of isolated points pricked out in terms of the taking of property; the freedom of speech, press, and religion; the right to keep and bear arms; the freedom from unreasonable searches and seizures; and so on. It is a rational continuum which, broadly speaking, includes a freedom from all substantial arbitrary impositions and purposeless restraints, . . . and which also recognizes, what a reasonable and sensitive judgment must, that certain interests require particularly careful scrutiny of the state needs asserted to justify their abridgment.

. . .

The inescapable fact is that adjudication of substantive due process claims may call upon the Court in interpreting the Constitution to exercise that same capacity which by tradition courts always have exercised: reasoned judgment. Its boundaries are not susceptible of expression as a simple rule. That does not mean we are free to invalidate state policy choices with which we disagree; yet neither does it permit us to shrink from the duties of our office. . . .

Men and women of good conscience can disagree, and we suppose some always shall disagree, about the profound moral and spiritual implications of terminating a pregnancy, even in its earliest stage. Some of us as individuals find abortion offensive to our most basic principles of morality, but that cannot control our decision. Our obligation is to define the liberty of all, not to mandate our own moral code. . . .

It was . . . personal liberty that *Roe* sought to protect. . . .

While we appreciate the weight of the arguments made on behalf of the State in the case before us, arguments which in their ultimate formulation conclude that *Roe* should be overruled, the reservations any of us may have in reaffirming the central holding of *Roe* are outweighed by the explication of individual liberty we have given combined with the force of *stare decisis*. We turn now to that doctrine.

III

The obligation to follow precedent begins with necessity, and a contrary necessity marks its outer limit. With Cardozo, we recognize that no judicial system could do society's work if it eyed each issue afresh in every case that raised it. Indeed, the very concept of the rule of law underlying our own Constitution requires such continuity over time that a respect for precedent is, by definition, indispensable. At the other extreme, a different necessity would make itself felt if a prior judicial ruling should come to be seen so clearly as error that its enforcement was for that very reason doomed.

. . .

So in this case we may inquire whether *Roe*'s central rule has been found unworkable; whether the rule's limitation on state power could be removed without serious inequity to those who have relied upon it or significant damage to the stability of the society governed by the rule in question; whether the law's growth in the intervening years has left *Roe*'s central rule a doctrinal anachronism discounted by society; and whether *Roe*'s premises of fact have so far changed in the ensuing two decades as to render its central holding somehow irrelevant or unjustifiable in dealing with the issue it addressed. . . .

The sum of the precedential inquiry to this point shows *Roe*'s underpinnings unweakened in any way affecting its central holding. While it has engendered disapproval, it has not been unworkable. An entire generation has come of age free to assume *Roe*'s concept of liberty in defining the capacity of women to act in society, and to make reproductive decisions; no erosion of principle going to liberty or personal autonomy has left *Roe*'s central holding a doctrinal remnant; *Roe* portends no developments at odds with other precedent for the analysis of personal liberty; and no changes of fact have rendered viability more or less appropriate as the point at which the balance of interests tips. Within the bounds of normal stare decisis analysis, then, and subject to the considerations on which it customarily turns, the stronger argument is for affirming *Roe*'s central holding, with whatever degree of personal reluctance any of us may have, not for overruling it.

In a less significant case, *stare decisis* analysis could, and would, stop at the point we have reached. But the sustained and widespread debate *Roe* has provoked calls for some comparison between that case and others of comparable dimension that have responded to national controversies and taken on the impress of the controversies addressed. Only two such decisional lines from the past century present themselves for examination, and in each instance the result reached by the Court accorded with the principles we apply today.

The first example is that line of cases identified with *Lochner v. New York*, which imposed substantive limitations on legislation limiting economic autonomy in favor of health and welfare regulation, adopting, in Justice Holmes' view, the theory of *laissez-faire*. *Id.* (Holmes, J., dissenting). The *Lochner* decisions were exemplified by *Adkins v. Children's Hospital of D.C.*, 261 U.S. 525 (1923), in which this Court held it to be an infringement of constitutionally protected liberty of contract to require the employers of adult women to satisfy minimum wage standards. Fourteen years later, *West Coast Hotel Co. v. Parrish* signalled the demise of *Lochner* by overruling *Adkins*. In the meantime, the Depression had come and, with it, the lesson that seemed unmistakable to most people by 1937, that the interpretation of contractual freedom protected in *Adkins* rested on fundamentally false factual assumptions about the capacity of a relatively unregulated market to satisfy minimal levels of human welfare. As Justice Jackson wrote of the constitutional crisis of 1937 shortly before he came on the bench, "The older world of *laissez-faire* was recognized everywhere outside the Court to be dead." The facts upon which the earlier case had premised a constitutional resolution of social controversy had proved to be untrue, and history's demonstration of their untruth not only justified but required the new choice of constitutional principle that *West Coast Hotel* announced. Of course, it was true that the Court lost something by its misperception, or its lack of prescience, and the Court-packing crisis only magnified the loss; but the clear demonstration that the facts of economic life were different from those previously assumed warranted the repudiation of the old law.

The second comparison that 20th century history invites is with the cases employing the separate-but-equal rule for applying the Fourteenth Amendment's equal protection guarantee. They began with *Plessy v. Ferguson*, holding that legislatively mandated racial segregation in public transportation works no denial of equal protection, rejecting the argument that racial separation enforced by the legal machinery of American society treats the black race as inferior. . . . As one commentator observed, the question before the Court in *Brown* was "whether discrimination inheres in that segregation which is imposed by law in the twentieth century in certain specific states in the American Union. And that question has meaning and can find an answer only on the ground of history and of common knowledge about the facts of life in the times and places aforesaid."

The Court in *Brown* addressed these facts of life by observing that whatever may have been the understanding in *Plessy*'s time of the power of segregation to stigmatize those who were segregated with a "badge of inferiority," it was clear by 1954 that legally sanctioned segregation had just such an effect, to the point that racially separate public educational facilities were deemed inherently unequal. Society's understanding of the facts upon which a constitutional ruling was sought in 1954 was thus fundamentally different from the basis claimed for the decision in 1896. While we think *Plessy* was wrong the day it was decided, see *Plessy* (Harlan, J., dissenting), we must also recognize that the *Plessy* Court's explanation for its decision was so clearly at odds with the facts apparent to the Court in 1954 that the decision to reexamine *Plessy* was on this ground alone not only justified but required.

West Coast Hotel and *Brown* each rested on facts, or an understanding of facts, changed from those which furnished the claimed justifications for the earlier constitutional resolutions. Each case was comprehensible as the Court's response to facts that the country could understand, or had come to understand already, but which the Court of an earlier day, as its own declarations disclosed, had not been able to perceive. As the decisions were thus comprehensible they were also defensible, not merely as the victories of one doctrinal school over another by dint of numbers (victories though they were), but as applications of constitutional principle to facts as they had not been seen by the Court before. In constitutional adjudication as elsewhere in life, changed circumstances may impose new obligations, and the thoughtful part of the Nation could accept each decision to overrule a prior case as a response to the Court's constitutional duty. . . .

      . . .

VI

Our Constitution is a covenant running from the first generation of Americans to us and then to future generations. It is a coherent succession. Each generation must learn anew that the Constitution's written terms embody ideas and aspirations that must survive more ages than one. We accept our responsibility not to retreat from interpreting the full meaning of the covenant in light of all of our precedents. We invoke it once again to define the freedom guaranteed by the Constitution's own promise, the promise of liberty.

------------------------------ ℘ ------------------------------

— 74 —

LIBERTY, PRIVACY, AND THE RIGHT TO ABORTION

Chief Justice William H. Rehnquist

℘

      . . .

We have held that a liberty interest protected under the Due Process Clause of the Fourteenth Amendment will be deemed fundamental if it is "implicit in the concept of ordered liberty." *Palko v. Connecticut.* . . .

In construing the phrase "liberty" incorporated in the Due Process Clause of the Fourteenth Amendment, we have recognized that its meaning extends beyond freedom from physical restraint. . . .

In *Roe v. Wade*, the Court recognized a "guarantee of personal privacy" which "is broad enough to encompass a woman's decision whether or not to terminate her pregnancy." We are now of the view that, in terming this right fundamental, the Court in *Roe* read the earlier opinions upon which it based its decision much too broadly. Unlike marriage, procreation and contraception, abortion "involves the purposeful termination of potential life." The abortion decision must therefore "be recognized as *sui generis*, different in kind from the others that the Court has protected under the rubric of personal or family privacy and autonomy." One cannot ignore the fact that a woman is not isolated in her pregnancy, and that the decision to abort necessarily involves the destruction of a fetus.

Nor do the historical traditions of the American people support the view that the right to terminate one's pregnancy is "fundamental." The common law which we inherited from England made abortion after "quickening" an offense. At the time of the adoption of the Fourteenth Amendment, statutory prohibitions or restrictions on abortion were commonplace; in 1868, at least 28 of the then-37 States and 8 Territories had statutes banning or limiting abortion. By the turn of the century virtually every State had a law prohibiting or restricting abortion on its books. By the middle of the present century, a liberalization trend had set in. But 21 of the restrictive abortion laws in effect in 1868 were still in effect in 1973 when *Roe* was decided, and an overwhelming majority of the States prohibited abortion unless necessary to preserve the life or health of the mother. On this record, it can scarcely be said that any deeply rooted tradition of relatively unrestricted abortion in our history supported the classification of the right to abortion as "fundamental" under the Due Process Clause of the Fourteenth Amendment. . . .

75

LIBERTY AND ABORTION: A STRICT CONSTRUCTIONIST'S VIEW

Justice Antonin Scalia

. . . Laws against bigamy . . . which entire societies of reasonable people disagree with—intrude upon men and women's liberty to marry and live with one another. But bigamy happens not to be a liberty specially "protected" by the Constitution.

That is, quite simply, the issue in this case: not whether the power of a woman to abort her unborn child is a "liberty" in the absolute sense; or even whether it is a liberty of great importance to many women. Of course it is both. The issue is whether it is a liberty protected by the Constitution of the United States. I am sure it is not. I reach that conclusion not because of anything so exalted as my views concerning the "concept of existence, of meaning, of the universe, and of the mystery of human life." Rather, I reach it for the same reason I reach the conclusion that bigamy is not constitutionally protected—because of two simple facts: (1) the Constitution says absolutely nothing about it, and (2) the longstanding traditions of American society have permitted it to be legally proscribed. . . .

The emptiness of the "reasoned judgment" that produced *Roe* is displayed in plain view by the fact that, after more than 19 years of effort by some of the brightest (and most determined) legal minds in the country, after more than 10 cases upholding abortion rights in this Court, and after dozens upon dozens of *amicus* briefs submitted in this and other cases, the best the Court can do to explain how it is that the word "liberty" *must* be thought to include the right to destroy human fetuses is to rattle off a collection of adjectives that simply decorate a value judgment and conceal a political choice. The right to abort, we are told, inheres in "liberty" because it is among "a person's most basic decisions," it involves a "most intimate and personal choic[e]," it is "central to personal dignity and autonomy," it "originate[s] within the zone of conscience and belief," it is "too intimate and personal" for state interference, it reflects "intimate views" of a "deep, personal character," it involves "intimate relationships," and notions of "personal autonomy and bodily integrity," and it concerns a particularly "'important decisio[n].'" But it is obvious to anyone applying "reasoned judgment" that the same adjectives can be applied to many forms of conduct that this Court . . . has held are *not* entitled to constitutional protection—because, like abortion, they are forms of conduct that have long been criminalized in American society. Those adjectives might be applied, for example, to homosexual sodomy, polygamy, adult incest, and suicide, all of which are equally "intimate" and "deep[ly] personal" decisions involving "personal autonomy and bodily integrity," and all of which can constitutionally be proscribed because it is our unquestionable constitutional tradition that they are proscribable. It is not reasoned judgment that supports the Court's decision; only personal predilection. . . .

[W]hether it would "subvert the Court's legitimacy" or not, the notion that we would decide a case differently from the way we otherwise would have in order to show that we can stand firm against public disapproval is frightening. It is a bad enough idea, even in the head of someone like me, who believes that the text of the Constitution, and our traditions, say what they say and there is no fiddling with them. But when it is in the mind of a Court that believes the Constitution has an evolving meaning; that the Ninth Amendment's reference to "othe[r]" rights is not a disclaimer, but a charter for action; and that the function of this Court is to "speak before all others for constitutional ideals" unrestrained by meaningful text or tradition—then the notion that the Court must adhere to a decision for as long as the decision faces "great opposition" and the Court is "under fire" acquires a character of almost czarist arrogance. We are offended by these marchers who descend upon us, every year on the anniversary of *Roe*, to protest our saying that the Constitution requires what our society has never thought the Constitution requires. These people who refuse to be "tested by following" must be taught a lesson. We have no Cossacks, but at least we can stubbornly refuse to abandon an erroneous opinion that we might otherwise change—to show how little they intimidate us. . . .

We should get out of this area, where we have no right to be, and where we do neither ourselves nor the country any good by remaining.

APPENDIX 1

THE DECLARATION OF INDEPENDENCE*

In CONGRESS, July 4, 1776,

The unanimous Declaration of the thirteen united States of America

When in the Course of human events it becomes necessary for one people to dissolve the political bands which have connected them with another, and to assume among the Powers of the earth, the separate and equal station to which the Laws of Nature and of Nature's God entitle them, a decent respect to the opinions of mankind requires that they should declare the causes which impel them to the separation.

We hold these truths to be self-evident, that all men are created equal, that they are endowed by their Creator with certain unalienable Rights, that among these are Life, Liberty and the pursuit of Happiness. That to secure these rights, Governments are instituted among Men, deriving their just powers from the consent of the governed. That whenever any Form of Government becomes destructive of these ends, it is the Right of the People to alter or to abolish it, and to institute new Government, laying its foundation on such principles and organizing its powers in such form, as to them shall seem most likely to effect their Safety and Happiness. Prudence, indeed, will dictate that Governments long established should not be changed for light and transient causes; and accordingly all experience hath shown, that mankind are more disposed to suffer, while evils are sufferable, than to right themselves by abolishing the forms to which they are accustomed. But when a long train of abuses and usurpations, pursuing invariably the same Object evinces a design to reduce them under absolute Despotism, it is their right, it is their duty, to throw off such Government, and to provide new Guards for their future security.—Such has been the patient sufferance of these Colonies; and such is now the necessity which constrains them to alter their former Systems of Government. The history of the present King of Great Britain is a history of repeated injuries and usurpations, all having in direct object the establishment of an absolute Tyranny over these States. To prove this, let Facts be submitted to a candid world.

He has refused his Assent to Laws, the most wholesome and necessary for the public good.

He has forbidden his Governors to pass Laws of immediate and pressing importance, unless suspended in their operation till his Assent should be obtained; and when so suspended, he has utterly neglected to attend to them.

He has refused to pass other Laws for the accommodation of large districts of people, unless those people would relinquish the right of Representation in the Legislature, a right inestimable to them and formidable to tyrants only.

He has called together legislative bodies at places unusual, uncomfortable, and distant from the depository of their Public Records, for the sole purpose of fatiguing them into compliance with his measures.

He has dissolved Representative Houses repeatedly, for opposing with manly firmness his invasions on the rights of the people.

He has refused for a long time, after such dissolutions, to cause others to be elected; whereby the Legislative powers, incapable of Annihilation, have returned to the People at large for their exercise; the State remaining in the mean time exposed to all the dangers of invasion from without, and convulsions within.

He has endeavored to prevent the population of these States; for that purpose obstructing the Laws for Naturalization of Foreigners; refusing to pass others to encourage their migration hither, and raising the conditions of new Appropriations of Lands.

He has obstructed the Administration of Justice, by refusing his Assent to Laws for establishing Judiciary powers.

He has made Judges dependent on his Will alone, for the tenure of their offices, and the amount and payment of their salaries.

He has erected a multitude of New Offices, and sent hither swarms of Officers to harass our People, and eat out their substance.

He has kept among us, in times of peace, Standing Armies without the Consent of our legislatures.

He has affected to render the Military independent of and superior to the Civil power.

He has combined with others to subject us to a jurisdiction foreign to our constitution, and unacknowledged by our laws; giving his Assent to their Acts of pretended Legislation:

For quartering large bodies of armed troops among us:

For protecting them, by a mock Trial, from Punishment for any Murders which they should commit on the Inhabitants of these States:

For cutting off our Trade with all parts of the world:

For imposing Taxes on us without our Consent:

For depriving us in many cases, of the benefits of Trial by Jury:

For transporting us beyond Seas to be tried for pretended offenses:

For abolishing the free System of English Laws in a neighbouring Province, establishing therein an Arbitrary government, and enlarging its Boundaries so as to render it at once an example and fit instrument for introducing the same absolute rule into these Colonies:

For taking away our Charters, abolishing our most valuable Laws, and altering fundamentally the Forms of our Governments:

For suspending our own Legislatures, and declaring themselves invested with Power to legislate for us in all cases whatsoever.

He has abdicated Government here, by declaring us out of his Protection and waging War against us.

He has plundered our seas, ravaged our Coasts, burnt our towns, and destroyed the Lives of our people.

He is at this time transporting large armies of foreign mercenaries to compleat the works of death, desolation and tyranny, already begun with circumstances of Cruelty & perfidy scarcely paralleled in the most barbarous ages, and totally unworthy the Head of a civilized nation.

He has constrained our fellow Citizens taken Captive on the high Seas to bear Arms against their Country, to become the executioners of their friends and Brethren, or to fall themselves by their Hands.

He has excited domestic insurrections amongst us, and has endeavored to bring on the inhabitants of our frontiers, the merciless Indian Savages, whose known rule of warfare, is an undistinguished destruction of all ages, sexes and conditions.

In every stage of these Oppressions We have Petitioned for Redress in the most humble terms: Our repeated Petitions have been answered only by repeated injury. A Prince, whose character is thus marked by every act which may define a Tyrant, is unfit to be the ruler of a free People.

Nor have We been wanting in attention to our British brethren. We have warned them from time to time of attempts by their legislature to extend an unwarrantable jurisdiction over us. We have reminded them of the circumstances of our emigration and settlement here. We have appealed to their native justice and magnanimity, and we have conjured them by the ties of our common kindred to disavow these usurpations, which, would inevitably interrupt our connections and correspondence. They too have been deaf to the voice of justice and consanguinity. We must, therefore, acquiesce in the necessity, which denounces our Separation, and hold them, as we hold the rest of mankind, Enemies in War, in Peace Friends.

We, therefore, the Representatives of the united States of America, in General Congress, Assembled, appealing to the Supreme Judge of the world for the rectitude of our intentions, do, in the Name, and by Authority of the good People of these Colonies, solemnly publish and declare, That these United Colonies are, and of Right ought to be, Free and Independent States; that they are Absolved from all Allegiance to the British-Crown, and that all political connection between them and the State of Great-Britain, is and ought to be totally dissolved; and that as Free and Independent States, they have full Power to levy War, conclude Peace, contract Alliances, establish Commerce, and to do all other Acts and Things which Independent States may of right do. And for the support of this Declaration, with a firm reliance on the Protection of Divine Providence, we mutually pledge to each other our Lives, our Fortunes, and our sacred Honor.

Signed by Order and in Behalf of the Congress,

John Hancock, President

Attest. Charles Thomson, Secretary

New-Hampshire.

Josiah Bartlett,   Matthew Thornton.

W^m.Wimple,

Massachusetts-Bay.

Sam^L Adams,   Robt Treat Paine,
John Adams,   Elbridge Gerry.

Rhode-Island.

Step. Hopkins,   William Ellery.

Connecticut.

Roger Sherman,   W^m. Williams,
Sam'^{El} Huntington,   Oliver Wolcott.

New-York.

Wm Floyd,   Fran^s Lewis,
Phil. Livingston, Lewis Morris.

New-Jersey.

Richd Stockton,   John Hart,
Jno. Witherspoon,   Abra. Clark.
Fra^s Hopkinson,

Pennsylvania.

Robt Morris,   Ja^s Smith,
Benjamin Rush,   Geo. Taylor,
Benja. Franklin,   James Wilson,
John Morton,   Geo. Ross.
Geo. Clymer,

Delaware.

Caesar Rodney,   Tho. M'kean.
Geo. Read

Maryland.

Samuel Chase,   Thos. Stone,
W^m. Paca,   Charles Caroll, of Carrollton.

Virginia.

George Wythe,   Thos. Nelson, j^r.,
Richard Henry Lee,   Francis Lightfoot Lee,
Th. Jefferson,   Carter Braxton.
Benj^a. Harrison,

North-Carolina.

W^m. Hooper,   John Penn.
Joseph Hewes,

South-Carolina.

Edward Rutledge,   Thomas Lynch, jun^r.,
Thos. Heyward, jun^r.,   Arthur Middleton.

Georgia.

Button Gwinnett,   Geo. Walton.
Lyman Hall,

*This text retains the spelling, capitalization, and punctuation of the original.

APPENDIX 2

THE CONSTITUTION OF THE UNITED STATES

We, the People of the United States, in Order to form a more perfect Union, establish Justice, insure domestic Tranquility, provide for the common defence, promote the general Welfare, and secure the Blessings of Liberty to ourselves and our Posterity, do ordain and establish this Constitution for the United States of America.

Article I

Section 1.

All legislative Powers herein granted shall be vested in a Congress of the United States, which shall consist of a Senate and House of Representatives.

Section 2.

1. The House of Representatives shall be composed of Members chosen every second Year by the People of the several States, and the Electors in each State shall have the Qualifications requisite for Electors of the most numerous Branch of the State Legislature.
2. No Person shall be a Representative who shall not have attained to the Age of twenty five Years, and been seven Years a Citizen of the United States, and who shall not, when elected, be an Inhabitant of that State in which he shall be chosen.
3. [Representatives and direct Taxes[1] shall be apportioned among the several States which may be included within this Union, according to their respective Numbers,

---

[1]The Sixteenth Amendment replaced this with respect to income taxes.

which shall be determined by adding to the whole Number of free Persons, including those bound to Service for a Term of Years, and excluding Indians not taxed, three fifths of all other Persons.][2] The actual Enumeration shall be made within three Years after the first Meeting of the Congress of the United States, and within every subsequent Term of ten years, in such Manner as they shall by Law direct. The Number of Representatives shall not exceed one for every thirty Thousand, but each State shall have at Least one Representative; and until such enumeration shall be made, the State of New-Hampshire shall be entitled to chuse three, Massachusetts eight, Rhode-Island and Providence Plantations one, Connecticut five, New-York six, New-Jersey four, Pennsylvania eight, Delaware one, Maryland six, Virginia ten, North-Carolina five, South-Carolina five, and Georgia three.

4. When vacancies happen in the Representation from any State, the Executive Authority thereof shall issue Writs of Election to fill such Vacancies.

5. The House of Representatives shall choose their Speaker and other Officers; and shall have the sole Power of Impeachment.

Section 3.

1. The Senate of the United States shall be composed of two Senators from each State, [chosen by the Legislature][3] thereof, for six Years; and each Senator shall have one Vote.

2. Immediately after they shall be assembled in Consequence of the first Election, they shall be divided as equally as may be into three Classes. The Seats of the Senators of the first Class shall be vacated at the Expiration of the second Year, of the second Class at the Expiration of the fourth Year, and of the third Class at the Expiration of the sixth Year, so that one third may be chosen every second Year; [and if Vacancies happen by Resignation, or otherwise, during the Recess of the Legislature of any State, the Executive thereof may make temporary Appointments until the next Meeting of the Legislature, which shall then fill such Vacancies].[4]

3. No person shall be a Senator who shall not have attained to the Age of thirty Years, and been nine Years a Citizen of the United States, and who shall not, when elected, be an Inhabitant of that State for which he shall be chosen.

4. The Vice President of the United States shall be President of the Senate, but shall have no Vote, unless they be equally divided.

5. The Senate shall choose their other Officers, and also a President pro tempore, in the absence of the Vice President, or when he shall exercise the Office of President of the United States.

6. The Senate shall have the sole Power to try all Impeachments. When sitting for that Purpose, they shall be on Oath or Affirmation. When the President of the United States is tried, the Chief Justice shall preside: And no Person shall be convicted without the Concurrence of two thirds of the Members present.

7. Judgment in Cases of Impeachment shall not extend further than to removal from Office, and disqualification to hold and enjoy any Office of honor, Trust or Profit under the United States: but the Party convicted shall nevertheless be liable and subject to Indictment, Trial, Judgment and Punishment, according to Law.

[2] Repealed by the Fourteenth Amendment.
[3] Repealed by the Seventeenth Amendment, Section 1.
[4] Changed by the Seventeenth Amendment.

Section 4.

1. The Times, Places and Manner of holding Elections for Senators and Representatives, shall be prescribed in each State by the Legislature thereof; but the Congress may at any time by Law make or alter such Regulations, except as to the Places of chusing Senators.
2. The Congress shall assemble at least once in every Year, and such Meeting shall [be on the first Monday in December,][5] unless they shall by Law appoint a different Day.

Section 5.

1. Each House shall be the Judge of the Elections, Returns and Qualifications of its own Members, and a Majority of each shall constitute a Quorum to do Business; but a smaller number may adjourn from day to day, and may be authorized to compel the Attendance of absent Members, in such Manner, and under such Penalties as each House may provide.
2. Each House may determine the Rules of its Proceedings, punish its Members for disorderly Behaviour, and, with the Concurrence of two thirds, expel a Member.
3. Each House shall keep a Journal of its Proceedings, and from time to time publish the same, excepting such Parts as may in their Judgment require Secrecy; and the Yeas and Nays of the Members of either House on any question shall, at the Desire of one fifth of those Present, be entered on the Journal.
4. Neither House, during the Session of Congress, shall, without the Consent of the other, adjourn for more than three days, nor to any other Place than that in which the two Houses shall be sitting.

Section 6.

1. The Senators and Representatives shall receive a Compensation for their Services, to be ascertained by Law, and paid out of the Treasury of the United States. They shall in all Cases, except Treason, Felony and Breach of the Peace, be privileged from Arrest during their Attendance at the Session of their respective Houses, and in going to and returning from the same; and for any Speech or Debate in either House, they shall not be questioned in any other Place.
2. No Senator or Representative shall, during the Time for which he was elected, be appointed to any civil Office under the Authority of the United States, which shall have been created, or the Emoluments whereof have been increased during such time; and no Person holding any Office under the United States, shall be a Member of either House during his Continuance in Office.

Section 7.

1. All Bills for raising Revenue shall originate in the House of Representatives; but the Senate may propose or concur with Amendments as on other Bills.
2. Every Bill which shall have passed the House of Representatives and the Senate, shall, before it become a Law, be presented to the President of the United States; If he ap-

---

[5]Changed by the Twentieth Amendment, Section 2.

prove he shall sign it, but if not he shall return it, with his Objections to that House in which it shall have originated, who shall enter the Objections at large on their Journal, and proceed to reconsider it. If after such Reconsideration two thirds of that House shall agree to pass the Bill, it shall be sent, together with the Objections, to the other House, by which it shall likewise be reconsidered, and if approved by two thirds of that House, it shall become a Law. But in all such Cases the Votes of both Houses shall be determined by Yeas and Nays, and the Names of the Persons voting for and against the Bill shall be entered on the Journal of each House respectively. If any Bill shall not be returned by the President within ten Days (Sundays excepted) after it shall have been presented to him, the Same shall be a Law, in like Manner as if he had signed it, unless the Congress by their Adjournment prevent its Return, in which Case it shall not be a Law.

3. Every Order, Resolution, or Vote to which the Concurrence of the Senate and House of Representatives may be necessary (except on a question of Adjournment) shall be presented to the President of the United States; and before the Same shall take Effect, shall be approved by him, or being disapproved by him, shall be repassed by two thirds of the Senate and House of Representatives, according to the Rules and Limitations prescribed in the Case of a Bill.

Section 8.

1. The Congress shall have Power To lay and collect Taxes, Duties, Imposts and Excises, to pay the Debts and provide for the common Defence and general Welfare of the United States; but all Duties, Imposts and Excises shall be uniform throughout the United States;
2. To borrow money on the credit of the United States;
3. To regulate Commerce with foreign Nations, and among the several States, and with the Indian Tribes;
4. To establish an uniform Rule of Naturalization, and uniform Laws on the subject of Bankruptcies throughout the United States;
5. To coin Money, regulate the Value thereof, and of foreign Coin, and fix the Standard of Weights and Measures;
6. To provide for the Punishment of counterfeiting the Securities and current Coin of the United States;
7. To establish Post Offices and post Roads;
8. To promote the Progress of Science and useful Arts, by securing for limited Times to Authors and Inventors the exclusive Right to their respective Writings and Discoveries;
9. To constitute Tribunals inferior to the supreme Court;
10. To define and punish Piracies and Felonies committed on the high Seas, and Offences against the Law of Nations;
11. To declare War, grant Letters of Marque and Reprisal, and make Rules concerning Captures on Land and Water;
12. To raise and support Armies, but no Appropriation of Money to that Use shall be for a longer Term than two Years;
13. To provide and maintain a Navy;
14. To make rules for the Government and Regulation of the land and naval Forces;
15. To provide for calling forth the Militia to execute the Laws of the Union, suppress Insurrections and repel Invasions;
16. To provide for organizing, arming, and disciplining the Militia, and for governing such Part of them as may be employed in the Service of the United States, reserving to the States respectively, the Appointment of the Officers, and the Authority of training the Militia according to the discipline prescribed by Congress;

That clause VIII .16

17. To exercise exclusive Legislation in all Cases whatsoever, over such District (not exceeding ten Miles square) as may, by Cession of particular States, and the acceptance of Congress, become the Seat of the Government of the United States, and to exercise like Authority over all Places purchased by the Consent of the Legislature of the State in which the Same shall be, for the Erection of Forts, Magazines, Arsenals, dock-Yards, and other needful Buildings;—And

18. To make all Laws which shall be necessary and proper for carrying into Execution the foregoing Powers, and all other Powers vested by this Constitution in the Government of the United States, or in any Department or Officer thereof.

Section 9.

1. The Migration or Importation of such Persons as any of the States now existing shall think proper to admit, shall not be prohibited by the Congress prior to the Year one thousand eight hundred and eight, but a Tax or duty may be imposed on such Importation, not exceeding ten dollars for each Person.
2. The Privilege of the Writ of Habeas Corpus shall not be suspended, unless when in Cases of Rebellion or Invasion the public Safety may require it.
3. No Bill of Attainder or ex post facto Law shall be passed.
4. No Capitation, or other direct, Tax shall be laid, unless in Proportion to the Census or Enumeration herein before directed to be taken.[6]
5. No Tax or Duty shall be laid on Articles exported from any State.
6. No Preference shall be given by any Regulation of Commerce or Revenue to the Ports of one State over those of another: nor shall Vessels bound to, or from, one State, be obliged to enter, clear, or pay Duties in another.
7. No Money shall be drawn from the Treasury, but in Consequence of Appropriations made by Law; and a regular Statement and Account of the Receipts and Expenditures of all public Money shall be published from time to time.
8. No Title of Nobility shall be granted by the United States: And no Person holding any Office of Profit or Trust under them, shall, without the Consent of the Congress, accept of any present, Emolument, Office, or Title, of any kind whatever, from any King, Prince, or foreign State.

Section 10.

1. No State shall enter into any Treaty, Alliance, or Confederation; grant Letters of Marque and Reprisal; coin Money; emit Bills of Credit; make any Thing but gold and silver Coin a Tender in Payment of Debts; pass any Bill of Attainder, ex post facto Law, or Law impairing the Obligation of Contracts, or grant any Title of Nobility.
2. No State shall, without the Consent of the Congress, lay any Imposts or Duties on Imports or Exports, except what may be absolutely necessary for executing its inspection Laws: and the net Produce of all Duties and Imposts, laid by any State on Imports or Exports, shall be for the Use of the Treasury of the United States; and all such Laws shall be subject to the Revision and Controul of the Congress.
3. No State shall, without the Consent of Congress, lay any duty of Tonnage, keep Troops, or Ships of War in time of Peace, enter into any Agreement or Compact with another

[6]Changed by the Sixteenth Amendment.

State, or with a foreign Power, or engage in War, unless actually invaded, or in such imminent Danger as will not admit of delay.

Article II

Section 1.

1. The executive Power shall be vested in a President of the United States of America. He shall hold his Office during the Term of four Years, and, together with the Vice President, chosen for the same Term, be elected, as follows:

2. Each State shall appoint, in such Manner as the Legislature thereof may direct, a Number of Electors, equal to the whole Number of Senators and Representatives to which the State may be entitled in the Congress; but no Senator or Representative, or Person holding an Office of Trust or Profit under the United States, shall be appointed an Elector.

    [The Electors shall meet in their respective States, and vote by Ballot for two persons, of whom one at least shall not be an Inhabitant of the same State with themselves. And they shall make a List of all the Persons voted for, and of the Number of Votes for each; which List they shall sign and certify, and transmit sealed to the Seat of the Government of the United States, directed to the President of the Senate. The President of the Senate shall, in the Presence of the Senate and House of Representatives, open all the Certificates, and the Votes shall then be counted. The Person having the greatest Number of Votes shall be the President, if such Number be a Majority of the whole Number of Electors appointed; and if there be more than one who have such Majority, and have an equal Number of Votes, then the House of Representatives shall immediately choose by Ballot one of them for President; and if no Person have a Majority, then from the five highest on the List the said House shall in like Manner choose the President. But in choosing the President, the Votes shall be taken by States, the Representation from each State having one Vote; A quorum for this Purpose shall consist of a Member or Members from two thirds of the States, and a Majority of all the States shall be necessary to a Choice. In every Case, after the Choice of the President, the Person having the greatest Number of Votes of the Electors shall be the Vice President. But if there should remain two or more who have equal Votes, the Senate shall choose from them by Ballot the Vice President.][7]

3. The Congress may determine the Time of choosing the electors, and the Day on which they shall give their Votes; which Day shall be the same throughout the United States.

4. No person except a natural born Citizen, or a Citizen of the United States, at the time of the Adoption of this Constitution, shall be eligible to the Office of President; neither shall any Person be eligible to that Office who shall not have attained to the Age of thirty five Years, and been fourteen Years a Resident within the United States.

5. In Case of the Removal of the President from Office, or of his Death, Resignation, or Inability to discharge the Powers and Duties of the said Office, the Same shall devolve on the Vice President, and the Congress may by Law provide for the Case of Removal, Death, Resignation or Inability, both of the President and Vice President, declaring what Officer shall then act as President, and such Officer shall act accordingly, until the Disability be removed, or a President shall be elected.[8]

---

[7]This paragraph was superseded in 1804 by the Twelfth Amendment.
[8]Changed by the Twenty-fifth Amendment.

6. The President shall, at stated Times, receive for his Services, a Compensation, which shall neither be increased nor diminished during the Period for which he shall have been elected, and he shall not receive within that Period any other Emolument from the United States, or any of them.

7. Before he enter on the Execution of his Office, he shall take the following Oath or Affirmation:—"I do solemnly swear (or affirm) that I will faithfully execute the Office of President of the United States, and will to the best of my Ability, preserve, protect and defend the Constitution of the United States."

Section 2.

1. The President shall be Commander in Chief of the Army and Navy of the United States, and of the Militia of the several States, when called into the actual Service of the United States; he may require the Opinion in writing, of the principal Officer in each of the executive Departments, upon any Subject relating to the Duties of their respective Offices, and he shall have Power to Grant Reprieves and Pardons for Offenses against the United States, except in Cases of Impeachment.

2. He shall have Power, by and with the Advice and Consent of the Senate, to make Treaties, provided two thirds of the Senators present concur; and he shall nominate, and by and with the Advice and Consent of the Senate, shall appoint Ambassadors, other public Ministers and Consuls, Judges of the supreme Court, and all other Officers of the United States, whose Appointments are not herein otherwise provided for, and which shall be established by Law: but the Congress may by Law vest the Appointment of such inferior Officers, as they think proper, in the President alone, in the Courts of Law, or in the Heads of Departments.

3. The President shall have Power to fill up all Vacancies that may happen during the Recess of the Senate, by granting Commissions which shall expire at the End of their next Session.

Section 3.

He shall from time to time give to the Congress Information of the State of the Union, and recommend to their Consideration such Measures as he shall judge necessary and expedient; he may, on extraordinary Occasions, convene both Houses, or either of them, and in Case of Disagreement between them, with Respect to the Time of Adjournment, he may adjourn them to such Time as he shall think proper; he shall receive Ambassadors and other public Ministers; he shall take Care that the Laws be faithfully executed, and shall Commission all the Officers of the United States.

Section 4.

The President, Vice President and all civil Officers of the United States, shall be removed from Office on Impeachment for, and Conviction of, Treason, Bribery, or other high Crimes and Misdemeanors.

Article III

Section 1.

The judicial Power of the United States, shall be vested in one supreme Court, and in such inferior Courts as the Congress may from time to time ordain and establish. The Judges, both of the supreme and inferior Courts, shall hold their Offices during good Behaviour, and shall, at stated Times, receive for their Services, a Compensation, which shall not be diminished during their Continuance in Office.

Section 2.

1. The judicial Power shall extend to all Cases, in Law and Equity, arising under this Constitution, the Laws of the United States, and Treaties made, or which shall be made, under their Authority;—to all Cases affecting Ambassadors, other public Ministers and Consuls;—to all Cases of admiralty and maritime Jurisdiction;—to Controversies to which the United States shall be a Party;—to Controversies between two or more States;—[between a State and Citizens of another State];[9]—between Citizens of different States;—between Citizens of the same State claiming Lands under Grants of different States, and [between a State, or the Citizens thereof, and foreign States, Citizens or Subjects].[10]

2. In all Cases affecting Ambassadors, other public Ministers and Consuls, and those in which a State shall be Party, the supreme Court shall have original Jurisdiction. In all the other Cases before mentioned, the supreme Court shall have appellate Jurisdiction, both as to Law and Fact, with such Exceptions, and under such Regulations as the Congress shall make.

3. The Trial of all Crimes, except in Cases of Impeachment, shall be by Jury; and such Trial shall be held in the State where the said Crimes shall have been committed: but when not committed within any state, the Trial shall be at such Place or Places as the Congress may by Law have directed.

Section 3.

1. Treason against the United States, shall consist only in levying War against them, or in adhering to their Enemies, giving them Aid and Comfort. No Person shall be convicted of Treason unless on the Testimony of two Witnesses to the same overt Act, or on Confession in open Court.

2. The Congress shall have power to declare the Punishment of Treason, but no Attainder of Treason shall work Corruption of Blood, or Forfeiture except during the Life of the Person attained.

Article IV

Section 1.

Full Faith and Credit shall be given in each State to the public Acts, Records, and judicial Proceedings of every other State. And the Congress may by general Laws prescribe the Manner in which such Acts, Records and Proceedings shall be proved, and the Effect thereof.

Section 2.

1. The Citizens of each State shall be entitled to all Privileges and Immunities of Citizens in the several States.

---

[9]Restricted by the Eleventh Amendment.
[10]Restricted by the Eleventh Amendment.

2. A Person charged in any State with Treason, Felony, or other Crime, who shall flee from Justice, and be found in another State, shall on demand of the executive Authority of the State from which he fled, be delivered up, to be removed to the State having Jurisdiction of the Crime.

3. [No Person held to Service or Labour in one State, under the Laws thereof, escaping into another, shall, in Consequence of any Law or Regulation therein, be discharged from such Service or Labour, but shall be delivered up on Claim of the Party to whom such Service or Labour may be due.][11]

Section 3.

1. New States may be admitted by the Congress into this Union; but no new State shall be formed or erected within the Jurisdiction of any other State; nor any State be formed by the Junction of two or more States, or Parts of States, without the Consent of the Legislatures of the States concerned as well as of the Congress.

2. The Congress shall have Power to dispose of and make all needful Rules and Regulations respecting the Territory or other Property belonging to the United States; and nothing in this Constitution shall be so construed as to Prejudice any Claims of the United States, or of any particular State.

Section 4.

The United States shall guarantee to every State in this Union a Republican Form of Government, and shall protect each of them against Invasion; and on Application of the Legislature, or of the Executive (when the Legislature cannot be convened) against domestic Violence.

Article V

The Congress, whenever two thirds of both Houses shall deem it necessary, shall propose Amendments to this Constitution, or, on the Application of the Legislatures of two thirds of the several States, shall call a Convention for proposing Amendments, which, in either Case, shall be valid to all Intents and Purposes, as Part of this Constitution, when ratified by the Legislature of three fourths of the several States, or by Conventions in three fourths thereof, as the one or the other Mode of Ratification may be proposed by the Congress; Provided that no Amendment which may be made prior to Year One thousand eight hundred and eight shall in any Manner affect the first and fourth Clauses in the Ninth Section of the first Article; and that no State, without its Consent, shall be deprived of its equal Suffrage in the Senate.

---

[11]This paragraph has been superseded by the Thirteenth Amendment.

Article VI

1. All Debts contracted and Engagements entered into, before the Adoption of this Constitution, shall be as valid against the United States under this Constitution, as under the Confederation.
2. This Constitution, and the Laws of the United States which shall be made in Pursuance thereof; and all Treaties made, or which shall be made, under the Authority of the United States, shall be the supreme Law of the Land; and the Judges in every State shall be bound thereby, any Thing in the Constitution or Laws of any State to the Contrary notwithstanding.
3. The Senators and Representatives before mentioned, and the Members of the several State Legislatures, and all executive and judicial Officers, both of the United States and of the several States, shall be bound by Oath or Affirmation, to support this Constitution; but no religious Test shall ever be required as a Qualification to any Office or public Trust under the United States.

Article VII

The Ratification of the conventions of nine States, shall be sufficient for the Establishment of this Constitution between the States so ratifying the Same.

DONE in Convention by the Unanimous Consent of the States present the Seventeenth Day of September in the Year of our Lord one thousand seven hundred and Eighty seven and of the Independence of the United States of America the Twelfth.

In Witness whereof We have hereunto subscribed our Names,

Go. Washington—

Presid't. and deputy from Virginia
Attest William Jackson, Secretary [followed by 38 names from 12 states]

Amendments

Articles in Addition to, and Amendment of, the Constitution of the United States of America, Proposed by Congress, and Ratified by the Legislatures of the Several States, Pursuant to the Fifth Article of the Original Constitution.

Article I[12]

Congress shall make no law respecting an establishment of religion, or prohibiting the free exercise thereof; or abridging the freedom of speech, or of the press; or the right of the people peaceably to assemble, and to petition the Government for a redress of grievances.

---

[12]The first ten amendments were adopted in 1791.

Article II

A well regulated Militia, being necessary to the security of a free State, the right of the people to keep and bear Arms, shall not be infringed.

Article III

No Soldier, shall, in time of peace he quartered in any house, without the consent of the Owner, nor in time of war, but in a manner to be prescribed by law.

Changing technologies

Article IV

The right of the people to be secure in their persons, houses, papers, and effects, against unreasonable searches and seizures, shall not be violated, and no Warrants shall issue, but upon probable cause, supported by Oath or affirmation, and particularly describing the place to be searched, and the persons or things to be seized.

Rise of permanent standing army + military justice

Article V

No person shall be held to answer for a capital, or otherwise infamous crime, unless on a presentment or indictment of a Grand Jury, except in cases arising in the land or naval forces, or in the Militia, when in actual service in time of War or public danger; nor shall any person be subject for the same offence to be twice put in jeopardy of life or limb; nor shall be compelled in any criminal case to be witness against himself, nor be deprived of life, liberty, or property, without due process of law; nor shall private property be taken for public use, without just compensation.

Article VI

In all criminal prosecutions, the accused shall enjoy the right to a speedy and public trial, by an impartial jury of the State and district wherein the crime shall have been committed, which district shall have been previously ascertained by law, and to be informed of the nature and cause of the accusation; to be confronted with the witnesses against him; to have compulsory process for obtaining witnesses in his favor, and to have the Assistance of Counsel for his defence.

Article VII

In suits at common law, where the value in controversy shall exceed twenty dollars, the right of trial by jury shall be preserved, and no fact tried by a jury, shall be otherwise reexamined in any Court of the United States, than according to the rules of the common law.

Article VIII

Excessive bail shall not be required, nor excessive fines imposed, nor cruel and unusual punishments inflicted.

Article IX

The enumeration in the Constitution, of certain rights, shall not be construed to deny or disparage others retained by the people.

Article X

The powers not delegated to the United States by the Constitution, nor prohibited by it to the States, are reserved to the States respectively, or to the people.

Article XI[13]

The Judicial power of the United States shall not be construed to extend to any suit in law or equity, commenced or prosecuted against one of the United States by Citizens of another State, or by Citizens or Subjects of any Foreign State.

Article XII[14]

The Electors shall meet in their respective states and vote by ballot for President and Vice-President, one of whom, at least, shall not be an inhabitant of the same state with themselves; they shall name in their ballots the person voted for as President, and in distinct ballots the person voted for as Vice-President, and they shall make distinct lists of all persons voted for as President, and of all persons voted for as Vice-President, and of the number of votes for each, which lists they shall sign and certify, and transmit sealed to the seat of the government of the United States, directed to the President of the Senate;—The President of the Senate shall, in presence of the Senate and House of Representatives, open all the certificates and the votes shall then be counted;—The person having the greatest number of votes for President, shall be the President, if such number be a majority of the whole number of Electors appointed; and if no person have such majority, then from the persons having the highest numbers not exceeding three on the list of those voted for as President, the House of Representatives shall choose immediately, by ballot, the President. But in choosing the President, the votes shall be taken by states, the representation from each state having one vote; a quorum for this purpose shall consist of a member or members

---

[13]Adopted in 1798.
[14]Adopted in 1804.

from two-thirds of the states, and a majority of all the states shall be necessary to a choice. [And if the House of Representatives shall not choose a President whenever the right of choice shall devolve upon them, before the fourth day of March next following, then the Vice-President shall act as President, as in the case of the death or other constitutional disability of the President].[15]—The person having the greatest number of votes as Vice-President, shall be the Vice-President, if such number be a majority of the whole number of Electors appointed, and if no person have a majority, then from the two highest numbers on the list, the Senate shall choose the Vice-President; a quorum for the purpose shall consist of two-thirds of the whole number of Senators, and a majority of the whole number shall be necessary to a choice. But no person constitutionally ineligible to the office of President shall be eligible to that of Vice-President of the United States.

Article XIII[16]

Section 1.

Neither slavery nor involuntary servitude, except as a punishment for crime whereof the party shall have been duly convicted, shall exist within the United States, or any place subject to their jurisdiction.

Section 2.

Congress shall have power to enforce this article by appropriate legislation.

Article XIV[17]

Section 1.

All persons born or naturalized in the United States, and subject to the jurisdiction thereof, are citizens of the United States and of the State wherein they reside. No state shall make or enforce any law which shall abridge the privileges or immunities of citizens of the United States; nor shall any State deprive any person of life, liberty, or property, without due process of law; nor deny to any person within its jurisdiction the equal protection of the laws.

Section 2.

Representatives shall be apportioned among the several States according to their respective numbers, counting the whole number of persons in each State, excluding Indians not taxed. But when the right to vote at any election for the choice of electors for President and Vice-

---

[15]Superseded by the Twentieth Amendment, Section 3.
[16]Adopted in 1865.
[17]Adopted in 1868.

President of the United States, Representatives in Congress, the Executive and Judicial officers of a State, or the members of the Legislature thereof, is denied to any of the male inhabitants of such State, being twenty-one years of age, and citizens of the United States, or in any way abridged, except for participation in rebellion, or other crime, the basis of representation therein shall be reduced in the proportion which the number of such male citizens shall bear to the whole number of male citizens twenty-one years of age in such State.

Section 3.

No person shall be a Senator or Representative in Congress, or elector of President and Vice-President, or hold any office, civil or military, under the United States, or under any State, who, having previously taken an oath, as a member of Congress, or as an officer of the United States, or as a member of any State legislature, or as an executive or judicial officer of any State, to support the Constitution of the United States, shall have engaged in insurrection or rebellion against the same, or given aid or comfort to the enemies thereof. But Congress may by a vote of two-thirds of each House, remove such disability.

Section 4.

The validity of the public debt of the United States, authorized by law, including debts incurred for payment of pensions and bounties for services in suppressing insurrection or rebellion, shall not be questioned. But neither the United States nor any State shall assume or pay any debt or obligation incurred in aid of insurrection or rebellion against the United States, or any claim for the loss or emancipation of any slave; but all such debts, obligations and claims shall be held illegal and void.

Section 5.

The Congress shall have power to enforce, by appropriate legislation, the provisions of this article.

Article XV[18]

Section 1.

The right of citizens of the United States to vote shall not be denied or abridged by the United States or by any State on account of race, color, or previous condition of servitude.

Section 2.

The Congress shall have power to enforce this article by appropriate legislation.

---

[18]Adopted in 1870.

Article XVI[19]

The Congress shall have power to lay and collect taxes on incomes, from whatever source derived, without apportionment among the several States, and without regard to any census or enumeration.

Article XVII[20]

The Senate of the United States shall be composed of two Senators from each State, elected by the people thereof, for six years; and each Senator shall have one vote. The electors in each State shall have the qualifications requisite for electors of the most numerous branch of the State legislatures.

When vacancies happen in the representation of any State in the Senate, the executive authority of such State shall issue writs of election to fill such vacancies: *Provided,* That the legislature of any State may empower the executive thereof to make temporary appointments until the people fill the vacancies by election as the legislature may direct.

This amendment shall not be so construed as to affect the election or term of any Senator chosen before it becomes valid as part of the Constitution.

Article XVIII[21]

Section 1.

After one year from the ratification of this article the manufacture, sale, or transportation of intoxicating liquors within, the importation thereof into, or the exportation thereof from the United States and all territory subject to the jurisdiction thereof for beverage purposes is hereby prohibited.

Section 2.

The Congress and the several States shall have concurrent power to enforce this article by appropriate legislation.

Section 3.

This article shall be inoperative unless it shall have been ratified as an amendment to the Constitution by the legislatures of the several States, as provided in the Constitution, within seven years from the date of the submission hereof to the States by the Congress.

---

[19]Adopted in 1913.
[20]Adopted in 1913.
[21]Adopted in 1919. Repealed by Section 1 of the Twenty-first Amendment.

Article XIX[22]

The right of citizens of the United States to vote shall not be denied or abridged by the United States or by any State on account of sex.

Congress shall have power to enforce this article by appropriate legislation.

Article XX[23]

Section 1.

The terms of the President and Vice-President shall end at noon on the 20th day of January, and the terms of Senators and Representatives at noon on the 3d day of January, of the years in which such terms would have ended if this article had not been ratified; and the terms of their successors shall then begin.

Section 2.

The Congress shall assemble at least once in every year, and such meeting shall begin at noon on the 3d day of January, unless they shall by law appoint a different day.

Section 3.

If, at the time fixed for the beginning of the term of the President, the president elect shall have died, the Vice-President elect shall become President. If a President shall not have been chosen before the time fixed for the beginning of his term, or if the President elect shall have failed to qualify, then the Vice-President elect shall act as President until a President shall have qualified; and the Congress may by law provide for the case wherein neither a President elect nor a Vice-President elect shall have qualified, declaring who shall then act as President, or the manner in which one who is to act shall be selected, and such person shall act accordingly until a President or Vice-President shall have qualified.

Section 4.

The Congress may by law provide for the case of the death of any of the persons from whom the House of Representatives may choose a President whenever the right of choice shall have devolved upon them, and for the case of the death of any of the persons from whom the Senate may choose a Vice-President whenever the right of choice shall have devolved upon them.

---

[22]Adopted in 1920.
[23]Adopted in 1933.

Section 5.

Section 1 and 2 shall take effect on the 15th day of October following the ratification of this article.

Section 6.

This article shall be inoperative unless it shall have been ratified as an amendment to the Constitution by the legislatures of three-fourths of the several States within seven years from the date of its submission.

Article XXI[24]

Section 1.

The eighteenth article of amendment to the Constitution of the United States is hereby repealed.

Section 2.

The transportation or importation into any State, Territory, or possession of the United States for delivery or use therein of intoxicating liquors, in violation of the laws thereof, is hereby prohibited.

Section 3.

This article shall be inoperative unless it shall have been ratified as an amendment to the Constitution by conventions in the several States, as provided in the Constitution, within seven years from the date of the submission hereof to the States by the Congress.

Article XXII[25]

Section 1.

No person shall be elected to the office of the President more than twice, and no person who has held the office of President, or acted as President, for more than two years of a term to which some other person was elected President shall be elected to the office of the President more than once. But this Article shall not apply to any person holding the office of President when this Article was proposed by the Congress, and shall not prevent any person who may be holding the office of President, or acting as President, during the term

---

[24]Adopted in 1933.
[25]Adopted in 1951.

within which this Article becomes operative from holding the office of President or acting as President during the remainder of such term.

Section 2.

This article shall be inoperative unless it shall have been ratified as an amendment to the Constitution by the legislatures of three-fourths of the several States within seven years from the date of its submission to the States by the Congress.

Article XXIII[26]

Section 1.

The District constituting the seat of Government of the United States shall appoint in such manner as the Congress may direct:

A number of electors of President and Vice-President equal to the whole number of Senators and Representatives in Congress to which the District would be entitled if it were a State, but in no event more than the least populous State; they shall be in addition to those appointed by the States, but they shall be considered, for the purposes of the election of President and Vice-President, to be electors appointed by a State; and they shall meet in the District and perform such duties as provided by the twelfth article of amendment.

Section 2.

The Congress shall have power to enforce this article by appropriate legislation.

Article XXIV[27]

Section 1.

The right of citizens of the United States to vote in any primary or other election for President or Vice-President, for electors for President or Vice-President, or for Senator or Representative in Congress, shall not be denied or abridged by the United States or any state by reasons of failure to pay any poll tax or other tax.

Section 2.

The Congress shall have power to enforce this article by appropriate legislation.

---

[26]Adopted in 1961.
[27]Adopted in 1964.

Article XXV[28]

Section 1.

In case of the removal of the President from office or of his death or resignation, the Vice-President shall become President.

Section 2.

Whenever there is a vacancy in the office of the Vice-President, the President shall nominate a Vice-President who shall take office upon confirmation by a majority vote of both Houses of Congress.

Section 3.

Whenever the President transmits to the President pro tempore of the Senate and the Speaker of the House of Representatives his written declaration that he is unable to discharge the powers and duties of his office, and until he transmits to them a written declaration to the contrary, such powers and duties shall be discharged by the Vice-President as Acting President.

Section 4.

Whenever the Vice-President and a majority of either the principal officers of the Executive departments or of such other body as Congress may by law provide transmit to the President pro tempore of the Senate and the Speaker of the House of Representatives their written declaration that the President is unable to discharge the powers and duties of his office, the Vice-President shall immediately assume the powers and duties of the office as Acting President.

Thereafter, when the President transmits to the President pro tempore of the Senate and the Speaker of the House of Representatives his written declaration that no inability exists, he shall resume the powers and duties of his office unless the Vice-President and a majority of either the principal officers of the Executive departments or of such other body as Congress may by law provide transmit within four days to the President pro tempore of the Senate and the Speaker of the House of Representatives their written declaration that the President is unable to discharge the powers and duties of his office. Thereupon Congress shall decide the issue, assembling within forty-eight hours for that purpose if not in session. If the Congress, within twenty-one days after receipt of the latter written declaration, or, if Congress is not in session, within twenty-one days after Congress is required to assemble, determines by two-thirds vote of both houses that the President is unable to discharge the powers and duties of his office, the Vice-President shall continue to discharge

---

[28]Adopted in 1967.

the same as Acting President; otherwise, the President shall resume the powers and duties of his office.

Article XXVI[29]

Section 1.

The right of citizens of the United States, who are 18 years of age or older, to vote shall not be denied or abridged by the United States or any state on account of age.

Section 2.

The Congress shall have power to enforce this article by appropriate legislation.

Article XXVII[30]

Section 1.

No law varying the compensation for services of the Senators and Representatives, shall take effect, until an election of Representatives shall have intervened.

---

[29]Adopted in 1971.
[30]Adopted in 1992.

CREDITS

∽

$$20$$
$$\times 1.8$$

$$16\ 6$$
$$2\ 0$$

$$3\ 6.0$$
$$+32 = 6.8$$

$$15$$
$$1.8$$

$$12\ 0$$
$$1\ 6$$

$$28.0\ +32 = 60$$